UNIVERSITY CASEBOOK SER

2018 SUPPLEMENT TO

CIVIL PROCEDURE

FOURTH EDITION

RULES, STATUTES, AND RECENT DEVELOPMENTS

THOMAS D. ROWE, JR.
Elvin R. Latty Professor of Law Emeritus
Duke University School of Law

SUZANNA SHERRY
Herman O. Loewenstein Professor of Law
Vanderbilt University Law School

JAY TIDMARSH
Judge James J. Clynes, Jr., Professor of Law
Notre Dame Law School

FOUNDATION
PRESS

444 Cedar Street, Suite 700
St. Paul, MN 55101
1-877-888-1330

Printed in the United States of America

ISBN: 978-1-64020-983-1

TABLE OF CONTENTS

TABLE OF CONTENTS iii
DEVELOPMENTS AND CLARIFICATIONS 1
RECENT SUPREME COURT CASE 11
Bristol-Myers Squibb Co. v. Superior Court of California 11
FEDERAL RULES OF CIVIL PROCEDURE (WITH SELECTED ADVISORY COMMITTEE NOTES) 17
FEDERAL RULES OF APPELLATE PROCEDURE: SELECTED SECTIONS 259
RULES OF THE SUPREME COURT OF THE UNITED STATES: SELECTED SECTIONS 267
UNITED STATES CODE: SELECTED SECTIONS 271
Title 28 271
Title 29 329
Title 42 330
UNITED STATES CONSTITUTION 333
PENDING AMENDMENTS TO THE FEDERAL RULES OF CIVIL PROCEDURE 353

DEVELOPMENTS AND CLARIFICATIONS

CHAPTER ONE: INTRODUCTION

Pages 3-4 (Note 4): Professor Michalski surveyed 1,200 judges and litigants to determine the procedural goals that they valued and those they did not. He reported a consensus on speed, cost, and privacy: no groups valued them highly. Beyond this agreement, differences emerged: federal judges valued fairness and participation, corporations valued accuracy and finality, and *pro se* litigants (i.e., those not represented by lawyers) rated accessibility and simplicity highly. The author concludes that favoring certain values may amount to favoring certain litigants. *See* Roger Michalski, *The Clash of Procedural Values*, 22 LEWIS & CLARK L. REV. — (forthcoming 2018), *available at* https://papers.ssrn.com/sol3/papers.cfm?abstract_id=3045381.

Pages 5-6 (Note 4): Due to an editing error, this Note is misnumbered. It should be Note 5.

CHAPTER TWO: PLEADING

Page 60 (Note 4): In a decision resting on grounds other than the pleading issues dealt with by the Second Circuit, the Supreme Court reversed and remanded *Turkmen* in *Ziglar v. Abbasi*, 582 U.S. —, 137 S. Ct. 1843 (2017). The Court held that the plaintiffs could not sue government officials for damages arising from any injuries that the detention policy caused. Claims that the warden allowed prison guards to abuse prisoners, however, survived for now. Disagreeing with the warden's argument that *Iqbal* barred the claims, the Court noted that the allegations of abuse, "assumed here to be true, . . . plausibly show the warden's deliberate indifference to the abuse." *Id.* at 1864. On remand, the court of appeals was instructed to determine whether a damages remedy was available against the warden.

Pages 61-62 (Note 6): A more recent article by Hubbard reaches conclusions similar to his earlier one. He suggests that *Twombly* and *Iqbal*

have not had a major effect on dismissal rates, the number of motions to dismiss, or settlement and filing patterns in cases in which plaintiffs are represented by lawyers. He does find some evidence of potentially major effects on *unrepresented* plaintiffs. William H.J. Hubbard, *The Effects of* Twombly *and* Iqbal, 14 J. EMPIRICAL LEGAL STUD. 474 (2017). *See also* Roger Michalski & Abby K. Wood, Twombly *and* Iqbal *at the State Level,* 14 J. EMP. LEG. STUD. 424 (2017) (comparing Nebraska, which raised pleading standards, to several other states that did not; finding no effects on plaintiffs' behavior, defense strategies, or judicial responses).

Page 63 (Note 8): As of April 2018, six states had adopted *Twombly*'s and *Iqbal*'s plausibility standard and 19 states had rejected or criticized it. *See* Zachary D. Clopton, *Procedural Retrenchment and the States*, 106 CALIF L. REV. 411, 425-26 (2018).

Page 72 (Note 8): When a nonprofit organization alleging that a defendant had financed ISIS terrorists was unable to serve him through traditional means, a federal court authorized service through Twitter, on which the defendant had an active presence. *See* St. Francis Assisi v. Kuwait Fin. House, 2016 WL 5725002 (N.D. Cal. Sept. 30, 2016). In a case involving service of process against a foreign defendant under the Hague Convention, the Supreme Court held that the Convention permits service by mail as long as the court issuing the process (in this case, a Texas state court) authorizes such service. *See* Water Splash, Inc. v. Menon, 581 U.S. —, 137 S. Ct. 1504 (2017).

Page 83 (Note 1): One article concludes that between May 2007 and May 2017, a majority (62%) of 925 district-court cases reaching the question (no court of appeals having yet ruled on the issue) held that *Twombly* and *Iqbal* do *not* apply to affirmative defenses. Brian Soucek & Remington B. Lamons, *Heightened Pleading Standards for Defendants: A Case Study of Court-Counting Precedent*, 70 ALA. L. REV — (forthcoming 2018), *available at* https://papers.ssrn.com/sol3/papers.cfm?abstract_id=3164416.

Pages 104-05 (Note 3): Although Rule 11(c)(4) limits sanctions to an appropriate deterrent, courts often recognize that the best deterrent is payment of the opponent's fees and costs. *See* Royce v. Michael R. Needle, P.C., 158 F. Supp. 3d 708, 713 (N.D. Ill. 2016) (noting that "[c]ompensation and deterrence are not only not mutually exclusive, they are sometimes compatible") (internal quotation marks omitted).

On March 10, 2017, the House of Representatives passed a bill that would roll back the balance struck in the 1993 amendments to Rule 11. The legislation would make Rule 11 sanctions mandatory, would eliminate the safe-harbor provision of Rule 11(c)(2), and (in addition to other appropriate sanctions) would require the payment of attorney's fees, expenses, and other costs to compensate parties injured by a Rule 11 violation. *See* Lawsuit Abuse Reduction Act, H.R. 720, 115th Cong. (2017). Prospects for passage in the Senate are uncertain.

Pages 106-07 (Note 8): In one of the largest Rule 11 sanctions cases ever, a four-judge panel sanctioned plaintiffs' lawyers $9.1 million for filing

meritless complaints against tobacco companies. The lawyers filed 3,700 cases, which had tentatively settled for $100 million. Of the filed lawsuits, 1,250 were frivolous, including 588 cases that were filed on behalf of dead clients. In addition to Rule 11, the court cited as a sanctioning authority 28 U.S.C. § 1927, because the lawyers vexatiously advocated for another 572 clients whose cases were subject to dismissal for failing to comply with a pretrial order. As an alternative to Rule 11 and § 1927, the court found that its inherent power authorized the sanctions. The court also referred the matter to the Florida State Bar to consider whether the lawyers violated their ethical responsibilities. The court did not, however, require one sanction that you might have thought about — disgorgement of the entire fee that the plaintiffs' lawyers earned in the litigation — even though the special master handling the case recommended it. *See In re* Engle Cases, 283 F. Supp. 3d 1174 (M.D. Fla. 2017).

CHAPTER THREE: DISCLOSURE AND DISCOVERY

Page 132 (Note 1): This note incompletely states the standard of review with respect to the decisions of magistrate judges. A district judge reviews de novo any legal determinations in a nondispositive motion that a magistrate judge decides under § 636(b)(1)(A), and also reviews de novo any findings or recommendations of the magistrate judge regarding any motion not listed in § 636(b)(1)(A). For factual or discretionary determinations that a magistrate judge makes in deciding any motion listed in § 636(b)(1)(A), however, the statute's stated standard of review — "clearly erroneous or contrary to law" — is more deferential. *See* Computer Econ., Inc. v. Gartner Grp., 50 F. Supp. 2d 980, 983 (S.D. Cal. 1999).

Page 169-70 (Note 4): In *Browder v. City of Albuquerque*, 187 F. Supp. 3d 1288 (D.N.M. 2016), the city had issued a cell phone to a police officer involved in a car accident with plaintiff's decedent. The plaintiff believed that the phone contained texts and other information showing that the police officer had fabricated his story about the accident. The city did not preserve the cell phone even after the plaintiff's lawyer requested that the phone be preserved. The court held that the city was obliged to preserve the phone from the date that it received the lawyer's letter, that it was grossly negligent in failing to do so, and that the plaintiff's case was prejudiced. As a sanction for the spoliation of evidence, the district court ordered the city to produce "all documents relevant to the . . . cell phone" — including documents that it was withholding under claims of work product and attorney-client privilege. The plaintiff was also allowed to tell the jury that the cell phone had not been preserved, but the court declined to issue an instruction that the jury could draw an adverse inference from this fact.

Page 171 (Note 8): In *Goodyear Tire & Rubber Co. v. Haeger*, 581 U.S. —, 137 S. Ct. 1178 (2017), the Court clarified some limits on courts' inherent powers to award attorney's fees as a sanction for bad-faith conduct. The award of attorney's fees "must be compensatory rather than punitive in

nature," and is thus limited to "those attorney's fees incurred because of the misconduct at issue."

CHAPTER FOUR: CASE MANAGEMENT, SETTLEMENT, AND ALTERNATIVE DISPUTE RESOLUTION

Page 218 (Note 6): The Supreme Court's *Campbell-Ewald* decision settled that a defendant's unaccepted full-satisfaction Rule 68 offer does not moot the plaintiff's individual claim, and the plaintiff can proceed to seek to be the group representative in a class or collective action. Numerous defendants have since turned to the alternative possibility mentioned — but not resolved — in the majority opinion, "whether the result would be different if a defendant deposits the full amount of the plaintiff's individual claim in an amount payable to the plaintiff, and the court then enters judgment for the plaintiff in that amount." So far, lower courts facing this situation have held, relying on language in the *Campbell-Ewald* opinion, that such plaintiffs must have a "fair opportunity to move for class certification." *See, e.g.*, Chen v. Allstate Ins. Co., 819 F.3d 1136, 1139 (9th Cir. 2016).

Page 233 (Note 2): The Court relied on *DirecTV* in *Kindred Nursing Centers v. Clark*, 581 U.S. —, 137 S. Ct. 1421 (2017). A Kentucky state court had held that a general power of attorney, one lacking specific authority to waive the principal's state constitutional rights to court access and jury trial, does not authorize the legal representative to enter into an arbitration agreement. The Supreme Court reversed, holding that "because the rule singles out arbitration agreements for disfavored treatment, . . . it violates the FAA." Only Justice Thomas dissented, on the ground that the FAA should not apply in state-court proceedings.

The Court relied on *Concepcion* and *Italian Colors* in rejecting an argument that the National Labor Relations Act's protection of workers' rights such as to bargain collectively "and to engage in other concerted activities for the purpose of . . . other mutual aid and protection," 29 U.S.C. § 157, invalidates waivers of class or collective proceedings in employment contracts with arbitration clauses. *See* Epic Systems Corp. v. Lewis, 584 U.S. —, 138 S. Ct. 1612 (2018). Employees who had signed contracts with such waiver provisions sought to bring collective federal-court actions for small individual claims of wage underpayment in violation of the federal Fair Labor Standards Act and analogous state laws. Justice Gorsuch's opinion for a five-Justice majority held that the NLRA should not be read to create an exception to the Federal Arbitration Act's general favoring of arbitration contracts' enforceability. Justice Ginsburg's dissent for herself and Justices Breyer, Sotomayor, and Kagan took a different view of the interpretation of the FAA and NLRA and cited the likely effects of the ruling, which means that employees' claims must be pursued in individual arbitrations rather than cost-effective class or collective actions, on enforcement of workers' rights. The majority replied, "The policy may be debatable but the law is

clear: Congress has instructed that arbitration agreements like those before us must be enforced as written."

CHAPTER FIVE: JUDGE AND JURY

Pages 246-47 (Note 4): The description of the statistics from the Eisenberg & Lanvers article was ambiguous. In the authors' study, summary-judgment motions were found to be successful in 5.0% to 10.9% of all of the cases filed in the three studied federal districts, not in 5.0% to 10.9% of the cases in which motions for summary judgment were filed. Put differently, a motion for summary judgment resolved between 5.0% and 10.9% of the total number of civil cases in the three districts.

Pages 247-48 (Note 6): Note that, as the Eleventh Circuit recently held, an affidavit "may preclude summary judgment even if it is self-serving and uncorroborated." U.S. v. Stein, 881 F.3d 853, 854 (11th Cir. 2018); *accord*, Payne v. Pauley, 337 F.3d 767, 772 (7th Cir. 2003).

CHAPTER SIX: APPEALS

Pages 314-15 (carryover paragraph): The quoted text from 28 U.S.C. § 1292(b) is missing one line. The correct quotation (with the missing text in bold) is: "a district judge, in making in a civil action an order not otherwise appealable under this section, shall be of opinion that such order involves a controlling question of law as to which there is substantial ground for difference of opinion and **that an immediate appeal from the order may materially advance the ultimate termination of the litigation, he shall so** state in writing in such order."

Page 315 (bullet item summarizing *Gelboim* case): The Supreme Court unanimously applied the *Gelboim* principle allowing immediate appeal to the slightly different context of cases consolidated under Rule 42(a) when one consolidated case goes to judgment, even though other consolidated cases remain pending. Hall v. Hall, 584 U.S. —, 138 S. Ct. 1118 (2018).

Page 318 (after first paragraph): The Supreme Court spoke generally to the standard of appellate review for trial courts' findings on mixed questions of law and fact in *U.S. Bank N.A. v. Village at Lakeridge, LLC*, 583 U.S. —, 138 S. Ct. 960 (2018), stating that the standard should differ depending on the type of appellate determination involved.

> Mixed questions are not all alike. . . . [S]ome require courts to expound on the law, particularly by amplifying on a broad legal standard. When that is so — when applying the law involves developing auxiliary legal principles of use in other cases — appellate courts should typically review a decision *de novo*. . . . But . . . other mixed questions immerse courts in case-specific factual issues—compelling them to marshal and weigh evidence, make credibility judgments, and otherwise address

> what we have . . . called "multifarious, fleeting, special, narrow facts that utterly resist generalization." And when that is so, appellate courts should usually review a decision with deference. . . . In short, the standard of review for a mixed question all depends — on whether answering it entails primarily legal or factual work.

Id. at 967.

CHAPTER SEVEN: JUDGMENTS

Page 329 (Note 2): Although not featured in general-media reporting on the case, possible claim preclusion played a significant role in the Supreme Court's June, 2016 abortion-rights decision, *Whole Woman's Health v. Hellerstedt*, 579 U.S. —, 136 S. Ct. 2292 (2016). Some providers had brought an earlier, pre-enforcement challenge to one provision of House Bill 2 (H.B. 2), adopted by the Texas Legislature in 2013. Two main provisions required doctors performing abortions to have admitting privileges at a hospital no more than 30 miles from the abortion facility (the "admitting-privileges requirement") and that the facility itself meet minimum state standards for ambulatory surgical centers (the "surgical-center requirement"). The Fifth Circuit upheld the challenged admitting-privileges requirement, and these plaintiffs did not seek Supreme Court review.

After the law took effect, another group of abortion providers, including some who had been plaintiffs in the prior litigation, brought a new challenge to both requirements. Justice Breyer's opinion for the Supreme Court held that claim preclusion did not bar the new challenge to the admitting-privileges requirement because changed circumstances once the law is enforced, showing the concreteness of the constitutional harms claimed, can give rise to a new claim. Nor did the rule against claim-splitting bar the challenge to the surgical-center requirement, because it is a distinct requirement giving rise to a distinct claim. Justice Alito's dissent, joined by Chief Justice Roberts and Justice Thomas, accused the majority of failing to be "scrupulously neutral" in applying regular preclusion rules.

Page 355 (after carryover paragraph): In *Janus v. American Federation of State, County, and Municipal Employees, Council 31*, 585 U.S. —, 2018 WL 3129785 (U.S. June 27, 2018), the Supreme Court overruled *Abood v. Detroit Bd. of Educ.*, 431 U.S. 209 (1977), which had permitted requiring non-union members to pay an "agency fee" to a union representing government workers for activities "germane" to the union's collective-bargaining activities, but not its political work The majority listed factors relevant to whether *stare decisis* should be observed: the quality of the prior decision's reasoning, its workability, subsequent legal and factual developments, and real-world reliance on the precedent.

CHAPTER EIGHT: JOINDER OF CLAIMS AND PARTIES

Page 403 (Note 4): In *Town of Chester v. Laroe Estates, Inc.*, 581 U.S. —, 137 S. Ct. 1645 (2017), the Supreme Court held that a plaintiff-intervenor must meet the Article III standing requirements if the intervenor seeks relief different from or beyond the relief sought by the plaintiff. As the Court said, "standing is not dispensed in gross," so "[f]or all relief sought, there must be a litigant with standing."

CHAPTER NINE: PERSONAL JURISDICTION AND VENUE

Pages 418-20 (Notes after *Pennoyer*): Professor Stephen Sachs has recently published an intriguing article suggesting that *Pennoyer* has been misunderstood, and that on the proper understanding it is entirely correct. Stephen E. Sachs, Pennoyer *Was Right*, 95 TEX. L. REV. 1249 (2017). He suggests that the Constitution (before the adoption of the Fourteenth Amendment) left questions of jurisdiction to "general law," about which state and federal courts could, and did, differ. Most of *Pennoyer*'s analysis was based on then-existing general law — that is, the customary principles followed by most courts domestically and internationally. The only thing the Fourteenth Amendment changed was that a judgment by a court lacking jurisdiction under the principles of general law was now void as a deprivation of liberty or property without due process, because it was issued by a court that had no authority to issue it. What the Fourteenth Amendment thus requires, according to Sachs, is "jurisdiction, full stop"; the Amendment didn't (and shouldn't be interpreted to) specify the rules determining whether jurisdiction actually exists.

Page 433 (Note 5): For an illustration of the limits on finding jurisdiction over a parent corporation based on the in-forum actions of the subsidiary, see *Williams v. Yamaha Motor Co.*, 851 F.3d 1015, 1021 (9th Cir. 2017): Parent and subsidiary corporations are"alter egos" of one another, and thus both subject to jurisdiction wherever either one has sufficient contacts, only if the plaintiff makes out a prima facie case "(1) that there is such unity of interest and ownership that the separate personalities of the two entities no longer exist and (2) that failure to disregard their separate identities would result in fraud or injustice." *See also* Anwar v. Dow Chem. Co., 876 F.3d 841 (6th Cir. 2017) (similar analysis).

Pages 447-48 (Note 1) & Page 466 (Note 6): Although *Insurance Corp.* rejected sovereignty as a basis for limits on personal jurisdiction, later cases seem to resurrect it. (In Note 6 on p. 466 of the Casebook, we point out how the plurality opinion in *J. McIntyre v. Nicastro* does so.) Notably, eight Justices recently joined an opinion containing a very strong endorsement of sovereignty as the primary underpinning of personal-jurisdiction doctrines:

> [T]he "primary concern" [in determining whether personal jurisdiction is present] is "the burden on the defendant." Assessing this burden obviously requires a court to consider the practical problems resulting

> from litigating in the forum, but it also encompasses the more abstract matter of submitting to the coercive power of a State that may have little legitimate interest in the claims in question. As we have put it, restrictions on personal jurisdiction "are more than a guarantee of immunity from inconvenient or distant litigation. They are a consequence of territorial limitations on the power of the respective States." "[T]he States retain many essential attributes of sovereignty, including, in particular, the sovereign power to try causes in their courts. The sovereignty of each State . . . implie[s] a limitation on the sovereignty of all its sister States." And at times, this federalism interest may be decisive. As we explained in *World–Wide Volkswagen,* "[e]ven if the defendant would suffer minimal or no inconvenience from being forced to litigate before the tribunals of another State; even if the forum State has a strong interest in applying its law to the controversy; even if the forum State is the most convenient location for litigation, the Due Process Clause, acting as an instrument of interstate federalism, may sometimes act to divest the State of its power to render a valid judgment."

Bristol-Myers Squibb Co. v. Superior Court, 582 U.S. —, 137 S. Ct. 1773, 1780-81 (2017) (*infra* p. 11). The *Bristol-Myers* Court did not mention *Insurance Corp. of Ireland.*

Page 473 (after Note 6): In *Bristol-Myers Squibb Co. v. Superior Court*, 582 U.S. —, 137 S. Ct. 1773 (2017) (*infra* p. 11), the Court weighed in on the required relationship between the claims and the contacts with the forum state. Numerous plaintiffs sued Bristol-Myers Squibb (BMS) in California state court for injuries caused by the BMS drug Plavix. Most of the plaintiffs were not California residents, had not bought Plavix in California, and had not suffered their injuries in California. The Court held that the fact that BMS also sold Plavix (and caused injuries) in California did not establish a sufficient connection between California and the non-California plaintiffs' claims. "What is needed — and what is lacking here — is a connection between the forum and the specific claims at issue." The California state courts therefore lacked specific personal jurisdiction over the non-Californians' claims. (Because BMS was not "at home" in California, there was no general personal jurisdiction either.)

Pages 484-85 (Notes after *Daimler*): The Court reaffirmed *Daimler*, reining in another state court, in *BNSF Ry. Co. v. Tyrrell*, 581 U.S. —, 137 S. Ct. 1549 (2017). That a railroad incorporated elsewhere and with its principal place of business elsewhere had some of its track and work force in Montana did not make it "at home" there for purposes of general personal jurisdiction over claims arising outside the state. The Court also made clear that the Due Process limit on state-court jurisdiction "does not vary with the type of claim asserted or business enterprise sued."

Page 504 (Note 4): For other cases following *Knowlton* and allowing personal jurisdiction on the basis of compliance with a state's registration statute, see *Kukich v. Electrolux Home Prods., Inc.*, 2017 WL 345856 (D. Md. 2017); *Bors v. Johnson & Johnson,* 208 F. Supp. 3d 648, 651-55 (E.D. Pa.

2016); *Mitchell v. Eli Lilly & Co.*, 159 F. Supp. 3d 967, 975-77 (E.D. Mo. 2016).

CHAPTER TEN: SUBJECT-MATTER JURISDICTION

Page 539 (Note 4): In *Lightfoot v. Cendant Mortgage Corp.*, 580 U.S. —, 137 S. Ct. 553 (2017), the Court held that not every sue-and-be-sued clause grants federal subject-matter jurisdiction. The case involved the Federal National Mortgage Association (Fannie Mae), whose federal charter authorizes it to be sue and be sued in "any court of competent jurisdiction." The Court interpreted this phrase, not present in the Red Cross's charter, as presuming an already-existing source of subject-matter jurisdiction.

Page 553 (Note 3): The Court recently reiterated that a finding of "insubstantiality" is not the same a finding of failure to state a claim for relief on the merits under *Ashcroft v. Iqbal* (Casebook p. 50) and *Bell Atlantic Corp. v. Twombly* (Casebook p. 39). Shapiro v. McManus, 577 U.S. —, 136 S. Ct. 450 (2015). The latter is "too demanding" a showing for jurisdictional purposes.

Page 586 (Note 7): The § 1367(c) discretion to decline supplemental discretion means that a court might dismiss a state claim even though it is within supplemental jurisdiction (for example, if all the federal claims have been dismissed). Presumably, the plaintiff can refile that claim in state court. But what happens if the statute of limitations has expired while the claim is pending in federal court? Section 1367(d) provides that the statute of limitations "shall be tolled" on a state claim brought in federal court under § 1367(a) "while the claim is pending and for a period of 30 days after it is dismissed." In *Artis v. District of Columbia*, 583 U.S. —, 138 S. Ct. 594 (2018), the Supreme Court interpreted this language to mean that the clock stops running entirely while the case is pending in federal court. Thus, if the federal case is filed with one year left on the statute of limitations, and the state claim is dismissed after the statute of limitations expires, the plaintiff has a year and 30 days to refile in state court.

CHAPTER TWELVE: CLASS ACTIONS

Page 660 (new paragraphs after the first full paragraph): The Supreme Court has promulgated amendments to Rules 23(b), -(e), and -(f). The most significant changes occur in Rule 23(e), which governs the settlement of class actions. The amendments specify the factors that a court must consider in determining whether to approve a class-action settlement and also require judicial approval of any payments made to objectors who agree to withdraw their objection or appeal. Unless Congress acts to halt the amendments, which seems unlikely, they will become effective on December 1, 2018. For the text of the amendments, see *infra* pp. 354-357.

There is also activity on the legislative front. A bill (entitled the Fairness in Class Action Litigation and Furthering Asbestos Claim Transparency Act of 2017) passed the House of Representatives on March 9, 2017. Among numerous changes to class actions and other devices often used in complex litigation, the bill requires that, in class actions seeking monetary relief, each class member suffer "the same type and scope of injury as the named class representative or representatives." The district court must make this determination when certifying a class, "based on a rigorous analysis of the evidence presented." *See* H.R. 985, 115th Cong. (2017). The bill's prospects in the Senate are uncertain.

Page 676 (Note 3): In *Jennings v. Rodriguez*, 583 U.S. —, 138 S. Ct. 830 (2018), the Court cited *Wal-Mart* to suggest another possible limit on the use of (b)(2) class actions. The principal dispute in *Jennings* was whether periodic bond hearings are required for immigrants detained for possible deportation. The Court's opinion, at times a plurality and at times a majority, held that the immigration provisions at issue gave no such right. That ruling opened up a new question: whether the Constitution provides such a right. The Court remanded the case, which had been filed as a class action on behalf of detainees, for consideration of this issue. At the very end of the majority opinion, the Court observed that the court of appeals should "consider whether a Rule 23(b)(2) class action continues to be the appropriate vehicle for respondents' claims in light of *Wal-Mart Stores, Inc. v. Dukes*." Because some class members could not successfully claim a constitutional right to a bond hearing, "it may no longer be true that the complained-of 'conduct is such that it can be enjoined or declared unlawful only as to all of the class members or as to none of them.' *Dukes*, 564 U.S. at 360." 138 S. Ct. at 851 (internal quotation marks omitted). The majority also questioned whether a (b)(2) class action could be maintained for the class members' claimed violation of due process because due process is flexible and requires procedural protections tailored to each particular situation.

Page 676 (Note 4): In *Microsoft Corp. v. Baker*, 582 U.S. —, 137 S. Ct. 1702 (2017), the Supreme Court rejected another device to obtain an immediate appeal of a district court's denial of class certification. In *Microsoft*, the court of appeals declined to permit a Rule 23(f) appeal when the district court denied class certification. The plaintiffs then voluntarily dismissed the case, and argued that this dismissal was a "final decision" under 28 U.S.C. § 1291 — thus allowing them to appeal the adverse class-certification decision. The Court unanimously rejected this maneuver. A majority of five Justices held that this tactic would vitiate the final-judgment rule and the limited exception in Rule 23(f). A concurrence of three Justices argued that the voluntary dismissal deprived the courts of Article III jurisdiction over the appeal because no case or controversy survived.

RECENT SUPREME COURT CASE

BRISTOL-MYERS SQUIBB CO. V. SUPERIOR COURT OF CALIFORNIA

582 U.S. —, 137 S. Ct. 1773 (2017)

■ JUSTICE ALITO delivered the opinion of the Court.

More than 600 plaintiffs, most of whom are not California residents, filed this civil action in a California state court against Bristol-Myers Squibb Company (BMS), asserting a variety of state-law claims based on injuries allegedly caused by a BMS drug called Plavix. The California Supreme Court held that the California courts have specific jurisdiction to entertain the nonresidents' claims. We now reverse.

I

A

BMS, a large pharmaceutical company, is incorporated in Delaware and headquartered in New York, and it maintains substantial operations in both New York and New Jersey. Over 50 percent of BMS's work force in the United States is employed in those two States.

BMS also engages in business activities in other jurisdictions, including California. Five of the company's research and laboratory facilities, which employ a total of around 160 employees, are located there. BMS also employs about 250 sales representatives in California and maintains a small state-government advocacy office in Sacramento.

One of the pharmaceuticals that BMS manufactures and sells is Plavix, a prescription drug that thins the blood and inhibits blood clotting. BMS did not develop Plavix in California, did not create a marketing strategy for Plavix in California, and did not manufacture, label, package, or work on the regulatory approval of the product in California. BMS instead engaged in all of these activities in either New York or New Jersey. But BMS does sell Plavix in California. Between 2006 and 2012, it sold almost 187 million Plavix pills in the State and took in more than $900 million from those sales. This amounts to a little over one percent of the company's nationwide sales revenue.

B

A group of plaintiffs — consisting of 86 California residents and 592 residents from 33 other States — filed eight separate complaints in California Superior Court, alleging that Plavix had damaged their health. All the complaints asserted 13 claims under California law, including products liability, negligent misrepresentation, and misleading advertising claims. The nonresident plaintiffs did not allege that they obtained Plavix through California physicians or from any other California source; nor did they claim that they were injured by Plavix or were treated for their injuries in California. . . . [The California Court of Appeal found] that the California courts had specific jurisdiction over the nonresidents' claims against BMS.

The California Supreme Court affirmed. The court unanimously agreed with the Court of Appeal [that general jurisdiction was lacking], but the court was divided on the question of specific jurisdiction. The majority applied a "sliding scale approach to specific jurisdiction." Under this approach, "the more wide ranging the defendant's forum contacts, the more readily is shown a connection between the forum contacts and the claim." Applying this test, the majority concluded that "BMS's extensive contacts with California" permitted the exercise of specific jurisdiction "based on a less direct connection between BMS's forum activities and plaintiffs' claims than might otherwise be required." This attenuated requirement was met, the majority found, because the claims of the nonresidents were similar in several ways to the claims of the California residents (as to which specific jurisdiction was uncontested). The court noted that "[b]oth the resident and nonresident plaintiffs' claims are based on the same allegedly defective product and the assertedly misleading marketing and promotion of that product. And while acknowledging that "there is no claim that Plavix itself was designed and developed in [BMS's California research facilities]," the court thought it significant that other research was done in the State.

Three justices dissented. "The claims of . . . nonresidents injured by their use of Plavix they purchased and used in other states," they wrote, "in no sense arise from BMS's marketing and sales of Plavix in California," and they found that the "mere similarity" of the residents' and nonresidents' claims was not enough. . . .

We granted certiorari to decide whether the California courts' exercise of jurisdiction in this case violates the Due Process Clause of the Fourteenth Amendment.

II

. . .

Since our seminal decision in *International Shoe* [Casebook, p. 420],our decisions have recognized two types of personal jurisdiction: "general" (sometimes called "all-purpose") jurisdiction and "specific" (sometimes called

"case-linked") jurisdiction. Goodyear [Dunlop Tires Operations, S.A. v. Brown, 564 U. S. 915, 919 (2011)]. . . .

. . . In order for a state court to exercise specific jurisdiction, "the *suit*" must "aris[e] out of or relat[e] to the defendant's contacts with the *forum*." In other words, there must be "an affiliation between the forum and the underlying controversy, principally, [an] activity or an occurrence that takes place in the forum State and is therefore subject to the State's regulation." *Id.* For this reason, "specific jurisdiction is confined to adjudication of issues deriving from, or connected with, the very controversy that establishes jurisdiction." *Id.* . . .

III

A

Our settled principles regarding specific jurisdiction control this case. In order for a court to exercise specific jurisdiction over a claim, there must be an "affiliation between the forum and the underlying controversy, principally, [an] activity or an occurrence that takes place in the forum State." *Id.* When there is no such connection, specific jurisdiction is lacking regardless of the extent of a defendant's unconnected activities in the State. *See id.* at 931 n.6 ("[E]ven regularly occurring sales of a product in a State do not justify the exercise of jurisdiction over a claim unrelated to those sales").

For this reason, the California Supreme Court's "sliding scale approach" is difficult to square with our precedents. Under the California approach, the strength of the requisite connection between the forum and the specific claims at issue is relaxed if the defendant has extensive forum contacts that are unrelated to those claims. Our cases provide no support for this approach, which resembles a loose and spurious form of general jurisdiction. For specific jurisdiction, a defendant's general connections with the forum are not enough. . . .

The present case illustrates the danger of the California approach. The State Supreme Court found that specific jurisdiction was present without identifying any adequate link between the State and the nonresidents' claims. As noted, the nonresidents were not prescribed Plavix in California, did not purchase Plavix in California, did not ingest Plavix in California, and were not injured by Plavix in California. The mere fact that *other* plaintiffs were prescribed, obtained, and ingested Plavix in California — and allegedly sustained the same injuries as did the nonresidents — does not allow the State to assert specific jurisdiction over the nonresidents' claims. As we have explained, "a defendant's relationship with a . . . third party, standing alone, is an insufficient basis for jurisdiction." Walden [v. Fiore, 571 U.S. 277 (2014)]. This remains true even when third parties (here, the plaintiffs who reside in California) can bring claims similar to those brought by the nonresidents. Nor is it sufficient — or even relevant — that BMS conducted research in California on matters unrelated to Plavix. What is

needed — and what is missing here — is a connection between the forum and the specific claims at issue. . . .

C

In a last ditch contention, respondents contend that BMS's "decision to contract with a California company [McKesson] to distribute [Plavix] nationally" provides a sufficient basis for personal jurisdiction. But as we have explained, "[t]he requirements of *International Shoe* . . . must be met as to each defendant over whom a state court exercises jurisdiction." In this case, it is not alleged that BMS engaged in relevant acts together with McKesson in California. Nor is it alleged that BMS is derivatively liable for McKesson's conduct in California. And the nonresidents "have adduced no evidence to show how or by whom the Plavix they took was distributed to the pharmacies that dispensed it to them." The bare fact that BMS contracted with a California distributor is not enough to establish personal jurisdiction in the State.

IV

Our straightforward application in this case of settled principles of personal jurisdiction will not result in the parade of horribles that respondents conjure up. Our decision does not prevent the California and out-of-state plaintiffs from joining together in a consolidated action in the States that have general jurisdiction over BMS. BMS concedes that such suits could be brought in either New York or Delaware. Alternatively, the plaintiffs who are residents of a particular State — for example, the 92 plaintiffs from Texas and the 71 from Ohio — could probably sue together in their home States. In addition, since our decision concerns the due process limits on the exercise of specific jurisdiction by a State, we leave open the question whether the Fifth Amendment imposes the same restrictions on the exercise of personal jurisdiction by a federal court. *See* Omni Capital Int'l, Ltd. v. Rudolf Wolff & Co., 484 U. S. 97, 102 n.5 (1987).

* * *

The judgment of the California Supreme Court is reversed, and the case is remanded for further proceedings not inconsistent with this opinion.

■ JUSTICE SOTOMAYOR, dissenting.

Three years ago, the Court imposed substantial curbs on the exercise of general jurisdiction in its decision in *Daimler AG v. Bauman*, 571 U. S. 117 (2014) [Casebook, p. 475]. Today, the Court takes its first step toward a similar contraction of specific jurisdiction by holding that a corporation that engages in a nationwide course of conduct cannot be held accountable in a state court by a group of injured people unless all of those people were injured in the forum State.

I fear the consequences of the Court's decision today will be substantial. The majority's rule will make it difficult to aggregate the claims of plaintiffs across the country whose claims may be worth little alone. It will make it impossible to bring a nationwide mass action in state court against defendants who are "at home" in different States. And it will result in piecemeal litigation and the bifurcation of claims. None of this is necessary. A core concern in this Court's personal jurisdiction cases is fairness. And there is nothing unfair about subjecting a massive corporation to suit in a State for a nationwide course of conduct that injures both forum residents and nonresidents alike. . . .

. . . Even absent a rigid requirement that a defendant's in-state conduct must actually cause a plaintiff's claim,[3] the upshot of today's opinion is that plaintiffs cannot join their claims together and sue a defendant in a State in which only some of them have been injured. That rule is likely to have consequences far beyond this case.

3. Bristol-Meyers urges such a rule upon us, but its adoption would have consequences far beyond those that follow from today's factbound opinion. Among other things, it might call into question whether even a plaintiff *injured* in a State by an item identical to those sold by a defendant in that State could avail himself of that State's courts to redress his injuries — a result specifically contemplated by *World-Wide Volkswagen Corp. v. Woodson*, 444 U.S. 286, 297 (1980) [Casebook, p. 439].

FEDERAL RULES OF CIVIL PROCEDURE FOR THE UNITED STATES DISTRICT COURTS

WITH

SELECTED ADVISORY COMMITTEE NOTES

I. SCOPE OF RULES; FORM OF ACTION 20
II. COMMENCING AN ACTION; SERVICE OF PROCESS, PLEADINGS, MOTIONS, AND ORDERS 21
III. PLEADINGS AND MOTIONS 48
IV. PARTIES 88
V. DISCLOSURES AND DISCOVERY 119
VI. TRIALS 193
VII. JUDGMENT 225
VIII. PROVISIONAL AND FINAL REMEDIES 240
IX. SPECIAL PROCEEDINGS 245
X. DISTRICT COURTS AND CLERKS: CONDUCTING BUSINESS; ISSUING ORDERS 252
XI. GENERAL PROVISIONS 254
SUPPLEMENTAL RULES FOR ADMIRALTY OR MARITIME CLAIMS AND ASSET FORFEITURE ACTIONS [OMITTED – ED.] 258

TITLE I. SCOPE OF RULES; FORM OF ACTION

Rule 1. Scope and Purpose 20
Rule 2. One Form of Action 20

TITLE II. COMMENCING AN ACTION; SERVICE OF PROCESS, PLEADINGS, MOTIONS, AND ORDERS

Rule 3. Commencing an Action 21
Rule 4. Summons 21
Rule 4.1. Serving Other Process 39
Rule 5. Serving and Filing Pleadings and Other Papers 39
Rule 5.1. Constitutional Challenge to a Statute — Notice, Certification, and Intervention 44
Rule 5.2. Privacy Protection for Filings Made with the Court 45
Rule 6. Computing and Extending Time; Time for Motion Papers 46

TITLE III. PLEADINGS AND MOTIONS

Rule 7. Pleadings Allowed; Form of Motions and Other Papers 48
Rule 7.1. Disclosure Statement 49
Rule 8. General Rules of Pleading 49
Rule 9. Pleading Special Matters 51
Rule 10. Form of Pleadings 53
Rule 11. Signing Pleadings, Motions, and Other Papers; Representations to the Court; Sanctions 53

Rule 12. Defenses and Objections: When and How Presented; Motion for Judgment on the Pleadings; Consolidating Motions; Waiving Defenses; Pretrial Hearing . . . 63
Rule 13. Counterclaim and Crossclaim . . . 67
Rule 14. Third-Party Practice . . . 69
Rule 15. Amended and Supplemental Pleadings . . . 70
Rule 16. Pretrial Conferences; Scheduling; Management . . . 74

TITLE IV. PARTIES

Rule 17. Plaintiff and Defendant; Capacity; Public Officers . . . 88
Rule 18. Joinder of Claims . . . 90
Rule 19. Required Joinder of Parties . . . 90
Rule 20. Permissive Joinder of Parties . . . 91
Rule 21. Misjoinder and Nonjoinder of Parties . . . 92
Rule 22. Interpleader . . . 92
Rule 23. Class Actions . . . 93
Rule 23.1. Derivative Actions . . . 116
Rule 23.2. Actions Relating to Unincorporated Associations . . . 117
Rule 24. Intervention . . . 117
Rule 25. Substitution of Parties . . . 118

TITLE V. DISCLOSURES AND DISCOVERY

Rule 26. Duty to Disclose; General Provisions Governing Discovery . . . 119
Rule 27. Depositions to Perpetuate Testimony . . . 155
Rule 28. Persons Before Whom Depositions May Be Taken . . . 157
Rule 29. Stipulations About Discovery Procedure . . . 158
Rule 30. Depositions by Oral Examination . . . 159
Rule 31. Depositions by Written Questions . . . 168
Rule 32. Using Depositions in Court Proceedings . . . 169
Rule 33. Interrogatories to Parties . . . 172
Rule 34. Producing Documents, Electronically Stored Information, and Tangible Things, or Entering onto Land, for Inspection and Other Purposes . . . 175
Rule 35. Physical and Mental Examinations . . . 180
Rule 36. Requests for Admission . . . 181
Rule 37. Failure to Make Disclosures or to Cooperate in Discovery; Sanctions . . . 183

TITLE VI. TRIALS

Rule 38. Right to a Jury Trial; Demand . . . 193
Rule 39. Trial by Jury or by the Court . . . 193
Rule 40. Scheduling Cases for Trial . . . 194
Rule 41. Dismissal of Actions . . . 194
Rule 42. Consolidation; Separate Trials . . . 195
Rule 43. Taking Testimony . . . 196
Rule 44. Proving an Official Record . . . 196
Rule 44.1. Determining Foreign Law . . . 197
Rule 45. Subpoena . . . 198
Rule 46. Objecting to a Ruling or Order . . . 208

Rule 47. Selecting Jurors 209
Rule 48. Number of Jurors; Verdict; Polling 209
Rule 49. Special Verdict; General Verdict and Questions 210
Rule 50. Judgment as a Matter of Law in a Jury Trial; Related Motion for a New Trial; Conditional Ruling 211
Rule 51. Instructions to the Jury; Objections; Preserving a Claim of Error 218
Rule 52. Findings and Conclusions by the Court; Judgment on Partial Findings 221
Rule 53. Masters 222

TITLE VII. JUDGMENT

Rule 54. Judgment; Costs 225
Rule 55. Default; Default Judgment 226
Rule 56. Summary Judgment 227
Rule 57. Declaratory Judgment 234
Rule 58. Entering Judgment 234
Rule 59. New Trial; Altering or Amending a Judgment 236
Rule 60. Relief from a Judgment or Order 236
Rule 61. Harmless Error 237
Rule 62. Stay of Proceedings to Enforce a Judgment 238
Rule 62.1. Indicative Ruling on a Motion for Relief That is Barred by a Pending Appeal 239
Rule 63. Judge's Inability to Proceed 239

TITLE VIII. PROVISIONAL AND FINAL REMEDIES

Rule 64. Seizing a Person or Property 240
Rule 65. Injunctions and Restraining Orders 240
Rule 65.1. Proceedings Against a Surety 242
Rule 66. Receivers 242
Rule 67. Deposit into Court 243
Rule 68. Offer of Judgment 243
Rule 69. Execution 244
Rule 70. Enforcing a Judgment for a Specific Act 244
Rule 71. Enforcing Relief for or Against a Nonparty 245

TITLE IX. SPECIAL PROCEEDINGS

Rule 71.1. Condemning Real or Personal Property 245
Rule 72. Magistrate Judges: Pretrial Order 250
Rule 73. Magistrate Judges: Trial by Consent; Appeal 251
Rule 74. [Abrogated] 252
Rule 75. [Abrogated] 252
Rule 76. [Abrogated] 252

TITLE X. DISTRICT COURTS AND CLERKS: CONDUCTING BUSINESS; ISSUING ORDERS

Rule 77. Conducting Business; Clerk's Authority; Notice of an Order or Judgment 252

Rule 78. Hearing Motions; Submission on Briefs 253
Rule 79. Records Kept by the Clerk 253
Rule 80. Stenographic Transcript as Evidence 254

TITLE XI. GENERAL PROVISIONS

Rule 81. Applicability of the Rules in General; Removed Actions 254
Rule 82. Jurisdiction and Venue Unaffected 257
Rule 83. Rules by District Courts; Judge's Directives 257
Rule 84. [Abrogated] 257
Rule 85. Title 258
Rule 86. Effective Dates 258

TITLE I. SCOPE OF RULES; FORM OF ACTION

Rule 1. Scope and Purpose

These rules govern the procedure in all civil actions and proceedings in the United States district courts, except as stated in Rule 81. They should be construed, administered, and employed by the court and the parties to secure the just, speedy, and inexpensive determination of every action and proceeding.

ADVISORY COMMITTEE NOTES

1993 Amendment

The purpose of this revision, adding the words "and administered" to the second sentence, is to recognize the affirmative duty of the court to exercise the authority conferred by these rules to ensure that civil litigation is resolved not only fairly, but also without undue cost or delay. As officers of the court, attorneys share this responsibility with the judge to whom the case is assigned.

2015 Amendment

Rule 1 is amended to emphasize that just as the court should construe and administer these rules to secure the just, speedy, and inexpensive determination of every action, so the parties share the responsibility to employ the rules in the same way. Most lawyers and parties cooperate to achieve these ends. But discussions of ways to improve the administration of civil justice regularly include pleas to discourage over-use, misuse, and abuse of procedural tools that increase cost and result in delay. Effective advocacy is consistent with — and indeed depends upon — cooperative and proportional use of procedure.

This amendment does not create a new or independent source of sanctions. Neither does it abridge the scope of any other of these rules.

Rule 2. One Form of Action

There is one form of action — the civil action.

TITLE II. COMMENCING AN ACTION; SERVICE OF PROCESS, PLEADINGS, MOTIONS, AND ORDERS

Rule 3. Commencing an Action

A civil action is commenced by filing a complaint with the court.

Rule 4. Summons

(a) Contents; Amendments.

(1) Contents. A summons must:

(A) name the court and the parties;

(B) be directed to the defendant;

(C) state the name and address of the plaintiff's attorney or — if unrepresented — of the plaintiff;

(D) state the time within which the defendant must appear and defend;

(E) notify the defendant that a failure to appear and defend will result in a default judgment against the defendant for the relief demanded in the complaint;

(F) be signed by the clerk; and

(G) bear the court's seal.

(2) *Amendments*. The court may permit a summons to be amended.

(b) Issuance. On or after filing the complaint, the plaintiff may present a summons to the clerk for signature and seal. If the summons is properly completed, the clerk must sign, seal, and issue it to the plaintiff for service on the defendant. A summons — or a copy of a summons that is addressed to multiple defendants — must be issued for each defendant to be served.

(c) Service.

(1) *In General*. A summons must be served with a copy of the complaint. The plaintiff is responsible for having the summons and complaint served within the time allowed by Rule 4(m) and must furnish the necessary copies to the person who makes service.

(2) *By Whom*. Any person who is at least 18 years old and not a party may serve a summons and complaint.

(3) *By a Marshal or Someone Specially Appointed*. At the plaintiff's request, the court may order that service be made by a

United States marshal or deputy marshal or by a person specially appointed by the court. The court must so order if the plaintiff is authorized to proceed in forma pauperis under 28 U.S.C. §1915 or as a seaman under 28 U.S.C. § 1916.

(d) Waiving Service.

(1) ***Requesting a Waiver***. An individual, corporation, or association that is subject to service under Rule 4(e), (f), or (h) has a duty to avoid unnecessary expenses of serving the summons. The plaintiff may notify such a defendant that an action has been commenced and request that the defendant waive service of a summons. The notice and request must:

(A) be in writing and be addressed:

(i) to the individual defendant; or

(ii) for a defendant subject to service under Rule 4(h), to an officer, a managing or general agent, or any other agent authorized by appointment or by law to receive service of process;

(B) name the court where the complaint was filed;

(C) be accompanied by a copy of the complaint, 2 copies of the waiver form appended to this Rule 4, and a prepaid means for returning the form;

(D) inform the defendant, using the form appended to this Rule 4, of the consequences of waiving and not waiving service;

(E) state the date when the request is sent;

(F) give the defendant a reasonable time of at least 30 days after the request was sent — or at least 60 days if sent to the defendant outside any judicial district of the United States — to return the waiver; and

(G) be sent by first-class mail or other reliable means.

(2) ***Failure to Waive***. If a defendant located within the United States fails, without good cause, to sign and return a waiver requested by a plaintiff located within the United States, the court must impose on the defendant:

(A) the expenses later incurred in making service; and

(B) the reasonable expenses, including attorney's fees, of any motion required to collect those service expenses.

(3) ***Time to Answer After a Waiver***. A defendant who, before being served with process, timely returns a waiver need not serve an answer to the complaint until 60 days after the request was sent — or

until 90 days after it was sent to the defendant outside any judicial district of the United States.

(4) ***Results of Filing a Waiver.*** When the plaintiff files a waiver, proof of service is not required and these rules apply as if a summons and complaint had been served at the time of filing the waiver.

(5) ***Jurisdiction and Venue Not Waived.*** Waiving service of a summons does not waive any objection to personal jurisdiction or to venue.

(e) Serving an Individual Within a Judicial District of the United States. Unless federal law provides otherwise, an individual — other than a minor, an incompetent person, or a person whose waiver has been filed — may be served in a judicial district of the United States by:

(1) following state law for serving a summons in an action brought in courts of general jurisdiction in the state where the district court is located or where service is made; or

(2) doing any of the following:

(A) delivering a copy of the summons and of the complaint to the individual personally;

(B) leaving a copy of each at the individual's dwelling or usual place of abode with someone of suitable age and discretion who resides there; or

(C) delivering a copy of each to an agent authorized by appointment or by law to receive service of process.

(f) Serving an Individual in a Foreign Country. Unless federal law provides otherwise, an individual — other than a minor, an incompetent person, or a person whose waiver has been filed — may be served at a place not within any judicial district of the United States:

(1) by any internationally agreed means of service that is reasonably calculated to give notice, such as those authorized by the Hague Convention on the Service Abroad of Judicial and Extrajudicial Documents;

(2) if there is no internationally agreed means, or if an international agreement allows but does not specify other means, by a method that is reasonably calculated to give notice:

(A) as prescribed by the foreign country's law for service in that country in an action in its courts of general jurisdiction;

(B) as the foreign authority directs in response to a letter rogatory or letter of request; or

(C) unless prohibited by the foreign country's law, by:

(i) delivering a copy of the summons and of the complaint to the individual personally; or

(ii) using any form of mail that the clerk addresses and sends to the individual and that requires a signed receipt; or

(3) by other means not prohibited by international agreement, as the court orders.

(g) Serving a Minor or an Incompetent Person. A minor or an incompetent person in a judicial district of the United States must be served by following state law for serving a summons or like process on such a defendant in an action brought in the courts of general jurisdiction of the state where service is made. A minor or an incompetent person who is not within any judicial district of the United States must be served in the manner prescribed by Rule 4(f)(2)(A), (f)(2)(B), or (f)(3).

(h) Serving a Corporation, Partnership, or Association. Unless federal law provides otherwise or the defendant's waiver has been filed, a domestic or foreign corporation, or a partnership or other unincorporated association that is subject to suit under a common name, must be served

(1) in a judicial district of the United States:

(A) in the manner prescribed by Rule 4(e)(1) for serving an individual; or

(B) by delivering a copy of the summons and of the complaint to an officer, a managing or general agent, or any other agent authorized by appointment or by law to receive service of process and — if the agent is one authorized by statute and the statute so requires — by also mailing a copy of each to the defendant; or

(2) at a place not within any judicial district of the United States, in any manner prescribed by Rule 4(f) for serving an individual, except personal delivery under (f)(2)(C)(i).

(i) Serving the United States and Its Agencies, Corporations, Officers, or Employees.

(1) ***United States***. To serve the United States, a party must:

(A) (i) deliver a copy of the summons and of the complaint to the United States attorney for the district where the action is brought — or to an assistant United States attorney or clerical employee whom the United States attorney designates in a writing filed with the court clerk — or

(ii) send a copy of each by registered or certified mail to the civil-process clerk at the United States attorney's office;

(B) send a copy of each by registered or certified mail to the Attorney General of the United States at Washington, D.C.; and

(C) if the action challenges an order of a nonparty agency or officer of the United States, send a copy of each by registered or certified mail to the agency or officer.

(2) ***Agency; Corporation; Officer or Employee Sued in an Official Capacity.*** To serve a United States agency or corporation, or a United States officer or employee sued only in an official capacity, a party must serve the United States and also send a copy of the summons and of the complaint by registered or certified mail to the agency, corporation, officer, or employee.

(3) ***Officer or Employee Sued Individually.*** To serve a United States officer or employee sued in an individual capacity for an act or omission occurring in connection with duties performed on the United States' behalf (whether or not the officer or employee is also sued in an official capacity), a party must serve the United States and also serve the officer or employee under Rule 4(e), (f), or (g).

(4) ***Extending Time.*** The court must allow a party a reasonable time to cure its failure to:

(A) serve a person required to be served under Rule 4(i)(2), if the party has served either the United States attorney or the Attorney General of the United States; or

(B) serve the United States under Rule 4(i)(3), if the party has served the United States officer or employee.

(j) Serving a Foreign, State, or Local Government.

(1) ***Foreign State.*** A foreign state or its political subdivision, agency, or instrumentality must be served in accordance with 28 U.S.C. § 1608.

(2) ***State or Local Government.*** A state, a municipal corporation, or any other state-created governmental organization that is subject to suit must be served by:

(A) delivering a copy of the summons and of the complaint to its chief executive officer; or

(B) serving a copy of each in the manner prescribed by that state's law for serving a summons or like process on such a defendant.

(k) Territorial Limits of Effective Service.

(1) ***In General.*** Serving a summons or filing a waiver of service establishes personal jurisdiction over a defendant:

(A) who is subject to the jurisdiction of a court of general jurisdiction in the state where the district court is located;

(B) who is a party joined under Rule 14 or 19 and is served within a judicial district of the United States and not more than 100 miles from where the summons was issued;

(C) when authorized by a federal statute.

(2) ***Federal Claim Outside State-Court Jurisdiction.*** For a claim that arises under federal law, serving a summons or filing a waiver of service establishes personal jurisdiction over a defendant if:

(A) the defendant is not subject to jurisdiction in any state's courts of general jurisdiction; and

(B) exercising jurisdiction is consistent with the United States Constitution and laws.

(*l*) Proving Service.

(1) ***Affidavit Required.*** Unless service is waived, proof of service must be made to the court. Except for service by a United States marshal or deputy marshal, proof must be by the server's affidavit.

(2) ***Service Outside the United States.*** Service not within any judicial district of the United States must be proved as follows:

(A) if made under Rule 4(f)(1), as provided in the applicable treaty or convention; or

(B) if made under Rule 4(f)(2) or (f)(3), by a receipt signed by the addressee, or by other evidence satisfying the court that the summons and complaint were delivered to the addressee.

(3) ***Validity of Service; Amending Proof.*** Failure to prove service does not affect the validity of service. The court may permit proof of service to be amended.

(m) Time Limit for Service. If a defendant is not served within 90 days after the complaint is filed, the court — on motion or on its own after notice to the plaintiff — must dismiss the action without prejudice against that defendant or order that service be made within a specified time. But if the plaintiff shows good cause for the failure, the court must extend the time for service for an appropriate period. This subdivision (m) does not apply to service in a foreign country under Rule 4(f), 4(h)(2), or 4(j)(1), or to service of a notice under Rule 71.1(d)(3)(A).

(n) Asserting Jurisdiction over Property or Assets.

(1) ***Federal Law.*** The court may assert jurisdiction over property if authorized by a federal statute. Notice to claimants of the property must be given as provided in the statute or by serving a summons under this rule.

(2) ***State Law***. On a showing that personal jurisdiction over a defendant cannot be obtained in the district where the action is brought by reasonable efforts to serve a summons under this rule, the court may assert jurisdiction over the defendant's assets found in the district. Jurisdiction is acquired by seizing the assets under the circumstances and in the manner provided by state law in that district.

Rule 4 Notice of a Lawsuit and Request to Waive Service of Summons.

(Caption)

To (*name the defendant or — if the defendant is a corporation, partnership, or association — name an officer or agent authorized to receive service*):

Why are you getting this?

A lawsuit has been filed against you, or the entity you represent, in this court under the number shown above. A copy of the complaint is attached.

This is not a summons, or an official notice from the court. It is a request that, to avoid expenses, you waive formal service of a summons by signing and returning the enclosed waiver. To avoid these expenses, you must return the signed waiver within (*give at least 30 days or at least 60 days if the defendant is outside any judicial district of the United States*) from the date shown below, which is the date this notice was sent. Two copies of the waiver form are enclosed, along with a stamped, self-addressed envelope or other prepaid means for returning one copy. You may keep the other copy.

What happens next?

If you return the signed waiver, I will file it with the court. The action will then proceed as if you had been served on the date the waiver is filed, but no summons will be served on you and you will have 60 days from the date this notice is sent (see the date below) to answer the complaint (or 90 days if this notice is sent to you outside any judicial district of the United States).

If you do not return the signed waiver within the time indicated, I will arrange to have the summons and complaint served on you. And I will ask the court to require you, or the entity you represent, to pay the expenses of making service.

Please read the enclosed statement about the duty to avoid unnecessary expenses.

I certify that this request is being sent to you on the date below.

Date: __________

____
(Signature of the attorney or unrepresented party)

____
(Printed name)

____
(Address)

____
(E-mail address)

____
(Telephone number)

Rule 4 Waiver of the Service of Summons.

(Caption)

To (*name the plaintiff's attorney or the unrepresented plaintiff*):

I have received your request to waive service of a summons in this action along with a copy of the complaint, two copies of this waiver form, and a prepaid means of returning one signed copy of the form to you.

I, or the entity I represent, agree to save the expense of serving a summons and complaint in this case.

I understand that I, or the entity I represent, will keep all defenses or objections to the lawsuit, the court's jurisdiction, and the venue of the action, but that I waive any objections to the absence of a summons or of service.

I also understand that I, or the entity I represent, must file and serve an answer or a motion under Rule 12 within 60 days from ____________________, the date when this request was sent (or 90 days if it was sent outside the United States). If I fail to do so, a default judgment will be entered against me or the entity I represent.

Date: __________

____
(Signature of the attorney or unrepresented party)

____
(Printed name)

____
(Address)

____
(E-mail address)

____

(Telephone number)

(Attach the following)

Duty to Avoid Unnecessary Expenses of Serving a Summons

Rule 4 of the Federal Rules of Civil Procedure requires certain defendants to cooperate in saving unnecessary expenses of serving a summons and complaint. A defendant who is located in the United States and who fails to return a signed waiver of service requested by a plaintiff located in the United States will be required to pay the expenses of service, unless the defendant shows good cause for the failure.

"Good cause" does not include a belief that the lawsuit is groundless, or that it has been brought in an improper venue, or that the court has no jurisdiction over this matter or over the defendant or the defendant's property.

If the waiver is signed and returned, you can still make these and all other defenses and objections, but you cannot object to the absence of a summons or of service.

If you waive service, then you must, within the time specified on the waiver form, serve an answer or a motion under Rule 12 on the plaintiff and file a copy with the court. By signing and returning the waiver form, you are allowed more time to respond than if a summons had been served.

ADVISORY COMMITTEE NOTES

1993 Amendment [citations omitted without notation — ED.]

. . .

Purposes of Revision. The general purpose of this revision is to facilitate the service of the summons and complaint. The revised rule explicitly authorizes a means for service of the summons and complaint on any defendant. While the methods of service so authorized always provide appropriate notice to persons against whom claims are made, effective service under this rule does not assure that personal jurisdiction has been established over the defendant served.

First, the revised rule authorizes the use of any means of service provided by the law not only of the forum state, but also of the state in which a defendant is served, unless the defendant is a minor or incompetent.

Second, the revised rule clarifies and enhances the cost-saving practice of securing the assent of the defendant to dispense with actual service of the summons and complaint. This practice was introduced to the rule in 1983 by an act of Congress authorizing "service-by-mail," a procedure that effects economic service with cooperation of the defendant. Defendants that magnify costs of service by requiring expensive service not necessary to achieve full notice of an action brought against them are required to bear the wasteful costs. This provision is made

available in actions against defendants who cannot be served in the districts in which the actions are brought.

Third, the revision reduces the hazard of commencing an action against the United States or its officers, agencies, and corporations. A party failing to effect service on all the offices of the United States as required by the rule is assured adequate time to cure defects in service.

Fourth, the revision calls attention to the important effect of the Hague Convention and other treaties bearing on service of documents in foreign countries and favors the use of internationally agreed means of service. In some respects, these treaties have facilitated service in foreign countries but are not fully known to the bar.

Finally, the revised rule extends the reach of federal courts to impose jurisdiction over the person of all defendant[s] against whom federal law claims are made and who can be constitutionally subjected to the jurisdiction of the courts of the United States. The present territorial limits on the effectiveness of service to subject a defendant to the jurisdiction of the court over the defendant's person are retained for all actions in which there is a state in which personal jurisdiction can be asserted consistently with state law and the Fourteenth Amendment. A new provision enables district courts to exercise jurisdiction, if permissible under the Constitution and not precluded by statute, when a federal claim is made against a defendant not subject to the jurisdiction of any single state.

The revised rule is reorganized to make its provisions more accessible to those not familiar with all of them. Additional subdivisions in this rule allow for more captions; several overlaps among subdivisions are eliminated; and several disconnected provisions are removed, to be relocated in a new Rule 4.1.

The Caption of the Rule. Prior to this revision, Rule 4 was entitled "Process" and applied to the service of not only the summons but also other process as well, although these are not covered by the revised rule. Service of process in eminent domain proceedings is governed by Rule 71A [now Rule 71.1 — ED.]. Service of a subpoena is governed by Rule 45, and service of papers such as orders, motions, notices, pleadings, and other documents is governed by Rule 5.

The revised rule is entitled "Summons" and applies only to that form of legal process. Unless service of the summons is waived, a summons must be served whenever a person is joined as a party against whom a claim is made. Those few provisions of the former rule which relate specifically to service of process other than a summons are relocated in Rule 4.1 in order to simplify the text of this rule.

Subdivision (a). Revised subdivision (a) contains most of the language of the former subdivision (b). The second sentence of the former subdivision (b) has been stricken, so that the federal court summons will be the same in all cases. Few states now employ, distinctive requirements of form for a summons and the applicability of such a requirement in federal court can only serve as a trap for an unwary party or attorney. A sentence is added to this subdivision authorizing an amendment of a summons. . . .

Subdivision (b). Revised subdivision (b) replaces the former subdivision (a). The revised text makes clear that the responsibility for filling in the summons falls on the plaintiff, not the clerk of the court. If there are multiple defendants, the

plaintiff may secure issuance of a summons for each defendant, or may serve copies of a single original bearing the names of multiple defendants if the addressee of the summons is effectively identified.

Subdivision (c). . . .

The 1983 revision of Rule 4 relieved the marshals' offices of much of the burden of serving the summons. Subdivision (c) eliminates the requirement for service by the marshal's office in actions in which the party seeking service is the United States. The United States, like other civil litigants, is now permitted to designate any person who is 18 years of age and not a party to serve its summons.

The court remains obligated to appoint a marshal, a deputy, or some other person to effect service of a summons in two classes of cases specified by statute: actions brought in forma pauperis or by a seaman. 28 U.S.C. §§ 1915, 1916. The court also retains discretion to appoint a process server on motion of a party. If a law enforcement presence appears to be necessary or advisable to keep the peace, the court should appoint a marshal or deputy or other official person to make the service. The Department of Justice may also call upon the Marshals Service to perform services in actions brought by the United States.

Subdivision (d). This text is new, but is substantially derived from the former subdivisions (c)(2)(C) and (D), added to the rule by Congress in 1983. The aims of the provision are to eliminate the costs of service of a summons on many parties and to foster cooperation among adversaries and counsel. The rule operates to impose upon the defendant those costs that could have been avoided if the defendant had cooperated reasonably in the manner prescribed. This device is useful in dealing with defendants who are furtive, who reside in places not easily reached by process servers, or who are outside the United States and can be served only at substantial and unnecessary expense. Illustratively, there is no useful purpose achieved by requiring a plaintiff to comply with all the formalities of service in a foreign country, including costs of translation, when suing a defendant manufacturer, fluent in English, whose products are widely distributed in the United States.

The former text described this process as service-by-mail. This language misled some plaintiffs into thinking that service could be effected by mail without the affirmative cooperation of the defendant. . . . It is more accurate to describe the communication sent to the defendant as a request for a waiver of formal service.

The request for waiver of service may be sent only to defendants subject to service under subdivision (e), (f), or (h). The United States is not expected to waive service for the reason that its mail receiving facilities are inadequate to assure that the notice is actually received by the correct person in the Department of Justice. The same principle is applied to agencies, corporations, and officers of the United States and to other governments and entities subject to service under subdivision (j). Moreover, there are policy reasons why governmental entities should not be confronted with the potential for bearing costs of service in cases in which they ultimately prevail. Infants or incompetent persons likewise are not called upon to waive service because, due to their presumed inability to understand the request and its consequences, they must generally be served through fiduciaries.

It was unclear whether the former rule authorized, mailing of a request for "acknowledgment of service" to defendants outside the forum state. See 1 R. Casad, Jurisdiction in Civil Actions (2d Ed.) 5-29, 30 (1991) and cases cited. But, as Professor Casad observed, there was no reason not to employ this device in an effort to obtain service outside the state, and there are many instances in which it was in fact so used, with respect both to defendants within the United States and to defendants in other countries.

The opportunity for waiver has distinct advantages to a foreign defendant. By waiving service, the defendant can reduce the costs that may ultimately be taxed against it if unsuccessful in the lawsuit, including the sometimes substantial expense of translation that may be wholly unnecessary for defendants fluent in English. Moreover, a foreign defendant that waives service is afforded substantially more time to defend against the action than if it had been formally served: under Rule 12, a defendant ordinarily has only 20 days after service in which to file its answer or raise objections by motion, but by signing a waiver it is allowed 90 days after the date the request for waiver was mailed in which to submit its defenses. Because of the additional time needed for mailing and the unreliability of some foreign mail services, a period of 60 days (rather than the 30 days required for domestic transmissions) is provided for a return of a waiver sent to a foreign country.

It is hoped that, since transmission of the notice and waiver forms is a private nonjudicial act, does not purport to effect service, and is not accompanied by any summons or directive from a court, use of the procedure will not offend foreign sovereignties, even those that have withheld their assent to formal service by mail or have objected to the "service-by-mail" provisions of the former rule. Unless the addressee consents, receipt of the request under the revised rule does not give rise to any obligation to answer the lawsuit, does not provide a basis for default judgment, and does not suspend the statute of limitations in those states where the period continues to run until service. Nor are there any adverse consequences to a foreign defendant, since the provisions for shifting the expense of service to a defendant that declines to waive service apply only if the plaintiff and defendant are both located in the United States.

With respect to a defendant located in a foreign country like the United Kingdom, which accepts documents in English, whose Central Authority acts promptly in effecting service, and whose policies discourage its residents from waiving formal service, there will be little reason for a plaintiff to send the notice and request under subdivision (d) rather than use convention methods. On the other hand, the procedure offers significant potential benefits to a plaintiff when suing a defendant that, though fluent in English, is located in a country where, as a condition to formal service under a convention, documents must be translated into another language or where formal service will be otherwise costly or time-consuming.

Paragraph (1) [now Rule 4(d)(5) — ED.] is explicit that a timely waiver of service of a summons does not prejudice the right of a defendant to object by means of a motion authorized by Rule 12(b)(2) to the absence of jurisdiction over the defendant's person, or to assert other defenses that may be available. The only

issues eliminated are those involving the sufficiency of the summons or the sufficiency of the method by which it is served.

Paragraph (2) [now Rule 4(d)(1) — ED.] states what the present rule implies: the defendant has a duty to avoid costs associated with the service of a summons not needed to inform the defendant regarding the commencement of an action. The text of the rule also sets forth the requirements for a Notice and Request for Waiver sufficient to put the cost-shifting provision in place. . . .

Paragraph (2)(A) [now Rule 4(d)(1)(A)(ii) — ED.] is explicit that a request for waiver of service by a corporate defendant must be addressed to a person qualified to receive service. The general mail rooms of large organizations cannot be required to identify the appropriate individual recipient for an institutional summons.

Paragraph (2)(B) [now Rule 4(d)(1)(G) — ED.] permits the use of alternatives to the United States mails in sending the Notice and Request. While private messenger services or electronic communications may be more expensive than the mail, they may be equally reliable and on occasion more convenient to the parties. Especially with respect to transmissions to foreign countries, alternative means may be desirable, for in some countries facsimile transmission is the most efficient and economical means of communication. If electronic means such as facsimile transmission are employed, the sender should maintain a record of the transmission to assure proof of transmission if receipt is denied, but a party receiving such a transmission has a duty to cooperate and cannot avoid liability for the resulting cost of formal service if the transmission is prevented at the point of receipt.

A defendant failing to comply with a request for waiver shall be given an opportunity to show good cause for the failure, but sufficient cause should be rare. It is not a good cause for failure to waive service that the claim is unjust or that the court lacks jurisdiction. Sufficient cause not to shift the cost of service would exist, however, if the defendant did not receive the request or was insufficiently literate in English to understand it. It should be noted that the provisions for shifting the cost of service apply only if the plaintiff and the defendant are both located in the United States, and accordingly a foreign defendant need not show "good cause" for its failure to waive service.

Paragraph (3) extends the time for answer if, before being served with process, the defendant waives formal service. The extension is intended to serve as an inducement to waive service and to assure that a defendant will not gain any delay be declining to waive service and thereby causing the additional time needed to effect service. By waiving service, a defendant is not called upon to respond to the complaint until 60 days from the date the notice was sent to it — 90 days if the notice was sent to a foreign country — rather than within the 20 day period from date of service specified in Rule 12.

Paragraph (4) clarifies the effective date of service when service is waived; the provision is needed to resolve an issue arising when applicable law requires service of process to toll the statute of limitations. Cf. Walker v. Armco Steel Corp., 446 U.S. 740 (1980).

The provisions in former subdivision (c)(2)(C)(ii) of this rule may have been misleading to some parties. Some plaintiffs, not reading the rule carefully, supposed that receipt by the defendant of the mailed complaint had the effect both of establishing the jurisdiction of the court over the defendant's person and of tolling the statute of limitations in actions in which service of the summons is required to toll the limitations period. The revised rule is clear that, if the waiver is not returned and filed, the limitations period under such a law is not tolled and the action will not otherwise proceed until formal service of process is effected.

Some state limitations laws may toll an otherwise applicable statute at the time when the defendant receives notice of the action. Nevertheless, the device of requested waiver of service is not suitable if a limitations period which is about to expire is not tolled by filing the action. Unless there is ample time, the plaintiff should proceed directly to the formal methods for service identified in subdivisions (e), (f), or (h).

The procedure of requesting waiver of service should also not be used if the time for service under subdivision (m) will expire before the date on which the waiver must be returned. While a plaintiff has been allowed additional time for service in that situation, the court could refuse a request for additional time unless the defendant appears to have evaded service pursuant to subdivision (e) or (h). It may be noted that the presumptive time limit for service under subdivision (m) does not apply to service in a foreign country.

Paragraph (5) [now Rule 4(d)(2) — ED.] is a cost-shifting provision retained from the former rule. The costs that may be imposed on the defendant could include, for example, the cost of the time of a process server required to make contact with a defendant residing in a guarded apartment house or residential development. The paragraph is explicit that the costs of enforcing the cost-shifting provision are themselves recoverable from a defendant who fails to return the waiver. In the absence of such a provision, the purpose of the rule would be frustrated by the cost of its enforcement, which is likely to be high in relation to the small benefit secured by the plaintiff.

Some plaintiffs may send a notice and request for waiver and, without waiting for return of the waiver, also proceed with efforts to effect formal service on the defendant. To discourage this practice, the cost-shifting provisions in paragraphs (2) and (5) [now Rules 4(d)(1)-(2) — ED.] are limited to costs of effecting service incurred after the time expires for the defendant to return the waiver. Moreover, by returning the waiver within the time allowed and before being served with process, a defendant receives the benefit of the longer period for responding to the complaint afforded for waivers under paragraph (3).

Subdivision (e). This subdivision replaces former subdivisions (c)(2)(C)(i) and (d)(1). It provides a means for service of summons on individuals within a judicial district of the United States. Together with subdivision (f), it provides for service on persons anywhere, subject to constitutional and statutory constraints.

Service of the summons under this subdivision does not conclusively establish the jurisdiction of the court over the person of the defendant. A defendant may assert the territorial limits of the court's reach set forth in subdivision (k), including the constitutional limitations that may be imposed by the Due Process Clause of the Fifth Amendment.

Paragraph (1) authorizes service in any judicial district in conformity with state law. This paragraph sets forth the language of former subdivision (c)(2)(C)(i), which authorized the use of the law of the state in which the district court sits, but adds as an alternative the use of the law of the state in which the service is effected.

Paragraph (2) retains the text of the former subdivision (d)(1) and authorizes the use of the familiar methods of personal or abode service or service on an authorized agent in any judicial district. . . .

Subdivision (f). This subdivision provides for service on individuals who are in a foreign country, replacing the former subdivision (i) that was added to Rule 4 in 1963. Reflecting the pattern of Rule 4 in incorporating state law limitations on the exercise of jurisdiction over persons, the former subdivision (i) limited service outside the United States to cases in which extraterritorial service was authorized by state or federal law. The new rule eliminates the requirement of explicit authorization. On occasion, service in a foreign country was held to be improper for lack of statutory authority. This authority, however, was found to exist by implication. Given the substantial increase in the number of international transactions and events that are the subject of litigation in federal courts, it is appropriate to infer a general legislative authority to effect service on defendants in a foreign country.

A secondary effect of this provision for foreign service of a federal summons is to facilitate the use of federal long-arm law in actions brought to enforce the federal law against defendants who cannot be served under any state law but who can be constitutionally subjected to the jurisdiction of the federal court. Such a provision is set forth in paragraph (2) of subdivision (k) of this rule, applicable only to persons not subject to the territorial jurisdiction of any particular state.

Paragraph (1) gives effect to the Hague Convention on the Service Abroad of Judicial and Extrajudicial Documents, which entered into force for the United States on February 10, 1969. See 28 U.S.C.A., Fed. R. Civ. P. 4 (Supp. 1986). This Convention is an important means of dealing with problems of service in a foreign country. Use of the Convention procedures, when available, is mandatory if documents must be transmitted abroad to effect service. . . . Therefore, this paragraph provides that, when service is to be effected outside a judicial district of the United States, the methods of service appropriate under an applicable treaty shall be employed if available and if the treaty so requires.

The Hague Convention furnishes safeguards against the abridgment of rights of parties through inadequate notice. Article 15 provides for verification of actual notice or a demonstration that process was served by a method prescribed by the internal laws of the foreign state before a default judgment may be entered. Article 16 of the Convention also enables the judge to extend the time for appeal after judgment if the defendant shows a lack of adequate notice either to defend or to appeal the judgment, or has disclosed a prima facie case on the merits.

The Hague Convention does not specify a time within which a foreign country's Central Authority must effect service, but Article 15 does provide that alternate methods may be used if a Central Authority does not respond within six months. Generally, a Central Authority can be expected to respond much more quickly than that limit might permit, but there have been occasions when the signatory state

was dilatory or refused to cooperate for substantive reasons. In such cases, resort may be had to the provision set forth in subdivision (f)(3). . . .

Paragraph (2) provides alternative methods for use when internationally agreed methods are not intended to be exclusive, or where there is no international agreement applicable. It contains most of the language formerly set forth in subdivision (i) of the rule. Service by methods that would violate foreign law is not generally authorized. Subparagraphs (A) and (B) prescribe the more appropriate methods for conforming to local practice or using a local authority. Subparagraph (C) prescribes other methods authorized by the former rule.

Paragraph (3) authorizes the court to approve other methods of service not prohibited by international agreements. The Hague Convention, for example, authorizes special forms of service in cases of urgency if convention methods will not permit service within the time required by the circumstances. Other circumstances that might justify the use of additional methods include the failure of the foreign country's Central Authority to effect service within the six-month period provided by the Convention, or the refusal of the Central Authority to serve a complaint seeking punitive damages or to enforce the antitrust laws of the United States. In such cases, the court may direct a special method of service not explicitly authorized by international agreement if not prohibited by the agreement. Inasmuch as our Constitution requires that reasonable notice be given, an earnest effort should be made to devise a method of communication that is consistent with due process and minimizes offense to foreign law. A court may in some instances specially authorize use of ordinary mail. Cf. Levin v. Ruby Trading Corp., 248 F. Supp. 537 (S.D.N.Y. 1965). . . .

Subdivision (i). This subdivision retains much of the text of former subdivisions (d)(4) and (d)(5). Paragraph (1) provides for service of a summons on the United States; it amends former subdivision (d)(4) to permit the United States attorney to be served by registered or certified mail. The rule does not authorize the use of the Notice and Request procedure of revised subdivision (d) when the United States is the defendant. To assure proper handling of mail in the United States attorney's office, the authorized mail service must be specifically addressed to the civil process clerk of the office of the United States attorney.

Paragraph (2) [now Rules 4(i)(2)-(3) — ED.] replaces former subdivision (d)(5). Paragraph (3) [now Rule 4(i)(4) — ED.] saves the plaintiff from the hazard of losing a substantive right because of failure to comply with the complex requirements of multiple service under this subdivision. That risk has proved to be more than nominal. This provision should be read in connection with the provisions of subdivision (c) of Rule 15 to preclude the loss of substantive rights against the United States or its agencies, corporations, or officers resulting from a plaintiff's failure to correctly identify and serve all the persons who should be named or served. . . .

Subdivision (k). This subdivision replaces the former subdivision (f), with no change in the title. Paragraph (1) retains the substance of the former rule in explicitly authorizing the exercise of personal jurisdiction over persons who can be reached under state long-arm law, the "100-mile bulge" provision added in 1963, or the federal interpleader act. Paragraph (1)(D) [now Rule 4(k)(1)(C) — ED.] is new, but merely calls attention to federal legislation that may provide for

nationwide or even world-wide service of process in cases arising under particular federal laws. Congress has provided for nationwide service of process and full exercise of territorial jurisdiction by all district courts with respect to specified federal actions.

Paragraph (2) is new. It authorizes the exercise of territorial jurisdiction over the person of any defendant against whom is made a claim arising under any federal law if that person is subject to personal jurisdiction in no state. This addition is a companion to the amendments made in revised subdivisions (e) and (f).

This paragraph corrects a gap in the enforcement of federal law. Under the former rule, a problem was presented when the defendant was a non-resident of the United States having contacts with the United States sufficient to justify the application of United States law and to satisfy federal standards of forum selection, but having insufficient contact with any single state to support jurisdiction under state long-arm legislation or meet the requirements of the Fourteenth Amendment limitation on state court territorial jurisdiction. In such cases, the defendant was shielded from the enforcement of federal law by the fortuity of a favorable limitation on the power of state courts, which was incorporated into the federal practice by the former rule. In this respect, the revision responds to the suggestion of the Supreme Court made in Omni Capital Int'l. v. Rudolf Wolff & Co., Ltd., 484 U.S. 97, 111 (1987).

There remain constitutional limitations on the exercise of territorial jurisdiction by federal courts over persons outside the United States. These restrictions arise from the Fifth Amendment rather than from the Fourteenth Amendment, which limits state-court reach and which was incorporated into federal practice by the reference to state law in the text of the former subdivision (e) that is deleted by this revision. The Fifth Amendment requires that any defendant have affiliating contacts with the United States sufficient to justify the exercise of personal jurisdiction over that party. There also may be a further Fifth Amendment constraint in that a plaintiff's forum selection might be so inconvenient to a defendant that it would be a denial of "fair play and substantial justice" required by the due process clause, even though the defendant had significant affiliating contacts with the United States. Compare World-Wide Volkswagen Corp. v. Woodson, 444 U.S. 286, 293-94 (1980); Insurance Corp. of Ireland v. Compagnie des Bauxites de Guinee, 456 U.S. 694, 702-03 (1982); Burger King Corp. v. Rudzewicz, 471 U.S. 462, 476-78 (1985); Asahi Metal Indus. v. Superior Court, 480 U.S. 102, 108-13 (1987).

This provision does not affect the operation of federal venue legislation. See generally 28 U.S.C. § 1391. Nor does it affect the operation of federal law providing for the change of venue. 28 U.S.C. §§ 1404, 1406. The availability of transfer for fairness and convenience under § 1404 should preclude most conflicts between the full exercise of territorial jurisdiction permitted by this rule and the Fifth Amendment requirement of "fair play and substantial justice."

The district court should be especially scrupulous to protect aliens who reside in a foreign country from forum selections so onerous that injustice could result. "[G]reat care and reserve should be exercised when extending our notions of personal jurisdiction into the international field." Asahi Metal Indus. v. Superior

Court, 480 U.S. 102, 115 (1987), quoting United States v. First Nat'l City Bank, 379 U.S. 378, 404 (1965) (Harlan, J., dissenting).

This narrow extension of the federal reach applies only if a claim is made against the defendant under federal law. It does not establish personal jurisdiction if the only claims are those arising under state law or the law of another country, even though there might be diversity or alienage subject matter jurisdiction as to such claims. If, however, personal jurisdiction is established under this paragraph with respect to a federal claim, then 28 U.S.C. § 1367(a) provides supplemental jurisdiction over related claims against that defendant, subject to the court's discretion to decline exercise of that jurisdiction under 28 U.S.C. § 1367(c).

Subdivision (*l*). This subdivision assembles in one place all the provisions of the present rule bearing on proof of service. No material change in the rule is effected. . . .

Subdivision (m). This subdivision retains much of the language of the present subdivision (j).

The new subdivision explicitly provides that the court shall allow additional time if there is good cause for the plaintiff's failure to effect service in the prescribed 120 [now 90 — ED.] days, and authorizes the court to relieve a plaintiff of the consequences of an application of this subdivision even if there is no good cause shown. Such relief formerly was afforded in some cases, partly in reliance on Rule 6(b). Relief may be justified, for example, if the applicable statute of limitations would bar the refiled action, or if the defendant is evading service or conceals a defect in attempted service. A specific instance of good cause is set forth in paragraph (3) [now Rule 4(i)(4) — ED.] of this rule, which provides for extensions if necessary to correct oversights in compliance with the requirements of multiple service in actions against the United States or its officers, agencies, and corporations. The district court should also take care to protect pro se plaintiffs from consequences of confusion or delay attending the resolution of an in forma pauperis petition. . . .

Subdivision (n). This subdivision provides for in rem and quasi-in-rem jurisdiction. Paragraph (1) incorporates any requirements of 28 U.S.C. § 1655 or similar provisions bearing on seizures or liens.

Paragraph (2) provides for other uses of quasi-in-rem jurisdiction but limits its use to exigent circumstances. Provisional remedies may be employed as a means to secure jurisdiction over the property of a defendant whose person is not within reach of the court, but occasions for the use of this provision should be rare, as where the defendant is a fugitive or assets are in imminent danger of disappearing. Until 1963, it was not possible under Rule 4 to assert jurisdiction in a federal court over the property of a defendant not personally served. The 1963 amendment to subdivision (e) authorized the use of state law procedures authorizing seizures of assets as a basis for jurisdiction. Given the liberal availability of long-arm jurisdiction, the exercise of power quasi-in-rem has become almost an anachronism. Circumstances too spare to affiliate the defendant to the forum state sufficiently to support long-arm jurisdiction over the defendant's person are also inadequate to support seizure of the defendant's assets fortuitously found within the state. Shaffer v. Heitner, 433 U.S. 186 (1977).

2015 Amendment

Subdivision (m). The presumptive time limit for serving a defendant is reduced from 120 to 90 days. This change, together with the shortened times for issuing a scheduling order set by amended Rule 16(b)(2), will reduce delay at the beginning of litigation. . . .

Rule 4.1. Serving Other Process

(a) In General. Process — other than a summons under Rule 4 or a subpoena under Rule 45 — must be served by a United States marshal or deputy marshal or by a person specially appointed for that purpose. It may be served anywhere within the territorial limits of the state where the district court is located and, if authorized by a federal statute, beyond those limits. Proof of service must be made under Rule 4(*l*).

(b) Enforcing Orders: Committing for Civil Contempt. An order committing a person for civil contempt of a decree or injunction issued to enforce federal law may be served and enforced in any district. Any other order in a civil-contempt proceeding may be served only in the state where the issuing court is located or elsewhere in the United States within 100 miles from where the order was issued.

Rule 5. Serving and Filing Pleadings and Other Papers

(a) Service: When Required.

(1) ***In General.*** Unless these rules provide otherwise, each of the following papers must be served on every party:

(A) an order stating that service is required;

(B) a pleading filed after the original complaint, unless the court orders otherwise under Rule 5(c) because there are numerous defendants;

(C) a discovery paper required to be served on a party, unless the court orders otherwise;

(D) a written motion, except one that may be heard ex parte; and

(E) a written notice, appearance, demand, or offer of judgment, or any similar paper.

(2) ***If a Party Fails to Appear.*** No service is required on a party who is in default for failing to appear. But a pleading that asserts a new claim for relief against such a party must be served on that party under Rule 4.

(3) ***Seizing Property***. If an action is begun by seizing property and no person is or need be named as a defendant, any service required before the filing of an appearance, answer, or claim must be made on the person who had custody or possession of the property when it was seized.

(b) Service: How Made.

(1) ***Serving an Attorney***. If a party is represented by an attorney, service under this rule must be made on the attorney unless the court orders service on the party.

(2) ***Service in General***. A paper is served under this rule by:

(A) handing it to the person;

(B) leaving it:

(i) at the person's office with a clerk or other person in charge or, if no one is in charge, in a conspicuous place in the office; or

(ii) if the person has no office or the office is closed, at the person's dwelling or usual place of abode with someone of suitable age and discretion who resides there;

(C) mailing it to the person's last known address — in which event service is complete upon mailing;

(D) leaving it with the court clerk if the person has no known address;

(E) sending it by electronic means if the person consented in writing — in which event service is complete upon transmission, but is not effective if the serving party learns that it did not reach the person to be served; or

(F) delivering it by any other means that the person consented to in writing — in which event service is complete when the person making service delivers it to the agency designated to make delivery.

(3) ***Using Court Facilities***. If a local rule so authorizes, a party may use the court's transmission facilities to make service under Rule 5(b)(2)(E).

(c) Serving Numerous Defendants.

(1) ***In General***. If an action involves an unusually large number of defendants, the court may, on motion or on its own, order that:

(A) defendants' pleadings and replies to them need not be served on other defendants;

(B) any crossclaim, counterclaim, avoidance, or affirmative defense in those pleadings and replies to them will be treated as denied or avoided by all other parties; and

(C) filing any such pleading and serving it on the plaintiff constitutes notice of the pleading to all parties.

(2) ***Notifying Parties.*** A copy of every such order must be served on the parties as the court directs.

(d) Filing.

(1) ***Required Filings; Certificate of Service.*** Any paper after the complaint that is required to be served — together with a certificate of service — must be filed within a reasonable time after service. But disclosures under Rule 26(a)(1) or (2) and the following discovery requests and responses must not be filed until they are used in the proceeding or the court orders filing: depositions, interrogatories, requests for documents or tangible things or to permit entry onto land, and requests for admission.

(2) ***How Filing Is Made — In General.*** A paper is filed by delivering it:

(A) to the clerk; or

(B) to a judge who agrees to accept it for filing, and who must then note the filing date on the paper and promptly send it to the clerk.

(3) ***Electronic Filing, Signing, or Verification.*** A court may, by local rule, allow papers to be filed, signed, or verified by electronic means that are consistent with any technical standards established by the Judicial Conference of the United States. A local rule may require electronic filing only if reasonable exceptions are allowed. A paper filed electronically in compliance with a local rule is a written paper for purposes of these rules.

(4) ***Acceptance by the Clerk.*** The clerk must not refuse to file a paper solely because it is not in the form prescribed by these rules or by a local rule or practice.

ADVISORY COMMITTEE NOTES

2000 Amendment

Subdivision (d). Rule 5(d) is amended to provide that disclosures under Rule 26(a)(1) and (2), and discovery requests and responses under Rules 30, 31, 33, 34, and 36 must not be filed until they are used in the action. "Discovery requests" includes deposition notices and "discovery responses" includes objections. The rule supersedes and invalidates local rules that forbid, permit, or require filing of these materials before they are used in the action. The former Rule 26(a)(4) requirement

that disclosures under Rule 26(a)(1) and (2) be filed has been removed. Disclosures under Rule 26(a)(3), however, must be promptly filed as provided in Rule 26(a)(3). Filings in connection with Rule 35 examinations, which involve a motion proceeding when the parties do not agree, are unaffected by these amendments.

Recognizing the costs imposed on parties and courts by required filing of discovery materials that are never used in an action, Rule 5(d) was amended in 1980 to authorize court orders that excuse filing. Since then, many districts have adopted local rules that excuse or forbid filing. In 1989 the Judicial Conference Local Rules Project concluded that these local rules were inconsistent with Rule 5(d), but urged the Advisory Committee to consider amending the rule. . . . The reality of nonfiling reflected in these local rules has even been assumed in drafting the national rules. In 1993, Rule 30(f)(1) was amended to direct that the officer presiding at a deposition file it with the court or send it to the attorney who arranged for the transcript or recording. The Committee Note explained that this alternative to filing was designed for "courts which direct that depositions not be automatically filed." Rule 30(f)(1) has been amended to conform to this change in Rule 5(d).

Although this amendment is based on widespread experience with local rules, and confirms the results directed by these local rules, it is designed to supersede and invalidate local rules. There is no apparent reason to have different filing rules in different districts. . . .

The amended rule provides that discovery materials and disclosures under Rule 26(a)(1) and (a)(2) must not be filed until they are "used in the proceeding." This phrase is meant to refer to proceedings in court. This filing requirement is not triggered by "use" of discovery materials in other discovery activities, such as depositions. In connection with proceedings in court, however, the rule is to be interpreted broadly; any use of discovery materials in court in connection with a motion, a pretrial conference under Rule 16, or otherwise, should be interpreted as use in the proceeding.

Once discovery or disclosure materials are used in the proceeding, the filing requirements of Rule 5(d) should apply to them. But because the filing requirement applies only with regard to materials that are used, only those parts of voluminous materials that are actually used need be filed. Any party would be free to file other pertinent portions of materials that are so used. *See* Fed. R. Evid. 106; *cf.* Rule 32(a)(4). If the parties are unduly sparing in their submissions, the court may order further filings. By local rule, a court could provide appropriate direction regarding the filing of discovery materials, such as depositions, that are used in proceedings. . . .

2001 Amendment

. . .

Subparagraph (D) of Rule 5(b)(2) [now Rule 5(b)(2)(E) — ED.] is new. It authorizes service by electronic means or any other means, but only if consent is obtained from the person served. The consent must be express, and cannot be implied from conduct. Early experience with electronic filing as authorized by Rule 5(d) is positive, supporting service by electronic means as well. Consent is required, however, because it is not yet possible to assume universal entry into the world of

electronic communication. Subparagraph (D) [now Rule 5(b)(2)(F) — ED.] also authorizes service by nonelectronic means. The Rule 5(b)(2)(B) [now Rule 5(b)(2)(C) — ED.] provision making mail service complete on mailing is extended in subparagraph (D) [now Rule 5(b)(2)(E) — ED.] to make service by electronic means complete on transmission; transmission is effected when the sender does the last act that must be performed by the sender. Service by other agencies is complete on delivery to the designated agency.

Finally, subparagraph (D) [now Rule 5(d)(3) — ED.] authorizes adoption of local rules providing for service through the court. Electronic case filing systems will come to include the capacity to make service by using the court's facilities to transmit all documents filed in the case. It may prove most efficient to establish an environment in which a party can file with the court, making use of the court's transmission facilities to serve the filed paper on all other parties. Transmission might be by such means as direct transmission of the paper, or by transmission of a notice of filing that includes an electronic link for direct access to the paper. Because service is under subparagraph (D) [now Rules 5(b)(2)(E)-(F) — ED.], consent must be obtained from the persons served.

Consent to service under Rule 5(b)(2)(D) [now Rules 5(b)(2)(E)-(F) — ED.] must be in writing, which can be provided by electronic means. Parties are encouraged to specify the scope and duration of the consent. The specification should include at least the persons to whom service should be made, the appropriate address or location for such service — such as the e-mail address or facsimile machine number, and the format to be used for attachments. A district court may establish a registry or other facility that allows advance consent to service by specified means for future actions.

Rule 6(e) [now Rule 6(d) — ED.] is amended to allow additional time to respond when service is made under Rule 5(b)(2)(D) [now Rules 5(b)(2)(E)-(F) — ED.]. The additional time does not relieve a party who consents to service under Rule 5(b)(2)(D) [now Rules 5(b)(2)(E)-(F) — ED.] of the responsibilities to monitor the facility designated for receiving service and to provide prompt notice of any address change.

Paragraph (3) [now Rule 5(b)(2)(D) — ED.] addresses a question that may arise from a literal reading of the provision that service by electronic means is complete on transmission. Electronic communication is rapidly improving, but lawyers report continuing failures of transmission, particularly with respect to attachments. Ordinarily the risk of non-receipt falls on the person being served, who has consented to this form of service. But the risk should not extend to situations in which the person attempting service learns that the attempted service in fact did not reach the person to be served. Given actual knowledge that the attempt failed, service is not effected. The person attempting service must either try again or show circumstances that justify dispensing with service.

Paragraph (3) [now Rule 5(b)(2)(D) — ED.] does not address the similar questions that may arise when a person attempting service learns that service by means other than electronic means in fact did not reach the person to be served. Case law provides few illustrations of circumstances in which a person attempting service actually knows that the attempt failed but seeks to act as if service had been made. This negative history suggests there is no need to address these

problems . . . . This silence does not imply any view on these issues, nor on the circumstances that justify various forms of judicial action even though service has not been made.

2006 Amendment

Amended Rule 5(e) [now Rule 5(d)(3) — ED.] acknowledges that many courts have required electronic filing by means of a standing order, procedures manual, or local rule. These local practices reflect the advantages that courts and most litigants realize from electronic filing. Courts that mandate electronic filing recognize the need to make exceptions when requiring electronic filing imposes a hardship on a party. Under amended Rule 5(e) [now Rule 5(d)(3) — ED.], a local rule that requires electronic filing must include reasonable exceptions, but Rule 5(e) [now Rule 5(d)(3) — ED.] does not define the scope of those exceptions. Experience with the local rules that have been adopted and that will emerge will aid in drafting new local rules and will facilitate gradual convergence on uniform exceptions, whether in local rules or in an amended Rule 5(e) [now Rule 5(d)(3) — ED.].

2007 Amendment

. . .

Rule 5(d)(2)(B) provides that "a" judge may accept a paper for filing, replacing the reference in former Rule 5(e) to "the" judge. Some courts do not assign a designated judge to each case, and it may be important to have another judge accept a paper for filing even when a case is on the individual docket of a particular judge. . . .

Rule 5.1. Constitutional Challenge to a Statute — Notice, Certification, and Intervention

(a) Notice by a Party. A party that files a pleading, written motion, or other paper drawing into question the constitutionality of a federal or state statute must promptly:

(1) file a notice of constitutional question stating the question and identifying the paper that raises it, if:

(A) a federal statute is questioned and the parties do not include the United States, one of its agencies, or one of its officers or employees in an official capacity; or

(B) a state statute is questioned and the parties do not include the state, one of its agencies, or one of its officers or employees in an official capacity; and

(2) serve the notice and paper on the Attorney General of the United States if a federal statute is questioned — or on the state attorney general if a state statute is questioned — either by certified or registered mail or by sending it to an electronic address designated by the attorney general for this purpose.

(b) Certification by the Court. The court must, under 28 U.S.C. § 2403, certify to the appropriate attorney general that a statute has been questioned.

(c) Intervention; Final Decision on the Merits. Unless the court sets a later time, the attorney general may intervene within 60 days after the notice is filed or after the court certifies the challenge, whichever is earlier. Before the time to intervene expires, the court may reject the constitutional challenge, but may not enter a final judgment holding the statute unconstitutional.

(d) No Forfeiture. A party's failure to file and serve the notice, or the court's failure to certify, does not forfeit a constitutional claim or defense that is otherwise timely asserted.

Rule 5.2. Privacy Protection for Filings Made with the Court

(a) Redacted Filings. Unless the court orders otherwise, in an electronic or paper filing with the court that contains an individual's social-security number, taxpayer-identification number, or birth date, the name of an individual known to be a minor, or a financial-account number, a party or nonparty making the filing may include only:

(1) the last four digits of the social-security number and taxpayer-identification number;

(2) the year of the individual's birth;

(3) the minor's initials; and

(4) the last four digits of the financial-account number.

(b) Exemptions from the Redaction Requirement. The redaction requirement does not apply to the following:

(1) a financial-account number that identifies the property allegedly subject to forfeiture in a forfeiture proceeding;

(2) the record of an administrative or agency proceeding;

(3) the official record of a state-court proceeding;

(4) the record of a court or tribunal, if that record was not subject to the redaction requirement when originally filed;

(5) a filing covered by Rule 5.2(c) or (d); and

(6) a pro se filing in an action brought under 28 U.S.C. §§ 2241, 2254, or 2255.

(c) Limitations on Remote Access to Electronic Files; Social-Security Appeals and Immigration Cases. Unless the court orders otherwise, in an action for benefits under the Social Security Act,

and in an action or proceeding relating to an order of removal, to relief from removal, or to immigration benefits or detention, access to an electronic file is authorized as follows:

(1) the parties and their attorneys may have remote electronic access to any part of the case file, including the administrative record;

(2) any other person may have electronic access to the full record at the courthouse, but may have remote electronic access only to:

(A) the docket maintained by the court; and

(B) an opinion, order, judgment, or other disposition of the court, but not any other part of the case file or the administrative record.

(d) Filings Made Under Seal. The court may order that a filing be made under seal without redaction. The court may later unseal the filing or order the person who made the filing to file a redacted version for the public record.

(e) Protective Orders. For good cause, the court may by order in a case:

(1) require redaction of additional information; or

(2) limit or prohibit a nonparty's remote electronic access to a document filed with the court.

(f) Option for Additional Unredacted Filing Under Seal. A person making a redacted filing may also file an unredacted copy under seal. The court must retain the unredacted copy as part of the record.

(g) Option for Filing a Reference List. A filing that contains redacted information may be filed together with a reference list that identifies each item of redacted information and specifies an appropriate identifier that uniquely corresponds to each item listed. The list must be filed under seal and may be amended as of right. Any reference in the case to a listed identifier will be construed to refer to the corresponding item of information.

(h) Waiver of Protection of Identifiers. A person waives the protection of Rule 5.2(a) as to the person's own information by filing it without redaction and not under seal.

Rule 6. Computing and Extending Time; Time for Motion Papers

(a) Computing Time. The following rules apply in computing any time period specified in these rules, in any local rule or court order, or in any statute that does not specify a method of computing time.

(1) ***Period Stated in Days or a Longer Unit.*** When the period is stated in days or a longer unit of time:

(A) exclude the day of the event that triggers the period;

(B) count every day, including intermediate Saturdays, Sundays, and legal holidays; and

(C) include the last day of the period, but if the last day is a Saturday, Sunday, or legal holiday, the period continues to run until the end of the next day that is not a Saturday, Sunday, or legal holiday.

(2) ***Period Stated in Hours.*** When the period is stated in hours:

(A) begin counting immediately on the occurrence of the event that triggers the period;

(B) count every hour, including hours during intermediate Saturdays, Sundays, and legal holidays; and

(C) if the period would end on a Saturday, Sunday, or legal holiday, the period continues to run until the same time on the next day that is not a Saturday, Sunday, or legal holiday.

(3) ***Inaccessibility of the Clerk's Office.*** Unless the court orders otherwise, if the clerk's office is inaccessible:

(A) on the last day for filing under Rule 6(a)(1), then the time for filing is extended to the first accessible day that is not a Saturday, Sunday, or legal holiday; or

(B) during the last hour for filing under Rule 6(a)(2), then the time for filing is extended to the same time on the first accessible day that is not a Saturday, Sunday, or legal holiday.

(4) ***"Last Day" Defined.*** Unless a different time is set by a statute, local rule, or court order, the last day ends:

(A) for electronic filing, at midnight in the court's time zone; and

(B) for filing by other means, when the clerk's office is scheduled to close.

(5) ***"Next Day" Defined.*** The "next day" is determined by continuing to count forward when the period is measured after an event and backward when measured before an event.

(6) ***"Legal Holiday" Defined.*** "Legal holiday" means:

(A) the day set aside by statute for observing New Year's Day, Martin Luther King Jr.'s Birthday, Washington's Birthday, Memorial Day, Independence Day, Labor Day, Columbus Day, Veterans' Day, Thanksgiving Day, or Christmas Day;

(B) any day declared a holiday by the President or Congress; and

(C) for periods that are measured after an event, any other day declared a holiday by the state where the district court is located.

(b) Extending Time.

(1) ***In General.*** When an act may or must be done within a specified time, the court may, for good cause, extend the time:

(A) with or without motion or notice if the court acts, or if a request is made, before the original time or its extension expires; or

(B) on motion made after the time has expired if the party failed to act because of excusable neglect.

2) ***Exceptions.*** A court must not extend the time to act under Rules 50(b) and (d), 52(b), 59(b), (d), and (e), and 60(b).

(c) Motions, Notices of Hearing, and Affidavits.

(1) ***In General.*** A written motion and notice of the hearing must be served at least 14 days before the time specified for the hearing, with the following exceptions:

(A) when the motion may be heard ex parte;

(B) when these rules set a different time; or

(C) when a court order — which a party may, for good cause, apply for ex parte — sets a different time.

(2) ***Supporting Affidavit.*** Any affidavit supporting a motion must be served with the motion. Except as Rule 59(c) provides otherwise, any opposing affidavit must be served at least 7 days before the hearing, unless the court permits service at another time.

(d) Additional Time After Certain Kinds of Service. When a party may or must act within a specified time after being served and service is made under Rule 5(b)(2)(C) (mail), (D) (leaving with the clerk), or (F) (other means consented to), 3 days are added after the period would otherwise expire under Rule 6(a).

TITLE III. PLEADINGS AND MOTIONS

Rule 7. Pleadings Allowed; Form of Motions and Other Papers

(a) Pleadings. Only these pleadings are allowed:

(1) a complaint;

(2) an answer to a complaint;

(3) an answer to a counterclaim designated as a counterclaim;

(4) an answer to a crossclaim;

(5) a third-party complaint;

(6) an answer to a third-party complaint; and

(7) if the court orders one, a reply to an answer.

(b) Motions and Other Papers.

(1) ***In General.*** A request for a court order must be made by motion. The motion must:

(A) be in writing unless made during a hearing or trial;

(B) state with particularity the grounds for seeking the order; and

(C) state the relief sought.

(2) ***Form.*** The rules governing captions and other matters of form in pleadings apply to motions and other papers.

Rule 7.1. Disclosure Statement

(a) Who Must File; Contents. A nongovernmental corporate party must file two copies of a disclosure statement that:

(1) identifies any parent corporation and any publicly held corporation owning 10% or more of its stock; or

(2) states that there is no such corporation.

(b) Time to File; Supplemental Filing. A party must:

(1) file the disclosure statement with its first appearance, pleading, petition, motion, response, or other request addressed to the court; and

(2) promptly file a supplemental statement if any required information changes.

Rule 8. General Rules of Pleading

(a) Claim for Relief. A pleading that states a claim for relief must contain:

(1) a short and plain statement of the grounds for the court's jurisdiction, unless the court already has jurisdiction and the claim needs no new jurisdictional support;

(2) a short and plain statement of the claim showing that the pleader is entitled to relief; and

(3) a demand for the relief sought, which may include relief in the alternative or different types of relief.

(b) Defenses; Admissions and Denials.

(1) ***In General.*** In responding to a pleading, a party must:

(A) state in short and plain terms its defenses to each claim asserted against it; and

(B) admit or deny the allegations asserted against it by an opposing party.

(2) ***Denials — Responding to the Substance.*** A denial must fairly respond to the substance of the allegation.

(3) ***General and Specific Denials.*** A party that intends in good faith to deny all the allegations of a pleading — including the jurisdictional grounds — may do so by a general denial. A party that does not intend to deny all the allegations must either specifically deny designated allegations or generally deny all except those specifically admitted.

(4) ***Denying Part of an Allegation.*** A party that intends in good faith to deny only part of an allegation must admit the part that is true and deny the rest.

(5) ***Lacking Knowledge or Information.*** A party that lacks knowledge or information sufficient to form a belief about the truth of an allegation must so state, and the statement has the effect of a denial.

(6) ***Effect of Failing to Deny.*** An allegation — other than one relating to the amount of damages — is admitted if a responsive pleading is required and the allegation is not denied. If a responsive pleading is not required, an allegation is considered denied or avoided.

(c) Affirmative Defenses.

(1) ***In General.*** In responding to a pleading, a party must affirmatively state any avoidance or affirmative defense, including:

- accord and satisfaction;
- arbitration and award;
- assumption of risk;
- contributory negligence;
- duress;
- estoppel;

- failure of consideration;
- fraud;
- illegality;
- injury by fellow servant;
- laches;
- license;
- payment;
- release;
- res judicata;
- statute of frauds;
- statute of limitations; and
- waiver.

(2) ***Mistaken Designation***. If a party mistakenly designates a defense as a counterclaim, or a counterclaim as a defense, the court must, if justice requires, treat the pleading as though it were correctly designated, and may impose terms for doing so.

(d) Pleading to Be Concise and Direct; Alternative Statements; Inconsistency.

(1) ***In General***. Each allegation must be simple, concise, and direct. No technical form is required.

(2) ***Alternative Statements of a Claim or Defense***. A party may set out two or more statements of a claim or defense alternatively or hypothetically, either in a single count or defense or in separate ones. If a party makes alternative statements, the pleading is sufficient if any one of them is sufficient.

(3) ***Inconsistent Claims or Defenses***. A party may state as many separate claims or defenses as it has, regardless of consistency.

(e) Construing Pleadings. Pleadings must be construed so as to do justice.

Rule 9. Pleading Special Matters

(a) Capacity or Authority to Sue; Legal Existence.

(1) ***In General.*** Except when required to show that the court has jurisdiction, a pleading need not allege:

(A) a party's capacity to sue or be sued;

(B) a party's authority to sue or be sued in a representative capacity; or

(C) the legal existence of an organized association of persons that is made a party.

(2) ***Raising Those Issues.*** To raise any of those issues, a party must do so by a specific denial, which must state any supporting facts that are peculiarly within the party's knowledge.

(b) Fraud or Mistake; Conditions of Mind. In alleging fraud or mistake, a party must state with particularity the circumstances constituting fraud or mistake. Malice, intent, knowledge, and other conditions of a person's mind may be alleged generally.

(c) Conditions Precedent. In pleading conditions precedent, it suffices to allege generally that all conditions precedent have occurred or been performed. But when denying that a condition precedent has occurred or been performed, a party must do so with particularity.

(d) Official Document or Act. In pleading an official document or official act, it suffices to allege that the document was legally issued or the act legally done.

(e) Judgment. In pleading a judgment or decision of a domestic or foreign court, a judicial or quasi-judicial tribunal, or a board or officer, it suffices to plead the judgment or decision without showing jurisdiction to render it.

(f) Time and Place. An allegation of time or place is material when testing the sufficiency of a pleading.

(g) Special Damages. If an item of special damage is claimed, it must be specifically stated.

(h) Admiralty or Maritime Claim.

(1) ***How Designated.*** If a claim for relief is within the admiralty or maritime jurisdiction and also within the court's subject-matter jurisdiction on some other ground, the pleading may designate the claim as an admiralty or maritime claim for purposes of Rules 14(c), 38(e), and 82 and the Supplemental Rules for Admiralty or Maritime Claims and Asset Forfeiture Actions. A claim cognizable only in the admiralty or maritime jurisdiction is an admiralty or maritime claim for those purposes, whether or not so designated.

(2) ***Designation for Appeal.*** A case that includes an admiralty or maritime claim within this subdivision (h) is an admiralty case within 28 U.S.C. § 1292(a)(3).

Rule 10. Form of Pleadings

(a) Caption; Names of Parties. Every pleading must have a caption with the court's name, a title, a file number, and a Rule 7(a) designation. The title of the complaint must name all the parties; the title of other pleadings, after naming the first party on each side, may refer generally to other parties.

(b) Paragraphs; Separate Statements. A party must state its claims or defenses in numbered paragraphs, each limited as far as practicable to a single set of circumstances. A later pleading may refer by number to a paragraph in an earlier pleading. If doing so would promote clarity, each claim founded on a separate transaction or occurrence — and each defense other than a denial — must be stated in a separate count or defense.

(c) Adoption by Reference; Exhibits. A statement in a pleading may be adopted by reference elsewhere in the same pleading or in any other pleading or motion. A copy of a written instrument that is an exhibit to a pleading is a part of the pleading for all purposes.

Rule 11. Signing Pleadings, Motions, and Other Papers; Representations to the Court; Sanctions

(a) Signature. Every pleading, written motion, and other paper must be signed by at least one attorney of record in the attorney's name — or by a party personally if the party is unrepresented. The paper must state the signer's address, e-mail address, and telephone number. Unless a rule or statute specifically states otherwise, a pleading need not be verified or accompanied by an affidavit. The court must strike an unsigned paper unless the omission is promptly corrected after being called to the attorney's or party's attention.

(b) Representations to the Court. By presenting to the court a pleading, written motion, or other paper — whether by signing, filing, submitting, or later advocating it — an attorney or unrepresented party certifies that to the best of the person's knowledge, information, and belief, formed after an inquiry reasonable under the circumstances:

(1) it is not being presented for any improper purpose, such as to harass, cause unnecessary delay, or needlessly increase the cost of litigation;

(2) the claims, defenses, and other legal contentions are warranted by existing law or by a nonfrivolous argument for extending, modifying, or reversing existing law or for establishing new law;

(3) the factual contentions have evidentiary support or, if specifically so identified, will likely have evidentiary support after a reasonable opportunity for further investigation or discovery; and

(4) the denials of factual contentions are warranted on the evidence or, if specifically so identified, are reasonably based on belief or a lack of information.

(c) Sanctions.

(1) ***In General.*** If, after notice and a reasonable opportunity to respond, the court determines that Rule 11(b) has been violated, the court may impose an appropriate sanction on any attorney, law firm, or party that violated the rule or is responsible for the violation. Absent exceptional circumstances, a law firm must be held jointly responsible for a violation committed by its partner, associate, or employee.

(2) ***Motion for Sanctions.*** A motion for sanctions must be made separately from any other motion and must describe the specific conduct that allegedly violates Rule 11(b). The motion must be served under Rule 5, but it must not be filed or be presented to the court if the challenged paper, claim, defense, contention, or denial is withdrawn or appropriately corrected within 21 days after service or within another time the court sets. If warranted, the court may award to the prevailing party the reasonable expenses, including attorney's fees, incurred for the motion.

(3) ***On the Court's Initiative.*** On its own, the court may order an attorney, law firm, or party to show cause why conduct specifically described in the order has not violated Rule 11(b).

(4) ***Nature of a Sanction.*** A sanction imposed under this rule must be limited to what suffices to deter repetition of the conduct or comparable conduct by others similarly situated. The sanction may include nonmonetary directives; an order to pay a penalty into court; or, if imposed on motion and warranted for effective deterrence, an order directing payment to the movant of part or all of the reasonable attorney's fees and other expenses directly resulting from the violation.

(5) ***Limitations on Monetary Sanctions.*** The court must not impose a monetary sanction:

(A) against a represented party for violating Rule 11(b)(2); or

(B) on its own, unless it issued the show-cause order under Rule 11(c)(3) before voluntary dismissal or settlement of the claims made by or against the party that is, or whose attorneys are, to be sanctioned.

(6) *Requirements for an Order*. An order imposing a sanction must describe the sanctioned conduct and explain the basis for the sanction.

(d) Inapplicability to Discovery. This rule does not apply to disclosures and discovery requests, responses, objections, and motions under Rules 26 through 37.

ADVISORY COMMITTEE NOTES

1983 Amendment [some citations omitted without notation — ED.]

Since its original promulgation, Rule 11 has provided for the striking of pleadings and the imposition of disciplinary sanctions to check abuses in the signing of pleadings. Its provisions have always applied to motions and other papers by virtue of incorporation by reference in Rule 7(b)(2). . . .

Experience shows that in practice Rule 11 has not been effective in deterring abuses. There has been considerable confusion as to (1) the circumstances that should trigger striking a pleading or motion or taking disciplinary action, (2) the standard of conduct expected of attorneys who sign pleadings and motions, and (3) the range of available and appropriate sanctions. The new language is intended to reduce the reluctance of courts to impose sanctions, by emphasizing the responsibilities of the attorney and reenforcing those obligations by the imposition of sanctions.

The amended rule attempts to deal with the problem by building upon and expanding the equitable doctrine permitting the court to award expenses, including attorney's fees, to a litigant whose opponent acts in bad faith in instituting or conducting litigation. See, e.g., *Roadway Express, Inc. v. Piper*, 447 U.S. 752 (1980); *Hall v. Cole*, 412 U.S. 1, 5 (1973). Greater attention by the district courts to pleading and motion abuses and the imposition of sanctions when appropriate, should discourage dilatory or abusive tactics and help to streamline the litigation process by lessening frivolous claims or defenses.

The expanded nature of the lawyer's certification in the fifth sentence of amended Rule 11 [with modifications, this sentence is now Rule 11(b) — ED.] recognizes that the litigation process may be abused for purposes other than delay.

The words "good ground to support" the pleading in the original rule were interpreted to have both factual and legal elements. They have been replaced by a standard of conduct that is more focused.

The new language stresses the need for some prefiling inquiry into both the facts and the law to satisfy the affirmative duty imposed by the rule. The standard is one of reasonableness under the circumstances. This standard is more stringent than the original good-faith formula and thus it is expected that a greater range of circumstances will trigger its violation.

The rule is not intended to chill an attorney's enthusiasm or creativity in pursuing factual or legal theories. The court is expected to avoid using the wisdom of hindsight and should test the signer's conduct by inquiring what was reasonable to believe at the time the pleading, motion, or other paper was submitted. Thus, what constitutes a reasonable inquiry may depend on such factors as how much

time for investigation was available to the signer; whether he had to rely on a client for information as to the facts underlying the pleading, motion, or other paper; whether the pleading, motion, or other paper was based on a plausible view of the law; or whether he depended on forwarding counsel or another member of the bar.

The rule does not require a party or an attorney to disclose privileged communications or work product in order to show that the signing of the pleading, motion, or other paper is substantially justified. The provisions of Rule 26(c), including appropriate orders after *in camera* inspection by the court, remain available to protect a party claiming privilege or work product protection.

Amended Rule 11 continues to apply to anyone who signs a pleading, motion, or other paper. Although the standard is the same for unrepresented parties, who are obliged themselves to sign the pleadings, the court has sufficient discretion to take account of the special circumstances that often arise in *pro se* situations. See *Haines v. Kerner*, 404 U.S. 519 (1972).

The provision in the original rule for striking pleadings and motions as sham and false has been deleted. The passage has rarely been utilized, and decisions thereunder have tended to confuse the issue of attorney honesty with the merits of the action. Motions under this provision generally present issues better dealt with under Rules 8, 12, or 56.

The former reference to the inclusion of scandalous or indecent matter, which is itself strong indication that an improper purpose underlies the pleading, motion, or other paper, also has been deleted as unnecessary. Such matter may be stricken under Rule 12(f) as well as dealt with under the more general language of amended Rule 11.

The text of the amended rule seeks to dispel apprehensions that efforts to obtain enforcement will be fruitless by insuring that the rule will be applied when properly invoked. The word "sanctions" in the caption, for example, stresses a deterrent orientation in dealing with improper pleadings, motions or other papers. This corresponds to the approach in imposing sanctions for discovery abuses. See *National Hockey League v. Metropolitan Hockey Club*, 427 U.S. 639 (1976) (per curiam). And the words "shall impose" in the last sentence [with modifications, including the change to "may impose," this language is now found Rules 11(c)(1) and -(4) — ED.] focus the court's attention on the need to impose sanctions for pleading and motion abuses. The court, however, retains the necessary flexibility to deal appropriately with violations of the rule. It has discretion to tailor sanctions to the particular facts of the case, with which it should be well acquainted.

The references in the former text to wilfulness as a prerequisite to disciplinary action has been deleted. However, in considering the nature and severity of the sanctions to be imposed, the court should take account of the state of the attorney's or party's actual or presumed knowledge when the pleading or other paper was signed. Thus, for example, when a party is not represented by counsel, the absence of legal advice is an appropriate factor to be considered.

Courts currently appear to believe they may impose sanctions on their own motion. Authority to do so has been made explicit in order to overcome the traditional reluctance of courts to intervene unless requested by one of the parties.

The detection and punishment of a violation of the signing requirement, encouraged by the amended rule, is part of the court's responsibility for securing the system's effective operation.

If the duty imposed by the rule is violated, the court should have the discretion to impose sanctions on either the attorney, the party the signing attorney represents, or both, or on an unrepresented party who signed the pleading, and the new rule so provides. Although Rule 11 has been silent on the point, courts have claimed the power to impose sanctions on an attorney personally, either by imposing costs or employing the contempt technique. This power has been used infrequently. The amended rule should eliminate any doubt as to the propriety of assessing sanctions against the attorney.

Even though it is the attorney whose signature violates the rule, it may be appropriate under the circumstances of the case to impose a sanction on the client. This modification brings Rule 11 in line with practice under Rule 37, which allows sanctions for abuses during discovery to be imposed upon the party, the attorney, or both.

A party seeking sanctions should give notice to the court and the offending party promptly upon discovering a basis for doing so. The time when sanctions are to be imposed rests in the discretion of the trial judge. However, it is anticipated that in the case of pleadings the sanctions issue under Rule 11 normally will be determined at the end of the litigation, and in the case of motions at the time when the motion is decided or shortly thereafter. The procedure obviously must comport with due process requirements. The particular format to be followed should depend on the circumstances of the situation and the severity of the sanction under consideration. In many situations the judge's participation in the proceedings provides him with full knowledge of the relevant facts and little further inquiry will be necessary.

To assure that the efficiencies achieved through more effective operation of the pleading regimen will not be offset by the cost of satellite litigation over the imposition of sanctions, the court must to the extent possible limit the scope of sanction proceedings to the record. Thus, discovery should be conducted only by leave of the court, and then only in extraordinary circumstances.

Although the encompassing reference to "other papers" in new Rule 11 literally includes discovery papers, the certification requirement in that context is governed by proposed new Rule 26(g). Discovery motions, however, fall within the ambit of Rule 11.

1993 Amendment

Purpose of revision. This revision is intended to remedy problems that have arisen in the interpretation and application of the 1983 revision of the rule. For empirical examination of experience under the 1983 rule, see, *e.g.,* New York State Bar Committee on Federal Courts, *Sanctions and Attorneys' Fees* (1987); T. Willging, *The Rule 11 Sanctioning Process* (1989); American Judicature Society, *Report of the Third Circuit Task Force on Federal Rule of Civil Procedure 11* (S. Burbank ed., 1989); E. Wiggins, T. Willging, and D. Stienstra, *Report on Rule 11* (Federal Judicial Center 1991). . . .

The rule retains the principle that attorneys and pro se litigants have an obligation to the court to refrain from conduct that frustrates the aims of Rule 1. The revision broadens the scope of this obligation, but places greater constraints on the imposition of sanctions and should reduce the number of motions for sanctions presented to the court. New subdivision (d) removes from the ambit of this rule all discovery requests, responses, objections, and motions subject to the provisions of Rule 26 through 37.

Subdivision (a). Retained in this subdivision are the provisions requiring signatures on pleadings, written motions, and other papers. Unsigned papers are to be received by the Clerk, but then are to be stricken if the omission of the signature is not corrected promptly after being called to the attention of the attorney or pro se litigant. Correction can be made by signing the paper on file or by submitting a duplicate that contains the signature. A court may require by local rule that papers contain additional identifying information regarding the parties or attorneys, such as telephone numbers to facilitate facsimile transmissions, though, as for omission of a signature, the paper should not be rejected for failure to provide such information.

The sentence in the former rule relating to the effect of answers under oath is no longer needed and has been eliminated. The provision in the former rule that signing a paper constitutes a certificate that it has been read by the signer also has been eliminated as unnecessary. The obligations imposed under subdivision (b) obviously require that a pleading, written motion, or other paper be read before it is filed or submitted to the court.

Subdivisions (b) and (c). These subdivisions restate the provisions requiring attorneys and pro se litigants to conduct a reasonable inquiry into the law and facts before signing pleadings, written motions, and other documents, and prescribing sanctions for violation of these obligations. The revision in part expands the responsibilities of litigants to the court, while providing greater constraints and flexibility in dealing with infractions of the rule. The rule continues to require litigants to "stop-and-think" before initially making legal or factual contentions. It also, however, emphasizes the duty of candor by subjecting litigants to potential sanctions for insisting upon a position after it is no longer tenable and by generally providing protection against sanctions if they withdraw or correct contentions after a potential violation is called to their attention.

The rule applies only to assertions contained in papers filed with or submitted to the court. It does not cover matters arising for the first time during oral presentations to the court, when counsel may make statements that would not have been made if there had been more time for study and reflection. However, a litigant's obligations with respect to the contents of these papers are not measured solely as of the time they are filed with or submitted to the court, but include reaffirming to the court and advocating positions contained in those pleadings and motions after learning that they cease to have any merit. For example, an attorney who during a pretrial conference insists on a claim or defense should be viewed as "presenting to the court" that contention and would be subject to the obligations of subdivision (b) measured as of that time. Similarly, if after a notice of removal is filed, a party urges in federal court the allegations of a pleading filed in state court (whether as claims, defenses, or in disputes regarding removal or remand),

it would be viewed as "presenting" — and hence certifying to the district court under Rule 11 — those allegations.

The certification with respect to allegations and other factual contentions is revised in recognition that sometimes a litigant may have good reason to believe that a fact is true or false but may need discovery, formal or informal, from opposing parties or third persons to gather and confirm the evidentiary basis for the allegation. Tolerance of factual contentions in initial pleadings by plaintiffs or defendants when specifically identified as made on information and belief does not relieve litigants from the obligation to conduct an appropriate investigation into the facts that is reasonable under the circumstances; it is not a license to join parties, make claims, or present defenses without any factual basis or justification. Moreover, if evidentiary support is not obtained after a reasonable opportunity for further investigation or discovery, the party has a duty under the rule not to persist with that contention. Subdivision (b) does not require a formal amendment to pleadings for which evidentiary support is not obtained, but rather calls upon a litigant not thereafter to advocate such claims or defenses.

The certification is that there is (or likely will be) "evidentiary support" for the allegation, not that the party will prevail with respect to its contention regarding the fact. That summary judgment is rendered against a party does not necessarily mean, for purposes of this certification, that it had no evidentiary support for its position. On the other hand, if a party has evidence with respect to a contention that would suffice to defeat a motion for summary judgment based thereon, it would have sufficient "evidentiary support" for purposes of Rule 11.

Denials of factual contentions involve somewhat different considerations. Often, of course, a denial is premised upon the existence of evidence contradicting the alleged fact. At other times a denial is permissible because, after an appropriate investigation, a party has no information concerning the matter or, indeed, has a reasonable basis for doubting the credibility of the only evidence relevant to the matter. A party should not deny an allegation it knows to be true; but it is not required, simply because it lacks contradictory evidence, to admit an allegation that it believes is not true.

The changes in subdivisions (b)(3) and (b)(4) will serve to equalize the burden of the rule upon plaintiffs and defendants, who under Rule 8(b) are in effect allowed to deny allegations by stating that from their initial investigation they lack sufficient information to form a belief as to the truth of the allegation. If, after further investigation or discovery, a denial is no longer warranted, the defendant should not continue to insist on that denial. While sometimes helpful, formal amendment of the pleadings to withdraw an allegation or denial is not required by subdivision (b).

Arguments for extensions, modifications, or reversals of existing law or for creation of new law do not violate subdivision (b)(2) provided they are "nonfrivolous." This establishes an objective standard, intended to eliminate any "empty-head pure-heart" justification for patently frivolous arguments. However, the extent to which a litigant has researched the issues and found some support for its theories even in minority opinions, in law review articles, or through consultation with other attorneys should certainly be taken into account in determining whether paragraph (2) has been violated. Although arguments for a

change of law are not required to be specifically so identified, a contention that is so identified should be viewed with greater tolerance under the rule.

The court has available a variety of possible sanctions to impose for violations, such as striking the offending paper; issuing an admonition, reprimand, or censure; requiring participation in seminars or other educational programs; ordering a fine payable to the court; referring the matter to disciplinary authorities (or, in the case of government attorneys, to the Attorney General, Inspector General, or agency head), etc. *See Manual for Complex Litigation, Second,* § 42.3. The rule does not attempt to enumerate the factors a court should consider in deciding whether to impose a sanction or what sanctions would be appropriate in the circumstances; but, for emphasis, it does specifically note that a sanction may be nonmonetary as well as monetary. Whether the improper conduct was willful, or negligent; whether it was part of a pattern of activity, or an isolated event; whether it infected the entire pleading, or only one particular count or defense; whether the person has engaged in similar conduct in other litigation; whether it was intended to injure; what effect it had on the litigation process in time or expense; whether the responsible person is trained in the law; what amount, given the financial resources of the responsible person, is needed to deter that person from repetition in the same case; what amount is needed to deter similar activity by other litigants: all of these may in a particular case be proper considerations. The court has significant discretion in determining what sanctions, if any, should be imposed for a violation, subject to the principle that the sanctions should not be more severe than reasonably necessary to deter repetition of the conduct by the offending person or comparable conduct by similarly situated persons.

Since the purpose of Rule 11 sanctions is to deter rather than to compensate, the rule provides that, if a monetary sanction is imposed, it should ordinarily be paid into court as a penalty. However, under unusual circumstances, particularly for (b)(1) violations, deterrence may be ineffective unless the sanction not only requires the person violating the rule to make a monetary payment, but also directs that some or all of this payment be made to those injured by the violation. Accordingly, the rule authorizes the court, if requested in a motion and if so warranted, to award attorney's fees to another party. Any such award to another party, however, should not exceed the expenses and attorneys' fees for the services directly and unavoidably caused by the violation of the certification requirement. If, for example, a wholly unsupportable count were included in a multi-count complaint or counterclaim for the purpose of needlessly increasing the cost of litigation to an impecunious adversary, any award of expenses should be limited to those directly caused by inclusion of the improper count, and not those resulting from the filing of the complaint or answer itself. The award should not provide compensation for services that could have been avoided by an earlier disclosure of evidence or an earlier challenge to the groundless claims or defenses. Moreover, partial reimbursement of fees may constitute a sufficient deterrent with respect to violations by persons having modest financial resources. In cases brought under statutes providing for fees to be awarded to prevailing parties, the court should not employ cost-shifting under this rule in a manner that would be inconsistent with the standards that govern the statutory award of fees, such as stated in *Christiansburg Garment Co. v. EEOC*, 434 U.S. 412 (1978).

The sanction should be imposed on the persons — whether attorneys, law firms, or parties — who have violated the rule or who may be determined to be responsible for the violation. The person signing, filing, submitting, or advocating a document has a nondelegable responsibility to the court, and in most situations is the person to be sanctioned for a violation. Absent exceptional circumstances, a law firm is to be held also responsible when, as a result of a motion under subdivision (c)(1)(A) [now Rule 11(c)(1) — ED.], one of its partners, associates, or employees is determined to have violated the rule. Since such a motion may be filed only if the offending paper is not withdrawn or corrected within 21 days after service of the motion, it is appropriate that the law firm ordinarily be viewed as jointly responsible under established principles of agency. This provision is designed to remove the restrictions of the former rule. *Cf. Pavelic & LeFlore v. Marvel Entertainment Group*, 493 U.S. 120 (1989) (1983 version of Rule 11 does not permit sanctions against law firm of attorney signing groundless complaint).

The revision permits the court to consider whether other attorneys in the firm, co-counsel, other law firms, or the party itself should be held accountable for their part in causing a violation. When appropriate, the court can make an additional inquiry in order to determine whether the sanction should be imposed on such persons, firms, or parties either in addition to or, in unusual circumstances, instead of the person actually making the presentation to the court. For example, such an inquiry may be appropriate in cases involving governmental agencies or other institutional parties that frequently impose substantial restrictions on the discretion of individual attorneys employed by it.

Sanctions that involve monetary awards (such as a fine or an award of attorney's fees) may not be imposed on a represented party for causing a violation of subdivision (b)(2), involving frivolous contentions of law. Monetary responsibility for such violations is more properly placed solely on the party's attorneys. With this limitation, the rule should not be subject to attack under the Rules Enabling Act. See *Willy v. Coastal Corp.*, [503] U.S. [131] (1992); *Business Guides, Inc. v. Chromatic Communications Enter. Inc.*, [498] U.S. [533] (1991). This restriction does not limit the court's power to impose sanctions or remedial orders that may have collateral financial consequences upon a party, such as dismissal of a claim, preclusion of a defense, or preparation of amended pleadings.

Explicit provision is made for litigants to be provided notice of the alleged violation and an opportunity to respond before sanctions are imposed. Whether the matter should be decided solely on the basis of written submissions or should be scheduled for oral argument (or, indeed, for evidentiary presentation) will depend on the circumstances. If the court imposes a sanction, it must, unless waived, indicate its reasons in a written order or on the record; the court should not ordinarily have to explain its denial of a motion for sanctions. Whether a violation has occurred and what sanctions, if any, to impose for a violation are matters committed to the discretion of the trial court; accordingly, as under current law, the standard for appellate review of these decisions will be for abuse of discretion. *See Cooter & Gell v. Hartmarx Corp.*, 496 U.S. 384 (1990) (noting, however, that an abuse would be established if the court based its ruling on an erroneous view of the law or on a clearly erroneous assessment of the evidence).

The revision leaves for resolution on a case-by-case basis, considering the particular circumstances involved, the question as to when a motion for violation of Rule 11 should be served and when, if filed, it should be decided. Ordinarily the motion should be served promptly after the inappropriate paper is filed, and, if delayed too long, may be viewed as untimely. In other circumstances, it should not be served until the other party has had a reasonable opportunity for discovery. Given the "safe harbor" provisions discussed below, a party cannot delay serving its Rule 11 motion until conclusion of the case (or judicial rejection of the offending contention).

Rule 11 motions should not be made or threatened for minor, inconsequential violations of the standards prescribed by subdivision (b). They should not be employed as a discovery device or to test the legal sufficiency or efficacy of allegations in the pleadings; other motions are available for those purposes. Nor should Rule 11 motions be prepared to emphasize the merits of a party's position, to exact an unjust settlement, to intimidate an adversary into withdrawing contentions that are fairly debatable, to increase the costs of litigation, to create a conflict of interest between attorney and client, or to seek disclosure of matters otherwise protected by the attorney-client privilege or the work-product doctrine. As under the prior rule, the court may defer its ruling (or its decision as to the identity of the persons to be sanctioned) until final resolution of the case in order to avoid immediate conflicts of interest and to reduce the disruption created if a disclosure of attorney-client communications is needed to determine whether a violation occurred or to identify the person responsible for the violation.

The rule provides that requests for sanctions must be made as a separate motion, *i.e.,* not simply included as an additional prayer for relief contained in another motion. The motion for sanctions is not, however, to be filed until at least 21 days (or such other period as the court may set) after being served. If, during this period, the alleged violation is corrected, as by withdrawing (whether formally or informally) some allegation or contention, the motion should not be filed with the court. These provisions are intended to provide a type of "safe harbor" against motions under Rule 11 in that a party will not be subject to sanctions on the basis of another party's motion unless, after receiving the motion, it refuses to withdraw that position or to acknowledge candidly that it does not currently have evidence to support a specified allegation. Under the former rule, parties were sometimes reluctant to abandon a questionable contention lest that be viewed as evidence of a violation of Rule 11; under the revision, the timely withdrawal of a contention will protect a party against a motion for sanctions.

To stress the seriousness of a motion for sanctions and to define precisely the conduct claimed to violate the rule, the revision provides that the "safe harbor" period begins to run only upon service of the motion. In most cases, however, counsel should be expected to give informal notice to the other party, whether in person or by a telephone call or letter, of a potential violation before proceeding to prepare and serve a Rule 11 motion.

As under former Rule 11, the filing of a motion for sanctions is itself subject to the requirements of the rule and can lead to sanctions. However, service of a cross motion under Rule 11 should rarely be needed since under the revision the court may award to the person who prevails on a motion under Rule 11 — whether

the movant or the target of the motion — reasonable expenses, including attorney's fees, incurred in presenting or opposing the motion.

The power of the court to act on its own initiative is retained, but with the condition that this be done through a show cause order. This procedure provides the person with notice and an opportunity to respond. The revision provides that a monetary sanction imposed after a court-initiated show cause order be limited to a penalty payable to the court and that it be imposed only if the show cause order is issued before any voluntary dismissal or an agreement of the parties to settle the claims made by or against the litigant. Parties settling a case should not be subsequently faced with an unexpected order from the court leading to monetary sanctions that might have affected their willingness to settle or voluntarily dismiss a case. Since show cause orders will ordinarily be issued only in situations that are akin to a contempt of court, the rule does not provide a "safe harbor" to a litigant for withdrawing a claim, defense, etc., after a show cause order has been issued on the court's own initiative. Such corrective action, however, should be taken into account in deciding what — if any — sanction to impose if, after consideration of the litigant's response, the court concludes that a violation has occurred.

Subdivision (d). Rules 26(g) and 37 establish certification standards and sanctions that apply to discovery disclosures, requests, responses, objections, and motions. It is appropriate that Rules 26 through 37, which are specially designed for the discovery process, govern such documents and conduct rather than the more general provisions of Rule 11. Subdivision (d) has been added to accomplish this result.

Rule 11 is not the exclusive source for control of improper presentations of claims, defenses, or contentions. It does not supplant statutes permitting awards of attorney's fees to prevailing parties or alter the principles governing such awards. It does not inhibit the court in punishing for contempt, in exercising its inherent powers, or in imposing sanctions, awarding expenses, or directing remedial action authorized under other rules or under 28 U.S.C. § 1927. *See Chambers v. NASCO*, [501] U.S. [32] (1991). Chambers cautions, however, against reliance upon inherent powers if appropriate sanctions can be imposed under provisions such as Rule 11, and the procedures specified in Rule 11 — notice, opportunity to respond, and findings — should ordinarily be employed when imposing a sanction under the court's inherent powers. Finally, it should be noted that Rule 11 does not preclude a party from initiating an independent action for malicious prosecution or abuse of process.

Rule 12. Defenses and Objections: When and How Presented; Motion for Judgment on the Pleadings; Consolidating Motions; Waiving Defenses; Pretrial Hearing

(a) Time to Serve a Responsive Pleading.

(1) ***In General.*** Unless another time is specified by this rule or a federal statute, the time for serving a responsive pleading is as follows:

(A) A defendant must serve an answer:

(i) within 21 days after being served with the summons and complaint; or

(ii) if it has timely waived service under Rule 4(d), within 60 days after the request for a waiver was sent, or within 90 days after it was sent to the defendant outside any judicial district of the United States.

(B) A party must serve an answer to a counterclaim or crossclaim within 21 days after being served with the pleading that states the counterclaim or crossclaim.

(C) A party must serve a reply to an answer within 21 days after being served with an order to reply, unless the order specifies a different time.

(2) ***United States and Its Agencies, Officers, or Employees Sued in an Official Capacity.*** The United States, a United States agency, or a United States officer or employee sued only in an official capacity must serve an answer to a complaint, counterclaim, or crossclaim within 60 days after service on the United States attorney.

(3) ***United States Officers or Employees Sued in an Individual Capacity.*** A United States officer or employee sued in an individual capacity for an act or omission occurring in connection with duties performed on the United States' behalf must serve an answer to a complaint, counterclaim, or crossclaim within 60 days after service on the officer or employee or service on the United States attorney, whichever is later.

(4) ***Effect of a Motion.*** Unless the court sets a different time, serving a motion under this rule alters these periods as follows:

(A) if the court denies the motion or postpones its disposition until trial, the responsive pleading must be served within 14 days after notice of the court's action; or

(B) if the court grants a motion for a more definite statement, the responsive pleading must be served within 14 days after the more definite statement is served.

(b) How to Present Defenses. Every defense to a claim for relief in any pleading must be asserted in the responsive pleading if one is required. But a party may assert the following defenses by motion:

(1) lack of subject-matter jurisdiction;

(2) lack of personal jurisdiction;

(3) improper venue;

(4) insufficient process;

(5) insufficient service of process;

(6) failure to state a claim upon which relief can be granted; and

(7) failure to join a party under Rule 19.

A motion asserting any of these defenses must be made before pleading if a responsive pleading is allowed. If a pleading sets out a claim for relief that does not require a responsive pleading, an opposing party may assert at trial any defense to that claim. No defense or objection is waived by joining it with one or more other defenses or objections in a responsive pleading or in a motion.

(c) Motion for Judgment on the Pleadings. After the pleadings are closed — but early enough not to delay trial — a party may move for judgment on the pleadings.

(d) Result of Presenting Matters Outside the Pleadings. If, on a motion under Rule 12(b)(6) or 12(c), matters outside the pleadings are presented to and not excluded by the court, the motion must be treated as one for summary judgment under Rule 56. All parties must be given a reasonable opportunity to present all the material that is pertinent to the motion.

(e) Motion for a More Definite Statement. A party may move for a more definite statement of a pleading to which a responsive pleading is allowed but which is so vague or ambiguous that the party cannot reasonably prepare a response. The motion must be made before filing a responsive pleading and must point out the defects complained of and the details desired. If the court orders a more definite statement and the order is not obeyed within 14 days after notice of the order or within the time the court sets, the court may strike the pleading or issue any other appropriate order.

(f) Motion to Strike. The court may strike from a pleading an insufficient defense or any redundant, immaterial, impertinent, or scandalous matter. The court may act:

(1) on its own; or

(2) on motion made by a party either before responding to the pleading or, if a response is not allowed, within 21 days after being served with the pleading.

(g) Joining Motions.

(1) ***Right to Join.*** A motion under this rule may be joined with any other motion allowed by this rule.

(2) ***Limitation on Further Motions.*** Except as provided in Rule 12(h)(2) or (3), a party that makes a motion under this rule must not

make another motion under this rule raising a defense or objection that was available to the party but omitted from its earlier motion.

(h) Waiving and Preserving Certain Defenses.

(1) ***When Some Are Waived.*** A party waives any defense listed in Rule 12(b)(2)-(5) by:

(A) omitting it from a motion in the circumstances described in Rule 12(g)(2); or

(B) failing to either:

(i) make it by motion under this rule; or

(ii) include it in a responsive pleading or in an amendment allowed by Rule 15(a)(1) as a matter of course.

(2) ***When to Raise Others.*** Failure to state a claim upon which relief can be granted, to join a person required by Rule 19(b), or to state a legal defense to a claim may be raised:

(A) in any pleading allowed or ordered under Rule 7(a);

(B) by a motion under Rule 12(c); or

(C) at trial.

(3) ***Lack of Subject-Matter Jurisdiction.*** If the court determines at any time that it lacks subject-matter jurisdiction, the court must dismiss the action.

(i) Hearing Before Trial. If a party so moves, any defense listed in Rule 12(b)(1)-(7) — whether made in a pleading or by motion — and a motion under Rule 12(c) must be heard and decided before trial unless the court orders a deferral until trial.

ADVISORY COMMITTEE NOTES

1966 Amendment [citations omitted without notation — ED.]

. . .

Subdivision (g). Subdivision (g) has forbidden a defendant who makes a preanswer motion under this rule from making a further motion presenting any defense or objection which was available to him at the time he made the first motion and which he could have included, but did not in fact include therein. Thus if the defendant moves before answer to dismiss the complaint for failure to state a claim, he is barred from making a further motion presenting the defense of improper venue, if that defense was available to him when he made his original motion. Amended subdivision (g) is to the same effect. This required consolidation of defenses and objections in a Rule 12 motion is salutary in that it works against piecemeal consideration of a case. For exceptions to the requirement of consolidation, see the last clause of subdivision (g) [now Rule 12(g)(2) — ED.], referring to new subdivision (h)(2).

Subdivision (h). The question has arisen whether an omitted defense which cannot be made the basis of a second motion may nevertheless be pleaded in the answer. If the clause "if he has made no motion," was read literally, it seemed that the omitted defense was waived and could not be pleaded in the answer. On the other hand, the clause might be read as adding nothing of substance to the preceding words; in that event it appeared that a defense was not waived by reason of being omitted from the motion and might be set up in the answer. The decisions were divided.

Amended subdivision(h)(1)(A) eliminates the ambiguity and states that certain specified defenses which were available to a party when he made a preanswer motion, but which he omitted from the motion, are waived. The specified defenses are lack of jurisdiction over the person, improper venue, insufficiency of process, and insufficiency of service of process (see Rule 12(b)(2)-(5)). A party who by motion invites the court to pass upon a threshold defense should bring forward all the specified defenses he then has and thus allow the court to do a reasonably complete job. The waiver reinforces the policy of subdivision (g) forbidding successive motions.

By amended subdivision (h)(1)(B), the specified defenses, even if not waived by the operation of (A), are waived by the failure to raise them by a motion under Rule 12 or in the responsive pleading or any amendment thereof to which the party is entitled as a matter of course. The specified defenses are of such a character that they should not be delayed and brought up for the first time by means of an application to the court to amend the responsive pleading.

Since the language of the subdivisions is made clear, the party is put on fair notice of the effect of his actions and omissions and can guard himself against unintended waiver. It is to be noted that while the defenses specified in subdivision (h)(1) are subject to waiver as there provided, the more substantial defenses of failure to state a claim upon which relief can be granted, failure to join a party indispensable under Rule 19, and failure to state a legal defense to a claim (see Rule 12(b)(6), (7), (f)), as well as the defense of lack of jurisdiction over the subject matter (see Rule 12(b)(1)), are expressly preserved against waiver by amended subdivision (h)(2) and (3).

Rule 13. Counterclaim and Crossclaim

(a) Compulsory Counterclaim.

(1) ***In General.*** A pleading must state as a counterclaim any claim that — at the time of its service — the pleader has against an opposing party if the claim:

(A) arises out of the transaction or occurrence that is the subject matter of the opposing party's claim; and

(B) does not require adding another party over whom the court cannot acquire jurisdiction.

(2) ***Exceptions.*** The pleader need not state the claim if:

(A) when the action was commenced, the claim was the subject of another pending action; or

(B) the opposing party sued on its claim by attachment or other process that did not establish personal jurisdiction over the pleader on that claim, and the pleader does not assert any counterclaim under this rule.

(b) Permissive Counterclaim. A pleading may state as a counterclaim against an opposing party any claim that is not compulsory.

(c) Relief Sought in a Counterclaim. A counterclaim need not diminish or defeat the recovery sought by the opposing party. It may request relief that exceeds in amount or differs in kind from the relief sought by the opposing party.

(d) Counterclaim Against the United States. These rules do not expand the right to assert a counterclaim — or to claim a credit — against the United States or a United States officer or agency.

(e) Counterclaim Maturing or Acquired After Pleading. The court may permit a party to file a supplemental pleading asserting a counterclaim that matured or was acquired by the party after serving an earlier pleading.

(f) [Abrogated.]

(g) Crossclaim Against a Coparty. A pleading may state as a crossclaim any claim by one party against a coparty if the claim arises out of the transaction or occurrence that is the subject matter of the original action or of a counterclaim, or if the claim relates to any property that is the subject matter of the original action. The crossclaim may include a claim that the coparty is or may be liable to the crossclaimant for all or part of a claim asserted in the action against the crossclaimant.

(h) Joining Additional Parties. Rules 19 and 20 govern the addition of a person as a party to a counterclaim or crossclaim.

(i) Separate Trials; Separate Judgments. If the court orders separate trials under Rule 42(b), it may enter judgment on a counterclaim or crossclaim under Rule 54(b) when it has jurisdiction to do so, even if the opposing party's claims have been dismissed or otherwise resolved.

ADVISORY COMMITTEE NOTES

2007 Amendment

. . .

The meaning of former Rule 13(b) is better expressed by deleting "not arising out of the transaction or occurrence that is the subject matter of the opposing party's claim." Both as a matter of intended meaning and current practice, a party may state as a permissive counterclaim a claim that does grow out of the same

transaction or occurrence as an opposing party's claim even though one of the exceptions in Rule 13(a) means the claim is not a compulsory counterclaim.

Rule 14. Third-Party Practice

(a) When a Defending Party May Bring in a Third Party.

(1) ***Timing of the Summons and Complaint.*** A defending party may, as third-party plaintiff, serve a summons and complaint on a nonparty who is or may be liable to it for all or part of the claim against it. But the third-party plaintiff must, by motion, obtain the court's leave if it files the third-party complaint more than 14 days after serving its original answer.

(2) ***Third-Party Defendant's Claims and Defenses.*** The person served with the summons and third-party complaint — the "third-party defendant":

(A) must assert any defense against the third-party plaintiff's claim under Rule 12;

(B) must assert any counterclaim against the third-party plaintiff under Rule 13(a), and may assert any counterclaim against the third-party plaintiff under Rule 13(b) or any crossclaim against another third-party defendant under Rule 13(g);

(C) may assert against the plaintiff any defense that the third-party plaintiff has to the plaintiff's claim; and

(D) may also assert against the plaintiff any claim arising out of the transaction or occurrence that is the subject matter of the plaintiff's claim against the third-party plaintiff.

(3) ***Plaintiff's Claims Against a Third-Party Defendant.*** The plaintiff may assert against the third-party defendant any claim arising out of the transaction or occurrence that is the subject matter of the plaintiff's claim against the third-party plaintiff. The third-party defendant must then assert any defense under Rule 12 and any counterclaim under Rule 13(a), and may assert any counterclaim under Rule 13(b) or any crossclaim under Rule 13(g).

(4) ***Motion to Strike, Sever, or Try Separately.*** Any party may move to strike the third-party claim, to sever it, or to try it separately.

(5) ***Third-Party Defendant's Claim Against a Nonparty.*** A third-party defendant may proceed under this rule against a nonparty who is or may be liable to the third-party defendant for all or part of any claim against it.

(6) ***Third-Party Complaint In Rem***. If it is within the admiralty or maritime jurisdiction, a third-party complaint may be in rem. In that event, a reference in this rule to the "summons" includes the warrant of arrest, and a reference to the defendant or third-party plaintiff includes, when appropriate, a person who asserts a right under Supplemental Rule C(6)(a)(i) in the property arrested.

(b) When a Plaintiff May Bring in a Third Party. When a claim is asserted against a plaintiff, the plaintiff may bring in a third party if this rule would allow a defendant to do so.

(c) Admiralty or Maritime Claim.

(1) ***Scope of Impleader***. If a plaintiff asserts an admiralty or maritime claim under Rule 9(h), the defendant or a person who asserts a right under Supplemental Rule C(6)(a)(i) may, as a third-party plaintiff, bring in a third-party defendant who may be wholly or partly liable — either to the plaintiff or to the third-party plaintiff — for remedy over, contribution, or otherwise on account of the same transaction, occurrence, or series of transactions or occurrences.

(2) ***Defending Against a Demand for Judgment for the Plaintiff***. The third-party plaintiff may demand judgment in the plaintiff's favor against the third-party defendant. In that event, the third-party defendant must defend under Rule 12 against the plaintiff's claim as well as the third-party plaintiff's claim; and the action proceeds as if the plaintiff had sued both the third-party defendant and the third-party plaintiff.

ADVISORY COMMITTEE NOTES

2007 Amendment

. . .

Former Rule 14 twice refers to counterclaims under Rule 13. In each case, the operation of Rule 13(a) depends on the state of the action at the time the pleading is filed. If plaintiff and third-party defendant have become opposing parties because one has made a claim for relief against the other, Rule 13(a) requires assertion of any counterclaim that grows out of the transaction or occurrence that is the subject matter of that claim. Rules 14(a)(2)(B) and (a)(3) reflect the distinction between compulsory and permissive counterclaims.

Rule 15. Amended and Supplemental Pleadings

(a) Amendments Before Trial.

(1) ***Amending as a Matter of Course***. A party may amend its pleading once as a matter of course within:

(A) 21 days after serving it, or

(B) if the pleading is one to which a responsive pleading is required, 21 days after service of a responsive pleading or 21 days after service of a motion under Rule 12(b), (e), or (f), whichever is earlier.

(2) ***Other Amendments.*** In all other cases, a party may amend its pleading only with the opposing party's written consent or the court's leave. The court should freely give leave when justice so requires.

(3) ***Time to Respond.*** Unless the court orders otherwise, any required response to an amended pleading must be made within the time remaining to respond to the original pleading or within 14 days after service of the amended pleading, whichever is later.

(b) Amendments During and After Trial.

(1) ***Based on an Objection at Trial.*** If, at trial, a party objects that evidence is not within the issues raised in the pleadings, the court may permit the pleadings to be amended. The court should freely permit an amendment when doing so will aid in presenting the merits and the objecting party fails to satisfy the court that the evidence would prejudice that party's action or defense on the merits. The court may grant a continuance to enable the objecting party to meet the evidence.

(2) ***For Issues Tried by Consent.*** When an issue not raised by the pleadings is tried by the parties' express or implied consent, it must be treated in all respects as if raised in the pleadings. A party may move — at any time, even after judgment — to amend the pleadings to conform them to the evidence and to raise an unpleaded issue. But failure to amend does not affect the result of the trial of that issue.

(c) Relation Back of Amendments.

(1) ***When an Amendment Relates Back.*** An amendment to a pleading relates back to the date of the original pleading when:

(A) the law that provides the applicable statute of limitations allows relation back;

(B) the amendment asserts a claim or defense that arose out of the conduct, transaction, or occurrence set out — or attempted to be set out — in the original pleading; or

(C) the amendment changes the party or the naming of the party against whom a claim is asserted, if Rule 15(c)(1)(B) is satisfied and if, within the period provided by Rule 4(m) for serving the summons and complaint, the party to be brought in by amendment:

(i) received such notice of the action that it will not be prejudiced in defending on the merits; and

(ii) knew or should have known that the action would have been brought against it, but for a mistake concerning the proper party's identity.

(2) ***Notice to the United States.*** When the United States or a United States officer or agency is added as a defendant by amendment, the notice requirements of Rule 15(c)(1)(C)(i) and (ii) are satisfied if, during the stated period, process was delivered or mailed to the United States attorney or the United States attorney's designee, to the Attorney General of the United States, or to the officer or agency.

(d) Supplemental Pleadings. On motion and reasonable notice, the court may, on just terms, permit a party to serve a supplemental pleading setting out any transaction, occurrence, or event that happened after the date of the pleading to be supplemented. The court may permit supplementation even though the original pleading is defective in stating a claim or defense. The court may order that the opposing party plead to the supplemental pleading within a specified time.

ADVISORY COMMITTEE NOTES

1991 Amendment [citations omitted without notation — ED.]

The rule has been revised to prevent parties against whom claims are made from taking unjust advantage of otherwise inconsequential pleading errors to sustain a limitations defense.

Paragraph (c)(1). This provision is new. It is intended to make it clear that the rule does not apply to preclude any relation back that may be permitted under the applicable limitations law. Generally, the applicable limitations law will be state law. If federal jurisdiction is based on the citizenship of the parties, the primary reference is the law of the state in which the district court sits. *Walker v. Armco Steel Corp.*, 446 U.S. 740 (1980). If federal jurisdiction is based on a federal question, the reference may be to the law of the state governing relations between the parties. *E.g., Board of Regents v. Tomanio*, 446 U.S. 478 (1980). In some circumstances, the controlling limitations law may be federal law. *E.g., West v. Conrail, Inc.*, [481 U.S. 35] (1987). Cf. *Burlington Northern R. Co. v. Woods*, 480 U.S. 1 (1987); *Stewart Organization v. Ricoh*, [487 U.S. 22] (1988). Whatever may be the controlling body of limitations law, if that law affords a more forgiving principle of relation back than the one provided in this rule, it should be available to save the claim. Accord, *Marshall v. Mulrenin,* 508 F.2d 39 (1st Cir. 1974). If *Schiavone v. Fortune*, [477 U.S. 21] (1986) implies the contrary, this paragraph is intended to make a material change in the rule.

Paragraph (c)(3). This paragraph has been revised to change the result in *Schiavone v. Fortune, supra,* with respect to the problem of a misnamed defendant. An intended defendant who is notified of an action within the period allowed by Rule 4(m) [present Rule 4(m) was proposed as part of these 1991 amendments but

was withdrawn by the Supreme Court; Rule 4(m) was ultimately promulgated in 1993 — ED.] for service of a summons and complaint may not under the revised rule defeat the action on account of a defect in the pleading with respect to the defendant's name, provided that the requirements of clauses (A) and (B) have been met. If the notice requirement is met within the Rule 4(m) [see above — ED.] period, a complaint may be amended at any time to correct a formal defect such as a misnomer or misidentification. On the basis of the text of the former rule, the Court reached a result in *Schiavone v. Fortune* that was inconsistent with the liberal pleading practices secured by Rule 8. See Bauer, Schiavone: *An Un-Fortuneate Illustration of the Supreme Court's Role as Interpreter of the Federal Rules of Civil Procedure,* 63 Notre Dame L.Rev. 720 (1988); Brussack, *Outrageous Fortune: The Case for Amending Rule 15(c) Again,* 61 S.Cal. L.Rev. 671 (1988); Lewis, *The Excessive History of Federal Rule 15(c) and Its Lessons for Civil Rules Revision,* 86 Mich.L.Rev. 1507 (1987).

In allowing a name-correcting amendment within the time allowed by Rule 4(m) [see above — ED.], this rule allows not only the 120 [now 90 — ED.] days specified in that rule, but also any additional time resulting from any extension ordered by the court pursuant to that rule, as may be granted, for example, if the defendant is a fugitive from service of the summons. . . .

2007 Amendment

Former Rule 15(c)(3)(A) called for notice of the "institution" of the action. Rule 15(c)(1)(C)(i) omits the reference to "institution" as potentially confusing. What counts is that the party to be brought in have notice of the existence of the action, whether or not the notice includes details as to its "institution."

2009 Amendment

. . .

Rule 15(a)(l) is amended to make three changes in the time allowed to make one amendment as a matter of course.

Former Rule 15(a) addressed amendment of a pleading to which a responsive pleading is required by distinguishing between the means used to challenge the pleading. Serving a responsive pleading terminated the right to amend. Serving a motion attacking the pleading did not terminate the right to amend, because a motion is not a "pleading" as defined in Rule 7. The right to amend survived beyond decision of the motion unless the decision expressly cut off the right to amend.

The distinction drawn in former Rule 15(a) is changed in two ways. First, the right to amend once as a matter of course terminates 21 days after service of a motion under Rule 12(b), (e), or (f). This provision will force the pleader to consider carefully and promptly the wisdom of amending to meet the arguments in the motion. A responsive amendment may avoid the need to decide the motion or reduce the number of issues to be decided, and will expedite determination of issues that otherwise might be raised seriatim. It also should advance other pretrial proceedings.

Second, the right to amend once as a matter of course is no longer terminated by service of a responsive pleading. The responsive pleading may point out issues

that the original pleader had not considered and persuade the pleader that amendment is wise. Just as amendment was permitted by former Rule 15(a) in response to a motion, so the amended rule permits one amendment as a matter of course in response to a responsive pleading. The right is subject to the same 21-day limit as the right to amend in response to a motion.

The 21-day periods to amend once as a matter of course after service of a responsive pleading or after service of a designated motion are not cumulative. If a responsive pleading is served after one of the designated motions is served, for example, there is no new 21-day period.

Finally, amended Rule 15(a)(l) extends from 20 to 21 days the period to amend a pleading to which no responsive pleading is allowed and omits the provision that cuts off the right if the action is on the trial calendar. Rule 40 no longer refers to a trial calendar, and many courts have abandoned formal trial calendars. It is more effective to rely on scheduling orders or other pretrial directions to establish time limits for amendment in the few situations that otherwise might allow one amendment as a matter of course at a time that would disrupt trial preparations. Leave to amend still can be sought under Rule 15(a)(2), or at and after trial under Rule 15(b). . . .

Rule 16. Pretrial Conferences; Scheduling; Management

(a) Purposes of a Pretrial Conference. In any action, the court may order the attorneys and any unrepresented parties to appear for one or more pretrial conferences for such purposes as:

(1) expediting disposition of the action;

(2) establishing early and continuing control so that the case will not be protracted because of lack of management;

(3) discouraging wasteful pretrial activities;

(4) improving the quality of the trial through more thorough preparation; and

(5) facilitating settlement.

(b) Scheduling.

(1) ***Scheduling Order***. Except in categories of actions exempted by local rule, the district judge — or a magistrate judge when authorized by local rule — must issue a scheduling order:

(A) after receiving the parties' report under Rule 26(f); or

(B) after consulting with the parties' attorneys and any unrepresented parties at a scheduling conference.

(2) ***Time to Issue***. The judge must issue the scheduling order as soon as practicable, but unless the judge finds good cause for delay, the judge must issue it within the earlier of 90 days after any defendant

has been served with the complaint or 60 days after any defendant has appeared.

(3) ***Contents of the Order.***

(A) ***Required Contents.*** The scheduling order must limit the time to join other parties, amend the pleadings, complete discovery, and file motions.

(B) ***Permitted Contents.*** The scheduling order may:

(i) modify the timing of disclosures under Rules 26(a) and 26(e)(1);

(ii) modify the extent of discovery;

(iii) provide for disclosure, discovery, or preservation of electronically stored information;

(iv) include any agreements the parties reach for asserting claims of privilege or of protection as trial-preparation material after information is produced, including agreements reached under Federal Rule of Evidence 502;

(v) direct that before moving for an order relating to discovery, the movant must request a conference with the court;

(vi) set dates for pretrial conferences and for trial; and

(vii) include other appropriate matters.

(4) ***Modifying a Schedule.*** A schedule may be modified only for good cause and with the judge's consent.

(c) Attendance and Matters for Consideration at a Pretrial Conference.

(1) ***Attendance.*** A represented party must authorize at least one of its attorneys to make stipulations and admissions about all matters that can reasonably be anticipated for discussion at a pretrial conference. If appropriate, the court may require that a party or its representative be present or reasonably available by other means to consider possible settlement.

(2) ***Matters for Consideration.*** At any pretrial conference, the court may consider and take appropriate action on the following matters:

(A) formulating and simplifying the issues, and eliminating frivolous claims or defenses;

(B) amending the pleadings if necessary or desirable;

(C) obtaining admissions and stipulations about facts and documents to avoid unnecessary proof, and ruling in advance on the admissibility of evidence;

(D) avoiding unnecessary proof and cumulative evidence, and limiting the use of testimony under Federal Rule of Evidence 702;

(E) determining the appropriateness and timing of summary adjudication under Rule 56;

(F) controlling and scheduling discovery, including orders affecting disclosures and discovery under Rule 26 and Rules 29 through 37;

(G) identifying witnesses and documents, scheduling the filing and exchange of any pretrial briefs, and setting dates for further conferences and for trial;

(H) referring matters to a magistrate judge or a master;

(I) settling the case and using special procedures to assist in resolving the dispute when authorized by statute or local rule;

(J) determining the form and content of the pretrial order;

(K) disposing of pending motions;

(L) adopting special procedures for managing potentially difficult or protracted actions that may involve complex issues, multiple parties, difficult legal questions, or unusual proof problems;

(M) ordering a separate trial under Rule 42(b) of a claim, counterclaim, crossclaim, third-party claim, or particular issue;

(N) ordering the presentation of evidence early in the trial on a manageable issue that might, on the evidence, be the basis for a judgment as a matter of law under Rule 50(a) or a judgment on partial findings under Rule 52(c);

(O) establishing a reasonable limit on the time allowed to present evidence; and

(P) facilitating in other ways the just, speedy, and inexpensive disposition of the action.

(d) Pretrial Orders. After any conference under this rule, the court should issue an order reciting the action taken. This order controls the course of the action unless the court modifies it.

(e) Final Pretrial Conference and Orders. The court may hold a final pretrial conference to formulate a trial plan, including a plan to facilitate the admission of evidence. The conference must be held as close to the start of trial as is reasonable, and must be attended by at least one

attorney who will conduct the trial for each party and by any unrepresented party. The court may modify the order issued after a final pretrial conference only to prevent manifest injustice.

(f) Sanctions.

(1) ***In General.*** On motion or on its own, the court may issue any just orders, including those authorized by Rule 37(b)(2)(A)(ii)-(vii), if a party or its attorney:

(A) fails to appear at a scheduling or other pretrial conference;

(B) is substantially unprepared to participate — or does not participate in good faith — in the conference; or

(C) fails to obey a scheduling or other pretrial order.

(2) ***Imposing Fees and Costs.*** Instead of or in addition to any other sanction, the court must order the party, its attorney, or both to pay the reasonable expenses — including attorney's fees — incurred because of any noncompliance with this rule, unless the noncompliance was substantially justified or other circumstances make an award of expenses unjust.

ADVISORY COMMITTEE NOTES

1983 Amendment [some citations omitted without notation — ED.]

Introduction

Rule 16 has not been amended since the Federal Rules were promulgated in 1938. In many respects, the rule has been a success. For example, there is evidence that pretrial conferences may improve the quality of justice rendered in the federal courts by sharpening the preparation and presentation of cases, tending to eliminate trial surprise, and improving, as well as facilitating, the settlement process. See 6 Wright & Miller, *Federal Practice and Procedure:* Civil § 1522 (1971). However, in other respects particularly with regard to case management, the rule has not always been as helpful as it might have been. Thus there has been a widespread feeling that amendment is necessary to encourage pretrial management that meets the needs of modern litigation. See *Report of the National Commission for the Review of Antitrust Laws and Procedures* (1979).

Major criticism of Rule 16 has centered on the fact that its application can result in over-regulation of some cases and under-regulation of others. In simple, run-of-the-mill cases, attorneys have found pretrial requirements burdensome. It is claimed that over-administration leads to a series of mini-trials that result in a waste of an attorney's time and needless expense to a client. Pollack, *Pretrial Procedures More Effectively Handled,* 65 F.R.D. 475 (1974). This is especially likely to be true when pretrial proceedings occur long before trial. At the other end of the spectrum, the discretionary character of Rule 16 and its orientation toward a single conference late in the pretrial process has led to under-administration of complex or protracted cases. Without judicial guidance beginning shortly after institution, these cases often become mired in discovery.

Four sources of criticism of pretrial have been identified. First, conferences often are seen as a mere exchange of legalistic contentions without any real analysis of the particular case. Second, the result frequently is nothing but a formal agreement on minutiae. Third, the conferences are seen as unnecessary and time-consuming in cases that will be settled before trial. Fourth, the meetings can be ceremonial and ritualistic, having little effect on the trial and being of minimal value, particularly when the attorneys attending the sessions are not the ones who will try the case or lack authority to enter into binding stipulations.

There also have been difficulties with the pretrial orders that issue following Rule 16 conferences. When an order is entered far in advance of trial, some issues may not be properly formulated. Counsel naturally are cautious and often try to preserve as many options as possible. If the judge who tries the case did not conduct the conference, he could find it difficult to determine exactly what was agreed to at the conference. But any insistence on a detailed order may be too burdensome, depending on the nature or posture of the case.

Given the significant changes in federal civil litigation since 1938 that are not reflected in Rule 16, it has been extensively rewritten and expanded to meet the challenges of modern litigation. Empirical studies reveal that when a trial judge intervenes personally at an early stage to assume judicial control over a case and to schedule dates for completion by the parties of the principal pretrial steps, the case is disposed of by settlement or trial more efficiently and with less cost and delay than when the parties are left to their own devices. Flanders, *Case Management and Court Management in United States District Courts* 17, Federal Judicial Center (1977). Thus, the rule mandates a pretrial scheduling order. However, although scheduling and pretrial conferences are encouraged in appropriate cases, they are not mandated.

Discussion

Subdivision (a); Pretrial Conferences; Objectives. The amended rule makes scheduling and case management an express goal of pretrial procedure. This is done in Rule 16(a) by shifting the emphasis away from a conference focused solely on the trial and toward a process of judicial management that embraces the entire pretrial phase, especially motions and discovery. In addition, the amendment explicitly recognizes some of the objectives of pretrial conferences and the powers that many courts already have assumed. Rule 16 thus will be a more accurate reflection of actual practice.

Subdivision (b); Scheduling and Planning. The most significant change in Rule 16 is the mandatory scheduling order described in Rule 16(b), which is based in part on Wisconsin Civil Procedure Rule 802.10. The idea of scheduling orders is not new. It has been used by many federal courts.

Although a mandatory scheduling order encourages the court to become involved in case management early in the litigation, it represents a degree of judicial involvement that is not warranted in many cases. Thus, subdivision (b) permits each district court to promulgate a local rule under Rule 83 exempting certain categories of cases in which the burdens of scheduling orders exceed the administrative efficiencies that would be gained. See Eastern District of Virginia, Local Rule 12(1). Logical candidates for this treatment include social security

disability matters, habeas corpus petitions, forfeitures, and reviews of certain administrative actions.

A scheduling conference may be requested either by the judge, a magistrate when authorized by district court rule, or a party within 120 days after the summons and complaint are filed. If a scheduling conference is not arranged within that time and the case is not exempted by local rule, a scheduling order must be issued under Rule 16(b), after some communication with the parties, which may be by telephone or mail rather than in person. The use of the term "judge" in subdivision (b) reflects the Advisory Committee's judgment that it is preferable that this task should be handled by a district judge rather than a magistrate, except when the magistrate is acting under 28 U.S.C. § 636(c). While personal supervision by the trial judge is preferred, the rule, in recognition of the impracticality or difficulty of complying with such a requirement in some districts, authorizes a district by local rule to delegate the duties to a magistrate. In order to formulate a practicable scheduling order, the judge, or a magistrate when authorized by district court rule, and attorneys are required to develop a timetable for the matters listed in Rule 16(b)(1)-(3) [now Rule 16(b)(3)(A) — ED.]. As indicated in Rule 16(b)(4)-(5)[with modifications, now Rule 16(b)(3)(B) — ED.], the order may also deal with a wide range of other matters. The rule is phrased permissively as to clauses (4) and (5), however, because scheduling these items at an early point may not be feasible or appropriate. Even though subdivision (b) relates only to scheduling, there is no reason why some of the procedural matters listed in Rule 16(c) cannot be addressed at the same time, at least when a scheduling conference is held.

Item (1) assures that at some point both the parties and the pleadings will be fixed, by setting a time within which joinder of parties shall be completed and the pleadings amended.

Item (2) requires setting time limits for interposing various motions that otherwise might be used as stalling techniques.

Item (3) deals with the problem of procrastination and delay by attorneys in a context in which scheduling is especially important-discovery. Scheduling the completion of discovery can serve some of the same functions as the conference described in Rule 26(f).

Item (4) refers to setting dates for conferences and for trial. Scheduling multiple pretrial conferences may well be desirable if the case is complex and the court believes that a more elaborate pretrial structure, such as that described in the *Manual for Complex Litigation,* should be employed. On the other hand, only one pretrial conference may be necessary in an uncomplicated case.

As long as the case is not exempted by local rule, the court must issue a written scheduling order even if no scheduling conference is called. The order, like pretrial orders under the former rule and those under new Rule 16(c), normally will "control the subsequent course of the action." See Rule 16(e). [The comparable language — "controls the course of the action" — is now found in Rule 16(d). — ED.] After consultation with the attorneys for the parties and any unrepresented parties — a formal motion is not necessary — the court may modify the schedule on a showing of good cause if it cannot reasonably be met despite the diligence of the party seeking the extension. Since the scheduling order is entered early in the

litigation, this standard seems more appropriate than a "manifest injustice" or "substantial hardship" test. Otherwise, a fear that extensions will not be granted may encourage counsel to request the longest possible periods for completing pleading, joinder, and discovery. Moreover, changes in the court's calendar sometimes will oblige the judge or magistrate when authorized by district court rule to modify the scheduling order.

The district courts undoubtedly will develop several prototype scheduling orders for different types of cases. In addition, when no formal conference is held, the court may obtain scheduling information by telephone, mail, or otherwise. In many instances this will result in a scheduling order better suited to the individual case than a standard order, without taking the time that would be required by a formal conference.

Rule 16(b) assures that the judge will take some early control over the litigation, even when its character does not warrant holding a scheduling conference. Despite the fact that the process of preparing a scheduling order does not always bring the attorneys and judge together, the fixing of time limits serves

> to stimulate litigants to narrow the areas of inquiry and advocacy to those they believe are truly relevant and material. Time limits not only compress the amount of time for litigation, they should also reduce the amount of resources invested in litigation. Litigants are forced to establish discovery priorities and thus to do the most important work first.

Report of the National Commission for the Review of Antitrust Laws and Procedures 28 (1979).

Thus, except in exempted cases, the judge or a magistrate when authorized by district court rule will have taken some action in every case within 120 days after the complaint is filed that notifies the attorneys that the case will be moving toward trial. Subdivision (b) is reenforced by subdivision (f), which makes it clear that the sanctions for violating a scheduling order are the same as those for violating a pretrial order.

Subdivision (c); Subjects to be Discussed at Pretrial Conferences. This subdivision expands upon the list of things that may be discussed at a pretrial conference that appeared in original Rule 16. The intention is to encourage better planning and management of litigation. Increased judicial control during the pretrial process accelerates the processing and termination of cases. Flanders, *Case Management and Court Management in United States District Courts*, 39 Federal Judicial Center (1977).

The reference in Rule 16(c)(1) to "formulation" [now "formulating," found in Rule 16(c)(2)(A) — ED.] is intended to clarify and confirm the court's power to identify the litigable issues. It has been added in the hope of promoting efficiency and conserving judicial resources by identifying the real issues prior to trial, thereby saving time and expense for everyone. The notion is emphasized by expressly authorizing the elimination of frivolous claims or defenses at a pretrial conference. There is no reason to require that this await a formal motion for summary judgment. Nor is there any reason for the court to wait for the parties to initiate the process called for in Rule 16(c)(1) [now Rule 16(c)(2)(A) — ED.].

The timing of any attempt at issue formulation is a matter of judicial discretion. In relatively simple cases it may not be necessary or may take the form of a stipulation between counsel or a request by the court that counsel work together to draft a proposed order.

Counsel bear a substantial responsibility for assisting the court in identifying the factual issues worthy of trial. If counsel fail to identify an issue for the court, the right to have the issue tried is waived. Although an order specifying the issues is intended to be binding, it may be amended at trial to avoid manifest injustice. See Rule 16(e). However, the rule's effectiveness depends on the court employing its discretion sparingly.

Clause (6) [now Rule 16(c)(2)(H) — ED.] acknowledges the widespread availability and use of magistrates. The corresponding provision in the original rule referred only to masters and limited the function of the reference to the making of "findings to be used as evidence" in a case to be tried to a jury. The new text is not limited and broadens the potential use of a magistrate to that permitted by the Magistrate's Act.

Clause (7) [now Rule 16(c)(2)(I) — ED.] explicitly recognizes that it has become commonplace to discuss settlement at pretrial conferences. Since it obviously eases crowded court dockets and results in savings to the litigants and the judicial system, settlement should be facilitated at as early a stage of the litigation as possible. Although it is not the purpose of Rule 16(b)(7) [probably should be "Rule 16(c)(7)," which is now found in Rule 16(c)(2)(I) — ED.] to impose settlement negotiations on unwilling litigants, it is believed that providing a neutral forum for discussing the subject might foster it. For instance, a judge to whom a case has been assigned may arrange, on his own motion or at a party's request, to have settlement conferences handled by another member of the court or by a magistrate. The rule does not make settlement conferences mandatory because they would be a waste of time in many cases. See Flanders, *Case Management and Court Management in the United States District Courts*, 39 Federal Judicial Center (1977). Requests for a conference from a party indicating a willingness to talk settlement normally should be honored, unless thought to be frivolous or dilatory.

A settlement conference is appropriate at any time. It may be held in conjunction with a pretrial or discovery conference, although various objectives of pretrial management, such as moving the case toward trial, may not always be compatible with settlement negotiations, and thus a separate settlement conference may be desirable.

In addition to settlement, Rule 16(c)(7) [now Rule 16(c)(2)(I) — ED.] refers to exploring the use of procedures other than litigation to resolve the dispute. This includes urging the litigants to employ adjudicatory techniques outside the courthouse. See, for example, the experiment described in *Green, Marks & Olson, Settling Large Case Litigation: An Alternative Approach*, 11 Loyola of L.A. L. Rev. 493 (1978).

Rule 16(c)(10) [now Rule 16(c)(2)(L) — ED.] authorizes the use of special pretrial procedures to expedite the adjudication of potentially difficult or protracted cases. Some district courts obviously have done so for many years. Clause 10 provides an explicit authorization for such procedures and encourages their use. No particular techniques have been described; the Committee felt that

flexibility and experience are the keys to efficient management of complex cases. Extensive guidance is offered in such documents as the *Manual for Complex Litigation*.

The rule simply identifies characteristics that make a case a strong candidate for special treatment. The four mentioned are illustrative, not exhaustive, and overlap to some degree. But experience has shown that one or more of them will be present in every protracted or difficult case and it seems desirable to set them out. See Kendig, *Procedures for Management of Non-Routine Cases,* 3 Hofstra L. Rev. 701 (1975).

The last sentence of subdivision (c) [with modifications, now Rule 16(c)(1) — ED.] is new. See Wisconsin Civil Procedure Rule 802.11(2). It has been added to meet one of the criticisms of the present practice described earlier and insure proper preconference preparation so that the meeting is more than a ceremonial or ritualistic event. The reference to "authority" [now "authorize" — ED.] is not intended to insist upon the ability to settle the litigation. Nor should the rule be read to encourage the judge conducting the conference to compel attorneys to enter into stipulations or to make admissions that they consider to be unreasonable, that touch on matters that could not normally have been anticipated to arise at the conference, or on subjects of a dimension that normally require prior consultation with and approval from the client.

Subdivision (d); Final Pretrial Conference [now Rule 16(e) — ED.]. This provision has been added to make it clear that the time between any final pretrial conference (which in a simple case may be the only pretrial conference) and trial should be as short as possible to be certain that the litigants make substantial progress with the case and avoid the inefficiency of having that preparation repeated when there is a delay between the last pretrial conference and trial. An optimum time of 10 days to two weeks has been suggested by one federal judge. Rubin, *The Managed Calendar: Some Pragmatic Suggestions About Achieving the Just, Speedy and Inexpensive Determination of Civil Cases in Federal Courts,* 4 Just. Sys. J. 135, 141 (1976). The Committee, however, concluded that it would be inappropriate to fix a precise time in the rule, given the numerous variables that could bear on the matter. Thus the timing has been left to the court's discretion.

At least one of the attorneys who will conduct the trial for each party must be present at the final pretrial conference. At this late date there should be no doubt as to which attorney or attorneys this will be. Since the agreements and stipulations made at this final conference will control the trial, the presence of lawyers who will be involved in it is especially useful to assist the judge in structuring the case, and to lead to a more effective trial.

Subdivision (e); Pretrial Orders [now Rule 16(d) and, in part, (e) — ED.]. Rule 16(e) does not substantially change the portion of the original rule dealing with pretrial orders. The purpose of an order is to guide the course of the litigation and the language of the original rule making that clear has been retained. No compelling reason has been found for major revision, especially since this portion of the rule has been interpreted and clarified by over forty years of judicial decisions with comparatively little difficulty. See 6 Wright & Miller, *Federal Practice and Procedure*: Civil §§ 1521-30 (1971). Changes in language therefore have been kept to a minimum to avoid confusion.

Since the amended rule encourages more extensive pretrial management than did the original, two or more conferences may be held in many cases. The language of Rule 16(e) recognizes this possibility and the corresponding need to issue more than one pretrial order in a single case.

Once formulated, pretrial orders should not be changed lightly; but total inflexibility is undesirable. The exact words used to describe the standard for amending the pretrial order probably are less important than the meaning given them in practice. By not imposing any limitation on the ability to modify a pretrial order, the rule reflects the reality that in any process of continuous management, what is done at one conference may have to be altered at the next. In the case of the final pretrial order, however, a more stringent standard is called for and the words "to prevent manifest injustice," which appeared in the original rule, have been retained. They have the virtue of familiarity and adequately describe the restraint the trial judge should exercise.

Many local rules make the plaintiff's attorney responsible for drafting a proposed pretrial order, either before or after the conference. Others allow the court to appoint any of the attorneys to perform the task, and others leave it to the court. Rule 16 has never addressed this matter. Since there is no consensus about which method of drafting the order works best and there is no reason to believe that nationwide uniformity is needed, the rule has been left silent on the point. See *Handbook for Effective Pretrial Procedure,* 37 F.R.D. 225 (1964).

Subdivision (f); Sanctions. Original Rule 16 did not mention the sanctions that might be imposed for failing to comply with the rule. However, courts have not hesitated to enforce it by appropriate measures. See, e.g., *Link v. Wabash R. Co.*, 370 U.S. 628 (1962) (district court's dismissal under Rule 41(b) after plaintiff's attorney failed to appear at a pretrial conference upheld); *Admiral Theatre Corp. v. Douglas Theatre*, 585 F.2d 877 (8th Cir. 1978) (district court has discretion to exclude exhibits or refuse to permit the testimony of a witness not listed prior to trial in contravention of its pretrial order).

To reflect that existing practice, and to obviate dependence upon Rule 41(b) or the court's inherent power to regulate litigation, *cf. Societe Internationale Pour Participations Industrielles et Commerciales, S.A. v. Rogers*, 357 U.S. 197 (1958), Rule 16(f) expressly provides for imposing sanctions on disobedient or recalcitrant parties, their attorneys, or both in four types of situations. Rodes, Ripple & Mooney, *Sanctions Imposable for Violations of the Federal Rules of Civil Procedure* 65-67, 80-84, Federal Judicial Center (1981). Furthermore, explicit reference to sanctions reenforces the rule's intention to encourage forceful judicial management.

Rule 16(f) incorporates portions of Rule 37(b)(2), which prescribes sanctions for failing to make discovery. This should facilitate application of Rule 16(f), since courts and lawyers already are familiar with the Rule 37 standards. Among the sanctions authorized by the new subdivision are: preclusion order, striking a pleading, staying the proceeding, default judgment, contempt, and charging a party, his attorney, or both with the expenses, including attorney's fees, caused by noncompliance. The contempt sanction, however, is only available for a violation of a court order. The references in Rule 16(f) are not exhaustive.

As is true under Rule 37(b)(2), the imposition of sanctions may be sought by either the court or a party. In addition, the court has discretion to impose whichever sanction it feels is appropriate under the circumstances. Its action is reviewable under the abuse-of-discretion standard. See *National Hockey League v. Metropolitan Hockey Club, Inc.*, 427 U.S. 639 (1976).

1993 Amendment

Subdivision (b). One purpose of this amendment is to provide a more appropriate deadline for the initial scheduling order required by the rule. The former rule directed that the order be entered within 120 days from the filing of the complaint. This requirement has created problems because Rule 4(m) allows 120 [now 90 — ED.]days for service and ordinarily at least one defendant should be available to participate in the process of formulating the scheduling order. The revision provides that the order is to be entered within 90 days after the date a defendant first appears (whether by answer or by a motion under Rule 12) or, if earlier (as may occur in some actions against the United States or if service is waived under Rule 4), within 120 days after service of the complaint on a defendant. The longer time provided by the revision is not intended to encourage unnecessary delays in entering the scheduling order. Indeed, in most cases the order can and should be entered at a much earlier date. Rather, the additional time is intended to alleviate problems in multi-defendant cases and should ordinarily be adequate to enable participation by all defendants initially named in the action.

In many cases the scheduling order can and should be entered before this deadline. However, when setting a scheduling conference, the court should take into account the effect this setting will have in establishing deadlines for the parties to meet under revised Rule 26(f) and to exchange information under revised Rule 26(a)(1). While the parties are expected to stipulate to additional time for making their disclosures when warranted by the circumstances, a scheduling conference held before defendants have had time to learn much about the case may result in diminishing the value of the Rule 26(f) meeting, the parties' proposed discovery plan, and indeed the conference itself.

New paragraph (4) [now Rule 16(b)(3)(B)(i)-(ii) — ED.] has been added to highlight that it will frequently be desirable for the scheduling order to include provisions relating to the timing of disclosures under Rule 26(a). While the initial disclosures required by Rule 26(a)(1) will ordinarily have been made before entry of the scheduling order, the timing and sequence for disclosure of expert testimony and of the witnesses and exhibits to be used at trial should be tailored to the circumstances of the case and is a matter that should be considered at the initial scheduling conference. Similarly, the scheduling order might contain provisions modifying the extent of discovery (*e.g.,* number and length of depositions) otherwise permitted under these rules or by a local rule.

The report from the attorneys concerning their meeting and proposed discovery plan, as required by revised Rule 26(f), should be submitted to the court before the scheduling order is entered. Their proposals, particularly regarding matters on which they agree, should be of substantial value to the court in setting the timing and limitations on discovery and should reduce the time of the court needed to conduct a meaningful conference under Rule 16(b). As under the prior rule, while

a scheduling order is mandated, a scheduling conference is not. However, in view of the benefits to be derived from the litigants and a judicial officer meeting in person, a Rule 16(b) conference should, to the extent practicable, be held in all cases that will involve discovery.

This subdivision, as well as subdivision (c)(8) [now Rule 16(c)(2)(H) — ED.], also is revised to reflect the new title of United States Magistrate Judges pursuant to the Judicial Improvements Act of 1990.

Subdivision (c). The primary purposes of the changes in subdivision (c) are to call attention to the opportunities for structuring of trial under Rules 42, 50, and 52 and to eliminate questions that have occasionally been raised regarding the authority of the court to make appropriate orders designed either to facilitate settlement or to provide for an efficient and economical trial. The prefatory language of this subdivision is revised to clarify the court's power to enter appropriate orders at a conference notwithstanding the objection of a party. Of course settlement is dependent upon agreement by the parties and, indeed, a conference is most effective and productive when the parties participate in a spirit of cooperation and mindful of their responsibilities under Rule 1.

Paragraph (4) [now Rule 16(c)(2)(D) — ED.] is revised to clarify that in advance of trial the court may address the need for, and possible limitations on, the use of expert testimony under Rule 702 of the Federal Rules of Evidence. Even when proposed expert testimony might be admissible under the standards of Rules 403 and 702 of the evidence rules, the court may preclude or limit such testimony if the cost to the litigants — which may include the cost to adversaries of securing testimony on the same subjects by other experts — would be unduly expensive given the needs of the case and the other evidence available at trial.

Paragraph (5) [now Rule 16(c)(2)(E) — ED.] is added (and the remaining paragraphs renumbered) in recognition that use of Rule 56 to avoid or reduce the scope of trial is a topic that can, and often should, be considered at a pretrial conference. Renumbered paragraph (11) [now Rule 16(c)(2)(K) — ED. enables the court to rule on pending motions for summary adjudication that are ripe for decision at the time of the conference. Often, however, the potential use of Rule 56 is a matter that arises from discussions during a conference. The court may then call for motions to be filed.

Paragraph (6) [now Rule 16(c)(2)(F) — ED.] is added to emphasize that a major objective of pretrial conferences should be to consider appropriate controls on the extent and timing of discovery. In many cases the court should also specify the times and sequence for disclosure of written reports from experts under revised Rule 26(a)(2)(B) and perhaps direct changes in the types of experts from whom written reports are required. Consideration should also be given to possible changes in the timing or form of the disclosure of trial witnesses and documents under Rule 26(a)(3).

Paragraph (9) [now Rule 16(c)(2)(I) — ED.] is revised to describe more accurately the various procedures that, in addition to traditional settlement conferences, may be helpful in settling litigation. Even if a case cannot immediately be settled, the judge and attorneys can explore possible use of alternative procedures such as mini-trials, summary jury trials, mediation, neutral evaluation, and nonbinding arbitration that can lead to consensual resolution of

the dispute without a full trial on the merits. The rule acknowledges the presence of statutes and local rules or plans that may authorize use of some of these procedures even when not agreed to by the parties. See 28 U.S.C. §§ 473(a)(6), 473(b)(4), 651-58; Section 104(b)(2), Pub. L. 101-650. The rule does not attempt to resolve questions as to the extent a court would be authorized to require such proceedings as an exercise of its inherent powers.

The amendment of paragraph (9) should be read in conjunction with the sentence added to the end of subdivision (c) [now Rule 16(c)(1) — ED.], authorizing the court to direct that, in appropriate cases, a responsible representative of the parties be present or available by telephone during a conference in order to discuss possible settlement of the case. The sentence refers to participation by a party or its representative. Whether this would be the individual party, an officer of a corporate party, a representative from an insurance carrier, or someone else would depend on the circumstances. Particularly in litigation in which governmental agencies or large amounts of money are involved, there may be no one with on-the-spot settlement authority, and the most that should be expected is access to a person who would have a major role in submitting a recommendation to the body or board with ultimate decision-making responsibility. The selection of the appropriate representative should ordinarily be left to the party and its counsel. Finally, it should be noted that the unwillingness of a party to be available, even by telephone, for a settlement conference may be a clear signal that the time and expense involved in pursuing settlement is likely to be unproductive and that personal participation by the parties should not be required.

The explicit authorization in the rule to require personal participation in the manner stated is not intended to limit the reasonable exercise of the court's inherent powers, *e.g., G. Heileman Brewing Co. v. Joseph Oat Corp.*, 871 F.2d 648 (7th Cir. 1989), or its power to require party participation under the Civil Justice Reform Act of 1990. See 28 U.S.C. § 473(b)(5) (civil justice expense and delay reduction plans adopted by district courts may include requirement that representatives "with authority to bind [parties] in settlement discussions" be available during settlement conferences).

New paragraphs (13) [now Rule 16(c)(2)(M) — ED.] and (14) [now Rule 16(c)(2)(N) — ED.] are added to call attention to the opportunities for structuring of trial under Rule 42 and under revised Rules 50 and 52.

Paragraph (15) [now Rule 16(c)(2)(O) — ED.] is also new. It supplements the power of the court to limit the extent of evidence under Rules 403 and 611(a) of the Federal Rules of Evidence, which typically would be invoked as a result of developments during trial. Limits on the length of trial established at a conference in advance of trial can provide the parties with a better opportunity to determine priorities and exercise selectivity in presenting evidence than when limits are imposed during trial. Any such limits must be reasonable under the circumstances, and ordinarily the court should impose them only after receiving appropriate submissions from the parties outlining the nature of the testimony expected to be presented through various witnesses, and the expected duration of direct and cross-examination.

2006 Amendment

The amendment to Rule 16(b) is designed to alert the court to the possible need to address the handling of discovery of electronically stored information early in the litigation if such discovery is expected to occur. Rule 26(f) is amended to direct the parties to discuss discovery of electronically stored information if such discovery is contemplated in the action. . . . In many instances, the court's involvement early in the litigation will help avoid difficulties that might otherwise arise.

Rule 16(b) is also amended to include among the topics that may be addressed in the scheduling order any agreements that the parties reach to facilitate discovery by minimizing the risk of waiver of privilege or work-product protection. Rule 26(f) is amended to add to the discovery plan the parties' proposal for the court to enter a case-management or other order adopting such an agreement. The parties may agree to various arrangements. For example, they may agree to initial provision of requested materials without waiver of privilege or protection to enable the party seeking production to designate the materials desired or protection for actual production, with the privilege review of only those materials to follow. Alternatively, they may agree that if privileged or protected information is inadvertently produced, the producing party may by timely notice assert the privilege or protection and obtain return of the materials without waiver. Other arrangements are possible. In most circumstances, a party who receives information under such an arrangement cannot assert that production of the information waived a claim of privilege or of protection as trial-preparation material.

An order that includes the parties' agreement may be helpful in avoiding delay and excessive cost in discovery. *See Manual for Complex Litigation (4th)* § 11.446. Rule 16(b)(6) [now Rule 16(b)(3)(B)(vi) — ED.] recognizes the propriety of including such agreements in the court's order. The rule does not provide the court with authority to enter such a case-management or other order without party agreement, or limit the court's authority to act on motion.

2015 Amendment

The provision for consulting at a scheduling conference by "telephone, mail, or other means" is deleted. A scheduling conference is more effective if the court and parties engage in direct simultaneous communication. The conference may be held in person, by telephone, or by more sophisticated electronic means.

The time to issue the scheduling order is reduced to the earlier of 90 days (not 120 days) after any defendant has been served, or 60 days (not 90 days) after any defendant has appeared. This change, together with the shortened time for making service under Rule 4(m), will reduce delay at the beginning of litigation. At the same time, a new provision recognizes that the court may find good cause to extend the time to issue the scheduling order. In some cases it may be that the parties cannot prepare adequately for a meaningful Rule 26(f) conference and then a scheduling conference in the time allowed. Litigation involving complex issues, multiple parties, and large organizations, public or private, may be more likely to need extra time to establish meaningful collaboration between counsel and the people who can supply the information needed to participate in a useful way. Because the time for the Rule 26(f) conference is geared to the time for the

scheduling conference or order, an order extending the time for the scheduling conference will also extend the time for the Rule 26(f) conference. But in most cases it will be desirable to hold at least a first scheduling conference in the time set by the rule.

Three items are added to the list of permitted contents in Rule 16(b)(3)(B).

The order may provide for preservation of electronically stored information, a topic also added to the provisions of a discovery plan under Rule 26(f)(3)(C). Parallel amendments of Rule 37(e) recognize that a duty to preserve discoverable information may arise before an action is filed.

The order also may include agreements incorporated in a court order under Evidence Rule 502 controlling the effects of disclosure of information covered by attorney-client privilege or work-product protection, a topic also added to the provisions of a discovery plan under Rule 26(f)(3)(D).

Finally, the order may direct that before filing a motion for an order relating to discovery the movant must request a conference with the court. Many judges who hold such conferences find them an efficient way to resolve most discovery disputes without the delay and burdens attending a formal motion, but the decision whether to require such conferences is left to the discretion of the judge in each case.

TITLE IV. PARTIES

Rule 17. Plaintiff and Defendant; Capacity; Public Officers

(a) Real Party in Interest.

(1) ***Designation in General.*** An action must be prosecuted in the name of the real party in interest. The following may sue in their own names without joining the person for whose benefit the action is brought:

(A) an executor;

(B) an administrator;

(C) a guardian;

(D) a bailee;

(E) a trustee of an express trust;

(F) a party with whom or in whose name a contract has been made for another's benefit; and

(G) a party authorized by statute.

(2) ***Action in the Name of the United States for Another's Use or Benefit.*** When a federal statute so provides, an action for another's use or benefit must be brought in the name of the United States.

(3) ***Joinder of the Real Party in Interest.*** The court may not dismiss an action for failure to prosecute in the name of the real party in interest until, after an objection, a reasonable time has been allowed for the real party in interest to ratify, join, or be substituted into the action. After ratification, joinder, or substitution, the action proceeds as if it had been originally commenced by the real party in interest.

(b) Capacity to Sue or Be Sued. Capacity to sue or be sued is determined as follows:

(1) for an individual who is not acting in a representative capacity, by the law of the individual's domicile;

(2) for a corporation, by the law under which it was organized; and

(3) for all other parties, by the law of the state where the court is located, except that:

(A) a partnership or other unincorporated association with no such capacity under that state's law may sue or be sued in its common name to enforce a substantive right existing under the United States Constitution or laws; and

(B) 28 U.S.C. §§ 754 and 959(a) govern the capacity of a receiver appointed by a United States court to sue or be sued in a United States court.

(c) Minor or Incompetent Person.

(1) ***With a Representative.*** The following representatives may sue or defend on behalf of a minor or an incompetent person:

(A) a general guardian;

(B) a committee;

(C) a conservator; or

(D) a like fiduciary.

(2) ***Without a Representative.*** A minor or an incompetent person who does not have a duly appointed representative may sue by a next friend or by a guardian ad litem. The court must appoint a guardian ad litem — or issue another appropriate order — to protect a minor or incompetent person who is unrepresented in an action.

(d) Public Officer's Title and Name. A public officer who sues or is sued in an official capacity may be designated by official title rather than by name, but the court may order that the officer's name be added.

Rule 18. Joinder of Claims

(a) In General. A party asserting a claim, counterclaim, crossclaim, or third-party claim may join, as independent or alternative claims, as many claims as it has against an opposing party.

(b) Joinder of Contingent Claims. A party may join two claims even though one of them is contingent on the disposition of the other; but the court may grant relief only in accordance with the parties' relative substantive rights. In particular, a plaintiff may state a claim for money and a claim to set aside a conveyance that is fraudulent as to that plaintiff, without first obtaining a judgment for the money.

Rule 19. Required Joinder of Parties

(a) Persons Required to Be Joined if Feasible.

(1) ***Required Party.*** A person who is subject to service of process and whose joinder will not deprive the court of subject-matter jurisdiction must be joined as a party if:

(A) in that person's absence, the court cannot accord complete relief among existing parties; or

(B) that person claims an interest relating to the subject of the action and is so situated that disposing of the action in the person's absence may:

(i) as a practical matter impair or impede the person's ability to protect the interest; or

(ii) leave an existing party subject to a substantial risk of incurring double, multiple, or otherwise inconsistent obligations because of the interest.

(2) ***Joinder by Court Order.*** If a person has not been joined as required, the court must order that the person be made a party. A person who refuses to join as a plaintiff may be made either a defendant or, in a proper case, an involuntary plaintiff.

(3) ***Venue.*** If a joined party objects to venue and the joinder would make venue improper, the court must dismiss that party.

(b) When Joinder Is Not Feasible. If a person who is required to be joined if feasible cannot be joined, the court must determine whether, in equity and good conscience, the action should proceed among the existing parties or should be dismissed. The factors for the court to consider include:

(1) the extent to which a judgment rendered in the person's absence might prejudice that person or the existing parties;

(2) the extent to which any prejudice could be lessened or avoided by:

(A) protective provisions in the judgment;

(B) shaping the relief; or

(C) other measures;

(3) whether a judgment rendered in the person's absence would be adequate; and

(4) whether the plaintiff would have an adequate remedy if the action were dismissed for nonjoinder.

(c) Pleading the Reasons for Nonjoinder. When asserting a claim for relief, a party must state:

(1) the name, if known, of any person who is required to be joined if feasible but is not joined; and

(2) the reasons for not joining that person.

(d) Exception for Class Actions. This rule is subject to Rule 23.

ADVISORY COMMITTEE NOTES

2007 Amendment

. . .

Former Rule 19(b) described the conclusion that an action should be dismissed for inability to join a Rule 19(a) party by carrying forward traditional terminology: "the absent person being thus regarded as indispensable." "Indispensable" was used only to express a conclusion reached by applying the tests of Rule 19(b). It has been discarded as redundant.

Rule 20. Permissive Joinder of Parties

(a) Persons Who May Join or Be Joined.

(1) ***Plaintiffs***. Persons may join in one action as plaintiffs if:

(A) they assert any right to relief jointly, severally, or in the alternative with respect to or arising out of the same transaction, occurrence, or series of transactions or occurrences; and

(B) any question of law or fact common to all plaintiffs will arise in the action.

(2) ***Defendants***. Persons — as well as a vessel, cargo, or other property subject to admiralty process in rem — may be joined in one action as defendants if:

(A) any right to relief is asserted against them jointly, severally, or in the alternative with respect to or arising out of the same transaction, occurrence, or series of transactions or occurrences; and

(B) any question of law or fact common to all defendants will arise in the action.

(3) ***Extent of Relief***. Neither a plaintiff nor a defendant need be interested in obtaining or defending against all the relief demanded. The court may grant judgment to one or more plaintiffs according to their rights, and against one or more defendants according to their liabilities.

(b) Protective Measures. The court may issue orders — including an order for separate trials — to protect a party against embarrassment, delay, expense, or other prejudice that arises from including a person against whom the party asserts no claim and who asserts no claim against the party.

Rule 21. Misjoinder and Nonjoinder of Parties

Misjoinder of parties is not a ground for dismissing an action. On motion or on its own, the court may at any time, on just terms, add or drop a party. The court may also sever any claim against a party.

Rule 22. Interpleader

(a) Grounds.

(1) ***By a Plaintiff***. Persons with claims that may expose a plaintiff to double or multiple liability may be joined as defendants and required to interplead. Joinder for interpleader is proper even though:

(A) the claims of the several claimants, or the titles on which their claims depend, lack a common origin or are adverse and independent rather than identical; or

(B) the plaintiff denies liability in whole or in part to any or all of the claimants.

(2) ***By a Defendant***. A defendant exposed to similar liability may seek interpleader through a crossclaim or counterclaim.

(b) Relation to Other Rules and Statutes. This rule supplements — and does not limit — the joinder of parties allowed by Rule 20. The remedy this rule provides is in addition to — and does not supersede or

limit — the remedy provided by 28 U.S.C. §§ 1335, 1397, and 2361. An action under those statutes must be conducted under these rules.

Rule 23. Class Actions

(a) Prerequisites. One or more members of a class may sue or be sued as representative parties on behalf of all members only if:

(1) the class is so numerous that joinder of all members is impracticable;

(2) there are questions of law or fact common to the class;

(3) the claims or defenses of the representative parties are typical of the claims or defenses of the class; and

(4) the representative parties will fairly and adequately protect the interests of the class.

(b) Types of Class Actions. A class action may be maintained if Rule 23(a) is satisfied and if:

(1) prosecuting separate actions by or against individual class members would create a risk of:

(A) inconsistent or varying adjudications with respect to individual class members that would establish incompatible standards of conduct for the party opposing the class; or

(B) adjudications with respect to individual class members that, as a practical matter, would be dispositive of the interests of the other members not parties to the individual adjudications or would substantially impair or impede their ability to protect their interests;

(2) the party opposing the class has acted or refused to act on grounds that apply generally to the class, so that final injunctive relief or corresponding declaratory relief is appropriate respecting the class as a whole; or

(3) the court finds that the questions of law or fact common to class members predominate over any questions affecting only individual members, and that a class action is superior to other available methods for fairly and efficiently adjudicating the controversy. The matters pertinent to these findings include:

(A) the class members' interests in individually controlling the prosecution or defense of separate actions;

(B) the extent and nature of any litigation concerning the controversy already begun by or against class members;

(C) the desirability or undesirability of concentrating the litigation of the claims in the particular forum; and

(D) the likely difficulties in managing a class action.

(c) Certification Order; Notice to Class Members; Judgment; Issues Classes; Subclasses.

(1) ***Certification Order.***

(A) *Time to Issue.* At an early practicable time after a person sues or is sued as a class representative, the court must determine by order whether to certify the action as a class action.

(B) *Defining the Class; Appointing Class Counsel.* An order that certifies a class action must define the class and the class claims, issues, or defenses, and must appoint class counsel under Rule 23(g).

(C) *Altering or Amending the Order.* An order that grants or denies class certification may be altered or amended before final judgment.

(2) ***Notice.***

(A) *For (b)(1) or (b)(2) Classes.* For any class certified under Rule 23(b)(1) or (b)(2), the court may direct appropriate notice to the class.

(B) *For (b)(3) Classes.* For any class certified under Rule 23(b)(3), the court must direct to class members the best notice that is practicable under the circumstances, including individual notice to all members who can be identified through reasonable effort. The notice must clearly and concisely state in plain, easily understood language:

(i) the nature of the action;

(ii) the definition of the class certified;

(iii) the class claims, issues, or defenses;

(iv) that a class member may enter an appearance through an attorney if the member so desires;

(v) that the court will exclude from the class any member who requests exclusion;

(vi) the time and manner for requesting exclusion; and

(vii) the binding effect of a class judgment on members under Rule 23(c)(3).

(3) ***Judgment.*** Whether or not favorable to the class, the judgment in a class action must:

(A) for any class certified under Rule 23(b)(1) or (b)(2), include and describe those whom the court finds to be class members; and

(B) for any class certified under Rule 23(b)(3), include and specify or describe those to whom the Rule 23(c)(2) notice was directed, who have not requested exclusion, and whom the court finds to be class members.

(4) ***Particular Issues.*** When appropriate, an action may be brought or maintained as a class action with respect to particular issues.

(5) ***Subclasses.*** When appropriate, a class may be divided into subclasses that are each treated as a class under this rule.

(d) Conducting the Action.

(1) ***In General.*** In conducting an action under this rule, the court may issue orders that:

(A) determine the course of proceedings or prescribe measures to prevent undue repetition or complication in presenting evidence or argument;

(B) require — to protect class members and fairly conduct the action — giving appropriate notice to some or all class members of:

(i) any step in the action;

(ii) the proposed extent of the judgment; or

(iii) the members' opportunity to signify whether they consider the representation fair and adequate, to intervene and present claims or defenses, or to otherwise come into the action;

(C) impose conditions on the representative parties or on intervenors;

(D) require that the pleadings be amended to eliminate allegations about representation of absent persons and that the action proceed accordingly; or

(E) deal with similar procedural matters.

(2) ***Combining and Amending Orders.*** An order under Rule 23(d)(1) may be altered or amended from time to time and may be combined with an order under Rule 16.

(e) Settlement, Voluntary Dismissal, or Compromise. The claims, issues, or defenses of a certified class may be settled, voluntarily dismissed, or compromised only with the court's approval. The following procedures apply to a proposed settlement, voluntary dismissal, or compromise:

(1) The court must direct notice in a reasonable manner to all class members who would be bound by the proposal.

(2) If the proposal would bind class members, the court may approve it only after a hearing and on finding that it is fair, reasonable, and adequate.

(3) The parties seeking approval must file a statement identifying any agreement made in connection with the proposal.

(4) If the class action was previously certified under Rule 23(b)(3), the court may refuse to approve a settlement unless it affords a new opportunity to request exclusion to individual class members who had an earlier opportunity to request exclusion but did not do so.

(5) Any class member may object to the proposal if it requires court approval under this subdivision (e); the objection may be withdrawn only with the court's approval.

(f) Appeals. A court of appeals may permit an appeal from an order granting or denying class-action certification under this rule if a petition for permission to appeal is filed with the circuit clerk within 14 days after the order is entered. An appeal does not stay proceedings in the district court unless the district judge or the court of appeals so orders.

(g) Class Counsel.

(1) ***Appointing Class Counsel***. Unless a statute provides otherwise, a court that certifies a class must appoint class counsel. In appointing class counsel, the court:

(A) must consider:

(i) the work counsel has done in identifying or investigating potential claims in the action;

(ii) counsel's experience in handling class actions, other complex litigation, and the types of claims asserted in the action;

(iii) counsel's knowledge of the applicable law; and

(iv) the resources that counsel will commit to representing the class;

(B) may consider any other matter pertinent to counsel's ability to fairly and adequately represent the interests of the class;

(C) may order potential class counsel to provide information on any subject pertinent to the appointment and to propose terms for attorney's fees and nontaxable costs;

(D) may include in the appointing order provisions about the award of attorney's fees or nontaxable costs under Rule 23(h); and

(E) may make further orders in connection with the appointment.

(2) ***Standard for Appointing Class Counsel.*** When one applicant seeks appointment as class counsel, the court may appoint that applicant only if the applicant is adequate under Rule 23(g)(1) and (4). If more than one adequate applicant seeks appointment, the court must appoint the applicant best able to represent the interests of the class.

(3) ***Interim Counsel.*** The court may designate interim counsel to act on behalf of a putative class before determining whether to certify the action as a class action.

(4) ***Duty of Class Counsel.*** Class counsel must fairly and adequately represent the interests of the class.

(h) Attorney's Fees and Nontaxable Costs. In a certified class action, the court may award reasonable attorney's fees and nontaxable costs that are authorized by law or by the parties' agreement. The following procedures apply:

(1) A claim for an award must be made by motion under Rule 54(d)(2), subject to the provisions of this subdivision (h), at a time the court sets. Notice of the motion must be served on all parties and, for motions by class counsel, directed to class members in a reasonable manner.

(2) A class member, or a party from whom payment is sought, may object to the motion.

(3) The court may hold a hearing and must find the facts and state its legal conclusions under Rule 52(a).

(4) The court may refer issues related to the amount of the award to a special master or a magistrate judge, as provided in Rule 54(d)(2)(D).

ADVISORY COMMITTEE NOTES

1966 Amendment [citations omitted without notation — ED.]

. . .

The amended rule describes in more practical terms the occasions for maintaining class actions; provides that all class actions maintained to the end as such will result in judgments including those whom the court finds to be members of the class, whether or not the judgment is favorable to the class; and refers to the measures which can be taken to assure the fair conduct of these actions.

Subdivision (a) states the prerequisites for maintaining any class action in terms of the numerousness of the class making joinder of the members impracticable, the existence of questions common to the class, and the desired

qualifications of the representative parties. These are necessary but not sufficient conditions for a class action. Subdivision (b) describes the additional elements which in varying situations justify the use of a class action.

Subdivision (b)(1). The difficulties which would be likely to arise if resort were had to separate actions by or against the individual members of the class here furnish the reasons for, and the principal key to, the propriety and value of utilizing the class-action device. The considerations stated under clauses (A) and (B) are comparable to certain of the elements which define the persons whose joinder in an action is desirable as stated in Rule 19(a), as amended.

Clause (A): One person may have rights against, or be under duties toward, numerous persons constituting a class, and be so positioned that conflicting or varying adjudications in lawsuits with individual members of the class might establish incompatible standards to govern his conduct. The class action device can be used effectively to obviate the actual or virtual dilemma which would thus confront the party opposing the class. The matter has been stated thus: "The felt necessity for a class action is greatest when the courts are called upon to order or sanction the alteration of the status quo in circumstances such that a large number of persons are in a position to call on a single person to alter the status quo, or to complain if it is altered, and the possibility exists that [the] actor might be called upon to act in inconsistent ways." To illustrate: Separate actions by individuals against a municipality to declare a bond issue invalid or condition or limit it, to prevent or limit the making of a particular appropriation or to compel or invalidate an assessment, might create a risk of inconsistent or varying determinations. In the same way, individual litigations of the rights and duties of riparian owners, or of landowners' rights and duties respecting a claimed nuisance, could create a possibility of incompatible adjudications. Actions by or against a class provide a ready and fair means of achieving unitary adjudication.

Clause (B): This clause takes in situations where the judgment in a nonclass action by or against an individual member of the class, while not technically concluding the other members, might do so as a practical matter. The vice of an individual action would lie in the fact that the other members of the class, thus practically concluded, would have had no representation in the lawsuit. In an action by policy holders against a fraternal benefit association attacking a financial reorganization of the society, it would hardly have been practical, if indeed it would have been possible, to confine the effects of a validation of the reorganization to the individual plaintiffs. Consequently a class action was called for with adequate representation of all members of the class. For much the same reason actions by shareholders to compel the declaration of a dividend[,] the proper recognition and handling of redemption or pre-emption rights, or the like (or actions by the corporation for corresponding declarations of rights), should ordinarily be conducted as class actions, although the matter has been much obscured by the insistence that each shareholder has an individual claim. The same reasoning applies to an action which charges a breach of trust by an indenture trustee or other fiduciary similarly affecting the members of a large class of security holders or other beneficiaries, and which requires an accounting or like measures to restore the subject of the trust.

In various situations an adjudication as to one or more members of the class will necessarily or probably have an adverse practical effect on the interests of other members who should therefore be represented in the lawsuit. This is plainly the case when claims are made by numerous persons against a fund insufficient to satisfy all claims. A class action by or against representative members to settle the validity of the claims as a whole, or in groups, followed by separate proof of the amount of each valid claim and proportionate distribution of the fund, meets the problem. The same reasoning applies to an action by a creditor to set aside a fraudulent conveyance by the debtor and to appropriate the property to his claim, when the debtor's assets are insufficient to pay all creditors' claims. Similar problems, however, can arise in the absence of a fund either present or potential. A negative or mandatory injunction secured by one of a numerous class may disable the opposing party from performing claimed duties toward the other members of the class or materially affect his ability to do so. An adjudication as to movie "clearances and runs" nominally affecting only one exhibitor would often have practical effects on all the exhibitors in the same territorial area. Assuming a sufficiently numerous class of exhibitors, a class action would be advisable. (Here representation of subclasses of exhibitors could become necessary; see subdivision (c)(3)(B) [probably should be "subdivision 23(c)(4)(B)," now found in Rule 23(c)(5) — ED.].)

Subdivision (b)(2). This subdivision is intended to reach situations where a party has taken action or refused to take action with respect to a class, and final relief of an injunctive nature or of a corresponding declaratory nature, settling the legality of the behavior with respect to the class as a whole, is appropriate. Declaratory relief "corresponds" to injunctive relief when as a practical matter it affords injunctive relief or serves as a basis for later injunctive relief. The subdivision does not extend to cases in which the appropriate final relief relates exclusively or predominantly to money damages. Action or inaction is directed to a class within the meaning of this subdivision even if it has taken effect or is threatened only as to one or a few members of the class, provided it is based on grounds which have general application to the class.

Illustrative are various actions in the civil-rights field where a party is charged with discriminating unlawfully against a class, usually one whose members are incapable of specific enumeration. Subdivision (b)(2) is not limited to civil-rights cases. Thus an action looking to specific or declaratory relief could be brought by a numerous class of purchasers, say retailers of a given description, against a seller alleged to have undertaken to sell to that class at prices higher than those set for other purchasers, say retailers of another description, when the applicable law forbids such a pricing differential. So also a patentee of a machine, charged with selling or licensing the machine on condition that purchasers or licensees also purchase or obtain licenses to use an ancillary unpatented machine, could be sued on a class basis by a numerous group of purchasers or licensees, or by a numerous group of competing sellers or licensors of the unpatented machine, to test the legality of the "tying" condition.

Subdivision (b)(3). In the situations to which this subdivision relates, class-action treatment is not as clearly called for as in those described above, but it may nevertheless be convenient and desirable depending upon the particular facts. Subdivision (b)(3) encompasses those cases in which a class action would achieve

economies of time, effort, and expense, and promote uniformity of decision as to persons similarly situated, without sacrificing procedural fairness or bringing about other undesirable results.

The court is required to find, as a condition of holding that a class action may be maintained under this subdivision, that the questions common to the class predominate over the questions affecting individual members. It is only where this predominance exists that economies can be achieved by means of the class-action device. In this view, a fraud perpetrated on numerous persons by the use of similar misrepresentations may be an appealing situation for a class action, and it may remain so despite the need, if liability is found, for separate determination of the damages suffered by individuals within the class. On the other hand, although having some common core, a fraud case may be unsuited for treatment as a class action if there was material variation in the representations made or in the kinds or degrees of reliance by the persons to whom they were addressed. A "mass accident" resulting in injuries to numerous persons is ordinarily not appropriate for a class action because of the likelihood that significant questions, not only of damages but of liability and defenses of liability, would be present, affecting the individuals in different ways. In these circumstances an action conducted nominally as a class action would degenerate in practice into multiple lawsuits separately tried. Private damage claims by numerous individuals arising out of concerted antitrust violations may or may not involve predominating common questions.

That common questions predominate is not itself sufficient to justify a class action under subdivision (b)(3), for another method of handling the litigious situation may be available which has greater practical advantages. Thus one or more actions agreed to by the parties as test or model actions may be preferable to a class action; or it may prove feasible and preferable to consolidate actions. Even when a number of separate actions are proceeding simultaneously, experience shows that the burdens on the parties and the courts can sometimes be reduced by arrangements for avoiding repetitious discovery or the like. Currently the Coordinating Committee on Multiple Litigation in the United States District Courts (a subcommittee of the Committee on Trial Practice and Technique of the Judicial Conference of the United States) is charged with developing methods for expediting such massive litigation. To reinforce the point that the court with the aid of the parties ought to assess the relative advantages of alternative procedures for handling the total controversy, subdivision (b)(3) requires, as a further condition of maintaining the class action, that the court shall find that that procedure is "superior" to the others in the particular circumstances.

Factors (A)-(D) are listed, non-exhaustively, as pertinent to the findings. The court is to consider the interests of individual members of the class in controlling their own litigations and carrying them on as they see fit.

In this connection the court should inform itself of any litigation actually pending by or against the individuals. The interests of individuals in conducting separate lawsuits may be so strong as to call for denial of a class action. On the other hand, these interests may be theoretic rather than practical; the class may have a high degree of cohesion and prosecution of the action through representatives would be quite unobjectionable, or the amounts at stake for

individuals may be so small that separate suits would be impracticable. The burden that separate suits would impose on the party opposing the class, or upon the court calendars, may also fairly be considered. (See the discussion, under subdivision (c)(2) below, of the right of members to be excluded from the class upon their request.)

Also pertinent is the question of the desirability of concentrating the trial of the claims in the particular forum by means of a class action, in contrast to allowing the claims to be litigated separately in forums to which they would ordinarily be brought. Finally, the court should consider the problems of management which are likely to arise in the conduct of a class action.

Subdivision (c)(1). In order to give clear definition to the action, this provision requires the court to determine, as early in the proceedings as may be practicable, whether an action brought as a class action is to be so maintained. The determination depends in each case on satisfaction of the terms of subdivision (a) and the relevant provisions of subdivision (b).

An order embodying a determination can be conditional; the court may rule, for example, that a class action may be maintained only if the representation is improved through intervention of additional parties of a stated type. A determination once made can be altered or amended before the decision on the merits if, upon fuller development of the facts, the original determination appears unsound. A negative determination means that the action should be stripped of its character as a class action. See subdivision (d)(4) [now Rule 23(d)(1)(D) — ED.]. Although an action thus becomes a nonclass action, the court may still be receptive to interventions before the decision on the merits so that the litigation may cover as many interests as can be conveniently handled; the questions whether the intervenors in the nonclass action shall be permitted to claim "ancillary" jurisdiction or the benefit of the date of the commencement of the action for purposes of the statute of limitations are to be decided by reference to the laws governing jurisdiction and limitations as they apply in particular contexts.

Whether the court should require notice to be given to members of the class of its intention to make a determination, or of the order embodying it, is left to the court's discretion under subdivision (d)(2) [now Rule 23(d)(1)(B) — ED.].

Subdivision (c)(2) [with modifications, now Rules 23(c)(2)(B) — ED.] makes special provision for class actions maintained under subdivision (b)(3). As noted in the discussion of the latter subdivision, the interests of the individuals in pursing their own litigations may be so strong here as to warrant denial of a class action altogether. Even when a class action is maintained under subdivision (b)(3), this individual interest is respected. Thus the court is required to direct notice to the members of the class of the right of each member to be excluded from the class upon his request. A member who does not request exclusion may, if he wishes, enter an appearance in the action through his counsel; whether or not he does so, the judgment in the action will embrace him.

The notice[,] setting forth the alternatives open to the members of the class, is to be the best practicable under the circumstances, and shall include individual notice to the members who can be identified through reasonable effort. (For further discussion of this notice, see the statement under subdivision (d)(2) below.)

Subdivision (c)(3). The judgment in a class action maintained as such to the end will embrace the class, that is, in a class action under subdivision (b)(1) or (b)(2), those found by the court to be class members; in a class action under subdivision (b)(3), those to whom the notice prescribed by subdivision (c)(2) was directed, excepting those who requested exclusion or who are ultimately found by the court not to be members of the class. The judgment has this scope whether it is favorable or unfavorable to the class. In a (b)(1) or (b)(2) action the judgment "describes" the members of the class, but need not specify the individual members; in a (b)(3) action the judgment "specifies" the individual members who have been identified and described the others.

Compare subdivision (c)(4) as to actions conducted as class actions only with respect to particular issues. Where the class-action character of the lawsuit is based solely on the existence of a "limited fund," the judgment, while extending to all claims of class members against the fund, has ordinarily left unaffected the personal claims of nonappearing members against the debtor.

Hitherto, in a few actions conducted as "spurious" class actions and thus nominally designed to extend only to parties and others intervening before the determination of liability, courts have held or intimated that class members might be permitted to intervene after a decision on the merits favorable to their interests, in order to secure the benefits of the decision for themselves, although they would presumably be unaffected by an unfavorable decision. See, as to the propriety of this so-called "one-way" intervention in "spurious" actions, the conflicting views expressed in [several lower-court cases]. Under proposed subdivision (c)(3), one-way intervention is excluded; the action will have been early determined to be a class or nonclass action, and in the former case the judgment, whether or not favorable, will include the class, as above stated.

Although thus declaring that the judgment in a class action includes the class, as defined, subdivision (c)(3) does not disturb the recognized principle that the court conducting the action cannot predetermine the *res judicata* effect of the judgment; this can be tested only in a subsequent action. The court, however, in framing the judgment in any suit brought as a class action, must decide what its extent or coverage shall be, and if the matter is carefully considered, questions of *res judicata* are less likely to be raised at a later time and if raised will be more satisfactorily answered.

Subdivision (c)(4) [now Rules 23(c)(4) and -(5) — ED.]. This provision recognizes that an action may be maintained as a class action as to particular issues only. For example, in a fraud or similar case the action may retain its "class" character only through the adjudication of liability to the class; the members of the class may thereafter be required to come in individually and prove the amounts of their respective claims.

Two or more classes may be represented in a single action. Where a class is found to include subclasses divergent in interest, the class may be divided correspondingly, and each subclass treated as a class.

Subdivision (d) is concerned with the fair and efficient conduct of the action and lists some types of orders which may be appropriate.

The court should consider how the proceedings are to be arranged in sequence, and what measures should be taken to simplify the proof and argument. See subdivision (d)(1) [now Rule 23(d)(1)(A) — ED.]. The orders resulting from this consideration, like the others referred to in subdivision (d), may be combined with a pretrial order under Rule 16, and are subject to modification as the case proceeds.

Subdivision (d)(2) [now Rule 23(d)(1)(B) — ED.] sets out a non-exhaustive list of possible occasions for orders requiring notice to the class. Such notice is not a novel conception. For example, in "limited fund" cases, members of the class have been notified to present individual claims after the basic class decision. Notice has gone to members of a class so that they might express any opposition to the representation, and notice may encourage interventions to improve the representation of the class. Notice has been used to poll members on a proposed modification of a consent decree.

Subdivision (d)(2) does not require notice at any stage, but rather calls attention to its availability and invokes the court's discretion. In the degree that there is cohesiveness or unity in the class and the representation is effective, the need for notice to the class will tend toward a minimum. These indicators suggest that notice under subdivision (d)(2) may be particularly useful and advisable in certain class actions maintained under subdivision (b)(3), for example, to permit members of the class to object to the representation. Indeed, under subdivision (c)(2) [now Rule 23(c)(2)(B) — ED.], notice must be ordered, and is not merely discretionary, to give the members in a subdivision (b)(3) class action an opportunity to secure exclusion from the class. This mandatory notice pursuant to subdivision (c)(2), together with any discretionary notice which the court may find it advisable to give under subdivision (d)(2), is designed to fulfill requirements of due process to which the class action procedure is of course subject.

Notice to members of the class, whenever employed under amended Rule 23, should be accommodated to the particular purpose but need not comply with the formalities for service of process. The fact that notice is given at one stage of the action does not mean that it must be given at subsequent stages. Notice is available fundamentally "for the protection of the members of the class or otherwise for the fair conduct of the action" [with modifications, this language is now found in Rule 23(d)(1)(B) — ED.] and should not be used merely as a device for the undesirable solicitation of claims.

In appropriate cases the court should notify interested government agencies of the pendency of the action or of particular steps therein.

Subdivision (d)(3) [now Rule 23(d)(1)(C) — ED.] reflects the possibility of conditioning the maintenance of a class action, e.g., on the strengthening of the representation, see subdivision (c)(1) above; and recognizes that the imposition of conditions on intervenors may be required for the proper and efficient conduct of the action. . . .

Subdivision (e) requires approval of the court, after notice, for the dismissal or compromise of any class action.

1998 Amendment

Subdivision (f). This permissive interlocutory appeal provision is adopted under the power conferred by 28 U.S.C. § 1292(e). Appeal from an order granting or denying class certification is permitted in the sole discretion of the court of appeals. No other type of Rule 23 order is covered by this provision. The court of appeals is given unfettered discretion whether to permit the appeal, akin to the discretion exercised by the Supreme Court in acting on a petition for certiorari. This discretion suggests an analogy to the provision in 28 U.S.C. § 1292(b) for permissive appeal on certification by a district court. Subdivision (f), however, departs from the § 1291(b) model in two significant ways. It does not require that the district court certify the certification ruling for appeal, although the district court often can assist the parties and court of appeals by offering advice on the desirability of appeal. And it does not include the potentially limiting requirements of § 1292(b) that the district court order "involve[ ] a controlling question of law as to which there is substantial ground for difference of opinion and that an immediate appeal from the order may materially advance the ultimate termination of the litigation.["]

The courts of appeals will develop standards for granting review that reflect the changing areas of uncertainty in class litigation. The Federal Judicial Center study supports the view that many suits with class-action allegations present familiar and almost routine issues that are no more worthy of immediate appeal than many other interlocutory rulings. Yet several concerns justify expansion of present opportunities to appeal. An order denying certification may confront the plaintiff with a situation in which the only sure path to appellate review is by proceeding to final judgment on the merits of an individual claim that, standing alone, is far smaller than the costs of litigation. An order granting certification, on the other hand, may force a defendant to settle rather than incur the costs of defending a class action and run the risk of potentially ruinous liability. These concerns can be met at low cost by establishing in the court of appeals a discretionary power to grant interlocutory review in cases that show appeal-worthy certification issues.

Permission to appeal may be granted or denied on the basis of any consideration that the court of appeals finds persuasive. Permission is most likely to be granted when the certification decision turns on a novel or unsettled question of law, or when, as a practical matter, the decision on certification is likely dispositive of the litigation.

The district court, having worked through the certification decision, often will be able to provide cogent advice on the factors that bear on the decision whether to permit appeal. This advice can be particularly valuable if the certification decision is tentative. Even as to a firm certification decision, a statement of reasons bearing on the probable benefits and costs of immediate appeal can help focus the court of appeals decision, and may persuade the disappointed party that an attempt to appeal would be fruitless.

The 10-day [now 14-day — ED.] period for seeking permission to appeal is designed to reduce the risk that attempted appeals will disrupt continuing proceedings. It is expected that the courts of appeals will act quickly in making the preliminary determination whether to permit appeal. Permission to appeal does

not stay trial court proceedings. A stay should be sought first from the trial court. If the trial court refuses a stay, its action and any explanation of its views should weigh heavily with the court of appeals. . . .

2003 Amendment [some citations omitted without notation — ED.]

Subdivision (c). Subdivision (c) is amended in several respects. The requirement that the court determine whether to certify a class "as soon as practicable after commencement of an action" is replaced by requiring determination "at an early practicable time." The notice provisions are substantially revised.

Paragraph (1). Subdivision (c)(1)(A) is changed to require that the determination whether to certify a class be made "at an early practicable time." The "as soon as practicable" exaction neither reflects prevailing practice nor captures the many valid reasons that may justify deferring the initial certification decision.

Time may be needed to gather information necessary to make the certification decision. Although an evaluation of the probable outcome on the merits is not properly part of the certification decision, discovery in aid of the certification decision often includes information required to identify the nature of the issues that actually will be presented at trial. In this sense it is appropriate to conduct controlled discovery into the "merits," limited to those aspects relevant to making the certification decision on an informed basis. Active judicial supervision may be required to achieve the most effective balance that expedites an informed certification determination without forcing an artificial and ultimately wasteful division between "certification discovery" and "merits discovery." A critical need is to determine how the case will be tried. An increasing number of courts require a party requesting class certification to present a "trial plan" that describes the issues likely to be presented at trial and tests whether they are susceptible of class-wide proof.

Other considerations may affect the timing of the certification decision. The party opposing the class may prefer to win dismissal or summary judgment as to the individual plaintiffs without certification and without binding the class that might have been certified. Time may be needed to explore designation of class counsel under Rule 23(g), recognizing that in many cases the need to progress toward the certification determination may require designation of interim counsel under Rule 23(g)(2)(A) [now Rule 23(g)(3) — ED.].

Although many circumstances may justify deferring the certification decision, active management may be necessary to ensure that the certification decision is not unjustifiably delayed.

Subdivision (c)(1)(C) reflects two amendments. The provision that a class certification "may be conditional" is deleted. A court that is not satisfied that the requirements of Rule 23 have been met should refuse certification until they have been met. The provision that permits alteration or amendment of an order granting or denying class certification is amended to set the cut-off point at final judgment rather than "the decision on the merits." This change avoids the possible ambiguity in referring to "the decision on the merits." Following a determination of liability, for example, proceedings to define the remedy may demonstrate the

need to amend the class definition or subdivide the class. In this setting the final judgment concept is pragmatic. It is not the same as the concept used for appeal purposes, but it should be flexible, particularly in protracted litigation.

The authority to amend an order under Rule 23(c)(1) before final judgment does not restore the practice of "one-way intervention" that was rejected by the 1966 revision of Rule 23. A determination of liability after certification, however, may show a need to amend the class definition. Decertification may be warranted after further proceedings.

If the definition of a class certified under Rule 23(b)(3) is altered to include members who have not been afforded notice and an opportunity to request exclusion, notice — including an opportunity to request exclusion — must be directed to the new class members under Rule 23(c)(2)(B).

Paragraph (2). The first change made in Rule 23(c)(2) is to call attention to the court's authority — already established in part by Rule 23(d)(2) [now Rule 23(d)(1)(B) — ED.] — to direct notice of certification to a Rule 23(b)(1) or (b)(2) class. The present rule expressly requires notice only in actions certified under Rule 23(b)(3). Members of classes certified under Rules 23(b)(1) or (b)(2) have interests that may deserve protection by notice.

The authority to direct notice to class members in a (b)(1) or (b)(2) class action should be exercised with care. For several reasons, there may be less need for notice than in a (b)(3) class action. There is no right to request exclusion from a (b)(1) or (b)(2) class. The characteristics of the class may reduce the need for formal notice. The cost of providing notice, moreover, could easily cripple actions that do not seek damages. The court may decide not to direct notice after balancing the risk that notice costs may deter the pursuit of class relief against the benefits of notice.

When the court does direct certification notice in a (b)(1) or (b)(2) class action, the discretion and flexibility established by subdivision (c)(2)(A) extend to the method of giving notice. Notice facilitates the opportunity to participate. Notice calculated to reach a significant number of class members often will protect the interests of all. Informal methods may prove effective. A simple posting in a place visited by many class members, directing attention to a source of more detailed information, may suffice. The court should consider the costs of notice in relation to the probable reach of inexpensive methods.

If a Rule 23(b)(3) class is certified in conjunction with a (b)(2) class, the (c)(2)(B) notice requirements must be satisfied as to the (b)(3) class.

The direction that class-certification notice be couched in plain, easily understood language is a reminder of the need to work unremittingly at the difficult task of communicating with class members. It is difficult to provide information about most class actions that is both accurate and easily understood by class members who are not themselves lawyers. Factual uncertainty, legal complexity, and the complication of class-action procedure raise the barriers high. The Federal Judicial Center has created illustrative clear-notice forms that provide a helpful starting point for actions similar to those described in the forms.

Subdivision (e). Subdivision (e) is amended to strengthen the process of reviewing proposed class-action settlements. Settlement may be a desirable means

of resolving a class action. But court review and approval are essential to assure adequate representation of class members who have not participated in shaping the settlement.

Paragraph (1). Subdivision (e)(1)(A) expressly recognizes the power of a class representative to settle class claims, issues, or defenses.

Rule 23(e)(1)(A) [now Rule 23(e) — ED.] resolves the ambiguity in former Rule 23(e)'s reference to dismissal or compromise of "a class action." That language could be — and at times was — read to require court approval of settlements with putative class representatives that resolved only individual claims. The new rule requires approval only if the claims, issues, or defenses of a certified class are resolved by a settlement, voluntary dismissal, or compromise.

Subdivision (e)(1)(B) [now Rule 23(e)(1) — ED.] carries forward the notice requirement of present Rule 23(e) when the settlement binds the class through claim or issue preclusion; notice is not required when the settlement binds only the individual class representatives. Notice of a settlement binding on the class is required either when the settlement follows class certification or when the decisions on certification and settlement proceed simultaneously.

Reasonable settlement notice may require individual notice in the manner required by Rule 23(c)(2)(B) for certification notice to a Rule 23(b)(3) class. Individual notice is appropriate, for example, if class members are required to take action — such as filing claims — to participate in the judgment, or if the court orders a settlement opt-out opportunity under Rule 23(e)(3) [now Rule 23(e)(4) — ED.].

Subdivision (e)(1)(C) [now Rule 23(e)(2) — ED.] confirms and mandates the already common practice of holding hearings as part of the process of approving settlement, voluntary dismissal, or compromise that would bind members of a class.

Subdivision (e)(1)(C) states the standard for approving a proposed settlement that would bind class members. The settlement must be fair, reasonable, and adequate. A helpful review of many factors that may deserve consideration is provided by *In re: Prudential Ins. Co. America Sales Practice Litigation Agent Actions,* 148 F.3d 283, 316-324 (3d Cir. 1998). Further guidance can be found in the *Manual for Complex Litigation.*

The court must make findings that support the conclusion that the settlement is fair, reasonable, and adequate. The findings must be set out in sufficient detail to explain to class members and the appellate court the factors that bear on applying the standard.

Settlement review also may provide an occasion to review the cogency of the initial class definition. The terms of the settlement themselves, or objections, may reveal divergent interests of class members and demonstrate the need to redefine the class or to designate subclasses. Redefinition of a class certified under Rule 23(b)(3) may require notice to new class members under Rule 23(c)(2)(B). See Rule 23(c)(1)(C).

Paragraph (2). Subdivision (e)(2) [now Rule 23(e)(3) — ED.] requires parties seeking approval of a settlement, voluntary dismissal, or compromise under Rule 23(e)(1) [now Rule 23(e), -(e)(1), and -(e)(2) — ED.] to file a statement identifying

any agreement made in connection with the settlement. This provision does not change the basic requirement that the parties disclose all terms of the settlement or compromise that the court must approve under Rule 23(e)(1). It aims instead at related undertakings that, although seemingly separate, may have influenced the terms of the settlement by trading away possible advantages for the class in return for advantages for others. Doubts should be resolved in favor of identification.

Further inquiry into the agreements identified by the parties should not become the occasion for discovery by the parties or objectors. The court may direct the parties to provide to the court or other parties a summary or copy of the full terms of any agreement identified by the parties. The court also may direct the parties to provide a summary or copy of any agreement not identified by the parties that the court considers relevant to its review of a proposed settlement. In exercising discretion under this rule, the court may act in steps, calling first for a summary of any agreement that may have affected the settlement and then for a complete version if the summary does not provide an adequate basis for review. A direction to disclose a summary or copy of an agreement may raise concerns of confidentiality. Some agreements may include information that merits protection against general disclosure. And the court must provide an opportunity to claim work-product or other protections.

Paragraph (3). Subdivision (e)(3) [now Rule 23(e)(4) — ED.] authorizes the court to refuse to approve a settlement unless the settlement affords class members a new opportunity to request exclusion from a class certified under Rule 23(b)(3) after settlement terms are known. An agreement by the parties themselves to permit class members to elect exclusion at this point by the settlement agreement may be one factor supporting approval of the settlement. Often there is an opportunity to opt out at this point because the class is certified and settlement is reached in circumstances that lead to simultaneous notice of certification and notice of settlement. In these cases, the basic opportunity to elect exclusion applies without further complication. In some cases, particularly if settlement appears imminent at the time of certification, it may be possible to achieve equivalent protection by deferring notice and the opportunity to elect exclusion until actual settlement terms are known. This approach avoids the cost and potential confusion of providing two notices and makes the single notice more meaningful. But notice should not be delayed unduly after certification in the hope of settlement.

Rule 23(e)(3) authorizes the court to refuse to approve a settlement unless the settlement affords a new opportunity to elect exclusion in a case that settles after a certification decision if the earlier opportunity to elect exclusion provided with the certification notice has expired by the time of the settlement notice. A decision to remain in the class is likely to be more carefully considered and is better informed when settlement terms are known.

The opportunity to request exclusion from a proposed settlement is limited to members of a (b)(3) class. Exclusion may be requested only by individual class members; no class member may purport to opt out other class members by way of another class action.

The decision whether to approve a settlement that does not allow a new opportunity to elect exclusion is confided to the court's discretion. The court may

make this decision before directing notice to the class under Rule 23(e)(1)(B) [now Rule 23(e)(1) — ED.] or after the Rule 23(e)(1)(C) [now Rule 23(e)(2) — ED.] hearing. Many factors may influence the court's decision. Among these are changes in the information available to class members since expiration of the first opportunity to request exclusion, and the nature of the individual class members' claims.

The terms set for permitting a new opportunity to elect exclusion from the proposed settlement of a Rule 23(b)(3) class action may address concerns of potential misuse. The court might direct, for example, that class members who elect exclusion are bound by rulings on the merits made before the settlement was proposed for approval. Still other terms or conditions may be appropriate.

Paragraph (4). Subdivision (e)(4) [now Rule 23(e)(5) — ED.] confirms the right of class members to object to a proposed settlement, voluntary dismissal, or compromise. The right is defined in relation to a disposition that, because it would bind the class, requires court approval under subdivision (e)(1)(C) [now Rule 23(e)(2) — ED.].

Subdivision (e)(4)(B) [now Rule 23(e)(5) — ED.] requires court approval for withdrawal of objections made under subdivision (e)(4)(A) [now Rule 23(e)(5) — ED.]. Review follows automatically if the objections are withdrawn on terms that lead to modification of the settlement with the class. Review also is required if the objector formally withdraws the objections. If the objector simply abandons pursuit of the objection, the court may inquire into the circumstances.

Approval under paragraph (4)(B) may be given or denied with little need for further inquiry if the objection and the disposition go only to a protest that the individual treatment afforded the objector under the proposed settlement is unfair because of factors that distinguish the objector from other class members. Different considerations may apply if the objector has protested that the proposed settlement is not fair, reasonable, or adequate on grounds that apply generally to a class or subclass. Such objections, which purport to represent class-wide interests, may augment the opportunity for obstruction or delay. If such objections are surrendered on terms that do not affect the class settlement or the objector's participation in the class settlement, the court often can approve withdrawal of the objections without elaborate inquiry.

Once an objector appeals, control of the proceeding lies in the court of appeals. The court of appeals may undertake review and approval of a settlement with the objector, perhaps as part of appeal settlement procedures, or may remand to the district court to take advantage of the district court's familiarity with the action and settlement.

Subdivision (g). Subdivision (g) is new. It responds to the reality that the selection and activity of class counsel are often critically important to the successful handling of a class action. Until now, courts have scrutinized proposed class counsel as well as the class representative under Rule 23(a)(4). This experience has recognized the importance of judicial evaluation of the proposed lawyer for the class, and this new subdivision builds on that experience rather than introducing an entirely new element into the class certification process. Rule 23(a)(4) will continue to call for scrutiny of the proposed class representative, while this subdivision will guide the court in assessing proposed class counsel as part of

the certification decision. This subdivision recognizes the importance of class counsel, states the obligation to represent the interests of the class, and provides a framework for selection of class counsel. The procedure and standards for appointment vary depending on whether there are multiple applicants to be class counsel. The new subdivision also provides a method by which the court may make directions from the outset about the potential fee award to class counsel in the event the action is successful.

Paragraph (1) sets out the basic requirement that class counsel be appointed if a class is certified and articulates the obligation of class counsel to represent the interests of the class, as opposed to the potentially conflicting interests of individual class members. It also sets out the factors the court should consider in assessing proposed class counsel.

Paragraph (1)(A) [now Rule23(g)(1) — ED.] requires that the court appoint class counsel to represent the class. Class counsel must be appointed for all classes, including each subclass that the court certifies to represent divergent interests.

Paragraph (1)(A) does not apply if "a statute provides otherwise." This recognizes that provisions of the Private Securities Litigation Reform Act of 1995, Pub. L. No. 104-67, 109 Stat. 737 (1995) (codified in various sections of 15 U.S.C.), contain directives that bear on selection of a lead plaintiff and the retention of counsel. This subdivision does not purport to supersede or to affect the interpretation of those provisions, or any similar provisions of other legislation.

Paragraph 1(B) [now Rule 23(g)(4) — ED.] recognizes that the primary responsibility of class counsel, resulting from appointment as class counsel, is to represent the best interests of the class. The rule thus establishes the obligation of class counsel, an obligation that may be different from the customary obligations of counsel to individual clients. Appointment as class counsel means that the primary obligation of counsel is to the class rather than to any individual members of it. The class representatives do not have an unfettered right to "fire" class counsel. In the same vein, the class representatives cannot command class counsel to accept or reject a settlement proposal. To the contrary, class counsel must determine whether seeking the court's approval of a settlement would be in the best interests of the class as a whole.

Paragraph (1)(C) [now Rules 23(g)(1)(A)-(E) — ED.] articulates the basic responsibility of the court to appoint class counsel who will provide the adequate representation called for by paragraph (1)(B) [now Rule 23(g)(4) — ED.]. It identifies criteria that must be considered and invites the court to consider any other pertinent matters. Although couched in terms of the court's duty, the listing also informs counsel seeking appointment about the topics that should be addressed in an application for appointment or in the motion for class certification.

The court may direct potential class counsel to provide additional information about the topics mentioned in paragraph (1)(C) [now Rules 23(g)(1)(A)-(C) and -(E)— ED.] or about any other relevant topic. For example, the court may direct applicants to inform the court concerning any agreements about a prospective award of attorney fees or nontaxable costs, as such agreements may sometimes be significant in the selection of class counsel. The court might also direct that potential class counsel indicate how parallel litigation might be coordinated or consolidated with the action before the court.

The court may also direct counsel to propose terms for a potential award of attorney fees and nontaxable costs. Attorney fee awards are an important feature of class action practice, and attention to this subject from the outset may often be a productive technique. Paragraph (2)(C) [now Rule 23(g)(1)(D) — ED.] therefore authorizes the court to provide directions about attorney fees and costs when appointing class counsel. Because there will be numerous class actions in which this information is not likely to be useful, the court need not consider it in all class actions.

Some information relevant to class counsel appointment may involve matters that include adversary preparation in a way that should be shielded from disclosure to other parties. An appropriate protective order may be necessary to preserve confidentiality.

In evaluating prospective class counsel, the court should weigh all pertinent factors. No single factor should necessarily be determinative in a given case. For example, the resources counsel will commit to the case must be appropriate to its needs, but the court should be careful not to limit consideration to lawyers with the greatest resources.

If, after review of all applicants, the court concludes that none would be satisfactory class counsel, it may deny class certification, reject all applications, recommend that an application be modified, invite new applications, or make any other appropriate order regarding selection and appointment of class counsel.

Paragraph (2) [now Rules 23(g)(1)(D), -(g)(2), and (g)(3) — ED.]. This paragraph sets out the procedure that should be followed in appointing class counsel. Although it affords substantial flexibility, it provides the framework for appointment of class counsel in all class actions. For counsel who filed the action, the materials submitted in support of the motion for class certification may suffice to justify appointment so long as the information described in paragraph (g)(1)(C) [now Rules 23(g)(1)(A)-(C) and -(E) — ED.] is included. If there are other applicants, they ordinarily would file a formal application detailing their suitability for the position.

In a plaintiff class action the court usually would appoint as class counsel only an attorney or attorneys who have sought appointment. Different considerations may apply in defendant class actions.

The rule states that the court should appoint "class counsel." In many instances, the applicant will be an individual attorney. In other cases, however, an entire firm, or perhaps numerous attorneys who are not otherwise affiliated but are collaborating on the action will apply. No rule of thumb exists to determine when such arrangements are appropriate; the court should be alert to the need for adequate staffing of the case, but also to the risk of overstaffing or an ungainly counsel structure.

Paragraph (2)(A) [now Rule 23(g)(3) — ED.] authorizes the court to designate interim counsel during the pre-certification period if necessary to protect the interests of the putative class. Rule 23(c)(1)(B) directs that the order certifying the class include appointment of class counsel. Before class certification, however, it will usually be important for an attorney to take action to prepare for the certification decision. The amendment to Rule 23(c)(1) recognizes that some

discovery is often necessary for that determination. It also may be important to make or respond to motions before certification. Settlement may be discussed before certification. Ordinarily, such work is handled by the lawyer who filed the action. In some cases, however, there may be rivalry or uncertainty that makes formal designation of interim counsel appropriate. Rule 23(g)(2)(A) [now Rule 23(g)(3) — ED.] authorizes the court to designate interim counsel to act on behalf of the putative class before the certification decision is made. Failure to make the formal designation does not prevent the attorney who filed the action from proceeding in it. Whether or not formally designated interim counsel, an attorney who acts on behalf of the class before certification must act in the best interests of the class as a whole. For example, an attorney who negotiates a pre-certification settlement must seek a settlement that is fair, reasonable, and adequate for the class.

Rule 23(c)(1) provides that the court should decide whether to certify the class "at an early practicable time," and directs that class counsel should be appointed in the order certifying the class. In some cases, it may be appropriate for the court to allow a reasonable period after commencement of the action for filing applications to serve as class counsel. The primary ground for deferring appointment would be that there is reason to anticipate competing applications to serve as class counsel. Examples might include instances in which more than one class action has been filed, or in which other attorneys have filed individual actions on behalf of putative class members. The purpose of facilitating competing applications in such a case is to afford the best possible representation for the class. Another possible reason for deferring appointment would be that the initial applicant was found inadequate, but it seems appropriate to permit additional applications rather than deny class certification.

Paragraph (2)(B) [now Rule 23(g)(2) — ED.] states the basic standard the court should use in deciding whether to certify the class and appoint class counsel in the single applicant situation — that the applicant be able to provide the representation called for by paragraph (1)(B) [now Rule 23(g)(4) — ED.] in light of the factors identified in paragraph (1)(C) [now Rules 23(g)(1)(A)-(C) and -(E) — ED.].

If there are multiple adequate applicants, paragraph (2)(B) [now Rule 23(g)(2) — ED.] directs the court to select the class counsel best able to represent the interests of the class. This decision should also be made using the factors outlined in paragraph (1)(C) [now Rules 23(g)(1)(A)-(C) and -(E) — ED.], but in the multiple applicant situation the court is to go beyond scrutinizing the adequacy of counsel and make a comparison of the strengths of the various applicants. As with the decision whether to appoint the sole applicant for the position, no single factor should be dispositive in selecting class counsel in cases in which there are multiple applicants. The fact that a given attorney filed the instant action, for example, might not weigh heavily in the decision if that lawyer had not done significant work identifying or investigating claims. Depending on the nature of the case, one important consideration might be the applicant's existing attorney-client relationship with the proposed class representative.

Paragraph (2)(C) [now Rule 23(g)(1)(D) — ED.] builds on the appointment process by authorizing the court to include provisions regarding attorney fees in

the order appointing class counsel. Courts may find it desirable to adopt guidelines for fees or nontaxable costs, or to direct class counsel to report to the court at regular intervals on the efforts undertaken in the action, to facilitate the court's later determination of a reasonable attorney fee.

Subdivision (h). Subdivision (h) is new. Fee awards are a powerful influence on the way attorneys initiate, develop, and conclude class actions. Class action attorney fee awards have heretofore been handled, along with all other attorney fee awards, under Rule 54(d)(2), but that rule is not addressed to the particular concerns of class actions. This subdivision is designed to work in tandem with new subdivision (g) on appointment of class counsel, which may afford an opportunity for the court to provide an early framework for an eventual fee award, or for monitoring the work of class counsel during the pendency of the action.

Subdivision (h) applies to "an action certified as a class action" [now "a certified class action" — ED.]. This includes cases in which there is a simultaneous proposal for class certification and settlement even though technically the class may not be certified unless the court approves the settlement pursuant to review under Rule 23(e). When a settlement is proposed for Rule 23(e) approval, either after certification or with a request for certification, notice to class members about class counsel's fee motion would ordinarily accompany the notice to the class about the settlement proposal itself.

This subdivision does not undertake to create new grounds for an award of attorney fees or nontaxable costs. Instead, it applies when such awards are authorized by law or by agreement of the parties. Against that background, it provides a format for all awards of attorney fees and nontaxable costs in connection with a class action, not only the award to class counsel. In some situations, there may be a basis for making an award to other counsel whose work produced a beneficial result for the class, such as attorneys who acted for the class before certification but were not appointed class counsel, or attorneys who represented objectors to a proposed settlement under Rule 23(e) or to the fee motion of class counsel. Other situations in which fee awards are authorized by law or by agreement of the parties may exist.

This subdivision authorizes an award of "reasonable" attorney fees and nontaxable costs. This is the customary term for measurement of fee awards in cases in which counsel may obtain an award of fees under the "common fund" theory that applies in many class actions, and is used in many fee-shifting statutes. Depending on the circumstances, courts have approached the determination of what is reasonable in different ways. In particular, there is some variation among courts about whether in "common fund" cases the court should use the lodestar or a percentage method of determining what fee is reasonable. The rule does not attempt to resolve the question whether the lodestar or percentage approach should be viewed as preferable.

Active judicial involvement in measuring fee awards is singularly important to the proper operation of the class-action process. Continued reliance on caselaw development of fee-award measures does not diminish the court's responsibility. In a class action, the district court must ensure that the amount and mode of payment of attorney fees are fair and proper whether the fees come from a common

fund or are otherwise paid. Even in the absence of objections, the court bears this responsibility.

Courts discharging this responsibility have looked to a variety of factors. One fundamental focus is the result actually achieved for class members, a basic consideration in any case in which fees are sought on the basis of a benefit achieved for class members. The Private Securities Litigation Reform Act of 1995 explicitly makes this factor a cap for a fee award in actions to which it applies. See 15 U.S.C. §§ 77z-1(a)(6); 78u-4(a)(6) (fee award should not exceed a "reasonable percentage of the amount of any damages and prejudgment interest actually paid to the class"). For a percentage approach to fee measurement, results achieved is the basic starting point.

In many instances, the court may need to proceed with care in assessing the value conferred on class members. Settlement regimes that provide for future payments, for example, may not result in significant actual payments to class members. In this connection, the court may need to scrutinize the manner and operation of any applicable claims procedure. In some cases, it may be appropriate to defer some portion of the fee award until actual payouts to class members are known. Settlements involving nonmonetary provisions for class members also deserve careful scrutiny to ensure that these provisions have actual value to the class. On occasion the court's Rule 23(e) review will provide a solid basis for this sort of evaluation, but in any event it is also important to assessing the fee award for the class.

At the same time, it is important to recognize that in some class actions the monetary relief obtained is not the sole determinant of an appropriate attorney fees award.

Any directions or orders made by the court in connection with appointing class counsel under Rule 23(g) should weigh heavily in making a fee award under this subdivision.

Courts have also given weight to agreements among the parties regarding the fee motion, and to agreements between class counsel and others about the fees claimed by the motion. Rule 54(d)(2)(B) provides: "If directed by the court, the motion shall also disclose the terms of any agreement with respect to fees to be paid for the services for which claim is made." [With modifications, this language is now found in Rules 54(d)(2)(B) and -(d)(2)(B)(iv) — ED.] The agreement by a settling party not to oppose a fee application up to a certain amount, for example, is worthy of consideration, but the court remains responsible to determine a reasonable fee. "Side agreements" regarding fees provide at least perspective pertinent to an appropriate fee award.

In addition, courts may take account of the fees charged by class counsel or other attorneys for representing individual claimants or objectors in the case. In determining a fee for class counsel, the court's objective is to ensure an overall fee that is fair for counsel and equitable within the class. In some circumstances individual fee agreements between class counsel and class members might have provisions inconsistent with those goals, and the court might determine that adjustments in the class fee award were necessary as a result.

Finally, it is important to scrutinize separately the application for an award covering nontaxable costs. If costs were addressed in the order appointing class counsel, those directives should be a presumptive starting point in determining what is an appropriate award.

Paragraph (1). Any claim for an award of attorney fees must be sought by motion under Rule 54(d)(2), which invokes the provisions for timing of appeal in Rule 58 and Appellate Rule 4. Owing to the distinctive features of class action fee motions, however, the provisions of this subdivision control disposition of fee motions in class actions, while Rule 54(d)(2) applies to matters not addressed in this subdivision.

The court should direct when the fee motion must be filed. For motions by class counsel in cases subject to court review of a proposed settlement under Rule 23(e), it would be important to require the filing of at least the initial motion in time for inclusion of information about the motion in the notice to the class about the proposed settlement that is required by Rule 23(e). In cases litigated to judgment, the court might also order class counsel's motion to be filed promptly so that notice to the class under this subdivision (h) can be given.

Besides service of the motion on all parties, notice of class counsel's motion for attorney fees must be "directed to the class in a reasonable manner" [now "directed to class members in a reasonable manner" — ED.]. Because members of the class have an interest in the arrangements for payment of class counsel whether that payment comes from the class fund or is made directly by another party, notice is required in all instances. In cases in which settlement approval is contemplated under Rule 23(e), notice of class counsel's fee motion should be combined with notice of the proposed settlement, and the provision regarding notice to the class is parallel to the requirements for notice under Rule 23(e). In adjudicated class actions, the court may calibrate the notice to avoid undue expense.

Paragraph (2). A class member and any party from whom payment is sought may object to the fee motion. Other parties — for example, nonsettling defendants — may not object because they lack a sufficient interest in the amount the court awards. The rule does not specify a time limit for making an objection. In setting the date objections are due, the court should provide sufficient time after the full fee motion is on file to enable potential objectors to examine the motion.

The court may allow an objector discovery relevant to the objections. In determining whether to allow discovery, the court should weigh the need for the information against the cost and delay that would attend discovery. See Rule 26(b)(2). One factor in determining whether to authorize discovery is the completeness of the material submitted in support of the fee motion, which depends in part on the fee measurement standard applicable to the case. If the motion provides thorough information, the burden should be on the objector to justify discovery to obtain further information.

Paragraph (3). Whether or not there are formal objections, the court must determine whether a fee award is justified and, if so, set a reasonable fee. The rule does not require a formal hearing in all cases. The form and extent of a hearing depend on the circumstances of the case. The rule does require findings and conclusions under Rule 52(a).

Paragraph (4). By incorporating Rule 54(d)(2), this provision gives the court broad authority to obtain assistance in determining the appropriate amount to award. In deciding whether to direct submission of such questions to a special master or magistrate judge, the court should give appropriate consideration to the cost and delay that such a process might entail.

2007 Amendment

. . .

Amended Rule 23(d)(2) carries forward the provisions of former Rule 23(d) that recognize two separate propositions. First, a Rule 23(d) order may be combined with a pretrial order under Rule 16. Second, the standard for amending the Rule 23(d) order continues to be the more open-ended standard for amending Rule 23(d) orders, not the more exacting standard for amending Rule 16 orders.

As part of the general restyling, intensifiers that provide emphasis but add no meaning are consistently deleted. Amended Rule 23(f) omits as redundant the explicit reference to court of appeals discretion in deciding whether to permit an interlocutory appeal. The omission does not in any way limit the unfettered discretion established by the original rule.

Rule 23.1. Derivative Actions

(a) Prerequisites. This rule applies when one or more shareholders or members of a corporation or an unincorporated association bring a derivative action to enforce a right that the corporation or association may properly assert but has failed to enforce. The derivative action may not be maintained if it appears that the plaintiff does not fairly and adequately represent the interests of shareholders or members who are similarly situated in enforcing the right of the corporation or association.

(b) Pleading Requirements. The complaint must be verified and must:

(1) allege that the plaintiff was a shareholder or member at the time of the transaction complained of, or that the plaintiff's share or membership later devolved on it by operation of law;

(2) allege that the action is not a collusive one to confer jurisdiction that the court would otherwise lack; and

(3) state with particularity:

(A) any effort by the plaintiff to obtain the desired action from the directors or comparable authority and, if necessary, from the shareholders or members; and

(B) the reasons for not obtaining the action or not making the effort.

(c) Settlement, Dismissal, and Compromise. A derivative action may be settled, voluntarily dismissed, or compromised only with the

court's approval. Notice of a proposed settlement, voluntary dismissal, or compromise must be given to shareholders or members in the manner that the court orders.

Rule 23.2. Actions Relating to Unincorporated Associations

This rule applies to an action brought by or against the members of an unincorporated association as a class by naming certain members as representative parties. The action may be maintained only if it appears that those parties will fairly and adequately protect the interests of the association and its members. In conducting the action, the court may issue any appropriate orders corresponding with those in Rule 23(d), and the procedure for settlement, voluntary dismissal, or compromise must correspond with the procedure in Rule 23(e).

Rule 24. Intervention

(a) Intervention of Right. On timely motion, the court must permit anyone to intervene who:

(1) is given an unconditional right to intervene by a federal statute; or

(2) claims an interest relating to the property or transaction that is the subject of the action, and is so situated that disposing of the action may as a practical matter impair or impede the movant's ability to protect its interest, unless existing parties adequately represent that interest.

(b) Permissive Intervention.

(1) ***In General.*** On timely motion, the court may permit anyone to intervene who:

(A) is given a conditional right to intervene by a federal statute; or

(B) has a claim or defense that shares with the main action a common question of law or fact.

(2) ***By a Government Officer or Agency.*** On timely motion, the court may permit a federal or state governmental officer or agency to intervene if a party's claim or defense is based on:

(A) a statute or executive order administered by the officer or agency; or

(B) any regulation, order, requirement, or agreement issued or made under the statute or executive order.

(3) ***Delay or Prejudice.*** In exercising its discretion, the court must consider whether the intervention will unduly delay or prejudice the adjudication of the original parties' rights.

(c) Notice and Pleading Required. A motion to intervene must be served on the parties as provided in Rule 5. The motion must state the grounds for intervention and be accompanied by a pleading that sets out the claim or defense for which intervention is sought.

ADVISORY COMMITTEE NOTES

1966 Amendment [citations omitted without notation — ED.]

. . .

The amendment provides that an applicant is entitled to intervene in an action when his position is comparable to that of a person under Rule 19(a)(2)(i) [now Rule 19(a)(1)(B)(i) — ED.], as amended, unless his interest is already adequately represented in the action by existing parties. The Rule 19(a)(2)(i) criterion imports practical considerations, and the deletion of the "bound" language similarly frees the rule from undue preoccupation with strict considerations of res judicata.

The representation whose adequacy comes into question under the amended rule is not confined to formal representation like that provided by a trustee for his beneficiary or a representative party in a class action for a member of the class. A party to an action may provide practical representation to the absentee seeking intervention although no such formal relationship exists between them, and the adequacy of this practical representation will then have to be weighed.

An intervention of right under the amended rule may be subject to appropriate conditions or restrictions responsive among other things to the requirements of efficient conduct of the proceedings.

Rule 25. Substitution of Parties

(a) Death.

(1) ***Substitution if the Claim Is Not Extinguished.*** If a party dies and the claim is not extinguished, the court may order substitution of the proper party. A motion for substitution may be made by any party or by the decedent's successor or representative. If the motion is not made within 90 days after service of a statement noting the death, the action by or against the decedent must be dismissed.

(2) ***Continuation Among the Remaining Parties.*** After a party's death, if the right sought to be enforced survives only to or against the remaining parties, the action does not abate, but proceeds in favor of or against the remaining parties. The death should be noted on the record.

(3) ***Service.*** A motion to substitute, together with a notice of hearing, must be served on the parties as provided in Rule 5 and on nonparties as provided in Rule 4. A statement noting death must be served in the same manner. Service may be made in any judicial district.

(b) Incompetency. If a party becomes incompetent, the court may, on motion, permit the action to be continued by or against the party's representative. The motion must be served as provided in Rule 25(a)(3).

(c) Transfer of Interest. If an interest is transferred, the action may be continued by or against the original party unless the court, on motion, orders the transferee to be substituted in the action or joined with the original party. The motion must be served as provided in Rule 25(a)(3).

(d) Public Officers; Death or Separation from Office. An action does not abate when a public officer who is a party in an official capacity dies, resigns, or otherwise ceases to hold office while the action is pending. The officer's successor is automatically substituted as a party. Later proceedings should be in the substituted party's name, but any misnomer not affecting the parties' substantial rights must be disregarded. The court may order substitution at any time, but the absence of such an order does not affect the substitution.

TITLE V. DISCLOSURES AND DISCOVERY

Rule 26. Duty to Disclose; General Provisions Governing Discovery

(a) Required Disclosures.

(1) ***Initial Disclosure.***

(A) *In General.* Except as exempted by Rule 26(a)(1)(B) or as otherwise stipulated or ordered by the court, a party must, without awaiting a discovery request, provide to the other parties:

(i) the name and, if known, the address and telephone number of each individual likely to have discoverable information — along with the subjects of that information — that the disclosing party may use to support its claims or defenses, unless the use would be solely for impeachment;

(ii) a copy — or a description by category and location — of all documents, electronically stored information, and tangible things that the disclosing party has in its possession, custody,

or control and may use to support its claims or defenses, unless the use would be solely for impeachment;

(iii) a computation of each category of damages claimed by the disclosing party — who must also make available for inspection and copying as under Rule 34 the documents or other evidentiary material, unless privileged or protected from disclosure, on which each computation is based, including materials bearing on the nature and extent of injuries suffered; and

(iv) for inspection and copying as under Rule 34, any insurance agreement under which an insurance business may be liable to satisfy all or part of a possible judgment in the action or to indemnify or reimburse for payments made to satisfy the judgment.

(B) *Proceedings Exempt from Initial Disclosure.* The following proceedings are exempt from initial disclosure:

(i) an action for review on an administrative record;

(ii) a petition for habeas corpus or any other proceeding to challenge a criminal conviction or sentence;

(iii) an action brought without an attorney by a person in the custody of the United States, a state, or a state subdivision;

(iv) an action to enforce or quash an administrative summons or subpoena;

(v) an action by the United States to recover benefit payments;

(vi) an action by the United States to collect on a student loan guaranteed by the United States;

(vii) a proceeding ancillary to a proceeding in another court; and

(viii) an action to enforce an arbitration award.

(C) *Time for Initial Disclosures — In General.* A party must make the initial disclosures at or within 14 days after the parties' Rule 26(f) conference unless a different time is set by stipulation or court order, or unless a party objects during the conference that initial disclosures are not appropriate in this action and states the objection in the proposed discovery plan. In ruling on the objection, the court must determine what disclosures, if any, are to be made and must set the time for disclosure.

(D) *Time for Initial Disclosures — For Parties Served or Joined Later.* A party that is first served or otherwise joined after the Rule

26(f) conference must make the initial disclosures within 30 days after being served or joined, unless a different time is set by stipulation or court order.

(E) *Basis for Initial Disclosure; Unacceptable Excuses.* A party must make its initial disclosures based on the information then reasonably available to it. A party is not excused from making its disclosures because it has not fully investigated the case or because it challenges the sufficiency of another party's disclosures or because another party has not made its disclosures.

(2) ***Disclosure of Expert Testimony.***

(A) *In General.* In addition to the disclosures required by Rule 26(a)(1), a party must disclose to the other parties the identity of any witness it may use at trial to present evidence under Federal Rule of Evidence 702, 703, or 705.

(B) *Witnesses Who Must Provide a Written Report.* Unless otherwise stipulated or ordered by the court, this disclosure must be accompanied by a written report — prepared and signed by the witness — if the witness is one retained or specially employed to provide expert testimony in the case or one whose duties as the party's employee regularly involve giving expert testimony. The report must contain:

(i) a complete statement of all opinions the witness will express and the basis and reasons for them;

(ii) the facts or data considered by the witness in forming them;

(iii) any exhibits that will be used to summarize or support them;

(iv) the witness's qualifications, including a list of all publications authored in the previous 10 years;

(v) a list of all other cases in which, during the previous 4 years, the witness testified as an expert at trial or by deposition; and

(vi) a statement of the compensation to be paid for the study and testimony in the case.

(C) *Witnesses Who Do Not Provide a Written Report.* Unless otherwise stipulated or ordered by the court, if the witness is not required to provide a written report, this disclosure must state:

(i) the subject matter on which the witness is expected to present evidence under Federal Rule of Evidence 702, 703, or 705; and

(ii) a summary of the facts and opinions to which the witness is expected to testify.

(D) *Time to Disclose Expert Testimony.* A party must make these disclosures at the times and in the sequence that the court orders. Absent a stipulation or a court order, the disclosures must be made:

(i) at least 90 days before the date set for trial or for the case to be ready for trial; or

(ii) if the evidence is intended solely to contradict or rebut evidence on the same subject matter identified by another party under Rule 26(a)(2)(B) or (C), within 30 days after the other party's disclosure.

(E) *Supplementing the Disclosure.* The parties must supplement these disclosures when required under Rule 26(e).

(3) ***Pretrial Disclosures.***

(A) *In General.* In addition to the disclosures required by Rule 26(a)(1) and (2), a party must provide to the other parties and promptly file the following information about the evidence that it may present at trial other than solely for impeachment:

(i) the name and, if not previously provided, the address and telephone number of each witness — separately identifying those the party expects to present and those it may call if the need arises;

(ii) the designation of those witnesses whose testimony the party expects to present by deposition and, if not taken stenographically, a transcript of the pertinent parts of the deposition; and

(iii) an identification of each document or other exhibit, including summaries of other evidence — separately identifying those items the party expects to offer and those it may offer if the need arises.

(B) *Time for Pretrial Disclosures; Objections.* Unless the court orders otherwise, these disclosures must be made at least 30 days before trial. Within 14 days after they are made, unless the court sets a different time, a party may serve and promptly file a list of the following objections: any objections to the use under Rule 32(a) of a deposition designated by another party under Rule 26(a)(3)(A)(ii); and any objection, together with the grounds for it, that may be made to the admissibility of materials identified under Rule 26(a)(3)(A)(iii). An objection not so made — except for one

under Federal Rule of Evidence 402 or 403 — is waived unless excused by the court for good cause.

(4) ***Form of Disclosures.*** Unless the court orders otherwise, all disclosures under Rule 26(a) must be in writing, signed, and served.

(b) Discovery Scope and Limits.

(1) ***Scope in General.*** Unless otherwise limited by court order, the scope of discovery is as follows: Parties may obtain discovery regarding any nonprivileged matter that is relevant to any party's claim or defense and proportional to the needs of the case, considering the importance of the issues at stake in the action, the amount in controversy, the parties' relative access to relevant information, the parties' resources, the importance of the discovery in resolving the issues, and whether the burden or expense of the proposed discovery outweighs its likely benefit. Information within this scope of discovery need not be admissible in evidence to be discoverable.

(2) ***Limitations on Frequency and Extent.***

(A) *When Permitted.* By order, the court may alter the limits in these rules on the number of depositions and interrogatories or on the length of depositions under Rule 30. By order or local rule, the court may also limit the number of requests under Rule 36.

(B) *Specific Limitations on Electronically Stored Information.* A party need not provide discovery of electronically stored information from sources that the party identifies as not reasonably accessible because of undue burden or cost. On motion to compel discovery or for a protective order, the party from whom discovery is sought must show that the information is not reasonably accessible because of undue burden or cost. If that showing is made, the court may nonetheless order discovery from such sources if the requesting party shows good cause, considering the limitations of Rule 26(b)(2)(C). The court may specify conditions for the discovery.

(C) *When Required.* On motion or on its own, the court must limit the frequency or extent of discovery otherwise allowed by these rules or by local rule if it determines that:

(i) the discovery sought is unreasonably cumulative or duplicative, or can be obtained from some other source that is more convenient, less burdensome, or less expensive;

(ii) the party seeking discovery has had ample opportunity to obtain the information by discovery in the action; or

(iii) the proposed discovery is outside the scope permitted by Rule 26(b)(1).

(3) ***Trial Preparation: Materials.***

(A) *Documents and Tangible Things.* Ordinarily, a party may not discover documents and tangible things that are prepared in anticipation of litigation or for trial by or for another party or its representative (including the other party's attorney, consultant, surety, indemnitor, insurer, or agent). But, subject to Rule 26(b)(4), those materials may be discovered if:

(i) they are otherwise discoverable under Rule 26(b)(1); and

(ii) the party shows that it has substantial need for the materials to prepare its case and cannot, without undue hardship, obtain their substantial equivalent by other means.

(B) *Protection Against Disclosure.* If the court orders discovery of those materials, it must protect against disclosure of the mental impressions, conclusions, opinions, or legal theories of a party's attorney or other representative concerning the litigation.

(C) *Previous Statement.* Any party or other person may, on request and without the required showing, obtain the person's own previous statement about the action or its subject matter. If the request is refused, the person may move for a court order, and Rule 37(a)(5) applies to the award of expenses. A previous statement is either:

(i) a written statement that the person has signed or otherwise adopted or approved; or

(ii) a contemporaneous stenographic, mechanical, electrical, or other recording — or a transcription of it — that recites substantially verbatim the person's oral statement.

(4) ***Trial Preparation: Experts.***

(A) *Deposition of an Expert Who May Testify.* A party may depose any person who has been identified as an expert whose opinions may be presented at trial. If Rule 26(a)(2)(B) requires a report from the expert, the deposition may be conducted only after the report is provided.

(B) *Trial-Preparation Protection for Draft Reports or Disclosures.* Rules 26(b)(3)(A) and (B) protect drafts of any report or disclosure required under Rule 26(a)(2), regardless of the form in which the draft is recorded.

(C) *Trial-Preparation Protection for Communications Between a Party's Attorney and Expert Witnesses.* Rules 26(b)(3)(A) and (B) protect communications between the party's attorney and any witness required to provide a report under Rule 26(a)(2)(B), regardless of the form of the communications, except to the extent that the communications:

(i) relate to compensation for the expert's study or testimony;

(ii) identify facts or data that the party's attorney provided and that the expert considered in forming the opinions to be expressed; or

(iii) identify assumptions that the party's attorney provided and that the expert relied on in forming the opinions to be expressed.

(D) *Expert Employed Only for Trial Preparation.* Ordinarily, a party may not, by interrogatories or deposition, discover facts known or opinions held by an expert who has been retained or specially employed by another party in anticipation of litigation or to prepare for trial and who is not expected to be called as a witness at trial. But a party may do so only:

(i) as provided in Rule 35(b); or

(ii) on showing exceptional circumstances under which it is impracticable for the party to obtain facts or opinions on the same subject by other means.

(E) *Payment.* Unless manifest injustice would result, the court must require that the party seeking discovery:

(i) pay the expert a reasonable fee for time spent in responding to discovery under Rule 26(b)(4)(A) or (D); and

(ii) for discovery under (D), also pay the other party a fair portion of the fees and expenses it reasonably incurred in obtaining the expert's facts and opinions.

(5) ***Claiming Privilege or Protecting Trial-Preparation Materials.***

(A) *Information Withheld.* When a party withholds information otherwise discoverable by claiming that the information is privileged or subject to protection as trial-preparation material, the party must:

(i) expressly make the claim; and

(ii) describe the nature of the documents, communications, or tangible things not produced or disclosed — and do so in a

manner that, without revealing information itself privileged or protected, will enable other parties to assess the claim.

(B) *Information Produced.* If information produced in discovery is subject to a claim of privilege or of protection as trial-preparation material, the party making the claim may notify any party that received the information of the claim and the basis for it. After being notified, a party must promptly return, sequester, or destroy the specified information and any copies it has; must not use or disclose the information until the claim is resolved; must take reasonable steps to retrieve the information if the party disclosed it before being notified; and may promptly present the information to the court under seal for a determination of the claim. The producing party must preserve the information until the claim is resolved.

(c) Protective Orders.

(1) ***In General.*** A party or any person from whom discovery is sought may move for a protective order in the court where the action is pending — or as an alternative on matters relating to a deposition, in the court for the district where the deposition will be taken. The motion must include a certification that the movant has in good faith conferred or attempted to confer with other affected parties in an effort to resolve the dispute without court action. The court may, for good cause, issue an order to protect a party or person from annoyance, embarrassment, oppression, or undue burden or expense, including one or more of the following:

(A) forbidding the disclosure or discovery;

(B) specifying terms, including time and place or the allocation of expenses, for the disclosure or discovery;

(C) prescribing a discovery method other than the one selected by the party seeking discovery;

(D) forbidding inquiry into certain matters, or limiting the scope of disclosure or discovery to certain matters;

(E) designating the persons who may be present while the discovery is conducted;

(F) requiring that a deposition be sealed and opened only on court order;

(G) requiring that a trade secret or other confidential research, development, or commercial information not be revealed or be revealed only in a specified way; and

(H) requiring that the parties simultaneously file specified documents or information in sealed envelopes, to be opened as the court directs.

(2) ***Ordering Discovery.*** If a motion for a protective order is wholly or partly denied, the court may, on just terms, order that any party or person provide or permit discovery.

(3) ***Awarding Expenses.*** Rule 37(a)(5) applies to the award of expenses.

(d) Timing and Sequence of Discovery.

(1) ***Timing.*** A party may not seek discovery from any source before the parties have conferred as required by Rule 26(f), except in a proceeding exempted from initial disclosure under Rule 26(a)(1)(B), or when authorized by these rules, by stipulation, or by court order.

(2) ***Early Rule 34 Requests.***

(A) *Time to Deliver.* More than 21 days after the summons and complaint are served on a party, a request under Rule 34 may be delivered:

(i) to that party by any other party, and

(ii) by that party to any plaintiff or to any other party that has been served.

(B) *When Considered Served.* The request is considered to have been served at the first Rule 26(f) conference.

(3) ***Sequence.*** Unless the parties stipulate or the court orders otherwise for the parties' and witnesses' convenience and in the interests of justice:

(A) methods of discovery may be used in any sequence; and

(B) discovery by one party does not require any other party to delay its discovery.

(e) Supplementing Disclosures and Responses.

(1) ***In General.*** A party who has made a disclosure under Rule 26(a) — or who has responded to an interrogatory, request for production, or request for admission — must supplement or correct its disclosure or response:

(A) in a timely manner if the party learns that in some material respect the disclosure or response is incomplete or incorrect, and if the additional or corrective information has not otherwise been made known to the other parties during the discovery process or in writing; or

(B) as ordered by the court.

(2) ***Expert Witness***. For an expert whose report must be disclosed under Rule 26(a)(2)(B), the party's duty to supplement extends both to information included in the report and to information given during the expert's deposition. Any additions or changes to this information must be disclosed by the time the party's pretrial disclosures under Rule 26(a)(3) are due.

(f) Conference of the Parties; Planning for Discovery.

(1) ***Conference Timing***. Except in a proceeding exempted from initial disclosure under Rule 26(a)(1)(B) or when the court orders otherwise, the parties must confer as soon as practicable — and in any event at least 21 days before a scheduling conference is to be held or a scheduling order is due under Rule 16(b).

(2) ***Conference Content; Parties' Responsibilities***. In conferring, the parties must consider the nature and basis of their claims and defenses and the possibilities for promptly settling or resolving the case; make or arrange for the disclosures required by Rule 26(a)(1); discuss any issues about preserving discoverable information; and develop a proposed discovery plan. The attorneys of record and all unrepresented parties that have appeared in the case are jointly responsible for arranging the conference, for attempting in good faith to agree on the proposed discovery plan, and for submitting to the court within 14 days after the conference a written report outlining the plan. The court may order the parties or attorneys to attend the conference in person.

(3) ***Discovery Plan***. A discovery plan must state the parties' views and proposals on:

(A) what changes should be made in the timing, form, or requirement for disclosures under Rule 26(a), including a statement of when initial disclosures were made or will be made;

(B) the subjects on which discovery may be needed, when discovery should be completed, and whether discovery should be conducted in phases or be limited to or focused on particular issues;

(C) any issues about disclosure, discovery, or preservation of electronically stored information, including the form or forms in which it should be produced;

(D) any issues about claims of privilege or of protection as trial-preparation materials, including — if the parties agree on a procedure to assert these claims after production — whether to ask the court to include their agreement in an order under Federal Rule of Evidence 502;

(E) what changes should be made in the limitations on discovery imposed under these rules or by local rule, and what other limitations should be imposed; and

(F) any other orders that the court should issue under Rule 26(c) or under Rule 16(b) and (c).

(4) ***Expedited Schedule.*** If necessary to comply with its expedited schedule for Rule 16(b) conferences, a court may by local rule:

(A) require the parties' conference to occur less than 21 days before the scheduling conference is held or a scheduling order is due under Rule 16(b); and

(B) require the written report outlining the discovery plan to be filed less than 14 days after the parties' conference, or excuse the parties from submitting a written report and permit them to report orally on their discovery plan at the Rule 16(b) conference.

(g) Signing Disclosures and Discovery Requests, Responses, and Objections.

(1) ***Signature Required; Effect of Signature.*** Every disclosure under Rule 26(a)(1) or (a)(3) and every discovery request, response, or objection must be signed by at least one attorney of record in the attorney's own name — or by the party personally, if unrepresented — and must state the signer's address, e-mail address, and telephone number. By signing, an attorney or party certifies that to the best of the person's knowledge, information, and belief formed after a reasonable inquiry:

(A) with respect to a disclosure, it is complete and correct as of the time it is made; and

(B) with respect to a discovery request, response, or objection, it is:

(i) consistent with these rules and warranted by existing law or by a nonfrivolous argument for extending, modifying, or reversing existing law, or for establishing new law;

(ii) not interposed for any improper purpose, such as to harass, cause unnecessary delay, or needlessly increase the cost of litigation; and

(iii) neither unreasonable nor unduly burdensome or expensive, considering the needs of the case, prior discovery in the case, the amount in controversy, and the importance of the issues at stake in the action.

(2) ***Failure to Sign.*** Other parties have no duty to act on an unsigned disclosure, request, response, or objection until it is signed,

and the court must strike it unless a signature is promptly supplied after the omission is called to the attorney's or party's attention.

(3) ***Sanction for Improper Certification.*** If a certification violates this rule without substantial justification, the court, on motion or on its own, must impose an appropriate sanction on the signer, the party on whose behalf the signer was acting, or both. The sanction may include an order to pay the reasonable expenses, including attorney's fees, caused by the violation.

ADVISORY COMMITTEE NOTES

1970 Amendment [citations omitted without notation — ED.]

. . .

Subdivision (b)(3) — Trial Preparation: Materials. Some of the most controversial and vexing problems to emerge from the discovery rules have arisen out of requests for the production of documents or things prepared in anticipation of litigation or for trial. The existing rules make no explicit provision for such materials. . . .

The rules are amended by eliminating the general requirement of "good cause" from Rule 34 but retaining a requirement of a special showing for trial preparation materials in this subdivision. The required showing is expressed, not in terms of "good cause" whose generality has tended to encourage confusion and controversy, but in terms of the elements of the special showing to be made: substantial need of the materials in the preparation of the case and inability without undue hardship to obtain the substantial equivalent of the materials by other means.

These changes conform to the holdings of the cases, when viewed in light of their facts. Apart from trial preparation, the fact that the materials sought are documentary does not in and of itself require a special showing beyond relevance and absence of privilege. The protective provisions are of course available, and if the party from whom production is sought raises a special issue of privacy (as with respect to income tax returns or grand jury minutes) or points to evidence primarily impeaching, or can show serious burden or expense, the court will exercise its traditional power to decide whether to issue a protective order. On the other hand, the requirement of a special showing for discovery of trial preparation materials reflects the view that each side's informal evaluation of its case should be protected, that each side should be encouraged to prepare independently, and that one side should not automatically have the benefit of the detailed preparatory work of the other side. . . .

Materials assembled in the ordinary course of business, or pursuant to public requirements unrelated to litigation, or for other nonlitigation purposes are not under the qualified immunity provided by this subdivision. No change is made in the existing doctrine, noted in the *Hickman* case, that one party may discover relevant facts known or available to the other party, even though such facts are contained in a document which is not itself discoverable.

Treatment of Lawyers; Special Protection of Mental Impressions, Conclusions, Opinions, and Legal Theories Concerning the Litigation. —

The courts are divided as to whether the work-product doctrine extends to the preparatory work only of lawyers. The *Hickman* case left this issue open since the statements in that case were taken by a lawyer. . . .

Subdivision (b)(3) reflects the trend of the cases by requiring a special showing, not merely as to materials prepared by an attorney, but also as to materials prepared in anticipation of litigation or preparation for trial by or for a party or any representative acting on his behalf. The subdivision then goes on to protect against disclosure the mental impressions, conclusions, opinions, or legal theories concerning the litigation of an attorney or other representative of a party. The *Hickman* opinion drew special attention to the need for protecting an attorney against discovery of memoranda prepared from recollection of oral interviews. The courts have steadfastly safeguarded against disclosure of lawyers' mental impressions and legal theories, as well as mental impressions and subjective evaluations of investigators and claim-agents. In enforcing this provision of the subdivision, the courts will sometimes find it necessary to order disclosure of a document but with portions deleted.

Rules 33 and 36 have been revised in order to permit discovery calling for opinions, contentions, and admissions relating not only to fact but also to the application of law to fact. Under those rules, a party and his attorney or other representative may be required to disclose, to some extent, mental impressions, opinions, or conclusions. But documents or parts of documents containing these matters are protected against discovery by this subdivision. Even though a party may ultimately have to disclose in response to interrogatories or requests to admit, he is entitled to keep confidential documents containing such matters prepared for internal use. . . .

1983 Amendment [citations omitted without notation — ED.]

Excessive discovery and evasion or resistance to reasonable discovery requests pose significant problems. Recent studies have made some attempt to determine the sources and extent of the difficulties. See Brazil, *Civil Discovery: Lawyers' Views of its Effectiveness, Principal Problems and Abuses,* American Bar Foundation (1980); Connolly, Holleman & Kuhlman, *Judicial Controls and the Civil Litigative Process: Discovery,* Federal Judicial Center (1978); Ellington, *A Study of Sanctions for Discovery Abuse,* Department of Justice (1979); Schroeder & Frank, *The Proposed Changes in the Discovery Rules,* 1978 Ariz. St. L.J. 475.

The purpose of discovery is to provide a mechanism for making relevant information available to the litigants. "Mutual knowledge of all the relevant facts gathered by both parties is essential to proper litigation." *Hickman v. Taylor,* 329 U.S. 495, 507 (1947). Thus the spirit of the rules is violated when advocates attempt to use discovery tools as tactical weapons rather than to expose the facts and illuminate the issues by overuse of discovery or unnecessary use of defensive weapons or evasive responses. All of this results in excessively costly and time-consuming activities that are disproportionate to the nature of the case, the amount involved, or the issues or values at stake.

Given our adversary tradition and the current discovery rules, it is not surprising that there are many opportunities, if not incentives, for attorneys to engage in discovery that, although authorized by the broad, permissive terms of the rules, nevertheless results in delay. See Brazil, *The Adversary Character of*

Civil Discovery: A Critique and Proposals for Change, 31 Vand. L. Rev. 1259 (1978). As a result, it has been said that the rules have "not infrequently [been] exploited to the disadvantage of justice." *Herbert v. Lando,* 441 U.S. 153, 179 (1979) (Powell, J., concurring). These practices impose costs on an already overburdened system and impede the fundamental goal of the "just, speedy, and inexpensive determination of every action." Fed. R. Civ. P. 1.

Subdivision (a); Discovery Methods. The deletion of the last sentence of Rule 26(a)(1) [probably should be "Rule 26(a)" — ED.], which provided that unless the court ordered otherwise under Rule 26(c) "the frequency of use" of the various discovery methods was not to be limited, is an attempt to address the problem of duplicative, redundant, and excessive discovery and to reduce it. The amendment, in conjunction with the changes in Rule 26(b)(1), is designed to encourage district judges to identify instances of needless discovery and to limit the use of the various discovery devices accordingly. The question may be raised by one of the parties, typically on a motion for a protective order, or by the court on its own initiative. It is entirely appropriate to consider a limitation on the frequency of use of discovery at a discovery conference under Rule 26(f) or at any other pretrial conference authorized by these rules. In considering the discovery needs of a particular case, the court should consider the factors described in Rule 26(b)(1).

Subdivision (b); Discovery Scope and Limits. Rule 26(b)(1) has been amended to add a sentence to deal with the problem of over-discovery. [The amendment referred to was later moved, with modifications, to Rule 26(b)(2)(C), and then returned to Rule 26(b)(1). — ED.] The objective is to guard against redundant or disproportionate discovery by giving the court authority to reduce the amount of discovery that may be directed to matters that are otherwise proper subjects of inquiry. The new sentence is intended to encourage judges to be more aggressive in identifying and discouraging discovery overuse. The grounds mentioned in the amended rule for limiting discovery reflect the existing practice of many courts in issuing protective orders under Rule 26(c).

The first element of the standard, Rule 26(b)(1)(i) [now Rule 26(b)(2)(C)(i) — ED.], is designed to minimize redundancy in discovery and encourage attorneys to be sensitive to the comparative costs of different methods of securing information. Subdivision (b)(1)(ii)) [now Rule 26(b)(2)(C)(ii) — ED.] also seeks to reduce repetitiveness and to oblige lawyers to think through their discovery activities in advance so that full utilization is made of each deposition, document request, or set of interrogatories. The elements of Rule 26(b)(1)(iii)) [now found in Rule 26(b)(1) — ED.] address the problem of discovery that is disproportionate to the individual lawsuit as measured by such matters as its nature and complexity, the importance of the issues at stake in a case seeking damages, the limitations on a financially weak litigant to withstand extensive opposition to a discovery program or to respond to discovery requests, and the significance of the substantive issues, as measured in philosophic, social, or institutional terms. Thus the rule recognizes that many cases in public policy spheres, such as employment practices, free speech, and other matters, may have importance far beyond the monetary amount involved. The court must apply the standards in an even-handed manner that will prevent use of discovery to wage a war of attrition or as a device to coerce a party, whether financially weak or affluent.

The rule contemplates greater judicial involvement in the discovery process and thus acknowledges the reality that it cannot always operate on a self-regulating basis. In an appropriate case the court could restrict the number of depositions, interrogatories, or the scope of a production request. But the court must be careful not to deprive a party of discovery that is reasonably necessary to afford a fair opportunity to develop and prepare the case.

The court may act on motion, or its own initiative. It is entirely appropriate to resort to the amended rule in conjunction with a discovery conference under Rule 26(f) or one of the other pretrial conferences authorized by the rules.

Subdivision (g); Signing of Discovery Requests, Responses, and Objections. Rule 26(g) imposes an affirmative duty to engage in pretrial discovery in a responsible manner that is consistent with the spirit and purposes of Rules 26 through 37. In addition, Rule 26(g) is designed to curb discovery abuse by explicitly encouraging the imposition of sanctions. The subdivision provides a deterrent to both excessive discovery and evasion by imposing a certification requirement that obliges each attorney to stop and think about the legitimacy of a discovery request, a response thereto, or an objection. The term "response" includes answers to interrogatories and to requests to admit as well as responses to production requests.

If primary responsibility for conducting discovery is to continue to rest with the litigants, they must be obliged to act responsibly and avoid abuse. With this in mind, Rule 26(g), which parallels the amendments to Rule 11, requires an attorney or unrepresented party to sign each discovery request, response, or objection. Motions relating to discovery are governed by Rule 11. However, since a discovery request, response, or objection usually deals with more specific subject matter than motions or papers, the elements that must be certified in connection with the former are spelled out more completely. The signature is a certification of the elements set forth in Rule 26(g).

Although the certification duty requires the lawyer to pause and consider the reasonableness of his request, response, or objection, it is not meant to discourage or restrict necessary and legitimate discovery. The rule simply requires that the attorney make a reasonable inquiry into the factual basis of his response, request, or objection.

The duty to make a "reasonable inquiry" is satisfied if the investigation undertaken by the attorney and the conclusions drawn therefrom are reasonable under the circumstances. It is an objective standard similar to the one imposed by Rule 11. See the Advisory Committee Note to Rule 11. In making the inquiry, the attorney may rely on assertions by the client and on communications with other counsel in the case as long as that reliance is appropriate under the circumstances. Ultimately, what is reasonable is a matter for the court to decide on the totality of the circumstances.

Rule 26(g) does not require the signing attorney to certify the truthfulness of the client's factual responses to a discovery request. Rather, the signature certifies that the lawyer has made a reasonable effort to assure that the client has provided all the information and documents available to him that are responsive to the discovery demand. Thus, the lawyer's certification under Rule 26(g) should be distinguished from other signature requirements in the rules, such as those in

Rules 30(e) and 33. [Changes to Rule 30(e) in 1993 eliminated the signature requirement under that rule in most cases. — ED.]

Nor does the rule require a party or an attorney to disclose privileged communications or work product in order to show that a discovery request, response, or objection is substantially justified. The provisions of Rule 26(c), including appropriate orders after *in camera* inspection by the court, remain available to protect a party claiming privilege or work product protection.

The signing requirement means that every discovery request, response, or objection should be grounded on a theory that is reasonable under the precedents or a good faith belief as to what should be the law. This standard is heavily dependent on the circumstances of each case. The certification speaks as of the time it is made. The duty to supplement discovery responses continues to be governed by Rule 26(e). . . .

1993 Amendment

Subdivision (a). Through the addition of paragraphs (1)-(4), this subdivision imposes on parties a duty to disclose, without awaiting formal discovery requests, certain basic information that is needed in most cases to prepare for trial or make an informed decision about settlement. The rule requires all parties (1) early in the case to exchange information regarding potential witnesses, documentary evidence, damages, and insurance, (2) at an appropriate time during the discovery period to identify expert witnesses and provide a detailed written statement of the testimony that may be offered at trial through specially retained experts, and (3) as the trial date approaches to identify the particular evidence that may be offered at trial. The enumeration in Rule 26(a) of items to be disclosed does not prevent a court from requiring by order or local rule that the parties disclose additional information without a discovery request. Nor are parties precluded from using traditional discovery methods to obtain further information regarding these matters, as for example asking an expert during a deposition about testimony given in other litigation beyond the four-year period specified in Rule 26(a)(2)(B) [now Rule 26(a)(2)(B)(v) — ED.].

A major purpose of the revision is to accelerate the exchange of basic information about the case and to eliminate the paper work involved in requesting such information, and the rule should be applied in a manner to achieve those objectives. . . .

The rule is based upon the experience of district courts that have required disclosure of some of this information through local rules, court-approved standard interrogatories, and standing orders. Most have required pretrial disclosure of the kind of information described in Rule 26(a)(3). Many have required written reports from experts containing information like that specified in Rule 26(a)(2)(B). While far more limited, the experience of the few state and federal courts that have required pre-discovery exchange of core information such as is contemplated in Rule 26(a)(1) indicates that savings in time and expense can be achieved, particularly if the litigants meet and discuss the issues in the case as a predicate for this exchange and if a judge supports the process, as by using the results to guide further proceedings in the case. Courts in Canada and the United Kingdom have for many years required disclosure of certain information without awaiting a request from an adversary.

Paragraph (1). As the functional equivalent of court-ordered interrogatories, this paragraph requires early disclosure, without need for any request, of four types of information that have been customarily secured early in litigation through formal discovery. The introductory clause permits the court, by local rule, to exempt all or particular types of cases from these disclosure requirement[s] or to modify the nature of the information to be disclosed. [The local-rule exemption was deleted in an amendment to Rule 26(a)(1). — ED.] . . . The disclosure obligations specified in paragraph (1) will not be appropriate for all cases, and it is expected that changes in these obligations will be made by the court or parties when the circumstances warrant. . . .

Paragraph (2). This paragraph imposes an additional duty to disclose information regarding expert testimony sufficiently in advance of trial that opposing parties have a reasonable opportunity to prepare for effective cross examination and perhaps arrange for expert testimony from other witnesses. . . .

Paragraph (2)(B) requires that persons retained or specially employed to provide expert testimony, or whose duties as an employee of the party regularly involve the giving of expert testimony, must prepare a detailed and complete written report, stating the testimony the witness is expected to present during direct examination, together with the reasons therefor. . . .

The report is to disclose the data and other information considered by the expert and any exhibits or charts that summarize or support the expert's opinions. Given this obligation of disclosure, litigants should no longer be able to argue that materials furnished to their experts to be used in forming their opinions — whether or not ultimately relied upon by the expert — are privileged or otherwise protected from disclosure when such persons are testifying or being deposed. . . .

Subdivision (e). This subdivision is revised to provide that the requirement for supplementation applies to all disclosures required by subdivisions (a)(1)-(3). Like the former rule, the duty, while imposed on a "party," applies whether the corrective information is learned by the client or by the attorney. Supplementations need not be made as each new item of information is learned but should be made at appropriate intervals during the discovery period, and with special promptness as the trial date approaches. It may be useful for the scheduling order to specify the time or times when supplementations should be made.

The revision also clarifies that the obligation to supplement responses to formal discovery requests applies to interrogatories, requests for production, and requests for admissions, but not ordinarily to deposition testimony. However, with respect to experts from whom a written report is required under subdivision (a)(2)(B), changes in the opinions expressed by the expert whether in the report or at a subsequent deposition are subject to a duty of supplemental disclosure under subdivision (e)(1) [now Rule 26(e)(2) — ED.].

The obligation to supplement disclosures and discovery responses applies whenever a party learns that its prior disclosures or responses are in some material respect incomplete or incorrect. There is, however, no obligation to provide supplemental or corrective information that has been otherwise made known to the parties in writing or during the discovery process, as when a witness

not previously disclosed is identified during the taking of a deposition or when an expert during a deposition corrects information contained in an earlier report.

Subdivision (f). This subdivision was added in 1980 to provide a party threatened with abusive discovery with a special means for obtaining judicial intervention other than through discrete motions under Rules 26(c) and 37(a). . . .

The desirability of some judicial control of discovery can hardly be doubted. Rule 16, as revised, requires that the court set a time for completion of discovery and authorizes various other orders affecting the scope, timing, and extent of discovery and disclosures. Before entering such orders, the court should consider the views of the parties, preferably by means of a conference, but at the least through written submissions. Moreover, it is desirable that the parties' proposals regarding discovery be developed through a process where they meet in person, informally explore the nature and basis of the issues, and discuss how discovery can be conducted most efficiently and economically.

. . . [F]ormer subdivision (f) envisioned the development of proposed discovery plans as an optional procedure to be used in relatively few cases. The revised rule directs that in all cases not exempted by local rule or special order the litigants must meet in person and plan for discovery. Following this meeting, the parties submit to the court their proposals for a discovery plan and can begin formal discovery. Their report will assist the court in seeing that the timing and scope of disclosures under revised Rule 26(a) and the limitations on the extent of discovery under these rules and local rules are tailored to the circumstances of the particular case. . . .

Subdivision (g). Paragraph (1) is added to require signatures on disclosures, a requirement that parallels the provisions of paragraph (2) with respect to discovery requests, responses, and objections. [Both requirements are now found in Rule 26(g)(1). — ED.] The provisions of paragraph (3) have been modified to be consistent with Rules 37(a)(4) [now Rule 37(a)(5) — ED.] and 37(c)(1); in combination, these rules establish sanctions for violation of the rules regarding disclosures and discovery matters. Amended Rule 11 no longer applies to such violations.

2000 Amendment [citations omitted without notation — ED.]

Purposes of amendments. The Rule 26(a)(1) initial disclosure provisions are amended to establish a nationally uniform practice. The scope of the disclosure obligation is narrowed to cover only information that the disclosing party may use to support its position. In addition, the rule exempts specified categories of proceedings from initial disclosure, and permits a party who contends that disclosure is not appropriate in the circumstances of the case to present its objections to the court, which must then determine whether disclosure should be made. Related changes are made in Rules 26(d) and (f).

The initial disclosure requirements added by the 1993 amendments permitted local rules directing that disclosure would not be required or altering its operation. The inclusion of the "opt out" provision reflected the strong opposition to initial disclosure felt in some districts, and permitted experimentation with differing disclosure rules in those districts that were favorable to disclosure. The local option also recognized that — partly in response to the first publication in 1991 of a

proposed disclosure rule — many districts had adopted a variety of disclosure programs under the aegis of the Civil Justice Reform Act. It was hoped that developing experience under a variety of disclosure systems would support eventual refinement of a uniform national disclosure practice. In addition, there was hope that local experience could identify categories of actions in which disclosure is not useful.

A striking array of local regimes in fact emerged for disclosure and related features introduced in 1993. . . .

The Committee has discerned widespread support for national uniformity. . . .

These amendments restore national uniformity to disclosure practice. . . .

Subdivision (a)(1). The amendments remove the authority to alter or opt out of the national disclosure requirements by local rule, invalidating not only formal local rules but also informal "standing" orders of an individual judge or court that purport to create exemptions from — or limit or expand — the disclosure provided under the national rule. *See* Rule 83. Case-specific orders remain proper, however, and are expressly required if a party objects that initial disclosure is not appropriate in the circumstances of the action. Specified categories of proceedings are excluded from initial disclosure under subdivision (a)(1)(E) [now Rule 26(a)(1)(B) — ED.]. In addition, the parties can stipulate to forgo disclosure, as was true before. But even in a case excluded by subdivision (a)(1)(E) or in which the parties stipulate to bypass disclosure, the court can order exchange of similar information in managing the action under Rule 16.

The initial disclosure obligation of subdivisions (a)(1)(A) and (B) [now Rules 26(a)(1)(A)(i)-(ii) — ED.] has been narrowed to identification of witnesses and documents that the disclosing party may use to support its claims or defenses. "Use" includes any use at a pretrial conference, to support a motion, or at trial. The disclosure obligation is also triggered by intended use in discovery, apart from use to respond to a discovery request; use of a document to question a witness during a deposition is a common example. The disclosure obligation attaches both to witnesses and documents a party intends to use and also to witnesses and to documents the party intends to use if — in the language of Rule 26(a)(3) — "the need arises."

A party is no longer obligated to disclose witnesses or documents, whether favorable or unfavorable, that it does not intend to use. The obligation to disclose information the party may use connects directly to the exclusion sanction of Rule 37(c)(1). Because the disclosure obligation is limited to material that the party may use, it is no longer tied to particularized allegations in the pleadings. Subdivision (e)(1), which is unchanged, requires supplementation if information later acquired would have been subject to the disclosure requirement. As case preparation continues, a party must supplement its disclosures when it determines that it may use a witness or document that it did not previously intend to use.

The disclosure obligation applies to "claims and defenses," and therefore requires a party to disclose information it may use to support its denial or rebuttal of the allegations, claim, or defense of another party. It thereby bolsters the requirements of Rule 11(b)(4), which authorizes denials "warranted on the

evidence," and disclosure should include the identity of any witness or document that the disclosing party may use to support such denials.

Subdivision (a)(3) presently excuses pretrial disclosure of information solely for impeachment. Impeachment information is similarly excluded from the initial disclosure requirement.

Subdivisions (a)(1)(C) and (D) [now Rules 26(a)(1)(A)(iii) and (iv) — ED.] are not changed. Should a case be exempted from initial disclosure by Rule 26(a)(1)(E) [now Rule 26(a)(1)(B) — ED.] or by agreement or order, the insurance information described by subparagraph (D) [now Rule 26(a)(1)(A)(iv) — ED.] should be subject to discovery, as it would have been under the principles of former Rule 26(b)(2), which was added in 1970 and deleted in 1993 as redundant in light of the new initial disclosure obligation.

New subdivision (a)(1)(E) [now Rule 26(a)(1)(B) — ED.] excludes eight specified categories of proceedings from initial disclosure. The objective of this listing is to identify cases in which there is likely to be little or no discovery, or in which initial disclosure appears unlikely to contribute to the effective development of the case. The list was developed after a review of the categories excluded by local rules in various districts from the operation of Rule 16(b) and the conference requirements of subdivision (f). . . . The descriptions in the rule are generic and are intended to be administered by the parties — and, when needed, the courts — with the flexibility needed to adapt to gradual evolution in the types of proceedings that fall within these general categories. The exclusion of an action for review on an administrative record, for example, is intended to reach a proceeding that is framed as an "appeal" based solely on an administrative record. The exclusion should not apply to a proceeding in a form that commonly permits admission of new evidence to supplement the record. . . .

Subdivision (a)(1)(E) is likely to exempt a substantial proportion of the cases in most districts from the initial disclosure requirement. Based on 1996 and 1997 case filing statistics, Federal Judicial Center staff estimate that, nationwide, these categories total approximately one-third of all civil filings.

The categories of proceedings listed in subdivision (a)(1)(E) are also exempted from the subdivision (f) conference requirement and from the subdivision (d) moratorium on discovery. Although there is no restriction on commencement of discovery in these cases, it is not expected that this opportunity will often lead to abuse since there is likely to be little or no discovery in most such cases. Should a defendant need more time to respond to discovery requests filed at the beginning of an exempted action, it can seek relief by motion under Rule 26(c) if the plaintiff is unwilling to defer the due date by agreement.

Subdivision (a)(1)(E)'s enumeration of exempt categories is exclusive. Although a case-specific order can alter or excuse initial disclosure, local rules or "standing" orders that purport to create general exemptions are invalid. *See* Rule 83.

The time for initial disclosure is extended to 14 days after the subdivision (f) conference unless the court orders otherwise. This change is integrated with corresponding changes requiring that the subdivision (f) conference be held 21 days before the Rule 16(b) scheduling conference or scheduling order, and that the report on the subdivision (f) conference be submitted to the court 14 days after the

meeting. These changes provide a more orderly opportunity for the parties to review the disclosures, and for the court to consider the report. In many instances, the subdivision (f) conference and the effective preparation of the case would benefit from disclosure before the conference, and earlier disclosure is encouraged.

The presumptive disclosure date does not apply if a party objects to initial disclosure during the subdivision (f) conference and states its objection in the subdivision (f) discovery plan. The right to object to initial disclosure is not intended to afford parties an opportunity to "opt out" of disclosure unilaterally. It does provide an opportunity for an objecting party to present to the court its position that disclosure would be "inappropriate in the circumstances of the action." Making the objection permits the objecting party to present the question to the judge before any party is required to make disclosure. The court must then rule on the objection and determine what disclosures — if any — should be made. Ordinarily, this determination would be included in the Rule 16(b) scheduling order, but the court could handle the matter in a different fashion. Even when circumstances warrant suspending some disclosure obligations, others — such as the damages and insurance information called for by subdivisions (a)(1)(C) and (D) [now Rules 26(a)(1)(A)(iii) and -(iv) — ED.] — may continue to be appropriate.

The presumptive disclosure date is also inapplicable to a party who is "first served or otherwise joined" after the subdivision (f) conference. This phrase refers to the date of service of a claim on a party in a defensive posture (such as a defendant or third-party defendant), and the date of joinder of a party added as a claimant or an intervenor. Absent court order or stipulation, a new party has 30 days in which to make its initial disclosures. But it is expected that later-added parties will ordinarily be treated the same as the original parties when the original parties have stipulated to forgo initial disclosure, or the court has ordered disclosure in a modified form.

Subdivision (a)(3). The amendment to Rule 5(d) forbids filing disclosures under subdivisions (a)(1) and (a)(2) until they are used in the proceeding, and this change is reflected in an amendment to subdivision (a)(4). Disclosures under subdivision (a)(3), however, may be important to the court in connection with the final pretrial conference or otherwise in preparing for trial. The requirement that objections to certain matters be filed points up the court's need to be provided with these materials. Accordingly, the requirement that subdivision (a)(3) materials be filed has been moved from subdivision (a)(4) to subdivision (a)(3), and it has also been made clear that they — and any objections — should be filed "promptly."

Subdivision (a)(4). The filing requirement has been removed from this subdivision. Rule 5(d) has been amended to provide that disclosures under subdivisions (a)(1) and (a)(2) must not be filed until used in the proceeding. Subdivision (a)(3) has been amended to require that the disclosures it directs, and objections to them, be filed promptly. Subdivision (a)(4) continues to require that all disclosures under subdivisions (a)(1), (a)(2), and (a)(3) be in writing, signed, and served. . . .

Subdivision (b)(1). In 1978, the Committee published for comment a proposed amendment, suggested by the Section of Litigation of the American Bar Association, to refine the scope of discovery by deleting the "subject matter" language. This proposal was withdrawn, and the Committee has since then made

other changes in the discovery rules to address concerns about overbroad discovery. Concerns about costs and delay of discovery have persisted nonetheless, and other bar groups have repeatedly renewed similar proposals for amendment to this subdivision to delete the "subject matter" language. Nearly one-third of the lawyers surveyed in 1997 by the Federal Judicial Center endorsed narrowing the scope of discovery as a means of reducing litigation expense without interfering with fair case resolutions. The Committee has heard that in some instances, particularly cases involving large quantities of discovery, parties seek to justify discovery requests that sweep far beyond the claims and defenses of the parties on the ground that they nevertheless have a bearing on the "subject matter" involved in the action.

. . . The court . . . retains authority to order discovery of any matter relevant to the subject matter involved in the action for good cause. [This authority was terminated in 2015. — ED.] The amendment is designed to involve the court more actively in regulating the breadth of sweeping or contentious discovery. The Committee has been informed repeatedly by lawyers that involvement of the court in managing discovery is an important method of controlling problems of inappropriately broad discovery. . . . Under the amended provisions, if there is an objection that discovery goes beyond material relevant to the parties' claims or defenses, the court would become involved to determine whether the discovery is relevant to the claims or defenses and, if not, whether good cause exists for authorizing it so long as it is relevant to the subject matter of the action. The good-cause standard warranting broader discovery is meant to be flexible.

The Committee intends that the parties and the court focus on the actual claims and defenses involved in the action. The dividing line between information relevant to the claims and defenses and that relevant only to the subject matter of the action cannot be defined with precision. A variety of types of information not directly pertinent to the incident in suit could be relevant to the claims or defenses raised in a given action. For example, other incidents of the same type, or involving the same product, could be properly discoverable under the revised standard. Information about organizational arrangements or filing systems of a party could be discoverable if likely to yield or lead to the discovery of admissible information. Similarly, information that could be used to impeach a likely witness, although not otherwise relevant to the claims or defenses, might be properly discoverable. In each instance, the determination whether such information is discoverable because it is relevant to the claims or defenses depends on the circumstances of the pending action.

The rule change signals to the court that it has the authority to confine discovery to the claims and defenses asserted in the pleadings, and signals to the parties that they have no entitlement to discovery to develop new claims or defenses that are not already identified in the pleadings. . . . The court may permit broader discovery in a particular case depending on the circumstances of the case, the nature of the claims and defenses, and the scope of the discovery requested.

The amendments also modify the provision regarding discovery of information not admissible in evidence. As added in 1946, this sentence was designed to make clear that otherwise relevant material could not be withheld because it was hearsay or otherwise inadmissible. The Committee was concerned that the

"reasonably calculated to lead to the discovery of admissible evidence" standard set forth in this sentence might swallow any other limitation on the scope of discovery. Accordingly, this sentence has been amended to clarify that information must be relevant to be discoverable, even though inadmissible, and that discovery of such material is permitted if reasonably calculated to lead to the discovery of admissible evidence. As used here, "relevant" means within the scope of discovery as defined in this subdivision, and it would include information relevant to the subject matter involved in the action if the court has ordered discovery to that limit based on a showing of good cause.

Finally, a sentence has been added calling attention to the limitations of subdivision (b)(2)(i), (ii), and (iii) [now found in Rules 26(b)(1) and 26(b)(2)(C)(i)-(ii) — ED.]. These limitations apply to discovery that is otherwise within the scope of subdivision (b)(1). The Committee has been told repeatedly that courts have not implemented these limitations with the vigor that was contemplated. This otherwise redundant cross-reference has been added to emphasize the need for active judicial use of subdivision (b)(2) to control excessive discovery. *Cf. Crawford-El v. Britton*, [523 U.S. 574, 598-99] (1998) (quoting Rule 26(b)(2)(iii) and stating that "Rule 26 vests the trial judge with broad discretion to tailor discovery narrowly").

Subdivision (b)(2). Rules 30, 31, and 33 establish presumptive national limits on the numbers of depositions and interrogatories. New Rule 30(d)(2) [now Rule 30(d)(1) — ED.] establishes a presumptive limit on the length of depositions. Subdivision (b)(2) is amended to remove the previous permission for local rules that establish different presumptive limits on these discovery activities. There is no reason to believe that unique circumstances justify varying these nationally-applicable presumptive limits in certain districts. The limits can be modified by court order or agreement in an individual action, but "standing" orders imposing different presumptive limits are not authorized. Because there is no national rule limiting the number of Rule 36 requests for admissions, the rule continues to authorize local rules that impose numerical limits on them. This change is not intended to interfere with differentiated case management in districts that use this technique by case-specific order as part of their Rule 16 process.

Subdivision (d). The amendments remove the prior authority to exempt cases by local rule from the moratorium on discovery before the subdivision (f) conference, but the categories of proceedings exempted from initial disclosure under subdivision (a)(1)(E) [now Rule 26(a)(1)(B) — ED.] are excluded from subdivision (d). The parties may agree to disregard the moratorium where it applies, and the court may so order in a case, but "standing" orders altering the moratorium are not authorized.

Subdivision (f). As in subdivision (d), the amendments remove the prior authority to exempt cases by local rule from the conference requirement. The Committee has been informed that the addition of the conference was one of the most successful changes made in the 1993 amendments, and it therefore has determined to apply the conference requirement nationwide. The categories of proceedings exempted from initial disclosure under subdivision (a)(1)(E) [now Rule 26(a)(1)(B) — ED.] are exempted from the conference requirement for the reasons that warrant exclusion from initial disclosure. The court may order that the

conference need not occur in a case where otherwise required, or that it occur in a case otherwise exempted by subdivision (a)(1)(E). "Standing" orders altering the conference requirement for categories of cases are not authorized.

The rule is amended to require only a "conference" of the parties, rather than a "meeting." There are important benefits to face-to-face discussion of the topics to be covered in the conference, and those benefits may be lost if other means of conferring were routinely used when face-to- face meetings would not impose burdens. Nevertheless, geographic conditions in some districts may exact costs far out of proportion to these benefits. The amendment allows the court by case-specific order to require a face-to-face meeting, but "standing" orders so requiring are not authorized.

As noted concerning the amendments to subdivision (a)(1), the time for the conference has been changed to at least 21 days before the Rule 16 scheduling conference, and the time for the report is changed to no more than 14 days after the Rule 26(f) conference. This should ensure that the court will have the report well in advance of the scheduling conference or the entry of the scheduling order.

Since Rule 16 was amended in 1983 to mandate some case management activities in all courts, it has included deadlines for Completing these tasks to ensure that all courts do so within a reasonable time. Rule 26(f) was fit into this scheme when it was adopted in 1993. It was never intended, however, that the national requirements that certain activities be completed by a certain time should delay case management in districts that move much faster than the national rules direct, and the rule is therefore amended to permit such a court to adopt a local rule that shortens the period specified for the completion of these tasks. . . .

2006 Amendment

Subdivision (a). Rule 26(a)(1)(B) [now Rule 26(a)(1)(A)(ii) — ED.] is amended to parallel Rule 34(a) by recognizing that a party must disclose electronically stored information as well as documents that it may use to support its claims or defenses. The term "electronically stored information" has the same broad meaning in Rule 26(a)(1) as in Rule 34(a). This amendment is consistent with the 1993 addition of Rule 26(a)(1)(B). The term "data compilations" is deleted as unnecessary because it is a subset of both documents and electronically stored information.

Subdivision (b)(2). The amendment to Rule 26(b)(2) is designed to address issues raised by difficulties in locating, retrieving, and providing discovery of some electronically stored information. Electronic storage systems often make it easier to locate and retrieve information. These advantages are properly taken into account in determining the reasonable scope of discovery in a particular case. But some sources of electronically stored information can be accessed only with substantial burden and cost. In a particular case, these burdens and costs may make the information on such sources not reasonably accessible.

It is not possible to define in a rule the different types of technological features that may affect the burdens and costs of accessing electronically stored information. Information systems are designed to provide ready access to information used in regular ongoing activities. They also may be designed so as to provide ready access to information that is not regularly used. But a system may

retain information on sources that are accessible only by incurring substantial burdens or costs. Subparagraph (B) is added to regulate discovery from such sources.

Under this rule, a responding party should produce electronically stored information that is relevant, not privileged, and reasonably accessible, subject to the (b)(2)(C) [now (b)(1) and (b)(2)(C)(i)-(ii) — ED.] limitations that apply to all discovery. The responding party must also identify, by category or type, the sources containing potentially responsive information that it is neither searching nor producing. The identification should, to the extent possible, provide enough detail to enable the requesting party to evaluate the burdens and costs of providing the discovery and the likelihood of finding responsive information on the identified sources.

A party's identification of sources of electronically stored information as not reasonably accessible does not relieve the party of its common-law or statutory duties to preserve evidence. Whether a responding party is required to preserve unsearched sources of potentially responsive information that it believes are not reasonably accessible depends on the circumstances of each case. It is often useful for the parties to discuss this issue early in discovery.

The volume of — and the ability to search — much electronically stored information means that in many cases the responding party will be able to produce information from reasonably accessible sources that will fully satisfy the parties' discovery needs. In many circumstances the requesting party should obtain and evaluate the information from such sources before insisting that the responding party search and produce information contained on sources that are not reasonably accessible. If the requesting party continues to seek discovery of information from sources identified as not reasonably accessible, the parties should discuss the burdens and costs of accessing and retrieving the information, the needs that may establish good cause for requiring all or part of the requested discovery even if the information sought is not reasonably accessible, and conditions on obtaining and producing the information that may be appropriate.

If the parties cannot agree whether, or on what terms, sources identified as not reasonably accessible should be searched and discoverable information produced, the issue may be raised either by a motion to compel discovery or by a motion for a protective order. The parties must confer before bringing either motion. If the parties do not resolve the issue and the court must decide, the responding party must show that the identified sources of information are not reasonably accessible because of undue burden or cost. The requesting party may need discovery to test this assertion. Such discovery might take the form of requiring the responding party to conduct a sampling of information contained on the sources identified as not reasonably accessible; allowing some form of inspection of such sources; or taking depositions of witnesses knowledgeable about the responding party's information systems.

Once it is shown that a source of electronically stored information is not reasonably accessible, the requesting party may still obtain discovery by showing good cause, considering the limitations of Rule 26(b)(2)(C) [now Rules 26(b)(1) and (b)(2)(C)(i)-(ii) — ED.] that balance the costs and potential benefits of discovery. The decision whether to require a responding party to search for and produce

information that is not reasonably accessible depends not only on the burdens and costs of doing so, but also on whether those burdens and costs can be justified in the circumstances of the case. Appropriate considerations may include: (1) the specificity of the discovery request; (2) the quantity of information available from other and more easily accessed sources; (3) the failure to produce relevant information that seems likely to have existed but is no longer available on more easily accessed sources; (4) the likelihood of finding relevant, responsive information that cannot be obtained from other, more easily accessed sources; (5) predictions as to the importance and usefulness of the further information; (6) the importance of the issues at stake in the litigation; and (7) the parties' resources.

The responding party has the burden as to one aspect of the inquiry — whether the identified sources are not reasonably accessible in light of the burdens and costs required to search for, retrieve, and produce whatever responsive information may be found. The requesting party has the burden of showing that its need for the discovery outweighs the burdens and costs of locating, retrieving, and producing the information. In some cases, the court will be able to determine whether the identified sources are not reasonably accessible and whether the requesting party has shown good cause for some or all of the discovery, consistent with the limitations of Rule 26(b)(2)(C) [now Rules 26(b)(1) and (b)(2)(C)(i)-(ii) — ED.], through a single proceeding or presentation. The good-cause determination, however, may be complicated because the court and parties may know little about what information the sources identified as not reasonably accessible might contain, whether it is relevant, or how valuable it may be to the litigation. In such cases, the parties may need some focused discovery, which may include sampling of the sources, to learn more about what burdens and costs are involved in accessing the information, what the information consists of, and how valuable it is for the litigation in light of information that can be obtained by exhausting other opportunities for discovery.

The good-cause inquiry and consideration of the Rule 26(b)(2)(C) [now Rules 26(b)(1) and (b)(2)(C)(i)-(ii) — ED.] limitations are coupled with the authority to set conditions for discovery. The conditions may take the form of limits on the amount, type, or sources of information required to be accessed and produced. The conditions may also include payment by the requesting party of part or all of the reasonable costs of obtaining information from sources that are not reasonably accessible. A requesting party's willingness to share or bear the access costs may be weighed by the court in determining whether there is good cause. But the producing party's burdens in reviewing the information for relevance and privilege may weigh against permitting the requested discovery.

The limitations of Rule 26(b)(2)(C) [now Rules 26(b)(1) and (b)(2)(C)(i)-(ii) — ED.] continue to apply to all discovery of electronically stored information, including that stored on reasonably accessible electronic sources.

Subdivision (b)(5). The Committee has repeatedly been advised that the risk of privilege waiver, and the work necessary to avoid it, add to the costs and delay of discovery. When the review is of electronically stored information, the risk of waiver, and the time and effort required to avoid it, can increase substantially because of the volume of electronically stored information and the difficulty in ensuring that all information to be produced has in fact been reviewed. Rule

26(b)(5)(A) provides a procedure for a party that has withheld information on the basis of privilege or protection as trial-preparation material to make the claim so that the requesting party can decide whether to contest the claim and the court can resolve the dispute. Rule 26(b)(5)(B) is added to provide a procedure for a party to assert a claim of privilege or trial-preparation material protection after information is produced in discovery in the action and, if the claim is contested, permit any party that received the information to present the matter to the court for resolution.

Rule 26(b)(5)(B) does not address whether the privilege or protection that is asserted after production was waived by the production. The courts have developed principles to determine whether, and under what circumstances, waiver results from inadvertent production of privileged or protected information. Rule 26(b)(5)(B) provides a procedure for presenting and addressing these issues. Rule 26(b)(5)(B) works in tandem with Rule 26(f), which is amended to direct the parties to discuss privilege issues in preparing their discovery plan, and which, with amended Rule 16(b), allows the parties to ask the court to include in an order any agreements the parties reach regarding issues of privilege or trial-preparation material protection. Agreements reached under Rule 26(f)(4) [now Rule 26(f)(3)(F) — ED.] and orders including such agreements entered under Rule 16(b)(6) [now Rule 16(b)(3)(B)(iv) — ED.] may be considered when a court determines whether a waiver has occurred. Such agreements and orders ordinarily control if they adopt procedures different from those in Rule 26(b)(5)(B).

A party asserting a claim of privilege or protection after production must give notice to the receiving party. That notice should be in writing unless the circumstances preclude it. Such circumstances could include the assertion of the claim during a deposition. The notice should be as specific as possible in identifying the information and stating the basis for the claim. Because the receiving party must decide whether to challenge the claim and may sequester the information and submit it to the court for a ruling on whether the claimed privilege or protection applies and whether it has been waived, the notice should be sufficiently detailed so as to enable the receiving party and the court to understand the basis for the claim and to determine whether waiver has occurred. Courts will continue to examine whether a claim of privilege or protection was made at a reasonable time when delay is part of the waiver determination under the governing law.

After receiving notice, each party that received the information must promptly return, sequester, or destroy the information and any copies it has. The option of sequestering or destroying the information is included in part because the receiving party may have incorporated the information in protected trial-preparation materials. No receiving party may use or disclose the information pending resolution of the privilege claim. The receiving party may present to the court the questions whether the information is privileged or protected as trial-preparation material, and whether the privilege or protection has been waived. If it does so, it must provide the court with the grounds for the privilege or protection specified in the producing party's notice, and serve all parties. In presenting the question, the party may use the content of the information only to the extent permitted by the applicable law of privilege, protection for trial-preparation material, and professional responsibility.

If a party disclosed the information to nonparties before receiving notice of a claim of privilege or protection as trial-preparation material, it must take reasonable steps to retrieve the information and to return it, sequester it until the claim is resolved, or destroy it.

Whether the information is returned or not, the producing party must preserve the information pending the court's ruling on whether the claim of privilege or of protection is properly asserted and whether it was waived. As with claims made under Rule 26(b)(5)(A), there may be no ruling if the other parties do not contest the claim.

Subdivision (f). Rule 26(f) is amended to direct the parties to discuss discovery of electronically stored information during their discovery-planning conference. The rule focuses on "issues relating to disclosure or discovery of electronically stored information" [now "issues about disclosure or discovery of electronically stored information" — ED.]; the discussion is not required in cases not involving electronic discovery, and the amendment imposes no additional requirements in those cases. When the parties do anticipate disclosure or discovery of electronically stored information, discussion at the outset may avoid later difficulties or ease their resolution.

When a case involves discovery of electronically stored information, the issues to be addressed during the Rule 26(f) conference depend on the nature and extent of the contemplated discovery and of the parties' information systems. It may be important for the parties to discuss those systems, and accordingly important for counsel to become familiar with those systems before the conference. With that information, the parties can develop a discovery plan that takes into account the capabilities of their computer systems. In appropriate cases identification of, and early discovery from, individuals with special knowledge of a party's computer systems may be helpful.

The particular issues regarding electronically stored information that deserve attention during the discovery planning stage depend on the specifics of the given case. *See Manual for Complex Litigation (4th)* § 40.25(2) (listing topics for discussion in a proposed order regarding meet-and-confer sessions). For example, the parties may specify the topics for such discovery and the time period for which discovery will be sought. They may identify the various sources of such information within a party's control that should be searched for electronically stored information. They may discuss whether the information is reasonably accessible to the party that has it, including the burden or cost of retrieving and reviewing the information. *See* Rule 26(b)(2)(B). Rule 26(f)(3) [now Rule 26(f)(3)(C) — ED.] explicitly directs the parties to discuss the form or forms in which electronically stored information might be produced. The parties may be able to reach agreement on the forms of production, making discovery more efficient. Rule 34(b) is amended to permit a requesting party to specify the form or forms in which it wants electronically stored information produced. If the requesting party does not specify a form, Rule 34(b) directs the responding party to state the forms it intends to use in the production. Early discussion of the forms of production may facilitate the application of Rule 34(b) by allowing the parties to determine what forms of production will meet both parties' needs. Early identification of disputes over the

forms of production may help avoid the expense and delay of searches or productions using inappropriate forms.

Rule 26(f) is also amended to direct the parties to discuss any issues regarding preservation of discoverable information during their conference as they develop a discovery plan. This provision applies to all sorts of discoverable information, but can be particularly important with regard to electronically stored information. The volume and dynamic nature of electronically stored information may complicate preservation obligations. The ordinary operation of computers involves both the automatic creation and the automatic deletion or overwriting of certain information. Failure to address preservation issues early in the litigation increases uncertainty and raises a risk of disputes.

The parties' discussion should pay particular attention to the balance between the competing needs to preserve relevant evidence and to continue routine operations critical to ongoing activities. Complete or broad cessation of a party's routine computer operations could paralyze the party's activities. *Cf. Manual for Complex Litigation (4th)* § 11.422 ("A blanket preservation order may be prohibitively expensive and unduly burdensome for parties dependent on computer systems for their day-to-day operations.") The parties should take account of these considerations in their discussions, with the goal of agreeing on reasonable preservation steps.

The requirement that the parties discuss preservation does not imply that courts should routinely enter preservation orders. A preservation order entered over objections should be narrowly tailored. Ex parte preservation orders should issue only in exceptional circumstances.

Rule 26(f) is also amended to provide that the parties should discuss any issues relating to assertions of privilege or of protection as trial-preparation materials, including whether the parties can facilitate discovery by agreeing on procedures for asserting claims of privilege or protection after production and whether to ask the court to enter an order that includes any agreement the parties reach. The Committee has repeatedly been advised about the discovery difficulties that can result from efforts to guard against waiver of privilege and work-product protection. Frequently parties find it necessary to spend large amounts of time reviewing materials requested through discovery to avoid waiving privilege. These efforts are necessary because materials subject to a claim of privilege or protection are often difficult to identify. A failure to withhold even one such item may result in an argument that there has been a waiver of privilege as to all other privileged materials on that subject matter. Efforts to avoid the risk of waiver can impose substantial costs on the party producing the material and the time required for the privilege review can substantially delay access for the party seeking discovery.

These problems often become more acute when discovery of electronically stored information is sought. The volume of such data, and the informality that attends use of e-mail and some other types of electronically stored information, may make privilege determinations more difficult, and privilege review correspondingly more expensive and time consuming. Other aspects of electronically stored information pose particular difficulties for privilege review. For example, production may be sought of information automatically included in electronic files but not apparent to the creator or to readers. Computer programs

may retain draft language, editorial comments, and other deleted matter (sometimes referred to as "embedded data" or "embedded edits") in an electronic file but not make them apparent to the reader. Information describing the history, tracking, or management of an electronic file (sometimes called "metadata") is usually not apparent to the reader viewing a hard copy or a screen image. Whether this information should be produced may be among the topics discussed in the Rule 26(f) conference. If it is, it may need to be reviewed to ensure that no privileged information is included, further complicating the task of privilege review.

Parties may attempt to minimize these costs and delays by agreeing to protocols that minimize the risk of waiver. They may agree that the responding party will provide certain requested materials for initial examination without waiving any privilege or protection — sometimes known as a "quick peek." The requesting party then designates the documents it wishes to have actually produced. This designation is the Rule 34 request. The responding party then responds in the usual course, screening only those documents actually requested for formal production and asserting privilege claims as provided in Rule 26(b)(5)(A). On other occasions, parties enter agreements — sometimes called "clawback agreements"— that production without intent to waive privilege or protection should not be a waiver so long as the responding party identifies the documents mistakenly produced, and that the documents should be returned under those circumstances. Other voluntary arrangements may be appropriate depending on the circumstances of each litigation. In most circumstances, a party who receives information under such an arrangement cannot assert that production of the information waived a claim of privilege or of protection as trial-preparation material.

Although these agreements may not be appropriate for all cases, in certain cases they can facilitate prompt and economical discovery by reducing delay before the discovering party obtains access to documents, and by reducing the cost and burden of review by the producing party. A case-management or other order including such agreements may further facilitate the discovery process. . . . Rule 16(b) is amended to recognize that the court may include such an agreement in a case-management or other order. If the parties agree to entry of such an order, their proposal should be included in the report to the court.

Rule 26(b)(5)(B) is added to establish a parallel procedure to assert privilege or protection as trial-preparation material after production, leaving the question of waiver to later determination by the court.

2007 Amendment

. . .

Former Rule 26(g)(1) did not call for striking an unsigned disclosure. The omission was an obvious drafting oversight. Amended Rule 26(g)(2) includes disclosures in the list of matters that the court must strike unless a signature is provided "promptly . . . after being called to the attorney's or party's attention."

Former Rule 26([g])(2)(A) referred to a "good faith" argument to extend existing law. Amended Rule 26([g])(1)(B)(i) changes this reference to a "nonfrivolous" argument to achieve consistency with Rule 11(b)(2). . . .

Rule 11(b)(2) recognizes that it is legitimate to argue for establishing new law. An argument to establish new law is equally legitimate in conducting discovery.

2010 Amendment

Rule 26. Rules 26(a)(2) and (b)(4) are amended to address concerns about expert discovery. The amendments to Rule 26(a)(2) require disclosure regarding expected expert testimony of those expert witnesses not required to provide expert reports and limit the expert report to facts or data (rather than "data or other information," as in the current rule) considered by the witness. Rule 26(b)(4) is amended to provide work-product protection against discovery regarding draft expert disclosures or reports and — with three specific exceptions — communications between expert witnesses and counsel.

In 1993, Rule 26(b)(4)(A) was revised to authorize expert depositions and Rule 26(a)(2) was added to provide disclosure, including — for many experts — an extensive report. Many courts read the disclosure provision to authorize discovery of all communications between counsel and expert witnesses and all draft reports. The Committee has been told repeatedly that routine discovery into attorney-expert communications and draft reports has had undesirable effects. Costs have risen. Attorneys may employ two sets of experts — one for purposes of consultation and another to testify at trial — because disclosure of their collaborative interactions with expert consultants would reveal their most sensitive and confidential case analyses. At the same time, attorneys often feel compelled to adopt a guarded attitude toward their interaction with testifying experts that impedes effective communication, and experts adopt strategies that protect against discovery but also interfere with their work.

Subdivision (a)(2)(B). Rule 26(a)(2)(B)(ii) is amended to provide that disclosure include all "facts or data considered by the witness in forming" the opinions to be offered, rather than the "data or other information" disclosure prescribed in 1993. This amendment is intended to alter the outcome in cases that have relied on the 1993 formulation in requiring disclosure of all attorney-expert communications and draft reports. The amendments to Rule 26(b)(4) make this change explicit by providing work-product protection against discovery regarding draft reports and disclosures or attorney-expert communications.

The refocus of disclosure on "facts or data" is meant to limit disclosure to material of a factual nature by excluding theories or mental impressions of counsel. At the same time, the intention is that "facts or data" be interpreted broadly to require disclosure of any material considered by the expert, from whatever source, that contains factual ingredients. The disclosure obligation extends to any facts or data "considered" by the expert in forming the opinions to be expressed, not only those relied upon by the expert.

Subdivision (a)(2)(C). Rule 26(a)(2)(C) is added to mandate summary disclosures of the opinions to be offered by expert witnesses who are not required to provide reports under Rule 26(a)(2)(B) and of the facts supporting those opinions. This disclosure is considerably less extensive than the report required by Rule 26(a)(2)(B). Courts must take care against requiring undue detail, keeping in mind that these witnesses have not been specially retained and may not be as responsive to counsel as those who have.

This amendment resolves a tension that has sometimes prompted courts to require reports under Rule 26(a)(2)(B) even from witnesses exempted from the report requirement. An (a)(2)(B) report is required only from an expert described in (a)(2)(B).

A witness who is not required to provide a report under Rule 26(a)(2)(B) may both testify as a fact witness and also provide expert testimony under Evidence Rule 702, 703, or 705. Frequent examples include physicians or other health care professionals and employees of a party who do not regularly provide expert testimony. Parties must identify such witnesses under Rule 26(a)(2)(A) and provide the disclosure required under Rule 26(a)(2)(C). The (a)(2)(C) disclosure obligation does not include facts unrelated to the expert opinions the witness will present. . . .

Subdivision (b)(4). Rule 26(b)(4)(B) is added to provide work-product protection under Rule 26(b)(3)(A) and (B) for drafts of expert reports or disclosures. This protection applies to all witnesses identified under Rule 26(a)(2)(A), whether they are required to provide reports under Rule 26(a)(2)(B) or are the subject of disclosure under Rule 26(a)(2)(C). It applies regardless of the form in which the draft is recorded, whether written, electronic, or otherwise. It also applies to drafts of any supplementation under Rule 26(e); *see* Rule 26(a)(2)(E).

Rule 26(b)(4)(C) is added to provide work-product protection for attorney-expert communications regardless of the form of the communications, whether oral, written, electronic, or otherwise. The addition of Rule 26(b)(4)(C) is designed to protect counsel's work product and ensure that lawyers may interact with retained experts without fear of exposing those communications to searching discovery. The protection is limited to communications between an expert witness required to provide a report under Rule 26(a)(2)(B) and the attorney for the party on whose behalf the witness will be testifying, including any "preliminary" expert opinions. Protected "communications" include those between the party's attorney and assistants of the expert witness. The rule does not itself protect communications between counsel and other expert witnesses, such as those for whom disclosure is required under Rule 26(a)(2)(C). The rule does not exclude protection under other doctrines, such as privilege or independent development of the work-product doctrine.

The most frequent method for discovering the work of expert witnesses is by deposition, but Rules 26(b)(4)(B) and (C) apply to all forms of discovery.

Rules 26(b)(4)(B) and (C) do not impede discovery about the opinions to be offered by the expert or the development, foundation, or basis of those opinions. For example, the expert's testing of material involved in litigation, and notes of any such testing, would not be exempted from discovery by this rule. Similarly, inquiry about communications the expert had with anyone other than the party's counsel about the opinions expressed is unaffected by the rule. Counsel are also free to question expert witnesses about alternative analyses, testing methods, or approaches to the issues on which they are testifying, whether or not the expert considered them in forming the opinions expressed. These discovery changes therefore do not affect the gatekeeping functions called for by *Daubert v. Merrell Dow Pharmaceuticals, Inc.*, 509 U.S. 579 (1993), and related cases.

The protection for communications between the retained expert and "the party's attorney" should be applied in a realistic manner, and often would not be

limited to communications with a single lawyer or a single law firm. For example, a party may be involved in a number of suits about a given product or service, and may retain a particular expert witness to testify on that party's behalf in several of the cases. In such a situation, the protection applies to communications between the expert witness and the attorneys representing the party in any of those cases. Similarly, communications with in-house counsel for the party would often be regarded as protected even if the in-house attorney is not counsel of record in the action. Other situations may also justify a pragmatic application of the "party's attorney" concept.

Although attorney-expert communications are generally protected by Rule 26(b)(4)(C), the protection does not apply to the extent the lawyer and the expert communicate about matters that fall within three exceptions. But the discovery authorized by the exceptions does not extend beyond those specific topics. Lawyer-expert communications may cover many topics and, even when the excepted topics are included among those involved in a given communication, the protection applies to all other aspects of the communication beyond the excepted topics.

First, under Rule 26(b)(4)(C)(i) attorney-expert communications regarding compensation for the expert's study or testimony may be the subject of discovery. In some cases, this discovery may go beyond the disclosure requirement in Rule 26(a)(2)(B)(vi). It is not limited to compensation for work forming the opinions to be expressed, but extends to all compensation for the study and testimony provided in relation to the action. Any communications about additional benefits to the expert, such as further work in the event of a successful result in the present case, would be included. This exception includes compensation for work done by a person or organization associated with the expert. The objective is to permit full inquiry into such potential sources of bias.

Second, under Rule 26(b)(4)(C)(ii) discovery is permitted to identify facts or data the party's attorney provided to the expert and that the expert considered in forming the opinions to be expressed. The exception applies only to communications "identifying" the facts or data provided by counsel; further communications about the potential relevance of the facts or data are protected.

Third, under Rule 26(b)(4)(C)(iii) discovery regarding attorney-expert communications is permitted to identify any assumptions that counsel provided to the expert and that the expert relied upon in forming the opinions to be expressed. For example, the party's attorney may tell the expert to assume the truth of certain testimony or evidence, or the correctness of another expert's conclusions. This exception is limited to those assumptions that the expert actually did rely on in forming the opinions to be expressed. More general attorney-expert discussions about hypotheticals, or exploring possibilities based on hypothetical facts, are outside this exception.

Under the amended rule, discovery regarding attorney-expert communications on subjects outside the three exceptions in Rule 26(b)(4)(C), or regarding draft expert reports or disclosures, is permitted only in limited circumstances and by court order. A party seeking such discovery must make the showing specified in Rule 26(b)(3)(A)(ii) — that the party has a substantial need for the discovery and cannot obtain the substantial equivalent without undue hardship. It will be rare for a party to be able to make such a showing given the broad disclosure and

discovery otherwise allowed regarding the expert's testimony. A party's failure to provide required disclosure or discovery does not show the need and hardship required by Rule 26(b)(3)(A); remedies are provided by Rule 37.

In the rare case in which a party does make this showing, the court must protect against disclosure of the attorney's mental impressions, conclusions, opinions, or legal theories under Rule 26(b)(3)(B). But this protection does not extend to the expert's own development of the opinions to be presented; those are subject to probing in deposition or at trial.

2015 Amendment

Rule 26(b)(1) is changed in several ways.

Information is discoverable under revised Rule 26(b)(1) if it is relevant to any party's claim or defense and is proportional to the needs of the case. The considerations that bear on proportionality are moved from present Rule 26(b)(2)(C)(iii), slightly rearranged and with one addition.

Most of what now appears in Rule 26(b)(2)(C)(iii) was first adopted in 1983. The 1983 provision was explicitly adopted as part of the scope of discovery defined by Rule 26(b)(1). Rule 26(b)(1) directed the court to limit the frequency or extent of use of discovery if it determined that "the discovery is unduly burdensome or expensive, taking into account the needs of the case, the amount in controversy, limitations on the parties' resources, and the importance of the issues at stake in the litigation." At the same time, Rule 26(g) was added. Rule 26(g) provided that signing a discovery request, response, or objection certified that the request, response, or objection was "not unreasonable or unduly burdensome or expensive, given the needs of the case, the discovery already had in the case, the amount in controversy, and the importance of the issues at stake in the litigation." The parties thus shared the responsibility to honor these limits on the scope of discovery. . . .

The clear focus of the 1983 provisions may have been softened, although inadvertently, by the amendments made in 1993. The 1993 Committee Note explained: "[F]ormer paragraph (b)(1) [was] subdivided into two paragraphs for ease of reference and to avoid renumbering of paragraphs (3) and (4)." Subdividing the paragraphs, however, was done in a way that could be read to separate the proportionality provisions as "limitations," no longer an integral part of the (b)(1) scope provisions. . . .

The 1993 amendments added two factors to the considerations that bear on limiting discovery: whether "the burden or expense of the proposed discovery outweighs its likely benefit," and "the importance of the proposed discovery in resolving the issues." . . .

The relationship between Rule 26(b)(1) and (2) was further addressed by an amendment made in 2000 that added a new sentence at the end of (b)(1): "All discovery is subject to the limitations imposed by Rule 26(b)(2)(i), (ii), and (iii)[now Rule 26(b)(2)(C)]." . . .

The present amendment restores the proportionality factors to their original place in defining the scope of discovery. This change reinforces the Rule 26(g) obligation of the parties to consider these factors in making discovery requests, responses, or objections.

Restoring the proportionality calculation to Rule 26(b)(1) does not change the existing responsibilities of the court and the parties to consider proportionality, and the change does not place on the party seeking discovery the burden of addressing all proportionality considerations.

Nor is the change intended to permit the opposing party to refuse discovery simply by making a boilerplate objection that it is not proportional. The parties and the court have a collective responsibility to consider the proportionality of all discovery and consider it in resolving discovery disputes.

The parties may begin discovery without a full appreciation of the factors that bear on proportionality. A party requesting discovery, for example, may have little information about the burden or expense of responding. A party requested to provide discovery may have little information about the importance of the discovery in resolving the issues as understood by the requesting party. Many of these uncertainties should be addressed and reduced in the parties' Rule 26(f) conference and in scheduling and pretrial conferences with the court. But if the parties continue to disagree, the discovery dispute could be brought before the court and the parties' responsibilities would remain as they have been since 1983. A party claiming undue burden or expense ordinarily has far better information — perhaps the only information — with respect to that part of the determination. A party claiming that a request is important to resolve the issues should be able to explain the ways in which the underlying information bears on the issues as that party understands them. The court's responsibility, using all the information provided by the parties, is to consider these and all the other factors in reaching a case-specific determination of the appropriate scope of discovery.

The direction to consider the parties' relative access to relevant information adds new text to provide explicit focus on considerations already implicit in present Rule 26(b)(2)(C)(iii). Some cases involve what often is called "information asymmetry." One party — often an individual plaintiff — may have very little discoverable information. The other party may have vast amounts of information, including information that can be readily retrieved and information that is more difficult to retrieve. In practice these circumstances often mean that the burden of responding to discovery lies heavier on the party who has more information, and properly so.

. . . [The information] explosion [of recent decades]has been exacerbated by the advent of e-discovery. The present amendment again reflects the need for continuing and close judicial involvement in the cases that do not yield readily to the ideal of effective party management. It is expected that discovery will be effectively managed by the parties in many cases. But there will be important occasions for judicial management, both when the parties are legitimately unable to resolve important differences and when the parties fall short of effective, cooperative management on their own.

It also is important to repeat the caution that the monetary stakes are only one factor, to be balanced against other factors. The 1983 Committee Note recognized "the significance of the substantive issues, as measured in philosophic, social, or institutional terms. Thus the rule recognizes that many cases in public policy spheres, such as employment practices, free speech, and other matters, may have importance far beyond the monetary amount involved." Many other substantive

areas also may involve litigation that seeks relatively small amounts of money, or no money at all, but that seeks to vindicate vitally important personal or public values.

So too, consideration of the parties' resources does not foreclose discovery requests addressed to an impecunious party, nor justify unlimited discovery requests addressed to a wealthy party. The 1983 Committee Note cautioned that "[t]he court must apply the standards in an even-handed manner that will prevent use of discovery to wage a war of attrition or as a device to coerce a party, whether financially weak or affluent."

The burden or expense of proposed discovery should be determined in a realistic way. This includes the burden or expense of producing electronically stored information. Computer-based methods of searching such information continue to develop, particularly for cases involving large volumes of electronically stored information. Courts and parties should be willing to consider the opportunities for reducing the burden or expense of discovery as reliable means of searching electronically stored information become available.

A portion of present Rule 26(b)(1) is omitted from the proposed revision. After allowing discovery of any matter relevant to any party's claim or defense, the present rule adds: "including the existence, description, nature, custody, condition, and location of any documents or other tangible things and the identity and location of persons who know of any discoverable matter." Discovery of such matters is so deeply entrenched in practice that it is no longer necessary to clutter the long text of Rule 26 with these examples. The discovery identified in these examples should still be permitted under the revised rule when relevant and proportional to the needs of the case. Framing intelligent requests for electronically stored information, for example, may require detailed information about another party's information systems and other information resources.

The amendment deletes the former provision authorizing the court, for good cause, to order discovery of any matter relevant to the subject matter involved in the action. The Committee has been informed that this language is rarely invoked. Proportional discovery relevant to any party's claim or defense suffices, given a proper understanding of what is relevant to a claim or defense. The distinction between matter relevant to a claim or defense and matter relevant to the subject matter was introduced in 2000. The 2000 Note offered three examples of information that, suitably focused, would be relevant to the parties' claims or defenses. The examples were "other incidents of the same type, or involving the same product"; "information about organizational arrangements or filing systems"; and "information that could be used to impeach a likely witness." Such discovery is not foreclosed by the amendments. Discovery that is relevant to the parties' claims or defenses may also support amendment of the pleadings to add a new claim or defense that affects the scope of discovery.

The former provision for discovery of relevant but inadmissible information that appears "reasonably calculated to lead to the discovery of admissible evidence" is also deleted. The phrase has been used by some, incorrectly, to define the scope of discovery. As the Committee Note to the 2000 amendments observed, use of the "reasonably calculated" phrase to define the scope of discovery "might swallow any other limitation on the scope of discovery." The 2000 amendments sought to

prevent such misuse by adding the word "Relevant" at the beginning of the sentence, making clear that "'relevant' means within the scope of discovery as defined in this subdivision . . . ." The "reasonably calculated" phrase has continued to create problems, however, and is removed by these amendments. It is replaced by the direct statement that "Information within this scope of discovery need not be admissible in evidence to be discoverable." Discovery of nonprivileged information not admissible in evidence remains available so long as it is otherwise within the scope of discovery.

Rule 26(b)(2)(C)(iii) is amended to reflect the transfer of the considerations that bear on proportionality to Rule 26(b)(1). The court still must limit the frequency or extent of proposed discovery, on motion or on its own, if it is outside the scope permitted by Rule 26(b)(1).

Rule 26(c)(1)(B) is amended to include an express recognition of protective orders that allocate expenses for disclosure or discovery. Authority to enter such orders is included in the present rule, and courts already exercise this authority. Explicit recognition will forestall the temptation some parties may feel to contest this authority. Recognizing the authority does not imply that cost-shifting should become a common practice. Courts and parties should continue to assume that a responding party ordinarily bears the costs of responding.

Rule 26(d)(2) is added to allow a party to deliver Rule 34 requests to another party more than 21 days after that party has been served even though the parties have not yet had a required Rule 26(f) conference. Delivery may be made by any party to the party that has been served, and by that party to any plaintiff and any other party that has been served. Delivery does not count as service; the requests are considered to be served at the first Rule 26(f) conference. Under Rule 34(b)(2)(A) the time to respond runs from service. This relaxation of the discovery moratorium is designed to facilitate focused discussion during the Rule 26(f) conference. Discussion at the conference may produce changes in the requests. The opportunity for advance scrutiny of requests delivered before the Rule 26(f) conference should not affect a decision whether to allow additional time to respond.

Rule 26(d)(3) is renumbered and amended to recognize that the parties may stipulate to case-specific sequences of discovery.

Rule 26(f)(3) is amended in parallel with Rule 16(b)(3) to add two items to the discovery plan — issues about preserving electronically stored information and court orders under Evidence Rule 502.

Rule 27. Depositions to Perpetuate Testimony

(a) Before an Action Is Filed.

(1) ***Petition***. A person who wants to perpetuate testimony about any matter cognizable in a United States court may file a verified petition in the district court for the district where any expected adverse party resides. The petition must ask for an order authorizing the petitioner to depose the named persons in order to perpetuate their

testimony. The petition must be titled in the petitioner's name and must show:

(A) that the petitioner expects to be a party to an action cognizable in a United States court but cannot presently bring it or cause it to be brought;

(B) the subject matter of the expected action and the petitioner's interest;

(C) the facts that the petitioner wants to establish by the proposed testimony and the reasons to perpetuate it;

(D) the names or a description of the persons whom the petitioner expects to be adverse parties and their addresses, so far as known; and

(E) the name, address, and expected substance of the testimony of each deponent.

(2) ***Notice and Service.*** At least 21 days before the hearing date, the petitioner must serve each expected adverse party with a copy of the petition and a notice stating the time and place of the hearing. The notice may be served either inside or outside the district or state in the manner provided in Rule 4. If that service cannot be made with reasonable diligence on an expected adverse party, the court may order service by publication or otherwise. The court must appoint an attorney to represent persons not served in the manner provided in Rule 4 and to cross-examine the deponent if an unserved person is not otherwise represented. If any expected adverse party is a minor or is incompetent, Rule 17(c) applies.

(3) ***Order and Examination.*** If satisfied that perpetuating the testimony may prevent a failure or delay of justice, the court must issue an order that designates or describes the persons whose depositions may be taken, specifies the subject matter of the examinations, and states whether the depositions will be taken orally or by written interrogatories. The depositions may then be taken under these rules, and the court may issue orders like those authorized by Rules 34 and 35. A reference in these rules to the court where an action is pending means, for purposes of this rule, the court where the petition for the deposition was filed.

(4) ***Using the Deposition.*** A deposition to perpetuate testimony may be used under Rule 32(a) in any later-filed district-court action involving the same subject matter if the deposition either was taken under these rules or, although not so taken, would be admissible in evidence in the courts of the state where it was taken.

(b) Pending Appeal.

(1) ***In General.*** The court where a judgment has been rendered may, if an appeal has been taken or may still be taken, permit a party to depose witnesses to perpetuate their testimony for use in the event of further proceedings in that court.

(2) ***Motion.*** The party who wants to perpetuate testimony may move for leave to take the depositions, on the same notice and service as if the action were pending in the district court. The motion must show:

(A) the name, address, and expected substance of the testimony of each deponent; and

(B) the reasons for perpetuating the testimony.

(3) ***Court Order.*** If the court finds that perpetuating the testimony may prevent a failure or delay of justice, the court may permit the depositions to be taken and may issue orders like those authorized by Rules 34 and 35. The depositions may be taken and used as any other deposition taken in a pending district-court action.

(c) Perpetuation by an Action. This rule does not limit a court's power to entertain an action to perpetuate testimony.

Rule 28. Persons Before Whom Depositions May Be Taken

(a) Within the United States.

(1) ***In General.*** Within the United States or a territory or insular possession subject to United States jurisdiction, a deposition must be taken before:

(A) an officer authorized to administer oaths either by federal law or by the law in the place of examination; or

(B) a person appointed by the court where the action is pending to administer oaths and take testimony.

(2) ***Definition of "Officer."*** The term "officer" in Rules 30, 31, and 32 includes a person appointed by the court under this rule or designated by the parties under Rule 29(a).

(b) In a Foreign Country.

(1) ***In General.*** A deposition may be taken in a foreign country:

(A) under an applicable treaty or convention;

(B) under a letter of request, whether or not captioned a "letter rogatory";

(C) on notice, before a person authorized to administer oaths either by federal law or by the law in the place of examination; or

(D) before a person commissioned by the court to administer any necessary oath and take testimony.

(2) ***Issuing a Letter of Request or a Commission.*** A letter of request, a commission, or both may be issued:

(A) on appropriate terms after an application and notice of it; and

(B) without a showing that taking the deposition in another manner is impracticable or inconvenient.

(3) ***Form of a Request, Notice, or Commission.*** When a letter of request or any other device is used according to a treaty or convention, it must be captioned in the form prescribed by that treaty or convention. A letter of request may be addressed "To the Appropriate Authority in [name of country]." A deposition notice or a commission must designate by name or descriptive title the person before whom the deposition is to be taken.

(4) ***Letter of Request — Admitting Evidence.*** Evidence obtained in response to a letter of request need not be excluded merely because it is not a verbatim transcript, because the testimony was not taken under oath, or because of any similar departure from the requirements for depositions taken within the United States.

(c) Disqualification. A deposition must not be taken before a person who is any party's relative, employee, or attorney; who is related to or employed by any party's attorney; or who is financially interested in the action.

Rule 29. Stipulations About Discovery Procedure

Unless the court orders otherwise, the parties may stipulate that:

(a) a deposition may be taken before any person, at any time or place, on any notice, and in the manner specified — in which event it may be used in the same way as any other deposition; and

(b) other procedures governing or limiting discovery be modified — but a stipulation extending the time for any form of discovery must have court approval if it would interfere with the time set for completing discovery, for hearing a motion, or for trial.

Rule 30. Depositions by Oral Examination

(a) When a Deposition May Be Taken.

(1) ***Without Leave.*** A party may, by oral questions, depose any person, including a party, without leave of court except as provided in Rule 30(a)(2). The deponent's attendance may be compelled by subpoena under Rule 45.

(2) ***With Leave.*** A party must obtain leave of court, and the court must grant leave to the extent consistent with Rule 26(b)(1) and (2):

(A) if the parties have not stipulated to the deposition and:

(i) the deposition would result in more than 10 depositions being taken under this rule or Rule 31 by the plaintiffs, or by the defendants, or by the third-party defendants;

(ii) the deponent has already been deposed in the case; or

(iii) the party seeks to take the deposition before the time specified in Rule 26(d), unless the party certifies in the notice, with supporting facts, that the deponent is expected to leave the United States and be unavailable for examination in this country after that time; or

(B) if the deponent is confined in prison.

(b) Notice of the Deposition; Other Formal Requirements.

(1) ***Notice in General.*** A party who wants to depose a person by oral questions must give reasonable written notice to every other party. The notice must state the time and place of the deposition and, if known, the deponent's name and address. If the name is unknown, the notice must provide a general description sufficient to identify the person or the particular class or group to which the person belongs.

(2) ***Producing Documents.*** If a subpoena duces tecum is to be served on the deponent, the materials designated for production, as set out in the subpoena, must be listed in the notice or in an attachment. The notice to a party deponent may be accompanied by a request under Rule 34 to produce documents and tangible things at the deposition.

(3) ***Method of Recording.***

(A) *Method Stated in the Notice.* The party who notices the deposition must state in the notice the method for recording the testimony. Unless the court orders otherwise, testimony may be recorded by audio, audiovisual, or stenographic means. The noticing party bears the recording costs. Any party may arrange to transcribe a deposition.

(B) *Additional Method.* With prior notice to the deponent and other parties, any party may designate another method for recording the testimony in addition to that specified in the original notice. That party bears the expense of the additional record or transcript unless the court orders otherwise.

(4) ***By Remote Means.*** The parties may stipulate — or the court may on motion order — that a deposition be taken by telephone or other remote means. For the purpose of this rule and Rules 28(a), 37(a)(2), and 37(b)(1), the deposition takes place where the deponent answers the questions.

(5) ***Officer's Duties.***

(A) *Before the Deposition.* Unless the parties stipulate otherwise, a deposition must be conducted before an officer appointed or designated under Rule 28. The officer must begin the deposition with an on-the-record statement that includes:

(i) the officer's name and business address;

(ii) the date, time, and place of the deposition;

(iii) the deponent's name;

(iv) the officer's administration of the oath or affirmation to the deponent; and

(v) the identity of all persons present.

(B) *Conducting the Deposition; Avoiding Distortion.* If the deposition is recorded nonstenographically, the officer must repeat the items in Rule 30(b)(5)(A)(i)-(iii) at the beginning of each unit of the recording medium. The deponent's and attorneys' appearance or demeanor must not be distorted through recording techniques.

(C) *After the Deposition.* At the end of a deposition, the officer must state on the record that the deposition is complete and must set out any stipulations made by the attorneys about custody of the transcript or recording and of the exhibits, or about any other pertinent matters.

(6) ***Notice or Subpoena Directed to an Organization.*** In its notice or subpoena, a party may name as the deponent a public or private corporation, a partnership, an association, a governmental agency, or other entity and must describe with reasonable particularity the matters for examination. The named organization must then designate one or more officers, directors, or managing agents, or designate other persons who consent to testify on its behalf; and it may set out the matters on which each person designated will testify. A subpoena must advise a nonparty organization of its duty to make this

designation. The persons designated must testify about information known or reasonably available to the organization. This paragraph (6) does not preclude a deposition by any other procedure allowed by these rules.

(c) Examination and Cross-Examination; Record of the Examination; Objections; Written Questions.

(1) ***Examination and Cross-Examination.*** The examination and cross-examination of a deponent proceed as they would at trial under the Federal Rules of Evidence, except Rules 103 and 615. After putting the deponent under oath or affirmation, the officer must record the testimony by the method designated under Rule 30(b)(3)(A). The testimony must be recorded by the officer personally or by a person acting in the presence and under the direction of the officer.

(2) ***Objections.*** An objection at the time of the examination — whether to evidence, to a party's conduct, to the officer's qualifications, to the manner of taking the deposition, or to any other aspect of the deposition — must be noted on the record, but the examination still proceeds; the testimony is taken subject to any objection. An objection must be stated concisely in a nonargumentative and nonsuggestive manner. A person may instruct a deponent not to answer only when necessary to preserve a privilege, to enforce a limitation ordered by the court, or to present a motion under Rule 30(d)(3).

(3) ***Participating Through Written Questions.*** Instead of participating in the oral examination, a party may serve written questions in a sealed envelope on the party noticing the deposition, who must deliver them to the officer. The officer must ask the deponent those questions and record the answers verbatim.

(d) Duration; Sanction; Motion to Terminate or Limit.

(1) ***Duration.*** Unless otherwise stipulated or ordered by the court, a deposition is limited to 1 day of 7 hours. The court must allow additional time consistent with Rule 26(b)(1) and (2) if needed to fairly examine the deponent or if the deponent, another person, or any other circumstance impedes or delays the examination.

(2) ***Sanction.*** The court may impose an appropriate sanction — including the reasonable expenses and attorney's fees incurred by any party — on a person who impedes, delays, or frustrates the fair examination of the deponent.

(3) ***Motion to Terminate or Limit.***

(A) *Grounds.* At any time during a deposition, the deponent or a party may move to terminate or limit it on the ground that it is being conducted in bad faith or in a manner that unreasonably

annoys, embarrasses, or oppresses the deponent or party. The motion may be filed in the court where the action is pending or the deposition is being taken. If the objecting deponent or party so demands, the deposition must be suspended for the time necessary to obtain an order.

(B) *Order*. The court may order that the deposition be terminated or may limit its scope and manner as provided in Rule 26(c). If terminated, the deposition may be resumed only by order of the court where the action is pending.

(C) *Award of Expenses*. Rule 37(a)(5) applies to the award of expenses.

(e) Review by the Witness; Changes.

(1) ***Review; Statement of Changes***. On request by the deponent or a party before the deposition is completed, the deponent must be allowed 30 days after being notified by the officer that the transcript or recording is available in which:

(A) to review the transcript or recording; and

(B) if there are changes in form or substance, to sign a statement listing the changes and the reasons for making them.

(2) ***Changes Indicated in the Officer's Certificate***. The officer must note in the certificate prescribed by Rule 30(f)(1) whether a review was requested and, if so, must attach any changes the deponent makes during the 30-day period.

(f) Certification and Delivery; Exhibits; Copies of the Transcript or Recording; Filing.

(1) ***Certification and Delivery***. The officer must certify in writing that the witness was duly sworn and that the deposition accurately records the witness's testimony. The certificate must accompany the record of the deposition. Unless the court orders otherwise, the officer must seal the deposition in an envelope or package bearing the title of the action and marked "Deposition of [witness's name]" and must promptly send it to the attorney who arranged for the transcript or recording. The attorney must store it under conditions that will protect it against loss, destruction, tampering, or deterioration.

(2) ***Documents and Tangible Things.***

(A) *Originals and Copies*. Documents and tangible things produced for inspection during a deposition must, on a party's request, be marked for identification and attached to the

deposition. Any party may inspect and copy them. But if the person who produced them wants to keep the originals, the person may:

(i) offer copies to be marked, attached to the deposition, and then used as originals — after giving all parties a fair opportunity to verify the copies by comparing them with the originals; or

(ii) give all parties a fair opportunity to inspect and copy the originals after they are marked — in which event the originals may be used as if attached to the deposition.

(B) *Order Regarding the Originals.* Any party may move for an order that the originals be attached to the deposition pending final disposition of the case.

(3) ***Copies of the Transcript or Recording.*** Unless otherwise stipulated or ordered by the court, the officer must retain the stenographic notes of a deposition taken stenographically or a copy of the recording of a deposition taken by another method. When paid reasonable charges, the officer must furnish a copy of the transcript or recording to any party or the deponent.

(4) ***Notice of Filing.*** A party who files the deposition must promptly notify all other parties of the filing.

(g) Failure to Attend a Deposition or Serve a Subpoena; Expenses. A party who, expecting a deposition to be taken, attends in person or by an attorney may recover reasonable expenses for attending, including attorney's fees, if the noticing party failed to:

(1) attend and proceed with the deposition; or

(2) serve a subpoena on a nonparty deponent, who consequently did not attend.

ADVISORY COMMITTEE NOTES

1993 Amendment

Subdivision (a). . . .

Paragraph (2)(A) [now Rule 30(a)(2)(A)(i) — ED.] is new. It provides a limit on the number of depositions the parties may take, absent leave of court or stipulation with the other parties. One aim of this revision is to assure judicial review under the standards stated in Rule 26(b)(2) [now Rule 26(b)(2)(C) — ED.] before any side will be allowed to take more than ten depositions in a case without agreement of the other parties. A second objective is to emphasize that counsel have a professional obligation to develop a mutual cost-effective plan for discovery in the case. Leave to take additional depositions should be granted when consistent with the principles of Rule 26(b)(2), and in some cases the ten-per-side limit should be reduced in accordance with those same principles. Consideration should ordinarily be given at the planning meeting of the parties under Rule 26(f) and at the time

of a scheduling conference under Rule 16(b) as to enlargements or reductions in the number of depositions, eliminating the need for special motions.

A deposition under Rule 30(b)(6) should, for purposes of this limit, be treated as a single deposition even though more than one person may be designated to testify.

In multi-party cases, the parties on any side are expected to confer and agree as to which depositions are most needed, given the presumptive limit on the number of depositions they can take without leave of court. If these disputes cannot be amicably resolved, the court can be requested to resolve the dispute or permit additional depositions.

Paragraph (2)(B) [now Rule 30(a)(2)(A)(ii) — ED.] is new. It requires leave of court if any witness is to be deposed in the action more than once. This requirement does not apply when a deposition is temporarily recessed for convenience of counsel or the deponent or to enable additional materials to be gathered before resuming the deposition. If significant travel costs would be incurred to resume the deposition, the parties should consider the feasibility of conducting the balance of the examination by telephonic means.

Paragraph (2)(C) [now Rule 30(a)(2)(A)(iii) — ED.] revises the second sentence of the former subdivision (a) as to when depositions may be taken. Consistent with the changes made in Rule 26(d), providing that formal discovery ordinarily not commence until after the litigants have met and conferred as directed in revised Rule 26(f), the rule requires leave of court or agreement of the parties if a deposition is to be taken before that time (except when a witness is about to leave the country).

Subdivision (b). The primary change in subdivision (b) is that parties will be authorized to record deposition testimony by nonstenographic means without first having to obtain permission of the court or agreement from other counsel. . . .

New paragraph (2) [now Rule 30(b)(3)(A) — ED.] confers on the party taking the deposition the choice of the method of recording, without the need to obtain prior court approval for one taken other than stenographically. A party choosing to record a deposition only by videotape or audiotape should understand that a transcript will be required by Rule 26(a)(3)(B) [now Rule 26(a)(3)(A)(ii) — ED.] and Rule 32(c) if the deposition is later to be offered as evidence at trial or on a dispositive motion under Rule 56. Objections to the nonstenographic recording of a deposition, when warranted by the circumstances, can be presented to the court under Rule 26(c).

Paragraph (3) [now Rule 30(b)(3)(B) — ED.] provides that other parties may arrange, at their own expense, for the recording of a deposition by a means (stenographic, visual, or sound) in addition to the method designated by the person noticing the deposition. The former provisions of this paragraph, relating to the court's power to change the date of a deposition, have been eliminated as redundant in view of Rule 26(c)(2) [now Rule 26(c)(1)(B) — ED.]. . . .

Paragraph (7) [now Rule 30(b)(4) — ED.] is revised to authorize the taking of a deposition not only by telephone but also by other remote electronic means, such as satellite television, when agreed to by the parties or authorized by the court.

Subdivision (c). Minor changes are made in this subdivision to reflect those made in subdivision (b) and to complement the new provisions of subdivision (d)(1) [now the final two sentences of Rule 30(c)(2) — ED.], aimed at reducing the number of interruptions during depositions.

In addition, the revision addresses a recurring problem as to whether other potential deponents can attend a deposition. Courts have disagreed, some holding that witnesses should be excluded through invocation of Rule 615 of the evidence rules, and others holding that witnesses may attend unless excluded by an order under Rule 26(c)(5) [now Rule 26(c)(1)(E) — ED.]. The revision provides that other witnesses are not automatically excluded from a deposition simply by the request of a party. Exclusion, however, can be ordered under Rule 26(c)(5) when appropriate; and, if exclusion is ordered, consideration should be given as to whether the excluded witnesses likewise should be precluded from reading, or being otherwise informed about, the testimony given in the earlier depositions. The revision addresses only the matter of attendance by potential deponents, and does not attempt to resolve issues concerning attendance by others, such as members of the public or press.

Subdivision (d). The first sentence of new paragraph (1) [now the second sentence of Rule 30(c)(2) — ED.] provides that any objections during a deposition must be made concisely and in a non-argumentative and non-suggestive manner. Depositions frequently have been unduly prolonged, if not unfairly frustrated, by lengthy objections and colloquy, often suggesting how the deponent should respond. While objections may, under the revised rule, be made during a deposition, they ordinarily should be limited to those that under Rule 32(d)(3) might be waived if not made at that time, *i.e.,* objections on grounds that might be immediately obviated, removed, or cured, such as to the form of a question or the responsiveness of an answer. Under Rule 32(b), other objections can, even without the so-called "usual stipulation" preserving objections, be raised for the first time at trial and therefore should be kept to a minimum during a deposition.

Directions to a deponent not to answer a question can be even more disruptive than objections. The second sentence of new paragraph (1) [now the final sentence of Rule 30(c)(2) — ED.] prohibits such directions except in the three circumstances indicated: to claim a privilege or protection against disclosure (*e.g.*, as work product), to enforce a court directive limiting the scope or length of permissible discovery, or to suspend a deposition to enable presentation of a motion under paragraph (3).

Paragraph (2) [with significant modifications, now Rules 30(d)(1) and -(2) — ED.] is added to this subdivision to dispel any doubts regarding the power of the court by order or local rule to establish limits on the length of depositions. The rule also explicitly authorizes the court to impose the cost resulting from obstructive tactics that unreasonably prolong a deposition on the person engaged in such obstruction. This sanction may be imposed on a non-party witness as well as a party or attorney, but is otherwise congruent with Rule 26(g).

It is anticipated that limits on the length of depositions prescribed by local rules would be presumptive only, subject to modification by the court or by agreement of the parties. Such modifications typically should be discussed by the parties in their meeting under Rule 26(f) and included in the scheduling order

required by Rule 16(b). Additional time, moreover, should be allowed under the revised rule when justified under the principles stated in Rule 26(b)(2) [now the final two sentences of Rule 26(b)(2)(C) — ED.]. To reduce the number of special motions, local rules should ordinarily permit — and indeed encourage — the parties to agree to additional time, as when, during the taking of a deposition, it becomes clear that some additional examination is needed.

Paragraph (3) authorizes appropriate sanctions not only when a deposition is unreasonably prolonged, but also when an attorney engages in other practices that improperly frustrate the fair examination of the deponent, such as making improper objections or giving directions not to answer prohibited by paragraph (1) [now the final two sentences of Rule 30(c)(2) — ED.]. In general, counsel should not engage in any conduct during a deposition that would not be allowed in the presence of a judicial officer. The making of an excessive number of unnecessary objections may itself constitute sanctionable conduct, as may the refusal of an attorney to agree with other counsel on a fair apportionment of the time allowed for examination of a deponent or a refusal to agree to a reasonable request for some additional time to complete a deposition, when that is permitted by the local rule or order. . . .

2000 Amendment

Subdivision (d). Paragraph (1) [now the final two sentences of Rule 30(c)(2) — ED.] has been amended to clarify the terms regarding behavior during depositions. The references to objections "to evidence" and limitations "on evidence" have been removed to avoid disputes about what is "evidence" and whether an objection is to, or a limitation is on, discovery instead. It is intended that the rule apply to any objection to a question or other issue arising during a deposition, and to any limitation imposed by the court in connection with a deposition, which might relate to duration or other matters.

The current rule places limitations on instructions that a witness not answer only when the instruction is made by a "party." Similar limitations should apply with regard to anyone who might purport to instruct a witness not to answer a question. Accordingly, the rule is amended to apply the limitation to instructions by any person. The amendment is not intended to confer new authority on nonparties to instruct witnesses to refuse to answer deposition questions. The amendment makes it clear that, whatever the legitimacy of giving such instructions, the nonparty is subject to the same limitations as parties.

Paragraph (2) [now Rule 30(d)(1) — ED.] imposes a presumptive durational limitation of one day of seven hours for any deposition. The Committee has been informed that overlong depositions can result in undue costs and delays in some circumstances. This limitation contemplates that there will be reasonable breaks during the day for lunch and other reasons, and that the only time to be counted is the time occupied by the actual deposition. For purposes of this durational limit, the deposition of each person designated under Rule 30(b)(6) should be considered a separate deposition. The presumptive duration may be extended, or otherwise altered, by agreement. Absent agreement, a court order is needed. The party seeking a court order to extend the examination, or otherwise alter the limitations, is expected to show good cause to justify such an order.

Parties considering extending the time for a deposition — and courts asked to order an extension — might consider a variety of factors. For example, if the witness needs an interpreter, that may prolong the examination. If the examination will cover events occurring over a long period of time, that may justify allowing additional time. In cases in which the witness will be questioned about numerous or lengthy documents, it is often desirable for the interrogating party to send copies of the documents to the witness sufficiently in advance of the deposition so that the witness can become familiar with them. Should the witness nevertheless not read the documents in advance, thereby prolonging the deposition, a court could consider that a reason for extending the time limit. If the examination reveals that documents have been requested but not produced, that may justify further examination once production has occurred. In multi-party cases, the need for each party to examine the witness may warrant additional time, although duplicative questioning should be avoided and parties with similar interests should strive to designate one lawyer to question about areas of common interest. Similarly, should the lawyer for the witness want to examine the witness, that may require additional time. Finally, with regard to expert witnesses, there may more often be a need for additional time — even after the submission of the report required by Rule 26(a)(2) — for full exploration of the theories upon which the witness relies.

It is expected that in most instances the parties and the witness will make reasonable accommodations to avoid the need for resort to the court. The limitation is phrased in terms of a single day on the assumption that ordinarily a single day would be preferable to a deposition extending over multiple days; if alternative arrangements would better suit the parties, they may agree to them. It is also assumed that there will be reasonable breaks during the day. Preoccupation with timing is to be avoided.

The rule directs the court to allow additional time where consistent with Rule 26(b)(2) [now Rule 26(b)(2)(C) — ED.] if needed for a fair examination of the deponent. In addition, if the deponent or another person impedes or delays the examination, the court must authorize extra time. The amendment makes clear that additional time should also be allowed where the examination is impeded by an "other circumstance," which might include a power outage, a health emergency, or other event.

In keeping with the amendment to Rule 26(b)(2), the provision added in 1993 granting authority to adopt a local rule limiting the time permitted for depositions has been removed. The court may enter a case-specific order directing shorter depositions for all depositions in a case or with regard to a specific witness. The court may also order that a deposition be taken for limited periods on several days.

Paragraph (3) [now Rule 30(d)(2) — ED.] includes sanctions provisions formerly included in paragraph (2). It authorizes the court to impose an appropriate sanction on any person responsible for an impediment that frustrated the fair examination of the deponent. This could include the deponent, any party, or any other person involved in the deposition. If the impediment or delay results from an "other circumstance" under paragraph (2) [now Rule 30(d)(1) — ED.], ordinarily no sanction would be appropriate. . . .

Subdivision (f)(1) [now Rule 30(f)(1) and -(2) — ED.][.] This subdivision is amended because Rule 5(d) has been amended to direct that discovery materials, including depositions, ordinarily should not be filed. The rule already has provisions directing that the lawyer who arranged for the transcript or recording preserve the deposition. Rule 5(d) provides that, once the deposition is used in the proceeding, the attorney must file it with the court. . . .

Rule 31. Depositions by Written Questions

(a) When a Deposition May Be Taken.

(1) ***Without Leave.*** A party may, by written questions, depose any person, including a party, without leave of court except as provided in Rule 31(a)(2). The deponent's attendance may be compelled by subpoena under Rule 45.

(2) ***With Leave.*** A party must obtain leave of court, and the court must grant leave to the extent consistent with Rule 26(b)(1) and (2):

(A) if the parties have not stipulated to the deposition and:

(i) the deposition would result in more than 10 depositions being taken under this rule or Rule 30 by the plaintiffs, or by the defendants, or by the third-party defendants;

(ii) the deponent has already been deposed in the case; or

(iii) the party seeks to take a deposition before the time specified in Rule 26(d); or

(B) if the deponent is confined in prison.

(3) ***Service; Required Notice.*** A party who wants to depose a person by written questions must serve them on every other party, with a notice stating, if known, the deponent's name and address. If the name is unknown, the notice must provide a general description sufficient to identify the person or the particular class or group to which the person belongs. The notice must also state the name or descriptive title and the address of the officer before whom the deposition will be taken.

(4) ***Questions Directed to an Organization.*** A public or private corporation, a partnership, an association, or a governmental agency may be deposed by written questions in accordance with Rule 30(b)(6).

(5) ***Questions from Other Parties.*** Any questions to the deponent from other parties must be served on all parties as follows: cross-questions, within 14 days after being served with the notice and direct questions; redirect questions, within 7 days after being served with cross-questions; and recross-questions, within 7 days after being

served with redirect questions. The court may, for good cause, extend or shorten these times.

(b) Delivery to the Officer; Officer's Duties. The party who noticed the deposition must deliver to the officer a copy of all the questions served and of the notice. The officer must promptly proceed in the manner provided in Rule 30(c), (e), and (f) to:

(1) take the deponent's testimony in response to the questions;

(2) prepare and certify the deposition; and

(3) send it to the party, attaching a copy of the questions and of the notice.

(c) Notice of Completion or Filing.

(1) ***Completion.*** The party who noticed the deposition must notify all other parties when it is completed.

(2) ***Filing.*** A party who files the deposition must promptly notify all other parties of the filing.

Rule 32. Using Depositions in Court Proceedings

(a) Using Depositions.

(1) ***In General.*** At a hearing or trial, all or part of a deposition may be used against a party on these conditions:

(A) the party was present or represented at the taking of the deposition or had reasonable notice of it;

(B) it is used to the extent it would be admissible under the Federal Rules of Evidence if the deponent were present and testifying; and

(C) the use is allowed by Rule 32(a)(2) through (8).

(2) ***Impeachment and Other Uses.*** Any party may use a deposition to contradict or impeach the testimony given by the deponent as a witness, or for any other purpose allowed by the Federal Rules of Evidence.

(3) ***Deposition of Party, Agent, or Designee.*** An adverse party may use for any purpose the deposition of a party or anyone who, when deposed, was the party's officer, director, managing agent, or designee under Rule 30(b)(6) or 31(a)(4).

(4) ***Unavailable Witness.*** A party may use for any purpose the deposition of a witness, whether or not a party, if the court finds:

(A) that the witness is dead;

(B) that the witness is more than 100 miles from the place of hearing or trial or is outside the United States, unless it appears that the witness's absence was procured by the party offering the deposition;

(C) that the witness cannot attend or testify because of age, illness, infirmity, or imprisonment;

(D) that the party offering the deposition could not procure the witness's attendance by subpoena; or

(E) on motion and notice, that exceptional circumstances make it desirable — in the interest of justice and with due regard to the importance of live testimony in open court — to permit the deposition to be used.

(5) ***Limitations on Use.***

(A) *Deposition Taken on Short Notice.* A deposition must not be used against a party who, having received less than 14 days' notice of the deposition, promptly moved for a protective order under Rule 26(c)(1)(B) requesting that it not be taken or be taken at a different time or place — and this motion was still pending when the deposition was taken.

(B) *Unavailable Deponent; Party Could Not Obtain an Attorney.* A deposition taken without leave of court under the unavailability provision of Rule 30(a)(2)(A)(iii) must not be used against a party who shows that, when served with the notice, it could not, despite diligent efforts, obtain an attorney to represent it at the deposition.

(6) ***Using Part of a Deposition***. If a party offers in evidence only part of a deposition, an adverse party may require the offeror to introduce other parts that in fairness should be considered with the part introduced, and any party may itself introduce any other parts.

(7) ***Substituting a Party***. Substituting a party under Rule 25 does not affect the right to use a deposition previously taken.

(8) ***Deposition Taken in an Earlier Action***. A deposition lawfully taken and, if required, filed in any federal- or state-court action may be used in a later action involving the same subject matter between the same parties, or their representatives or successors in interest, to the same extent as if taken in the later action. A deposition previously taken may also be used as allowed by the Federal Rules of Evidence.

(b) Objections to Admissibility. Subject to Rules 28(b) and 32(d)(3), an objection may be made at a hearing or trial to the admission of any

deposition testimony that would be inadmissible if the witness were present and testifying.

(c) Form of Presentation. Unless the court orders otherwise, a party must provide a transcript of any deposition testimony the party offers, but may provide the court with the testimony in nontranscript form as well. On any party's request, deposition testimony offered in a jury trial for any purpose other than impeachment must be presented in nontranscript form, if available, unless the court for good cause orders otherwise.

(d) Waiver of Objections.

(1) ***To the Notice.*** An objection to an error or irregularity in a deposition notice is waived unless promptly served in writing on the party giving the notice.

(2) ***To the Officer's Qualification.*** An objection based on disqualification of the officer before whom a deposition is to be taken is waived if not made:

(A) before the deposition begins; or

(B) promptly after the basis for disqualification becomes known or, with reasonable diligence, could have been known.

(3) ***To the Taking of the Deposition.***

(A) *Objection to Competence, Relevance, or Materiality.* An objection to a deponent's competence — or to the competence, relevance, or materiality of testimony — is not waived by a failure to make the objection before or during the deposition, unless the ground for it might have been corrected at that time.

(B) *Objection to an Error or Irregularity.* An objection to an error or irregularity at an oral examination is waived if:

(i) it relates to the manner of taking the deposition, the form of a question or answer, the oath or affirmation, a party's conduct, or other matters that might have been corrected at that time; and

(ii) it is not timely made during the deposition.

(C) *Objection to a Written Question.* An objection to the form of a written question under Rule 31 is waived if not served in writing on the party submitting the question within the time for serving responsive questions or, if the question is a recross-question, within 7 days after being served with it.

(4) ***To Completing and Returning the Deposition.*** An objection to how the officer transcribed the testimony — or prepared, signed, certified, sealed, endorsed, sent, or otherwise dealt with the deposition — is waived unless a motion to suppress is made promptly after the

error or irregularity becomes known or, with reasonable diligence, could have been known.

Rule 33. Interrogatories to Parties

(a) In General.

(1) ***Number***. Unless otherwise stipulated or ordered by the court, a party may serve on any other party no more than 25 written interrogatories, including all discrete subparts. Leave to serve additional interrogatories may be granted to the extent consistent with Rule 26(b)((2).

(2) ***Scope***. An interrogatory may relate to any matter that may be inquired into under Rule 26(b). An interrogatory is not objectionable merely because it asks for an opinion or contention that relates to fact or the application of law to fact, but the court may order that the interrogatory need not be answered until designated discovery is complete, or until a pretrial conference or some other time.

(b) Answers and Objections.

(1) ***Responding Party***. The interrogatories must be answered:

(A) by the party to whom they are directed; or

(B) if that party is a public or private corporation, a partnership, an association, or a governmental agency, by any officer or agent, who must furnish the information available to the party.

(2) ***Time to Respond***. The responding party must serve its answers and any objections within 30 days after being served with the interrogatories. A shorter or longer time may be stipulated to under Rule 29 or be ordered by the court.

(3) ***Answering Each Interrogatory***. Each interrogatory must, to the extent it is not objected to, be answered separately and fully in writing under oath.

(4) ***Objections***. The grounds for objecting to an interrogatory must be stated with specificity. Any ground not stated in a timely objection is waived unless the court, for good cause, excuses the failure.

(5) ***Signature***. The person who makes the answers must sign them, and the attorney who objects must sign any objections.

(c) Use. An answer to an interrogatory may be used to the extent allowed by the Federal Rules of Evidence.

(d) Option to Produce Business Records. If the answer to an interrogatory may be determined by examining, auditing, compiling,

abstracting, or summarizing a party's business records (including electronically stored information), and if the burden of deriving or ascertaining the answer will be substantially the same for either party, the responding party may answer by:

(1) specifying the records that must be reviewed, in sufficient detail to enable the interrogating party to locate and identify them as readily as the responding party could; and

(2) giving the interrogating party a reasonable opportunity to examine and audit the records and to make copies, compilations, abstracts, or summaries.

ADVISORY COMMITTEE NOTES

1980 Amendment

Subdivision (c) [now subdivision (d) — ED.]. The Committee is advised that parties upon whom interrogatories are served have occasionally responded by directing the interrogating party to a mass of business records or by offering to make all of their records available, justifying the response by the option provided by this subdivision. Such practices are an abuse of the option. A party who is permitted by the terms of this subdivision to offer records for inspection in lieu of answering an interrogatory should offer them in a manner than permits the same direct and economical access that is available to the party. If the information sought exists in the form of compilations, abstracts or summaries then available to the responding party, those should be made available to the interrogating party. The final sentence is added to make it clear that a responding party has the duty to specify, by category and location, the records from which answers to interrogatories can be derived.

1993 Amendment

Purpose of Revision. The purpose of this revision is to reduce the frequency and increase the efficiency of interrogatory practice. The revision is based on experience with local rules. For ease of reference, subdivision (a) is divided into two subdivisions and the remaining subdivisions renumbered.

Subdivision (a). Revision of this subdivision limits interrogatory practice. Because Rule 26(a)(1)-(3) requires disclosure of much of the information previously obtained by this form of discovery, there should be less occasion to use it. Experience in over half of the district courts has confirmed that limitations on the number of interrogatories are useful and manageable. Moreover, because the device can be costly and may be used as a means of harassment, it is desirable to subject its use to the control of the court consistent with the principles stated in Rule 26(b)(2) [now Rule 26(b)(2)(C) — ED.], particularly in multi-party cases where it has not been unusual for the same interrogatory to be propounded to a party by more than one of its adversaries.

Each party is allowed to serve 25 interrogatories upon any other party, but must secure leave of court (or a stipulation from the opposing party) to serve a larger number. Parties cannot evade this presumptive limitation through the device of joining as "subparts" questions that seek information about discrete

separate subjects. However, a question asking about communications of a particular type should be treated as a single interrogatory even though it requests that the time, place, persons present, and contents be stated separately for each such communication.

As with the number of depositions authorized by Rule 30, leave to serve additional interrogatories is to be allowed when consistent with Rule 26(b)(2). The aim is not to prevent needed discovery, but to provide judicial scrutiny before parties make potentially excessive use of this discovery device. In many cases it will be appropriate for the court to permit a larger number of interrogatories in the scheduling order entered under Rule 16(b).

Unless leave of court is obtained, interrogatories may not be served prior to the meeting [now "conference" — ED.] of the parties under Rule 26(f).

When a case with outstanding interrogatories exceeding the number permitted by this rule is removed to federal court, the interrogating party must seek leave allowing the additional interrogatories, specify which twenty-five are to be answered, or resubmit interrogatories that comply with the rule. Moreover, under Rule 26(d), the time for response would be measured from the date of the parties' meeting under Rule 26(f). See Rule 81(c), providing that these rules govern procedures after removal.

Subdivision (b). A separate subdivision is made of the former second paragraph of subdivision (a). Language is added to paragraph (1) [now Rule 33(b)(3) — ED.] of this subdivision to emphasize the duty of the responding party to provide full answers to the extent not objectionable. If, for example, an interrogatory seeking information about numerous facilities or products is deemed objectionable, but an interrogatory seeking information about a lesser number of facilities or products would not have been objectionable, the interrogatory should be answered with respect to the latter even though an objection is raised as to the balance of the facilities or products. Similarly, the fact that additional time may be needed to respond to some questions (or to some aspects of questions) should not justify a delay in responding to those questions (or other aspects of questions) that can be answered within the prescribed time.

Paragraph (4) is added to make clear that objections must be specifically justified, and that unstated or untimely grounds for objection ordinarily are waived. Note also the provisions of revised Rule 26(b)(5) [now Rule 26(b)(5)(A) — ED.], which require a responding party to indicate when it is withholding information under a claim of privilege or as trial preparation materials.

These provisions should be read in light of Rule 26(g), authorizing the court to impose sanctions on a party and attorney making an unfounded objection to an interrogatory. . . .

2006 Amendment

Rule 33(d) is amended to parallel Rule 34(a) by recognizing the importance of electronically stored information. The term "electronically stored information" has the same broad meaning in Rule 33(d) as in Rule 34(a). Much business information is stored only in electronic form; the Rule 33(d) option should be available with respect to such records as well.

Special difficulties may arise in using electronically stored information, either due to its form or because it is dependent on a particular computer system. Rule 33(d) allows a responding party to substitute access to documents or electronically stored information for an answer only if the burden of deriving the answer will be substantially the same for either party. Rule 33(d) states that a party electing to respond to an interrogatory by providing electronically stored information must ensure that the interrogating party can locate and identify it "as readily as can the party served" [now "as readily as the responding party could," found in Rule 33(d)(1) — ED.] and that the responding party must give the interrogating party a "reasonable opportunity to examine, audit, or inspect" [now "examine or audit," found in Rule 33(d)(2) — ED.] the information. Depending on the circumstances, satisfying these provisions with regard to electronically stored information may require the responding party to provide some combination of technical support, information on application software, or other assistance. The key question is whether such support enables the interrogating party to derive or ascertain the answer from the electronically stored information as readily as the responding party. A party that wishes to invoke Rule 33(d) by specifying electronically stored information may be required to provide direct access to its electronic information system, but only if that is necessary to afford the requesting party an adequate opportunity to derive or ascertain the answer to the interrogatory. In that situation, the responding party's need to protect sensitive interests of confidentiality or privacy may mean that it must derive or ascertain and provide the answer itself rather than invoke Rule 33(d).

Rule 34. Producing Documents, Electronically Stored Information, and Tangible Things, or Entering onto Land, for Inspection and Other Purposes

(a) In General. A party may serve on any other party a request within the scope of Rule 26(b):

(1) to produce and permit the requesting party or its representative to inspect, copy, test, or sample the following items in the responding party's possession, custody, or control:

(A) any designated documents or electronically stored information — including writings, drawings, graphs, charts, photographs, sound recordings, images, and other data or data compilations — stored in any medium from which information can be obtained either directly or, if necessary, after translation by the responding party into a reasonably usable form; or

(B) any designated tangible things; or

(2) to permit entry onto designated land or other property possessed or controlled by the responding party, so that the requesting party may inspect, measure, survey, photograph, test, or sample the property or any designated object or operation on it.

(b) Procedure.

(1) ***Contents of the Request.*** The request:

(A) must describe with reasonable particularity each item or category of items to be inspected;

(B) must specify a reasonable time, place, and manner for the inspection and for performing the related acts; and

(C) may specify the form or forms in which electronically stored information is to be produced.

(2) ***Responses and Objections.***

(A) *Time to Respond.* The party to whom the request is directed must respond in writing within 30 days after being served or — if the request was delivered under Rule 26(d)(2) — within 30 days after the parties' first Rule 26(f) conference. A shorter or longer time may be stipulated to under Rule 29 or be ordered by the court.

(B) *Responding to Each Item.* For each item or category, the response must either state that inspection and related activities will be permitted as requested or state with specificity the grounds for objecting to the request, including the reasons. The responding party may state that it will produce copies of documents or of electronically stored information instead of permitting inspection. The production must then be completed no later than the time for inspection specified in the request or another reasonable time specified in the response.

(C) *Objections.* An objection must state whether any responsive materials are being withheld on the basis of that objection. An objection to part of a request must specify the part and permit inspection of the rest.

(D) *Responding to a Request for Production of Electronically Stored Information.* The response may state an objection to a requested form for producing electronically stored information. If the responding party objects to a requested form — or if no form was specified in the request — the party must state the form or forms it intends to use.

(E) *Producing the Documents or Electronically Stored Information.* Unless otherwise stipulated or ordered by the court, these procedures apply to producing documents or electronically stored information:

(i) A party must produce documents as they are kept in the usual course of business or must organize and label them to correspond to the categories in the request;

(ii) If a request does not specify a form for producing electronically stored information, a party must produce it in a form or forms in which it is ordinarily maintained or in a reasonably usable form or forms; and

(iii) A party need not produce the same electronically stored information in more than one form.

(c) Nonparties. As provided in Rule 45, a nonparty may be compelled to produce documents and tangible things or to permit an inspection.

ADVISORY COMMITTEE NOTES

2006 Amendment

Subdivision (a). As originally adopted, Rule 34 focused on discovery of "documents" and "things." In 1970, Rule 34(a) was amended to include discovery of data compilations, anticipating that the use of computerized information would increase. Since then, the growth in electronically stored information and in the variety of systems for creating and storing such information has been dramatic. Lawyers and judges interpreted the term "documents" to include electronically stored information because it was obviously improper to allow a party to evade discovery obligations on the basis that the label had not kept pace with changes in information technology. But it has become increasingly difficult to say that all forms of electronically stored information, many dynamic in nature, fit within the traditional concept of a "document." Electronically stored information may exist in dynamic databases and other forms far different from fixed expression on paper. Rule 34(a) is amended to confirm that discovery of electronically stored information stands on equal footing with discovery of paper documents. The change clarifies that Rule 34 applies to information that is fixed in a tangible form and to information that is stored in a medium from which it can be retrieved and examined. At the same time, a Rule 34 request for production of "documents" should be understood to encompass, and the response should include, electronically stored information unless discovery in the action has clearly distinguished between electronically stored information and "documents."

Discoverable information often exists in both paper and electronic form, and the same or similar information might exist in both. The items listed in Rule 34(a) show different ways in which information may be recorded or stored. Images, for example, might be hard-copy documents or electronically stored information. The wide variety of computer systems currently in use, and the rapidity of technological change, counsel against a limiting or precise definition of electronically stored information. Rule 34(a)(1) is expansive and includes any type of information that is stored electronically. A common example often sought in discovery is electronic communications, such as e-mail. The rule covers — either as documents or as electronically stored information — information "stored in any medium," to encompass future developments in computer technology. Rule 34(a)(1) is intended to be broad enough to cover all current types of computer-based information, and flexible enough to encompass future changes and developments.

References elsewhere in the rules to "electronically stored information" should be understood to invoke this expansive approach. A companion change is made to

Rule 33(d), making it explicit that parties choosing to respond to an interrogatory by permitting access to responsive records may do so by providing access to electronically stored information. More generally, the term used in Rule 34(a)(1) appears in a number of other amendments, such as those to Rules 26(a)(1), 26(b)(2), 26(b)(5)(B), 26(f), 34(b), 37(f) [now Rule 37(e) — ED.], and 45. In each of these rules, electronically stored information has the same broad meaning it has under Rule 34(a)(1). References to "documents" appear in discovery rules that are not amended, including Rules 30(f), 36(a), and 37(c)(2). These references should be interpreted to include electronically stored information as circumstances warrant.

The term "electronically stored information" is broad, but whether material that falls within this term should be produced, and in what form, are separate questions that must be addressed under Rules 26(b), 26(c), and 34(b).

The Rule 34(a) requirement that, if necessary, a party producing electronically stored information translate it into reasonably usable form does not address the issue of translating from one human language to another.

Rule 34(a)(1) is also amended to make clear that parties may request an opportunity to test or sample materials sought under the rule in addition to inspecting and copying them. That opportunity may be important for both electronically stored information and hard-copy materials. The current rule is not clear that such testing or sampling is authorized; the amendment expressly permits it. As with any other form of discovery, issues of burden and intrusiveness raised by requests to test or sample can be addressed under Rules 26(b)(2) and 26(c). Inspection or testing of certain types of electronically stored information or of a responding party's electronic information system may raise issues of confidentiality or privacy. The addition of testing and sampling to Rule 34(a) with regard to documents and electronically stored information is not meant to create a routine right of direct access to a party's electronic information system, although such access might be justified in some circumstances. Courts should guard against undue intrusiveness resulting from inspecting or testing such systems.

Rule 34(a)(1) is further amended to make clear that tangible things must — like documents and land sought to be examined — be designated in the request.

Subdivision (b). Rule 34(b) provides that a party must produce documents as they are kept in the usual course of business or must organize and label them to correspond with the categories in the discovery request. The production of electronically stored information should be subject to comparable requirements to protect against deliberate or inadvertent production in ways that raise unnecessary obstacles for the requesting party. Rule 34(b) is amended to ensure similar protection for electronically stored information.

The amendment to Rule 34(b) permits the requesting party to designate the form or forms in which it wants electronically stored information produced. The form of production is more important to the exchange of electronically stored information than of hard-copy materials, although a party might specify hard copy as the requested form. Specification of the desired form or forms may facilitate the orderly, efficient, and cost-effective discovery of electronically stored information. The rule recognizes that different forms of production may be appropriate for different types of electronically stored information. . . . The rule therefore provides

that the requesting party may ask for different forms of production for different types of electronically stored information.

The rule does not require that the requesting party choose a form or forms of production. The requesting party may not have a preference. In some cases, the requesting party may not know what form the producing party uses to maintain its electronically stored information, although Rule 26(f)(3) is amended to call for discussion of the form of production in the parties' prediscovery conference. . . .

If the requesting party is not satisfied with the form stated by the responding party, or if the responding party has objected to the form specified by the requesting party, the parties must meet and confer under Rule 37(a)(2)(B) [now deleted, but in substance still found in Rule 37(a)(5)(A)(i) — ED.] in an effort to resolve the matter before the requesting party can file a motion to compel. If they cannot agree and the court resolves the dispute, the court is not limited to the forms initially chosen by the requesting party, stated by the responding party, or specified in this rule for situations in which there is no court order or party agreement.

If the form of production is not specified by party agreement or court order, the responding party must produce electronically stored information either in a form or forms in which it is ordinarily maintained or in a form or forms that are reasonably usable. Rule 34(a) requires that, if necessary, a responding party "translate" information it produces into a "reasonably usable" form. Under some circumstances, the responding party may need to provide some reasonable amount of technical support, information on application software, or other reasonable assistance to enable the requesting party to use the information. The rule does not require a party to produce electronically stored information in the form it which it is ordinarily maintained, as long as it is produced in a reasonably usable form. But the option to produce in a reasonably usable form does not mean that a responding party is free to convert electronically stored information from the form in which it is ordinarily maintained to a different form that makes it more difficult or burdensome for the requesting party to use the information efficiently in the litigation. If the responding party ordinarily maintains the information it is producing in a way that makes it searchable by electronic means, the information should not be produced in a form that removes or significantly degrades this feature.

Some electronically stored information may be ordinarily maintained in a form that is not reasonably usable by any party. One example is "legacy" data that can be used only by superseded systems. The questions whether a producing party should be required to convert such information to a more usable form, or should be required to produce it at all, should be addressed under Rule 26(b)(2)(B).

Whether or not the requesting party specified the form of production, Rule 34(b) provides that the same electronically stored information ordinarily need be produced in only one form.

2015 Amendment

Several amendments are made in Rule 34, aimed at reducing the potential to impose unreasonable burdens by objections to requests to produce.

Rule 34(b)(2)(A) is amended to fit with new Rule 26(d)(2). The time to respond to a Rule 34 request delivered before the parties' Rule 26(f) conference is 30 days after the first Rule 26(f) conference.

Rule 34(b)(2)(B) is amended to require that objections to Rule 34 requests be stated with specificity. This provision adopts the language of Rule 33(b)(4), eliminating any doubt that less specific objections might be suitable under Rule 34. The specificity of the objection ties to the new provision in Rule 34(b)(2)(C) directing that an objection must state whether any responsive materials are being withheld on the basis of that objection. An objection may state that a request is overbroad, but if the objection recognizes that some part of the request is appropriate the objection should state the scope that is not overbroad. Examples would be a statement that the responding party will limit the search to documents or electronically stored information created within a given period of time prior to the events in suit, or to specified sources. When there is such an objection, the statement of what has been withheld can properly identify as matters "withheld" anything beyond the scope of the search specified in the objection.

Rule 34(b)(2)(B) is further amended to reflect the common practice of producing copies of documents or electronically stored information rather than simply permitting inspection. . . .

Rule 34(b)(2)(C) is amended to provide that an objection to a Rule 34 request must state whether anything is being withheld on the basis of the objection. This amendment should end the confusion that frequently arises when a producing party states several objections and still produces information, leaving the requesting party uncertain whether any relevant and responsive information has been withheld on the basis of the objections. The producing party does not need to provide a detailed description or log of all documents withheld, but does need to alert other parties to the fact that documents have been withheld and thereby facilitate an informed discussion of the objection. An objection that states the limits that have controlled the search for responsive and relevant materials qualifies as a statement that the materials have been "withheld."

Rule 35. Physical and Mental Examinations

(a) Order for an Examination.

(1) ***In General.*** The court where the action is pending may order a party whose mental or physical condition — including blood group — is in controversy to submit to a physical or mental examination by a suitably licensed or certified examiner. The court has the same authority to order a party to produce for examination a person who is in its custody or under its legal control.

(2) ***Motion and Notice; Contents of the Order.*** The order:

(A) may be made only on motion for good cause and on notice to all parties and the person to be examined; and

(B) must specify the time, place, manner, conditions, and scope of the examination, as well as the person or persons who will perform it.

(b) Examiner's Report.

(1) ***Request by the Party or Person Examined.*** The party who moved for the examination must, on request, deliver to the requester a copy of the examiner's report, together with like reports of all earlier examinations of the same condition. The request may be made by the party against whom the examination order was issued or by the person examined.

(2) ***Contents.*** The examiner's report must be in writing and must set out in detail the examiner's findings, including diagnoses, conclusions, and the results of any tests.

(3) ***Request by the Moving Party.*** After delivering the reports, the party who moved for the examination may request — and is entitled to receive — from the party against whom the examination order was issued like reports of all earlier or later examinations of the same condition. But those reports need not be delivered by the party with custody or control of the person examined if the party shows that it could not obtain them.

(4) ***Waiver of Privilege.*** By requesting and obtaining the examiner's report, or by deposing the examiner, the party examined waives any privilege it may have — in that action or any other action involving the same controversy — concerning testimony about all examinations of the same condition.

(5) ***Failure to Deliver a Report.*** The court on motion may order — on just terms — that a party deliver the report of an examination. If the report is not provided, the court may exclude the examiner's testimony at trial.

(6) ***Scope.*** This subdivision (b) applies also to an examination made by the parties' agreement, unless the agreement states otherwise. This subdivision does not preclude obtaining an examiner's report or deposing an examiner under other rules.

Rule 36. Requests for Admission

(a) Scope and Procedure.

(1) ***Scope.*** A party may serve on any other party a written request to admit, for purposes of the pending action only, the truth of any matters within the scope of Rule 26(b)(1) relating to:

(A) facts, the application of law to fact, or opinions about either; and

(B) the genuineness of any described documents.

(2) ***Form; Copy of a Document***. Each matter must be separately stated. A request to admit the genuineness of a document must be accompanied by a copy of the document unless it is, or has been, otherwise furnished or made available for inspection and copying.

(3) ***Time to Respond; Effect of Not Responding***. A matter is admitted unless, within 30 days after being served, the party to whom the request is directed serves on the requesting party a written answer or objection addressed to the matter and signed by the party or its attorney. A shorter or longer time for responding may be stipulated to under Rule 29 or be ordered by the court.

(4) ***Answer***. If a matter is not admitted, the answer must specifically deny it or state in detail why the answering party cannot truthfully admit or deny it. A denial must fairly respond to the substance of the matter; and when good faith requires that a party qualify an answer or deny only a part of a matter, the answer must specify the part admitted and qualify or deny the rest. The answering party may assert lack of knowledge or information as a reason for failing to admit or deny only if the party states that it has made reasonable inquiry and that the information it knows or can readily obtain is insufficient to enable it to admit or deny.

(5) ***Objections***. The grounds for objecting to a request must be stated. A party must not object solely on the ground that the request presents a genuine issue for trial.

(6) ***Motion Regarding the Sufficiency of an Answer or Objection***. The requesting party may move to determine the sufficiency of an answer or objection. Unless the court finds an objection justified, it must order that an answer be served. On finding that an answer does not comply with this rule, the court may order either that the matter is admitted or that an amended answer be served. The court may defer its final decision until a pretrial conference or a specified time before trial. Rule 37(a)(5) applies to an award of expenses.

(b) Effect of an Admission; Withdrawing or Amending It. A matter admitted under this rule is conclusively established unless the court, on motion, permits the admission to be withdrawn or amended. Subject to Rule 16(e), the court may permit withdrawal or amendment if it would promote the presentation of the merits of the action and if the court is not persuaded that it would prejudice the requesting party in

maintaining or defending the action on the merits. An admission under this rule is not an admission for any other purpose and cannot be used against the party in any other proceeding.

Rule 37. Failure to Make Disclosures or to Cooperate in Discovery; Sanctions

(a) Motion for an Order Compelling Disclosure or Discovery.

(1) ***In General.*** On notice to other parties and all affected persons, a party may move for an order compelling disclosure or discovery. The motion must include a certification that the movant has in good faith conferred or attempted to confer with the person or party failing to make disclosure or discovery in an effort to obtain it without court action.

(2) ***Appropriate Court.*** A motion for an order to a party must be made in the court where the action is pending. A motion for an order to a nonparty must be made in the court where the discovery is or will be taken.

(3) ***Specific Motions.***

(A) *To Compel Disclosure.* If a party fails to make a disclosure required by Rule 26(a), any other party may move to compel disclosure and for appropriate sanctions.

(B) *To Compel a Discovery Response.* A party seeking discovery may move for an order compelling an answer, designation, production, or inspection. This motion may be made if:

(i) a deponent fails to answer a question asked under Rule 30 or 31;

(ii) a corporation or other entity fails to make a designation under Rule 30(b)(6) or 31(a)(4);

(iii) a party fails to answer an interrogatory submitted under Rule 33; or

(iv) a party fails to produce documents or fails to respond that inspection will be permitted — or fails to permit inspection — as requested under Rule 34.

(C) *Related to a Deposition.* When taking an oral deposition, the party asking a question may complete or adjourn the examination before moving for an order.

(4) ***Evasive or Incomplete Disclosure, Answer, or Response.*** For purposes of this subdivision (a), an evasive or incomplete

disclosure, answer, or response must be treated as a failure to disclose, answer, or respond.

(5) ***Payment of Expenses; Protective Orders.***

(A) *If the Motion Is Granted (or Disclosure or Discovery Is Provided After Filing).* If the motion is granted — or if the disclosure or requested discovery is provided after the motion was filed — the court must, after giving an opportunity to be heard, require the party or deponent whose conduct necessitated the motion, the party or attorney advising that conduct, or both to pay the movant's reasonable expenses incurred in making the motion, including attorney's fees. But the court must not order this payment if:

(i) the movant filed the motion before attempting in good faith to obtain the disclosure or discovery without court action;

(ii) the opposing party's nondisclosure, response, or objection was substantially justified; or

(iii) other circumstances make an award of expenses unjust.

(B) *If the Motion Is Denied.* If the motion is denied, the court may issue any protective order authorized under Rule 26(c) and must, after giving an opportunity to be heard, require the movant, the attorney filing the motion, or both to pay the party or deponent who opposed the motion its reasonable expenses incurred in opposing the motion, including attorney's fees. But the court must not order this payment if the motion was substantially justified or other circumstances make an award of expenses unjust.

(C) *If the Motion Is Granted in Part and Denied in Part.* If the motion is granted in part and denied in part, the court may issue any protective order authorized under Rule 26(c) and may, after giving an opportunity to be heard, apportion the reasonable expenses for the motion.

(b) Failure to Comply with a Court Order.

(1) ***Sanctions Sought in the District Where the Deposition Is Taken.*** If the court where the discovery is taken orders a deponent to be sworn or to answer a question and the deponent fails to obey, the failure may be treated as contempt of court. If a deposition-related motion is transferred to the court where the action is pending, and that court orders a deponent to be sworn or to answer a question and the deponent fails to obey, the failure may be treated as contempt of either the court where the discovery is taken or the court where the action is pending.

(2) ***Sanctions Sought in the District Where the Action Is Pending.***

(A) *For Not Obeying a Discovery Order.* If a party or a party's officer, director, or managing agent — or a witness designated under Rule 30(b)(6) or 31(a)(4) — fails to obey an order to provide or permit discovery, including an order under Rule 26(f), 35, or 37(a), the court where the action is pending may issue further just orders. They may include the following:

(i) directing that the matters embraced in the order or other designated facts be taken as established for purposes of the action, as the prevailing party claims;

(ii) prohibiting the disobedient party from supporting or opposing designated claims or defenses, or from introducing designated matters in evidence;

(iii) striking pleadings in whole or in part;

(iv) staying further proceedings until the order is obeyed;

(v) dismissing the action or proceeding in whole or in part;

(vi) rendering a default judgment against the disobedient party; or

(vii) treating as contempt of court the failure to obey any order except an order to submit to a physical or mental examination.

(B) *For Not Producing a Person for Examination.* If a party fails to comply with an order under Rule 35(a) requiring it to produce another person for examination, the court may issue any of the orders listed in Rule 37(b)(2)(A)(i)-(vi), unless the disobedient party shows that it cannot produce the other person.

(C) *Payment of Expenses.* Instead of or in addition to the orders above, the court must order the disobedient party, the attorney advising that party, or both to pay the reasonable expenses, including attorney's fees, caused by the failure, unless the failure was substantially justified or other circumstances make an award of expenses unjust.

(c) Failure to Disclose, to Supplement an Earlier Response, or to Admit.

(1) ***Failure to Disclose or Supplement.*** If a party fails to provide information or identify a witness as required by Rule 26(a) or (e), the party is not allowed to use that information or witness to supply evidence on a motion, at a hearing, or at a trial, unless the failure was substantially justified or is harmless. In addition to or instead of this

sanction, the court, on motion and after giving an opportunity to be heard:

(A) may order payment of the reasonable expenses, including attorney's fees, caused by the failure;

(B) may inform the jury of the party's failure; and

(C) may impose other appropriate sanctions, including any of the orders listed in Rule 37(b)(2)(A)(i)-(vi).

(2) ***Failure to Admit.*** If a party fails to admit what is requested under Rule 36 and if the requesting party later proves a document to be genuine or the matter true, the requesting party may move that the party who failed to admit pay the reasonable expenses, including attorney's fees, incurred in making that proof. The court must so order unless:

(A) the request was held objectionable under Rule 36(a);

(B) the admission sought was of no substantial importance;

(C) the party failing to admit had a reasonable ground to believe that it might prevail on the matter; or

(D) there was other good reason for the failure to admit.

(d) Party's Failure to Attend Its Own Deposition, Serve Answers to Interrogatories, or Respond to a Request for Inspection.

(1) ***In General.***

(A) *Motion; Grounds for Sanctions.* The court where the action is pending may, on motion, order sanctions if:

(i) a party or a party's officer, director, or managing agent — or a person designated under Rule 30(b)(6) or 31(a)(4) — fails, after being served with proper notice, to appear for that person's deposition; or

(ii) a party, after being properly served with interrogatories under Rule 33 or a request for inspection under Rule 34, fails to serve its answers, objections, or written response.

(B) *Certification.* A motion for sanctions for failing to answer or respond must include a certification that the movant has in good faith conferred or attempted to confer with the party failing to act in an effort to obtain the answer or response without court action.

(2) ***Unacceptable Excuse for Failing to Act.*** A failure described in Rule 37(d)(1)(A) is not excused on the ground that the discovery sought was objectionable, unless the party failing to act has a pending motion for a protective order under Rule 26(c).

(3) ***Types of Sanctions***. Sanctions may include any of the orders listed in Rule 37(b)(2)(A)(i)-(vi). Instead of or in addition to these sanctions, the court must require the party failing to act, the attorney advising that party, or both to pay the reasonable expenses, including attorney's fees, caused by the failure, unless the failure was substantially justified or other circumstances make an award of expenses unjust.

(e) Failure to Preserve Electronically Stored Information. If electronically stored information that should have been preserved in the anticipation or conduct of litigation is lost because a party failed to take reasonable steps to preserve it, and it cannot be restored or replaced through additional discovery, the court:

(1) upon finding prejudice to another party from loss of the information, may order measures no greater than necessary to cure the prejudice; or

(2) only upon finding that the party acted with the intent to deprive another party of the information's use in the litigation may:

(A) presume that the lost information was unfavorable to the party;

(B) instruct the jury that it may or must presume the information was unfavorable to the party; or

(C) dismiss the action or enter a default judgment.

(f) Failure to Participate in Framing a Discovery Plan. If a party or its attorney fails to participate in good faith in developing and submitting a proposed discovery plan as required by Rule 26(f), the court may, after giving an opportunity to be heard, require that party or attorney to pay to any other party the reasonable expenses, including attorney's fees, caused by the failure.

ADVISORY COMMITTEE NOTES

2006 Amendment

Subdivision (f) [now subdivision (e) — ED.]. Subdivision (f) is new. It focuses on a distinctive feature of computer operations, the routine alteration and deletion of information that attends ordinary use. Many steps essential to computer operation may alter or destroy information, for reasons that have nothing to do with how that information might relate to litigation. As a result, the ordinary operation of computer systems creates a risk that a party may lose potentially discoverable information without culpable conduct on its part. Under Rule 37(f), absent exceptional circumstances, sanctions cannot be imposed for loss of electronically stored information resulting from the routine, good-faith operation of an electronic information system. . . .

Rule 37(f) applies to information lost due to the routine operation of an information system only if the operation was in good faith. Good faith in the routine operation of an information system may involve a party's intervention to modify or suspend certain features of that routine operation to prevent the loss of information, if that information is subject to a preservation obligation. A preservation obligation may arise from many sources, including common law, statutes, regulations, or a court order in the case. The good faith requirement of Rule 37(f) means that a party is not permitted to exploit the routine operation of an information system to thwart discovery obligations by allowing that operation to continue in order to destroy specific stored information that it is required to preserve. When a party is under a duty to preserve information because of pending or reasonably anticipated litigation, intervention in the routine operation of an information system is one aspect of what is often called a "litigation hold." Among the factors that bear on a party's good faith in the routine operation of an information system are the steps the party took to comply with a court order in the case or party agreement requiring preservation of specific electronically stored information.

Whether good faith would call for steps to prevent the loss of information on sources that the party believes are not reasonably accessible under Rule 26(b)(2) depends on the circumstances of each case. One factor is whether the party reasonably believes that the information on such sources is likely to be discoverable and not available from reasonably accessible sources.

The protection provided by Rule 37(f) applies only to sanctions "under these rules." It does not affect other sources of authority to impose sanctions or rules of professional responsibility.

This rule restricts the imposition of "sanctions." It does not prevent a court from making the kinds of adjustments frequently used in managing discovery if a party is unable to provide relevant responsive information. For example, a court could order the responding party to produce an additional witness for deposition, respond to additional interrogatories, or make similar attempts to provide substitutes or alternatives for some or all of the lost information.

2015 Amendment

Subdivision (a). Rule 37(a)(3)(B)(iv) is amended to reflect the common practice of producing copies of documents or electronically stored information rather than simply permitting inspection. . . .

Subdivision (e). Present Rule 37(e), adopted in 2006, provides: "Absent exceptional circumstances, a court may not impose sanctions under these rules on a party for failing to provide electronically stored information lost as a result of the routine, good-faith operation of an electronic information system." This limited rule has not adequately addressed the serious problems resulting from the continued exponential growth in the volume of such information. Federal circuits have established significantly different standards for imposing sanctions or curative measures on parties who fail to preserve electronically stored information. These developments have caused litigants to expend excessive effort and money on preservation in order to avoid the risk of severe sanctions if a court finds they did not do enough.

New Rule 37(e) replaces the 2006 rule. It authorizes and specifies measures a court may employ if information that should have been preserved is lost, and specifies the findings necessary to justify these measures. It therefore forecloses reliance on inherent authority or state law to determine when certain measures should be used. The rule does not affect the validity of an independent tort claim for spoliation if state law applies in a case and authorizes the claim.

The new rule applies only to electronically stored information, also the focus of the 2006 rule. It applies only when such information is lost. Because electronically stored information often exists in multiple locations, loss from one source may often be harmless when substitute information can be found elsewhere.

The new rule applies only if the lost information should have been preserved in the anticipation or conduct of litigation and the party failed to take reasonable steps to preserve it. Many court decisions hold that potential litigants have a duty to preserve relevant information when litigation is reasonably foreseeable. Rule 37(e) is based on this common-law duty; it does not attempt to create a new duty to preserve. The rule does not apply when information is lost before a duty to preserve arises.

In applying the rule, a court may need to decide whether and when a duty to preserve arose. Courts should consider the extent to which a party was on notice that litigation was likely and that the information would be relevant. A variety of events may alert a party to the prospect of litigation. Often these events provide only limited information about that prospective litigation, however, so that the scope of information that should be preserved may remain uncertain. It is important not to be blinded to this reality by hindsight arising from familiarity with an action as it is actually filed.

Although the rule focuses on the common-law obligation to preserve in the anticipation or conduct of litigation, courts may sometimes consider whether there was an independent requirement that the lost information be preserved. Such requirements arise from many sources — statutes, administrative regulations, an order in another case, or a party's own information-retention protocols. The court should be sensitive, however, to the fact that such independent preservation requirements may be addressed to a wide variety of concerns unrelated to the current litigation. The fact that a party had an independent obligation to preserve information does not necessarily mean that it had such a duty with respect to the litigation, and the fact that the party failed to observe some other preservation obligation does not itself prove that its efforts to preserve were not reasonable with respect to a particular case.

The duty to preserve may in some instances be triggered or clarified by a court order in the case. Preservation orders may become more common, in part because Rules 16(b)(3)(B)(iii) and 26(f)(3)(C) are amended to encourage discovery plans and orders that address preservation. Once litigation has commenced, if the parties cannot reach agreement about preservation issues, promptly seeking judicial guidance about the extent of reasonable preservation may be important.

The rule applies only if the information was lost because the party failed to take reasonable steps to preserve the information. Due to the ever-increasing volume of electronically stored information and the multitude of devices that generate such information, perfection in preserving all relevant electronically

stored information is often impossible. As under the current rule, the routine, good-faith operation of an electronic information system would be a relevant factor for the court to consider in evaluating whether a party failed to take reasonable steps to preserve lost information, although the prospect of litigation may call for reasonable steps to preserve information by intervening in that routine operation. This rule recognizes that "reasonable steps" to preserve suffice; it does not call for perfection. The court should be sensitive to the party's sophistication with regard to litigation in evaluating preservation efforts; some litigants, particularly individual litigants, may be less familiar with preservation obligations than others who have considerable experience in litigation.

Because the rule calls only for reasonable steps to preserve, it is inapplicable when the loss of information occurs despite the party's reasonable steps to preserve. For example, the information may not be in the party's control. Or information the party has preserved may be destroyed by events outside the party's control — the computer room may be flooded, a "cloud" service may fail, a malign software attack may disrupt a storage system, and so on. Courts may, however, need to assess the extent to which a party knew of and protected against such risks.

Another factor in evaluating the reasonableness of preservation efforts is proportionality. The court should be sensitive to party resources; aggressive preservation efforts can be extremely costly, and parties (including governmental parties) may have limited staff and resources to devote to those efforts. A party may act reasonably by choosing a less costly form of information preservation, if it is substantially as effective as more costly forms. It is important that counsel become familiar with their clients' information systems and digital data — including social media — to address these issues. A party urging that preservation requests are disproportionate may need to provide specifics about these matters in order to enable meaningful discussion of the appropriate preservation regime.

When a party fails to take reasonable steps to preserve electronically stored information that should have been preserved in the anticipation or conduct of litigation, and the information is lost as a result, Rule 37(e) directs that the initial focus should be on whether the lost information can be restored or replaced through additional discovery. Nothing in the rule limits the court's powers under Rules 16 and 26 to authorize additional discovery. Orders under Rule 26(b)(2)(B) regarding discovery from sources that would ordinarily be considered inaccessible or under Rule 26(c)(1)(B) on allocation of expenses may be pertinent to solving such problems. If the information is restored or replaced, no further measures should be taken. At the same time, it is important to emphasize that efforts to restore or replace lost information through discovery should be proportional to the apparent importance of the lost information to claims or defenses in the litigation. For example, substantial measures should not be employed to restore or replace information that is marginally relevant or duplicative.

Subdivision (e)(1). This subdivision applies only if information should have been preserved in the anticipation or conduct of litigation, a party failed to take reasonable steps to preserve the information, information was lost as a result, and the information could not be restored or replaced by additional discovery. In addition, a court may resort to (e)(1) measures only "upon finding prejudice to

another party from loss of the information." An evaluation of prejudice from the loss of information necessarily includes an evaluation of the information's importance in the litigation.

The rule does not place a burden of proving or disproving prejudice on one party or the other. Determining the content of lost information may be a difficult task in some cases, and placing the burden of proving prejudice on the party that did not lose the information may be unfair. In other situations, however, the content of the lost information may be fairly evident, the information may appear to be unimportant, or the abundance of preserved information may appear sufficient to meet the needs of all parties. Requiring the party seeking curative measures to prove prejudice may be reasonable in such situations. The rule leaves judges with discretion to determine how best to assess prejudice in particular cases.

Once a finding of prejudice is made, the court is authorized to employ measures "no greater than necessary to cure the prejudice." The range of such measures is quite broad if they are necessary for this purpose. There is no all-purpose hierarchy of the severity of various measures; the severity of given measures must be calibrated in terms of their effect on the particular case. But authority to order measures no greater than necessary to cure prejudice does not require the court to adopt measures to cure every possible prejudicial effect. Much is entrusted to the court's discretion.

In an appropriate case, it may be that serious measures are necessary to cure prejudice found by the court, such as forbidding the party that failed to preserve information from putting on certain evidence, permitting the parties to present evidence and argument to the jury regarding the loss of information, or giving the jury instructions to assist in its evaluation of such evidence or argument, other than instructions to which subdivision (e)(2) applies. Care must be taken, however, to ensure that curative measures under subdivision (e)(1) do not have the effect of measures that are permitted under subdivision (e)(2) only on a finding of intent to deprive another party of the lost information's use in the litigation. An example of an inappropriate (e)(1) measure might be an order striking pleadings related to, or precluding a party from offering any evidence in support of, the central or only claim or defense in the case. On the other hand, it may be appropriate to exclude a specific item of evidence to offset prejudice caused by failure to preserve other evidence that might contradict the excluded item of evidence.

Subdivision (e)(2). This subdivision authorizes courts to use specified and very severe measures to address or deter failures to preserve electronically stored information, but only on finding that the party that lost the information acted with the intent to deprive another party of the information's use in the litigation. It is designed to provide a uniform standard in federal court for use of these serious measures when addressing failure to preserve electronically stored information. It rejects cases such as *Residential Funding Corp. v. DeGeorge Financial Corp.*, 306 F.3d 99 (2d Cir. 2002), that authorize the giving of adverse-inference instructions on a finding of negligence or gross negligence.

Adverse-inference instructions were developed on the premise that a party's intentional loss or destruction of evidence to prevent its use in litigation gives rise to a reasonable inference that the evidence was unfavorable to the party

responsible for loss or destruction of the evidence. Negligent or even grossly negligent behavior does not logically support that inference. Information lost through negligence may have been favorable to either party, including the party that lost it, and inferring that it was unfavorable to that party may tip the balance at trial in ways the lost information never would have. The better rule for the negligent or grossly negligent loss of electronically stored information is to preserve a broad range of measures to cure prejudice caused by its loss, but to limit the most severe measures to instances of intentional loss or destruction.

Similar reasons apply to limiting the court's authority to presume or infer that the lost information was unfavorable to the party who lost it when ruling on a pretrial motion or presiding at a bench trial. Subdivision (e)(2) limits the ability of courts to draw adverse inferences based on the loss of information in these circumstances, permitting them only when a court finds that the information was lost with the intent to prevent its use in litigation.

Subdivision (e)(2) applies to jury instructions that permit or require the jury to presume or infer that lost information was unfavorable to the party that lost it. Thus, it covers any instruction that directs or permits the jury to infer from the loss of information that it was in fact unfavorable to the party that lost it. The subdivision does not apply to jury instructions that do not involve such an inference. For example, subdivision (e)(2) would not prohibit a court from allowing the parties to present evidence to the jury concerning the loss and likely relevance of information and instructing the jury that it may consider that evidence, along with all the other evidence in the case, in making its decision. These measures, which would not involve instructing a jury it may draw an adverse inference from loss of information, would be available under subdivision (e)(1) if no greater than necessary to cure prejudice. In addition, subdivision (e)(2) does not limit the discretion of courts to give traditional missing evidence instructions based on a party's failure to present evidence it has in its possession at the time of trial.

Subdivision (e)(2) requires a finding that the party acted with the intent to deprive another party of the information's use in the litigation. This finding may be made by the court when ruling on a pretrial motion, when presiding at a bench trial, or when deciding whether to give an adverse inference instruction at trial. If a court were to conclude that the intent finding should be made by a jury, the court's instruction should make clear that the jury may infer from the loss of the information that it was unfavorable to the party that lost it only if the jury first finds that the party acted with the intent to deprive another party of the information's use in the litigation. If the jury does not make this finding, it may not infer from the loss that the information was unfavorable to the party that lost it.

Subdivision (e)(2) does not include a requirement that the court find prejudice to the party deprived of the information. This is because the finding of intent required by the subdivision can support not only an inference that the lost information was unfavorable to the party that intentionally destroyed it, but also an inference that the opposing party was prejudiced by the loss of information that would have favored its position. Subdivision (e)(2) does not require any further finding of prejudice.

Courts should exercise caution, however, in using the measures specified in (e)(2). Finding an intent to deprive another party of the lost information's use in the litigation does not require a court to adopt any of the measures listed in subdivision (e)(2). The remedy should fit the wrong, and the severe measures authorized by this subdivision should not be used when the information lost was relatively unimportant or lesser measures such as those specified in subdivision (e)(1) would be sufficient to redress the loss.

TITLE VI. TRIALS

Rule 38. Right to a Jury Trial; Demand

(a) Right Preserved. The right of trial by jury as declared by the Seventh Amendment to the Constitution — or as provided by a federal statute — is preserved to the parties inviolate.

(b) Demand. On any issue triable of right by a jury, a party may demand a jury trial by:

(1) serving the other parties with a written demand — which may be included in a pleading — no later than 14 days after the last pleading directed to the issue is served; and

(2) filing the demand in accordance with Rule 5(d).

(c) Specifying Issues. In its demand, a party may specify the issues that it wishes to have tried by a jury; otherwise, it is considered to have demanded a jury trial on all the issues so triable. If the party has demanded a jury trial on only some issues, any other party may — within 14 days after being served with the demand or within a shorter time ordered by the court — serve a demand for a jury trial on any other or all factual issues triable by jury.

(d) Waiver; Withdrawal. A party waives a jury trial unless its demand is properly served and filed. A proper demand may be withdrawn only if the parties consent.

(e) Admiralty and Maritime Claims. These rules do not create a right to a jury trial on issues in a claim that is an admiralty or maritime claim under Rule 9(h).

Rule 39. Trial by Jury or by the Court

(a) When a Demand Is Made. When a jury trial has been demanded under Rule 38, the action must be designated on the docket as a jury action. The trial on all issues so demanded must be by jury unless:

(1) the parties or their attorneys file a stipulation to a nonjury trial or so stipulate on the record; or

(2) the court, on motion or on its own, finds that on some or all of those issues there is no federal right to a jury trial.

(b) When No Demand Is Made. Issues on which a jury trial is not properly demanded are to be tried by the court. But the court may, on motion, order a jury trial on any issue for which a jury might have been demanded.

(c) Advisory Jury; Jury Trial by Consent. In an action not triable of right by a jury, the court, on motion or on its own:

(1) may try any issue with an advisory jury; or

(2) may, with the parties' consent, try any issue by a jury whose verdict has the same effect as if a jury trial had been a matter of right, unless the action is against the United States and a federal statute provides for a nonjury trial.

Rule 40. Scheduling Cases for Trial

Each court must provide by rule for scheduling trials. The court must give priority to actions entitled to priority by a federal statute.

Rule 41. Dismissal of Actions

(a) Voluntary Dismissal.

(1) ***By the Plaintiff.***

(A) *Without a Court Order*. Subject to Rules 23(e), 23.1(c), 23.2, and 66 and any applicable federal statute, the plaintiff may dismiss an action without a court order by filing:

(i) a notice of dismissal before the opposing party serves either an answer or a motion for summary judgment; or

(ii) a stipulation of dismissal signed by all parties who have appeared.

(B) *Effect*. Unless the notice or stipulation states otherwise, the dismissal is without prejudice. But if the plaintiff previously dismissed any federal- or state-court action based on or including the same claim, a notice of dismissal operates as an adjudication on the merits.

(2) ***By Court Order; Effect.*** Except as provided in Rule 41(a)(1), an action may be dismissed at the plaintiff's request only by court order, on terms that the court considers proper. If a defendant has

pleaded a counterclaim before being served with the plaintiff's motion to dismiss, the action may be dismissed over the defendant's objection only if the counterclaim can remain pending for independent adjudication. Unless the order states otherwise, a dismissal under this paragraph (2) is without prejudice.

(b) Involuntary Dismissal; Effect. If the plaintiff fails to prosecute or to comply with these rules or a court order, a defendant may move to dismiss the action or any claim against it. Unless the dismissal order states otherwise, a dismissal under this subdivision (b) and any dismissal not under this rule — except one for lack of jurisdiction, improper venue, or failure to join a party under Rule 19 — operates as an adjudication on the merits.

(c) Dismissing a Counterclaim, Crossclaim, or Third-Party Claim. This rule applies to a dismissal of any counterclaim, crossclaim, or third-party claim. A claimant's voluntary dismissal under Rule 41(a)(1)(A)(i) must be made:

(1) before a responsive pleading is served; or

(2) if there is no responsive pleading, before evidence is introduced at a hearing or trial.

(d) Costs of a Previously Dismissed Action. If a plaintiff who previously dismissed an action in any court files an action based on or including the same claim against the same defendant, the court:

(1) may order the plaintiff to pay all or part of the costs of that previous action; and

(2) may stay the proceedings until the plaintiff has complied.

Rule 42. Consolidation; Separate Trials

(a) Consolidation. If actions before the court involve a common question of law or fact, the court may:

(1) join for hearing or trial any or all matters at issue in the actions;

(2) consolidate the actions; or

(3) issue any other orders to avoid unnecessary cost or delay.

(b) Separate Trials. For convenience, to avoid prejudice, or to expedite and economize, the court may order a separate trial of one or more separate issues, claims, crossclaims, counterclaims, or third-party claims. When ordering a separate trial, the court must preserve any federal right to a jury trial.

Rule 43. Taking Testimony

(a) In Open Court. At trial, the witnesses' testimony must be taken in open court unless a federal statute, the Federal Rules of Evidence, these rules, or other rules adopted by the Supreme Court provide otherwise. For good cause in compelling circumstances and with appropriate safeguards, the court may permit testimony in open court by contemporaneous transmission from a different location.

(b) Affirmation Instead of an Oath. When these rules require an oath, a solemn affirmation suffices.

(c) Evidence on a Motion. When a motion relies on facts outside the record, the court may hear the matter on affidavits or may hear it wholly or partly on oral testimony or on depositions.

(d) Interpreter. The court may appoint an interpreter of its choosing; fix reasonable compensation to be paid from funds provided by law or by one or more parties; and tax the compensation as costs.

Rule 44. Proving an Official Record

(a) Means of Proving.

(1) *Domestic Record.* Each of the following evidences an official record — or an entry in it — that is otherwise admissible and is kept within the United States, any state, district, or commonwealth, or any territory subject to the administrative or judicial jurisdiction of the United States:

(A) an official publication of the record; or

(B) a copy attested by the officer with legal custody of the record — or by the officer's deputy — and accompanied by a certificate that the officer has custody. The certificate must be made under seal:

(i) by a judge of a court of record in the district or political subdivision where the record is kept; or

(ii) by any public officer with a seal of office and with official duties in the district or political subdivision where the record is kept.

(2) *Foreign Record.*

(A) *In General.* Each of the following evidences a foreign official record — or an entry in it — that is otherwise admissible:

(i) an official publication of the record; or

(ii) the record — or a copy — that is attested by an authorized person and is accompanied either by a final certification of genuineness or by a certification under a treaty or convention to which the United States and the country where the record is located are parties.

(B) *Final Certification of Genuineness.* A final certification must certify the genuineness of the signature and official position of the attester or of any foreign official whose certificate of genuineness relates to the attestation or is in a chain of certificates of genuineness relating to the attestation. A final certification may be made by a secretary of a United States embassy or legation; by a consul general, vice consul, or consular agent of the United States; or by a diplomatic or consular official of the foreign country assigned or accredited to the United States.

(C) *Other Means of Proof.* If all parties have had a reasonable opportunity to investigate a foreign record's authenticity and accuracy, the court may, for good cause, either:

(i) admit an attested copy without final certification; or

(ii) permit the record to be evidenced by an attested summary with or without a final certification.

(b) Lack of a Record. A written statement that a diligent search of designated records revealed no record or entry of a specified tenor is admissible as evidence that the records contain no such record or entry. For domestic records, the statement must be authenticated under Rule 44(a)(1). For foreign records, the statement must comply with (a)(2)(C)(ii).

(c) Other Proof. A party may prove an official record — or an entry or lack of an entry in it — by any other method authorized by law.

Rule 44.1. Determining Foreign Law

A party who intends to raise an issue about a foreign country's law must give notice by a pleading or other writing. In determining foreign law, the court may consider any relevant material or source, including testimony, whether or not submitted by a party or admissible under the Federal Rules of Evidence. The court's determination must be treated as a ruling on a question of law.

Rule 45. Subpoena

(a) In General.

(1) ***Form and Contents.***

(A) *Requirements — In General.* Every subpoena must:

(i) state the court from which it issued;

(ii) state the title of the action and its civil-action number;

(iii) command each person to whom it is directed to do the following at a specified time and place: attend and testify; produce designated documents, electronically stored information, or tangible things in that person's possession, custody, or control; or permit the inspection of premises; and

(iv) set out the text of Rule 45(c) and (d).

(B) *Command to Attend a Deposition — Notice of the Recording Method.* A subpoena commanding attendance at a deposition must state the method for recording the testimony.

(C) *Combining or Separating a Command to Produce or to Permit Inspection; Specifying the Form for Electronically Stored Information.* A command to produce documents, electronically stored information, or tangible things or to permit the inspection of premises may be included in a subpoena commanding attendance at a deposition, hearing, or trial, or may be set out in a separate subpoena. A subpoena may specify the form or forms in which electronically stored information is to be produced.

(D) *Command to Produce; Included Obligations.* A command in a subpoena to produce documents, electronically stored information, or tangible things requires the responding party to permit inspection, copying, testing, or sampling of the materials.

(2) ***Issuing Court***. A subpoena must issue from the court where the action is pending.

(3) ***Issued by Whom***. The clerk must issue a subpoena, signed but otherwise in blank, to a party who requests it. That party must complete it before service. An attorney also may issue and sign a subpoena if the attorney is authorized to practice in the issuing court.

(4) Notice to Other Parties Before Service. If the subpoena commands the production of documents, electronically stored information, or tangible things or the inspection of premises before trial, then before it is served on the person to whom it is directed, a notice and a copy of the subpoena must be served on each party.

(b) Service.

(1) ***By Whom and How; Tendering Fees.*** Any person who is at least 18 years old and not a party may serve a subpoena. Serving a subpoena requires delivering a copy to the named person and, if the subpoena requires that person's attendance, tendering the fees for 1 day's attendance and the mileage allowed by law. Fees and mileage need not be tendered when the subpoena issues on behalf of the United States or any of its officers or agencies.

(2) ***Service in the United States.*** A subpoena may be served at any place within the United States.

(3) ***Service in a Foreign Country.*** 28 U.S.C. § 1783 governs issuing and serving a subpoena directed to a United States national or resident who is in a foreign country.

(4) ***Proof of Service.*** Proving service, when necessary, requires filing with the issuing court a statement showing the date and manner of service and the names of the persons served. The statement must be certified by the server.

(c) Place of Compliance.

(1) ***For a Trial, Hearing, or Deposition.*** A subpoena may command a person to attend a trial, hearing, or deposition only as follows:

(A) within 100 miles of where the person resides, is employed, or regularly transacts business in person; or

(B) within the state where the person resides, is employed, or regularly transacts business in person, if the person

(i) is a party or a party's officer; or

(ii) is commanded to attend a trial and would not incur substantial expense.

(2) ***For Other Discovery.*** A subpoena may command:

(A) production of documents or electronically stored information, or tangible things at a place within 100 miles of where the person resides, is employed, or regularly transacts business in person; and

(B) inspection of premises, at the premises to be inspected.

(d) Protecting a Person Subject to a Subpoena; Enforcement.

(1) ***Avoiding Undue Burden or Expense; Sanctions.*** A party or attorney responsible for issuing and serving a subpoena must take reasonable steps to avoid imposing undue burden or expense on a person subject to the subpoena. The court for the district where

compliance is required must enforce this duty and impose an appropriate sanction — which may include lost earnings and reasonable attorney's fees — on a party or attorney who fails to comply.

(2) *Command to Produce Materials or Permit Inspection.*

(A) *Appearance Not Required.* A person commanded to produce documents, electronically stored information, or tangible things, or to permit the inspection of premises, need not appear in person at the place of production or inspection unless also commanded to appear for a deposition, hearing, or trial.

(B) *Objections.* A person commanded to produce documents or tangible things or to permit inspection may serve on the party or attorney designated in the subpoena a written objection to inspecting, copying, testing or sampling any or all of the materials or to inspecting the premises — or to producing electronically stored information in the form or forms requested. The objection must be served before the earlier of the time specified for compliance or 14 days after the subpoena is served. If an objection is made, the following rules apply:

(i) At any time, on notice to the commanded person, the serving party may move the court for the district where compliance is required for an order compelling production or inspection.

(ii) These acts may be required only as directed in the order, and the order must protect a person who is neither a party nor a party's officer from significant expense resulting from compliance.

(3) *Quashing or Modifying a Subpoena.*

(A) *When Required.* On timely motion, the court for the district where compliance is required must quash or modify a subpoena that:

(i) fails to allow a reasonable time to comply;

(ii) requires a person to comply beyond the geographical limits specified in Rule 45(c);

(iii) requires disclosure of privileged or other protected matter, if no exception or waiver applies; or

(iv) subjects a person to undue burden.

(B) *When Permitted.* To protect a person subject to or affected by a subpoena, the court for the district where compliance is required may, on motion, quash or modify the subpoena if it requires:

(i) disclosing a trade secret or other confidential research, development, or commercial information;

(ii) disclosing an unretained expert's opinion or information that does not describe specific occurrences in dispute and results from the expert's study that was not requested by a party.

(C) *Specifying Conditions as an Alternative.* In the circumstances described in Rule 45(c)(3)(B), the court may, instead of quashing or modifying a subpoena, order appearance or production under specified conditions if the serving party:

(i) shows a substantial need for the testimony or material that cannot be otherwise met without undue hardship; and

(ii) ensures that the subpoenaed person will be reasonably compensated.

(e) Duties in Responding to a Subpoena.

(1) ***Producing Documents or Electronically Stored Information.*** These procedures apply to producing documents or electronically stored information:

(A) *Documents.* A person responding to a subpoena to produce documents must produce them as they are kept in the ordinary course of business or must organize and label them to correspond to the categories in the demand.

(B) *Form for Producing Electronically Stored Information Not Specified.* If a subpoena does not specify a form for producing electronically stored information, the person responding must produce it in a form or forms in which it is ordinarily maintained or in a reasonably usable form or forms.

(C) *Electronically Stored Information Produced in Only One Form.* The person responding need not produce the same electronically stored information in more than one form.

(D) *Inaccessible Electronically Stored Information.* The person responding need not provide discovery of electronically stored information from sources that the person identifies as not reasonably accessible because of undue burden or cost. On motion to compel discovery or for a protective order, the person responding must show that the information is not reasonably accessible because of undue burden or cost. If that showing is made, the court may nonetheless order discovery from such sources if the requesting party shows good cause, considering the limitations of Rule 26(b)(2)(C). The court may specify conditions for the discovery.

(2) *Claiming Privilege or Protection.*

(A) *Information Withheld.* A person withholding subpoenaed information under a claim that it is privileged or subject to protection as trial-preparation material must:

(i) expressly make the claim; and

(ii) describe the nature of the withheld documents, communications, or tangible things in a manner that, without revealing information itself privileged or protected, will enable the parties to assess the claim.

(B) *Information Produced.* If information produced in response to a subpoena is subject to a claim of privilege or of protection as trial-preparation material, the person making the claim may notify any party that received the information of the claim and the basis for it. After being notified, a party must promptly return, sequester, or destroy the specified information and any copies it has; must not use or disclose the information until the claim is resolved; must take reasonable steps to retrieve the information if the party disclosed it before being notified; and may promptly present the information under seal to the court for the district where compliance is required for a determination of the claim. The person who produced the information must preserve the information until the claim is resolved.

(f) *Transferring a Subpoena-Related Motion*. When the court where compliance is required did not issue the subpoena, it may transfer a motion under this rule to the issuing court if the person subject to the subpoena consents or if the court finds exceptional circumstances. Then, if the attorney for a person subject to a subpoena is authorized to practice in the court where the motion was made, the attorney may file papers and appear on the motion as an officer of the issuing court. To enforce its order, the issuing court may transfer the order to the court where the motion was made.

(g) Contempt. The court for the district where compliance is required — and also, after a motion is transferred, the issuing court — may hold in contempt a person who, having been served, fails without adequate excuse to obey the subpoena or an order related to it.

ADVISORY COMMITTEE NOTES

1991 Amendment [some citations omitted without notation — ED.]

Purposes of Revision. The purposes of this revision are (1) to clarify and enlarge the protections afforded persons who are required to assist the court by giving information or evidence; (2) to facilitate access outside the deposition procedure provided by Rule 30 to documents and other information in the

possession of persons who are not parties; (3) to facilitate service of subpoenas for depositions or productions of evidence at places distant from the district in which an action is proceeding; (4) to enable the court to compel a witness found within the state in which the court sits to attend trial; (5) to clarify the organization of the text of the rule.

Subdivision (a). This subdivision is amended in seven significant respects.

First, Paragraph (a)(3) modifies the requirement that a subpoena be issued by the clerk of court. Provision is made for the issuance of subpoenas by attorneys as officers of the court. This revision perhaps culminates an evolution. Subpoenas were long issued by specific order of the court. As this became a burden to the court, general orders were made authorizing clerks to issue subpoenas on request. Since 1948, they have been issued in blank by the clerk of any federal court to any lawyer, the clerk serving as stationer to the bar. In allowing counsel to issue the subpoena, the rule is merely a recognition of present reality.

Although the subpoena is in a sense the command of the attorney who completes the form, defiance of a subpoena is nevertheless an act in defiance of a court order and exposes the defiant witness to contempt sanctions. In *ICC v. Brimson,* 154 U.S. 447 (1894), the Court upheld a statute directing federal courts to issue subpoenas to compel testimony before the ICC. In *CAB v. Hermann,* 353 U.S. 322 (1957), the Court approved as established practice the issuance of administrative subpoenas as a matter of absolute agency right. And in *NLRB v. Warren Co.,* 350 U.S. 107 (1955), the Court held that the lower court had no discretion to withhold sanctions against a contemnor who violated such subpoenas. . . . This revision makes the rule explicit that the attorney acts as an officer of the court in issuing and signing subpoenas.

Necessarily accompanying the evolution of this power of the lawyer as officer of the court is the development of increased responsibility and liability for the misuse of this power. The latter development is reflected in the provisions of subdivision (c) of this rule, and also in the requirement imposed by paragraph (3) of this subdivision that the attorney issuing a subpoena must sign it.

Second, Paragraph (a)(3) authorizes attorneys in distant districts to serve as officers authorized to issue commands in the name of the court. Any attorney permitted to represent a client in a federal court, even one admitted pro haec vice, has the same authority as a clerk to issue a subpoena from any federal court for the district in which the subpoena is served and enforced. In authorizing attorneys to issue subpoenas from distant courts, the amended rule effectively authorizes service of a subpoena anywhere in the United States by an attorney representing any party. This change is intended to ease the administrative burdens of inter-district law practice. The former rule resulted in delay and expense caused by the need to secure forms from clerks' offices some distance from the place at which the action proceeds. This change does not enlarge the burden on the witness.

Pursuant to Paragraph (a)(2), a subpoena for a deposition must still issue from the court in which the deposition or production would be compelled. Accordingly, a motion to quash such a subpoena if it overbears the limits of the subpoena power must, as under the previous rule, be presented to the court for the district in which the deposition would occur. Likewise, the court in whose name the subpoena is issued is responsible for its enforcement.

Third, in order to relieve attorneys of the need to secure an appropriate seal to affix to a subpoena issued as an officer of a distant court, the requirement that a subpoena be under seal is abolished by the provisions of Paragraph (a)(1).

Fourth, Paragraph (a)(1) authorizes the issuance of a subpoena to compel a non-party to produce evidence independent of any deposition. This revision spares the necessity of a deposition of the custodian of evidentiary material required to be produced. A party seeking additional production from a person subject to such a subpoena may serve an additional subpoena requiring additional production at the same time and place.

Fifth, Paragraph (a)(2) makes clear that the person subject to the subpoena is required to produce materials in that person's control whether or not the materials are located within the district or within the territory within which the subpoena can be served. The non-party witness is subject to the same scope of discovery under this rule as that person would be as a party to whom a request is addressed pursuant to Rule 34.

Sixth, Paragraph (a)(1) requires that the subpoena include a statement of the rights and duties of witnesses by setting forth in full the text of the new subdivisions (c) and (d).

Seventh, the revised rule authorizes the issuance of a subpoena to compel the inspection of premises in the possession of a non-party. Rule 34 has authorized such inspections of premises in the possession of a party as discovery compelled under Rule 37, but prior practice required an independent proceeding to secure such relief ancillary to the federal proceeding when the premises were not in the possession of a party. Practice in some states has long authorized such use of a subpoena for this purpose without apparent adverse consequence.

Subdivision (b). Paragraph (b)(1) retains the text of the former subdivision (c) with minor changes.

The reference to the United States marshal and deputy marshal is deleted because of the infrequency of the use of these officers for this purpose. Inasmuch as these officers meet the age requirement, they may still be used if available.

A provision requiring service of prior notice pursuant to Rule 5 of compulsory pretrial production or inspection has been added to paragraph (b)(1). The purpose of such notice is to afford other parties an opportunity to object to the production or inspection, or to serve a demand for additional documents or things. . . .

Subdivision (c). This provision is new and states the rights of witnesses. It is not intended to diminish rights conferred by Rules 26-37 or any other authority.

Paragraph (c)(1) gives specific application to the principle stated in Rule 26(g) and specifies liability for earnings lost by a non-party witness as a result of a misuse of the subpoena. No change in existing law is thereby effected. Abuse of a subpoena is an actionable tort, and the duty of the attorney to the non-party is also embodied in Model Rule of Professional Conduct 4.4. The liability of the attorney is correlative to the expanded power of the attorney to issue subpoenas. The liability may include the cost of fees to collect attorneys' fees owed as a result of a breach of this duty.

Paragraph (c)(2) retains language from the former subdivision (b) and paragraph (d)(1). The 10-day period for response to a subpoena is extended to 14

days to avoid the complex calculations associated with short time periods under Rule 6 and to allow a bit more time for such objections to be made.

A non-party required to produce documents or materials is protected against significant expense resulting from involuntary assistance to the court. This provision applies, for example, to a non-party required to provide a list of class members. The court is not required to fix the costs in advance of production, although this will often be the most satisfactory accommodation to protect the party seeking discovery from excessive costs. In some instances, it may be preferable to leave uncertain costs to be determined after the materials have been produced, provided that the risk of uncertainty is fully disclosed to the discovering party.

Paragraph (c)(3) explicitly authorizes the quashing of a subpoena as a means of protecting a witness from misuse of the subpoena power. It replaces and enlarges on the former subdivision (b) of this rule and tracks the provisions of Rule 26(c). While largely repetitious, this rule is addressed to the witness who may read it on the subpoena, where it is required to be printed by the revised paragraph (a)(1) of this rule.

Subparagraph (c)(3)(A) identifies those circumstances in which a subpoena must be quashed or modified. It restates the former provisions with respect to the limits of mandatory travel that are set forth in the former paragraphs (d)(2) and (e)(1), with one important change. Under the revised rule, a federal court can compel a witness to come from any place in the state to attend trial, whether or not the local state law so provides. This extension is subject to the qualification provided in the next paragraph, which authorizes the court to condition enforcement of a subpoena compelling a non-party witness to bear substantial expense to attend trial. The traveling non-party witness may be entitled to reasonable compensation for the time and effort entailed.

Clause (c)(3)(A)(iv) requires the court to protect all persons from undue burden imposed by the use of the subpoena power. Illustratively, it might be unduly burdensome to compel an adversary to attend trial as a witness if the adversary is known to have no personal knowledge of matters in dispute, especially so if the adversary would be required to incur substantial travel burdens.

Subparagraph (c)(3)(B) identifies circumstances in which a subpoena should be quashed unless the party serving the subpoena shows a substantial need and the court can devise an appropriate accommodation to protect the interests of the witness. An additional circumstance in which such action is required is a request for costly production of documents; that situation is expressly governed by subparagraph (b)(2)(B) [probably should read "(c)(2)(B)" — ED.].

Clause (c)(3)(B)(i) authorizes the court to quash, modify, or condition a subpoena to protect the person subject to or affected by the subpoena from unnecessary or unduly harmful disclosures of confidential information. It corresponds to Rule 26(c)(7).

Clause (c)(3)(B)(ii) provides appropriate protection for the intellectual property of the non-party witness; it does not apply to the expert retained by a party, whose information is subject to the provisions of Rule 26(b)(4). A growing problem has been the use of subpoenas to compel the giving of evidence and information by

unretained experts. Experts are not exempt from the duty to give evidence, even if they cannot be compelled to prepare themselves to give effective testimony, but compulsion to give evidence may threaten the intellectual property of experts denied the opportunity to bargain for the value of their services. Arguably the compulsion to testify can be regarded as a "taking" of intellectual property. The rule establishes the right of such persons to withhold their expertise, at least unless the party seeking it makes the kind of showing required for a conditional denial of a motion to quash as provided in the final sentence of subparagraph (c)(3)(B); that requirement is the same as that necessary to secure work product under Rule 26(b)(3) and gives assurance of reasonable compensation. The Rule thus approves the accommodation of competing interests exemplified in *United States v. Columbia Broadcasting Systems Inc.,* 666 F.2d 364 (9th Cir, 1982).

As stated in *Kaufman v. Edelstein,* 539 F.2d 811, 822 (2d Cir, 1976), the district court's discretion in these matters should be informed by "the degree to which the expert is being called because of his knowledge of facts relevant to the case rather than in order to give opinion testimony; the difference between testifying to a previously formed or expressed opinion and forming a new one; the possibility that, for other reasons, the witness is a unique expert; the extent to which the calling party is able to show the unlikelihood that any comparable witness will willingly testify; and the degree to which the witness is able to show that he has been oppressed by having continually to testify . . . ."

Clause (c)(3)(B)(iii) protects non-party witnesses who may be burdened to perform the duty to travel in order to provide testimony at trial. The provision requires the court to condition a subpoena requiring travel of more than 100 miles on reasonable compensation.

Subdivision (d). This provision is new. Paragraph (d)(1) [now Rule 45(d)(1)(A) — ED.] extends to non-parties the duty imposed on parties by the last paragraph of Rule 34(b), which was added in 1980.

Paragraph (d)(2) [now Rule 45(d)(2)(A) — ED.] is new . . . . Its purpose is to provide a party whose discovery is constrained by a claim of privilege or work product protection with information sufficient to evaluate such a claim and to resist if it seems unjustified. The person claiming a privilege or protection cannot decide the limits of that party's own entitlement.

A party receiving a discovery request who asserts a privilege or protection but fails to disclose that claim is at risk of waiving the privilege or protection. A person claiming a privilege or protection who fails to provide adequate information about the privilege or protection claim to the party seeking the information is subject to an order to show cause why the person should not be held in contempt under subdivision (e). Motions for such orders and responses to motions are subject to the sanctions provisions of Rules 7 and 11.

A person served a subpoena that is too broad may be faced with a burdensome task to provide full information regarding all that person's claims to privilege or work product protection. Such a person is entitled to protection that may be secured through an objection made pursuant to paragraph (c)(2).

Subdivision (e). This provision retains most of the language of the former subdivision (f).

"Adequate cause" [this phrase has been deleted from Rule 45(e), but the related phrase "adequate excuse" remains — ED.] for a failure to obey a subpoena remains undefined. In at least some circumstances, a non-party might be guilty of contempt for refusing to obey a subpoena even though the subpoena manifestly overreaches the appropriate limits of the subpoena power. But, because the command of the subpoena is not in fact one uttered by a judicial officer, contempt should be very sparingly applied when the non-party witness has been overborne by a party or attorney. The language added to subdivision (f) is intended to assure that result where a non-party has been commanded, on the signature of an attorney, to travel greater distances than can be compelled pursuant to this rule.

2006 Amendment

Rule 45 is amended to conform the provisions for subpoenas to changes in other discovery rules, largely related to discovery of electronically stored information.... Rule 45(a)(1)(C) is amended to recognize that electronically stored information, as defined in Rule 34(a), can also be sought by subpoena. . . .

As with discovery of electronically stored information from parties, complying with a subpoena for such information may impose burdens on the responding person. Rule 45(c) provides protection against undue impositions on nonparties. For example, Rule 45(c)(1) directs that a party serving a subpoena "shall [now "must" — ED.] take reasonable steps to avoid imposing undue burden or expense on a person subject to the subpoena," and Rule 45(c)(2)(B) permits the person served with the subpoena to object to it and directs that an order requiring compliance "shall [now "must" — ED.] protect a person who is neither a party nor a party's officer from significant expense resulting from" compliance. Rule 45(d)(1)(D) is added to provide that the responding person need not provide discovery of electronically stored information from sources the party identifies as not reasonably accessible, unless the court orders such discovery for good cause, considering the limitations of Rule 26(b)(2)(C), on terms that protect a nonparty against significant expense. A parallel provision is added to Rule 26(b)(2).

Rule 45(a)(1)(B) is also amended, as is Rule 34(a), to provide that a subpoena is available to permit testing and sampling as well as inspection and copying. As in Rule 34, this change recognizes that on occasion the opportunity to perform testing or sampling may be important, both for documents and for electronically stored information. Because testing or sampling may present particular issues of burden or intrusion for the person served with the subpoena, however, the protective provisions of Rule 45(c) should be enforced with vigilance when such demands are made. Inspection or testing of certain types of electronically stored information or of a person's electronic information system may raise issues of confidentiality or privacy. The addition of sampling and testing to Rule 45(a) with regard to documents and electronically stored information is not meant to create a routine right of direct access to a person's electronic information system, although such access might be justified in some circumstances. Courts should guard against undue intrusiveness resulting from inspecting or testing such systems.

Rule 45(d)(2) is amended, as is Rule 26(b)(5), to add a procedure for assertion of privilege or of protection as trial-preparation materials after production.

2013 Amendment

Rule 45 was extensively amended in 1991. The goal of the present amendments is to clarify and simplify the rule. The amendments recognize the court where the action is pending as the issuing court, permit nationwide service of a subpoena, and collect in a new subdivision (c) the previously scattered provisions regarding place of compliance. These changes resolve a conflict that arose after the 1991 amendment about a court's authority to compel a party or party officer to travel long distances to testify at trial; such testimony may now be required only as specified in new Rule 45(c). In addition, the amendments introduce authority in new Rule 45(f) for the court where compliance is required to transfer a subpoena-related motion to the court where the action is pending in exceptional circumstances or on consent by agreement of the parties and the person subject to the subpoena or in exceptional circumstances.

Subdivision (f). Subdivision (f) is new. . . .

Subpoenas are essential to obtain discovery from nonparties. To protect local nonparties, local resolution of disputes about subpoenas is assured by the limitations of Rule 45(c) and the requirements in Rules 45(d) and (e) that motions be made in the court in which compliance is required under Rule 45(c). But transfer to the court where the action is pending is sometimes warranted. If the person subject to the subpoena consents to transfer, Rule 45(f) provides that the court where compliance is required may do so.

In the absence of consent, the court may transfer in exceptional circumstances, and the proponent of transfer bears the burden of showing that such circumstances are present. The prime concern should be avoiding burdens on local nonparties subject to subpoenas, and it should not be assumed that the issuing court is in a superior position to resolve subpoena-related motions. In some circumstances, however, transfer may be warranted in order to avoid disrupting the issuing court's management of the underlying litigation, as when that court has already ruled on issues presented by the motion or the same issues are likely to arise in discovery in many districts. Transfer is appropriate only if such interests outweigh the interests of the nonparty served with the subpoena in obtaining local resolution of the motion. Judges in compliance districts may find it helpful to consult with the judge in the issuing court presiding over the underlying case while addressing subpoena-related motions. . . .

After transfer, the court where the action is pending will decide the motion. If the court rules that discovery is not justified, that should end the matter. If the court orders further discovery, it is possible that retransfer may be important to enforce the order.

Rule 46. Objecting to a Ruling or Order

A formal exception to a ruling or order is unnecessary. When the ruling or order is requested or made, a party need only state the action that it wants the court to take or objects to, along with the grounds for the request or objection. Failing to object does not prejudice a party who had no opportunity to do so when the ruling or order was made.

Rule 47. Selecting Jurors

(a) Examining Jurors. The court may permit the parties or their attorneys to examine prospective jurors or may itself do so. If the court examines the jurors, it must permit the parties or their attorneys to make any further inquiry it considers proper, or must itself ask any of their additional questions it considers proper.

(b) Peremptory Challenges. The court must allow the number of peremptory challenges provided by 28 U.S.C. § 1870.

(c) Excusing a Juror. During trial or deliberation, the court may excuse a juror for good cause.

Rule 48. Number of Jurors; Verdict; Polling

(a) Number of Jurors. A jury must begin with at least 6 and no more than 12 members, and each juror must participate in the verdict unless excused under Rule 47(c).

(b) Verdict. Unless the parties stipulate otherwise, the verdict must be unanimous and must be returned by a jury of at least 6 members.

(c) Polling. After a verdict is returned but before the jury is discharged, the court must on a party's request, or may on its own, poll the jurors individually. If the poll reveals a lack of unanimity or lack of assent by the number of jurors that the parties stipulated to, the court may direct the jury to deliberate further or may order a new trial.

ADVISORY COMMITTEE NOTES

1991 Amendment [citation omitted without notation — ED.]

. . .

It appears that the minimum size of a jury consistent with the Seventh Amendment is six. *Cf. Ballew v. Georgia*, 435 U.S. 223 (1978) (holding that a conviction based on a jury of less than six is a denial of due process of law). If the parties agree to trial before a smaller jury, a verdict can be taken, but the parties should not other than in exceptional circumstances be encouraged to waive the right to a jury of six, not only because of the constitutional stature of the right, but also because smaller juries are more erratic and less effective in serving to distribute responsibility for the exercise of judicial power.

Because the institution of the alternate juror has been abolished by the proposed revision of Rule 47, it will ordinarily be prudent and necessary, in order to provide for sickness or disability among jurors, to seat more than six jurors. The use of jurors in excess of six increases the representativeness of the jury and harms no interest of a party.

If the court takes the precaution of seating a jury larger than six, an illness occurring during the deliberation period will not result in a mistrial, as it did

formerly, because all seated jurors will participate in the verdict and a sufficient number will remain to render a unanimous verdict of six or more.

In exceptional circumstances, as where a jury suffers depletions during trial and deliberation that are greater than can reasonably be expected, the parties may agree to be bound by a verdict rendered by fewer than six jurors. The court should not, however, rely upon the availability of such an agreement, for the use of juries smaller than six is problematic for reasons fully explained in *Ballew v. Georgia*, supra.

2009 Amendment

Jury polling is added as new subdivision (c), which is drawn from Criminal Rule 31(d) with minor revisions to reflect Civil Rules Style and the parties' opportunity to stipulate to a nonunanimous verdict.

Rule 49. Special Verdict; General Verdict and Questions

(a) Special Verdict.

(1) ***In General.*** The court may require a jury to return only a special verdict in the form of a special written finding on each issue of fact. The court may do so by:

(A) submitting written questions susceptible of a categorical or other brief answer;

(B) submitting written forms of the special findings that might properly be made under the pleadings and evidence; or

(C) using any other method that the court considers appropriate.

(2) ***Instructions.*** The court must give the instructions and explanations necessary to enable the jury to make its findings on each submitted issue.

(3) ***Issues Not Submitted.*** A party waives the right to a jury trial on any issue of fact raised by the pleadings or evidence but not submitted to the jury unless, before the jury retires, the party demands its submission to the jury. If the party does not demand submission, the court may make a finding on the issue. If the court makes no finding, it is considered to have made a finding consistent with its judgment on the special verdict.

(b) General Verdict with Answers to Written Questions.

(1) ***In General.*** The court may submit to the jury forms for a general verdict, together with written questions on one or more issues of fact that the jury must decide. The court must give the instructions and explanations necessary to enable the jury to render a general

verdict and answer the questions in writing, and must direct the jury to do both.

(2) ***Verdict and Answers Consistent.*** When the general verdict and the answers are consistent, the court must approve, for entry under Rule 58, an appropriate judgment on the verdict and answers.

(3) ***Answers Inconsistent with the Verdict.*** When the answers are consistent with each other but one or more is inconsistent with the general verdict, the court may:

(A) approve, for entry under Rule 58, an appropriate judgment according to the answers, notwithstanding the general verdict;

(B) direct the jury to further consider its answers and verdict; or

(C) order a new trial.

(4) ***Answers Inconsistent with Each Other and the Verdict.*** When the answers are inconsistent with each other and one or more is also inconsistent with the general verdict, judgment must not be entered; instead, the court must direct the jury to further consider its answers and verdict, or must order a new trial.

Rule 50. Judgment as a Matter of Law in a Jury Trial; Related Motion for a New Trial; Conditional Ruling

(a) Judgment as a Matter of Law.

(1) ***In General.*** If a party has been fully heard on an issue during a jury trial and the court finds that a reasonable jury would not have a legally sufficient evidentiary basis to find for the party on that issue, the court may:

(A) resolve the issue against the party; and

(B) grant a motion for judgment as a matter of law against the party on a claim or defense that, under the controlling law, can be maintained or defeated only with a favorable finding on that issue.

(2) ***Motion.*** A motion for judgment as a matter of law may be made at any time before the case is submitted to the jury. The motion must specify the judgment sought and the law and facts that entitle the movant to the judgment.

(b) Renewing the Motion After Trial; Alternative Motion for a New Trial. If the court does not grant a motion for judgment as a matter of law made under Rule 50(a), the court is considered to have submitted the action to the jury subject to the court's later deciding the legal questions raised by the motion. No later than 28 days after the entry of

judgment — or if the motion addresses a jury issue not decided by a verdict, no later than 28 days after the jury was discharged — the movant may file a renewed motion for judgment as a matter of law and may include an alternative or joint request for a new trial under Rule 59. In ruling on the renewed motion, the court may:

(1) allow judgment on the verdict, if the jury returned a verdict;

(2) order a new trial; or

(3) direct the entry of judgment as a matter of law.

(c) Granting the Renewed Motion; Conditional Ruling on a Motion for a New Trial.

(1) ***In General.*** If the court grants a renewed motion for judgment as a matter of law, it must also conditionally rule on any motion for a new trial by determining whether a new trial should be granted if the judgment is later vacated or reversed. The court must state the grounds for conditionally granting or denying the motion for a new trial.

(2) ***Effect of a Conditional Ruling.*** Conditionally granting the motion for a new trial does not affect the judgment's finality; if the judgment is reversed, the new trial must proceed unless the appellate court orders otherwise. If the motion for a new trial is conditionally denied, the appellee may assert error in that denial; if the judgment is reversed, the case must proceed as the appellate court orders.

(d) Time for a Losing Party's New-Trial Motion. Any motion for a new trial under Rule 59 by a party against whom judgment as a matter of law is rendered must be filed no later than 28 days after the entry of the judgment.

(e) Denying the Motion for Judgment as a Matter of Law; Reversal on Appeal. If the court denies the motion for judgment as a matter of law, the prevailing party may, as appellee, assert grounds entitling it to a new trial should the appellate court conclude that the trial court erred in denying the motion. If the appellate court reverses the judgment, it may order a new trial, direct the trial court to determine whether a new trial should be granted, or direct the entry of judgment.

ADVISORY COMMITTEE NOTES

1963 Amendment [citations omitted without notation — ED.]

Subdivision (a). The practice, after the court has granted a motion for a directed verdict, of requiring the jury to express assent to a verdict they did not reach by their own deliberations serves no useful purpose and may give offense to the members of the jury. The final sentence of the subdivision, added by amendment, provides that the court's order granting a motion for a directed verdict

is effective in itself, and that no action need be taken by the foreman or other members of the jury. No change is intended in the standard to be applied in deciding the motion. To assure this interpretation, and in the interest of simplicity, the traditional term, "directed verdict," is retained.

Subdivision (b). A motion for judgment notwithstanding the verdict will not lie unless it was preceded by a motion for a directed verdict made at the close of all the evidence.

The amendment of the second sentence of this subdivision sets the time limit for making the motion for judgment n.o.v. at 10 days [now 28 days — ED.] after the entry of judgment, rather than 10 days after the reception of the verdict. Thus the time provision is made consistent with that contained in Rule 59(b) (time for motion for new trial) and Rule 52(b) (time for motion to amend findings by the court).

Subdivision (c) deals with the situation where a party joins a motion for a new trial with his motion for judgment n.o.v., or prays for a new trial in the alternative, and the motion for judgment n.o.v. is granted. The procedure to be followed in making rulings on the motion for the new trial, and the consequences of the rulings thereon, were partly set out in *Montgomery Ward & Co. v. Duncan,* 311 U.S. 243, 253 (1940), and have been further elaborated in later cases. See *Cone v. West Virginia Pulp & Paper Co.,* 330 U.S. 212 (1947); *Globe Liquor Co., Inc. v. San Roman,* 332 U.S. 571 (1948); *Fountain v. Filson,* 336 U.S. 681 (1949); *Johnson v. New York, N.H. & H.R.R. Co.*, 344 U.S. 48 (1952). However, courts as well as counsel have often misunderstood the procedure, and it will be helpful to summarize the proper practice in the text of the rule. The amendments do not alter the effects of a jury verdict or the scope of appellate review.

In the situation mentioned, subdivision (c)(1) requires that the court make a "conditional" ruling on the new-trial motion, i.e., a ruling which goes on the assumption that the motion for judgment n.o.v. was erroneously granted and will be reversed or vacated; and the court is required to state its grounds for the conditional ruling. Subdivision (c)(1) [now Rule 50(c)(2) — ED.]then spells out the consequences of a reversal of the judgment in the light of the conditional ruling on the new-trial motion.

If the motion for new trial has been conditionally granted, and the judgment is reversed, "the new trial shall proceed unless the appellate court has otherwise ordered." [With modifications, this language is now contained in Rule 50(c)(2) — ED.] The party against whom the judgment n.o.v. was entered below may, as appellant, besides seeking to overthrow that judgment, also attack the conditional grant of the new trial. And the appellate court, if it reverses the judgment n.o.v., may in an appropriate case also reverse the conditional grant of the new trial and direct that judgment be entered on the verdict.

If the motion for a new trial has been conditionally denied, and the judgment is reversed, "subsequent proceedings shall be in accordance with the order of the appellate court" [now "the case must proceed as the appellate court orders," *see* Fed. R. Civ. P. 50(c)(2) — ED.] The party in whose favor judgment n.o.v. was entered below may, as appellee, besides seeking to uphold that judgment, also urge on the appellate court that the trial court committed error in conditionally denying the new trial. The appellee may assert this error in his brief, without taking a

cross-appeal. If the appellate court concludes that the judgment cannot stand, but accepts the appellee's contention that there was error in the conditional denial of the new trial, it may order a new trial in lieu of directing the entry of judgment upon the verdict.

Subdivision (c)(2) [now Rule 50(d) — ED.], which also deals with the situation where the trial court has granted the motion for judgment n.o.v., states that the verdict-winner may apply to the trial court for a new trial pursuant to Rule 59 after the judgment n.o.v. has been entered against him. In arguing to the trial court in opposition to the motion for judgment n.o.v., the verdict-winner may, and often will, contend that he is entitled, at the least, to a new trial, and the court has a range of discretion to grant a new trial or (where plaintiff won the verdict) to order a dismissal of the action without prejudice instead of granting judgment n.o.v. See *Cone v. West Virginia Pulp & Paper Co.,* supra, 330 U.S. at 217, 218. Subdivision (c)(2) is a reminder that the verdict-winner is entitled, even after entry of judgment n.o.v. against him, to move for a new trial in the usual course. If in these circumstances the motion is granted, the judgment is superseded.

In some unusual circumstances, however, the grant of the new-trial motion may be only conditional, and the judgment will not be superseded. See the situation in *Tribble v. Bruin,* 279 F.2d 424 (4th Cir. 1960) (upon a verdict for plaintiff, defendant moves for and obtains judgment n.o.v.; plaintiff moves for a new trial on the ground of inadequate damages; trial court might properly have granted plaintiff's motion, conditional upon reversal of the judgment n.o.v.).

Even if the verdict-winner makes no motion for a new trial, he is entitled upon his appeal from the judgment n.o.v. not only to urge that that judgment should be reversed and judgment entered upon the verdict, but that errors were committed during the trial which at the least entitle him to a new trial.

Subdivision (d) [now Rule 50(e) — ED.] deals with the situation where judgment has been entered on the jury verdict, the motion for judgment n.o.v. and any motion for a new trial having been denied by the trial court. The verdict-winner, as appellee, besides seeking to uphold the judgment may urge upon the appellate court that in case the trial court is found to have erred in entering judgment on the verdict, there are grounds for granting him a new trial instead of directing the entry of judgment for his opponent. In appropriate cases the appellate court is not precluded from itself directing that a new trial be had. See *Weade v. Dichmann, Wright & Pugh, Inc.,* 337 U.S. 801 (1949). Nor is it precluded in proper cases from remanding the case for a determination by the trial court as to whether a new trial should be granted. The latter course is advisable where the grounds urged are suitable for the exercise of trial court discretion.

Subdivision (d) does not attempt a regulation of all aspects of the procedure where the motion for judgment n.o.v. and any accompanying motion for a new trial are denied, since the problems have not been fully canvassed in the decisions and the procedure is in some respects still in a formative stage. It is, however, designed to give guidance on certain important features of the practice.

1991 Amendment [citations omitted without notation — ED.]

Subdivision (a). The revision of this subdivision aims to facilitate the exercise by the court of its responsibility to assure the fidelity of its judgment to the

controlling law, a responsibility imposed by the Due Process Clause of the Fifth Amendment. *Cf. Galloway v. United States,* 319 U.S. 372 (1943).

The revision abandons the familiar terminology of *direction of verdict* for several reasons. The term is misleading as a description of the relationship between judge and jury. It is also freighted with anachronisms some of which are the subject of the text of former subdivision (a) of this rule that is deleted in this revision. Thus, it should not be necessary to state in the text of this rule that a motion made pursuant to it is not a waiver of the right to jury trial, and only the antiquities of directed verdict practice suggest that it might have been. The term "judgment as a matter of law" is an almost equally familiar term and appears in the text of Rule 56; its use in Rule 50 calls attention to the relationship between the two rules. Finally, the change enables the rule to refer to preverdict and post-verdict motions with a terminology that does not conceal the common identity of two motions made at different times in the proceeding.

If a motion is denominated a motion for directed verdict or for judgment notwithstanding the verdict, the party's error is merely formal. Such a motion should be treated as a motion for judgment as a matter of law in accordance with this rule.

Paragraph (a)(1) articulates the standard for the granting of a motion for judgment as a matter of law. It effects no change in the existing standard. That existing standard was not expressed in the former rule, but was articulated in long-standing case law. *See generally* Cooper, *Directions for Directed Verdicts: A Compass for Federal Courts,* 55 MINN. L. REV. 903 (1971). The expressed standard makes clear that action taken under the rule is a performance of the court's duty to assure enforcement of the controlling law and is not an intrusion on any responsibility for factual determinations conferred on the jury by the Seventh Amendment or any other provision of federal law. Because this standard is also used as a reference point for entry of summary judgment under [Rule] 56(a), it serves to link the two related provisions.

The revision authorizes the court to perform its duty to enter judgment as a matter of law at any time during the trial, as soon as it is apparent that either party is unable to carry a burden of proof that is essential to that party's case. Thus, the second sentence of paragraph (a)(1) authorizes the court to consider a motion for judgment as a matter of law as soon as a party has completed a presentation on a fact essential to that party's case. [N.B. The language referred to was subsequently moved to the first clause of Rule 50(a)(1) — ED.] Such early action is appropriate when economy and expedition will be served. In no event, however, should the court enter judgment against a party who has not been apprised of the materiality of the dispositive fact and been afforded an opportunity to present any available evidence bearing on that fact. In order further to facilitate the exercise of the authority provided by this rule, Rule 16 is also revised to encourage the court to schedule an order of trial that proceeds first with a presentation on an issue that is likely to be dispositive, if such an issue is identified in the course of pretrial. Such scheduling can be appropriate where the court is uncertain whether favorable action should be taken under Rule 56. Thus, the revision affords the court the alternative of denying a motion for summary judgment while scheduling a separate trial of the issue under Rule 42(b) or

scheduling the trial to begin with a presentation on that essential fact which the opposing party seems unlikely to be able to maintain.

Paragraph (a)(2) retains the requirement that a motion for judgment be made prior to the close of the trial, subject to renewal after a jury verdict has been rendered. The purpose of this requirement is to assure the responding party an opportunity to cure any deficiency in that party's proof that may have been overlooked until called to the party's attention by a late motion for judgment. Cf. *Farley Transp. Co. v. Santa Fe Trail Transp. Co.,* 786 F.2d 1342 (9th Cir. 1986) ("If the moving party is then permitted to make a later attack on the evidence through a motion for judgment notwithstanding the verdict or an appeal, the opposing party may be prejudiced by having lost the opportunity to present additional evidence before the case was submitted to the jury"). At one time, this requirement was held to be of constitutional stature, being compelled by the Seventh Amendment. Cf. *Slocum v. New York Insurance Co.,* 228 U.S. 364 (1913). But cf. *Baltimore & Carolina Line v. Redman,* 295 U.S. 654 (1935).

The second sentence of paragraph (a)(2) does impose a requirement that the moving party articulate the basis on which a judgment as a matter of law might be rendered. The articulation is necessary to achieve the purpose of the requirement that the motion be made before the case is submitted to the jury, so that the responding party may seek to correct any overlooked deficiencies in the proof. The revision thus alters the result in cases in which courts have used various techniques to avoid the requirement that a motion for a directed verdict be made as a predicate to a motion for judgment notwithstanding the verdict. . . . The information required with the motion may be supplied by explicit reference to materials and argument previously supplied to the court. . . .

This subdivision deals only with the entry of judgment and not with the resolution of particular factual issues as a matter of law. The court may, as before, properly refuse to instruct a jury to decide an issue if a reasonable jury could on the evidence presented decide that issue in only one way.

Subdivision (b). This provision retains the concept of the former rule that the post-verdict motion is a renewal of an earlier motion made at the close of the evidence. One purpose of this concept was to avoid any question arising under the Seventh Amendment. *Montgomery Ward & Co. v. Duncan,* 311 U.S. 243 (1940). It remains useful as a means of defining the appropriate issue posed by the post-verdict motion. A post-trial motion for judgment can be granted only on grounds advanced in the pre-verdict motion.

Often it appears to the court or to the moving party that a motion for judgment as a matter of law made at the close of the evidence should be reserved for a post-verdict decision. This is so because a jury verdict for the moving party moots the issue and because a preverdict ruling gambles that a reversal may result in a new trial that might have been avoided. For these reasons, the court may often wisely decline to rule on a motion for judgment as a matter of law made at the close of the evidence, and it is not inappropriate for the moving party to suggest such a postponement of the ruling until after the verdict has been rendered.

In ruling on such a motion, the court should disregard any jury determination for which there is no legally sufficient evidentiary basis enabling a reasonable jury to make it. The court may then decide such issues as a matter of law and enter

judgment if all other material issues have been decided by the jury on the basis of legally sufficient evidence, or by the court as a matter of law.

The revised rule is intended for use in this manner with Rule 49. Thus, the court may combine facts established as a matter of law either before trial under Rule 56 or at trial on the basis of the evidence presented with other facts determined by the jury under instructions provided under Rule 49 to support a proper judgment under this rule.

This provision also retains the former requirement that a post-trial motion under the rule must be made within 10 days [now 28 days — ED.] after entry of a contrary judgment. The renewed motion must be served and filed as provided by Rule 5. A purpose of this requirement is to meet the requirements of F.R. App. P. 4(a)(4). . . .

1995 Amendment

The only change, other than stylistic, intended by this revision is to prescribe a uniform explicit time for filing of post-judgment motions under this rule — no later than 10 days after entry of the judgment [now 28 days — ED.]. Previously, there was an inconsistency in the wording of Rules 50, 52, and 59 with respect to whether certain post-judgment motions had to be filed, or merely served, during that period. This inconsistency caused special problems when motions for a new trial were joined with other post-judgment motions. These motions affect the finality of the judgment, a matter often of importance to third persons as well as the parties and the court. The Committee believes that each of these rules should be revised to require filing before end of the 10-day [now 28-day — ED.] period. Filing is an event that can be determined with certainty from court records. . . .

2006 Amendment

. . .

Rule 50(b) is amended to permit renewal of any Rule 50(a) motion for judgment as a matter of law, deleting the requirement that a motion be made at the close of all the evidence. Because the Rule 50(b) motion is only a renewal of the preverdict motion, it can be granted only on grounds advanced in the preverdict motion. The earlier motion informs the opposing party of the challenge to the sufficiency of the evidence and affords a clear opportunity to provide additional evidence that may be available. The earlier motion also alerts the court to the opportunity to simplify the trial by resolving some issues, or even all issues, without submission to the jury. This fulfillment of the functional needs that underlie present Rule 50(b) also satisfies the Seventh Amendment. Automatic reservation of the legal questions raised by the motion conforms to the decision in *Baltimore & Carolina Line v. Redman*, 297 U.S. 654 (1935).

This change responds to many decisions that have begun to move away from requiring a motion for judgment as a matter of law at the literal close of all the evidence. Although the requirement has been clearly established for several decades, lawyers continue to overlook it. The courts are slowly working away from the formal requirement. The amendment establishes the functional approach that courts have been unable to reach under the present rule and makes practice more consistent and predictable.

Many judges expressly invite motions at the close of all the evidence. The amendment is not intended to discourage this useful practice.

Finally, an explicit time limit is added for making a posttrial motion when the trial ends without a verdict or with a verdict that does not dispose of all issues suitable for resolution by verdict. The motion must be made no later than 10 days [now 28 days — ED.] after the jury was discharged.

2007 Amendment

. . .

Amended Rule 50(e) identifies the appellate court's authority to direct the entry of judgment. This authority was not described in former Rule 50(d), but was recognized in *Weisgram v. Marley Co.*, 528 U.S. 440 (2000), and in *Neely v. Martin K. Eby Construction Company*, 386 U.S. 317 (1967). When Rule 50(d) was drafted in 1963, the Committee Note stated that "[s]ubdivision (d) does not attempt a regulation of all aspects of the procedure where the motion for judgment n.o.v. and any accompanying motion for a new trial are denied . . . ." Express recognition of the authority to direct entry of judgment does not otherwise supersede this caution.

Rule 51. Instructions to the Jury; Objections; Preserving a Claim of Error

(a) Requests.

(1) ***Before or at the Close of the Evidence***. At the close of the evidence or at any earlier reasonable time that the court orders, a party may file and furnish to every other party written requests for the jury instructions it wants the court to give.

(2) ***After the Close of the Evidence***. After the close of the evidence, a party may:

(A) file requests for instructions on issues that could not reasonably have been anticipated by an earlier time that the court set for requests; and

(B) with the court's permission, file untimely requests for instructions on any issue.

(b) Instructions. The court:

(1) must inform the parties of its proposed instructions and proposed action on the requests before instructing the jury and before final jury arguments;

(2) must give the parties an opportunity to object on the record and out of the jury's hearing before the instructions and arguments are delivered; and

(3) may instruct the jury at any time before the jury is discharged.

(c) Objections.

(1) ***How to Make.*** A party who objects to an instruction or the failure to give an instruction must do so on the record, stating distinctly the matter objected to and the grounds for the objection.

(2) ***When to Make.*** An objection is timely if:

(A) a party objects at the opportunity provided under Rule 51(b)(2); or

(B) a party was not informed of an instruction or action on a request before that opportunity to object, and the party objects promptly after learning that the instruction or request will be, or has been, given or refused.

(d) Assigning Error; Plain Error.

(1) ***Assigning Error.*** A party may assign as error:

(A) an error in an instruction actually given, if that party properly objected; or

(B) a failure to give an instruction, if that party properly requested it and — unless the court rejected the request in a definitive ruling on the record — also properly objected.

(2) ***Plain Error.*** A court may consider a plain error in the instructions that has not been preserved as required by Rule 51(d)(1) if the error affects substantial rights.

ADVISORY COMMITTEE NOTES

2003 Amendment

Rule 51 is revised to capture many of the interpretations that have emerged in practice. The revisions in text will make uniform the conclusions reached by a majority of decisions on each point. . . .

Scope. Rule 51 governs instructions to the trial jury on the law that governs the verdict. A variety of other instructions cannot practicably be brought within Rule 51. Among these instructions are preliminary instructions to a venire, and cautionary or limiting instructions delivered in immediate response to events at trial.

Requests. Subdivision (a) governs requests. Apart from the plain error doctrine recognized in subdivision (d)(2), a court is not obliged to instruct the jury on issues raised by the evidence unless a party requests an instruction. The revised rule recognizes the court's authority to direct that requests be submitted before trial.

The close-of-the-evidence deadline may come before trial is completed on all potential issues. Trial may be formally bifurcated or may be sequenced in some less formal manner. The close of the evidence is measured by the occurrence of two events: completion of all intended evidence on an identified phase of the trial and impending submission to the jury with instructions.

The risk in directing a pretrial request deadline is that trial evidence may raise new issues or reshape issues the parties thought they had understood. Courts need not insist on pretrial requests in all cases. Even if the request time is set before trial or early in the trial, subdivision (a)(2)(A) permits requests after the close of the evidence to address issues that could not reasonably have been anticipated at the earlier time for requests set by the court.

Subdivision (a)(2)(B) expressly recognizes the court's discretion to act on an untimely request. The most important consideration in exercising the discretion confirmed by subdivision (a)(2)(B) is the importance of the issue to the case — the closer the issue lies to the "plain error" that would be recognized under subdivision (d)(2), the better the reason to give an instruction. The cogency of the reason for failing to make a timely request also should be considered. To be considered under subdivision (a)(2)(B) a request should be made before final instructions and before final jury arguments. What is a "final" instruction and argument depends on the sequence of submitting the case to the jury. If separate portions of the case are submitted to the jury in sequence, the final arguments and final instructions are those made on submitting to the jury the portion of the case addressed by the arguments and instructions.

Instructions. Subdivision (b)(1) requires the court to inform the parties, before instructing the jury and before final jury arguments related to the instruction, of the proposed instructions as well as the proposed action on instruction requests. The time limit is addressed to final jury arguments to reflect the practice that allows interim argument s during trial in complex cases; it may not be feasible to develop final instructions before such interim arguments. It is enough that counsel know of the intended instructions before making final arguments addressed to the issue. If the trial is sequenced or bifurcated, the final arguments addressed to an issue may occur before the close of the entire trial.

Subdivision (b)(2) complements subdivision (b)(1) by carrying forward the opportunity to object established by present Rule 51. It makes explicit the opportunity to object on the record, ensuring a clear memorial of the objection.

Subdivision (b)(3) reflects common practice by authorizing instructions at any time after trial begins and before the jury is discharged.

Objections. Subdivision (c) states the right to object to an instruction or the failure to give an instruction. It carries forward the formula of present Rule 51 requiring that the objection state distinctly the matter objected to and the grounds of the objection, and makes explicit the requirement that the objection be made on the record. The provisions on the time to object make clear that it is timely to object promptly after learning of an instruction or action on a request when the court has not provided advance information as required by subdivision (b)(1). The need to repeat a request by way of objection is continued by new subdivision (d)(1)(B) except where the court made a definitive ruling on the record.

Preserving a claim of error and plain error. Many cases hold that a proper request for a jury instruction is not alone enough to preserve the right to appeal failure to give the instruction. The request must be renewed by objection. This doctrine is appropriate when the court may not have sufficiently focused on the request, or may believe that the request has been granted in substance although in different words. But this doctrine may also prove a trap for the unwary who fail

to add an objection after the court has made it clear that the request has been considered and rejected on the merits. Subdivision (d)(1)(B) establishes authority to review the failure to grant a timely request, despite a failure to add an objection, when the court has made a definitive ruling on the record rejecting the request.

Many circuits have recognized that an error not preserved under Rule 51 may be reviewed in exceptional circumstances. The language adopted to capture these decisions in subdivision (d)(2) is borrowed from Criminal Rule 52. Although the language is the same, the context of civil litigation often differs from the context of criminal prosecution; actual application of the plain-error standard takes account of the differences. The Supreme Court has summarized application of Criminal Rule 52 as involving four elements: (1) there must be an error; (2) the error must be plain; (3) the error must affect substantial rights; and (4) the error must seriously affect the fairness, integrity, or public reputation of judicial proceedings. Johnson v. U.S., 520 U.S. 461, 466-467, 469-470 (1997).

The court's duty to give correct jury instructions in a civil action is shaped by at least four factors.

The factor most directly implied by a "plain" error rule is the obviousness of the mistake. The importance of the error is a second major factor. The costs of correcting an error reflect a third factor that is affected by a variety of circumstances. In a case that seems close to the fundamental error line, account also may be taken of the impact a verdict may have on nonparties.

Rule 52. Findings and Conclusions by the Court; Judgment on Partial Findings

(a) Findings and Conclusions.

(1) ***In General.*** In an action tried on the facts without a jury or with an advisory jury, the court must find the facts specially and state its conclusions of law separately. The findings and conclusions may be stated on the record after the close of the evidence or may appear in an opinion or a memorandum of decision filed by the court. Judgment must be entered under Rule 58.

(2) ***For an Interlocutory Injunction.*** In granting or refusing an interlocutory injunction, the court must similarly state the findings and conclusions that support its action.

(3) ***For a Motion.*** The court is not required to state findings or conclusions when ruling on a motion under Rule 12 or 56 or, unless these rules provide otherwise, on any other motion.

(4) ***Effect of a Master's Findings.*** A master's findings, to the extent adopted by the court, must be considered the court's findings.

(5) ***Questioning the Evidentiary Support.*** A party may later question the sufficiency of the evidence supporting the findings,

whether or not the party requested findings, objected to them, moved to amend them, or moved for partial findings.

(6) ***Setting Aside the Findings***. Findings of fact, whether based on oral or other evidence, must not be set aside unless clearly erroneous, and the reviewing court must give due regard to the trial court's opportunity to judge the witnesses' credibility.

(b) Amended or Additional Findings. On a party's motion filed no later than 28 days after the entry of judgment, the court may amend its findings — or make additional findings — and may amend the judgment accordingly. The motion may accompany a motion for a new trial under Rule 59.

(c) Judgment on Partial Findings. If a party has been fully heard on an issue during a nonjury trial and the court finds against the party on that issue, the court may enter judgment against the party on a claim or defense that, under the controlling law, can be maintained or defeated only with a favorable finding on that issue. The court may, however, decline to render any judgment until the close of the evidence. A judgment on partial findings must be supported by findings of fact and conclusions of law as required by Rule 52(a).

Rule 53. Masters

(a) Appointment.

(1) ***Scope***. Unless a statute provides otherwise, a court may appoint a master only to:

(A) perform duties consented to by the parties;

(B) hold trial proceedings and make or recommend findings of fact on issues to be decided without a jury if appointment is warranted by:

(i) some exceptional condition; or

(ii) the need to perform an accounting or resolve a difficult computation of damages; or

(C) address pretrial and posttrial matters that cannot be effectively and timely addressed by an available district judge or magistrate judge of the district.

(2) ***Disqualification***. A master must not have a relationship to the parties, attorneys, action, or court that would require disqualification of a judge under 28 U.S.C. § 455, unless the parties, with the court's approval, consent to the appointment after the master discloses any potential grounds for disqualification.

(3) ***Possible Expense or Delay***. In appointing a master, the court must consider the fairness of imposing the likely expenses on the parties and must protect against unreasonable expense or delay.

(b) Order Appointing a Master.

(1) ***Notice***. Before appointing a master, the court must give the parties notice and an opportunity to be heard. Any party may suggest candidates for appointment.

(2) ***Contents***. The appointing order must direct the master to proceed with all reasonable diligence and must state:

(A) the master's duties, including any investigation or enforcement duties, and any limits on the master's authority under Rule 53(c);

(B) the circumstances, if any, in which the master may communicate ex parte with the court or a party;

(C) the nature of the materials to be preserved and filed as the record of the master's activities;

(D) the time limits, method of filing the record, other procedures, and standards for reviewing the master's orders, findings, and recommendations; and

(E) the basis, terms, and procedure for fixing the master's compensation under Rule 53(g).

(3) ***Issuing***. The court may issue the order only after:

(A) the master files an affidavit disclosing whether there is any ground for disqualification under 28 U.S.C. § 455; and

(B) if a ground is disclosed, the parties, with the court's approval, waive the disqualification.

(4) ***Amending***. The order may be amended at any time after notice to the parties and an opportunity to be heard.

(c) Master's Authority.

(1) ***In General.*** Unless the appointing order directs otherwise, a master may:

(A) regulate all proceedings;

(B) take all appropriate measures to perform the assigned duties fairly and efficiently; and

(C) if conducting an evidentiary hearing, exercise the appointing court's power to compel, take, and record evidence.

(2) ***Sanctions***. The master may by order impose on a party any noncontempt sanction provided by Rule 37 or 45, and may recommend a contempt sanction against a party and sanctions against a nonparty.

(d) Master's Orders. A master who issues an order must file it and promptly serve a copy on each party. The clerk must enter the order on the docket.

(e) Master's Reports. A master must report to the court as required by the appointing order. The master must file the report and promptly serve a copy on each party, unless the court orders otherwise.

(f) Action on the Master's Order, Report, or Recommendations.

(1) ***Opportunity for a Hearing; Action in General***. In acting on a master's order, report, or recommendations, the court must give the parties notice and an opportunity to be heard; may receive evidence; and may adopt or affirm, modify, wholly or partly reject or reverse, or resubmit to the master with instructions.

(2) ***Time to Object or Move to Adopt or Modify***. A party may file objections to — or a motion to adopt or modify — the master's order, report, or recommendations no later than 21 days after a copy is served, unless the court sets a different time.

(3) ***Reviewing Factual Findings***. The court must decide de novo all objections to findings of fact made or recommended by a master, unless the parties, with the court's approval, stipulate that:

(A) the findings will be reviewed for clear error; or

(B) the findings of a master appointed under Rule 53(a)(1)(A) or (C) will be final.

(4) ***Reviewing Legal Conclusions***. The court must decide de novo all objections to conclusions of law made or recommended by a master.

(5) ***Reviewing Procedural Matters***. Unless the appointing order establishes a different standard of review, the court may set aside a master's ruling on a procedural matter only for an abuse of discretion.

(g) Compensation.

(1) ***Fixing Compensation***. Before or after judgment, the court must fix the master's compensation on the basis and terms stated in the appointing order, but the court may set a new basis and terms after giving notice and an opportunity to be heard.

(2) ***Payment***. The compensation must be paid either:

(A) by a party or parties; or

(B) from a fund or subject matter of the action within the court's control.

(3) ***Allocating Payment.*** The court must allocate payment among the parties after considering the nature and amount of the controversy, the parties' means, and the extent to which any party is more responsible than other parties for the reference to a master. An interim allocation may be amended to reflect a decision on the merits.

(h) Appointing a Magistrate Judge. A magistrate judge is subject to this rule only when the order referring a matter to the magistrate judge states that the reference is made under this rule.

TITLE VII. JUDGMENT

Rule 54. Judgment; Costs

(a) Definition; Form. "Judgment" as used in these rules includes a decree and any order from which an appeal lies. A judgment should not include recitals of pleadings, a master's report, or a record of prior proceedings.

(b) Judgment on Multiple Claims or Involving Multiple Parties. When an action presents more than one claim for relief — whether as a claim, counterclaim, crossclaim, or third-party claim — or when multiple parties are involved, the court may direct entry of a final judgment as to one or more, but fewer than all, claims or parties only if the court expressly determines that there is no just reason for delay. Otherwise, any order or other decision, however designated, that adjudicates fewer than all the claims or the rights and liabilities of fewer than all the parties does not end the action as to any of the claims or parties and may be revised at any time before the entry of a judgment adjudicating all the claims and all the parties' rights and liabilities.

(c) Demand for Judgment; Relief to Be Granted. A default judgment must not differ in kind from, or exceed in amount, what is demanded in the pleadings. Every other final judgment should grant the relief to which each party is entitled, even if the party has not demanded that relief in its pleadings.

(d) Costs; Attorney's Fees.

(1) ***Costs Other Than Attorney's Fees.*** Unless a federal statute, these rules, or a court order provides otherwise, costs — other than attorney's fees — should be allowed to the prevailing party. But costs against the United States, its officers, and its agencies may be imposed only to the extent allowed by law. The clerk may tax costs on 14 days' notice. On motion served within the next 7 days, the court may review the clerk's action.

(2) ***Attorney's Fees.***

(A) *Claim to Be by Motion.* A claim for attorney's fees and related nontaxable expenses must be made by motion unless the substantive law requires those fees to be proved at trial as an element of damages.

(B) *Timing and Contents of the Motion.* Unless a statute or a court order provides otherwise, the motion must:

(i) be filed no later than 14 days after the entry of judgment;

(ii) specify the judgment and the statute, rule, or other grounds entitling the movant to the award;

(iii) state the amount sought or provide a fair estimate of it; and

(iv) disclose, if the court so orders, the terms of any agreement about fees for the services for which the claim is made.

(C) *Proceedings.* Subject to Rule 23(h), the court must, on a party's request, give an opportunity for adversary submissions on the motion in accordance with Rule 43(c) or 78. The court may decide issues of liability for fees before receiving submissions on the value of services. The court must find the facts and state its conclusions of law as provided in Rule 52(a).

(D) *Special Procedures by Local Rule; Reference to a Master or a Magistrate Judge.* By local rule, the court may establish special procedures to resolve fee-related issues without extensive evidentiary hearings. Also, the court may refer issues concerning the value of services to a special master under Rule 53 without regard to the limitations of Rule 53(a)(1), and may refer a motion for attorney's fees to a magistrate judge under Rule 72(b) as if it were a dispositive pretrial matter.

(E) *Exceptions.* Subparagraphs (A)-(D) do not apply to claims for fees and expenses as sanctions for violating these rules or as sanctions under 28 U.S.C. § 1927.

Rule 55. Default; Default Judgment

(a) Entering a Default. When a party against whom a judgment for affirmative relief is sought has failed to plead or otherwise defend, and that failure is shown by affidavit or otherwise, the clerk must enter the party's default.

(b) Entering a Default Judgment.

(1) ***By the Clerk.*** If the plaintiff's claim is for a sum certain or a sum that can be made certain by computation, the clerk — on the plaintiff's request, with an affidavit showing the amount due — must enter judgment for that amount and costs against a defendant who has been defaulted for not appearing and who is neither a minor nor an incompetent person.

(2) ***By the Court.*** In all other cases, the party must apply to the court for a default judgment. A default judgment may be entered against a minor or incompetent person only if represented by a general guardian, conservator, or other like fiduciary who has appeared. If the party against whom a default judgment is sought has appeared personally or by a representative, that party or its representative must be served with written notice of the application at least 7 days before the hearing. The court may conduct hearings or make referrals — preserving any federal statutory right to a jury trial — when, to enter or effectuate judgment, it needs to:

(A) conduct an accounting;

(B) determine the amount of damages;

(C) establish the truth of any allegation by evidence; or

(D) investigate any other matter.

(c) Setting Aside a Default or a Default Judgment. The court may set aside an entry of default for good cause, and it may set aside a final default judgment under Rule 60(b).

(d) Judgment Against the United States. A default judgment may be entered against the United States, its officers, or its agencies only if the claimant establishes a claim or right to relief by evidence that satisfies the court.

Rule 56. Summary Judgment

(a) Motion for Summary Judgment or Partial Summary Judgment. A party may move for summary judgment, identifying each claim or defense — or the part of each claim or defense — on which summary judgment is sought. The court shall grant summary judgment if the movant shows that there is no genuine dispute as to any material fact and the movant is entitled to judgment as a matter of law. The court should state on the record the reasons for granting or denying the motion.

(b) Time to File a Motion. Unless a different time is set by local rule or the court orders otherwise, a party may file a motion for summary judgment at any time until 30 days after the close of all discovery.

(c) Procedures.

(1) ***Supporting Factual Positions.*** A party asserting that a fact cannot be or is genuinely disputed must support the assertion by:

(A) citing to particular parts of materials in the record, including depositions, documents, electronically stored information, affidavits or declarations, stipulations (including those made for purposes of the motion only), admissions, interrogatory answers, or other materials; or

(B) showing that the materials cited do not establish the absence or presence of a genuine dispute, or that an adverse party cannot produce admissible evidence to support the fact.

(2) ***Objection That a Fact Is Not Supported by Admissible Evidence.*** A party may object that the material cited to support or dispute a fact cannot be presented in a form that would be admissible in evidence.

(3) ***Materials Not Cited.*** The court need consider only the cited materials, but it may consider other materials in the record.

(4) ***Affidavits or Declarations.*** An affidavit or declaration used to support or oppose a motion must be made on personal knowledge, set out facts that would be admissible in evidence, and show that the affiant or declarant is competent to testify on the matters stated.

(d) When Facts Are Unavailable to the Nonmovant. If a nonmovant shows by affidavit or declaration that, for specified reasons, it cannot present facts essential to justify its opposition, the court may:

(1) defer considering the motion or deny it;

(2) allow time to obtain affidavits or declarations or to take discovery; or

(3) issue any other appropriate order.

(e) Failing to Properly Support or Address a Fact. If a party fails to properly support an assertion of fact or fails to properly address another party's assertion of fact as required by Rule 56(c), the court may:

(1) give an opportunity to properly support or address the fact;

(2) consider the fact undisputed for purposes of the motion;

(3) grant summary judgment if the motion and supporting materials — including the facts considered undisputed — show that the movant is entitled to it; or

(4) issue any other appropriate order.

(f) Judgment Independent of the Motion. After giving notice and a reasonable time to respond, the court may:

(1) grant summary judgment for a nonmovant;

(2) grant the motion on grounds not raised by a party; or

(3) consider summary judgment on its own after identifying for the parties material facts that may not be genuinely in dispute.

(g) Failing to Grant All the Requested Relief. If the court does not grant all the relief requested by the motion, it may enter an order stating any material fact — including an item of damages or other relief — that is not genuinely in dispute and treating the fact as established in the case.

(h) Affidavit or Declaration Submitted in Bad Faith. If satisfied that an affidavit or declaration under this rule is submitted in bad faith or solely for delay, the court — after notice and a reasonable time to respond — may order the submitting party to pay the other party the reasonable expenses, including attorney's fees, it incurred as a result. An offending party or attorney may also be held in contempt or subjected to other appropriate sanctions.

ADVISORY COMMITTEE NOTES

1963 Amendment [citations omitted without notation — ED.]

. . .

Subdivision (e) [now with alterations subdivision (c) — ED.]. . . .

. . . [In some cases, a] party supports his motion for summary judgment by affidavits or other evidentiary matter sufficient to show that there is no genuine issue as to a material fact. The adverse party, in opposing the motion, does not produce any evidentiary matter, or produces some but not enough to establish that there is a genuine issue for trial. Instead, the adverse party rests on averments of his pleadings which on their face present an issue. In this situation Third Circuit cases have taken the view that summary judgment must be denied, at least if the averments are "well-pleaded," and not suppositious, conclusory, or ultimate.

The very mission of the summary judgment procedure is to pierce the pleadings and to assess the proof in order to see whether there is a genuine need for trial. The Third Circuit doctrine, which permits the pleadings themselves to stand in the way of granting an otherwise justified summary judgment, is incompatible with the basic purpose of the rule.

It is hoped that the amendment will contribute to the more effective utilization of the salutary device of summary judgment.

The amendment is not intended to derogate from the solemnity of the pleadings. Rather it recognizes that, despite the best efforts of counsel to make his pleadings accurate, they may be overwhelmingly contradicted by the proof available to his adversary. . . .

2007 Amendment

. . .

Former Rule 56(c), (d), and (e) stated circumstances in which summary judgment "shall be rendered," the court "shall if practicable" ascertain facts existing without substantial controversy, and "if appropriate, shall" enter summary judgment. In each place "shall" is changed to "should." It is established that although there is no discretion to enter summary judgment when there is a genuine issue as to any material fact, there is discretion to deny summary judgment when it appears that there is no genuine issue as to any material fact. Kennedy v. Silas Mason Co., 334 U.S. 249, 256-257 (1948). . . . "Should" in amended Rule 56(c) [now Rule 56(a), with "shall" replacing "should" in 2010 — ED.] recognizes that courts will seldom exercise the discretion to deny summary judgment when there is no genuine issue as to any material fact. Similarly sparing exercise of this discretion is appropriate under Rule 56(e)(2) [now Rule 56(c)(1) and -(e) — ED.]. Rule 56(d)(1) [now Rule 56(g) — ED.], on the other hand, reflects the more open-ended discretion to decide whether it is practicable to determine what material facts are not genuinely at issue.

Former Rule 56(d) used a variety of different phrases to express the Rule 56(c) standard for summary judgment — that there is no genuine issue as to any material fact. Amended Rule 56(d) [now Rule 56(g) — ED.] adopts terms directly parallel to Rule 56(c).

2009 Amendment

The timing provisions for summary judgment are outmoded. They are consolidated and substantially revised in new subdivision (c)(1) [now Rule 56(a) — ED.]. The new rule allows a party to move for summary judgment at any time, even as early as the commencement of the action. If the motion seems premature both subdivision (c)(1) [now Rule 56(b) — ED.] and Rule 6(b) allow the court to extend the time to respond. The rule does set a presumptive deadline at 30 days after the close of all discovery.

The presumptive timing rules are default provisions that may be altered by an order in the case or by local rule. Scheduling orders are likely to supersede the rule provisions in most cases, deferring summary-judgment motions until a stated time or establishing different deadlines. Scheduling orders tailored to the needs of the specific case, perhaps adjusted as it progresses, are likely to work better than default rules. A scheduling order may be adjusted to adopt the parties' agreement on timing, or may require that discovery and motions occur in stages — including separation of expert-witness discovery from other discovery.

Local rules may prove useful when local docket conditions or practices are incompatible with the general Rule 56 timing provisions.

If a motion for summary judgment is filed before a responsive pleading is due from a party affected by the motion, the time for responding to the motion is 21 days after the responsive pleading is due.

2010 Amendment [citation omitted without notation — ED.]

Rule 56 is revised to improve the procedures for presenting and deciding summary-judgment motions and to make the procedures more consistent with

those already used in many courts. The standard for granting summary judgment remains unchanged. The language of subdivision (a) continues to require that there be no genuine dispute as to any material fact and that the movant be entitled to judgment as a matter of law. The amendments will not affect continuing development of the decisional law construing and applying these phrases.

Subdivision (a). Subdivision (a) carries forward the summary-judgment standard expressed in former subdivision (c), changing only one word — genuine "issue" becomes genuine "dispute." "Dispute" better reflects the focus of a summary-judgment determination. As explained below, "shall" also is restored to the place it held from 1938 to 2007.

The first sentence is added to make clear at the beginning that summary judgment may be requested not only as to an entire case but also as to a claim, defense, or part of a claim or defense. The subdivision caption adopts the common phrase "partial summary judgment" to describe disposition of less than the whole action, whether or not the order grants all the relief requested by the motion.

"Shall" is restored to express the direction to grant summary judgment. The word "shall" in Rule 56 acquired significance over many decades of use. Rule 56 was amended in 2007 to replace "shall" with "should" as part of the Style Project, acting under a convention that prohibited any use of "shall." Comments on proposals to amend Rule 56, as published in 2008, have shown that neither of the choices available under the Style Project conventions — "must" or "should" — is suitable in light of the case law on whether a district court has discretion to deny summary judgment when there appears to be no genuine dispute as to any material fact. Compare *Anderson v. Liberty Lobby, Inc.*, 477 U.S. 242, 255 (1986) ("Neither do we suggest that the trial courts should act other than with caution in granting summary judgment or that the trial court may not deny summary judgment in a case in which there is reason to believe that the better course would be to proceed to a full trial. *Kennedy v. Silas Mason Co.*, 334 U.S. 249 . . . (1948)[."),] with *Celotex Corp. v. Catrett*, 477 U.S. 317, 322 (1986) ("In our view, the plain language of Rule 56(c) mandates the entry of summary judgment, after adequate time for discovery and upon motion, against a party who fails to make a showing sufficient to establish the existence of an element essential to that party's case, and on which that party will bear the burden of proof at trial."). Eliminating "shall" created an unacceptable risk of changing the summary-judgment standard. Restoring "shall" avoids the unintended consequences of any other word.

Subdivision (a) also adds a new direction that the court should state on the record the reasons for granting or denying the motion. Most courts recognize this practice. Among other advantages, a statement of reasons can facilitate an appeal or subsequent trial-court proceedings. It is particularly important to state the reasons for granting summary judgment. The form and detail of the statement of reasons are left to the court's discretion.

The statement on denying summary judgment need not address every available reason. But identification of central issues may help the parties to focus further proceedings.

Subdivision (b). The timing provisions in former subdivisions (a) and (c) are superseded. Although the rule allows a motion for summary judgment to be filed at the commencement of an action, in many cases the motion will be premature

until the nonmovant has had time to file a responsive pleading or other pretrial proceedings have been had. Scheduling orders or other pretrial orders can regulate timing to fit the needs of the case.

Subdivision (c). Subdivision (c) is new. It establishes a common procedure for several aspects of summary-judgment motions synthesized from similar elements developed in the cases or found in many local rules.

Subdivision (c)(1) addresses the ways to support an assertion that a fact can or cannot be genuinely disputed. It does not address the form for providing the required support. Different courts and judges have adopted different forms including, for example, directions that the support be included in the motion, made part of a separate statement of facts, interpolated in the body of a brief or memorandum, or provided in a separate statement of facts included in a brief or memorandum.

Subdivision (c)(1)(A) describes the familiar record materials commonly relied upon and requires that the movant cite the particular parts of the materials that support its fact positions. Materials that are not yet in the record — including materials referred to in an affidavit or declaration — must be placed in the record. Once materials are in the record, the court may, by order in the case, direct that the materials be gathered in an appendix, a party may voluntarily submit an appendix, or the parties may submit a joint appendix. The appendix procedure also may be established by local rule. Pointing to a specific location in an appendix satisfies the citation requirement. So too it may be convenient to direct that a party assist the court in locating materials buried in a voluminous record.

Subdivision (c)(1)(B) recognizes that a party need not always point to specific record materials. One party, without citing any other materials, may respond or reply that materials cited to dispute or support a fact do not establish the absence or presence of a genuine dispute. And a party who does not have the trial burden of production may rely on a showing that a party who does have the trial burden cannot produce admissible evidence to carry its burden as to the fact.

Subdivision (c)(2) provides that a party may object that material cited to support or dispute a fact cannot be presented in a form that would be admissible in evidence. The objection functions much as an objection at trial, adjusted for the pretrial setting. The burden is on the proponent to show that the material is admissible as presented or to explain the admissible form that is anticipated. There is no need to make a separate motion to strike. If the case goes to trial, failure to challenge admissibility at the summary-judgment stage does not forfeit the right to challenge admissibility at trial.

Subdivision (c)(3) reflects judicial opinions and local rules provisions stating that the court may decide a motion for summary judgment without undertaking an independent search of the record. Nonetheless, the rule also recognizes that a court may consider record materials not called to its attention by the parties.

Subdivision (c)(4) carries forward some of the provisions of former subdivision (e)(1). Other provisions are relocated or omitted. The requirement that a sworn or certified copy of a paper referred to in an affidavit or declaration be attached to the affidavit or declaration is omitted as unnecessary given the requirement in subdivision (c)(1)(A) that a statement or dispute of fact be supported by materials in the record.

A formal affidavit is no longer required. 28 U.S.C. § 1746 allows a written unsworn declaration, certificate, verification, or statement subscribed in proper form as true under penalty of perjury to substitute for an affidavit.

Subdivision (d). Subdivision (d) carries forward without substantial change the provisions of former subdivision (f).

A party who seeks relief under subdivision (d) may seek an order deferring the time to respond to the summary-judgment motion.

Subdivision (e). Subdivision (e) addresses questions that arise when a party fails to support an assertion of fact or fails to properly address another party's assertion of fact as required by Rule 56(c). As explained below, summary judgment cannot be granted by default even if there is a complete failure to respond to the motion, much less when an attempted response fails to comply with Rule 56(c) requirements. Nor should it be denied by default even if the movant completely fails to reply to a nonmovant's response. Before deciding on other possible action, subdivision (e)(1) recognizes that the court may afford an opportunity to properly support or address the fact. In many circumstances this opportunity will be the court's preferred first step.

Subdivision (e)(2) authorizes the court to consider a fact as undisputed for purposes of the motion when response or reply requirements are not satisfied. This approach reflects the "deemed admitted" provisions in many local rules. The fact is considered undisputed only for purposes of the motion; if summary judgment is denied, a party who failed to make a proper Rule 56 response or reply remains free to contest the fact in further proceedings. And the court may choose not to consider the fact as undisputed, particularly if the court knows of record materials that show grounds for genuine dispute.

Subdivision (e)(3) recognizes that the court may grant summary judgment only if the motion and supporting materials — including the facts considered undisputed under subdivision (e)(2) — show that the movant is entitled to it. Considering some facts undisputed does not of itself allow summary judgment. If there is a proper response or reply as to some facts, the court cannot grant summary judgment without determining whether those facts can be genuinely disputed. Once the court has determined the set of facts — both those it has chosen to consider undisputed for want of a proper response or reply and any that cannot be genuinely disputed despite a procedurally proper response or reply — it must determine the legal consequences of these facts and permissible inferences from them.

Subdivision (e)(4) recognizes that still other orders may be appropriate. The choice among possible orders should be designed to encourage proper presentation of the record. Many courts take extra care with pro se litigants, advising them of the need to respond and the risk of losing by summary judgment if an adequate response is not filed. And the court may seek to reassure itself by some examination of the record before granting summary judgment against a pro se litigant.

Subdivision (f). Subdivision (f) brings into Rule 56 text a number of related procedures that have grown up in practice. After giving notice and a reasonable time to respond the court may grant summary judgment for the nonmoving party;

grant a motion on legal or factual grounds not raised by the parties; or consider summary judgment on its own. In many cases it may prove useful first to invite a motion; the invited motion will automatically trigger the regular procedure of subdivision (c).

Subdivision (g). Subdivision (g) applies when the court does not grant all the relief requested by a motion for summary judgment. It becomes relevant only after the court has applied the summary-judgment standard carried forward in subdivision (a) to each claim, defense, or part of a claim or defense, identified by the motion. Once that duty is discharged, the court may decide whether to apply the summary-judgment standard to dispose of a material fact that is not genuinely in dispute. The court must take care that this determination does not interfere with a party's ability to accept a fact for purposes of the motion only. A nonmovant, for example, may feel confident that a genuine dispute as to one or a few facts will defeat the motion, and prefer to avoid the cost of detailed response to all facts stated by the movant. This position should be available without running the risk that the fact will be taken as established under subdivision (g) or otherwise found to have been accepted for other purposes.

If it is readily apparent that the court cannot grant all the relief requested by the motion, it may properly decide that the cost of determining whether some potential fact disputes may be eliminated by summary disposition is greater than the cost of resolving those disputes by other means, including trial. Even if the court believes that a fact is not genuinely in dispute it may refrain from ordering that the fact be treated as established. The court may conclude that it is better to leave open for trial facts and issues that may be better illuminated by the trial of related facts that must be tried in any event.

Subdivision (h). Subdivision (h) carries forward former subdivision (g) with three changes. Sanctions are made discretionary, not mandatory, reflecting the experience that courts seldom invoke the independent Rule 56 authority to impose sanctions. In addition, the rule text is expanded to recognize the need to provide notice and a reasonable time to respond. Finally, authority to impose other appropriate sanctions also is recognized.

Rule 57. Declaratory Judgment

These rules govern the procedure for obtaining a declaratory judgment under 28 U.S.C. § 2201. Rules 38 and 39 govern a demand for a jury trial. The existence of another adequate remedy does not preclude a declaratory judgment that is otherwise appropriate. The court may order a speedy hearing of a declaratory-judgment action.

Rule 58. Entering Judgment

(a) Separate Document. Every judgment and amended judgment must be set out in a separate document, but a separate document is not required for an order disposing of a motion:

(1) for judgment under Rule 50(b);

(2) to amend or make additional findings under Rule 52(b);

(3) for attorney's fees under Rule 54;

(4) for a new trial, or to alter or amend the judgment, under Rule 59; or

(5) for relief under Rule 60.

(b) Entering Judgment.

(1) ***Without the Court's Direction.*** Subject to Rule 54(b) and unless the court orders otherwise, the clerk must, without awaiting the court's direction, promptly prepare, sign, and enter the judgment when:

(A) the jury returns a general verdict;

(B) the court awards only costs or a sum certain; or

(C) the court denies all relief.

(2) ***Court's Approval Required.*** Subject to Rule 54(b), the court must promptly approve the form of the judgment, which the clerk must promptly enter, when:

(A) the jury returns a special verdict or a general verdict with answers to written questions; or

(B) the court grants other relief not described in this subdivision (b).

(c) Time of Entry. For purposes of these rules, judgment is entered at the following times:

(1) if a separate document is not required, when the judgment is entered in the civil docket under Rule 79(a); or

(2) if a separate document is required, when the judgment is entered in the civil docket under Rule 79(a) and the earlier of these events occurs:

(A) it is set out in a separate document; or

(B) 150 days have run from the entry in the civil docket.

(d) Request for Entry. A party may request that judgment be set out in a separate document as required by Rule 58(a).

(e) Cost or Fee Awards. Ordinarily, the entry of judgment may not be delayed, nor the time for appeal extended, in order to tax costs or award fees. But if a timely motion for attorney's fees is made under Rule 54(d)(2), the court may act before a notice of appeal has been filed and become effective to order that the motion have the same effect under Federal Rule of Appellate Procedure 4(a)(4) as a timely motion under Rule 59.

Rule 59. New Trial; Altering or Amending a Judgment

(a) In General.

(1) ***Grounds for New Trial.*** The court may, on motion, grant a new trial on all or some of the issues — and to any party — as follows:

(A) after a jury trial, for any reason for which a new trial has heretofore been granted in an action at law in federal court; or

(B) after a nonjury trial, for any reason for which a rehearing has heretofore been granted in a suit in equity in federal court.

(2) ***Further Action After a Nonjury Trial.*** After a nonjury trial, the court may, on motion for a new trial, open the judgment if one has been entered, take additional testimony, amend findings of fact and conclusions of law or make new ones, and direct the entry of a new judgment.

(b) Time to File a Motion for a New Trial. A motion for a new trial must be filed no later than 28 days after the entry of judgment.

(c) Time to Serve Affidavits. When a motion for a new trial is based on affidavits, they must be filed with the motion. The opposing party has 14 days after being served to file opposing affidavits. The court may permit reply affidavits.

(d) New Trial on the Court's Initiative or for Reasons Not in the Motion. No later than 28 days after the entry of judgment, the court, on its own, may order a new trial for any reason that would justify granting one on a party's motion. After giving the parties notice and an opportunity to be heard, the court may grant a timely motion for a new trial for a reason not stated in the motion. In either event, the court must specify the reasons in its order.

(e) Motion to Alter or Amend a Judgment. A motion to alter or amend a judgment must be filed no later than 28 days after the entry of the judgment.

Rule 60. Relief from a Judgment or Order

(a) Corrections Based on Clerical Mistakes; Oversights and Omissions. The court may correct a clerical mistake or a mistake arising from oversight or omission whenever one is found in a judgment, order, or other part of the record. The court may do so on motion or on its own, with or without notice. But after an appeal has been docketed in the appellate court and while it is pending, such a mistake may be corrected only with the appellate court's leave.

(b) Grounds for Relief from a Final Judgment, Order, or Proceeding. On motion and just terms, the court may relieve a party or its legal representative from a final judgment, order, or proceeding for the following reasons:

(1) mistake, inadvertence, surprise, or excusable neglect;

(2) newly discovered evidence that, with reasonable diligence, could not have been discovered in time to move for a new trial under Rule 59(b);

(3) fraud (whether previously called intrinsic or extrinsic), misrepresentation, or misconduct by an opposing party;

(4) the judgment is void;

(5) the judgment has been satisfied, released or discharged; it is based on an earlier judgment that has been reversed or vacated; or applying it prospectively is no longer equitable; or

(6) any other reason that justifies relief.

(c) Timing and Effect of the Motion.

(1) ***Timing***. A motion under Rule 60(b) must be made within a reasonable time — and for reasons (1), (2), and (3) no more than a year after the entry of the judgment or order or the date of the proceeding.

(2) ***Effect on Finality***. The motion does not affect the judgment's finality or suspend its operation.

(d) Other Powers to Grant Relief. This rule does not limit a court's power to:

(1) entertain an independent action to relieve a party from a judgment, order, or proceeding;

(2) grant relief under 28 U.S.C. § 1655 to a defendant who was not personally notified of the action; or

(3) set aside a judgment for fraud on the court.

(e) Bills and Writs Abolished. The following are abolished: bills of review, bills in the nature of bills of review, and writs of coram nobis, coram vobis, and audita querela.

Rule 61. Harmless Error

Unless justice requires otherwise, no error in admitting or excluding evidence — or any other error by the court or a party — is ground for granting a new trial, for setting aside a verdict, or for vacating, modifying, or otherwise disturbing a judgment or order. At every stage of the

proceeding, the court must disregard all errors and defects that do not affect any party's substantial rights.

Rule 62. Stay of Proceedings to Enforce a Judgment

(a) Automatic Stay; Exceptions for Injunctions, Receiverships, and Patent Accountings. Except as stated in this rule, no execution may issue on a judgment, nor may proceedings be taken to enforce it, until 14 days have passed after its entry. But unless the court orders otherwise, the following are not stayed after being entered, even if an appeal is taken:

(1) an interlocutory or final judgment in an action for an injunction or a receivership; or

(2) a judgment or order that directs an accounting in an action for patent infringement.

(b) Stay Pending the Disposition of a Motion. On appropriate terms for the opposing party's security, the court may stay the execution of a judgment — or any proceedings to enforce it — pending disposition of any of the following motions:

(1) under Rule 50, for judgment as a matter of law;

(2) under Rule 52(b), to amend the findings or for additional findings;

(3) under Rule 59, for a new trial or to alter or amend a judgment; or

(4) under Rule 60, for relief from a judgment or order.

(c) Injunction Pending an Appeal. While an appeal is pending from an interlocutory order or final judgment that grants, dissolves, or denies an injunction, the court may suspend, modify, restore, or grant an injunction on terms for bond or other terms that secure the opposing party's rights. If the judgment appealed from is rendered by a statutory three-judge district court, the order must be made either:

(1) by that court sitting in open session; or

(2) by the assent of all its judges, as evidenced by their signatures.

(d) Stay with Bond on Appeal. If an appeal is taken, the appellant may obtain a stay by supersedeas bond, except in an action described in Rule 62(a)(1) or (2). The bond may be given upon or after filing the notice of appeal or after obtaining the order allowing the appeal. The stay takes effect when the court approves the bond.

(e) Stay Without Bond on an Appeal by the United States, Its Officers, or Its Agencies. The court must not require a bond, obligation, or other security from the appellant when granting a stay on an appeal by

the United States, its officers, or its agencies or on an appeal directed by a department of the federal government.

(f) Stay in Favor of a Judgment Debtor Under State Law. If a judgment is a lien on the judgment debtor's property under the law of the state where the court is located, the judgment debtor is entitled to the same stay of execution the state court would give.

(g) Appellate Court's Power Not Limited. This rule does not limit the power of the appellate court or one of its judges or justices:

(1) to stay proceedings — or suspend, modify, restore, or grant an injunction — while an appeal is pending; or

(2) to issue an order to preserve the status quo or the effectiveness of the judgment to be entered.

(h) Stay with Multiple Claims or Parties. A court may stay the enforcement of a final judgment entered under Rule 54(b) until it enters a later judgment or judgments, and may prescribe terms necessary to secure the benefit of the stayed judgment for the party in whose favor it was entered.

Rule 62.1. Indicative Ruling on a Motion for Relief That is Barred by a Pending Appeal

(a) Relief Pending Appeal. If a timely motion is made for relief that the court lacks authority to grant because of an appeal that has been docketed and is pending, the court may:

(1) defer considering the motion;

(2) deny the motion; or

(3) state either that it would grant the motion if the court of appeals remands for that purpose or that the motion raises a substantial issue.

(b) Notice to the Court of Appeals. The movant must promptly notify the circuit clerk under Federal Rule of Appellate Procedure 12.1 if the district court states that it would grant the motion or that the motion raises a substantial issue.

(c) Remand. The district court may decide the motion if the court of appeals remands for that purpose.

Rule 63. Judge's Inability to Proceed

If a judge conducting a hearing or trial is unable to proceed, any other judge may proceed upon certifying familiarity with the record and

determining that the case may be completed without prejudice to the parties. In a hearing or a nonjury trial, the successor judge must, at a party's request, recall any witness whose testimony is material and disputed and who is available to testify again without undue burden. The successor judge may also recall any other witness.

TITLE VIII. PROVISIONAL AND FINAL REMEDIES

Rule 64. Seizing a Person or Property

(a) Remedies Under State Law — In General. At the commencement of and throughout an action, every remedy is available that, under the law of the state where the court is located, provides for seizing a person or property to secure satisfaction of the potential judgment. But a federal statute governs to the extent it applies.

(b) Specific Kinds of Remedies. The remedies available under this rule include the following — however designated and regardless of whether state procedure requires an independent action:

- arrest;
- attachment;
- garnishment;
- replevin;
- sequestration; and
- other corresponding or equivalent remedies.

Rule 65. Injunctions and Restraining Orders

(a) Preliminary Injunction.

(1) ***Notice.*** The court may issue a preliminary injunction only on notice to the adverse party.

(2) ***Consolidating the Hearing with the Trial on the Merits.*** Before or after beginning the hearing on a motion for a preliminary injunction, the court may advance the trial on the merits and consolidate it with the hearing. Even when consolidation is not ordered, evidence that is received on the motion and that would be admissible at trial becomes part of the trial record and need not be repeated at trial. But the court must preserve any party's right to a jury trial.

(b) Temporary Restraining Order.

(1) ***Issuing Without Notice.*** The court may issue a temporary restraining order without written or oral notice to the adverse party or its attorney only if:

(A) specific facts in an affidavit or a verified complaint clearly show that immediate and irreparable injury, loss, or damage will result to the movant before the adverse party can be heard in opposition; and

(B) the movant's attorney certifies in writing any efforts made to give notice and the reasons why it should not be required.

(2) ***Contents; Expiration.*** Every temporary restraining order issued without notice must state the date and hour it was issued; describe the injury and state why it is irreparable; state why the order was issued without notice; and be promptly filed in the clerk's office and entered in the record. The order expires at the time after entry — not to exceed 14 days — that the court sets, unless before that time the court, for good cause, extends it for a like period or the adverse party consents to a longer extension. The reasons for an extension must be entered in the record.

(3) ***Expediting the Preliminary-Injunction Hearing.*** If the order is issued without notice, the motion for a preliminary injunction must be set for hearing at the earliest possible time, taking precedence over all other matters except hearings on older matters of the same character. At the hearing, the party who obtained the order must proceed with the motion; if the party does not, the court must dissolve the order.

(4) ***Motion to Dissolve.*** On 2 days' notice to the party who obtained the order without notice — or on shorter notice set by the court — the adverse party may appear and move to dissolve or modify the order. The court must then hear and decide the motion as promptly as justice requires.

(c) Security. The court may issue a preliminary injunction or a temporary restraining order only if the movant gives security in an amount that the court considers proper to pay the costs and damages sustained by any party found to have been wrongfully enjoined or restrained. The United States, its officers, and its agencies are not required to give security.

(d) Contents and Scope of Every Injunction and Restraining Order.

(1) ***Contents.*** Every order granting an injunction and every restraining order must:

(A) state the reasons why it issued;

(B) state its terms specifically; and

(C) describe in reasonable detail — and not by referring to the complaint or other document — the act or acts restrained or required.

(2) ***Persons Bound***. The order binds only the following who receive actual notice of it by personal service or otherwise:

(A) the parties;

(B) the parties' officers, agents, servants, employees, and attorneys; and

(C) other persons who are in active concert or participation with anyone described in Rule 65(d)(2)(A) or (B).

(e) Other Laws Not Modified. These rules do not modify the following:

(1) any federal statute relating to temporary restraining orders or preliminary injunctions in actions affecting employer and employee;

(2) 28 U.S.C. § 2361, which relates to preliminary injunctions in actions of interpleader or in the nature of interpleader; or

(3) 28 U.S.C. § 2284, which relates to actions that must be heard and decided by a three-judge district court.

(f) Copyright Impoundment. This rule applies to copyright-impoundment proceedings.

Rule 65.1. Proceedings Against a Surety

Whenever these rules (including the Supplemental Rules for Admiralty or Maritime Claims and Asset Forfeiture Actions) require or allow a party to give security, and security is given through a bond or other undertaking with one or more sureties, each surety submits to the court's jurisdiction and irrevocably appoints the court clerk as its agent for receiving service of any papers that affect its liability on the bond or undertaking. The surety's liability may be enforced on motion without an independent action. The motion and any notice that the court orders may be served on the court clerk, who must promptly mail a copy of each to every surety whose address is known.

Rule 66. Receivers

These rules govern an action in which the appointment of a receiver is sought or a receiver sues or is sued. But the practice in administering an

estate by a receiver or a similar court-appointed officer must accord with the historical practice in federal courts or with a local rule. An action in which a receiver has been appointed may be dismissed only by court order.

Rule 67. Deposit into Court

(a) Depositing Property. If any part of the relief sought is a money judgment or the disposition of a sum of money or some other deliverable thing, a party — on notice to every other party and by leave of court — may deposit with the court all or part of the money or thing, whether or not that party claims any of it. The depositing party must deliver to the clerk a copy of the order permitting deposit.

(b) Investing and Withdrawing Funds. Money paid into court under this rule must be deposited and withdrawn in accordance with 28 U.S.C. §§ 2041 and 2042 and any like statute. The money must be deposited in an interest-bearing account or invested in a court-approved, interest-bearing instrument.

Rule 68. Offer of Judgment

(a) Making an Offer; Judgment on an Accepted Offer. At least 14 days before the date set for trial, a party defending against a claim may serve on an opposing party an offer to allow judgment on specified terms, with the costs then accrued. If, within 14 days after being served, the opposing party serves written notice accepting the offer, either party may then file the offer and notice of acceptance, plus proof of service. The clerk must then enter judgment.

(b) Unaccepted Offer. An unaccepted offer is considered withdrawn, but it does not preclude a later offer. Evidence of an unaccepted offer is not admissible except in a proceeding to determine costs.

(c) Offer After Liability is Determined. When one party's liability to another has been determined but the extent of liability remains to be determined by further proceedings, the party held liable may make an offer of judgment. It must be served within a reasonable time — but at least 14 days — before the date set for a hearing to determine the extent of liability.

(d) Paying Costs After an Unaccepted Offer. If the judgment that the offeree finally obtains is not more favorable than the unaccepted offer, the offeree must pay the costs incurred after the offer was made.

Rule 69. Execution

(a) In General.

(1) ***Money Judgment; Applicable Procedure.*** A money judgment is enforced by a writ of execution, unless the court directs otherwise. The procedure on execution — and in proceedings supplementary to and in aid of judgment or execution — must accord with the procedure of the state where the court is located, but a federal statute governs to the extent it applies.

(2) ***Obtaining Discovery.*** In aid of the judgment or execution, the judgment creditor or a successor in interest whose interest appears of record may obtain discovery from any person — including the judgment debtor — as provided in these rules or by the procedure of the state where the court is located.

(b) Against Certain Public Officers. When a judgment has been entered against a revenue officer in the circumstances stated in 28 U.S.C. § 2006, or against an officer of Congress in the circumstances stated in 2 U.S.C. § 118, the judgment must be satisfied as those statutes provide.

Rule 70. Enforcing a Judgment for a Specific Act

(a) Party's Failure to Act; Ordering Another to Act. If a judgment requires a party to convey land, to deliver a deed or other document, or to perform any other specific act and the party fails to comply within the time specified, the court may order the act to be done — at the disobedient party's expense — by another person appointed by the court. When done, the act has the same effect as if done by the party.

(b) Vesting Title. If the real or personal property is within the district, the court — instead of ordering a conveyance — may enter a judgment divesting any party's title and vesting it in others. That judgment has the effect of a legally executed conveyance.

(c) Obtaining a Writ of Attachment or Sequestration. On application by a party entitled to performance of an act, the clerk must issue a writ of attachment or sequestration against the disobedient party's property to compel obedience.

(d) Obtaining a Writ of Execution or Assistance. On application by a party who obtains a judgment or order for possession, the clerk must issue a writ of execution or assistance.

(e) Holding in Contempt. The court may also hold the disobedient party in contempt.

Rule 71. Enforcing Relief for or Against a Nonparty

When an order grants relief for a nonparty or may be enforced against a nonparty, the procedure for enforcing the order is the same as for a party.

TITLE IX. SPECIAL PROCEEDINGS

Rule 71.1. Condemning Real or Personal Property

(a) Applicability of Other Rules. These rules govern proceedings to condemn real and personal property by eminent domain, except as this rule provides otherwise.

(b) Joinder of Properties. The plaintiff may join separate pieces of property in a single action, no matter whether they are owned by the same persons or sought for the same use.

(c) Complaint.

(1) *Caption*. The complaint must contain a caption as provided in Rule 10(a). The plaintiff must, however, name as defendants both the property — designated generally by kind, quantity, and location — and at least one owner of some part of or interest in the property.

(2) *Contents*. The complaint must contain a short and plain statement of the following:

(A) the authority for the taking;

(B) the uses for which the property is to be taken;

(C) a description sufficient to identify the property;

(D) the interests to be acquired; and

(E) for each piece of property, a designation of each defendant who has been joined as an owner or owner of an interest in it.

(3) *Parties*. When the action commences, the plaintiff need join as defendants only those persons who have or claim an interest in the property and whose names are then known. But before any hearing on compensation, the plaintiff must add as defendants all those persons who have or claim an interest and whose names have become known or can be found by a reasonably diligent search of the records, considering both the property's character and value and the interests to be acquired. All others may be made defendants under the designation "Unknown Owners."

(4) *Procedure*. Notice must be served on all defendants as provided in Rule 71.1(d), whether they were named as defendants when the action commenced or were added later. A defendant may answer as provided in Rule 71.1(e). The court, meanwhile, may order any distribution of a deposit that the facts warrant.

(5) *Filing; Additional Copies*. In addition to filing the complaint, the plaintiff must give the clerk at least one copy for the defendants' use and additional copies at the request of the clerk or a defendant.

(d) Process.

(1) *Delivering Notice to the Clerk*. On filing a complaint, the plaintiff must promptly deliver to the clerk joint or several notices directed to the named defendants. When adding defendants, the plaintiff must deliver to the clerk additional notices directed to the new defendants.

(2) *Contents of the Notice*.

(A) *Main Contents*. Each notice must name the court, the title of the action, and the defendant to whom it is directed. It must describe the property sufficiently to identify it, but need not describe any property other than that to be taken from the named defendant. The notice must also state:

(i) that the action is to condemn property;

(ii) the interest to be taken;

(iii) the authority for the taking;

(iv) the uses for which the property is to be taken;

(v) that the defendant may serve an answer on the plaintiff's attorney within 21 days after being served with the notice;

(vi) that the failure to so serve an answer constitutes consent to the taking and to the court's authority to proceed with the action and fix the compensation; and

(vii) that a defendant who does not serve an answer may file a notice of appearance.

(B) *Conclusion*. The notice must conclude with the name, telephone number, and e-mail address of the plaintiff's attorney and an address within the district in which the action is brought where the attorney may be served.

(3) *Serving the Notice*.

(A) *Personal Service*. When a defendant whose address is known resides within the United States or a territory subject to the

administrative or judicial jurisdiction of the United States, personal service of the notice (without a copy of the complaint) must be made in accordance with Rule 4.

(B) *Service by Publication.*

(i) A defendant may be served by publication only when the plaintiff's attorney files a certificate stating that the attorney believes the defendant cannot be personally served, because after diligent inquiry within the state where the complaint is filed, the defendant's place of residence is still unknown or, if known, that it is beyond the territorial limits of personal service. Service is then made by publishing the notice — once a week for at least three successive weeks — in a newspaper published in the county where the property is located or, if there is no such newspaper, in a newspaper with general circulation where the property is located. Before the last publication, a copy of the notice must also be mailed to every defendant who cannot be personally served but whose place of residence is then known. Unknown owners may be served by publication in the same manner by a notice addressed to "Unknown Owners."

(ii) Service by publication is complete on the date of the last publication. The plaintiff's attorney must prove publication and mailing by a certificate, attach a printed copy of the published notice, and mark on the copy the newspaper's name and the dates of publication.

(4) ***Effect of Delivery and Service.*** Delivering the notice to the clerk and serving it have the same effect as serving a summons under Rule 4.

(5) ***Proof of Service; Amending the Proof or Notice.*** Rule 4(l) governs proof of service. The court may permit the proof or the notice to be amended.

(e) Appearance or Answer.

(1) ***Notice of Appearance.*** A defendant that has no objection or defense to the taking of its property may serve a notice of appearance designating the property in which it claims an interest. The defendant must then be given notice of all later proceedings affecting the defendant.

(2) ***Answer.*** A defendant that has an objection or defense to the taking must serve an answer within 21 days after being served with the notice. The answer must:

(A) identify the property in which the defendant claims an interest;

(B) state the nature and extent of the interest; and

(C) state all the defendant's objections and defenses to the taking.

(3) ***Waiver of Other Objections and Defenses; Evidence on Compensation.*** A defendant waives all objections and defenses not stated in its answer. No other pleading or motion asserting an additional objection or defense is allowed. But at the trial on compensation, a defendant — whether or not it has previously appeared or answered — may present evidence on the amount of compensation to be paid and may share in the award.

(f) Amending Pleadings. Without leave of court, the plaintiff may — as often as it wants — amend the complaint at any time before the trial on compensation. But no amendment may be made if it would result in a dismissal inconsistent with Rule 71.1(i)(1) or (2). The plaintiff need not serve a copy of an amendment, but must serve notice of the filing, as provided in Rule 5(b), on every affected party who has appeared and, as provided in Rule 71.1(d), on every affected party who has not appeared. In addition, the plaintiff must give the clerk at least one copy of each amendment for the defendants' use, and additional copies at the request of the clerk or a defendant. A defendant may appear or answer in the time and manner and with the same effect as provided in Rule 71.1(e).

(g) Substituting Parties. If a defendant dies, becomes incompetent, or transfers an interest after being joined, the court may, on motion and notice of hearing, order that the proper party be substituted. Service of the motion and notice on a nonparty must be made as provided in Rule 71.1(d)(3).

(h) Trial of the Issues.

(1) ***Issues Other Than Compensation; Compensation.*** In an action involving eminent domain under federal law, the court tries all issues, including compensation, except when compensation must be determined:

(A) by any tribunal specially constituted by a federal statute to determine compensation; or

(B) if there is no such tribunal, by a jury when a party demands one within the time to answer or within any additional time the court sets, unless the court appoints a commission.

(2) ***Appointing a Commission; Commission's Powers and Report.***

(A) *Reasons for Appointing.* If a party has demanded a jury, the court may instead appoint a three-person commission to determine compensation because of the character, location, or quantity of the property to be condemned or for other just reasons.

(B) *Alternate Commissioners.* The court may appoint up to two additional persons to serve as alternate commissioners to hear the case and replace commissioners who, before a decision is filed, the court finds unable or disqualified to perform their duties. Once the commission renders its final decision, the court must discharge any alternate who has not replaced a commissioner.

(C) *Examining the Prospective Commissioners.* Before making its appointments, the court must advise the parties of the identity and qualifications of each prospective commissioner and alternate, and may permit the parties to examine them. The parties may not suggest appointees, but for good cause may object to a prospective commissioner or alternate.

(D) *Commission's Powers and Report.* A commission has the powers of a master under Rule 53(c). Its action and report are determined by a majority. Rule 53(d), (e), and (f) apply to its action and report.

(i) Dismissal of the Action or a Defendant.

(1) ***Dismissing the Action.***

(A) *By the Plaintiff.* If no compensation hearing on a piece of property has begun, and if the plaintiff has not acquired title or a lesser interest or taken possession, the plaintiff may, without a court order, dismiss the action as to that property by filing a notice of dismissal briefly describing the property.

(B) *By Stipulation.* Before a judgment is entered vesting the plaintiff with title or a lesser interest in or possession of property, the plaintiff and affected defendants may, without a court order, dismiss the action in whole or in part by filing a stipulation of dismissal. And if the parties so stipulate, the court may vacate a judgment already entered.

(C) *By Court Order.* At any time before compensation has been determined and paid, the court may, after a motion and hearing, dismiss the action as to a piece of property. But if the plaintiff has already taken title, a lesser interest, or possession as to any part of it, the court must award compensation for the title, lesser interest, or possession taken.

(2) ***Dismissing a Defendant.*** The court may at any time dismiss a defendant who was unnecessarily or improperly joined.

(3) ***Effect***. A dismissal is without prejudice unless otherwise stated in the notice, stipulation, or court order.

(j) Deposit and Its Distribution.

(1) ***Deposit***. The plaintiff must deposit with the court any money required by law as a condition to the exercise of eminent domain and may make a deposit when allowed by statute.

(2) ***Distribution; Adjusting Distribution***. After a deposit, the court and attorneys must expedite the proceedings so as to distribute the deposit and to determine and pay compensation. If the compensation finally awarded to a defendant exceeds the amount distributed to that defendant, the court must enter judgment against the plaintiff for the deficiency. If the compensation awarded to a defendant is less than the amount distributed to that defendant, the court must enter judgment against that defendant for the overpayment.

(k) Condemnation Under a State's Power of Eminent Domain. This rule governs an action involving eminent domain under state law. But if state law provides for trying an issue by jury — or for trying the issue of compensation by jury or commission or both — that law governs.

(*l*) Costs. Costs are not subject to Rule 54(d).

Rule 72. Magistrate Judges: Pretrial Order

(a) Nondispositive Matters. When a pretrial matter not dispositive of a party's claim or defense is referred to a magistrate judge to hear and decide, the magistrate judge must promptly conduct the required proceedings and, when appropriate, issue a written order stating the decision. A party may serve and file objections to the order within 14 days after being served with a copy. A party may not assign as error a defect in the order not timely objected to. The district judge in the case must consider timely objections and modify or set aside any part of the order that is clearly erroneous or is contrary to law.

(b) Dispositive Motions and Prisoner Petitions.

(1) ***Findings and Recommendations***. A magistrate judge must promptly conduct the required proceedings when assigned, without the parties' consent, to hear a pretrial matter dispositive of a claim or defense or a prisoner petition challenging the conditions of confinement. A record must be made of all evidentiary proceedings and may, at the magistrate judge's discretion, be made of any other proceedings. The magistrate judge must enter a recommended

disposition, including, if appropriate, proposed findings of fact. The clerk must promptly mail a copy to each party.

(2) ***Objections***. Within 14 days after being served with a copy of the recommended disposition, a party may serve and file specific written objections to the proposed findings and recommendations. A party may respond to another party's objections within 14 days after being served with a copy. Unless the district judge orders otherwise, the objecting party must promptly arrange for transcribing the record, or whatever portions of it the parties agree to or the magistrate judge considers sufficient.

(3) ***Resolving Objections***. The district judge must determine de novo any part of the magistrate judge's disposition that has been properly objected to. The district judge may accept, reject, or modify the recommended disposition; receive further evidence; or return the matter to the magistrate judge with instructions.

Rule 73. Magistrate Judges: Trial by Consent; Appeal

(a) Trial by Consent. When authorized under 28 U.S.C. § 636(c), a magistrate judge may, if all parties consent, conduct a civil action or proceeding, including a jury or nonjury trial. A record must be made in accordance with 28 U.S.C. § 636(c)(5).

(b) Consent Procedure.

(1) ***In General***. When a magistrate judge has been designated to conduct civil actions or proceedings, the clerk must give the parties written notice of their opportunity to consent under 28 U.S.C. § 636(c). To signify their consent, the parties must jointly or separately file a statement consenting to the referral. A district judge or magistrate judge may be informed of a party's response to the clerk's notice only if all parties have consented to the referral.

(2) ***Reminding the Parties About Consenting***. A district judge, magistrate judge, or other court official may remind the parties of the magistrate judge's availability, but must also advise them that they are free to withhold consent without adverse substantive consequences.

(3) ***Vacating a Referral***. On its own for good cause — or when a party shows extraordinary circumstances — the district judge may vacate a referral to a magistrate judge under this rule.

(c) Appealing a Judgment. In accordance with 28 U.S.C. § 636(c)(3), an appeal from a judgment entered at a magistrate judge's direction may be taken to the court of appeals as would any other appeal from a district-court judgment.

Rule 74. [Abrogated.]

Rule 75. [Abrogated.]

Rule 76. [Abrogated.]

TITLE X. DISTRICT COURTS AND CLERKS: CONDUCTING BUSINESS; ISSUING ORDERS

Rule 77. Conducting Business; Clerk's Authority; Notice of an Order or Judgment

(a) When Court Is Open. Every district court is considered always open for filing any paper, issuing and returning process, making a motion, or entering an order.

(b) Place for Trial and Other Proceedings. Every trial on the merits must be conducted in open court and, so far as convenient, in a regular courtroom. Any other act or proceeding may be done or conducted by a judge in chambers, without the attendance of the clerk or other court official, and anywhere inside or outside the district. But no hearing — other than one ex parte — may be conducted outside the district unless all the affected parties consent.

(c) Clerk's Office Hours; Clerk's Orders.

(1) ***Hours.*** The clerk's office — with a clerk or deputy on duty — must be open during business hours every day except Saturdays, Sundays, and legal holidays. But a court may, by local rule or order, require that the office be open for specified hours on Saturday or a particular legal holiday other than one listed in Rule 6(a)(4)(A).

(2) ***Orders.*** Subject to the court's power to suspend, alter, or rescind the clerk's action for good cause, the clerk may:

(A) issue process;

(B) enter a default;

(C) enter a default judgment under Rule 55(b)(1); and

(D) act on any other matter that does not require the court's action.

(d) Serving Notice of an Order or Judgment.

(1) ***Service.*** Immediately after entering an order or judgment, the clerk must serve notice of the entry, as provided in Rule 5(b), on each

party who is not in default for failing to appear. The clerk must record the service on the docket. A party also may serve notice of the entry as provided in Rule 5(b).

(2) ***Time to Appeal Not Affected by Lack of Notice.*** Lack of notice of the entry does not affect the time for appeal or relieve — or authorize the court to relieve — a party for failing to appeal within the time allowed, except as allowed by Federal Rule of Appellate Procedure (4)(a).

Rule 78. Hearing Motions; Submission on Briefs

(a) Providing a Regular Schedule for Oral Hearings. A court may establish regular times and places for oral hearings on motions.

(b) Providing for Submission on Briefs. By rule or order, the court may provide for submitting and determining motions on briefs, without oral hearings.

Rule 79. Records Kept by the Clerk

(a) Civil Docket.

(1) ***In General.*** The clerk must keep a record known as the "civil docket" in the form and manner prescribed by the Director of the Administrative Office of the United States Courts with the approval of the Judicial Conference of the United States. The clerk must enter each civil action in the docket. Actions must be assigned consecutive file numbers, which must be noted in the docket where the first entry of the action is made.

(2) ***Items to be Entered.*** The following items must be marked with the file number and entered chronologically in the docket:

(A) papers filed with the clerk;

(B) process issued, and proofs of service or other returns showing execution; and

(C) appearances, orders, verdicts, and judgments.

(3) ***Contents of Entries; Jury Trial Demanded.*** Each entry must briefly show the nature of the paper filed or writ issued, the substance of each proof of service or other return, and the substance and date of entry of each order and judgment. When a jury trial has been properly demanded or ordered, the clerk must enter the word "jury" in the docket.

(b) Civil Judgments and Orders. The clerk must keep a copy of every final judgment and appealable order; of every order affecting title to or a lien on real or personal property; and of any other order that the court directs to be kept. The clerk must keep these in the form and manner prescribed by the Director of the Administrative Office of the United States Courts with the approval of the Judicial Conference of the United States.

(c) Indexes; Calendars. Under the court's direction, the clerk must:

(1) keep indexes of the docket and of the judgments and orders described in Rule 79(b); and

(2) prepare calendars of all actions ready for trial, distinguishing jury trials from nonjury trials.

(d) Other Records. The clerk must keep any other records required by the Director of the Administrative Office of the United States Courts with the approval of the Judicial Conference of the United States.

Rule 80. Stenographic Transcript as Evidence

If stenographically reported testimony at a hearing or trial is admissible in evidence at a later trial, the testimony may be proved by a transcript certified by the person who reported it.

TITLE XI. GENERAL PROVISIONS

Rule 81. Applicability of the Rules in General; Removed Actions

(a) Applicability to Particular Proceedings.

(1) ***Prize Proceedings***. These rules do not apply to prize proceedings in admiralty governed by 10 U.S.C. §§ 7651–7681.

(2) ***Bankruptcy***. These rules apply to bankruptcy proceedings to the extent provided by the Federal Rules of Bankruptcy Procedure.

(3) ***Citizenship***. These rules apply to proceedings for admission to citizenship to the extent that the practice in those proceedings is not specified in federal statutes and has previously conformed to the practice in civil actions. The provisions of 8 U.S.C. § 1451 for service by publication and for answer apply in proceedings to cancel citizenship certificates.

(4) ***Special Writs***. These rules apply to proceedings for habeas corpus and for quo warranto to the extent that the practice in those proceedings:

(A) is not specified in a federal statute, the Rules Governing Section 2254 Cases, or the Rules Governing Section 2255 Cases; and

(B) has previously conformed to the practice in civil actions.

(5) ***Proceedings Involving a Subpoena.*** These rules apply to proceedings to compel testimony or the production of documents through a subpoena issued by a United States officer or agency under a federal statute, except as otherwise provided by statute, by local rule, or by court order in the proceedings.

(6) ***Other Proceedings.*** These rules, to the extent applicable, govern proceedings under the following laws, except as these laws provide other procedures:

(A) 7 U.S.C. §§ 292, 499g(c), for reviewing an order of the Secretary of Agriculture;

(B) 9 U.S.C., relating to arbitration;

(C) 15 U.S.C. § 522, for reviewing an order of the Secretary of the Interior;

(D) 15 U.S.C. § 715d(c), for reviewing an order denying a certificate of clearance;

(E) 29 U.S.C. §§ 159, 160, for enforcing an order of the National Labor Relations Board;

(F) 33 U.S.C. §§ 918, 921, for enforcing or reviewing a compensation order under the Longshore and Harbor Workers' Compensation Act; and

(G) 45 U.S.C. § 159, for reviewing an arbitration award in a railway-labor dispute.

(b) Scire Facias and Mandamus. The writs of scire facias and mandamus are abolished. Relief previously available through them may be obtained by appropriate action or motion under these rules.

(c) Removed Actions.

(1) ***Applicability.*** These rules apply to a civil action after it is removed from a state court.

(2) ***Further Pleading.*** After removal, repleading is unnecessary unless the court orders it. A defendant who did not answer before removal must answer or present other defenses or objections under these rules within the longest of these periods:

(A) 21 days after receiving — through service or otherwise — a copy of the initial pleading stating the claim for relief;

(B) 21 days after being served with the summons for an initial pleading on file at the time of service; or

(C) 7 days after the notice of removal is filed.

(3) ***Demand for a Jury Trial.***

(A) *As Affected by State Law.* A party who, before removal, expressly demanded a jury trial in accordance with state law need not renew the demand after removal. If the state law did not require an express demand for a jury trial, a party need not make one after removal unless the court orders the parties to do so within a specified time. The court must so order at a party's request and may so order on its own. A party who fails to make a demand when so ordered waives a jury trial.

(B) *Under Rule 38.* If all necessary pleadings have been served at the time of removal, a party entitled to a jury trial under Rule 38 must be given one if the party serves a demand within 14 days after:

(i) it files a notice of removal; or

(ii) it is served with a notice of removal filed by another party.

(d) Law Applicable.

(1) ***"State Law" Defined.*** When these rules refer to state law, the term "law" includes the state's statutes and the state's judicial decisions.

(2) ***"State" Defined.*** The term "state" includes, where appropriate, the District of Columbia and any United States commonwealth or territory.

(3) ***"Federal Statute" Defined in the District of Columbia.*** In the United States District Court for the District of Columbia, the term "federal statute" includes any Act of Congress that applies locally to the District.

ADVISORY COMMITTEE NOTES

2007 Amendment

. . .

Former Rule 81(e), drafted before the decision in *Erie R.R. v. Tompkins*, 304 U.S. 64 (1938), defined state law to include "the statutes of that state and the state judicial decisions construing them." The *Erie* decision reinterpreted the Rules of Decision Act, now 28 U.S.C. § 1652, recognizing that the "laws" of the states include the common law established by judicial decisions. Long-established practice reflects this understanding, looking to state common law as well as statutes and court rules when a Civil Rule directs use of state law. Amended Rule

81(d)(1) adheres to this practice, including all state judicial decisions, not only those that construe state statutes.

Rule 82. Jurisdiction and Venue Unaffected

These rules do not extend or limit the jurisdiction of the district courts or the venue of actions in those courts. An admiralty or maritime claim under Rule 9(h) is governed by 28 U.S.C. § 1390.

Rule 83. Rules by District Courts; Judge's Directives

(a) Local Rules.

(1) ***In General.*** After giving public notice and an opportunity for comment, a district court, acting by a majority of its district judges, may adopt and amend rules governing its practice. A local rule must be consistent with — but not duplicate — federal statutes and rules adopted under 28 U.S.C. §§ 2072 and 2075, and must conform to any uniform numbering system prescribed by the Judicial Conference of the United States. A local rule takes effect on the date specified by the district court and remains in effect unless amended by the court or abrogated by the judicial council of the circuit. Copies of rules and amendments must, on their adoption, be furnished to the judicial council and the Administrative Office of the United States Courts and be made available to the public.

(2) ***Requirement of Form.*** A local rule imposing a requirement of form must not be enforced in a way that causes a party to lose any right because of a nonwillful failure to comply.

(b) Procedure When There Is No Controlling Law. A judge may regulate practice in any manner consistent with federal law, rules adopted under 28 U.S.C. §§ 2072 and 2075, and the district's local rules. No sanction or other disadvantage may be imposed for noncompliance with any requirement not in federal law, federal rules, or the local rules unless the alleged violator has been furnished in the particular case with actual notice of the requirement.

Rule 84. [Abrogated]

ADVISORY COMMITTEE NOTES

2015 Amendment

Rule 84 was adopted when the Civil Rules were established in 1938 "to indicate, subject to the provisions of these rules, the simplicity and brevity of

statement which the rules contemplate." The purpose of providing illustrations for the rules, although useful when the rules were adopted, has been fulfilled. Accordingly, recognizing that there are many alternative sources for forms, including the website of the Administrative Office of the United States Courts, the websites of many district courts, and local law libraries that contain many commercially published forms, Rule 84 and the Appendix of Forms are no longer necessary and have been abrogated. The abrogation of Rule 84 does not alter existing pleading standards or otherwise change the requirements of Civil Rule 8.

Rule 85. Title

These rules may be cited as the Federal Rules of Civil Procedure.

Rule 86. Effective Dates

(a) In General. These rules and any amendments take effect at the time specified by the Supreme Court, subject to 28 U.S.C. § 2074. They govern:

(1) proceedings in an action commenced after their effective date; and

(2) proceedings after that date in an action then pending unless:

(A) the Supreme Court specifies otherwise; or

(B) the court determines that applying them in a particular action would be infeasible or work an injustice.

(b) December 1, 2007 Amendments. If any provision in Rules 1-5.1, 6-73, or 77-86 conflicts with another law, priority in time for the purpose of 28 U.S.C. § 2072(b) is not affected by the amendments taking effect on December 1, 2007.

* * * * * * *

SUPPLEMENTAL RULES FOR ADMIRALTY OR MARITIME CLAIMS AND ASSET FORFEITURE ACTIONS

[Omitted.]

FEDERAL RULES OF APPELLATE PROCEDURE: SELECTED SECTIONS

TITLE I. APPLICABILITY OF RULES

Rule 1. Scope of Rules; Title

(a) Scope of Rules.

(1) These rules govern procedure in the United States courts of appeals.

(2) When these rules provide for filing a motion or other document in the district court, the procedure must comply with the practice of the district court. . . .

(c) Title. These rules are to be known as the Federal Rules of Appellate Procedure.

TITLE II. APPEAL FROM A JUDGMENT OR ORDER OF A DISTRICT COURT

Rule 3. Appeal as of Right — How Taken

(a) Filing the Notice of Appeal.

(1) An appeal permitted by law as of right from a district court to a court of appeals may be taken only by filing a notice of appeal with the district clerk within the time allowed by Rule 4. . . .

(3) An appeal from a judgment by a magistrate judge in a civil case is taken in the same way as an appeal from any other district court judgment.

(4) An appeal by permission under 28 U.S.C. § 1292(b) . . . may be taken only in the manner prescribed by Rule[ ] 5 . . . .

(c) Contents of the Notice of Appeal.

(1) The notice of appeal must:

(A) specify the party or parties taking the appeal by naming each one in the caption or body of the notice, but an attorney representing more than one party may describe those parties with such terms as "all plaintiffs," "the defendants," "the plaintiffs A, B, et al.," or "all defendants except X";

(B) designate the judgment, order, or part thereof being appealed; and

(C) name the court to which the appeal is taken. . . .

(3) In a class action, whether or not the class has been certified, the notice of appeal is sufficient if it names one person qualified to bring the appeal as representative of the class.

(4) An appeal must not be dismissed for informality of form or title of the notice of appeal, or for failure to name a party whose intent to appeal is otherwise clear from the notice. . . .

(d) Serving the Notice of Appeal.

(1) The district clerk must serve notice of the filing of a notice of appeal by mailing a copy to each party's counsel of record — excluding the appellant's — or, if a party is proceeding pro se, to the party's last known address. . . . The clerk must promptly send a copy of the notice of appeal and of the docket entries — and any later docket entries — to the clerk of the court of appeals named in the notice. The district clerk must note, on each copy, the date when the notice of appeal was filed.

(e) Payment of Fees. Upon filing a notice of appeal, the appellant must pay the district clerk all required fees. The district clerk receives the appellate docket fee on behalf of the court of appeals.

Rule 4. Appeal as of Right — When Taken

(a) Appeal in a Civil Case.

(1) ***Time for Filing a Notice of Appeal.***

(A) In a civil case, except as provided in Rules 4(a)(1)(B), 4(a)(4), and 4(c), the notice of appeal required by Rule 3 must be filed with the district clerk within 30 days after the entry of judgment or order appealed from.

(B) The notice of appeal may be filed by any party within 60 days after entry of the judgment or order appealed from if one of the parties is:

(i) the United States;

(ii) a United States agency;

(iii) a United States officer or employee sued in an official capacity; or

(iv) a current or former United States officer or employee sued in an individual capacity for an act or omission occurring

in connection with duties performed on the United States' behalf — including all instances in which the United States represents that person when the judgment or order is entered or files the appeal for that person. . . .

(2) ***Filing Before Entry of Judgment.*** A notice of appeal filed after the court announces a decision or order — but before the entry of the judgment or order — is treated as filed on the date of and after the entry.

(3) ***Multiple Appeals.*** If one party timely files a notice of appeal, any other party may file a notice of appeal within 14 days after the date when the first notice was filed, or within the time otherwise prescribed by this Rule 4(a), whichever period ends later.

(4) ***Effect of a Motion on a Notice of Appeal.***

(A) If a party files in the district court any of the following motions under the Federal Rules of Civil Procedure — and does so within the time allowed by those rules — the time to file an appeal runs for all parties from the entry of the order disposing of the last such remaining motion:

(i) for judgment under Rule 50(b);

(ii) to amend or make additional factual findings under Rule 52(b), whether or not granting the motion would alter the judgment;

(iii) for attorney's fees under Rule 54 if the district court extends the time to appeal under Rule 58;

(iv) to alter or amend the judgment under Rule 59;

(v) for a new trial under Rule 59; or

(vi) for relief under Rule 60 if the motion is filed no later than 28 days after the judgment is entered.

(B) **(i)** If a party files a notice of appeal after the court announces or enters a judgment — but before it disposes of any motion listed in Rule 4(a)(4)(A) — the notice becomes effective to appeal a judgment or order, in whole or in part, when the order disposing of the last such remaining motion is entered.

(ii) A party intending to challenge an order disposing of any motion listed in Rule 4(a)(4)(A), or a judgment's alteration or amendment upon such a motion, must file a notice of appeal, or an amended notice of appeal — in compliance with Rule 3(c) — within the time prescribed by this Rule measured from the entry of the order disposing of the last such remaining motion.

(iii) No additional fee is required to file an amended notice.

(5) ***Motion for Extension of Time.***

(A) The district court may extend the time to file a notice of appeal if:

(i) a party so moves no later than 30 days after the time prescribed by this Rule 4(a) expires; and

(ii) regardless of whether its motion is filed before or during the 30 days after the time prescribed by this Rule 4(a) expires, that party shows excusable neglect or good cause.

(B) A motion filed before the expiration of the time prescribed in Rule 4(a)(1) or (3) may be ex parte unless the court requires otherwise. If the motion is filed after the expiration of the prescribed time, notice must be given to the other parties in accordance with local rules.

(C) No extension under this Rule 4(a)(5) may exceed 30 days after the prescribed time or 14 days after the date when the order granting the motion is entered, whichever is later.

(6) ***Reopening the Time to File an Appeal.*** The district court may reopen the time to file an appeal for a period of 14 days after the date when its order to reopen is entered, but only if all the following conditions are satisfied:

(A) the court finds that the moving party did not receive notice under Federal Rule of Civil Procedure 77(d) of the entry of the judgment or order sought to be appealed within 21 days after entry;

(B) the motion is filed within 180 days after the judgment or order is entered or within 14 days after the moving party receives notice under Federal Rule of Civil Procedure 77(d) of the entry, whichever is earlier; and

(C) the court finds that no party would be prejudiced.

(7) ***Entry Defined.***

(A) A judgment or order is entered for purposes of this Rule 4(a):

(i) if Federal Rule of Civil Procedure 58(a) does not require a separate document, when the judgment or order is entered in the civil docket under Federal Rule of Civil Procedure 79(a); or

(ii) if Federal Rule of Civil Procedure 58(a) requires a separate document, when the judgment or order is entered in

the civil docket under Federal Rule of Civil Procedure 79(a) and when the earlier of these events occurs:

- the judgment or order is set forth on a separate document, or
- 150 days have run from entry of the judgment or order in the civil docket under Federal Rule of Civil Procedure 79(a).

(B) A failure to set forth a judgment or order on a separate document when required by Federal Rule of Civil Procedure 58(a) does not affect the validity of an appeal from that judgment or order. . . .

(d) Mistaken Filing in the Court of Appeals. If a notice of appeal in either a civil or a criminal case is mistakenly filed in the court of appeals, the clerk of that court must note on the notice the date when it was received and send it to the district clerk. The notice is then considered filed in the district court on the date so noted.

Rule 5. Appeal by Permission

(a) Petition for Permission to Appeal.

(1) To request permission to appeal when an appeal is within the court of appeals' discretion, a party must file a petition for permission to appeal. The petition must be filed with the circuit clerk with proof of service on all other parties to the district-court action.

(2) The petition must be filed within the time specified by the statute or rule authorizing the appeal or, if no such time is specified, within the time provided by Rule 4(a) for filing a notice of appeal.

(3) If a party cannot petition for appeal unless the district court first enters an order granting permission to do so or stating that the necessary conditions are met, the district court may amend its order, either on its own or in response to a party's motion, to include the required permission or statement. In that event, the time to petition runs from entry of the amended order.

(b) Contents of the Petition; Answer or Cross-Petition; Oral Argument.

(1) The petition must include the following:

(A) the facts necessary to understand the question presented;

(B) the question itself;

(C) the relief sought;

(D) the reasons why the appeal should be allowed and is authorized by a statute or rule; and

(E) an attached copy of:

(i) the order, decree, or judgment complained of and any related opinion or memorandum, and

(ii) any order stating the district court's permission to appeal or finding that the necessary conditions are met.

(2) A party may file an answer in opposition or a cross-petition within 10 days after the petition is served. . . .

TITLE VII. GENERAL PROVISIONS

Rule 35. En Banc Determination

(a) When Hearing or Rehearing En Banc May Be Ordered. A majority of the circuit judges who are in regular active service and who are not disqualified may order that an appeal or other proceeding be heard or reheard by the court of appeals en banc. An en banc hearing or rehearing is not favored and ordinarily will not be ordered unless:

(1) en banc consideration is necessary to secure or maintain uniformity of the court's decisions; or

(2) the proceeding involves a question of exceptional importance. . . .

(c) Time for Petition for Hearing or Rehearing En Banc. A petition that an appeal be heard initially en banc must be filed by the date when the appellee's brief is due. A petition for a rehearing en banc must be filed within the time prescribed by Rule 40 for filing a petition for rehearing. . . .

(e) Response. No response may be filed to a petition for an en banc consideration unless the court orders a response. . . .

Rule 38. Frivolous Appeal — Damages and Costs

If a court of appeals determines that an appeal is frivolous, it may, after a separately filed motion or notice from the court and reasonable opportunity to respond, award just damages and single or double costs to the appellee.

Rule 40. Petition for Panel Rehearing

(a) Time to File; Contents; Answer; Action by the Court if Granted.

(1) ***Time***. Unless the time is shortened or extended by order or local rule, a petition for panel rehearing may be filed within 14 days after entry of judgment. But in a civil case, unless an order shortens or extends the time, the petition may be filed by any party within 45 days after entry of judgment if one of the parties is:

(A) the United States;

(B) a United States agency;

(C) a United States officer or employee sued in an official capacity; or

(D) a current or former United States officer or employee sued in an individual capacity for an act or omission occurring in connection with duties performed on the United States' behalf — including all instances in which the United States represents that person when the court of appeals' judgment is entered or files the petition for that person.

(2) ***Contents***. The petition must state with particularity each point of law or fact that the petitioner believes the court has overlooked or misapprehended and must argue in support of the petition. Oral argument is not permitted.

(3) ***Answer***. Unless the court requests, no answer to a petition for panel rehearing is permitted. But ordinarily rehearing will not be granted in the absence of such a request.

(4) ***Action by the Court***. If a petition for panel rehearing is granted, the court may do any of the following:

(A) make a final disposition of the case without reargument;

(B) restore the case to the calendar for reargument or resubmission; or

(C) issue any other appropriate order. . . .

RULES OF THE SUPREME COURT OF THE UNITED STATES: SELECTED SECTIONS

PART I. THE COURT

Rule 3. Term

The Court holds a continuous annual Term commencing on the first Monday in October and ending on the day before the first Monday in October of the following year. See 28 U.S.C. § 2. At the end of each Term, all cases pending on the docket are continued to the next Term.

Rule 4. Sessions and Quorum

1. Open sessions of the Court are held beginning at 10 a.m. on the first Monday in October of each year, and thereafter as announced by the Court. Unless it orders otherwise, the Court sits to hear arguments from 10 a.m. until noon and from 1 p.m. until 3 p.m.

2. Six Members of the Court constitute a quorum. See 28 U.S.C. § 1. In the absence of a quorum on any day appointed for holding a session of the Court, the Justices attending — or if no Justice is present, the Clerk or a Deputy Clerk — may announce that the Court will not meet until there is a quorum.

3. When appropriate, the Court will direct the Clerk or the Marshal to announce recesses.

PART III. JURISDICTION ON WRIT OF CERTIORARI

Rule 10. Considerations Governing Review on Certiorari

Review on a writ of certiorari is not a matter of right, but of judicial discretion. A petition for a writ of certiorari will be granted only for compelling reasons. The following, although neither controlling nor fully measuring the Court's discretion, indicate the character of the reasons the Court considers:

(a) a United States court of appeals has entered a decision in conflict with the decision of another United States court of appeals on the same important matter; has decided an important federal question in a way that conflicts with a decision by a state court of last resort; or has so far departed from the accepted and usual course of judicial

proceedings, or sanctioned such a departure by a lower court, as to call for an exercise of this Court's supervisory power;

(b) a state court of last resort has decided an important federal question in a way that conflicts with the decision of another state court of last resort or of a United States court of appeals;

(c) a state court or a United States court of appeals has decided an important question of federal law that has not been, but should be, settled by this Court, or has decided an important federal question in a way that conflicts with relevant decisions of this Court.

A petition for a writ of certiorari is rarely granted when the asserted error consists of erroneous factual findings or the misapplication of a properly stated rule of law.

Rule 11. Certiorari to a United States Court of Appeals Before Judgment

A petition for a writ of certiorari to review a case pending in a United States court of appeals, before judgment is entered in that court, will be granted only upon a showing that the case is of such imperative public importance as to justify deviation from normal appellate practice and to require immediate determination in this Court. See 28 U.S.C. § 2101(e).

Rule 13. Review on Certiorari: Time for Petitioning

1. Unless otherwise provided by law, a petition for a writ of certiorari to review a judgment in any case, civil or criminal, entered by a state court of last resort or a United States court of appeals (including the United States Court of Appeals for the Armed Forces) is timely when it is filed with the Clerk of this Court within 90 days after entry of the judgment. A petition for a writ of certiorari seeking review of a judgment of a lower state court that is subject to discretionary review by the state court of last resort is timely when it is filed with the Clerk within 90 days after entry of the order denying discretionary review.

2. The Clerk will not file any petition for a writ of certiorari that is jurisdictionally out of time. See, *e.g.*, 28 U.S.C. § 2101(c).

3. The time to file a petition for a writ of certiorari runs from the date of entry of the judgment or order sought to be reviewed, and not from the issuance date of the mandate (or its equivalent under local practice). But if a petition for rehearing is timely filed in the lower court by any party, or if the lower court appropriately entertains an untimely petition for rehearing or *sua sponte* considers rehearing, the time to file the petition for

a writ of certiorari for all parties (whether or not they requested rehearing or joined in the petition for rehearing) runs from the date of the denial of the petition for rehearing or, if the petition for rehearing is granted, the subsequent entry of judgment.

4. A cross-petition for a writ of certiorari is timely when it is filed with the Clerk as provided in paragraphs 1, 3, and 5 of this Rule, or in Rule 12.5. However, a conditional cross-petition (which except for Rule 12.5 would be untimely) will not be granted unless another party's timely petition for a writ of certiorari is granted.

5. For good cause, a Justice may extend the time to file a petition for a writ of certiorari for a period not exceeding 60 days. An application to extend the time to file shall set out the basis for jurisdiction in this Court, identify the judgment sought to be reviewed, include a copy of the opinion and any order respecting rehearing, and set out specific reasons why an extension of time is justified. The application must be filed with the Clerk at least 10 days before the date the petition is due, except in extraordinary circumstances. The application must clearly identify each party for whom an extension is being sought, as any extension that might be granted would apply solely to the party or parties named in the application. For the time and manner of presenting the application, see Rules 21, 22, 30, and 33.2. An application to extend the time to file a petition for a writ of certiorari is not favored.

Rule 16. Disposition of a Petition for a Writ of Certiorari

1. After considering the documents [filed regarding a petition for certiorari], the Court will enter an appropriate order. The order may be a summary disposition on the merits.

2. Whenever the Court grants a petition for a writ of certiorari, the Clerk will prepare, sign, and enter an order to that effect and will notify forthwith counsel of record and the court whose judgment is to be reviewed. The case then will be scheduled for briefing and oral argument. If the record has not previously been filed in this Court, the Clerk will request the clerk of the court having possession of the record to certify and transmit it. A formal writ will not issue unless specially directed.

3. Whenever the Court denies a petition for a writ of certiorari, the Clerk will prepare, sign, and enter an order to that effect and will notify forthwith counsel of record and the court whose judgment was sought to be reviewed. The order of denial will not be suspended pending disposition of a petition for rehearing except by order of the Court or a Justice.

PART IV. OTHER JURISDICTION

Rule 18. Appeal from a United States District Court

1. When a direct appeal from a decision of a United States district court is authorized by law, the appeal is commenced by filing a notice of appeal with the clerk of the district court within the time provided by law after entry of the judgment sought to be reviewed. The time to file may not be extended. The notice of appeal shall specify the parties taking the appeal, designate the judgment, or part thereof, appealed from and the date of its entry, and specify the statute or statutes under which the appeal is taken. . . .

Rule 19. Procedure on a Certified Question

1. A United States court of appeals may certify to this Court a question or proposition of law on which it seeks instruction for the proper decision of a case. The certificate shall contain a statement of the nature of the case and the facts on which the question or proposition of law arises. Only questions or propositions of law may be certified, and they shall be stated separately and with precision. The certificate shall be prepared as required by Rule 33.2 and shall be signed by the clerk of the court of appeals.

2. When a question is certified by a United States court of appeals, this Court, on its own motion or that of a party, may consider and decide the entire matter in controversy. See 28 U.S.C. § 1254(2). . . .

Rule 20. Procedure on a Petition for an Extraordinary Writ

1. Issuance by the Court of an extraordinary writ authorized by 28 U.S.C. § 1651(a) is not a matter of right, but of discretion sparingly exercised. To justify the granting of any such writ, the petition must show that the writ will be in aid of the Court's appellate jurisdiction, that exceptional circumstances warrant the exercise of the Court's discretionary powers, and that adequate relief cannot be obtained in any other form or from any other court. . . .

UNITED STATES CODE: SELECTED SECTIONS

TITLE 28. JUDICIARY AND JUDICIAL PROCEDURE

PART I — ORGANIZATION OF COURTS

CHAPTER 1 — SUPREME COURT

§ 1. Number of justices; quorum

The Supreme Court of the United States shall consist of a Chief Justice of the United States and eight associate justices, any six of whom shall constitute a quorum.

CHAPTER 3 — COURTS OF APPEALS

§ 41. Number and composition of circuits

The thirteen judicial circuits of the United States are constituted as follows:

Circuits	*Composition*
District of Columbia	District of Columbia.
First	Maine, Massachusetts, New Hampshire, Puerto Rico, Rhode Island.
Second	Connecticut, New York, Vermont.
Third	Delaware, New Jersey, Pennsylvania, Virgin Islands.
Fourth	Maryland, North Carolina, South Carolina, Virginia, West Virginia.
Fifth	District of the Canal Zone, Louisiana, Mississippi, Texas.
Sixth	Kentucky, Michigan, Ohio, Tennessee.
Seventh	Illinois, Indiana, Wisconsin.
Eighth	Arkansas, Iowa, Minnesota, Missouri, Nebraska, North Dakota, South Dakota.

Ninth	Alaska, Arizona, California, Idaho, Montana, Nevada, Oregon, Washington, Guam, Hawaii.
Tenth	Colorado, Kansas, New Mexico, Oklahoma, Utah, Wyoming.
Eleventh	Alabama, Florida, Georgia.
Federal	All Federal judicial districts.

§ 43. Creation and composition of courts

(a) There shall be in each circuit a court of appeals, which shall be a court of record, known as the United States Court of Appeals for the circuit.

(b) Each court of appeals shall consist of the circuit judges of the circuit in regular active service. The circuit justice and justices or judges designated or assigned shall be competent to sit as judges of the court.

§ 46. Assignment of judges; panels; hearings; quorum

(a) Circuit judges shall sit on the court and its panels in such order and at such times as the court directs.

(b) In each circuit the court may authorize the hearing and determination of cases and controversies by separate panels, each consisting of three judges, at least a majority of whom shall be judges of that court, unless such judges cannot sit because recused or disqualified, or unless the chief judge of that court certifies that there is an emergency including, but not limited to, the unavailability of a judge of the court because of illness. . . .

(c) Cases and controversies shall be heard and determined by a court or panel of not more than three judges . . . unless a hearing or rehearing before the court in banc is ordered by a majority of the circuit judges of the circuit who are in regular active service. A court in banc shall consist of all circuit judges in regular active service [with limited exceptions].

CHAPTER 5 — DISTRICT COURTS

§ 132. Creation and composition of district courts

(a) There shall be in each judicial district a district court which shall be a court of record known as the United States District Court for the district.

(b) Each district court shall consist of the district judge or judges for the district in regular active service. Justices or judges designated or assigned shall be competent to sit as judges of the court.

(c) Except as otherwise provided by law, or rule or order of court, the judicial power of a district court with respect to any action, suit or proceeding may be exercised by a single judge, who may preside alone and hold a regular or special session of court at the same time other sessions are held by other judges.

§ 144. Bias or prejudice of judge

Whenever a party to any proceeding in a district court makes and files a timely and sufficient affidavit that the judge before whom the matter is pending has a personal bias or prejudice either against him or in favor of any adverse party, such judge shall proceed no further therein, but another judge shall be assigned to hear such proceeding.

The affidavit shall state the facts and the reasons for the belief that bias or prejudice exists, and shall be filed not less than ten days before the beginning of the term at which the proceeding is to be heard, or good cause shall be shown for failure to file it within such time. A party may file only one such affidavit in any case. It shall be accompanied by a certificate of counsel of record stating that it is made in good faith.

CHAPTER 13 — ASSIGNMENT OF JUDGES TO OTHER COURTS

§ 291. Circuit judges

(a) The Chief Justice of the United States may, in the public interest, designate and assign temporarily any circuit judge to act as circuit judge in another circuit upon request by the chief judge or circuit justice of such circuit.

(b) The chief judge of a circuit or the circuit justice may, in the public interest, designate and assign temporarily any circuit judge within the circuit, including a judge designated and assigned to temporary duty therein, to hold a district court in any district within the circuit.

§ 292. District judges

(a) The chief judge of a circuit may designate and assign one or more district judges within the circuit to sit upon the court of appeals or a division thereof whenever the business of that court so requires. Such

designations or assignments shall be in conformity with the rules or orders of the court of appeals of the circuit.

(b) The chief judge of a circuit may, in the public interest, designate and assign temporarily any district judge of the circuit to hold a district court in any district within the circuit. . . .

(d) The Chief Justice of the United States may designate and assign temporarily a district judge of one circuit for service in another circuit, either in a district court or court of appeals, upon presentation of a certificate of necessity by the chief judge or circuit justice of the circuit wherein the need arises. . . .

CHAPTER 21 — GENERAL PROVISIONS APPLICABLE TO COURTS AND JUDGES

§ 451. Definitions

As used in this title:

The term "court of the United States" includes the Supreme Court of the United States, courts of appeals, district courts constituted by chapter 5 of this title, including the Court of International Trade and any court created by Act of Congress the judges of which are entitled to hold office during good behavior.

The terms "district court" and "district court of the United States" mean the courts constituted by chapter 5 of this title.

The term "judge of the United States" includes judges of the courts of appeals, district courts, Court of International Trade and any court created by Act of Congress, the judges of which are entitled to hold office during good behavior.

The term "justice of the United States" includes the Chief Justice of the United States and the associate justices of the Supreme Court.

The term "district" and "judicial district" mean the districts enumerated in Chapter 5 of this title.

The term "department" means one of the executive departments enumerated in section 1 of Title 5, unless the context shows that such term was intended to describe the executive, legislative, or judicial branches of the government.

The term "agency" includes any department, independent establishment, commission, administration, authority, board or bureau of the United States or any corporation in which the United States has a

proprietary interest, unless the context shows that such term was intended to be used in a more limited sense.

§ 452. Courts always open; powers unrestricted by expiration of sessions

All courts of the United States shall be deemed always open for the purpose of filing proper papers, issuing and returning process, and making motions and orders.

The continued existence or expiration of a session of a court in no way affects the power of the court to do any act or take any proceeding.

§ 453. Oaths of justices and judges

Each justice or judge of the United States shall take the following oath or affirmation before performing the duties of his office: "I, _______ _______, do solemnly swear (or affirm) that I will administer justice without respect to persons, and do equal right to the poor and to the rich, and that I will faithfully and impartially discharge and perform all the duties incumbent upon me as _______ under the Constitution and laws of the United States. So help me God."

§ 454. Practice of law by justices and judges

Any justice or judge appointed under the authority of the United States who engages in the practice of law is guilty of a high misdemeanor.

§ 455. Disqualification of justice, judge, or magistrate judge

(a) Any justice, judge, or magistrate judge of the United States shall disqualify himself in any proceeding in which his impartiality might reasonably be questioned.

(b) He shall also disqualify himself in the following circumstances:

(1) Where he has a personal bias or prejudice concerning a party, or personal knowledge of disputed evidentiary facts concerning the proceeding;

(2) Where in private practice he served as lawyer in the matter in controversy, or a lawyer with whom he previously practiced law served during such association as a lawyer concerning the matter, or the judge or such lawyer has been a material witness concerning it;

(3) Where he has served in governmental employment and in such capacity participated as counsel, adviser or material witness concerning the proceeding or expressed an opinion concerning the merits of the particular case in controversy;

(4) He knows that he, individually or as a fiduciary, or his spouse or minor child residing in his household, has a financial interest in the subject matter in controversy or in a party to the proceeding, or any other interest that could be substantially affected by the outcome of the proceeding;

(5) He or his spouse, or a person within the third degree of relationship to either of them, or the spouse of such a person:

(i) Is a party to the proceeding, or an officer, director, or trustee of a party;

(ii) Is acting as a lawyer in the proceeding;

(iii) Is known by the judge to have an interest that could be substantially affected by the outcome of the proceeding;

(iv) Is to the judge's knowledge likely to be a material witness in the proceeding.

(c) A judge should inform himself about his personal and fiduciary financial interests, and make a reasonable effort to inform himself about the personal financial interests of his spouse and minor children residing in his household.

(d) For the purposes of this section the following words or phrases shall have the meaning indicated:

(1) "proceeding" includes pretrial, trial, appellate review, or other stages of litigation;

(2) the degree of relationship is calculated according to the civil law system;

(3) "fiduciary" includes such relationships as executor, administrator, trustee, and guardian;

(4) "financial interest" means ownership of a legal or equitable interest, however small, or a relationship as director, adviser, or other active participant in the affairs of a party, except that:

(i) Ownership in a mutual or common investment fund that holds securities is not a "financial interest" in such securities unless the judge participates in the management of the fund;

(ii) An office in an educational, religious, charitable, fraternal, or civic organization is not a "financial interest" in securities held by the organization;

(iii) The proprietary interest of a policyholder in a mutual insurance company, of a depositor in a mutual savings association, or a similar proprietary interest, is a "financial interest" in the

organization only if the outcome of the proceeding could substantially affect the value of the interest;

(iv) Ownership of government securities is a "financial interest" in the issuer only if the outcome of the proceeding could substantially affect the value of the securities.

(e) No justice, judge, or magistrate judge shall accept from the parties to the proceeding a waiver of any ground for disqualification enumerated in subsection (b). Where the ground for disqualification arises only under subsection (a), waiver may be accepted provided it is preceded by a full disclosure on the record of the basis for disqualification.

(f) Notwithstanding the preceding provisions of this section, if any justice, judge, magistrate judge, or bankruptcy judge to whom a matter has been assigned would be disqualified, after substantial judicial time has been devoted to the matter, because of the appearance or discovery, after the matter was assigned to him or her, that he or she individually or as a fiduciary, or his or her spouse or minor child residing in his or her household, has a financial interest in a party (other than an interest that could be substantially affected by the outcome), disqualification is not required if the justice, judge, magistrate judge, bankruptcy judge, spouse or minor child, as the case may be, divests himself or herself of the interest that provides the grounds for the disqualification.

PART III — COURT OFFICERS AND EMPLOYEES

CHAPTER 43 — UNITED STATES MAGISTRATE JUDGES

§ 631. Appointment and tenure

(a) The judges of each United States district court and the district courts of the Virgin Islands, Guam, and the Northern Mariana Islands shall appoint United States magistrate judges in such numbers and to serve at such locations within the judicial districts as the Judicial Conference may determine under this chapter. In the case of a magistrate judge appointed by the district court of the Virgin Islands, Guam, or the Northern Mariana Islands, this chapter shall apply as though the court appointing such a magistrate judge were a United States district court. Where there is more than one judge of a district court, the appointment, whether an original appointment or a reappointment, shall be by the concurrence of a majority of all the judges of such district court, and when there is no such concurrence, then by the chief judge. Where the conference deems it desirable, a magistrate judge may be designated to serve in one

or more districts adjoining the district for which he is appointed. Such a designation shall be made by the concurrence of a majority of the judges of each of the district courts involved and shall specify the duties to be performed by the magistrate judge in the adjoining district or districts. . . .

(e) The appointment of any individual as a full-time magistrate judge shall be for a term of eight years, and the appointment of any individuals as a part-time magistrate judge shall be for a term of four years . . .

§ 636. Jurisdiction, powers, and temporary assignment

. . .

(b) (1) Notwithstanding any provision of law to the contrary —

(A) a judge may designate a magistrate judge to hear and determine any pretrial matter pending before the court, except a motion for injunctive relief, for judgment on the pleadings, for summary judgment, to dismiss or quash an indictment or information made by the defendant, to suppress evidence in a criminal case, to dismiss or to permit maintenance of a class action, to dismiss for failure to state a claim upon which relief can be granted, and to involuntarily dismiss an action. A judge of the court may reconsider any pretrial matter under this subparagraph (A) where it has been shown that the magistrate judge's order is clearly erroneous or contrary to law.

(B) a judge may also designate a magistrate judge to conduct hearings, including evidentiary hearings, and to submit to a judge of the court proposed findings of fact and recommendations for the disposition, by a judge of the court, of any motion excepted in subparagraph (A), of applications for posttrial relief made by individuals convicted of criminal offenses and of prisoner petitions challenging conditions of confinement.

(C) the magistrate judge shall file his proposed findings and recommendations under subparagraph (B) with the court and a copy shall forthwith be mailed to all parties.

Within fourteen days after being served with a copy, any party may serve and file written objections to such proposed findings and recommendations as provided by rules of court. A judge of the court shall make a de novo determination of those portions of the report or specified proposed findings or recommendations to which objection is made. A judge of the court may accept, reject, or modify, in whole or in part, the findings or recommendations made by the magistrate judge. The judge may also receive further evidence or recommit the matter to the magistrate judge with instructions. . . .

(3) A magistrate judge may be assigned such additional duties as are not inconsistent with the Constitution and laws of the United States. . . .

(c) Notwithstanding any provision of law to the contrary —

(1) Upon the consent of the parties, a full-time United States magistrate judge or a part-time United States magistrate judge who serves as a full-time judicial officer may conduct any or all proceedings in a jury or nonjury civil matter and order the entry of judgment in the case, when specially designated to exercise such jurisdiction by the district court or courts he serves. . . .

(2) If a magistrate judge is designated to exercise civil jurisdiction under paragraph (1) of this subsection, the clerk of court shall, at the time the action is filed, notify the parties of the availability of a magistrate judge to exercise such jurisdiction. The decision of the parties shall be communicated to the clerk of court. Thereafter, either the district court judge or the magistrate judge may again advise the parties of the availability of the magistrate judge, but in so doing, shall also advise the parties that they are free to withhold consent without adverse substantive consequences. Rules of court for the reference of civil matters to magistrate judges shall include procedures to protect the voluntariness of the parties' consent.

(3) Upon entry of judgment in any case referred under paragraph (1) of this subsection, an aggrieved party may appeal directly to the appropriate United States court of appeals from the judgment of the magistrate judge in the same manner as an appeal from any other judgment of a district court. The consent of the parties allows a magistrate judge designated to exercise civil jurisdiction under paragraph (1) of this subsection to direct the entry of a judgment of the district court in accordance with the Federal Rules of Civil Procedure. Nothing in this paragraph shall be construed as a limitation of any party's right to seek review by the Supreme Court of the United States.

(4) The court may, for good cause shown on its own motion, or under extraordinary circumstances shown by any party, vacate a reference of a civil matter to a magistrate judge under this subsection. . . .

(d) The practice and procedure for the trial of cases before officers serving under this chapter shall conform to rules promulgated by the Supreme Court pursuant to section 2072 of this title. . . .

CHAPTER 44 — ALTERNATIVE DISPUTE RESOLUTION

§ 651. Authorization of alternative dispute resolution

(a) DEFINITION. — For purposes of this chapter, an alternative dispute resolution process includes any process or procedure, other than an adjudication by a presiding judge, in which a neutral third party participates to assist in the resolution of issues in controversy, through processes such as early neutral evaluation, mediation, minitrial, and arbitration as provided in sections 654 through 658.

(b) AUTHORITY. — Each United States district court shall authorize, by local rule adopted under section 2071(a), the use of alternative dispute resolution processes in all civil actions, including adversary proceedings in bankruptcy, in accordance with this chapter, except that the use of arbitration may be authorized only as provided in section 654. Each United States district court shall devise and implement its own alternative dispute resolution program, by local rule adopted under section 2071(a), to encourage and promote the use of alternative dispute resolution in its district.

(c) EXISTING ALTERNATIVE DISPUTE RESOLUTION PROGRAMS. — In those courts where an alternative dispute resolution program is in place on the date of the enactment of the Alternative Dispute Resolution Act of 1998, the court shall examine the effectiveness of that program and adopt such improvements to the program as are consistent with the provisions and purposes of this chapter. . . .

§ 652. Jurisdiction

(a) CONSIDERATION OF ALTERNATIVE DISPUTE RESOLUTION IN APPROPRIATE CASES. — Notwithstanding any provision of law to the contrary and except as provided in subsections (b) and (c), each district court shall, by local rule adopted under section 2071(a), require that litigants in all civil cases consider the use of an alternative dispute resolution process at an appropriate stage in the litigation. Each district court shall provide litigants in all civil cases with at least one alternative dispute resolution process, including, but not limited to, mediation, early neutral evaluation, minitrial, and arbitration as authorized in sections 654 through 658. Any district court that elects to require the use of alternative dispute resolution in certain cases may do so only with respect to mediation, early neutral evaluation, and, if the parties consent, arbitration.

(b) ACTIONS EXEMPTED FROM CONSIDERATION OF ALTERNATIVE DISPUTE RESOLUTION. — Each district court may exempt from the requirements of this section specific cases or categories of cases in which use of alternative

dispute resolution would not be appropriate. In defining these exemptions, each district court shall consult with members of the bar, including the United States Attorney for that district. . . .

(d) CONFIDENTIALITY PROVISIONS. — Until such time as rules are adopted under chapter 131 of this title providing for the confidentiality of alternative dispute resolution processes under this chapter, each district court shall, by local rule adopted under section 2071(a), provide for the confidentiality of the alternative dispute resolution processes and to prohibit disclosure of confidential dispute resolution communications.

§ 654. Arbitration

(a) REFERRAL OF ACTIONS TO ARBITRATION. — Notwithstanding any provision of law to the contrary and except as provided in subsections (a), (b), and (c) of section 652 and subsection (d) of this section, a district court may allow the referral to arbitration of any civil action (including any adversary proceeding in bankruptcy) pending before it when the parties consent, except that referral to arbitration may not be made where —

(1) the action is based on an alleged violation of a right secured by the Constitution of the United States;

(2) jurisdiction is based in whole or in part on section 1343 of this title; or

(3) the relief sought consists of money damages in an amount greater than $150,000.

(b) SAFEGUARDS IN CONSENT CASES. — Until such time as rules are adopted under chapter 131 of this title relating to procedures described in this subsection, the district court shall, by local rule adopted under section 2071(a), establish procedures to ensure that any civil action in which arbitration by consent is allowed under subsection (a) —

(1) consent to arbitration is freely and knowingly obtained; and

(2) no party or attorney is prejudiced for refusing to participate in arbitration.

§ 657. Arbitration award and judgment

(a) FILING AND EFFECT OF ARBITRATION AWARD. — An arbitration award made by an arbitrator under this chapter, along with proof of service of such award on the other party by the prevailing party or by the plaintiff, shall be filed promptly after the arbitration hearing is concluded with the clerk of the district court that referred the case to arbitration. Such award shall be entered as the judgment of the court after the time has expired for requesting a trial de novo. The judgment so entered shall be subject to the same provisions of law and shall have the same force and

effect as a judgment of the court in a civil action, except that the judgment shall not be subject to review in any other court by appeal or otherwise.

(b) SEALING OF ARBITRATION AWARD. — The district court shall provide, by local rule adopted under section 2071(a), that the contents of any arbitration award made under this chapter shall not be made known to any judge who might be assigned to the case until the district court has entered final judgment in the action or the action has otherwise terminated.

(c) TRIAL DE NOVO OF ARBITRATION AWARDS. —

(1) TIME FOR FILING DEMAND. — Within 30 days after the filing of an arbitration award with a district court under subsection (a), any party may file a written demand for a trial de novo in the district court.

(2) ACTION RESTORED TO COURT DOCKET. — Upon a demand for a trial de novo, the action shall be restored to the docket of the court and treated for all purposes as if it had not been referred to arbitration.

(3) EXCLUSION OF EVIDENCE OF ARBITRATION. — The court shall not admit at the trial de novo any evidence that there has been an arbitration proceeding, the nature or amount of any award, or any other matter concerning the conduct of the arbitration proceeding, unless —

(A) the evidence would otherwise be admissible in the court under the Federal Rules of Evidence; or

(B) the parties have otherwise stipulated.

PART IV — JURISDICTION AND VENUE

CHAPTER 81 — SUPREME COURT

§ 1251. Original jurisdiction

(a) The Supreme Court shall have original and exclusive jurisdiction of all controversies between two or more States.

(b) The Supreme Court shall have original but not exclusive jurisdiction of:

(1) All actions or proceedings to which ambassadors, other public ministers, consuls, or vice consuls of foreign states are parties;

(2) All controversies between the United States and a State;

(3) All actions or proceedings by a State against the citizens of another State or against aliens.

§ 1253. Direct appeals from decisions of three-judge courts

Except as otherwise provided by law, any party may appeal to the Supreme Court from an order granting or denying, after notice and hearing, an interlocutory or permanent injunction in any civil action, suit or proceeding required by any Act of Congress to be heard and determined by a district court of three judges.

§ 1254. Courts of appeals; certiorari; certified questions

Cases in the courts of appeals may be reviewed by the Supreme Court by the following methods:

(1) By writ of certiorari granted upon the petition of any party to any civil or criminal case, before or after rendition of judgment or decree;

(2) By certification at any time by a court of appeals of any question of law in any civil or criminal case as to which instructions are desired, and upon such certification the Supreme Court may give binding instructions or require the entire record to be sent up for decision of the entire matter in controversy.

§ 1257. State courts; certiorari

(a) Final judgments or decrees rendered by the highest court of a State in which a decision could be had, may be reviewed by the Supreme Court by writ of certiorari where the validity of a treaty or statute of the United States is drawn in question or where the validity of a statute of any State is drawn in question on the ground of its being repugnant to the Constitution, treaties, or laws of the United States, or where any title, right, privilege, or immunity is specially set up or claimed under the Constitution or the treaties or statutes of, or any commission held or authority exercised under, the United States.

(b) For the purposes of this section, the term "highest court of a State" includes the District of Columbia Court of Appeals.

§ 1258. Supreme Court of Puerto Rico; certiorari

Final judgments or decrees rendered by the Supreme Court of the Commonwealth of Puerto Rico may be reviewed by the Supreme Court by writ of certiorari where the validity of a treaty or statute of the United States is drawn in question or where the validity of a statute of the Commonwealth of Puerto Rico is drawn in question on the ground of its being repugnant to the Constitution, treaties, or laws of the United States, or where any title, right, privilege, or immunity is specially set up or claimed under the Constitution or the treaties or statutes of, or any commission held or authority exercised under, the United States.

§ 1259. Court of Appeals for the Armed Forces; certiorari

Decisions of the United States Court of Appeals for the Armed Forces may be reviewed by the Supreme Court by writ of certiorari in the following cases:

(1) Cases reviewed by the Court of Appeals for the Armed Forces under section 867(a)(1) of title 10.

(2) Cases certified to the Court of Appeals for the Armed Forces by the Judge Advocate General under section 867(a)(2) of title 10.

(3) Cases in which the Court of Appeals for the Armed Forces granted a petition for review under section 867(a)(3) of title 10.

(4) Cases, other than those described in paragraphs (1), (2), and (3) of this subsection, in which the Court of Appeals for the Armed Forces granted relief.

CHAPTER 83 — COURTS OF APPEALS

§ 1291. Final decisions of district courts

The courts of appeals (other than the United States Court of Appeals for the Federal Circuit) shall have jurisdiction of appeals from all final decisions of the district courts of the United States, the United States District Court for the District of the Canal Zone, the District Court of Guam, and the District Court of the Virgin Islands, except where a direct review may be had in the Supreme Court. The jurisdiction of the United States Court of Appeals for the Federal Circuit shall be limited to the jurisdiction described in sections 1292(c) and (d) and 1295 of this title.

§ 1292. Interlocutory decisions

(a) Except as provided in subsections (c) and (d) of this section, the courts of appeals shall have jurisdiction of appeals from:

(1) Interlocutory orders of the district courts of the United States, the United States District Court for the District of the Canal Zone, the District Court of Guam, and the District Court of the Virgin Islands, or of the judges thereof, granting, continuing, modifying, refusing or dissolving injunctions, or refusing to dissolve or modify injunctions, except where a direct review may be had in the Supreme Court;

(2) Interlocutory orders appointing receivers, or refusing orders to wind up receiverships or to take steps to accomplish the purposes thereof, such as directing sales or other disposals of property;

(3) Interlocutory decrees of such district courts or the judges thereof determining the rights and liabilities of the parties to admiralty cases in which appeals from final decrees are allowed.

(b) When a district judge, in making in a civil action an order not otherwise appealable under this section, shall be of the opinion that such order involves a controlling question of law as to which there is substantial ground for difference of opinion and that an immediate appeal from the order may materially advance the ultimate termination of the litigation, he shall so state in writing in such order. The Court of Appeals which would have jurisdiction of an appeal of such action may thereupon, in its discretion, permit an appeal to be taken from such order, if application is made to it within ten days after the entry of the order: *Provided, however,* That application for an appeal hereunder shall not stay proceedings in the district court unless the district judge or the Court of Appeals or a judge thereof shall so order. . . .

(c) The United States Court of Appeals for the Federal Circuit shall have exclusive jurisdiction —

(1) of an appeal from an interlocutory order or decree described in subsection (a) or (b) of this section in any case over which the court would have jurisdiction of an appeal under section 1295 of this title; and

(2) of an appeal from a judgment in a civil action for patent infringement which would otherwise be appealable to the United States Court of Appeals for the Federal Circuit and is final except for an accounting.

(d) [Omitted.]

(e) The Supreme Court may prescribe rules, in accordance with section 2072 of this title, to provide for an appeal of an interlocutory decision to the courts of appeals that is not otherwise provided for under subsection (a), (b), (c), or (d).

§ 1294. Circuits in which decisions reviewable

Except as provided in sections 1292(c), 1292(d), and 1295 of this title, appeals from reviewable decisions of the district and territorial courts shall be taken to the courts of appeals as follows:

(1) From a district court of the United States to the court of appeals for the circuit embracing the district;

(2) From the United States District Court for the District of the Canal Zone, to the Court of Appeals for the Fifth Circuit;

(3) From the District Court of the Virgin Islands, to the Court of Appeals for the Third Circuit;

(4) From the District Court of Guam, to the Court of Appeals for the Ninth Circuit.

§ 1295. Jurisdiction of the United States Court of Appeals for the Federal Circuit

(a) The United States Court of Appeals for the Federal Circuit shall have exclusive jurisdiction [of appeals from final decisions of the district courts "in any civil action arising under, or in any civil action in which a party has asserted a compulsory counterclaim arising under, any Act of Congress relating to patents or plant variety protection"; of appeals in government-contract disputes; and of appeals in various other matters.]

CHAPTER 85 — DISTRICT COURTS; JURISDICTION

§ 1331. Federal question

The district courts shall have original jurisdiction of all civil actions arising under the Constitution, laws, or treaties of the United States.

§ 1332. Diversity of citizenship; amount in controversy; costs

(a) The district courts shall have original jurisdiction of all civil actions where the matter in controversy exceeds the sum or value of $75,000, exclusive of interest and costs, and is between —

(1) citizens of different States;

(2) citizens of a State and citizens or subjects of a foreign state, except that the district courts shall not have original jurisdiction under this subsection of an action between citizens of a State and citizens or subjects of a foreign state who are lawfully admitted for permanent residence in the United States and are domiciled in the same State;

(3) citizens of different States and in which citizens or subjects of a foreign state are additional parties; and

(4) a foreign state, defined in section 1603(a) of this title [part of the Foreign Sovereign Immunities Act, not included in this supplement — ED.], as plaintiff and citizens of a State or of different States.

(b) Except when express provision therefor is otherwise made in a statute of the United States, where the plaintiff who files the case originally in the Federal courts is finally adjudged to be entitled to recover less than the sum or value of $75,000, computed without regard to any

setoff or counterclaim to which the defendant may be adjudged to be entitled, and exclusive of interest and costs, the district court may deny costs to the plaintiff and, in addition, may impose costs on the plaintiff.

(c) For the purposes of this section and section 1441 of this title —

(1) a corporation shall be deemed to be a citizen of every State and foreign state by which it has been incorporated and of the State or foreign state where it has its principal place of business, except that in any direct action against the insurer of a policy or contract of liability insurance, whether incorporated or unincorporated, to which action the insured is not joined as a party-defendant, such insurer shall be deemed a citizen of —

(A) every State and foreign state of which the insured is a citizen;

(B) every State and foreign state by which the insurer has been incorporated; and

(C) the State or foreign state where the insurer has its principal place of business; and

(2) the legal representative of the estate of a decedent shall be deemed to be a citizen only of the same State as the decedent, and the legal representative of an infant or incompetent shall be deemed to be a citizen only of the same State as the infant or incompetent.

(d) (1) In this subsection —

(A) the term "class" means all of the class members in a class action;

(B) the term "class action" means any civil action filed under rule 23 of the Federal Rules of Civil Procedure or similar State statute or rule of judicial procedure authorizing an action to be brought by 1 or more representative persons as a class action;

(C) the term "class certification order" means an order issued by a court approving the treatment of some or all aspects of a civil action as a class action; and

(D) the term "class members" means the persons (named or unnamed) who fall within the definition of the proposed or certified class in a class action.

(2) The district courts shall have original jurisdiction of any civil action in which the matter in controversy exceeds the sum or value of $5,000,000, exclusive of interest and costs, and is a class action in which —

(A) any member of a class of plaintiffs is a citizen of a State different from any defendant;

(B) any member of a class of plaintiffs is a foreign state or a citizen or subject of a foreign state and any defendant is a citizen of a State; or

(C) any member of a class of plaintiffs is a citizen of a State and any defendant is a foreign state or a citizen or subject of a foreign state.

(3) A district court may, in the interests of justice and looking at the totality of the circumstances, decline to exercise jurisdiction under paragraph (2) over a class action in which greater than one-third but less than two-thirds of the members of all proposed plaintiff classes in the aggregate and the primary defendants are citizens of the State in which the action was originally filed based on consideration of —

(A) whether the claims asserted involve matters of national or interstate interest;

(B) whether the claims asserted will be governed by laws of the State in which the action was originally filed or by the laws of other States;

(C) whether the class action has been pleaded in a manner that seeks to avoid Federal jurisdiction;

(D) whether the action was brought in a forum with a distinct nexus with the class members, the alleged harm, or the defendants;

(E) whether the number of citizens of the State in which the action was originally filed in all proposed plaintiff classes in the aggregate is substantially larger than the number of citizens from any other State, and the citizenship of the other members of the proposed class is dispersed among a substantial number of States; and

(F) whether, during the 3-year period preceding the filing of that class action, 1 or more other class actions asserting the same or similar claims on behalf of the same or other persons have been filed.

(4) A district court shall decline to exercise jurisdiction under paragraph (2) —

(A) (i) over a class action in which —

(I) greater than two-thirds of the members of all proposed plaintiff classes in the aggregate are citizens of the State in which the action was originally filed;

(II) at least 1 defendant is a defendant —

(aa) from whom significant relief is sought by members of the plaintiff class;

(bb) whose alleged conduct forms a significant basis for the claims asserted by the proposed plaintiff class; and

(cc) who is a citizen of the State in which the action was originally filed; and

(III) principal injuries resulting from the alleged conduct or any related conduct of each defendant were incurred in the State in which the action was originally filed; and

(ii) during the 3-year period preceding the filing of that class action, no other class action has been filed asserting the same or similar factual allegations against any of the defendants on behalf of the same or other persons; or

(B) two-thirds or more of the members of all proposed plaintiff classes in the aggregate, and the primary defendants, are citizens of the State in which the action was originally filed.

(5) Paragraphs (2) through (4) shall not apply to any class action in which —

(A) the primary defendants are States, State officials, or other governmental entities against whom the district court may be foreclosed from ordering relief; or

(B) the number of members of all proposed plaintiff classes in the aggregate is less than 100.

(6) In any class action, the claims of the individual class members shall be aggregated to determine whether the matter in controversy exceeds the sum or value of $5,000,000, exclusive of interest and costs.

(7) Citizenship of the members of the proposed plaintiff classes shall be determined for purposes of paragraphs (2) through (6) as of the date of filing of the complaint or amended complaint, or, if the case stated by the initial pleading is not subject to Federal jurisdiction, as of the date of service by plaintiffs of an amended pleading, motion, or other paper, indicating the existence of Federal jurisdiction.

(8) This subsection shall apply to any class action before or after the entry of a class certification order by the court with respect to that action.

(9) Paragraph (2) shall not apply to any class action that solely involves a claim —

(A) concerning a covered security as defined under 16(f)(3) of the Securities Act of 1933 (15 U.S.C. 78p(f)(3)) and section 28(f)(5)(E) of the Securities Exchange Act of 1934 (15 U.S.C. 78bb(f)(5)(E));

(B) that relates to the internal affairs or governance of a corporation or other form of business enterprise and that arises under or by virtue of the laws of the State in which such corporation or business enterprise is incorporated or organized; or

(C) that relates to the rights, duties (including fiduciary duties), and obligations relating to or created by or pursuant to any security (as defined under section 2(a)(1) of the Securities Act of 1933 (15 U.S.C. 77b(a)(1)) and the regulations issued thereunder).

(10) For purposes of this subsection and section 1453, an unincorporated association shall be deemed to be a citizen of the State where it has its principal place of business and the State under whose laws it is organized.

(11)(A) For purposes of this subsection and section 1453, a mass action shall be deemed to be a class action removable under paragraphs (2) through (10) if it otherwise meets the provisions of those paragraphs.

(B) (i) As used in subparagraph (A), the term "mass action" means any civil action (except a civil action within the scope of section 1711(2)) in which monetary relief claims of 100 or more persons are proposed to be tried jointly on the ground that the plaintiffs' claims involve common questions of law or fact, except that jurisdiction shall exist only over those plaintiffs whose claims in a mass action satisfy the jurisdictional amount requirements under subsection (a).

(ii) As used in subparagraph (A), the term "mass action" shall not include any civil action in which —

(I) all of the claims in the action arise from an event or occurrence in the State in which the action was filed, and that allegedly resulted in injuries in that State or in States contiguous to that State;

(II) the claims are joined upon motion of a defendant;

(III) all of the claims in the action are asserted on behalf of the general public (and not on behalf of individual claimants or members of a purported class) pursuant to a State statute specifically authorizing such action; or

(IV) the claims have been consolidated or coordinated solely for pretrial proceedings.

(C) (i) Any action(s) removed to Federal court pursuant to this subsection shall not thereafter be transferred to any other court pursuant to section 1407, or the rules promulgated thereunder, unless a majority of the plaintiffs in the action request transfer pursuant to section 1407.

(ii) This subparagraph will not apply —

(I) to cases certified pursuant to rule 23 of the Federal Rules of Civil Procedure; or

(II) if plaintiffs propose that the action proceed as a class action pursuant to rule 23 of the Federal Rules of Civil Procedure.

(D) The limitations periods on any claims asserted in a mass action that is removed to Federal court pursuant to this subsection shall be deemed tolled during the period that the action is pending in Federal court.

(e) The word "States", as used in this section, includes the Territories, the District of Columbia, and the Commonwealth of Puerto Rico.

§ 1333. Admiralty, maritime and prize cases

The district courts shall have original jurisdiction, exclusive of the courts of the States, of:

(1) Any civil case of admiralty or maritime jurisdiction, saving to suitors in all cases all other remedies to which they are otherwise entitled.

(2) Any prize brought into the United States and all proceedings for the condemnation of property taken as prize.

§ 1334. Bankruptcy cases and proceedings

(a) Except as provided in subsection (b) of this section, the district courts shall have original and exclusive jurisdiction of all cases under title 11.

(b) Except as provided in subsection (e)(2), and notwithstanding any Act of Congress that confers exclusive jurisdiction on a court or courts other than the district courts, the district courts shall have original but not exclusive jurisdiction of all civil proceedings arising under title 11, or arising in or related to cases under title 11.

(c) (1) Except with respect to a case under chapter 15 of title 11, nothing in this section prevents a district court in the interest of justice, or in the interest of comity with State courts or respect for

State law, from abstaining from hearing a particular proceeding arising under title 11 or arising in or related to a case under title 11.

(2) Upon timely motion of a party in a proceeding based upon a State law claim or State law cause of action, related to a case under title 11 but not arising under title 11 or arising in a case under title 11, with respect to which an action could not have been commenced in a court of the United States absent jurisdiction under this section, the district court shall abstain from hearing such proceeding if an action is commenced, and can be timely adjudicated, in a State forum of appropriate jurisdiction.

(d) Any decision to abstain or not to abstain made under subsection (c) (other than a decision not to abstain in a proceeding described in subsection (c)(2)) is not reviewable by appeal or otherwise by the court of appeals under section 158(d), 1291, or 1292 of this title or by the Supreme Court of the United States under section 1254 of this title. Subsection (c) and this subsection shall not be construed to limit the applicability of the stay provided for by section 362 of title 11, United States Code, as such section applies to an action affecting the property of the estate in bankruptcy. . . .

§ 1335. Interpleader

(a) The district courts shall have original jurisdiction of any civil action of interpleader or in the nature of interpleader filed by any person, firm, or corporation, association, or society having in his or its custody or possession money or property of the value of $500 or more, or having issued a note, bond, certificate, policy of insurance, or other instrument of value or amount of $500 or more, or providing for the delivery or payment or the loan of money or property of such amount or value, or being under any obligation written or unwritten to the amount of $500 or more, if

(1) Two or more adverse claimants, of diverse citizenship as defined in subsection (a) or (d) of section 1332 of this title, are claiming or may claim to be entitled to such money or property, or to any one or more of the benefits arising by virtue of any note, bond, certificate, policy or other instrument, or arising by virtue of any such obligation; and if (2) the plaintiff has deposited such money or property or has paid the amount of or the loan or other value of such instrument or the amount due under such obligation into the registry of the court, there to abide the judgment of the court, or has given bond payable to the clerk of the court in such amount and with such surety as the court or judge may deem proper, conditioned upon the compliance by the plaintiff with the future order or judgment of the court with respect to the subject matter of the controversy.

(b) Such an action may be entertained although the titles or claims of the conflicting claimants do not have a common origin, or are not identical, but are adverse to and independent of one another.

§ 1337. Commerce and antitrust regulations; amount in controversy, costs

(a) The district courts shall have original jurisdiction of any civil action or proceeding arising under any Act of Congress regulating commerce or protecting trade and commerce against restraints and monopolies: *Provided, however*, That the district courts shall have original jurisdiction of an action brought under section 11706 or 14706 of title 49, only if the matter in controversy for each receipt or bill of lading exceeds $10,000, exclusive of interest and costs.

(b) Except when express provision therefor is otherwise made in a statute of the United States, where a plaintiff who files the case under section 11706 or 14706 of title 49, originally in the Federal courts is finally adjudged to be entitled to recover less than the sum or value of $10,000, computed without regard to any setoff or counterclaim to which the defendant may be adjudged to be entitled, and exclusive of any interest and costs, the district court may deny costs to the plaintiff and, in addition, may impose costs on the plaintiff. . . .

§ 1338. Patents, plant variety protection, copyrights, mask works, designs, trademarks, and unfair competition

(a) The district courts shall have original jurisdiction of any civil action arising under any Act of Congress relating to patents, plant variety protection, copyrights and trademarks. No State court shall have jurisdiction over any claim for relief arising under any Act of Congress relating to patents, plant variety protection, or copyrights. For purposes of this subsection, the term "State" includes any State of the United States, the District of Columbia, the Commonwealth of Puerto Rico, the United States Virgin Islands, American Samoa, Guam, and the Northern Mariana Islands.

(b) The district courts shall have original jurisdiction of any civil action asserting a claim of unfair competition when joined with a substantial and related claim under the copyright, patent, plant variety protection or trademark laws. . . .

§ 1341. Taxes by States

The district courts shall not enjoin, suspend or restrain the assessment, levy or collection of any tax under State law where a plain, speedy and efficient remedy may be had in the courts of such State.

§ 1343. Civil rights and elective franchise

(a) The district courts shall have original jurisdiction of any civil action authorized by law to be commenced by any person:

(1) To recover damages for injury to his person or property, or because of the deprivation of any right or privilege of a citizen of the United States, by any act done in furtherance of any conspiracy mentioned in section 1985 of Title 42;

(2) To recover damages from any person who fails to prevent or to aid in preventing any wrongs mentioned in section 1985 of Title 42 which he had knowledge were about to occur and power to prevent;

(3) To redress the deprivation, under color of any State law, statute, ordinance, regulation, custom or usage, of any right, privilege or immunity secured by the Constitution of the United States or by any Act of Congress providing for equal rights of citizens or of all persons within the jurisdiction of the United States;

(4) To recover damages or to secure equitable or other relief under any Act of Congress providing for the protection of civil rights, including the right to vote.

(b) For purposes of this section —

(1) the District of Columbia shall be considered to be a State; and

(2) any Act of Congress applicable exclusively to the District of Columbia shall be considered to be a statute of the District of Columbia.

§ 1345. United States as plaintiff

Except as otherwise provided by Act of Congress, the district courts shall have original jurisdiction of all civil actions, suits or proceedings commenced by the United States, or by any agency or officer thereof expressly authorized to sue by Act of Congress.

§ 1346. United States as defendant

(a) The district courts shall have original jurisdiction, concurrent with the United States Court of Federal Claims, of:

(1) Any civil action against the United States for the recovery of any internal-revenue tax alleged to have been erroneously or illegally assessed or collected, or any penalty claimed to have been collected without authority or any sum alleged to have been excessive or in any manner wrongfully collected under the internal-revenue laws;

(2) Any other civil action or claim against the United States, not exceeding $10,000 in amount, founded either upon the Constitution, or

any Act of Congress, or any regulation of an executive department, or upon any express or implied contract with the United States, or for liquidated or unliquidated damages in cases not sounding in tort [subject to certain exceptions].

(b) (1) Subject to the provisions of chapter 171 of this title, the district courts, together with the United States District Court for the District of the Canal Zone and the District Court of the Virgin Islands, shall have exclusive jurisdiction of civil actions on claims against the United States, for money damages, accruing on and after January 1, 1945, for injury or loss of property, or personal injury or death caused by the negligent or wrongful act or omission of any employee of the Government while acting within the scope of his office or employment, under circumstances where the United States, if a private person, would be liable to the claimant in accordance with the law of the place where the act or omission occurred. . . .

§ 1358. Eminent domain

The district courts shall have original jurisdiction of all proceedings to condemn real estate for the use of the United States or its departments or agencies.

§ 1359. Parties collusively joined or made

A district court shall not have jurisdiction of a civil action in which any party, by assignment or otherwise, has been improperly or collusively made or joined to invoke the jurisdiction of such court.

§ 1361. Action to compel an officer of the United States to perform his duty

The district courts shall have original jurisdiction of any action in the nature of mandamus to compel an officer or employee of the United States or any agency thereof to perform a duty owed to the plaintiff.

§ 1367. Supplemental jurisdiction

(a) Except as provided in subsections (b) and (c) or as expressly provided otherwise by Federal statute, in any civil action of which the district courts have original jurisdiction, the district courts shall have supplemental jurisdiction over all other claims that are so related to claims in the action within such original jurisdiction that they form part of the same case or controversy under Article III of the United States Constitution. Such supplemental jurisdiction shall include claims that involve the joinder or intervention of additional parties.

(b) In any civil action of which the district courts have original jurisdiction founded solely on section 1332 of this title, the district courts shall not have supplemental jurisdiction under subsection (a) over claims by plaintiffs against persons made parties under Rule 14, 19, 20, or 24 of the Federal Rules of Civil Procedure, or over claims by persons proposed to be joined as plaintiffs under Rule 19 of such rules, or seeking to intervene as plaintiffs under Rule 24 of such rules, when exercising supplemental jurisdiction over such claims would be inconsistent with the jurisdictional requirements of section 1332.

(c) The district courts may decline to exercise supplemental jurisdiction over a claim under subsection (a) if —

(1) the claim raises a novel or complex issue of State law,

(2) the claim substantially predominates over the claim or claims over which the district court has original jurisdiction,

(3) the district court has dismissed all claims over which it has original jurisdiction, or

(4) in exceptional circumstances, there are other compelling reasons for declining jurisdiction.

(d) The period of limitations for any claim asserted under subsection (a), and for any other claim in the same action that is voluntarily dismissed at the same time as or after the dismissal of the claim under subsection (a), shall be tolled while the claim is pending and for a period of 30 days after it is dismissed unless State law provides for a longer tolling period.

(e) As used in this section, the term "State" includes the District of Columbia, the Commonwealth of Puerto Rico, and any territory or possession of the United States.

§ 1369. Multiparty, multiforum jurisdiction

(a) IN GENERAL. — The district courts shall have original jurisdiction of any civil action involving minimal diversity between adverse parties that arises from a single accident, where at least 75 natural persons have died in the accident at a discrete location, if —

(1) a defendant resides in a State and a substantial part of the accident took place in another State or other location, regardless of whether that defendant is also a resident of the State where a substantial part of the accident took place;

(2) any two defendants reside in different States, regardless of whether such defendants are also residents of the same State or States; or

(3) substantial parts of the accident took place in different States.

(b) LIMITATION OF JURISDICTION OF DISTRICT COURTS. — The district court shall abstain from hearing any civil action described in subsection (a) in which —

(1) the substantial majority of all plaintiffs are citizens of a single State of which the primary defendants are also citizens; and

(2) the claims asserted will be governed primarily by the laws of that State.

(c) SPECIAL RULES AND DEFINITIONS. — For purposes of this section —

(1) minimal diversity exists between adverse parties if any party is a citizen of a State and any adverse party is a citizen of another State, a citizen or subject of a foreign state, or a foreign state as defined in section 1603(a) of this title [part of the Foreign Sovereign Immunities Act, not included in this supplement — ED.];

(2) a corporation is deemed to be a citizen of any State, and a citizen or subject of any foreign state, in which it is incorporated or has its principal place of business, and is deemed to be a resident of any State in which it is incorporated or licensed to do business or is doing business;

(3) the term "injury" means —

(A) physical harm to a natural person; and

(B) physical damage to or destruction of tangible property, but only if physical harm described in subparagraph (A) exists;

(4) the term "accident" means a sudden accident, or a natural event culminating in an accident, that results in death incurred at a discrete location by at least 75 natural persons; and

(5) the term "State" includes the District of Columbia, the Commonwealth of Puerto Rico, and any territory or possession of the United States.

(d) INTERVENING PARTIES. — In any action in a district court which is or could have been brought, in whole or in part, under this section, any person with a claim arising from the accident described in subsection (a) shall be permitted to intervene as a party plaintiff in the action, even if that person could not have brought an action in a district court as an original matter.

(e) NOTIFICATION OF JUDICIAL PANEL ON MULTIDISTRICT LITIGATION. — A district court in which an action under this section is pending shall promptly notify the judicial panel on multidistrict litigation of the pendency of the action.

CHAPTER 87 — DISTRICT COURTS; VENUE

§ 1390. Scope

(a) VENUE DEFINED. — As used in this chapter, the term "venue" refers to the geographic specification of the proper court or courts for the litigation of a civil action that is within the subject-matter jurisdiction of the district courts in general, and does not refer to any grant or restriction of subject-matter jurisdiction providing for a civil action to be adjudicated only by the district court for a particular district or districts.

(b) EXCLUSION OF CERTAIN CASES. — Except as otherwise provided by law, this chapter shall not govern the venue of a civil action in which the district court exercises the jurisdiction conferred by section 1333, except that such civil actions may be transferred between district courts as provided in this chapter.

(c) CLARIFICATION REGARDING CASES REMOVED FROM STATE COURTS. — This chapter shall not determine the district court to which a civil action pending in a State court may be removed, but shall govern the transfer of an action so removed as between districts and divisions of the United States district courts.

§ 1391. Venue generally

(a) APPLICABILITY OF SECTION. — Except as otherwise provided by law —

(1) this section shall govern the venue of all civil actions brought in district courts of the United States; and

(2) the proper venue for a civil action shall be determined without regard to whether the action is local or transitory in nature.

(b) VENUE IN GENERAL. — A civil action may be brought in —

(1) a judicial district in which any defendant resides, if all defendants are residents of the State in which the district is located;

(2) a judicial district in which a substantial part of the events or omissions giving rise to the claim occurred, or a substantial part of property that is the subject of the action is situated; or

(3) if there is no district in which an action may otherwise be brought as provided in this section, any judicial district in which any defendant is subject to the court's personal jurisdiction with respect to such action.

(c) RESIDENCY. — For all venue purposes —

(1) a natural person, including an alien lawfully admitted for permanent residence in the United States, shall be deemed to reside in the judicial district in which that person is domiciled;

(2) an entity with the capacity to sue and be sued in its common name under applicable law, whether or not incorporated, shall be deemed to reside, if a defendant, in any judicial district in which such defendant is subject to the court's personal jurisdiction with respect to the civil action in question and, if a plaintiff, only in the judicial district in which it maintains its principal place of business; and

(3) a defendant not resident in the United States may be sued in any judicial district, and the joinder of such a defendant shall be disregarded in determining where the action may be brought with respect to other defendants.

(d) RESIDENCY OF CORPORATIONS IN STATES WITH MULTIPLE DISTRICTS. — For purposes of venue under this chapter, in a State which has more than one judicial district and in which a defendant that is a corporation is subject to personal jurisdiction at the time an action is commenced, such corporation shall be deemed to reside in any district in that State within which its contacts would be sufficient to subject it to personal jurisdiction if that district were a separate State, and, if there is no such district, the corporation shall be deemed to reside in the district within which it has the most significant contacts.

(e) ACTIONS WHERE DEFENDANT IS OFFICER OR EMPLOYEE OF THE UNITED STATES. —

(1) IN GENERAL. — A civil action in which a defendant is an officer or employee of the United States or any agency thereof acting in his official capacity or under color of legal authority, or an agency of the United States, or the United States, may, except as otherwise provided by law, be brought in any judicial district in which (A) a defendant in the action resides, (B) a substantial part of the events or omissions giving rise to the claim occurred, or a substantial part of property that is the subject of the action is situated, or (C) the plaintiff resides if no real property is involved in the action. Additional persons may be joined as parties to any such action in accordance with the Federal Rules of Civil Procedure and with such other venue requirements as would be applicable if the United States or one of its officers, employees, or agencies were not a party.

(2) SERVICE. — The summons and complaint in such an action shall be served as provided by the Federal Rules of Civil Procedure except that the delivery of the summons and complaint to the officer or agency as required by the rules may be made by certified mail beyond the territorial limits of the district in which the action is brought. . . .

(g) MULTIPARTY, MULTIFORUM LITIGATION. — A civil action in which jurisdiction of the district court is based upon section 1369 of this title may

be brought in any district in which any defendant resides or in which a substantial part of the accident giving rise to the action took place.

§ 1397. Interpleader

Any civil action of interpleader or in the nature of interpleader under section 1335 of this title may be brought in the judicial district in which one or more of the claimants reside.

§ 1400. Patents and copyrights, mask works, and designs

(a) Civil actions, suits, or proceedings arising under any Act of Congress relating to copyrights or exclusive rights in mask works or designs may be instituted in the district in which the defendant or his agent resides or may be found.

(b) Any civil action for patent infringement may be brought in the judicial district where the defendant resides, or where the defendant has committed acts of infringement and has a regular and established place of business.

§ 1404. Change of venue

(a) For the convenience of parties and witnesses, in the interest of justice, a district court may transfer any civil action to any other district or division where it might have been brought or to any district or division to which all parties have consented.

(b) Upon motion, consent or stipulation of all parties, any action, suit or proceeding of a civil nature or any motion or hearing thereof, may be transferred, in the discretion of the court, from the division in which pending to any other division in the same district. Transfer of proceedings in rem brought by or on behalf of the United States may be transferred under this section without the consent of the United States where all other parties request transfer.

(c) A district court may order any civil action to be tried at any place within the division in which it is pending. . . .

§ 1406. Cure or waiver of defects

(a) The district court of a district in which is filed a case laying venue in the wrong division or district shall dismiss, or if it be in the interest of justice, transfer such case to any district or division in which it could have been brought.

(b) Nothing in this chapter shall impair the jurisdiction of a district court of any matter involving a party who does not interpose timely and sufficient objection to the venue. . . .

§ 1407. Multidistrict litigation

(a) When civil actions involving one or more common questions of fact are pending in different districts, such actions may be transferred to any district for coordinated or consolidated pretrial proceedings. Such transfers shall be made by the judicial panel on multidistrict litigation authorized by this section upon its determination that transfers for such proceedings will be for the convenience of parties and witnesses and will promote the just and efficient conduct of such actions. Each action so transferred shall be remanded by the panel at or before the conclusion of such pretrial proceedings to the district from which it was transferred unless it shall have been previously terminated: *Provided, however*, That the panel may separate any claim, cross-claim, counter-claim, or third-party claim and remand any of such claims before the remainder of the action is remanded.

(b) Such coordinated or consolidated pretrial proceedings shall be conducted by a judge or judges to whom such actions are assigned by the judicial panel on multidistrict litigation. For this purpose, upon request of the panel, a circuit judge or a district judge may be designated and assigned temporarily for service in the transferee district by the Chief Justice of the United States or the chief judge of the circuit, as may be required, in accordance with the provisions of chapter 13 of this title. With the consent of the transferee district court, such actions may be assigned by the panel to a judge or judges of such district. The judge or judges to whom such actions are assigned, the members of the judicial panel on multidistrict litigation, and other circuit and district judges designated when needed by the panel may exercise the powers of a district judge in any district for the purpose of conducting pretrial depositions in such coordinated or consolidated pretrial proceedings.

(c) Proceedings for the transfer of an action under this section may be initiated by —

(i) the judicial panel on multidistrict litigation upon its own initiative, or

(ii) motion filed with the panel by a party in any action in which transfer for coordinated or consolidated pretrial proceedings under this section may be appropriate. A copy of such motion shall be filed in the district court in which the moving party's action is pending.

The panel shall give notice to the parties in all actions in which transfers for coordinated or consolidated pretrial proceedings are contemplated, and such notice shall specify the time and place of any hearing to determine whether such transfer shall be made. Orders of the panel to set a hearing and other orders of the panel issued prior to the order either directing or denying transfer shall be filed in the office of the clerk of the district court in which a transfer hearing is to be or has been

held. The panel's order of transfer shall be based upon a record of such hearing at which material evidence may be offered by any party to an action pending in any district that would be affected by the proceedings under this section, and shall be supported by findings of fact and conclusions of law based upon such record. Orders of transfer and such other orders as the panel may make thereafter shall be filed in the office of the clerk of the district court of the transferee district and shall be effective when thus filed. The clerk of the transferee district court shall forthwith transmit a certified copy of the panel's order to transfer to the clerk of the district court from which the action is being transferred. An order denying transfer shall be filed in each district wherein there is a case pending in which the motion for transfer has been made.

(d) The judicial panel on multidistrict litigation shall consist of seven circuit and district judges designated from time to time by the Chief Justice of the United States, no two of whom shall be from the same circuit. The concurrence of four members shall be necessary to any action by the panel.

(e) No proceedings for review of any order of the panel may be permitted except by extraordinary writ pursuant to the provisions of title 28, section 1651, United States Code. Petitions for an extraordinary writ to review an order of the panel to set a transfer hearing and other orders of the panel issued prior to the order either directing or denying transfer shall be filed only in the court of appeals having jurisdiction over the district in which a hearing is to be or has been held. Petitions for an extraordinary writ to review an order to transfer or orders subsequent to transfer shall be filed only in the court of appeals having jurisdiction over the transferee district. There shall be no appeal or review of an order of the panel denying a motion to transfer for consolidated or coordinated proceedings.

(f) The panel may prescribe rules for the conduct of its business not inconsistent with Acts of Congress and the Federal Rules of Civil Procedure.

(g) Nothing in this section shall apply to any action in which the United States is a complainant arising under the antitrust laws. . . .

(h) Notwithstanding the provisions of section 1404 or subsection (f) of this section, the judicial panel on multidistrict litigation may consolidate and transfer with or without the consent of the parties, for both pretrial purposes and for trial, any action brought under section 4C of the Clayton Act.

CHAPTER 89 — DISTRICT COURTS; REMOVAL OF CASES FROM STATE COURTS

§ 1441. Removal of civil actions

(a) GENERALLY. — Except as otherwise expressly provided by Act of Congress, any civil action brought in a State court of which the district courts of the United States have original jurisdiction, may be removed by the defendant or the defendants, to the district court of the United States for the district and division embracing the place where such action is pending.

(b) REMOVAL BASED ON DIVERSITY OF CITIZENSHIP. —

(1) In determining whether a civil action is removable on the basis of the jurisdiction under section 1332(a) of this title, the citizenship of defendants sued under fictitious names shall be disregarded.

(2) A civil action otherwise removable solely on the basis of the jurisdiction under section 1332(a) of this title may not be removed if any of the parties in interest properly joined and served as defendants is a citizen of the State in which such action is brought.

(c) JOINDER OF FEDERAL LAW CLAIMS AND STATE LAW CLAIMS. —

(1) If a civil action includes —

(A) a claim arising under the Constitution, laws, or treaties of the United States (within the meaning of section 1331 of this title), and

(B) a claim not within the original or supplemental jurisdiction of the district court or a claim that has been made nonremovable by statute,

the entire action may be removed if the action would be removable without the inclusion of the claim described in subparagraph (B).

(2) Upon removal of an action described in paragraph (1), the district court shall sever from the action all claims described in paragraph (1)(B) and shall remand the severed claims to the State court from which the action was removed. Only defendants against whom a claim described in paragraph (1)(A) has been asserted are required to join in or consent to the removal under paragraph (1). . . .

(e) MULTIPARTY, MULTIFORUM JURISDICTION. —

(1) Notwithstanding the provisions of subsection (b) of this section, a defendant in a civil action in a State court may remove the action to the district court of the United States for the district and division embracing the place where the action is pending if —

(A) the action could have been brought in a United States district court under section 1369 of this title; or

(B) the defendant is a party to an action which is or could have been brought, in whole or in part, under section 1369 in a United States district court and arises from the same accident as the action in State court, even if the action to be removed could not have been brought in a district court as an original matter.

The removal of an action under this subsection shall be made in accordance with section 1446 of this title, except that a notice of removal may also be filed before trial of the action in State court within 30 days after the date on which the defendant first becomes a party to an action under section 1369 in a United States district court that arises from the same accident as the action in State court, or at a later time with leave of the district court.

(2) Whenever an action is removed under this subsection and the district court to which it is removed or transferred under section 1407(j) has made a liability determination requiring further proceedings as to damages, the district court shall remand the action to the State court from which it had been removed for the determination of damages, unless the court finds that, for the convenience of parties and witnesses and in the interest of justice, the action should be retained for the determination of damages.

(3) Any remand under paragraph (2) shall not be effective until 60 days after the district court has issued an order determining liability and has certified its intention to remand the removed action for the determination of damages. An appeal with respect to the liability determination of the district court may be taken during that 60-day period to the court of appeals with appellate jurisdiction over the district court. In the event a party files such an appeal, the remand shall not be effective until the appeal has been finally disposed of. Once the remand has become effective, the liability determination shall not be subject to further review by appeal or otherwise.

(4) Any decision under this subsection concerning remand for the determination of damages shall not be reviewable by appeal or otherwise.

(5) An action removed under this subsection shall be deemed to be an action under section 1369 and an action in which jurisdiction is based on section 1369 of this title for purposes of this section and sections 1407, 1697, and 1785 of this title.

(6) Nothing in this subsection shall restrict the authority of the district court to transfer or dismiss an action on the ground of inconvenient forum.

(f) DERIVATIVE REMOVAL JURISDICTION. — The court to which a civil action is removed under this section is not precluded from hearing and determining any claim in such civil action because the State court from which such civil action is removed did not have jurisdiction over that claim.

§ 1442. Federal officers or agencies sued or prosecuted

(a) A civil action or criminal prosecution that is commenced in a State court and that is against or directed to any of the following may be removed by them to the district court of the United States for the district and division embracing the place wherein it is pending:

(1) The United States or any agency thereof or any officer (or any person acting under that officer) of the United States or of any agency thereof, in an official or individual capacity, for or relating to any act under color of such office or on account of any right, title or authority claimed under any Act of Congress for the apprehension or punishment of criminals or the collection of the revenue.

(2) A property holder whose title is derived from any such officer, where such action or prosecution affects the validity of any law of the United States.

(3) Any officer of the courts of the United States, for or relating to any act under color of office or in the performance of his duties;

(4) Any officer of either House of Congress, for or relating to any act in the discharge of his official duty under an order of such House.

(b) A personal action commenced in any State court by an alien against any citizen of a State who is, or at the time the alleged action accrued was, a civil officer of the United States and is a nonresident of such State, wherein jurisdiction is obtained by the State court by personal service of process, may be removed by the defendant to the district court of the United States for the district and division in which the defendant was served with process.

(c) As used in subsection (a), the terms "civil action" and "criminal prosecution" include any proceeding (whether or not ancillary to another proceeding) to the extent that in such proceeding a judicial order, including a subpoena for testimony or documents, is sought or issued. If removal is sought for a proceeding described in the previous sentence, and there is no other basis for removal, only that proceeding may be removed to the district court.

§ 1442a. Members of armed forces sued or prosecuted

A civil or criminal prosecution in a court of a State of the United States against a member of the armed forces of the United States on account of an act done under color of his office or status, or in respect to which he claims any right, title, or authority under a law of the United States respecting the armed forces thereof, or under the law of war, may at any time before the trial or final hearing thereof be removed for trial into the district court of the United States for the district where it is pending in the manner prescribed by law, and it shall thereupon be entered on the docket of the district court, which shall proceed as if the cause had been originally commenced therein and shall have full power to hear and determine the cause.

§ 1443. Civil rights cases

Any of the following civil actions or criminal prosecutions, commenced in a State court may be removed by the defendant to the district court of the United States for the district and division embracing the place wherein it is pending:

(1) Against any person who is denied or cannot enforce in the courts of such State a right under any law providing for the equal civil rights of citizens of the United States, or of all persons within the jurisdiction thereof;

(2) For any act under color of authority derived from any law providing for equal rights, or for refusing to do any act on the ground that it would be inconsistent with such law.

§ 1445. Nonremovable actions

(a) A civil action in any State court against a railroad or its receivers or trustees, arising under sections 1-4 and 5-10 of the Act of April 22, 1908 (45 U.S.C. 51-54, 55-60), may not be removed to any district court of the United States.

(b) A civil action in any State court against a carrier or its receivers or trustees to recover damages for delay, loss, or injury of shipments, arising under section 11706 or 14706 of title 49, may not be removed to any district court of the United States unless the matter in controversy exceeds $10,000, exclusive of interest and costs.

(c) A civil action in any State court arising under the workmen's compensation laws of such State may not be removed to any district court of the United States.

(d) A civil action in any State court arising under section 40302 of the Violence Against Women Act of 1994 may not be removed to any district court of the United States.

§ 1446. Procedure for removal of civil actions

(a) GENERALLY. — A defendant or defendants desiring to remove any civil action from a State court shall file in the district court of the United States for the district and division within which such action is pending a notice of removal signed pursuant to Rule 11 of the Federal Rules of Civil Procedure and containing a short and plain statement of the grounds for removal, together with a copy of all process, pleadings, and orders served upon such defendant or defendants in such action.

(b) REQUIREMENTS; GENERALLY. —

(1) The notice of removal of a civil action or proceeding shall be filed within 30 days after the receipt by the defendant, through service or otherwise, of a copy of the initial pleading setting forth the claim for relief upon which such action or proceeding is based, or within 30 days after the service of summons upon the defendant if such initial pleading has then been filed in court and is not required to be served on the defendant, whichever period is shorter.

(2) (A) When a civil action is removed solely under section 1441(a), all defendants who have been properly joined and served must join in or consent to the removal of the action.

(B) Each defendant shall have 30 days after receipt by or service on that defendant of the initial pleading or summons described in paragraph (1) to file the notice of removal.

(C) If defendants are served at different times, and a later-served defendant files a notice of removal, any earlier-served defendant may consent to the removal even though that earlier-served defendant did not previously initiate or consent to removal.

(3) Except as provided in subsection (c), if the case stated by the initial pleading is not removable, a notice of removal may be filed within 30 days after receipt by the defendant, through service or otherwise, of a copy of an amended pleading, motion, order or other paper from which it may first be ascertained that the case is one which is or has become removable.

(c) REQUIREMENTS; REMOVAL BASED ON DIVERSITY OF CITIZENSHIP. —

(1) A case may not be removed under subsection (b)(3) on the basis of jurisdiction conferred by section 1332 more than 1 year after commencement of the action, unless the district court finds that the

plaintiff has acted in bad faith in order to prevent a defendant from removing the action.

(2) If removal of a civil action is sought on the basis of the jurisdiction conferred by section 1332(a), the sum demanded in good faith in the initial pleading shall be deemed to be the amount in controversy, except that —

(A) the notice of removal may assert the amount in controversy if the initial pleading seeks —

(i) nonmonetary relief; or

(ii) a money judgment, but the State practice either does not permit demand for a specific sum or permits recovery of damages in excess of the amount demanded; and

(B) removal of the action is proper on the basis of an amount in controversy asserted under subparagraph (A) if the district court finds, by the preponderance of the evidence, that the amount in controversy exceeds the amount specified in section 1332(a).

(3) (A) If the case stated by the initial pleading is not removable solely because the amount in controversy does not exceed the amount specified in section 1332(a), information relating to the amount in controversy in the record of the State proceeding, or in responses to discovery, shall be treated as an "other paper" under subsection (b)(3).

(B) If the notice of removal is filed more than 1 year after commencement of the action and the district court finds that the plaintiff deliberately failed to disclose the actual amount in controversy to prevent removal, that finding shall be deemed bad faith under paragraph (1).

(d) NOTICE TO ADVERSE PARTIES AND STATE COURT. — Promptly after the filing of such notice of removal of a civil action the defendant or defendants shall give written notice thereof to all adverse parties and shall file a copy of the notice with the clerk of such State court, which shall effect the removal and the State court shall proceed no further unless and until the case is remanded. . . .

§ 1447. Procedure after removal generally

(a) In any case removed from a State court, the district court may issue all necessary orders and process to bring before it all proper parties whether served by process issued by the State court or otherwise.

(b) It may require the removing party to file with its clerk copies of all records and proceedings in such State court or may cause the same to be brought before it by writ of certiorari issued to such State court.

(c) A motion to remand the case on the basis of any defect other than lack of subject matter jurisdiction must be made within 30 days after the filing of the notice of removal under section 1446(a). If at any time before final judgment it appears that the district court lacks subject matter jurisdiction, the case shall be remanded. An order remanding the case may require payment of just costs and any actual expenses, including attorney fees, incurred as a result of the removal. A certified copy of the order of remand shall be mailed by the clerk to the clerk of the State court. The State court may thereupon proceed with such case.

(d) An order remanding a case to the State court from which it was removed is not reviewable on appeal or otherwise, except that an order remanding a case to the State court from which it was removed pursuant to section 1442 or 1443 of this title shall be reviewable by appeal or otherwise.

(e) If after removal the plaintiff seeks to join additional defendants whose joinder would destroy subject matter jurisdiction, the court may deny joinder, or permit joinder and remand the action to the State court.

§ 1448. Process after removal

In all cases removed from any State court to any district court of the United States in which any one or more of the defendants has not been served with process or in which the service has not been perfected prior to removal, or in which process served proves to be defective, such process or service may be completed or new process issued in the same manner as in cases originally filed in such district court.

This section shall not deprive any defendant upon whom process is served after removal of his right to move to remand the case.

§ 1453. Removal of class actions

(a) DEFINITIONS. — In this section, the terms “class”, “class action”, “class certification order”, and “class member” shall have the meanings given such terms under section 1332(d)(1).

(b) IN GENERAL. — A class action may be removed to a district court of the United States in accordance with section 1446 (except that the 1-year limitation under section 1446(c)(1) shall not apply), without regard to whether any defendant is a citizen of the State in which the action is brought, except that such action may be removed by any defendant without the consent of all defendants.

(c) REVIEW OF REMAND ORDERS. —

(1) IN GENERAL. — Section 1447 shall apply to any removal of a case under this section, except that notwithstanding section 1447(d), a court of appeals may accept an appeal from an order of a district court granting or denying a motion to remand a class action to the State court from which it was removed if application is made to the court of appeals not more than 10 days after entry of the order.

(2) TIME PERIOD FOR JUDGMENT. — If the court of appeals accepts an appeal under paragraph (1), the court shall complete all action on such appeal, including rendering judgment, not later than 60 days after the date on which such appeal was filed, unless an extension is granted under paragraph (3).

(3) EXTENSION OF TIME PERIOD. — The court of appeals may grant an extension of the 60-day period described in paragraph (2) if —

(A) all parties to the proceeding agree to such extension, for any period of time; or

(B) such extension is for good cause shown and in the interests of justice, for a period not to exceed 10 days.

(4) DENIAL OF APPEAL. — If a final judgment on the appeal under paragraph (1) is not issued before the end of the period described in paragraph (2), including any extension under paragraph (3), the appeal shall be denied.

(d) EXCEPTION. — This section shall not apply to any class action that solely involves —

(1) a claim concerning a covered security as defined under section 16(f)(3) of the Securities Act of 1933 (15 U.S.C. 78p(f)(3)) and section 28(f)(5)(E) of the Securities Exchange Act of 1934 (15 U.S.C. 78bb(f)(5)(E));

(2) a claim that relates to the internal affairs or governance of a corporation or other form of business enterprise and arises under or by virtue of the laws of the State in which such corporation or business enterprise is incorporated or organized; or

(3) a claim that relates to the rights, duties (including fiduciary duties), and obligations relating to or created by or pursuant to any security (as defined under section 2(a)(1) of the Securities Act of 1933 (15 U.S.C. 77b(a)(1)) and the regulations issued thereunder).

§ 1454. Patent, plant variety protection, and copyright cases

(a) IN GENERAL. — A civil action in which any party asserts a claim for relief arising under any Act of Congress relating to patents, plant variety

protection, or copyrights may be removed to the district court of the United States for the district and division embracing the place where the action is pending.

(b) SPECIAL RULES. — The removal of an action under this section shall be made in accordance with section 1446, except that if the removal is based solely on this section —

(1) the action may be removed by any party; and

(2) the time limitations contained in section 1446(b) may be extended at any time for cause shown.

(c) CLARIFICATION OF JURISDICTION IN CERTAIN CASES. — The court to which a civil action is removed under this section is not precluded from hearing and determining any claim in the civil action because the State court from which the civil action is removed did not have jurisdiction over that claim.

(d) REMAND. — If a civil action is removed solely under this section, the district court —

(1) shall remand all claims that are neither a basis for removal under subsection (a) nor within the original or supplemental jurisdiction of the district court under any Act of Congress; and

(2) may, under the circumstances specified in section 1367(c), remand any claims within the supplemental jurisdiction of the district court under section 1367.

CHAPTER 99 — GENERAL PROVISIONS

§ 1631. Transfer to cure want of jurisdiction

Whenever a civil action is filed in a court as defined in section 610 of this title or an appeal, including a petition for review of administrative action, is noticed for or filed with such a court and that court finds that there is a want of jurisdiction, the court shall, if it is in the interest of justice, transfer such action or appeal to any other such court in which the action or appeal could have been brought at the time it was filed or noticed, and the action or appeal shall proceed as if it had been filed in or noticed for the court to which it is transferred on the date upon which it was actually filed in or noticed for the court from which it is transferred.

PART V — PROCEDURE

CHAPTER 111 — GENERAL PROVISIONS

§ 1651. Writs

(a) The Supreme Court and all courts established by Act of Congress may issue all writs necessary or appropriate in aid of their respective jurisdictions and agreeable to the usages and principles of law. . . .

§ 1652. State laws as rules of decision

The laws of the several states, except where the Constitution or treaties of the United States or Acts of Congress otherwise require or provide, shall be regarded as rules of decision in civil actions in the courts of the United States, in cases where they apply.

§ 1653. Amendment of pleadings to show jurisdiction

Defective allegations of jurisdiction may be amended, upon terms, in the trial or appellate courts.

§ 1655. Lien enforcement; absent defendants

In an action in a district court to enforce any lien upon or claim to, or to remove any incumbrance or lien or cloud upon the title to, real or personal property within the district, where any defendant cannot be served within the State, or does not voluntarily appear, the court may order the absent defendant to appear or plead by a day certain.

Such order shall be served on the absent defendant personally if practicable, wherever found, and also upon the person or persons in possession or charge of such property, if any. Where personal service is not practicable, the order shall be published as the court may direct, not less than once a week for six consecutive weeks.

If an absent defendant does not appear or plead within the time allowed, the court may proceed as if the absent defendant had been served with process within the State, but any adjudication shall, as regards the absent defendant without appearance, affect only the property which is the subject of the action. When a part of the property is within another district, but within the same state, such action may be brought in either district.

Any defendant not so personally notified may, at any time within one year after final judgment, enter his appearance, and thereupon the court shall set aside the judgment and permit such defendant to plead on payment of such costs as the court deems just.

CHAPTER 113 — PROCESS

§ 1696. Service in foreign and international litigation

(a) The district court of the district in which a person resides or is found may order service upon him of any document issued in connection with a proceeding in a foreign or international tribunal. The order may be made pursuant to a letter rogatory issued, or request made, by a foreign or international tribunal or upon application of any interested person and shall direct the manner of service. Service pursuant to this subsection does not, of itself, require the recognition or enforcement in the United States of a judgment, decree, or order rendered by a foreign or international tribunal.

(b) This section does not preclude service of such a document without an order of court.

§ 1697. Service in multiparty, multiforum actions

When the jurisdiction of the district court is based in whole or in part upon section 1369 of this title, process, other than subpoenas, may be served at any place within the United States, or anywhere outside the United States if otherwise permitted by law.

CHAPTER 114 — CLASS ACTIONS

§ 1711. Definitions

In this chapter:

(1) CLASS. — The term "class" means all of the class members in a class action.

(2) CLASS ACTION. — The term "class action" means any civil action filed in a district court of the United States under rule 23 of the Federal Rules of Civil Procedure or any civil action that is removed to a district court of the United States that was originally filed under a State statute or rule of judicial procedure authorizing an action to be brought by 1 or more representatives as a class action.

(3) CLASS COUNSEL. — The term "class counsel" means the persons who serve as the attorneys for the class members in a proposed or certified class action.

(4) CLASS MEMBERS. — The term "class members" means the persons (named or unnamed) who fall within the definition of the proposed or certified class in a class action.

(5) PLAINTIFF CLASS ACTION. — The term "plaintiff class action" means a class action in which class members are plaintiffs.

(6) PROPOSED SETTLEMENT. — The term "proposed settlement" means an agreement regarding a class action that is subject to court approval and that, if approved, would be binding on some or all class members.

§ 1712. Coupon settlements

(a) CONTINGENT FEES IN COUPON SETTLEMENTS. — If a proposed settlement in a class action provides for a recovery of coupons to a class member, the portion of any attorney's fee award to class counsel that is attributable to the award of the coupons shall be based on the value to class members of the coupons that are redeemed.

(b) OTHER ATTORNEY'S FEE AWARDS IN COUPON SETTLEMENTS. —

(1) IN GENERAL. — If a proposed settlement in a class action provides for a recovery of coupons to class members, and a portion of the recovery of the coupons is not used to determine the attorney's fee to be paid to class counsel, any attorney's fee award shall be based upon the amount of time class counsel reasonably expended working on the action.

(2) COURT APPROVAL. — Any attorney's fee under this subsection shall be subject to approval by the court and shall include an appropriate attorney's fee, if any, for obtaining equitable relief, including an injunction, if applicable. Nothing in this subsection shall be construed to prohibit application of a lodestar with a multiplier method of determining attorney's fees.

(c) ATTORNEY'S FEE AWARDS CALCULATED ON A MIXED BASIS IN COUPON SETTLEMENTS. — If a proposed settlement in a class action provides for an award of coupons to class members and also provides for equitable relief, including injunctive relief —

(1) that portion of the attorney's fee to be paid to class counsel that is based upon a portion of the recovery of the coupons shall be calculated in accordance with subsection (a); and

(2) that portion of the attorney's fee to be paid to class counsel that is not based upon a portion of the recovery of the coupons shall be calculated in accordance with subsection (b).

(d) SETTLEMENT VALUATION EXPERTISE. — In a class action involving the awarding of coupons, the court may, in its discretion upon the motion of a party, receive expert testimony from a witness qualified to provide information on the actual value to the class members of the coupons that are redeemed.

(e) JUDICIAL SCRUTINY OF COUPON SETTLEMENTS. — In a proposed settlement under which class members would be awarded coupons, the court may approve the proposed settlement only after a hearing to determine whether, and making a written finding that, the settlement is fair, reasonable, and adequate for class members. The court, in its discretion, may also require that a proposed settlement agreement provide for the distribution of a portion of the value of unclaimed coupons to 1 or more charitable or governmental organizations, as agreed to by the parties. The distribution and redemption of any proceeds under this subsection shall not be used to calculate attorneys' fees under this section.

§ 1713. Protection against loss by class members

The court may approve a proposed settlement under which any class member is obligated to pay sums to class counsel that would result in a net loss to the class member only if the court makes a written finding that nonmonetary benefits to the class member substantially outweigh the monetary loss.

§ 1714. Protection against discrimination based on geographic location

The court may not approve a proposed settlement that provides for the payment of greater sums to some class members than to others solely on the basis that the class members to whom the greater sums are to be paid are located in closer geographic proximity to the court.

§ 1715. Notifications to appropriate Federal and State officials

(a) DEFINITIONS. —

(1) APPROPRIATE FEDERAL OFFICIAL. — In this section, the term "appropriate Federal official" means —

(A) the Attorney General of the United States; or

(B) in any case in which the defendant is a Federal depository institution, a State depository institution, a depository institution holding company, a foreign bank, or a nondepository institution subsidiary of the foregoing (as such terms are defined in section 3 of the Federal Deposit Insurance Act (12 U.S.C. 1813)), the person who has the primary Federal regulatory or supervisory responsibility with respect to the defendant, if some or all of the matters alleged in the class action are subject to regulation or supervision by that person.

(2) APPROPRIATE STATE OFFICIAL. — In this section, the term "appropriate State official" means the person in the State who has the

primary regulatory or supervisory responsibility with respect to the defendant, or who licenses or otherwise authorizes the defendant to conduct business in the State, if some or all of the matters alleged in the class action are subject to regulation by that person. If there is no primary regulator, supervisor, or licensing authority, or the matters alleged in the class action are not subject to regulation or supervision by that person, then the appropriate State official shall be the State attorney general.

(b) IN GENERAL. — Not later than 10 days after a proposed settlement of a class action is filed in court, each defendant that is participating in the proposed settlement shall serve upon the appropriate State official of each State in which a class member resides and the appropriate Federal official, a notice of the proposed settlement consisting of —

(1) a copy of the complaint and any materials filed with the complaint and any amended complaints (except such materials shall not be required to be served if such materials are made electronically available through the Internet and such service includes notice of how to electronically access such material);

(2) notice of any scheduled judicial hearing in the class action;

(3) any proposed or final notification to class members of —

(A) (i) the members' rights to request exclusion from the class action; or

(ii) if no right to request exclusion exists, a statement that no such right exists; and

(B) a proposed settlement of a class action;

(4) any proposed or final class action settlement;

(5) any settlement or other agreement contemporaneously made between class counsel and counsel for the defendants;

(6) any final judgment or notice of dismissal;

(7) (A) if feasible, the names of class members who reside in each State and the estimated proportionate share of the claims of such members to the entire settlement to that State's appropriate State official; or

(B) if the provision of information under subparagraph (A) is not feasible, a reasonable estimate of the number of class members residing in each State and the estimated proportionate share of the claims of such members to the entire settlement; and

(8) any written judicial opinion relating to the materials described under subparagraphs (3) through (6).

(c) DEPOSITORY INSTITUTIONS NOTIFICATION. —

(1) FEDERAL AND OTHER DEPOSITORY INSTITUTIONS. — In any case in which the defendant is a Federal depository institution, a depository institution holding company, a foreign bank, or a non-depository institution subsidiary of the foregoing, the notice requirements of this section are satisfied by serving the notice required under subsection (b) upon the person who has the primary Federal regulatory or supervisory responsibility with respect to the defendant, if some or all of the matters alleged in the class action are subject to regulation or supervision by that person.

(2) STATE DEPOSITORY INSTITUTIONS. — In any case in which the defendant is a State depository institution (as that term is defined in section 3 of the Federal Deposit Insurance Act (12 U.S.C. 1813)), the notice requirements of this section are satisfied by serving the notice required under subsection (b) upon the State bank supervisor (as that term is defined in section 3 of the Federal Deposit Insurance Act (12 U.S.C. 1813)) of the State in which the defendant is incorporated or chartered, if some or all of the matters alleged in the class action are subject to regulation or supervision by that person, and upon the appropriate Federal official.

(d) FINAL APPROVAL. — An order giving final approval of a proposed settlement may not be issued earlier than 90 days after the later of the dates on which the appropriate Federal official and the appropriate State official are served with the notice required under subsection (b).

(e) NONCOMPLIANCE IF NOTICE NOT PROVIDED. —

(1) IN GENERAL. — A class member may refuse to comply with and may choose not to be bound by a settlement agreement or consent decree in a class action if the class member demonstrates that the notice required under subsection (b) has not been provided.

(2) LIMITATION. — A class member may not refuse to comply with or to be bound by a settlement agreement or consent decree under paragraph (1) if the notice required under subsection (b) was directed to the appropriate Federal official and to either the State attorney general or the person that has primary regulatory, supervisory, or licensing authority over the defendant.

(3) APPLICATION OF RIGHTS. — The rights created by this subsection shall apply only to class members or any person acting on a class member's behalf, and shall not be construed to limit any other rights affecting a class member's participation in the settlement.

(f) RULE OF CONSTRUCTION. — Nothing in this section shall be construed to expand the authority of, or impose any obligations, duties, or responsibilities upon, Federal or State officials.

CHAPTER 115 — EVIDENCE; DOCUMENTARY

§ 1738. State and Territorial statutes and judicial proceedings; full faith and credit

The Acts of the legislature of any State, Territory, or Possession of the United States, or copies thereof, shall be authenticated by affixing the seal of such State, Territory or Possession thereto.

The records and judicial proceedings of any court of any such State, Territory or Possession, or copies thereof, shall be proved or admitted in other courts within the United States and its Territories and Possessions by the attestation of the clerk and seal of the court annexed, if a seal exists, together with a certificate of a judge of the court that the said attestation is in proper form.

Such Acts, records and judicial proceedings or copies thereof, so authenticated, shall have the same full faith and credit in every court within the United States and its Territories and Possessions as they have by law or usage in the courts of such State, Territory or Possession from which they are taken.

CHAPTER 117 — EVIDENCE; DEPOSITIONS

§ 1781. Transmittal of letter rogatory or request

(a) The Department of State has power, directly, or through suitable channels —

(1) to receive a letter rogatory issued, or request made, by a foreign or international tribunal, to transmit it to the tribunal, officer, or agency in the United States to whom it is addressed, and to receive and return it after execution; and

(2) to receive a letter rogatory issued, or request made, by a tribunal in the United States, to transmit it to the foreign or international tribunal, officer, or agency to whom it is addressed, and to receive and return it after execution.

(b) This section does not preclude —

(1) the transmittal of a letter rogatory or request directly from a foreign or international tribunal to the tribunal, officer, or agency in

the United States to whom it is addressed and its return in the same manner; or

(2) the transmittal of a letter rogatory or request directly from a tribunal in the United States to the foreign or international tribunal, officer, or agency to whom it is addressed and its return in the same manner.

§ 1782. Assistance to foreign and international tribunals and to litigants before such tribunals

(a) The district court of the district in which a person resides or is found may order him to give his testimony or statement or to produce a document or other thing for use in a proceeding in a foreign or international tribunal, including criminal investigations conducted before formal accusation. The order may be made pursuant to a letter rogatory issued, or request made, by a foreign or international tribunal or upon the application of any interested person and may direct that the testimony or statement be given, or the document or other thing be produced, before a person appointed by the court. By virtue of his appointment, the person appointed has power to administer any necessary oath and take the testimony or statement. The order may prescribe the practice and procedure, which may be in whole or part the practice and procedure of the foreign country or the international tribunal, for taking the testimony or statement or producing the document or other thing. To the extent that the order does not prescribe otherwise, the testimony or statement shall be taken, and the document or other thing produced, in accordance with the Federal Rules of Civil Procedure.

A person may not be compelled to give his testimony or statement or to produce a document or other thing in violation of any legally applicable privilege.

(b) This chapter does not preclude a person within the United States from voluntarily giving his testimony or statement, or producing a document or other thing, for use in a proceeding in a foreign or international tribunal before any person and in any manner acceptable to him.

§ 1783. Subpoena of person in foreign country

(a) A court of the United States may order the issuance of a subpoena requiring the appearance as a witness before it, or before a person or body designated by it, of a national or resident of the United States who is in a foreign country, or requiring the production of a specified document or other thing by him, if the court finds that particular testimony or the production of the document or other thing by him is necessary in the

interest of justice, and, in other than a criminal action or proceeding, if the court finds, in addition, that it is not possible to obtain his testimony in admissible form without his personal appearance or to obtain the production of the document or other thing in any other manner.

(b) The subpoena shall designate the time and place for the appearance or for the production of the document or other thing. Service of the subpoena and any order to show cause, rule, judgment, or decree authorized by this section or by section 1784 of this title shall be effected in accordance with the provisions of the Federal Rules of Civil Procedure relating to service of process on a person in a foreign country. The person serving the subpoena shall tender to the person to whom the subpoena is addressed his estimated necessary travel and attendance expenses, the amount of which shall be determined by the court and stated in the order directing the issuance of the subpoena.

§ 1785. Subpoenas in multiparty, multiforum actions

When the jurisdiction of the district court is based in whole or in part upon section 1369 of this title, a subpoena for attendance at a hearing or trial may, if authorized by the court upon motion for good cause shown, and upon such terms and conditions as the court may impose, be served at any place within the United States, or anywhere outside the United States if otherwise permitted by law.

CHAPTER 121 — JURIES; TRIAL BY JURY

§ 1861. Declaration of policy

It is the policy of the United States that all litigants in Federal courts entitled to trial by jury shall have the right to grand and petit juries selected at random from a fair cross section of the community in the district or division wherein the court convenes. It is further the policy of the United States that all citizens shall have the opportunity to be considered for service on grand and petit juries in the district courts of the United States, and shall have an obligation to serve as jurors when summoned for that purpose.

§ 1862. Discrimination prohibited

No citizen shall be excluded from service as a grand or petit juror in the district courts of the United States or in the Court of International Trade on account of race, color, religion, sex, national origin, or economic status.

§ 1863. Plan for random jury selection

(a) Each United States district court shall devise and place into operation a written plan for random selection of grand and petit jurors that shall be designed to achieve the objectives of sections 1861 and 1862 of this title, and that shall otherwise comply with the provisions of this title. The plan shall be placed into operation after approval by a reviewing panel consisting of the members of the judicial council of the circuit and either the chief judge of the district whose plan is being reviewed or such other active district judge of that district as the chief judge of the district may designate. The panel shall examine the plan to ascertain that it complies with the provisions of this title. If the reviewing panel finds that the plan does not comply, the panel shall state the particulars in which the plan fails to comply and direct the district court to present within a reasonable time an alternative plan remedying the defect or defects. Separate plans may be adopted for each division or combination of divisions within a judicial district. The district court may modify a plan at any time and it shall modify the plan when so directed by the reviewing panel. The district court shall promptly notify the panel, the Administrative Office of the United States Courts, and the Attorney General of the United States, of the initial adoption and future modifications of the plan by filing copies therewith. Modifications of the plan made at the instance of the district court shall become effective after approval by the panel. Each district court shall submit a report on the jury selection process within its jurisdiction to the Administrative Office of the United States Courts in such form and at such times as the Judicial Conference of the United States may specify. The Judicial Conference of the United States may, from time to time, adopt rules and regulations governing the provisions and the operation of the plans formulated under this title. . . .

§ 1865. Qualifications for jury service

(a) The chief judge of the district court, or such other district court judge as the plan may provide, on his initiative or upon recommendation of the clerk or jury commission, or the clerk under supervision of the court if the court's jury selection plan so authorizes, shall determine solely on the basis of information provided on the juror qualification form and other competent evidence whether a person is unqualified for, or exempt, or to be excused from jury service. The clerk shall enter such determination in the space provided on the juror qualification form and in any alphabetical list of names drawn from the master jury wheel. If a person did not appear in response to a summons, such fact shall be noted on said list.

(b) In making such determination the chief judge of the district court, or such other district court judge as the plan may provide, or the clerk if

the court's jury selection plan so provides, shall deem any person qualified to serve on grand and petit juries in the district court unless he —

(1) is not a citizen of the United States eighteen years old who has resided for a period of one year within the judicial district;

(2) is unable to read, write, and understand the English language with a degree of proficiency sufficient to fill out satisfactorily the juror qualification form;

(3) is unable to speak the English language;

(4) is incapable, by reason of mental or physical infirmity, to render satisfactory jury service; or

(5) has a charge pending against him for the commission of, or has been convicted in a State or Federal court of record of, a crime punishable by imprisonment for more than one year and his civil rights have not been restored.

§ 1867. Challenging compliance with selection procedures

. . .

(c) In civil cases, before the voir dire examination begins, or within seven days after the party discovered or could have discovered, by the exercise of diligence, the grounds therefor, whichever is earlier, any party may move to stay the proceedings on the ground of substantial failure to comply with the provisions of this title in selecting the petit jury.

(d) Upon motion filed under subsection . . . (c) of this section, containing a sworn statement of facts which, if true, would constitute a substantial failure to comply with the provisions of this title, the moving party shall be entitled to present in support of such motion the testimony of the jury commission or clerk, if available, any relevant records and papers not public or otherwise available used by the jury commissioner or clerk, and any other relevant evidence. . . . If the court determines that there has been a substantial failure to comply with the provisions of this title in selecting the petit jury, the court shall stay the proceedings pending the selection of a petit jury in conformity with this title.

(e) The procedures prescribed by this section shall be the exclusive means by which . . . a party in a civil case may challenge any jury on the ground that such jury was not selected in conformity with the provisions of this title. Nothing in this section shall preclude any person or the United States from pursuing any other remedy, civil or criminal, which may be available for the vindication or enforcement of any law prohibiting discrimination on account of race, color, religion, sex, national origin or economic status in the selection of persons for service on grand or petit juries.

§ 1870. Challenges

In civil cases, each party shall be entitled to three peremptory challenges. Several defendants or several plaintiffs may be considered as a single party for the purposes of making challenges, or the court may allow additional peremptory challenges and permit them to be exercised separately or jointly.

All challenges for cause or favor, whether to the array or panel or to individual jurors, shall be determined by the court.

CHAPTER 123 — FEES AND COSTS

§ 1920. Taxation of costs

A judge or clerk of any court of the United States may tax as costs the following:

(1) Fees of the clerk and marshal;

(2) Fees of the court reporter for all or any part of the stenographic transcript necessarily obtained for use in the case;

(3) Fees and disbursements for printing and witnesses;

(4) Fees for exemplification and copies of papers necessarily obtained for use in the case;

(5) Docket fees under section 1923 of this title;

(6) Compensation of court appointed experts, compensation of interpreters, and salaries, fees, expenses, and costs of special interpretation services under section 1828 of this title.

A bill of costs shall be filed in the case and, upon allowance, included in the judgment or decree.

§ 1927. Counsel's liability for excessive costs

Any attorney or other person admitted to conduct cases in any court of the United States or any Territory thereof who so multiplies the proceedings in any case unreasonably and vexatiously may be required by the court to satisfy personally the excess costs, expenses, and attorneys' fees reasonably incurred because of such conduct.

CHAPTER 125 — PENDING ACTIONS AND JUDGMENTS

§ 1963. Registration of judgments for enforcement in other districts

A judgment in an action for the recovery of money or property entered in any court of appeals, district court, bankruptcy court, or in the Court of International Trade may be registered by filing a certified copy of the judgment in any other district or, with respect to the Court of International Trade, in any judicial district, when the judgment has become final by appeal or expiration of the time for appeal or when ordered by the court that entered the judgment for good cause shown. Such a judgment entered in favor of the United States may be so registered any time after judgment is entered. A judgment so registered shall have the same effect as a judgment of the district court of the district where registered and may be enforced in like manner.

A certified copy of the satisfaction of any judgment in whole or in part may be registered in like manner in any district in which the judgment is a lien.

The procedure prescribed under this section is in addition to other procedures provided by law for the enforcement of judgments.

PART VI — PARTICULAR PROCEEDINGS

CHAPTER 131 — RULES OF COURTS

§ 2071. Rule-making power generally

(a) The Supreme Court and all courts established by Act of Congress may from time to time prescribe rules for the conduct of their business. Such rules shall be consistent with Acts of Congress and rules of practice and procedure prescribed under section 2072 of this title.

(b) Any rule prescribed by a court, other than the Supreme Court, under subsection (a) shall be prescribed only after giving appropriate public notice and an opportunity for comment. Such rule shall take effect upon the date specified by the prescribing court and shall have such effect on pending proceedings as the prescribing court may order.

(c) (1) A rule of a district court prescribed under subsection (a) shall remain in effect unless modified or abrogated by the judicial council of the relevant circuit.

(2) Any other rule prescribed by a court other than the Supreme Court under subsection (a) shall remain in effect unless modified or abrogated by the Judicial Conference.

(d) Copies of rules prescribed under subsection (a) by a district court shall be furnished to the judicial council, and copies of all rules prescribed by a court other than the Supreme Court under subsection (a) shall be furnished to the Director of the Administrative Office of the United States Courts and made available to the public.

(e) If the prescribing court determines that there is an immediate need for a rule, such court may proceed under this section without public notice and opportunity for comment, but such court shall promptly thereafter afford such notice and opportunity for comment.

(f) No rule may be prescribed by a district court other than under this section.

§ 2072. Rules of procedure and evidence; power to prescribe

(a) The Supreme Court shall have the power to prescribe general rules of practice and procedure and rules of evidence for cases in the United States district courts (including proceedings before magistrate judges thereof) and courts of appeals.

(b) Such rules shall not abridge, enlarge or modify any substantive right. All laws in conflict with such rules shall be of no further force or effect after such rules have taken effect.

(c) Such rules may define when a ruling of a district court is final for the purposes of appeal under section 1291 of this title.

§ 2073. Rules of procedure and evidence; method of prescribing

(a) (1) The Judicial Conference shall prescribe and publish the procedures for the consideration of proposed rules under this section.

(2) The Judicial Conference may authorize the appointment of committees to assist the Conference by recommending rules to be prescribed under sections 2072 . . . of this title. Each such committee shall consist of members of the bench and the professional bar, and trial and appellate judges.

(b) The Judicial Conference shall authorize the appointment of a standing committee on rules of practice, procedure, and evidence under subsection (a) of this section. Such standing committee shall review each recommendation of any other committees so appointed and recommend to the Judicial Conference rules of practice, procedure, and evidence and such changes in rules proposed by a committee appointed under subsection

(a)(2) of this section as may be necessary to maintain consistency and otherwise promote the interest of justice.

(c) (1) Each meeting for the transaction of business under this chapter by any committee appointed under this section shall be open to the public, except when the committee so meeting, in open session and with a majority present, determines that it is in the public interest that all or part of the remainder of the meeting on that day shall be closed to the public, and states the reason for so closing the meeting. Minutes of each meeting for the transaction of business under this chapter shall be maintained by the committee and made available to the public, except that any portion of such minutes, relating to a closed meeting and made available to the public, may contain such deletions as may be necessary to avoid frustrating the purposes of closing the meeting.

(2) Any meeting for the transaction of business under this chapter, by a committee appointed under this section, shall be preceded by sufficient notice to enable all interested persons to attend.

(d) In making a recommendation under this section or under section 2072 . . ., the body making that recommendation shall provide a proposed rule, an explanatory note on the rule, and a written report explaining the body's action, including any minority or other separate views.

(e) Failure to comply with this section does not invalidate a rule prescribed under section 2072 . . . of this title.

§ 2074. Rules of procedure and evidence; submission to Congress; effective date

(a) The Supreme Court shall transmit to the Congress not later than May 1 of the year in which a rule prescribed under section 2072 is to become effective a copy of the proposed rule. Such rule shall take effect no earlier than December 1 of the year in which such rule is so transmitted unless otherwise provided by law. The Supreme Court may fix the extent such rule shall apply to proceedings then pending, except that the Supreme Court shall not require the application of such rule to further proceedings then pending to the extent that, in the opinion of the court in which such proceedings are pending, the application of such rule in such proceedings would not be feasible or would work injustice, in which event the former rule applies.

(b) Any such rule creating, abolishing, or modifying an evidentiary privilege shall have no force or effect unless approved by Act of Congress.

CHAPTER 133 — REVIEW — MISCELLANEOUS PROVISIONS

§ 2111. Harmless error

On the hearing of any appeal or writ of certiorari in any case, the court shall give judgment after an examination of the record without regard to errors or defects which do not affect the substantial rights of the parties.

PART VI — PARTICULAR PROCEEDINGS

CHAPTER 151 — DECLARATORY JUDGMENTS

§ 2201. Creation of remedy

(a) In a case of actual controversy within its jurisdiction, except with respect to Federal taxes other than actions brought under section 7428 of the Internal Revenue Code of 1986, a proceeding under section 505 or 1146 of title 11, or in any civil action involving an antidumping or countervailing duty proceeding regarding a class or kind of merchandise of a free trade area country (as defined in section 516A(f)(10) of the Tariff Act of 1930), as determined by the administering authority, any court of the United States, upon the filing of an appropriate pleading, may declare the rights and other legal relations of any interested party seeking such declaration, whether or not further relief is or could be sought. Any such declaration shall have the force and effect of a final judgment or decree and shall be reviewable as such. . . .

§ 2202. Further relief

Further necessary or proper relief based on a declaratory judgment or decree may be granted, after reasonable notice and hearing, against any adverse party whose rights have been determined by such judgment.

CHAPTER 155 — INJUNCTIONS; THREE-JUDGE COURTS

§ 2283. Stay of State court proceedings

A court of the United States may not grant an injunction to stay proceedings in a State court except as expressly authorized by Act of Congress, or where necessary in aid of its jurisdiction, or to protect or effectuate its judgments.

CHAPTER 159 — INTERPLEADER

§ 2361. Process and procedure

In any civil action of interpleader or in the nature of interpleader under section 1335 of this title, a district court may issue its process for all claimants and enter its order restraining them from instituting or prosecuting any proceeding in any State or United States court affecting the property, instrument or obligation involved in the interpleader action until further order of the court. Such process and order shall be returnable at such time as the court or judge thereof directs, and shall be addressed to and served by the United States marshals for the respective districts where the claimants reside or may be found.

Such district court shall hear and determine the case, and may discharge the plaintiff from further liability, make the injunction permanent, and make all appropriate orders to enforce its judgment.

CHAPTER 190 — MISCELLANEOUS

§ 5001. Civil action for death or personal injury in a place subject to exclusive jurisdiction of United States

(a) DEATH. — In the case of the death of an individual by the neglect or wrongful act of another in a place subject to the exclusive jurisdiction of the United States within a State, a right of action shall exist as though the place were under the jurisdiction of the State in which the place is located.

(b) PERSONAL INJURY. — In a civil action brought to recover on account of an injury sustained in a place described in subsection (a), the rights of the parties shall be governed by the law of the State in which the place is located.

* * * * *

TITLE 29. LABOR

CHAPTER 14 — AGE DISCRIMINATION IN EMPLOYMENT

§ 623. Prohibition of age discrimination

(a) **Employer practices**

It shall be unlawful for an employer —

(1) to fail or refuse to hire or to discharge any individual or otherwise discriminate against any individual with respect to his compensation, terms, conditions, or privileges of employment, because of such individual's age;

(2) to limit, segregate, or classify his employees in any way which would deprive or tend to deprive any individual of employment opportunities or otherwise adversely affect his status as an employee, because of such individual's age; or

(3) to reduce the wage rate of any employee in order to comply with this chapter. . . .

* * * * *

TITLE 42. THE PUBLIC HEALTH AND WELFARE

CHAPTER 21 — CIVIL RIGHTS

§ 1983. Civil action for deprivation of rights

Every person who, under color of any statute, ordinance, regulation, custom, or usage, of any State or Territory or the District of Columbia, subjects, or causes to be subjected, any citizen of the United States or other person within the jurisdiction thereof to the deprivation of any rights, privileges, or immunities secured by the Constitution and laws, shall be liable to the party injured in an action at law, suit in equity, or other proper proceeding for redress, except that in any action brought against a judicial officer for an act or omission taken in such officer's judicial capacity, injunctive relief shall not be granted unless a declaratory decree was violated or declaratory relief was unavailable. For the purposes of this section, any Act of Congress applicable exclusively to the District of Columbia shall be considered to be a statute of the District of Columbia.

§ 1988. Proceedings in vindication of civil rights

(a) **Applicability of statutory and common law**

The jurisdiction in civil and criminal matters conferred on the district courts by the provisions of titles 13, 24, and 70 of the Revised Statutes for the protection of all persons in the United States in their civil rights, and for their vindication, shall be exercised and enforced in conformity with the laws of the United States, so far as such laws are suitable to carry the same into effect; but in all cases where they are not adapted to the object, or are deficient in the provisions necessary to furnish suitable remedies and punish offenses against law, the common law, as modified and changed by the constitution and statutes of the State wherein the court having jurisdiction of such civil or criminal cause is held, so far as the same is not inconsistent with the Constitution and laws of the United States, shall be extended to and govern the said courts in the trial and disposition of the cause, and, if it is of a criminal nature, in the infliction of punishment on the party found guilty.

(b) **Attorney's fees**

In any action or proceeding to enforce a provision of [section 1983 or various other listed civil rights statutes], the court, in its discretion, may allow the prevailing party, other than the United States, a reasonable attorney's fee as part of the costs, except that in any action brought against

a judicial officer for an act or omission taken in such officer's judicial capacity such officer shall not be held liable for any costs, including attorney's fees, unless such action was clearly in excess of such officer's jurisdiction.

(c) **Expert fees**

In awarding an attorney's fee under subsection (b) of this section in any action or proceeding to enforce a provision of section 1981 or 1981a of this title, the court, in its discretion, may include expert fees as part of the attorney's fee.

§ 2000e-2. Unlawful employment practices

(a) **Employer practices**

It shall be an unlawful employment practice for an employer —

(1) to fail or refuse to hire or to discharge any individual, or otherwise to discriminate against any individual with respect to his compensation, terms, conditions, or privileges of employment, because of such individual's race, color, religion, sex, or national origin; or

(2) to limit, segregate, or classify his employees or applicants for employment in any way which would deprive or tend to deprive any individual of employment opportunities or otherwise adversely affect his status as an employee, because of such individual's race, color, religion, sex, or national origin. . . .

UNITED STATES CONSTITUTION

PREAMBLE

WE THE PEOPLE of the United States, in Order to form a more perfect Union, establish Justice, insure domestic Tranquility, provide for the common defence, promote the general Welfare, and secure the Blessings of Liberty to ourselves and our Posterity, do ordain and establish this CONSTITUTION for the United States of America.

ARTICLE I.

SECTION 1. All legislative Powers herein granted shall be vested in a Congress of the United States, which shall consist of a Senate and House of Representatives.

SECTION 2. The House of Representatives shall be composed of Members chosen every second Year by the People of the several States, and the Electors in each State shall have the Qualifications requisite for Electors of the most numerous Branch of the State Legislature.

No Person shall be a Representative who shall not have attained to the Age of twenty five Years, and been seven Years a Citizen of the United States, and who shall not, when elected, be an Inhabitant of that State in which he shall be chosen.

Representatives and direct Taxes shall be apportioned among the several States which may be included within this Union, according to their respective Numbers, which shall be determined by adding to the whole Number of free Persons, including those bound to Service for a Term of Years, and excluding Indians not taxed, three fifths of all other Persons. The actual Enumeration shall be made within three Years after the first Meeting of the Congress of the United States, and within every subsequent Term of ten Years, in such Manner as they shall by Law direct. The Number of Representatives shall not exceed one for every thirty Thousand, but each State shall have at Least one Representative; and until such enumeration shall be made, the State of New Hampshire shall be entitled to chuse three, Massachusetts eight, Rhode Island and Providence Plantations one, Connecticut five, New York six, New Jersey four, Pennsylvania eight, Delaware one, Maryland six, Virginia ten, North Carolina five, South Carolina five, and Georgia three.

When vacancies happen in the Representation from any State, the Executive Authority thereof shall issue Writs of Election to fill such Vacancies.

The House of Representatives shall chuse their Speaker and other Officers; and shall have the sole Power of Impeachment.

SECTION 3. The Senate of the United States shall be composed of two Senators from each State, chosen by the Legislature thereof, for six Years; and each Senator shall have one Vote.

Immediately after they shall be assembled in Consequence of the first Election, they shall be divided as equally as may be into three Classes. The Seats of the Senators of the first Class shall be vacated at the Expiration of the second Year, of the second Class at the Expiration of the fourth Year, and of the third Class at the Expiration of the sixth Year, so that one third may be chosen every second Year; and if Vacancies happen by Resignation, or otherwise, during the Recess of the Legislature of any State, the Executive thereof may make temporary Appointments until the next Meeting of the Legislature, which shall then fill such Vacancies.

No Person shall be a Senator who shall not have attained to the Age of thirty Years, and been nine Years a Citizen of the United States, and who shall not, when elected, be an Inhabitant of that State for which he shall be chosen.

The Vice President of the United States shall be President of the Senate, but shall have no Vote, unless they be equally divided.

The Senate shall chuse their other Officers, and also a President pro tempore, in the Absence of the Vice President, or when he shall exercise the Office of President of the United States.

The Senate shall have the sole Power to try all Impeachments. When sitting for that Purpose, they shall be on Oath or Affirmation. When the President of the United States is tried, the Chief Justice shall preside: And no Person shall be convicted without the Concurrence of two thirds of the Members present.

Judgment in Cases of Impeachment shall not extend further than to removal from Office, and disqualification to hold and enjoy any Office of honor, Trust or Profit under the United States: but the Party convicted shall nevertheless be liable and subject to Indictment, Trial, Judgment and Punishment, according to Law.

SECTION 4. The Times, Places and Manner of holding Elections for Senators and Representatives, shall be prescribed in each State by the Legislature thereof; but the Congress may at any time by Law make or alter such Regulations, except as to the Places of chusing Senators.

The Congress shall assemble at least once in every Year, and such Meeting shall be on the first Monday in December, unless they shall by Law appoint a different Day.

SECTION 5. Each House shall be the Judge of the Elections, Returns and Qualifications of its own Members, and a Majority of each shall

constitute a Quorum to do Business; but a smaller Number may adjourn from day to day, and may be authorized to compel the Attendance of absent Members, in such Manner, and under such Penalties as each House may provide.

Each House may determine the Rules of its Proceedings, punish its Members for disorderly Behaviour, and, with the Concurrence of two thirds, expel a Member.

Each House shall keep a Journal of its Proceedings, and from time to time publish the same, excepting such Parts as may in their Judgment require Secrecy; and the Yeas and Nays of the Members of either House on any question shall, at the Desire of one fifth of those Present, be entered on the Journal.

Neither House, during the Session of Congress, shall, without the Consent of the other, adjourn for more than three days, nor to any other Place than that in which the two Houses shall be sitting.

SECTION 6. The Senators and Representatives shall receive a Compensation for their Services, to be ascertained by Law, and paid out of the Treasury of the United States. They shall in all Cases, except Treason, Felony and Breach of the Peace, be privileged from Arrest during their Attendance at the Session of their respective Houses, and in going to and returning from the same; and for any Speech or Debate in either House, they shall not be questioned in any other Place.

No Senator or Representative shall, during the Time for which he was elected, be appointed to any civil Office under the Authority of the United States, which shall have been created, or the Emoluments whereof shall have been encreased during such time; and no Person holding any Office under the United States, shall be a Member of either House during his Continuance in Office.

SECTION 7. All Bills for raising Revenue shall originate in the House of Representatives; but the Senate may propose or concur with Amendments as on other Bills.

Every Bill which shall have passed the House of Representatives and the Senate, shall, before it become a Law, be presented to the President of the United States; If he approve he shall sign it, but if not he shall return it, with his Objections to that House in which it shall have originated, who shall enter the Objections at large on their Journal, and proceed to reconsider it. If after such Reconsideration two thirds of that House shall agree to pass the Bill, it shall be sent, together with the Objections, to the other House, by which it shall likewise be reconsidered, and if approved by two thirds of that House, it shall become a Law. But in all such Cases the Votes of both Houses shall be determined by Yeas and Nays, and the

Names of the Persons voting for and against the Bill shall be entered on the Journal of each House respectively. If any Bill shall not be returned by the President within ten Days (Sundays excepted) after it shall have been presented to him, the Same shall be a Law, in like Manner as if he had signed it, unless the Congress by their Adjournment prevent its Return, in which Case it shall not be a Law.

Every Order, Resolution, or Vote to which the Concurrence of the Senate and House of Representatives may be necessary (except on a question of Adjournment) shall be presented to the President of the United States; and before the Same shall take Effect, shall be approved by him, or being disapproved by him, shall be repassed by two thirds of the Senate and House of Representatives, according to the Rules and Limitations prescribed in the Case of a Bill.

SECTION 8. The Congress shall have Power To lay and collect Taxes, Duties, Imposts and Excises, to pay the Debts and provide for the common Defence and general Welfare of the United States; but all Duties, Imposts and Excises shall be uniform throughout the United States;

To borrow Money on the credit of the United States;

To regulate Commerce with foreign Nations, and among the several States, and with the Indian Tribes;

To establish an uniform Rule of Naturalization, and uniform Laws on the subject of Bankruptcies throughout the United States;

To coin Money, regulate the Value thereof, and of foreign Coin, and fix the Standard of Weights and Measures;

To provide for the Punishment of counterfeiting the Securities and current Coin of the United States;

To establish Post Offices and post Roads;

To promote the Progress of Science and useful Arts, by securing for limited Times to Authors and Inventors the exclusive Right to their respective Writings and Discoveries;

To constitute Tribunals inferior to the supreme Court;

To define and punish Piracies and Felonies committed on the high Seas, and Offences against the Law of Nations;

To declare War, grant Letters of Marque and Reprisal, and make Rules concerning Captures on Land and Water;

To raise and support Armies, but no Appropriation of Money to that Use shall be for a longer Term than two Years;

To provide and maintain a Navy;

To make Rules for the Government and Regulation of the land and naval Forces;

To provide for calling forth the Militia to execute the Laws of the Union, suppress Insurrections and repel Invasions;

To provide for organizing, arming, and disciplining, the Militia, and for governing such Part of them as may be employed in the Service of the United States, reserving to the States respectively, the Appointment of the Officers, and the Authority of training the Militia according to the discipline prescribed by Congress;

To exercise exclusive Legislation in all Cases whatsoever, over such District (not exceeding ten Miles square) as may, by Cession of particular States, and the Acceptance of Congress, become the Seat of the Government of the United States, and to exercise like Authority over all Places purchased by the Consent of the Legislature of the State in which the Same shall be, for the Erection of Forts, Magazines, Arsenals, dock-Yards, and other needful Buildings; — And

To make all Laws which shall be necessary and proper for carrying into Execution the foregoing Powers, and all other Powers vested by this Constitution in the Government of the United States, or in any Department or Officer thereof.

SECTION 9. The Migration or Importation of such Persons as any of the States now existing shall think proper to admit, shall not be prohibited by the Congress prior to the Year one thousand eight hundred and eight, but a Tax or duty may be imposed on such Importation, not exceeding ten dollars for each Person.

The Privilege of the Writ of Habeas Corpus shall not be suspended, unless when in Cases of Rebellion or Invasion the public Safety may require it.

No Bill of Attainder or ex post facto Law shall be passed.

No Capitation, or other direct, Tax shall be laid, unless in Proportion to the Census or Enumeration herein before directed to be taken.

No Tax or Duty shall be laid on Articles exported from any State.

No Preference shall be given by any Regulation of Commerce or Revenue to the Ports of one State over those of another: nor shall Vessels bound to, or from, one State, be obliged to enter, clear, or pay Duties in another.

No Money shall be drawn from the Treasury, but in Consequence of Appropriations made by Law; and a regular Statement and Account of the Receipts and Expenditures of all public Money shall be published from time to time.

No Title of Nobility shall be granted by the United States: And no Person holding any Office of Profit or Trust under them, shall, without the Consent of the Congress, accept of any present, Emolument, Office, or Title, of any kind whatever, from any King, Prince, or foreign State.

SECTION 10. No State shall enter into any Treaty, Alliance, or Confederation; grant Letters of Marque and Reprisal; coin Money; emit Bills of Credit; make any Thing but gold and silver Coin a Tender in Payment of Debts; pass any Bill of Attainder, ex post facto Law, or Law impairing the Obligation of Contracts, or grant any Title of Nobility.

No State shall, without the Consent of the Congress, lay any Imposts or Duties on Imports or Exports, except what may be absolutely necessary for executing it's inspection Laws: and the net Produce of all Duties and Imposts, laid by any State on Imports or Exports, shall be for the Use of the Treasury of the United States; and all such Laws shall be subject to the Revision and Controul of the Congress.

No State shall, without the Consent of Congress, lay any Duty of Tonnage, keep Troops, or Ships of War in time of Peace, enter into any Agreement or Compact with another State, or with a foreign Power, or engage in War, unless actually invaded, or in such imminent Danger as will not admit of delay.

ARTICLE II.

SECTION 1. The executive Power shall be vested in a President of the United States of America. He shall hold his Office during the Term of four Years, and, together with the Vice President, chosen for the same Term, be elected, as follows

Each State shall appoint, in such Manner as the Legislature thereof may direct, a Number of Electors, equal to the whole Number of Senators and Representatives to which the State may be entitled in the Congress: but no Senator or Representative, or Person holding an Office of Trust or Profit under the United States, shall be appointed an Elector.

The Electors shall meet in their respective States, and vote by Ballot for two Persons, of whom one at least shall not be an Inhabitant of the same State with themselves. And they shall make a List of all the Persons voted for, and of the Number of Votes for each; which List they shall sign and certify, and transmit sealed to the Seat of the Government of the United States, directed to the President of the Senate. The President of the Senate shall, in the Presence of the Senate and House of Representatives, open all the Certificates, and the Votes shall then be counted. The Person having the greatest Number of Votes shall be the President, if such Number be a Majority of the whole Number of Electors appointed; and if

there be more than one who have such Majority, and have an equal Number of Votes, then the House of Representatives shall immediately chuse by Ballot one of them for President; and if no Person have a Majority, then from the five highest on the List the said House shall in like Manner chuse the President. But in chusing the President, the Votes shall be taken by States, the Representation from each State having one Vote; a quorum for this Purpose shall consist of a Member or Members from two thirds of the States, and a Majority of all the States shall be necessary to a Choice. In every Case, after the Choice of the President, the Person having the greatest Number of Votes of the Electors shall be the Vice President. But if there should remain two or more who have equal Votes, the Senate shall chuse from them by Ballot the Vice President.

The Congress may determine the Time of chusing the Electors, and the Day on which they shall give their Votes; which Day shall be the same throughout the United States.

No Person except a natural born Citizen, or a Citizen of the United States, at the time of the Adoption of this Constitution, shall be eligible to the Office of President; neither shall any Person be eligible to that Office who shall not have attained to the Age of thirty five Years, and been fourteen Years a Resident within the United States.

In Case of the Removal of the President from Office, or of his Death, Resignation, or Inability to discharge the Powers and Duties of the said Office, the Same shall devolve on the Vice President, and the Congress may by Law provide for the Case of Removal, Death, Resignation or Inability, both of the President and Vice President, declaring what Officer shall then act as President, and such Officer shall act accordingly, until the Disability be removed, or a President shall be elected.

The President shall, at stated Times, receive for his Services, a Compensation, which shall neither be encreased nor diminished during the Period for which he shall have been elected, and he shall not receive within that Period any other Emolument from the United States, or any of them.

Before he enter on the Execution of his Office, he shall take the following Oath or Affirmation: — "I do solemnly swear (or affirm) that I will faithfully execute the Office of President of the United States, and will to the best of my Ability, preserve, protect and defend the Constitution of the United States."

SECTION 2. The President shall be Commander in Chief of the Army and Navy of the United States, and of the Militia of the several States, when called into the actual Service of the United States; he may require the Opinion, in writing, of the principal Officer in each of the executive Departments, upon any Subject relating to the Duties of their respective

Offices, and he shall have Power to grant Reprieves and Pardons for Offences against the United States, except in Cases of Impeachment.

He shall have Power, by and with the Advice and Consent of the Senate, to make Treaties, provided two thirds of the Senators present concur; and he shall nominate, and by and with the Advice and Consent of the Senate, shall appoint Ambassadors, other public Ministers and Consuls, Judges of the supreme Court, and all other Officers of the United States, whose Appointments are not herein otherwise provided for, and which shall be established by Law: but the Congress may by Law vest the Appointment of such inferior Officers, as they think proper, in the President alone, in the Courts of Law, or in the Heads of Departments.

The President shall have Power to fill up all Vacancies that may happen during the Recess of the Senate, by granting Commissions which shall expire at the End of their next Session.

SECTION 3. He shall from time to time give to the Congress Information of the State of the Union, and recommend to their Consideration such Measures as he shall judge necessary and expedient; he may, on extraordinary Occasions, convene both Houses, or either of them, and in Case of Disagreement between them, with Respect to the Time of Adjournment, he may adjourn them to such Time as he shall think proper; he shall receive Ambassadors and other public Ministers; he shall take Care that the Laws be faithfully executed, and shall Commission all the Officers of the United States.

SECTION 4. The President, Vice President and all civil Officers of the United States, shall be removed from Office on Impeachment for, and Conviction of, Treason, Bribery, or other high Crimes and Misdemeanors.

ARTICLE III.

SECTION 1. The judicial Power of the United States, shall be vested in one supreme Court, and in such inferior Courts as the Congress may from time to time ordain and establish. The Judges, both of the supreme and inferior Courts, shall hold their Offices during good Behaviour, and shall, at stated Times, receive for their Services, a Compensation, which shall not be diminished during their Continuance in Office.

SECTION 2. The judicial Power shall extend to all Cases, in Law and Equity, arising under this Constitution, the Laws of the United States, and Treaties made, or which shall be made, under their Authority; — to all Cases affecting Ambassadors, other public Ministers and Consuls; — to all Cases of admiralty and maritime Jurisdiction; — to Controversies to which the United States shall be a Party; — to Controversies between two or more States; — between a State and Citizens of another State; — between

Citizens of different States; — between Citizens of the same State claiming Lands under Grants of different States, and between a State, or the Citizens thereof, and foreign States, Citizens or Subjects.

In all Cases affecting Ambassadors, other public Ministers and Consuls, and those in which a State shall be Party, the supreme Court shall have original Jurisdiction. In all the other Cases before mentioned, the supreme Court shall have appellate Jurisdiction, both as to Law and Fact, with such Exceptions, and under such Regulations as the Congress shall make.

The Trial of all Crimes, except in Cases of Impeachment, shall be by Jury; and such Trial shall be held in the State where the said Crimes shall have been committed; but when not committed within any State, the Trial shall be at such Place or Places as the Congress may by Law have directed.

SECTION 3. Treason against the United States, shall consist only in levying War against them, or in adhering to their Enemies, giving them Aid and Comfort. No Person shall be convicted of Treason unless on the Testimony of two Witnesses to the same overt Act, or on Confession in open Court.

The Congress shall have Power to declare the Punishment of Treason, but no Attainder of Treason shall work Corruption of Blood, or Forfeiture except during the Life of the Person attainted.

ARTICLE IV.

SECTION 1. Full Faith and Credit shall be given in each State to the public Acts, Records, and judicial Proceedings of every other State. And the Congress may by general Laws prescribe the Manner in which such Acts, Records and Proceedings shall be proved, and the Effect thereof.

SECTION 2. The Citizens of each State shall be entitled to all Privileges and Immunities of Citizens in the several States.

A Person charged in any State with Treason, Felony, or other Crime, who shall flee from Justice, and be found in another State, shall on Demand of the executive Authority of the State from which he fled, be delivered up, to be removed to the State having Jurisdiction of the Crime.

No Person held to Service or Labour in one State, under the Laws thereof, escaping into another, shall, in Consequence of any Law or Regulation therein, be discharged from such Service or Labour, but shall be delivered up on Claim of the Party to whom such Service or Labour may be due.

SECTION 3. New States may be admitted by the Congress into this Union; but no new State shall be formed or erected within the Jurisdiction

of any other State; nor any State be formed by the Junction of two or more States, or Parts of States, without the Consent of the Legislatures of the States concerned as well as of the Congress.

The Congress shall have Power to dispose of and make all needful Rules and Regulations respecting the Territory or other Property belonging to the United States; and nothing in this Constitution shall be so construed as to Prejudice any Claims of the United States, or of any particular State.

SECTION 4. The United States shall guarantee to every State in this Union a Republican Form of Government, and shall protect each of them against Invasion; and on Application of the Legislature, or of the Executive (when the Legislature cannot be convened) against domestic Violence.

ARTICLE V.

The Congress, whenever two thirds of both Houses shall deem it necessary, shall propose Amendments to this Constitution, or, on the Application of the Legislatures of two thirds of the several States, shall call a Convention for proposing Amendments, which, in either Case, shall be valid to all Intents and Purposes, as Part of this Constitution, when ratified by the Legislatures of three fourths of the several States, or by Conventions in three fourths thereof, as the one or the other Mode of Ratification may be proposed by the Congress; Provided that no Amendment which may be made prior to the Year One thousand eight hundred and eight shall in any Manner affect the first and fourth Clauses in the Ninth Section of the first Article; and that no State, without its Consent, shall be deprived of its equal Suffrage in the Senate.

ARTICLE VI.

All Debts contracted and Engagements entered into, before the Adoption of this Constitution, shall be as valid against the United States under this Constitution, as under the Confederation.

This Constitution, and the Laws of the United States which shall be made in Pursuance thereof; and all Treaties made, or which shall be made, under the Authority of the United States, shall be the supreme Law of the Land; and the Judges in every State shall be bound thereby, any Thing in the Constitution or Laws of any State to the Contrary notwithstanding.

The Senators and Representatives before mentioned, and the Members of the several State Legislatures, and all executive and judicial Officers, both of the United States and of the several States, shall be bound by Oath or Affirmation, to support this Constitution; but no religious Test shall

ever be required as a Qualification to any Office or public Trust under the United States.

ARTICLE VII.

The Ratification of the Conventions of nine States, shall be sufficient for the Establishment of this Constitution between the States so ratifying the Same.

Done in Convention by the Unanimous Consent of the States present the Seventeenth Day of September in the Year of Our Lord one thousand seven hundred and Eighty seven and of the Independence of the United States of America the Twelfth. IN WITNESS whereof We have hereunto subscribed our Names.

GO. WASHINGTON — *Presidt.*
and deputy from Virginia

[Signatories omitted.]

* * * * *

ARTICLES IN ADDITION TO, AND AMENDMENT OF, THE CONSTITUTION OF THE UNITED STATES OF AMERICA, PROPOSED BY CONGRESS, AND RATIFIED BY THE LEGISLATURES OF THE SEVERAL STATES, PURSUANT TO THE FIFTH ARTICLE OF THE ORIGINAL CONSTITUTION

AMENDMENT I [1791]

Congress shall make no law respecting an establishment of religion, or prohibiting the free exercise thereof; or abridging the freedom of speech, or of the press; or the right of the people peaceably to assemble, and to petition the Government for a redress of grievances.

AMENDMENT II [1791]

A well regulated Militia, being necessary to the security of a free State, the right of the people to keep and bear Arms, shall not be infringed.

AMENDMENT III [1791]

No Soldier shall, in time of peace be quartered in any house, without the consent of the Owner, nor in time of war, but in a manner to be prescribed by law.

AMENDMENT IV [1791]

The right of the people to be secure in their persons, houses, papers, and effects, against unreasonable searches and seizures, shall not be violated, and no Warrants shall issue, but upon probable cause, supported by Oath or affirmation, and particularly describing the place to be searched, and the persons or things to be seized.

AMENDMENT V [1791]

No person shall be held to answer for a capital, or otherwise infamous crime, unless on a presentment or indictment of a Grand Jury, except in cases arising in the land or naval forces, or in the Militia, when in actual service in time of War or public danger; nor shall any person be subject for the same offence to be twice put in jeopardy of life or limb; nor shall be compelled in any criminal case to be a witness against himself, nor be deprived of life, liberty, or property, without due process of law; nor shall private property be taken for public use, without just compensation.

AMENDMENT VI [1791]

In all criminal prosecutions, the accused shall enjoy the right to a speedy and public trial, by an impartial jury of the State and district wherein the crime shall have been committed, which district shall have been previously ascertained by law, and to be informed of the nature and cause of the accusation; to be confronted with the witnesses against him; to have compulsory process for obtaining witnesses in his favor, and to have the Assistance of Counsel for his defence.

AMENDMENT VII [1791]

In Suits at common law, where the value in controversy shall exceed twenty dollars, the right of trial by jury shall be preserved, and no fact tried by a jury, shall be otherwise re-examined in any Court of the United States, than according to the rules of the common law.

AMENDMENT VIII [1791]

Excessive bail shall not be required, nor excessive fines imposed, nor cruel and unusual punishments inflicted.

AMENDMENT IX [1791]

The enumeration in the Constitution, of certain rights, shall not be construed to deny or disparage others retained by the people.

AMENDMENT X [1791]

The powers not delegated to the United States by the Constitution, nor prohibited by it to the States, are reserved to the States respectively, or to the people.

AMENDMENT XI [1798]

The Judicial power of the United States shall not be construed to extend to any suit in law or equity, commenced or prosecuted against one of the United States by Citizens of another State, or by Citizens or Subjects of any Foreign State.

AMENDMENT XII [1804]

The Electors shall meet in their respective states, and vote by ballot for President and Vice-President, one of whom, at least, shall not be an inhabitant of the same state with themselves; they shall name in their ballots the person voted for as President, and in distinct ballots the person voted for as Vice-President, and they shall make distinct lists of all persons voted for as President, and of all persons voted for as Vice-President, and of the number of votes for each, which lists they shall sign and certify, and transmit sealed to the seat of the government of the United States, directed to the President of the Senate; — The President of the Senate shall, in the presence of the Senate and House of Representatives, open all the certificates and the votes shall then be counted; — The person having the greatest number of votes for President, shall be the President, if such number be a majority of the whole number of Electors appointed; and if no person have such majority, then from the persons having the highest numbers not exceeding three on the list of those voted for as President, the House of Representatives shall choose immediately, by ballot, the President. But in choosing the President, the votes shall be taken by states, the representation from each state having one vote; a quorum for this purpose shall consist of a member or members from two-thirds of the states, and a majority of all the states shall be necessary to a choice. And if the House of Representatives shall not choose a President whenever the right of choice shall devolve upon them, before the fourth day of March next following, then the Vice-President shall act as President, as in the

case of the death or other constitutional disability of the President. — The person having the greatest number of votes as Vice-President, shall be the Vice-President, if such number be a majority of the whole number of Electors appointed, and if no person have a majority, then from the two highest numbers on the list, the Senate shall choose the Vice-President; a quorum for the purpose shall consist of two-thirds of the whole number of Senators, and a majority of the whole number shall be necessary to a choice. But no person constitutionally ineligible to the office of President shall be eligible to that of Vice-President of the United States.

AMENDMENT XIII [1865]

SECTION 1. Neither slavery nor involuntary servitude, except as a punishment for crime whereof the party shall have been duly convicted, shall exist within the United States, or any place subject to their jurisdiction.

SECTION 2. Congress shall have power to enforce this article by appropriate legislation.

AMENDMENT XIV [1868]

SECTION 1. All persons born or naturalized in the United States, and subject to the jurisdiction thereof, are citizens of the United States and of the State wherein they reside. No State shall make or enforce any law which shall abridge the privileges or immunities of citizens of the United States; nor shall any State deprive any person of life, liberty, or property, without due process of law; nor deny to any person within its jurisdiction the equal protection of the laws.

SECTION 2. Representatives shall be apportioned among the several States according to their respective numbers, counting the whole number of persons in each State, excluding Indians not taxed. But when the right to vote at any election for the choice of electors for President and Vice President of the United States, Representatives in Congress, the Executive and Judicial officers of a State, or the members of the Legislature thereof, is denied to any of the male inhabitants of such State, being twenty-one years of age, and citizens of the United States, or in any way abridged, except for participation in rebellion, or other crime, the basis of representation therein shall be reduced in the proportion which the number of such male citizens shall bear to the whole number of male citizens twenty-one years of age in such State.

SECTION 3. No person shall be a Senator or Representative in Congress, or elector of President and Vice President, or hold any office, civil or

military, under the United States, or under any State, who, having previously taken an oath, as a member of Congress, or as an officer of the United States, or as a member of any State legislature, or as an executive or judicial officer of any State, to support the Constitution of the United States, shall have engaged in insurrection or rebellion against the same, or given aid or comfort to the enemies thereof. But Congress may by a vote of two-thirds of each House, remove such disability.

SECTION 4. The validity of the public debt of the United States, authorized by law, including debts incurred for payment of pensions and bounties for services in suppressing insurrection or rebellion, shall not be questioned. But neither the United States nor any State shall assume or pay any debt or obligation incurred in aid of insurrection or rebellion against the United States, or any claim for the loss or emancipation of any slave; but all such debts, obligations and claims shall be held illegal and void.

SECTION 5. The Congress shall have power to enforce, by appropriate legislation, the provisions of this article.

AMENDMENT XV [1870]

SECTION 1. The right of citizens of the United States to vote shall not be denied or abridged by the United States or by any State on account of race, color, or previous condition of servitude.

SECTION 2. The Congress shall have power to enforce this article by appropriate legislation.

AMENDMENT XVI [1913]

The Congress shall have power to lay and collect taxes on incomes, from whatever source derived, without apportionment among the several States, and without regard to any census or enumeration.

AMENDMENT XVII [1913]

The Senate of the United States shall be composed of two Senators from each State, elected by the people thereof, for six years; and each Senator shall have one vote. The electors in each State shall have the qualifications requisite for electors of the most numerous branch of the State legislatures.

When vacancies happen in the representation of any State in the Senate, the executive authority of such State shall issue writs of election to fill such vacancies: *Provided*, That the legislature of any State may

empower the executive thereof to make temporary appointments until the people fill the vacancies by election as the legislature may direct.

This Article shall not be so construed as to affect the election or term of any Senator chosen before it becomes valid as part of the Constitution.

AMENDMENT XVIII [1919]

SECTION 1. After one year from the ratification of this article the manufacture, sale, or transportation of intoxicating liquors within, the importation thereof into, or the exportation thereof from the United States and all territory subject to the jurisdiction thereof for beverage purposes is hereby prohibited.

SECTION 2. The Congress and the several States shall have concurrent power to enforce this article by appropriate legislation.

SECTION 3. This article shall be inoperative unless it shall have been ratified as an amendment to the Constitution by the legislatures of the several States, as provided in the Constitution, within seven years from the date of the submission hereof to the States by the Congress.

AMENDMENT XIX [1920]

The right of citizens of the United States to vote shall not be denied or abridged by the United States or by any State on account of sex.

Congress shall have power to enforce this article by appropriate legislation.

AMENDMENT XX [1933]

SECTION 1. The terms of the President and Vice President shall end at noon on the 20th day of January, and the terms of Senators and Representatives at noon on the 3d day of January, of the years in which such terms would have ended if this article had not been ratified; and the terms of their successors shall then begin.

SECTION 2. The Congress shall assemble at least once in every year, and such meeting shall begin at noon on the 3d day of January, unless they shall by law appoint a different day.

SECTION 3. If, at the time fixed for the beginning of the term of the President, the President elect shall have died, the Vice President elect shall become President. If a President shall not have been chosen before the time fixed for the beginning of his term, or if the President elect shall have failed to qualify, then the Vice President elect shall act as President

until a President shall have qualified; and the Congress may by law provide for the case wherein neither a President elect nor a Vice President elect shall have qualified, declaring who shall then act as President, or the manner in which one who is to act shall be selected, and such person shall act accordingly until a President or Vice President shall have qualified.

SECTION 4. The Congress may by law provide for the case of the death of any of the persons from whom the House of Representatives may choose a President whenever the right of choice shall have devolved upon them, and for the case of the death of any of the persons from whom the Senate may choose a Vice President whenever the right of choice shall have devolved upon them.

SECTION 5. Sections 1 and 2 shall take effect on the 15th day of October following the ratification of this article.

SECTION 6. This article shall be inoperative unless it shall have been ratified as an amendment to the Constitution by the legislatures of three-fourths of the several States within seven years from the date of its submission.

AMENDMENT XXI [1933]

SECTION 1. The eighteenth article of amendment to the Constitution of the United States is hereby repealed.

SECTION 2. The transportation or importation into any State, Territory, or possession of the United States for delivery or use therein of intoxicating liquors, in violation of the laws thereof, is hereby prohibited.

SECTION 3. This article shall be inoperative unless it shall have been ratified as an amendment to the Constitution by conventions in the several States, as provided in the Constitution, within seven years from the date of the submission hereof to the States by the Congress.

AMENDMENT XXII [1951]

SECTION 1. No person shall be elected to the office of the President more than twice, and no person who has held the office of President, or acted as President, for more than two years of a term to which some other person was elected President shall be elected to the office of the President more than once. But this article shall not apply to any person holding the office of President when this article was proposed by the Congress, and shall not prevent any person who may be holding the office of President, or acting as President, during the term within which this article becomes operative from holding the office of President or acting as President during the remainder of such term.

SECTION 2. This article shall be inoperative unless it shall have been ratified as an amendment to the Constitution by the legislatures of three-fourths of the several states within seven years from the date of its submission to the states by the Congress.

AMENDMENT XXIII [1961]

SECTION 1. The District constituting the seat of government of the United States shall appoint in such manner as the Congress may direct: A number of electors of President and Vice President equal to the whole number of Senators and Representatives in Congress to which the District would be entitled if it were a state, but in no event more than the least populous state; they shall be in addition to those appointed by the states, but they shall be considered, for the purposes of the election of President and Vice President, to be electors appointed by a state; and they shall meet in the District and perform such duties as provided by the twelfth article of amendment.

SECTION 2. The Congress shall have power to enforce this article by appropriate legislation.

AMENDMENT XXIV [1964]

SECTION 1. The right of citizens of the United States to vote in any primary or other election for President or Vice President, for electors for President or Vice President, or for Senator or Representative in Congress, shall not be denied or abridged by the United States or any state by reason of failure to pay any poll tax or other tax.

SECTION 2. The Congress shall have power to enforce this article by appropriate legislation.

AMENDMENT XXV [1967]

SECTION 1. In case of the removal of the President from office or of his death or resignation, the Vice President shall become President.

SECTION 2. Whenever there is a vacancy in the office of the Vice President, the President shall nominate a Vice President who shall take office upon confirmation by a majority vote of both Houses of Congress.

SECTION 3. Whenever the President transmits to the President pro tempore of the Senate and the Speaker of the House of Representatives his written declaration that he is unable to discharge the powers and duties of his office, and until he transmits to them a written declaration to the

contrary, such powers and duties shall be discharged by the Vice President as Acting President.

SECTION 4. Whenever the Vice President and a majority of either the principal officers of the executive departments or of such other body as Congress may by law provide, transmit to the President pro tempore of the Senate and the Speaker of the House of Representatives their written declaration that the President is unable to discharge the powers and duties of his office, the Vice President shall immediately assume the powers and duties of the office as Acting President.

Thereafter, when the President transmits to the President pro tempore of the Senate and the Speaker of the House of Representatives his written declaration that no inability exists, he shall resume the powers and duties of his office unless the Vice President and a majority of either the principal officers of the executive department or of such other body as Congress may by law provide, transmit within four days to the President pro tempore of the Senate and the Speaker of the House of Representatives their written declaration that the President is unable to discharge the powers and duties of his office. Thereupon Congress shall decide the issue, assembling within forty-eight hours for that purpose if not in session. If the Congress, within twenty-one days after receipt of the latter written declaration, or, if Congress is not in session, within twenty-one days after Congress is required to assemble, determines by two-thirds vote of both Houses that the President is unable to discharge the powers and duties of his office, the Vice President shall continue to discharge the same as Acting President; otherwise, the President shall resume the powers and duties of his office.

AMENDMENT XXVI [1971]

SECTION 1. The right of citizens of the United States, who are 18 years of age or older, to vote, shall not be denied or abridged by the United States or any state on account of age.

SECTION 2. The Congress shall have the power to enforce this article by appropriate legislation.

AMENDMENT XXVII [1992]*

No law varying the compensation for the services of the Senators and Representatives shall take effect until an election of Representatives shall have intervened.

* This amendment was proposed by Congress in 1789 as one of the original amendments constituting the Bill of Rights. The last of the requisite three-quarters of state legislatures ratified the amendment in 1992. — ED.

PENDING AMENDMENTS TO THE FEDERAL RULES OF CIVIL PROCEDURE*

Rule 5. Serving and Filing Pleadings and Other Papers

* * * * *

(b) Service: How Made.

* * * * *

(2) ***Service in General.*** A paper is served under this rule by:

(A) handing it to the person;

* * * * *

(E) sending it to a registered user by filing it with the court's electronic-filing system or sending it by other electronic means ~~if~~that the person consented to in writing — in either of which events service is complete upon ~~transmission~~filing or sending, but is not effective if the ~~serving party~~filer or sender learns that it did not reach the person to be served; or

* * * * *

(3) ***Using Court Facilities.*** ~~If a local rule so authorizes, a party may use the court's transmission facilities to make service under Rule 5(b)(2)(E).~~ [Abrogated (Apr. 26, 2018, eff. Dec. 1, 2018.)]

* * * * *

(d) Filing.

(1) ***Required Filings; Certificate of Service.***

(A) *Papers after the Complaint.* Any paper after the complaint that is required to be served~~— together with a certificate of service —~~ must be filed ~~within~~no later than a reasonable time after service. But disclosures under Rule 26(a)(1) or (2) and the following discovery requests and responses must not be filed until they are used in the proceeding or the court orders filing: depositions, interrogatories, requests for documents or tangible things or to permit entry onto land, and requests for admission.

(B) *Certificate of Service.* No certificate of service is required when a paper is served by filing it with the court's electronic-filing system. When a paper that is required to be served is served by other means:

* On April 26, 2018, the Supreme Court adopted these amendments to the Federal Rules of Civil Procedure and, pursuant to 28 U.S.C. § 2074(a), transmitted them to Congress. They will take effect on December 1, 2018, unless Congress enacts legislation disapproving, delaying, or modifying them. Deletions to the existing Federal Rules are ~~struck through~~; additions are underlined. — ED.

(i) if the paper is filed, a certificate of service must be filed with it or within a reasonable time after service; and

(ii) if the paper is not filed, a certificate of service need not be filed unless filing is required by court order or by local rule.

(2) ***Nonelectronic FilingHow Filing Is Made — In General.*** A paper not filed electronically is filed by delivering it:

(A) to the clerk; or

(B) to a judge who agrees to accept it for filing, and who must then note the filing date on the paper and promptly send it to the clerk.

(3) ***Electronic Filing, and Signing, or Verification.*** A court may, by local rule, allow papers to be filed, signed, or verified by electronic means that are consistent with any technical standards established by the Judicial Conference of the United States. A local rule may require electronic filing only if reasonable exceptions are allowed.

(A) By a Represented Person — Generally Required; Exceptions. A person represented by an attorney must file electronically, unless nonelectronic filing is allowed by the court for good cause or is allowed or required by local rule.

(B) By an Unrepresented Person — When Allowed or Required. A person not represented by an attorney:

(i) may file electronically only if allowed by court order or by local rule; and

(ii) may be required to file electronically only by court order, or by a local rule that includes reasonable exceptions.

(C) Signing. A filing made through a person's electronic-filing account and authorized by that person, together with that person's name on a signature block, constitutes the person's signature.

(D) Same as a Written Paper. A paper filed electronically in compliance with a local ruleis a written paper for purposes of these rules.

* * * * *

Rule 23. Class Actions

* * * * *

(c) Certification Order; Notice to Class Members; Judgment; Issues Classes; Subclasses.

* * * * *

(2) Notice.

* * * * *

(B) *For (b)(3) Classes.* For any class certified under Rule 23(b)(3) — or upon ordering notice under Rule 23(e)(1) to a class proposed to be certified for purposes of settlement under Rule 23(b)(3) — the court must direct to class members the best notice that is practicable under the circumstances, including individual notice to all members who can be identified through reasonable effort. The notice may be by one or more of the following: United States mail, electronic means, or other appropriate means. The notice must clearly and concisely state in plain, easily understood language:

* * * * *

(e) Settlement, Voluntary Dismissal, or Compromise. The claims, issues, or defenses of a certified class — or a class proposed to be certified for purposes of settlement — may be settled, voluntarily dismissed, or compromised only with the court's approval. The following procedures apply to a proposed settlement, voluntary dismissal, or compromise:

(1) ***Notice to the Class.***

(A) *Information That Parties Must Provide to the Court.* The parties must provide the court with information sufficient to enable it to determine whether to give notice of the proposal to the class.

(B) *Grounds for a Decision to Give Notice.* The court must direct notice in a reasonable manner to all class members who would be bound by the proposal if giving notice is justified by the parties' showing that the court will likely be able to:

(i) approve the proposal under Rule 23(e)(2); and

(ii) certify the class for purposes of judgment on the proposal.

(2) **Approval of the Proposal.** If the proposal would bind class members~~ under Rule 23(c)(3)~~, the court may approve it only after a hearing and only on finding that it is fair, reasonable, and adequate after considering whether:

(A) the class representatives and class counsel have adequately represented the class;

(B) the proposal was negotiated at arm's length;

(C) the relief provided for the class is adequate, taking into account:

(i) the costs, risks, and delay of trial and appeal;

(ii) the effectiveness of any proposed method of distributing relief to the class, including the method of processing class-member claims;

(iii) the terms of any proposed award of attorney's fees, including timing of payment; and

(iv) any agreement required to be identified under Rule 23(e)(3); and

(D) the proposal treats class members equitably relative to each other.

(3) Identifying Agreements. The parties seeking approval must file a statement identifying any agreement made in connection with the proposal.

(4) New Opportunity to Be Excluded. If the class action was previously certified under Rule 23(b)(3), the court may refuse to approve a settlement unless it affords a new opportunity to request exclusion to individual class members who had an earlier opportunity to request exclusion but did not do so.

(5) ***Class-Member Objections.***

(A) In General. Any class member may object to the proposal if it requires court approval under this subdivision (e)~~; the objection may be withdrawn only with the court's approval~~. The objection must state whether it applies only to the objector, to a specific subset of the class, or to the entire class, and also state with specificity the grounds for the objection.

(B) *Court Approval Required for Payment in Connection with an Objection.* Unless approved by the court after a hearing, no payment or other consideration may be provided in connection with:

(i) forgoing or withdrawing an objection, or

(ii) forgoing, dismissing, or abandoning an appeal from a judgment approving the proposal.

(C) *Procedure for Approval After an Appeal.* If approval under Rule 23(e)(5)(B) has not been obtained before an appeal is docketed in the court of appeals, the procedure of Rule 62.1 applies while the appeal remains pending.

(f) Appeals. A court of appeals may permit an appeal from an order granting or denying class-action certification under this rule, but not from an order under Rule 23(e)(1). ~~if a petition for permission to appeal is filed~~ A party must file a petition for permission to appeal with the circuit clerk within 14 days after the order is entered, or within 45 days after the order

is entered if any party is the United States, a United States agency, or a United States officer or employee sued for an act or omission occurring in connection with duties performed on the United States' behalf. An appeal does not stay proceedings in the district court unless the district judge or the court of appeals so orders.

* * * * *

Rule 62. Stay of Proceedings to Enforce a Judgment

(a) Automatic Stay~~; Exceptions for Injunctions, Receiverships, and Patent Accountings~~. Except as provided in Rule 62(c) and (d),~~stated in this rule, no~~ execution ~~may issue~~on a judgment~~, nor may~~ and proceedings ~~be taken~~to enforce it~~;~~ are stayed for 30 days ~~until 14 days have passed~~after its entry, unless the court orders otherwise.~~ But unless the court orders otherwise, the following are not stayed after being entered, even if an appeal is taken:~~

~~(1) an interlocutory or final judgment in an action for an injunction or a receivership; or~~

~~(2) a judgment or order that directs an accounting in an action for patent infringement.~~

~~**(b) Stay Pending the Disposition of a Motion.** On appropriate terms for the opposing party's security, the court may stay the execution of a judgment — or any proceedings to enforce it — pending disposition of any of the following motions:~~

~~(1) under Rule 50, for judgment as a matter of law;~~

~~(2) under Rule 52(b), to amend the findings or for additional findings;~~

~~(3) under Rule 59, for a new trial or to alter or amend a judgment; or~~

~~(4) under Rule 60, for relief from a judgment or order.~~

(b) Stay by Bond or Other Security. At any time after judgment is entered, a party may obtain a stay by providing a bond or other security. The stay takes effect when the court approves the bond or other security and remains in effect for the time specified in the bond or other security.

(c) Stay of an Injunction, Receivership, or Patent Accounting Order. Unless the court orders otherwise, the following are not stayed after being entered, even if an appeal is taken:

(1) an interlocutory or final judgment in an action for an injunction or receivership; or

(2) a judgment or order that directs an accounting in an action for patent infringement.

(d~~c~~) Injunction Pending an Appeal. While an appeal is pending from an interlocutory order or final judgment that grants, continues, modifies, refuses, dissolves, or ~~denies~~refuses to dissolve or modify an injunction, the court may suspend, modify, restore, or grant an injunction on terms for bond or other terms that secure the opposing party's rights. If the judgment appealed from is rendered by a statutory three-judge district court, the order must be made either:

(1) by that court sitting in open session; or

(2) by the assent of all its judges, as evidenced by their signatures.

~~**(d) Stay with Bond on Appeal**. If an appeal is taken, the appellant may obtain a stay by supersedeas bond, except in an action described in Rule 62(a)(1) or (2). The bond may be given upon or after filing the notice of appeal or after obtaining the order allowing the appeal. The stay takes effect when the court approves the bond.~~

* * * * *

Rule 65.1. Proceedings Against a ~~Surety~~Security Provider

Whenever these rules (including the Supplemental Rules for Admiralty or Maritime Claims and Asset Forfeiture Actions) require or allow a party to give security, and security is given ~~through a bond or other undertaking~~with one or more ~~sureties~~security providers, each ~~surety~~provider submits to the court's jurisdiction and irrevocably appoints the court clerk as its agent for receiving service of any papers that affect its liability on the ~~bond or undertaking~~security. The ~~surety's~~security provider's liability may be enforced on motion without an independent action. The motion and any notice that the court orders may be served on the court clerk, who must promptly ~~mail~~send a copy of each to every ~~surety~~security provider whose address is known.

At My Portuguese Table

Azorean Cooking and More

by Maria Lawton

ISBN: 978-1-942155-79-9
Library of Congress Control Number:
2024905573

Published by
azorean greenbean
An imprint of
Peter E. Randall Publisher
5 Greenleaf Woods Drive, #102
Portsmouth, New Hampshire 03801
www.perpublisher.com

Edited by Bob Lawton, Lilia Cabral-Bernard, Monica Bensaude Fernandes, and Vanessa Gonsalvas

Book design by Tim Holtz

www.Azoreangreenbean.com

Printed in the United States of America

Dedication

This book is dedicated to my dear Avó & Madrinha, Filomena.

She is the woman who taught me to never give up on my dreams, no matter what. She would say, "Sempre Para a Frente" which means "Always Forward." Those words have kept me moving forward in times of my life when it would have been easier to just let go and give up.

I have always felt blessed to have been her granddaughter, as well as her godchild, and we both felt a strong bond with each other. Even now, many years after her passing, I can still feel her presence cheering me on to keep going.

When I was young, she would say to me "you are all mine" and I didn't think twice about it. I heard the story of when I was born and while my dad ran out in the middle of a stormy night to get the midwife, my Madrinha stayed alongside my mother. I guess I was in a hurry to greet this world, and as my grandmother would say . . . she caught me.

I was held by her first and I am, and will always be, forever hers.

My maternal grandparents, Filomena & João

Hello Dear Reader,

I am beyond excited and deeply grateful that you have chosen to bring more of my family's recipes into your home. Your support means the world to me, and I hope you find as much joy in recreating these dishes as I have in sharing them with you. Cooking and sharing meals with family and friends create memories that last a lifetime. So, gather your loved ones and make every meal a cherished memory.

This book has once again been a labor of love, and I am thrilled to share it with you. Since writing my first cookbook, so many wonderful things have happened. We started filming and producing not one but two seasons of the multi-award-winning series "Maria's Portuguese Table" on PBS. This series has been my love letter to my culture, and I am incredibly grateful that it has made television history as the first on PBS to showcase the vibrant and rich culture of Portugal.

This achievement reflects my journey, which is deeply rooted in the sacrifices and bravery of my parents, who immigrated from the island of São Miguel to the United States, giving up everything for their children. Everything I do honors them and ensures their bravery was not in vain.

Thank you for being a part of my journey. Your support and enthusiasm inspire me every day. I encourage you to not only enjoy these recipes but also to write down and share your own family recipes. By doing so, you create a legacy of love and tradition for future generations.

With heartfelt gratitude,

Maria

My Roots

My roots run deep, a connection to the earth,
Anchoring my soul in a place of my birth,
Like a tree's roots, I stand tall and strong,
Grounded and still, where I belong.

Traveling deep within, I find my own space,
There's no need for fear, for it's all within me.
I embrace it fully, for it's my heritage and birthright.
I am rooted, I am strong, I am grounded from where I came from.

—Maria Lawton
Written in 2019, Terra Nostra Botanical Garden

My favorite tree, a Metrosideros Excelsa, at Terra Nostra Garden, Furnas, São Miguel Azores

Desserts

Beer Biscuits 128
Pumpkin Spice Biscuits 130
Green Tea Cookies 132
Dona Amelia's Queen Cakes 134
Pumpkin Scones 136
Vanilla and Cream Cake 140
Water Cake 142
Carrot Cake 144
Rosa's Cake 146
Sponge Cake 148
Orange Cake 150
Salazar's Cake—The One Egg Cake 152
Chocolate Maria Biscuit Cake 155
Coconut Tarts 158
Chocolate Tart with Maria Biscuit/Cookie Crust 160
Orange Tarts 162
Bread Pudding with Pineapple & Meringue Topping 164
Malassada Bread Pudding 166
Fruit Salad 168
Hot and Cold—No Churn Homemade Ice Cream 170
Christmas Cake 174

Other Favorites

Cake Toppings 178
Pumpkin Jam 180
Orange Jam 184
Roasted Tomato Jam 186
Infused Butter 188
Chouriço Butter 190
Saffron vs Safflower 194
Mozambique Seasoning 195
Classic Portuguese Rub 195
Homemade Vanilla 196
Vanilla Sugar 197
Tea Time 198
Lemon Tea 199

Index 200
About the Author 203

Soups, Sides, and Appetizers

Sopas, Acompanhamentos e Entradas

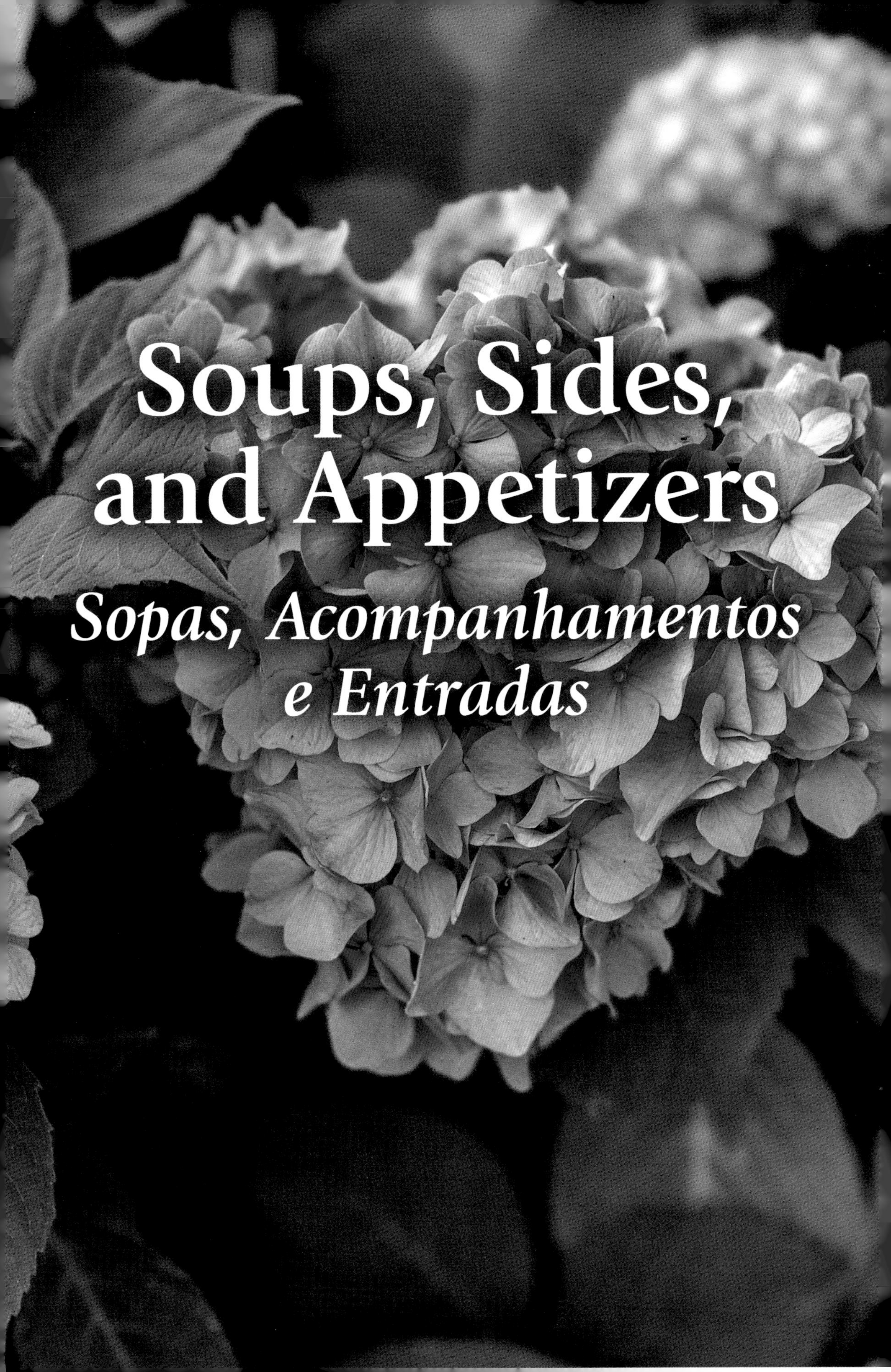

Soup with Dumplings

Sopa de Netos

This soup recipe was a favorite of my grandmother Filomena, and it was shared with me by my Aunt Lilia and my Uncle John. Some years ago the three of us were sitting around their dining room table and reminiscing about my maternal grandparents. Both were wonderful parents and grandparents, and their stories were always wonderful to hear, along with lots of laughing for some of the antics my grandmother would be up to. It's funny how my memories of them as a granddaughter differ from my Uncle John's memories of them as parents. They were stricter with their children than their grandchildren, so some stories didn't even sound like them to me . . . but I guess my children will probably say the same about me, too!

We started talking about food, which is an almost certain subject in my family and my Uncle John mentioned this soup with dumplings was a favorite of my grandmother. The word "Netos" when translated means grandchildren, so right away it was something I wanted to try making myself. It's funny that when I was growing up I never saw either my parents or grandparents making this soup, but after speaking with my sister Isabel she did remember eating it too. This soup is definitely a hardy and humble meal. Made with collard greens aka chouves, lard, sometimes cabbage, sometimes potatoes, and water. Lard was used to add flavor when there was no pork available. Only on some occasions they would add a chouriço sausage. Then, with some corn flour, salt and a little broth from the soup, little dumplings were made and added.

Some weeks later I made the soup for my husband and I, and it was delicious . . . of course now we can add more ingredients to the soup. I made sure to bring a big bowl of the soup to my aunt and uncle, and they said it tasted just as they remembered, but even better!

Ingredients:

Serves 4–6

1 bunch collard greens, chopped

1 small head cabbage or half of a large head, chopped

2 potatoes, peeled and chopped into large cubes

2 tablespoons lard, or butter

1 pound chouriço sausage

Salt to taste

2 chicken bouillon cubes

Water 6–8 cups

1–1½ cups fine white corn flour

continued on page 4

Sopa de Netos continued from page 2

Directions:

Remove any thick center stems and fibrous veins from the collard greens, chop and leave aside. In a large stock pot, add chopped potatoes, lard, sausage, bouillon cubes and water and bring to a rapid boil. Lower the heat to a gentle boil and add the chopped cabbage, salt, and once again bring to a boil; then add the collard greens and let it cook for 10 minutes.

Make sure to test the broth and see if it needs more salt. Note that using chouriço and bouillon cubes adds more salt so taste test for saltiness . . . but it's good to taste to be sure as well as to see if the potatoes are cooked. (My grandmother liked it when the potatoes would fall apart and almost thicken the broth, but if you don't want that you can remove the potatoes and keep aside to add back when the dumplings are cooked.)

In the meantime, while the soup is still on the heat and almost done, we can now make the dumplings:

In a large bowl, add the cornflour, pinch of salt and mix together.

Using a soup ladle, add the broth slowly, just a little at a time, into the bowl.

Stir everything together until the flour becomes a consistency good enough to form a ball. If it's too thin, add a little more flour; if it's too thick, add more broth.

Once the mixture is cool enough to hold in your hands, knead the dough together into a large ball. Then, pull a little of the dough and roll it in your hands (just like when you form meatballs). I actually used a small cookie scoop and rolled them up. If the dough gets stuck to your hands just wet your hands with warm water and that should do the trick to keep rolling. The smaller the dumpling rolls, the quicker they will cook. So after rolling them all out and saving them aside on a plate, you will add all the balls into the soup and let them cook for 8–10 minutes. They tend to sink when you put them in the soup, but as they cook they should rise to the top.

Taste test one of the dumplings to make sure it's cooked through . . . once that's done, if you have removed the potatoes you can add them back. Remove the chouriço, cut into rounds and add back into the soup . . . now serve!

Make sure to enjoy this delicious hearty soup that's actually perfect for cold winter nights in the Northeast. . . . Oh, and don't forget the wine! Filomena would definitely approve.

Holy Ghost Feast

This feast has been a part of Azorean tradition since settlers first arrived to the islands from the mainland. The Holy Ghost Soup is known as the *Sopa do Espírito Santo*, and is a tradition celebrating the Feast of the Holy Spirit. According to the legend, Portugal was suffering a great famine, and Portugal's Queen Isabel made a promise to the Holy Ghost that she would sell her crowns and jewels to feed the poor if the famine came to an end. When the famine ended, she did as she promised and fed the people with what is now known as "The Holy Ghost Soup," creating a tradition of thanksgiving that is still celebrated today.

The Holy Ghost Feast takes place on each of the seven Sundays following Easter, where thousands of people gather in celebration. The seven Sundays are known as "Domingas" with the seventh being Pentecost Sunday. The celebration first begins in the homes of the lay members of the Brotherhood or "Irmandade." One randomly chosen member of the Brotherhood, called the Mordomo, coordinates, organizes, and authorizes all funds and necessary aspects leading up to the Feast. For the seven Sundays, members of the Brotherhood are randomly picked to host the Holy Ghost crown and scepter in their homes.

Personally, I remember seeing the large silver crown and scepter that represented the Holy Spirit being delivered to my family's home. A room would be cleared out and a makeshift altar set up for the crown to be placed on, then the room would be decorated with lots of flowers and enough seating for all the guests. Each night during that week our home would be open to everyone to offer special prayers in honor of the Holy Ghost, followed by the singing of hymns, and ending with refreshments. At the end of the week, the celebration would move to the home of the next Dominga host.

This picture is of one of my daughters on the way to be crowned alongside my nieces, nephews, and other extended cousins during the Holy Ghost procession to the church.

The highlight of the entire observance is a three-day festival that begins on the Friday night just before the Seventh

Dominga, the "Blessing of the Meat and Bread." At this time, a portion of beef and bread is blessed by a priest and distributed to each member of the Brotherhood present. In my family, my parents, with other families, would donate the meat used to create the Holy Ghost Soup. In the Azores, the celebration takes place in the Império, or the Holy Ghost House. This is when large crowds gather to bring gifts and offerings such as desserts, flowers, and more.

On Trinity, or the seventh Sunday, there is a procession to honor the Holy Ghost. A child is chosen to be crowned Emperor, which my oldest daughter, as well as many nieces and nephews, have been honored with. In some communities a woman is chosen to represent Queen Isabel, and she and her court join the procession. The final event is the drawing of names for those who will be next year's Dominga sponsors. After the procession, the festa begins! Then comes the best part: the tradition of charity and feeding the poor. A bowl of soup is served to everyone who attends, and seating is at a very, very long table. Also provided are massa and arroz doce (sweet bread and rice pudding) as dessert.

During this feast, there is a deep passion and expression of charity, faith, and devotion. For many Azoreans, it is a way to come together as one and unite, in addition to keeping them connected to their homeland and honoring their roots.

This is just one example of an Império (Holy Ghost House), this Império da Caridade is on the island of Terceira, Azores.

Holy Ghost Soup

Sopas do Espírito Santo

This is my cousin Laureana's recipe, and it makes enough for 8–10 people.

When I serve this recipe, I use 3 soup tureens, which makes a wonderful presentation that everyone loves!

Ingredients:

1½ pounds beef shanks or beef short ribs

2½ pounds boneless chuck roast

2 large onions, chopped

3 garlic cloves, minced

1 head cabbage, chopped

5 whole black peppercorns

Salt to taste

3 sprigs mint, washed

1 loaf Portuguese bread at least 2 days old, sliced

Cheesecloth or spice ball

continued on page 8

Holy Ghost Soup continued from page 7

Directions:

In a large bowl, place all the meat and rinse very well. Then place the meat in a clean bowl and sprinkle salt over each piece and refrigerate for at least 3 hours or overnight, for best results.

Fill a large stockpot a little more than halfway with water. Add the onions, garlic, and the meat (making sure to rinse off some of the salt). Next, wrap the peppercorns in a tied pouch of cheesecloth or in a spice ball and add to the pot. Bring the water to a boil and then reduce the heat to simmer for 2–3 hours or until the meat is tender.

Once the meat is cooked and tender, remove it from the pot and place it on a large serving platter. Let the meat cool down enough to be able to handle without burning your hands while shredding. While the meat is out of the pan you can taste test the broth and adjust with more water and salt as desired. Also, make sure to skim fat from the meat broth and discard the spice bag of peppercorns. Add the chopped cabbage and let it cook for another 30 minutes or until tender.

While the cabbage is cooking, start shredding the meat. Make sure to remove all the bones and excess fat and then leave aside.

In the meantime, start setting up the soup tureens. In each tureen add the sliced bread, making sure that each is almost filled to the top. Then add a sprig of mint on top of the bread. Add a layer of the shredded meat on top of the mint. If you have extra shredded meat, place it on a smaller platter and put it on top of the table for those that want to add more meat to their soup.

Last but not least, ladle in the broth with the cooked cabbage over everything. Keep ladling in all the broth. . . . Trust me, the bread will soak up the broth.

Cover the soup tureens and leave aside for about 10 minutes.

Before serving make sure to remove the sprigs of mint from each tureen.

Then serve with a nice glass of red house wine or new wine such as (vinho de cheiro).

Then a toast to all the souls, "para as almas."

Bean Soup

Sopa de feijão

The following is my mom's recipe, and she would make it especially for my dad. My dad loved soup, and every day he would have a very large bowl of it. Every week would bring a different soup depending on the season, but bean soup was one of his favorites in any season. I can see him now, heating up the soup and cutting up slices of bread to add to the bottom of the bowl. Then he would pour the soup and let some of the bread soak up the soup. He would add a small splash of wine into the soup before he began to eat it. As you might guess, I would sometimes have him make me a small bowl the exact same way and then we would eat together. It's memories like these that come to mind when I make even the simplest thing; of special moments shared. The smells, the taste . . . it all brings me back to that wonderful table.

Ingredients:

Makes 6–8 servings

2 15.5 oz cans white kidney beans, rinsed
1 large onion, chopped
1 pound potatoes, chopped
½ pound carrots, chopped
1 link chouriço
4 cups kale, finely chopped
Salt and pepper to taste
Olive oil

Directions:

In a medium saucepan, add the rinsed beans and enough water to cover them. Even though the canned beans are already cooked, I like to simmer them over medium heat for a good 10 minutes. Use a slotted spoon to remove almost half of the whole beans and leave aside. With the remaining beans in the pan, use an immersion blender to puree them, then leave aside. You'll have both the whole beans and pureed beans waiting to go into the stock pot.

Using a large stock pot, add enough olive oil to cover the bottom of the pan, then add onions, potatoes, carrots, salt, pepper, and chouriço. Then fill the pot with enough water to cover everything. Over medium to high heat bring the water to a boil, then lower the heat to a low simmer and continue until the carrots and potatoes break when you stick a fork in them. Once that happens, you need to add the kale and cook for 5 minutes, then remove from heat. Then remove the link of chouriço and cut into rounds and place back into the soup pan. Next, add the pureed beans and the whole beans into the stock pot, and stir everything together. . . . The pureed beans will make the broth of the soup creamy. That's as easy as it gets and it's really delicious.

continued on page 10

Bean Soup continued from page 9

Using dry beans

This recipe can be made with dry beans, but the shortcut for this recipe is using canned beans. If you decide to use dry beans, you will want to soak them the night before. Before you do, though, look through the kidney beans and remove any shriveled, damaged, or broken pieces. Sometimes I have even found small stones, so it's important to check.

After the dry beans have been inspected, place them in a large bowl. Make sure the bowl is big enough to account for the beans expanding during soaking! I go by this rule: for every 1 pound of beans, soak in 6–8 cups of water. Let the dry beans soak for at least 8 hours or overnight. Then drain the soaked beans and add to a large pot. Cover the beans with water, add an onion, a garlic clove, a couple of bay leaves and bring to a boil.

Next you are going to skim the top to get rid of any foam that rises to the surface. Then reduce the heat to a simmer and cover. Let them cook for 1 to 1½ hours, making sure to stir every once in a while. To test if the beans are cooked, use a large spoon to press one of the beans up against the pot: if it breaks apart easily it's cooked. The cooked beans have a creamy texture, and don't worry if some of the beans split open while cooking.

Please note: make sure to remove bay leaves before serving.

Green Soup

Caldo Verde

This recipe came from my Tia Lilia. Although this is not a traditional way of making caldo verde, it is delicious and now a staple in my home. Since my dad liked the traditional rustic kale soup, it was very rare for my mom to make this updated version. I have come to enjoy this soup and appreciate it for how simple and flavorful it is. My husband loves this soup as well, so even though it's the perfect soup to take the chill away on a cold day, he loves eating this soup year round.

Ingredients:

Makes 6–8 servings

1 pound collard greens or flat kale, rinsed and cleaned
½ pound chouriço
1 pound potatoes, peeled and diced
8 cups water or chicken stock
2 medium yellow onions, finely chopped
1 stick butter
¼ cup milk
4 garlic cloves, minced
Olive oil
Kosher salt
Freshly ground white pepper

Directions:

Remove any thick center stems and fibrous veins from your collard greens. Stack several of the collard green leaves, and roll them lengthwise into a tight cigar shape, and cut crosswise into very-thin slices, also known as a chiffonade slicing technique. Repeat with the rest of the greens and set aside.

Using a 6 quart stockpot, add enough olive oil to cover the bottom of the pot. Over medium heat, add the chopped onions and sauté until translucent. Add the minced garlic and sauté together. Pour in the water or chicken stock and add the diced potatoes and the whole chouriço. Do not slice the chouriço yet, but make sure to pierce the casing or else the chouriço casing can burst open.

Bring this to a boil over high heat. Reduce the heat to medium–low, cover and simmer until the potatoes are cooked tender for about 15–20 minutes.

Remove the chouriço, let it cool down, remove the casings and slice it into ¼-inch-thick slices.

Remove all the potatoes into a large bowl and add butter, milk, salt and pepper to taste and mash the potatoes. If you think you need more liquid, add more broth from the pot.

Return the mashed potatoes back into the pot, stir into the broth and bring it back to a boil. Turn the heat to low. Add the thin sliced collard greens and stir together. Let it simmer uncovered for 10 minutes or until tender.

Taste your broth and if you feel like it needs more flavor, season again with salt and pepper. Add the slices of chouriço into the soup.

To serve, ladle the soup into bowls, making sure each bowl has a few of the sliced chouriços and top it off with a drizzle of olive oil.

Milk Soup

Sopa de Leite

This recipe is one of the most traditional breakfast dishes you can find. When I was growing up I'd see my dad having this for breakfast every once in a while; he loved it! Truly, it was a comfort food for him from his days as a child, growing up with his family. My mom and my sisters on the other hand, who also grew up eating milk soup, never cared for it. I guess it all depends on how you remember it. . . . They remember it being made with cornbread, and I only remember my dad using whatever type of leftover bread or rolls (pops) we had on hand.

This soup is definitely a humble breakfast. It was made up entirely of leftovers, days old bread, milk, honey/sugar and slices of whatever fruit you might have on hand. In our home, my dad liked adding a sliced banana. Keep in mind that not so long ago sugar and honey were often expensive for many Portuguese households. Using sliced fruit would have added the sweetness it needs, but feel free to add any sweetness to your own! This simple breakfast made of leftovers shows the humility that our Portuguese ancestors showcased.

Ingredients:

Serves 1

2–3 cups milk
Sliced and cubed days old bread
1 banana, sliced
Sugar/honey

Directions:

In a bowl, add the cubed bread.

In a saucepan over medium heat, warm up the milk and sugar.

Pour warm milk over the bread and let it soak up the liquid.

Top it off with sliced banana.

Now sit back and enjoy.

Porridge

Papas/Papinhas

I had a certain routine when I was young; as soon as I returned from school I dropped everything in my first floor apartment, gave my dad a kiss, and rushed upstairs to my grandparent's apartment. It seemed like each day something special would be waiting for me all the way up on the second floor! My grandmother, Filomena, had the sweetest tooth and I was never disappointed. On especially cold days she would have Papinhas made and ready. It's funny to think that when I was young I really thought I was having pudding, especially when she would add chocolate cocoa powder to it. Simply put, what little kid wouldn't want a plate of warm chocolate pudding waiting for them as soon as they came home from school! I loved it.

But now I know how wrong I was . . . Papas is a porridge. It is a very filling and "sticks to your ribs" kind of comfort food. It came with the promise that it had the ability to cure whatever ails you. Feeling a little under the weather? Then papas would help! Feeling a little weak? An egg yolk would be added during the cooking. Feeling cold and you need to warm up? Papas to the rescue! To this day, a dish of papas brings back such wonderful, loving memories of my grandparents.

I have two recipes: one uses all purpose flour; the other cornstarch. My grandmother would make either one; I guess it depended on what she had in her cabinet.

Papas recipe, using all-purpose flour

Ingredients:

Makes 2 servings

2 cups milk
½ cup all-purpose flour
⅓ cup granulated sugar
Small pinch of salt
Sugar/Cinnamon to taste

Directions:

In a small bowl, mix together flour, sugar, and salt. Leave aside. In a saucepan, add milk and bring the milk close to a boil over medium heat. Add the flour mixture and whisk everything together. Continue to whisk until the mixture thickens and just begins to boil. Pour the mixture onto two plates; let it cool for a few minutes.

Then sprinkle it with sugar and cinnamon to taste!

Papas de Maizena recipe, using cornstarch

Ingredients:

Makes 2 servings

2 cups milk
4 tablespoons cornstarch
⅓ cup granulated sugar
Small pinch of salt
Sugar/Cinnamon to taste

Directions:

In a small bowl, mix together cornstarch, sugar, and salt. Leave aside. In a saucepan, add milk and over medium heat bring the milk close to a boil. Add the cornstarch mixture and whisk everything together. Continue to whisk until the mixture thickens and just begins to boil. Pour the mixture onto two plates; let it cool for a few minutes.

Then sprinkle it with sugar and cinnamon to taste!

Variations to the recipe:

- For chocolate porridge add 2–3 tablespoons of chocolate cocoa powder to mix.
- For added protein add one beaten egg yolk and make sure to mix in very quickly to temper the egg so that it doesn't turn into a scrambled egg.
- For vanilla flavor, add 1 teaspoon pure vanilla extract to the milk.

On a side note: Once I became a mom and my children were babies, I made something even simpler than papas for them. It quickly became a favorite and it was so easy: I would crumble Maria Cookies or digestive biscuits and add warm milk or some orange juice and sliced bananas. It's wonderful to know that they will always have this as a childhood food memory.

Beans, Beans and more Beans!!

Beans play a central role in Portugal's gastronomy because of their versatility and nutritional value. Whether enjoyed in classic Portuguese dishes or creatively reinvented in modern cuisine, beans continue to be a beloved and an integral part of Portuguese menus, reflecting the country's rich history and many regional influences.

Beans were originally introduced to Portugal from the Americas, and have since become a staple piece in many dishes. Portugal's diverse regions have contributed to a wide range of bean based dishes. In the north of Portugal, you'll find dishes like Arroz de Feijão, while in the Azores, you'll find many variations of bean stews. There are even bean tarts! While Portugal is a small country, the regional variations of dishes highlight the diversity of our culture and food.

Chickpeas and various types of white and red beans have historically been an essential part of the Portuguese diet due to their affordability. Growing up, I can't remember any time when we didn't have beans served in one form or another, especially since my father loved eating them. Because of its important role in our diet, beans provided a reliable source of sustenance for many people, especially in rural areas. Beans can provide varying and healthy meals throughout the year. Broad beans are often harvested in the spring, while the harvest of chickpeas and other beans occurs in late summer and early fall.

Portuguese cooking often places an emphasis on nutrition. Beans are a valuable source of protein, and even if they aren't the main dish, you will almost always find them as a side in any Portuguese household. Because of their versatility and affordability, Portuguese families would grow them in their own backyards. Many of our bean dishes have influenced cultures all around the world.

Fava Bean pods freshly picked, shelled, and dried.

Young Fava Broad Bean Stew

Fava guisada com chouriço e ovos escalfados

This dish was a summer staple in my home when the garden was filled with lots of broad beans, aka fava beans. Sometimes my mom would make it using fresh peas and fresh green beans. I love it no matter which fresh vegetable is in season. It's a very simple dish to make, and one you'll have as a standby when you need to serve those quick meals.

Ingredients:

Serves 4–6

2 pounds fresh green fava beans, deshelled
1 medium onion, finely chopped
1 pound chouriço or linguiça, cut into rounds
1 tablespoon crushed red hot pepper sauce (pimenta moída)
Salt and pepper to taste
4 tablespoons olive oil
Eggs

Directions:

Using a dutch oven pan, add enough olive oil to cover bottom; over medium heat sauté the onions. Once the onions have become translucent add sausage rounds and sauté them for 5 minutes; add salt and pepper to taste (as well as a spoonful of hot red crushed pepper if you like it hot!). Now add the fresh fava beans and stir together.

Next, add enough water to cover the beans and bring to a boil, then lower and simmer until the beans are cooked to your liking. This can take from 10–30 minutes depending on the size, obviously smaller beans will cook the quickest. It's best to test them every 10–15 minutes by pressing one or two beans against the side of the pan. If it collapses easily, meaning the inside bean is cooked, they're done. The easier they collapse, the mushier they are. Keep that in mind, and cook them longer if you prefer mushy beans.

The final step is to crack one egg per person over the top of the stewed fava beans.

Cover the pan and remove it from the heat to let the eggs cook in the steam (you're poaching the egg). Let it poach to your liking: some people like their eggs a little runny . . . so it's up to you for how long to keep the eggs covered and poaching.

It's that simple! I enjoy this dish with some fresh crusty bread and a nice glass of wine.

Quick Stewed Beans

Feijão Guisado Rápido

This recipe is quick, simple, and perfect for those moments when we need a fast meal or an added side dish. My husband loves this dish and he sometimes fries a couple of eggs to eat along with. It's simple, but it's also very filling and is a pure comfort food.

Ingredients:

Serves 4–6

½ cup olive oil

4 tablespoons butter (half a stick)

Two small onions, finely chopped

1 pound round cut Portuguese sausage such as linguiça or chouriço with casings removed

5 to 6 garlic cloves, minced

¼ cup tomato paste

3 (1 lb and 13 oz) cans or (9 cups of cooked butter beans) drained and rinsed

Paprika to taste

Salt and pepper to taste

2 cups liquid either water or chicken broth, as well as wine or a combination

⅓ cup chopped parsley

Grated São Jorge cheese or any aged cheese of choice

Directions:

In a large skillet, heat the olive oil and butter over medium-high heat. Add the chopped onions and sauté until translucent, then add the chopped sausage and sauté for 5 to 6 minutes. Add the garlic and sauté together for another couple of minutes, making sure to reduce the heat to prevent the garlic from burning.

Stir in the tomato paste, and then add the beans, paprika, salt, and pepper. Pour in the liquid, stir well and bring to a low simmer. Keep stirring until it begins to thicken, for approximately 10 to 15 minutes. If your skillet is ovenproof, you can also place the skillet into a 350°F oven and bake for about 15 minutes until the top is toasted to a golden color.

Stir in the chopped parsley, and lastly, add some grated, aged cheese.

My Mom's Baked Beans

Feijão Assado da Minha Mãe

As I write this recipe I can envision my mom in the kitchen preparing this for my family. She used a very large, blue enameled baking pan just for this dish. The house would be filled with these amazing scents, and the anticipation left everyone giddy with excitement. We knew that we would have baked beans to accompany our meat dishes, but other times we loved eating it with a fried egg on top, or maybe as a baked bean sandwich. Yes . . . we would cut a pop seco in half and stuff it with the baked beans! Everyone, and I mean everyone, in my family loves this recipe and making it now is definitely something I don't take lightly.

I know that I am not my mother, whose cooking was on another level, but I try to recreate these baked beans the best I can, and I can honestly say that I have accomplished it with this recipe. When I wrote my first cookbook, I was completely unable to share this particular recipe. . . . As soon as I would start to write it out I would become a weepy mess, and I had to leave it out. Additionally, it took me several years to perfect the flavor, and my sister Isabel helped me with the small yet important steps that I seemed to have missed. Every time I make this recipe, I can feel my mom with me. It's as if she's making sure that I get it right. I can only imagine what she would have thought of it: she probably would say that I needed to add more salt, but all I know is that it's exactly like she would have made it.

Before you start making this recipe, please make sure to get all your ingredients together. I think it's best made the day before you serve it, as I think it gives the dish more time to concentrate its flavor.

Before cooking any beans, you want to examine and clean them thoroughly. It's important to rinse well and look for any "foreign" materials. Discard and remove any shriveled, damaged, or broken pieces, as well as any small stones. I suggest soaking the beans overnight.

I go by this rule: for every 1 pound of beans, soak in 6–8 cups of water overnight.

Make sure you use a large enough bowl to give room for the beans to expand.

continued on page 26

My Mom's Baked Beans continued from page 24

Ingredients:

Serves 10–12

2 pounds chouriço sausages
¾ pounds smoked pork belly
2 pound bag of navy beans, soaked the previous night
2 sticks butter (1 cup of butter)
1 extra large sweet onion, chopped
1 large bunch parsley, chopped
4 tablespoons olive oil
1–2 tablespoons red hot peppers (pimenta moída), chopped
1 heaping tablespoon onion powder
1 heaping tablespoon garlic powder
1 heaping tablespoon ground cinnamon
1 heaping tablespoon paprika
Salt and pepper to taste

Directions:

Begin by filling a stockpot halfway with water. Place beans in the pot and season them with salt, olive oil, and chopped red hot peppers. Add chopped onion to the pot and boil for 1 hour. If the water has evaporated before the beans are cooked, you can add additional hot water: do not add cold water as it will stop the cooking process. In the last 15 minutes of the beans cooking, add the whole chouriços to the pot and continue to cook. Depending on your preference, you can add a couple chicken bouillon cubes for additional flavor when cooking the beans.

In a separate pot, add the pork belly and enough water to cover it. Over medium heat, boil and cook the pork belly until you can stick a knife through to cut easily. Note: once you start to boil the pork it will first harden. You want to make sure to boil it until the meat becomes soft. This is a long process, and can even take a few hours depending on the thickness.

Once cooked, leave aside to cool. *Tip: I sometimes do this the day before, since it sometimes takes a couple of hours to cook, then I refrigerate. Then the next day, it's easily cut into small pieces.

Once the beans are cooked, remove them from the pot and put them in a roasting pan. Take out the chouriço and shred into small bits on top of the beans. Chop bacon back into small pieces and place into the pan as well. Do not worry about the fat as it will melt into the beans. Season the beans and chouriço with the parsley and 1 stick of butter (½ cup) along with the salt, pepper, onion powder, garlic powder, ground cinnamon, and paprika. Stir everything in the baking pan thoroughly.

Bake covered for 1 hour at 350°F and then uncovered for 40 minutes, stirring each time. If you find that the beans have dried out during the process, you can add the other stick of butter, and mix well together. Taste and adjust any seasonings if needed.

Now it's ready to serve, or let it cool and refrigerate to serve the following day.

I hope that you and your family enjoy this recipe as much as we do.

Rice

Rice has become a staple piece in our Portuguese gastronomy thanks to the Moorish invasion of mainland Portugal. Although it was introduced in the 8th century, it was over a decade before rice fields began to spread all over the country. Today, they can be seen in several districts on mainland Portugal, but its production heavily relies on the temperature, available water, and sunshine. While there are many different varieties, Portugal mainly cultivates Carolino and Agulha.

Agulha is a long grained Indica rice that is often found in oven baked dishes, while Carolino is a short grain used for creamy dishes and desserts. Interestingly, Portugal is the largest consumer of rice in all of Europe. Since it is so easy to cook with and adaptable to flavors, you can use it as a side dish, main dish, or as its own ingredient in different soups and desserts. Arroz de marisco, arroz de tomate, arroz doce, and so many more are just a small start of what Portugal's rice has to offer.

Butter Rice

Arroz de Manteiga

Growing up, pretty much every other dinner had a side dish of rice, so it's no surprise just how much I love rice. Heck, one of my favorite desserts is even rice pudding!

This recipe is not only delicious, but is also so easy to make. Trust me that you'll be making it often for your family and friends as a side dish, too. The serving size is ½ cup per person, and this recipe will give you three cups of rice. So it's perfect for 4 people, but the recipe can be doubled or tripled for extra servings.

Ingredients: **Serves 4**

1 cup rice, rinsed well
2 cups chicken broth
Salt to taste
½ cup of butter*

Directions:

First and foremost, rinse the rice. I place my rice in a bowl, and I run cold tap water over it, and you can quickly see that the water becomes very cloudy. After filling up the bowl, I stir the rice with my hands. Then I drain the water, and I repeat this as often as needed until the water is clear and not cloudy. Besides removing dirt, dust, bugs(!), etc . . . sometimes I have even found small pebbles while washing it too.

Leave the thoroughly rinsed rice aside. In a large saucepan over medium heat, add chicken broth and salt and bring to a boil. Once it begins to boil, add butter and allow the butter to melt. Then once it starts to boil again, add and stir in the rice and let it come to a light simmer. Once it starts to simmer, lower the heat, cover the saucepan, and let it cook.

This step will take 15–25 minutes depending if you're making a small or large batch. Make sure half way through the cooking process to uncover the saucepan and check if the rice has absorbed all the liquid; if it has you should add a little more liquid. Once the rice is cooked, remove the saucepan from heat and let it sit for a few minutes longer. Then fluff the rice, and taste it. I have, on some occasions, added another ¼ cup of butter into the rice before serving, especially if I think the flavor of butter could be enhanced. It is called butter rice for a reason!

*Note that the picture is of butter rice, with sauteed onions and linguiça on top.

Tomato Rice

Arroz de Tomate

Tomato rice was something that my mom would make, especially as a side dish when serving fish. Personally, I love it served with all meat dishes as well as fish dishes. My mom would especially make this during the summer when our garden tomatoes were abundant. When fresh tomatoes weren't available, she would use canned and chopped, kitchen ready tomatoes. The one thing my mom would add that is not usually in the traditional Tomato Rice recipe, is a couple of tablespoons of tomato paste. Besides adding a deep red color, it absolutely adds a much deeper tomato flavor to the rice. Also, like my mom, I like my tomato rice on the dry-side, without extra broth. With the added broth, the rice dish is called Arroz Malandrinho which means Naughty Rice! Trust me, there's nothing naughty about it, except if you like your rice on the fluffy side.

Ingredients:

Serves 4

4–5 medium tomatoes, peeled, deseeded and chopped (if tomatoes are not in season, you can use a 14 oz can of chopped kitchen ready tomatoes)
1 cup rice, rinsed well
2 cups chicken broth
1 medium onion, chopped
5–6 garlic cloves, minced
2 tablespoons butter
2 tablespoons tomato paste
Olive oil
Salt and pepper to taste

Directions:

In a Dutch oven pan, cover the bottom of the pan with olive oil. Over medium-high heat, add the chopped onions, salt, and pepper and sauté until the onions become translucent. Add garlic and quickly sauté together. Add in the chicken broth and tomato paste and stir together. Then add the chopped fresh tomatoes, and once it begins to boil, add in rice and butter and stir together. Once it begins to boil again, lower the heat to a simmer. Cook until the rice is done, or for about 20+ minutes. When done, take off the heat and leave aside.

If you test the rice and it is still uncooked after all this time, please add a bit more liquid, and continue to cook until the liquid is once again absorbed, and the rice is tender.

Codfish Rice

Arroz de Bacalhau

Ingredients:

Serves 2

1 pound codfish, cleaned and desalted
2 cups rice, rinsed and cleaned
1 cup fish broth
1 onion, finely chopped
1 garlic clove, minced
Paprika
Pimenta moída or another hot pepper sauce of choice
Salt and pepper to taste
2 bay leaves
Parsley
Olive oil

Directions:

In a medium stock pan, add cod fish, bay leaves and enough water to cover. Over high heat, bring to a simmer, and cook for 10–12 minutes. Once cooked, remove from the water and gently flake the fish. Reserve the water and leave aside.

In a Dutch oven, add enough olive oil to cover the bottom of the pan. Over medium-high heat, add the chopped onions, salt and pepper and sauté until the onions become translucent. Add garlic, paprika, and pimenta moída and quickly sauté together.

If you're not a fan of spicy heat, you can omit the pimenta moída. Add in 2 cups of reserved fish broth and stir together. Bring to a boil.

Once it begins to boil, add in the rice and flaked codfish and let the water reach a high simmer. Once it begins to boil again, lower the heat to a low simmer and cover. Usually this will take 15–25 minutes, depending if you're making a small or large batch. Half way through the cooking process uncover the saucepan to check if the rice has absorbed all the liquid. If it has, you might need to add a little more fish broth to the rice. Once the rice is cooked, remove the saucepan from heat and let it sit for a few minutes longer. Now fluff the rice, and taste it.

Top off with parsley and enjoy!

When I made this dish, fresh peas were in season and I had some cooked peas already in my refrigerator, so I decided to add them as a topping.

Sausages

Salsichas

Sausages can be quite tricky, especially Portuguese region-specific sausages. Portuguese sausages are cured and are also "*enchidos & fumados,*" or "stuffed and smoked." They are a perfect representation of very traditional Portuguese food prep. Because there were no refrigeration methods, it was important to preserve the meat through smoking. And if pork ran short during the cooking process, any leftover meats that were on-hand were added.

Although pork is the most prominent ingredient, Portuguese sausages are actually very diverse. . . .

- Alheira—Originally made with no pork and originally invented by the Jewish communities of Portugal during the Portuguese Inquisition. Now you'll find alheira that is made of pork, chicken, and a seasoned blend of other meats. Grill (or oven bake for an extra layer of crispiness) and serve with boiled potatoes or just a Portuguese roll.
- Chouriço—While many confuse chouriço and linguiça, any Portuguese person will tell you they are two completely different sausages. Compared to linguiça, chouriço is fattier and often has a strong smoked and mild spicy taste. It is made with beef casings and is thought to be more versatile than linguiça. It can be grilled, broiled, and roasted and is featured in a variety of Portuguese dishes.
- Linguiça—The one distinctive difference linguiça has from chouriço is its pig casings. It is smaller compared to chouriço and has a more mild flavor that is perfect for beginners. Similar to chouriço, it can be served with nearly anything!
- Farinheira—Derived from the Portuguese word *farinha*, or flour, it is known as the flour sausage. Although it may look similar to chouriço or linguiça, it has very little meaty flavor. Similar to alheira, it is believed that it once had little to no pork as it originated from the Jewish people of Portugal.
- Morcela—Morcela, or blood sausage, is the perfect representation of the culture behind wasting nothing and using all of the pig. While the idea may be off-putting, it is actually delicious! Morcela is seen in many dishes, but it is unique in

being a common breakfast side. When eating morcela, it is traditional to serve with pineapple, as it's said that eating pineapple helps with digestion.

- Salpicão/Paio—Paio was not historically a common sausage for the normal Portuguese family, since the sausage was considered very expensive due to only using pork loin as its main ingredient. Now it is a favorite for many Portuguese and non-Portuguese. It can be served with a side of bread or included in bean stew.
- Presunto—Although it is not a sausage, presunto is a staple piece in Portuguese households. It is dry cured ham that is fatty and thinly sliced to create a salty and sweet meaty flavor. There are several variations of presunto depending on the origin, but all are made from the leg of a pig. This is delicious served on its own or as a component for a charcuterie board.
- Barriga Fumada—Also known as Portuguese smoked pork belly bacon, barriga fumada was often rendered for lard. The rest is crackling, and it's perfect for a snack or an ingredient that can be added to any dish for flavor!

Homemade Smoked Chouriço

Chouriço Fumado Caseiro

Growing up in the Azores, I remember my parents would make homemade sausages every year. Family and friends would show up at our home to help with the slaughtering of the pig, or "*matança do porco*." While the adults were busy tending to everything that needed to be done, I distracted myself with my cousins by playing hide and seek. Honestly, I never really had an interest in their traditions until I got older.

Since my parents and so many in the community moved to the United States and found Portuguese sausages to be easily accessible, the tradition of making our own sausages slowly ended. I know of a few people on both the east and west coasts that still do this, but they are becoming very rare to find.

Some years ago, I bought an electric smoker with the intention of learning to make my own homemade sausage. Unfortunately, I couldn't find the right recipe or anyone that would teach me the exact steps. Luckily for me, while speaking to my friend Jessica I found out that her parents, who are from Serra da Estrela in the mainland, still make sausage each year. So when they offered me the opportunity to make smoked chouriço with them, I took it.

This is Senhora Isabel Coelho's family recipe:

Ingredients:

12 pounds pork butt
3 heaping tablespoons kosher salt
3 heaping tablespoons minced garlic
5 heaping tablespoons paprika
5 heaping tablespoons spicy hot crushed peppers (pimenta moída)
1½ cups red wine
1½ cups white wine
Hog casings (I ordered from my local butcher)
Cotton kitchen rope

Directions:

Remove the cap and trim off any excess fat from the pork butt. Cut the pork into small pieces, roughly a ¼–½ inch size. In a very large bowl, mix the pork with all of the dry ingredients thoroughly. Cover the bowl and leave in the refrigerator for 3 days. Within those 3 days, you want to mix the chouriço twice a day, such as every morning and every evening.

On the third day, you will add both wines first thing in the morning and let marinate a few more hours. Now that the meat has fully

continued on page 38

Homemade Smoked Chouriço continued from page 36

marinated, you will need to prepare the casings. You can choose natural or artificial casings, but personally I like using natural hog casings.

Rinse and clean casings several times with warm water first, then in a mixture of salt and either vinegar or lemon juice to ensure they are properly cleaned. You should soak the casings for at least one hour, changing out the water multiple times. Then try to turn the casings inside out and repeat the washing to make sure they're fully clean. Once cleaned, cut the casing to the size of your preferred sausage. Tightly tie one end of the casing with the kitchen rope, and fill casings by hand using a funnel tailored to making sausages. When you tie one end, you want to make sure the string is long enough in order to tie to the opposite side. When you do this, the sausage should look similar to a closed letter "U."

Using a three prong sausage pricker I purchased (I know my ancestors used sewing needles) you want to prick the casing after stuffing so it will allow air to escape, as well as to make sure the casings will not explode during the heat and smoking process. Once you're done with all the stuffing, tying, and pricking, please make sure to run the sausages under cold water to make sure they are clean before you smoke them.

Now comes the fun part: smoking. The old-fashioned way would be to light a fire in a smokehouse and let the chouriço smoke above the fire for 3–4 days.

Since the town we live in doesn't allow this type of smoking, we chose to smoke our chouriço in an electric smoker. We set the smoker to 200°F and smoked the chouriço for 6 hours. After the first 3 hours, we added applewood into the hopper.

Each electric smoker is different, so you will need to adjust it to your preferences. We chose applewood because of its mild flavor. Once it's smoked, they are ready to be used in your cooking . . . any remaining sausages can either be stored in the refrigerator or freezer.

It may be labor intensive, but it is absolutely worth every bite!

Chouriço Croquettes

Rissóis de chouriço

This recipe came from both my cousins Ana and Laureana. I know for the most part we only see shrimp and codfish as a filling, but they also make different fillings using ground meats and tuna . . . so why not use ground chouriço!

When my cousin Laureana was visiting us some years back, we actually made these in my home kitchen. It was so easy and delicious and since then I have used the dough recipe and have filled it with just about any leftover I had in the refrigerator. . . . I've even made a pizza one for my children and stuffed it with a little basil-seasoned tomato sauce, pepperoni and cheese. Everyone loved it.

Using this recipe, I made 30 rissóis . . . but depending on how big or small you make your rissóis will determine quantity.

Dough Ingredients:

2 tablespoons salted butter
1 cup flour
1 cup water
Salt and pepper to taste

Chouriço Filling:

1 pound finely ground chouriço
1 small onion, finely chopped
1 garlic clove, minced
2 tablespoons butter
1 tablespoon flour
1 teaspoon paprika
Salt and pepper to taste
Little bit of water (tablespoon or two)

Putting it all together:

3–4 eggs, beaten
Breadcrumbs (plain or seasoned)
Oil for deep frying (I like using Canola)

Directions:

In a saucepan, over medium high heat, add a cup of water with 2 tablespoons butter, salt and pepper, and bring to a boil.

Just when the water begins to boil, remove from heat and add 1 cup of flour.

Stir with a wooden spoon to get the dough to pull away from the sides of the saucepan and form a ball.

If the dough is on the wet side, place the saucepan back on the stovetop on medium

continued on page 40

Chouriço Croquettes continued from page 39

heat, and continue to stir until the dough has dried some more.

Remove the dough onto a floured surface and knead the dough until a nice smooth ball of dough is formed. Once that happens, let the dough rest while you start making the filling.

In a frying pan, over medium to high heat, add the butter and onion and cook until translucent.

Then add garlic, paprika, salt and pepper, and a little bit of water and bring to a simmer.

Add the chouriço, stir together, then add the tablespoon of flour to help thicken.

Continue to cook until it thickens, then remove from heat and set aside.

When the dough is cool, on a floured surface roll it out using a rolling pin and cut it into rounds by using a large cup or glass . . . I actually used a pierogi cutter to make mine, but my cousin used a large tea cup to cut the rolled out round of dough. Place a full teaspoon of the filling in the middle, fold in half, pressing the edges together. Next, dip the rissóis in beaten eggs and then breadcrumbs. Now you have two choices: fry them all up and/or freeze them.

If you decide to freeze some for another occasion, well, that's perfect . . . but don't forget them in the freezer! They'll need to be fried and eaten within a month of making them.

I just layer them on a cookie sheet and freeze them for at least three hours, then I place them in freezer bags. Pre-freezing keeps them from sticking together.

When it's time to deep fry them up . . . . Using a heavy bottom pan or fryer, heat the oil to 375° F. Fry them until they are a golden color, which should take a few minutes. Use a kitchen utensil of some sort to flip them midway through to make sure each side gets a similar color. I like to fry about 3–4 at a time, that gives them room in the fryer. Once fried, remove and place them on a plate lined with paper towels to help absorb extra oil. Just let them cool off a little before you bite into them . . . you'll be tempted to bite them right away but you don't want to burn your mouth! Trust me . . . I learned that lesson the hard way!

Charcuterie Board

Who knew that there was a name for it? I've seen this display of goodies all my life at almost every family party. We would fill up the entire table with beautiful arrays of tasty food. Family photos were never of us, but of the mountains of food! It wasn't just about feeding, but it was also about presentation.

There are no strict ingredients to making a charcuterie board.

Simply add whatever your heart desires!

Ingredients:

Sliced cured meat
Cooked assorted Portuguese sausages
Hard/soft cheeses
Pickles and pickled onions
All types of nuts
Olives and lupini beans
Dips, jams, and spreads
Vegetables
Fresh and dried fruits
Breads and crackers

Directions:

Sort and organize ingredients into an aesthetically pleasing array on the board.

Feel free to add as many components as you may like, as long as you are sure to dress it up. This is perfect for entertaining your guests before lunch or dinner.

Oh and one last thing.... Don't forget the wine!

Breakfast, the day begins

Pequeno almoço, o dia começa

When visiting family in São Miguel, my mornings tend to start at a very slow pace. I usually wake up to the sound of the bakery van delivering fresh bread to the house; two loud horn beeps announcing their delivery. My cousin's wife, Ana, goes out for the bread, then places the following day's order before the van goes to the next home for delivery. It's really quite wonderful to have warm, freshly baked bread being delivered to your home each day, something I truly miss back in the States.

When I finally do make it to the breakfast table, I'll find a table of food waiting. From still oven-warm bread ready to be slathered with butter, to fresh fruit, homemade fruit jams, slices of ham, fried blood sausage, and farm eggs along with several cheeses—soft, firm or spreadable—that are truly delicious.

My cousin told me that on our island there are two cows for every person. When traveling the island, you can see them freely grazing along the lush, green pastures and I think you can taste just how happy they are by the milk that they produce.

The cheeses waiting on the breakfast table include homemade queijo fresco with its soft, silky texture and served with chopped red hot peppers on top. There is also the savory and buttery taste of the queijo Nova Açores flavored with garlic and parsley. Then, last but not least, from the island of São Jorge is São Jorge cheese. This is a semi-hard cheese made from unpasteurized cow's milk. It's so good that it has the DOP (Protected Designation of Origin) status. Cheese wheels are aged from 3 months to 36 months. I love tasting and guessing the age . . . I find that at 3 months the cheese is softer with a salty flavor, but as they age the cheese becomes firmer and extra sharp in flavor. I actually love them all!

As I enjoy my breakfast with a hot cup of coffee, I start planning my day on this wonderful Island. I want to make sure I don't miss out on anything!

Freshly baked bread delivered to my cousin's home first thing in the morning.

On a side note regarding ordering coffee. . . . Coffee is served anywhere and any time and you will find it is part of a daily ritual for the majority of the Azorean population.

Here's what you need to know about ordering coffee in Portugal

- Café—which you may know as an espresso, or a short black coffee served in a demitasse cup.
- Abatanado—this is a long and weak coffee served in a medium cup, similar to a weak American coffee.
- Café pingado—an espresso with a drop of milk.
- Garoto—Portuguese for "little boy," and it's an espresso with milk in a small cup.
- Meia de leite—this is a medium cup of coffee with milk (half milk, half coffee). The size of the cup is the same as the abatanado. It literally means "half (cup) of milk."
- Galão—A tall glass with black coffee and ¾ milk, similar to a latte. It is served very hot and can burn your fingers when you are trying to hold it. So be very careful.
- Cappuccino—coffee traditionally prepared with espresso, hot milk, and steamed milk foam.

Taro Root

Inhames

Taro is thought to be one of the earliest cultivated plants. Because the land is so fertile in the Azores, taro is easily grown in abundance, especially in the fajãs, ravines, and valleys. It was introduced to the Azores in the 1600s from Southeast Asia and immediately became a staple piece in the diets of many peasants. It is rich in nutrients and provided relief during times of famine in the Azores.

During great economic stress in the late 1600s, the crown looked for ways to tax new products to expand its economy. While they mainly focused on meats and cereals, they created the "dízimo das miunças e ervagens," or a "tithe or tax on greens." This tithe imposed a tax on green plants. Since taro root was considered food for the peasants, it was not subject to this tax. After some time, certain villages were informed that they would have to pay the tax, resulting in what is now called the Taro Revolt. Many of the inhabitants on the island of São Jorge, in the municipality of Calheta and Topo, refused to pay the tax and protested against this demand but were arrested. Those who were not arrested formed a mob outside of

the Church of Nossa Senhora das Neves where they threatened physical retaliation until the prisoners were released. Despite their short-lived success, the rebels and their supporters were sent to Lisbon to be prosecuted. Some rebels were able to escape their sentencing, but their belongings were seized to pay off their debts. Many of the prisoners who were unable to escape, were subject to famine, disease, and death. As many years passed, those who were still consequently suffering from poverty were forced to emigrate to Brazil or the United States.

Here's an example of different taro roots. . . . The hourglass-shaped taro root originates from Furnas, while the softball shaped taro root originates from Bretanha, both in São Miguel, Azores. The smallest taro root, or inhames, are called minhotos and are grown in California. For those not familiar with Taro root, they are starchy tubers that once were used as a substitute for potatoes. There are some people who even call taro roots, "dasheen." Besides boiling and then frying them alongside chouriço, they are used for soups and stews and even desserts. One of my favorite variations was a Lent dinner dish using leftover inhames that were sliced, sautéd with olive oil, garlic, calda de pimenta, wine, vinegar and topped off with some sunny side up eggs.

2006
Junta de Freguesia

Breads

Pães

Taro Root Rolls

Pão de Inhames

I can honestly say that when I was growing up I did not eat taro root. It could also have been that during that time taro root was not being imported into the United States. But once it did become available my parents would always pick them up at the Portuguese markets. If you have ever seen them in the market, they are a type of dasheen. Even though some people call taro root a yam, it is not. Both the taro and yam are starchy root vegetables, yet they come from different botanical families and have distinct characteristics. Taro root can be found in tropical regions, and grown in volcanic wetlands, so besides being grown in the Azores, it's also grown in places like Hawaii.

Taro root can be a great substitute for potatoes and can be used in any way in which potatoes are used, whether mashed, fried, baked or boiled. Some say that they have a nutty flavor, and the texture is a combination of chestnuts and potatoes. In my home, my parents loved eating them boiled to go along with fish. Or, one of my favorite ways was when they would boil them for Friday's fish dinner and leave enough for leftovers which would be sliced and fried the next day. Then we would serve the fried taro slices along with fried chouriço for a quick Saturday lunch.

My Tia Lilia, who loves using potatoes in her baking, shared this recipe with me using taro root instead of potatoes for these delicious rolls. One thing she told me is that when you cook the *inhame*/taro root, make sure that you season the water with salt, and to boil them with the skin on. Only after they are fork tender and cooked, you can peel off the skin with a sharp knife.

Ingredients:

Makes a dozen rolls

- 1 cup cooked mashed taro
- ¼ cup lard
- 1 large egg
- ¼ cup whole milk
- 1½ cups all-purpose flour
- 1 tablespoon baking powder
- 2 tablespoons sugar
- ½ teaspoon salt

Directions:

Preheat the oven at 350°F

Line a baking sheet with parchment paper and leave aside.

In a large pot of water add 2 large taro roots, salt and bring to a boil. Once it's fork tender, drain out the water and let the taro cool. Once it's cooled off enough to handle, using a

continued on page 54

Taro Root Rolls continued from page 52

sharp knife peel off the skin. Add the peeled taro into a medium bowl, and with a potato masher, mash the taro with the lard and leave aside. In a small bowl, beat together the egg and milk, leave aside.

In a large bowl, add the flour, baking powder, salt, and sugar. Using a whisk, make sure to blend everything together thoroughly. Create a well in the center and add the mashed taro, along with the egg and milk. Using your hands, mix everything together.

Now, lightly flour your baking mat or kitchen counter and place the dough on it. Pat the dough down to ½ inch thickness. Using a biscuit cutter (or a drinking glass) cut the dough. If the dough starts to stick to the cutter or glass, just make sure that you press the glass on flour before you cut into the dough. Place the biscuits on the baking sheet and bake for 20–25 minutes.

Once baked, remove and cool a bit before serving.

Personally, I love it warm, along with a pat of butter . . . delicious!

Olive Bread

Pão de Azeitona

Growing up, we always had jars and cans filled with olives in our pantry, and of course we had bowls of black and green olives on our table. My dad especially loved any type of olive, yet I was never a big olive fan until I was older. Now, I love them so much that I could make a meal of bread, butter, cheese, olives, and wine. . . . So when I was served slices of *Pão de Azeitona,* I wondered why it took me so long to enjoy this delicious bread.

It's no surprise to find out that olives have been cultivated in Portugal for over 2000 years, and that they were first introduced to us by the Romans, then further developed by the Moors. Besides enjoying the whole fruit, olives have been made into amazing oils, which are crucial in flavoring most of our traditional dishes as well as in some desserts and breads. . . . This recipe has the best of both using olives and olive oil in its ingredients. I actually made this recipe several times just to make sure that it was as good as I remembered it, and let me tell you, it's been amazing every time!

The dough comes together so well and the actual bread is soft in texture, so much so that I have made the bread plain (without olives) and then stuffing it with slices of linguiça and eaten it as a sandwich. Every time it's spot on. I can honestly say that it's my go-to recipe for bread.

One other note I need to make about this bread recipe is that you must specifically use bread flour, which has a higher gluten content. In Portugal, the type of flour they use to make this bread is Type 80. In this specific recipe you do not want to use all purpose flour, which has a lower gluten level and will result in a different consistency.

This recipe makes one large round loaf, or two medium logs or 6–8 small baguette-size logs.

Ingredients:

3¾ cups bread flour, (don't over fill)
1½ teaspoons salt
1 packet (¼ oz) of active dry yeast
(I used Fleischmann's Rapid Rise)
2 tablespoons extra virgin olive oil
1½ cups warm water
1 tablespoon granulated sugar
1½ cups black or green olives, pitted and sliced
Cornmeal, for dusting
Extra olive oil for greasing bowl and your hands

continued on page 56

Olive Bread continued from page 55

Directions:

Always start by preparing and measuring out all your ingredients.

In a small bowl, whisk together the warm water, sugar and the packet of yeast. Leave aside for 15–20 minutes for yeast to proof and it begins to bubble. This is to ensure that the yeast is active and viable for baking.

In a large bowl, add the flour and salt and whisk together, then create a well in the center and pour in the activated yeast mixture, and olive oil. Using a wooden spoon or your hands, gently work the flour into the wet ingredients until a rough dough ball forms. Once that happens, transfer the dough onto a clean floured surface. Using your hands (which I rub with more olive oil so the dough doesn't stick to my hands), knead the dough for a good 10–15 minutes, or until it becomes smooth and elastic. If the dough is too sticky, add a little more flour, and if dry, add a little bit more olive oil.

Next, take the dough and flatten out before spreading out the sliced olives. Then fold the dough over the olives and knead gently to distribute the sliced olives evenly throughout.

Place the dough in a large greased bowl, cover with plastic wrap, and let rise in a draft-free warm spot in the kitchen for 1½–2 hours or until it's doubled in size.

Once it's doubled in size, punch down the dough and once again place the dough on a clean, lightly floured surface, and shape the dough into what form you want. I chose to divide the dough in half and I created two medium loafs. . . . Place the dough onto a baking tray dusted with cornmeal. Once again, cover and let rise for another 45 minutes, or until it has doubled in size.

While the dough is going through its second rise, start preheating the oven to 430° F: you want that oven to be really hot.

Once the dough has risen for the second time, but before you place it in the oven, make a few shallow slashes on the surface with a very sharp knife. Bake the bread in the preheated oven for 30–35 minutes, or until golden brown, or if you hear a hollow sound if you tap the bottom of the baked bread.

Once it's baked, remove and let it cool completely on a wire rack 30–45 minutes before cutting into it. I know you'll be tempted to cut into it beforehand . . . but really try not to!

On the first day of baking this bread, the outside has a good crunch and soft fluffy center. The next day, if you have any leftovers, the outside will be softer in texture and the inside will still be soft and fluffy.

So now that this special recipe has been shared, I just know that you are going to just love it. Don't be afraid to bake bread from scratch; once you make this recipe, you'll be convinced of how simple it really is.

Homemade Bread

Pão Caseiro

Pão Caseiro means "bread made at home." They're usually large-sized, rustic round loaves with a crispy outside crust and a soft texture on the inside. Growing up in the U.S. my mom would bake bread only once in a blue moon. We were very lucky to live just a very short walking distance to a wonderful Portuguese bakery, so almost every day we had fresh baked bread in our home. We would always have *papo-secos* (Portuguese pops) and Vienna bread during the week, but on the weekend, the bakery would make corn bread and Pão Caseiro. My mom explained that to make a great tasting Pão Caseiro you really need to have a yeast sponge made and ready to start the bread. She said that when we lived in São Miguel she would bake bread every day, so she would always have a yeast sponge ready in her kitchen cabinet. Of course, when we would have these conversations, I had no idea what she was talking about and no recipes were ever exchanged. All I remember her saying was "it was lots of work."

Many years after my mom's passing, I found myself sitting at my Aunt Ines' kitchen table in São Miguel and learning every step of baking Pão Caseiro from her; her's is the same recipe my mom would have used. The key to the recipe was having yeast made a day ahead of time and saved until it was needed. Using this method gives the bread a better texture and flavor than your usual bread. The breads were also baked in fire-heated stone ovens, but I don't have a bread oven in my kitchen. I have found that by using a large pizza baking stone dusted with corn flour will give me a crispier outer crust.

This recipe makes one loaf, but it can be easily doubled.

Ingredients for the yeast sponge:

1 cup lukewarm water
1 teaspoon active dry yeast
2 cups all-purpose flour

Directions for the yeast sponge:

(To be made the night before baking your bread)

Using a large bowl, pour in the water and yeast and mix well. Then stir in the flour and make sure everything gets mixed well together. Cover the bowl with a couple of tea towels and keep in a draft-free area to let the yeast ferment overnight.

continued on page 62

Homemade Bread continued from page 60

Ingredients for the dough:

1 cup lukewarm water
1 teaspoon active dry yeast
3 very full cups all-purpose flour
3 teaspoons salt
Pre-made yeast sponge

Directions for the dough:

In a large bowl, pour the water and active dry yeast and whisk well together. Add in the yeast sponge and stir together. Next add in the flour a little at a time and stir together until it becomes too hard to handle: you must use your hands to mix! Remove the dough from the bowl onto a floured surface and use your hands to continue to knead the dough for at least 5 minutes or until the dough feels smooth and elastic to the touch. If the dough is too soft, add a little more flour; if it's too dry, add a little more lukewarm water.

Grease the large bowl with softened butter and put the dough back in, cover it with a couple of tea towels and let it rise in a draft-free place until the dough has doubled in size, usually about 1 to 2 hours.

After the dough has doubled in size, remove it from the bowl and place onto a floured surface. Start shaping the dough by punching it and deflating it. Keep kneading and create a large circle out of it. Once it's at the shape you're happy with, place the dough on a floured surface, cover it, and let it rise again until it doubles in size. That takes about 1–2 hours.

About a half hour before the dough is ready, preheat the oven at 400°F. Move the rack to the middle of the oven and remove any extra racks. If you're using a baking stone, place it in the oven at this point to allow it to become nice and hot. When the dough is ready, transfer the dough onto the center of the stone. If you are not using a baking stone, place the ready dough on a floured baking pan instead. Using a very sharp knife or blade, slash a cross on the top of the loaf and bake for 50–60 minutes.

You can test to see if the bread is baked by carefully removing the bread and tapping on the bottom; if it sounds hollow, it's done.

Transfer the loaf onto a rack and let it cool before cutting into it.

Portuguese English Muffins

Bolos Lêvedos

Bolos Lêvedos are a Portuguese version of an English muffin, but better. I find them to be slightly sweet and delicious right out of the package, untoasted. Many people have them toasted the next day with jam and butter. Bolos lêvedos compliment any brunch meal, a midday snack, and they even work great as sandwich bread for an egg sandwich, BLT, or with cranberry chicken salad on top.

This recipe is said to be over a few hundred years old, and it came from my brother-in-law's mother. Senhora Rosalina Pimentel learned it from her mom, who learned it from her mom, who learned it from her mom, and well, you get the idea! The Pimentel family came from the area in São Miguel where this recipe originated, so it is as original as it gets.

Senhora Rosalina shared the recipe with my mom, which I found tucked inside my mom's notebook of assorted recipes. I shared it in my first book, and I also got to share it on the first season of my PBS series. It's one of the most-asked recipe requests I get, so I figured that I would share again.

After several years of making this for my family, I learned a few tricks along the way. One is that I start my dough the night before I plan on making them, and I let the first rise take place in the refrigerator overnight. Then I let the dough come to room temperature before following the rest of the steps listed in the recipe below. My good friend Cindy, who is a trained pastry chef, gave me this helpful hint about making the dough the night before. I even use this tip when making any brioche style dough. Once you try it, you'll wonder why no one ever shared it before. . . .

Ingredients:

3 packets (¼ oz each) of active dry yeast (I use Fleischmann's Rapid Rise)

1 cup lukewarm water

3 heaping cups and 3 tablespoons of sugar

5 pounds all-purpose flour

12 eggs (room temperature)

2 cups whole or 2% milk

2 sticks butter (room temperature)

1 tablespoon salt, dissolved in a tablespoon of warm water

1 lemon rind, grated

continued on page 64

Portuguese English Muffins continued from page 63

Directions:

Dissolve the yeast packets in lukewarm water (not too warm or it will kill the yeast). Stir in 3 tablespoons of sugar. Mix well and leave aside, allowing time for the yeast to proof by bubbling. (This is to ensure that the yeast is active and viable for baking.)

In your mixer bowl, add eggs and 3 cups of sugar. Mix until the color is a light cream and the consistency is just as creamy. Set aside. In a saucepan, add milk and butter, stirring until the butter is melted and milk is warmed. Set aside.

In a very large bowl, add flour and create a well in the center. Pour the melted butter and milk into the well and mix with the flour. Add lemon zest and salt, continuing to stir. Add the creamed eggs and sugar and continue to mix well. Don't be afraid to start using your hands if the mixture becomes too hard for the mixing spoon. Then, add the yeast that has proofed. Mix together and knead the dough for 15 minutes in the large bowl.

Then cover the bowl with a cloth and leave aside until the dough rises. (Hint: To help the dough rise faster, I usually turn on my oven to add a little more warmth to the kitchen, and then place the covered bowl on the counter next to the oven.) It usually takes 2–3 hours for the dough to rise.

After the dough rises:

Begin to take pieces of the dough out of the bowl and roll in your hands, forming balls the size of a medium orange. Make sure you dust your hands with flour as you do this since the dough is sticky.

Place the balls of dough on a floured cookie sheet and dust lightly with flour before covering with a cloth and allowing them to rise a second time, usually 4 hours.

After the dough rises, take each ball of dough and pat them down with flour-dusted hands to shape them to the desired size.

Dust a cast iron skillet with flour. (Resist the urge to use oil—I know it sounds funny, but trust me!) Set the stove top temperature to low to medium heat. If it's any hotter, the flour (and muffins) will burn.

Place the flattened dough on the skillet one at a time and allow it to slowly cook, turning it occasionally to make sure it doesn't burn. Use a toothpick to test and see if it is cooked through. This recipe makes 24 Bolos Lêvedos.

I have also used my electric skillet to make this recipe. . . . It's not traditional, but it's very easy and you can make more than one at a time.

Enjoy!

Crackling Bread

Bolo de Forno com Torresmos

My mom made this bread whenever she had leftover fried pork belly. She often made it on Saturdays as a weekend treat. It was one of my dad's favorite dishes, paired with *morcela*/blood sausage and fried eggs. This recipe is from a close family friend, Rosa Barbosa, who makes it almost identically to my mom's recipe. It brings back childhood memories, and I hope you all like it as much as I do!

Ingredients:

1 cup fried pork belly, finely chopped
1 cup white corn flour
½ cup all purpose flour
1 tablespoon lard
1 tablespoon sugar
1 teaspoon baking powder
½ teaspoon salt
Warm water

Directions:

If you have access to a Portuguese market, you can buy fried pork belly directly from them. If not, you will need to make it. Make sure that you buy strips of pork belly that are fatty with just a small portion of meat in order to get the most flavor. Finely chop it, then fry pork belly in a deep skillet over medium heat. Place pork belly in a single layer, seasoning with salt and pepper. The pork belly will begin to render and fry in its own fat.

You want to make sure to continuously stir the pieces so that it fries evenly. Once fried, place the pork belly pieces on a paper towel to blot any excess grease. For a more in-depth tutorial, you can visit my recipe for fried pork belly in my first book, *Azorean Cooking: From My Table To Yours*. Once the fried pork belly pieces cool off, start cutting them into smaller pieces and leave aside.

Preheat the oven to 350° F. Combine all of your dry ingredients in a large mixing bowl and mix thoroughly with enough warm water to form a dough. Add in the chopped pieces of fried pork belly and lard and mix thoroughly once again. Separate the dough in half to form two balls. You can, of course, separate them into smaller pieces depending on the quantity you want to make. On a greased baking tray, press the balls of dough down to form a disk shape. Each piece should be no thicker than 1 inch. Bake in the oven for 30 minutes +/- or until golden brown. Once it gets golden, Rosa recommends shutting the oven off and leaving the crackling bread inside of the oven 15 minutes +/- for the bread to dry up and become crispy.

Rosa also recommended that you can substitute the fried pork belly with caçoila (pulled pork), which I have tried and it's absolutely delicious too!

Pão

Rosa's Sweet Bread continued from page 72

Directions:

Start by gathering all the ingredients, then proof the yeast by making the yeast sponge. Mix all of the yeast sponge ingredients together in a small bowl. While waiting for the yeast to bubble up and double in size, you can begin putting together the rest of the recipe.

In a saucepan, heat together the milk, salt, butter and scald the milk . . . but don't bring to a boil. Take off the heat and leave aside.

In a large bowl, beat eggs with the sugar until it has a creamy consistency, then leave aside. In a very large bowl add in all of the flour and create a well in the center. Pour milk, butter, and salt into the well and start mixing. Then pour in the egg mixture and continue to mix. Lastly, add oil and yeast sponge into the dough and continue kneading together until the dough is smooth.

Knead the dough really well, using a slight slapping and hitting motion. We want to avoid any lumps so be sure to check constantly. Once well kneaded, cover the dough in the bowl and let it rest for a half hour.

After the half hour has passed, knead the dough again, bringing the sides of the dough up to the middle and punching it down again. Continue that several times before sprinkling the top of the dough and sides of the bowl with flour. Cover the bowl of dough with towels or blankets to keep warm and away from drafts. Let the dough rise until it doubles in size. This can take awhile, sometimes 5 hours or more depending on temperature, as well as weather.

Grease the baking pans (I use 9 inches in diameter, 3 inches high) well with butter and set aside. Once the dough has doubled in size, flour or grease your hands first, then punch down the dough, kneading it several times. Constantly flour or oil your hands lightly before you grab the dough and rip off appropriate sized pieces. Once the pans are filled with the dough, you need to cover them once again and keep away from drafts and let it rise in the pans until it doubles in size.

Once the dough has doubled in the pans, it's time to preheat your oven to 400° F. In a small bowl, beat the eggs and milk together. Using a kitchen brush, lightly coat the tops of the loaves with the egg mixture. Place the raw loaves in the oven and reduce the temperature to 350° F. Bake for the first 20 minutes at this temperature, then reduce the heat again to 300° F and continue baking until done.

Please note that every oven temperature runs differently. In my oven, sweetbread bakes for an hour depending on the size of the loaf. But it can take 90 minutes or more with bigger pans of dough. . . . Please insert a cake tester when the timer goes off, just to be sure. Also, this recipe makes 5 to 6, 9-inch round loaves, but will make more or less depending on the size of your baking pans.

Lanche, Not Lunch

"Lanche" as well as "Merenda" in Portuguese refers to a light meal or snack. Although it may sound like lunch, it is not. In Portuguese culture, "lanche" can include a variety of foods such as sandwiches, pastries, or small bites enjoyed between main meals. It's a convenient and casual way to satisfy hunger during the day without eating a full meal. The idea of lanche is deeply ingrained in Portuguese social gatherings and traditions. It often accompanies moments of socializing, whether it's during a coffee break, a casual meeting with friends, or as part of a family gathering. Portuguese lanche has a diversity of options, whether it be a pastel de nata, a small sandwich, or even some bread and jam with tea.

Picture courtesy of Vanessa Gonsalves

Viewpoint of Daybreak

Miradouro da Ponta da Madrugada

While on one of my visits to São Miguel, I really wanted to welcome the new day by watching the sunrise. I was told that the best spot to see it is in the northeastern part of the island, called Nordeste. I was inspired to go even knowing it involved getting up at 4:30 in the morning and driving for over an hour to be at the special point by 6:00 am. If that was not daunting enough, several family members had told me that the previous mornings had been very cloudy and that we faced the same forecast. We were probably not going to be able to see the sun behind the clouds at all. Despite that, I really didn't need much convincing, nor did anyone else as we were all onboard for this adventure. I just knew the sun would shine for us: my island always takes care of me.

So at 4:30 in the morning, in pitch darkness, my cousin, João and his wife Ana drove my husband Bob and I to the special point in Nordeste called Miradouro da Ponta da Madrugada. Once we reached this beautiful rest area garden overlooking the ocean, we bundled up, then patiently waited for the sun to make its appearance.

Slowly, but surely, the sky started opening up with light. A bright golden light lined the sky first, and then it turned to a dark purple, so regal. Then before we knew it, the whole sky turned to bright purple with bright yellow light pushing through the clouds. Finally the sun made its glorious appearance. The sun felt so close to us, as if the ocean was the only thing between us. It was a special moment that was not only breathtaking but very emotional for me, as the sunrise seemed to personally welcome us to another day on my beautiful island.

Then, after it showed its amazing splendor . . . the sun became covered in clouds.

I knew that my island would take care of me and show me what I wanted to see . . . it's a connection that I have always had with this place that I came from. I truly believe that you can leave our islands, but our islands never leave you.

That day I was beyond grateful for the gift that I received and will never forget it. Yes, to me, it was a gift from my island.

Entrées

Pratos Principais

Tomato Quiche

Quiche de Tomate

Summer is all about fresh grown vegetables, and to me there is nothing like garden tomatoes. I love them so much and try to include them in all my summer meals. When there's a particularly big bounty, I try to come up with as many new recipes as I can. But whenever I have a chance to pick up even a few more tomatoes at the local farmer's market, I'll often simply make some tomato pie/quiche for my family. It's really delicious and so easy to make.

Ingredients:

Serves 4

4 large garden tomatoes, sliced thin
5 large eggs
1 cup milk
½ cup heavy cream
1 small onion, chopped
3 garlic cloves, minced
4 tablespoons butter
Salt and pepper to taste
1 package Pie Crust Deep Dish 9-Inch or a package of refrigerated pie crust. Do not pre-bake the crust.

Directions:

Preheat oven to 375°F. In a large bowl, beat the eggs well together, then add the milk, cream, salt and pepper to taste. Leave aside.

Over medium heat, using a large skillet, add the butter, onion, garlic, salt and pepper to taste. Sauté everything together until the onions become wilted and translucent, then set aside until cooled.

In the meantime add several layers of sliced tomatoes into the piecrust and leave aside. Pour the egg mixture into the skillet of sautéd onions, and mix together well.

Lastly, pour and ladle the egg mixture over the sliced tomatoes and bake in the oven for 30 minutes, then turn down the oven to 350°F and bake for another 15 minutes.

Remove from the oven and let cool before serving. . . . Enjoy!

Linguiça Bake

Caçarola de Linguiça

This is not a traditional recipe I grew up with, but it's one that I make often when I have leftover bread and everyone loves it! My children actually ask me to make this when they're staying overnight during the holidays. I hope that you get to make it for your family to enjoy as well.

Ingredients:

Serves 4

1 pound sausage, chopped into small pieces
1–2 sweet onions, chopped into small pieces
6–8 slices day old bread, cubed
2 cups shredded cheese (mozzarella, cheddar, or São Jorge) optional
6 large eggs
2 cups milk
Salt and pepper to taste
Olive oil

Directions:

Lightly grease a 10x10 inch baking dish and place the cubed bread evenly throughout the dish and set aside.

In a large deep skillet, cover the bottom of the pan with some olive oil and on medium/high heat, sauté the onions and sausage until onions are translucent. Season with salt and pepper to taste. Drain off extra grease if needed and then layer over the cubed bread. At this point if you choose to add the shredded cheese, spread the shredded cheese over the top and set aside.

In a large bowl, beat well the eggs, milk, salt and pepper and pour over everything. Make sure that you press down on the bread, to help it absorb the egg mixture.

Cover and refrigerate at least 8 hours or best overnight.

The next morning:

Preheat the oven to 350°F and remove the baking dish from the refrigerator at least 15 minutes before baking.

Bake for 50–60 minutes depending on the oven or until a knife inserted in the center comes out clean.

Let it cool off for a few minutes before serving. Enjoy!

(As you can see in this picture, I decided to not add cheese to the topping.)

Scrambled Eggs with Tomatoes and Onions

Ovos Mexidos com Tomate e Cebola

Growing up, my mom would always make this dish for our family as a quick breakfast or lunch. We often had extra eggs and tomatoes during the summer so it was a perfect option when we wanted something simple and easy. You can of course put any other vegetables or toppings you may like, but tomatoes and onions will always bring me back home.

Ingredients:

Serves 4

4–6 large tomatoes, skinned, seeded and chopped (canned are fine if tomatoes aren't in season or you need to save time)

1–2 large sweet onion, cut in half and sliced thin in half-moon or chopped

6 large eggs

1 teaspoon hot chopped peppers (pimenta moída)

Salt and pepper to taste

6 tablespoons olive oil, or enough to cover bottom of pan

Directions:

In a medium bowl, beat together the eggs and season with salt and pepper to taste. Set aside.

In a large deep skillet, heat the oil over medium heat. Add the onions and sauté them until they turn a nice light golden color, about 10–12 minutes. Add the tomatoes and hot chopped peppers and continue to sauté together with the onions for another 5+ minutes.

Add the beaten eggs to the skillet and fold them into tomato and onion and continue to gently stir until the eggs are cooked. Serve it with some great crusty bread and a glass of wine.

Tuna with Tomato Rice

Atum com Arroz de Tomate

Ingredients:

Serves 4

2 cans tuna, drained
1 cup rice, rinsed
2 cups chicken broth
1 medium onion, chopped
5–6 garlic cloves, minced
2 tablespoons butter
2 tablespoons tomato paste
1 small bunch parsley
Olive oil
Salt and pepper to taste

Directions:

Cover the bottom of a Dutch oven pan with olive oil. Over medium-high heat, add your chopped onions, salt and pepper and sauté until the onions become translucent. Add the garlic and quickly sauté together. Add in the chicken broth and tomato paste and stir together. Once it begins to boil, add in rice and butter and stir together. Once it begins to boil again, lower the heat to a simmer. Cook until the rice is done, or for about 20–30 minutes. When done, take off the heat and leave aside.

In a medium bowl, mix together the tuna fish, parsley, salt and pepper. Add everything into the pan of rice and mix thoroughly.

Preheat your oven to 350° F. Add the tuna and rice mixture into a greased baking dish and bake for 15 minutes. Serve with a fresh garden salad!

(Sometimes I like to eat this dish right after I mix the tuna into the cooked rice, skipping the baking entirely. But, my husband likes it better after it's been in the oven. So you'll just have to make it for your family and then decide which way you like it the best.)

Chickpea and Tuna Salad

Salada de Grão de Bico e Atum

This is a quick and easy salad my mom would make during the summer season. She would serve it over fresh garden greens from our very own backyard garden. It was perfect for those hot summer days when you don't feel like turning your oven or stove top on. My parents would sometimes substitute tuna packed in water, but I find that you can't compare the taste of tuna packed in oil. I can honestly say that this salad would be made differently every time depending on what my mom had in the pantry or leftover in the refrigerator. Sometimes she wouldn't have potatoes on hand so instead she used cooked carrots or green beans. Feel free to add or omit to your liking. . . . Trust me, this will be one of your favorite summer meals.

Ingredients:

Serves 4

2 cans chickpeas
2 cans tuna in oil
1 small red onion
4 eggs, hard boiled
1 bunch parsley
1 large can black olives
Cooked potatoes
Tomatoes
Olive oil
Salt to taste

Directions:

Make sure to drain the water from the chickpeas and taste one chickpea. Sometimes they are under-cooked and you'll need to boil them for a few minutes in salted water before you can use them as an ingredient. But most of the time they are perfect to eat straight out of the can.

After rinsing the chickpeas, transfer them into a large bowl. Finely chop the onion and parsley and add them together along with the chickpeas.

Drain the oil from the tuna and add it to the bowl. My dad wouldn't drain it because he liked the extra oil in his salad, but of course that is up to you! My dad would like it with all the ingredients tossed well together. Personally I like them separated, just like in the picture. I do that since not everyone likes onions or tomatoes and this allows them to take what they like. Personally, I love to add olives and potatoes, too.

Lastly, season the salad with salt, black pepper and drizzle olive oil to your taste.

You can slice the boiled eggs into small pieces, or just cut them in half and add them to the top of your salad.

Grilled Tuna

Atum Grelhado

This tuna steak is such an easy dish, and another typical summer favorite meal of ours. Since it is so easy you can alter the spices and seasonings to your own taste, but marinating is key. Every time I've made it, it has come out delicious, but please be cautious with your cooking times. A quick 4–5 minutes on each side is perfect for me . . . but if you overcook it, it will be dry. Tuna tends to cook quite quickly, and my husband likes it for 3 minutes on each side, so if you haven't grilled fresh tuna before you might have to test it out at 3 minutes, and add back on the grill if needed so that it's perfect for your liking.

Ingredients:

Serving for 2

2 tuna steaks
2–3 garlic cloves, chopped
1+/- tablespoon hot crushed red pepper sauce (pimenta moída)
4 tablespoons olive oil
Juice of 1 lemon
Chopped parsley
Salt and pepper to taste

Directions:

Season the tuna steaks with chopped garlic, hot pepper sauce, olive oil, lemon juice, chopped parsley, salt, and pepper. As always, please season to your taste.

Marinate for at least 1 hour, if not more, before grilling.

When ready to grill, make sure to place the tuna steaks over the hottest part of the grill. It's important to know your cooking times for each side. Personally I like my tuna medium to medium well . . . so 4½ minutes to 5 minutes on each side is perfect for me. My husband on the other hand loves it medium rare and that's about 3 minutes on each side tops! The timing is just a quick half minute here or there, but the difference is huge.

Obviously, whenever cooking and in doubt, it's always good to use a food thermometer and the internal temperature for cooked fish should be at 145°F.

My Tia Lilia's Fish Stew

Caldeirada de Peixe

Ingredients:

Serves 6

4 tablespoons olive oil

2 large sweet onions, thinly sliced

4 garlic cloves, minced

1 bunch parsley, chopped

3 pounds assorted fish, cut into medium pieces

(I use ½ pound per person, and a combination of fresh cod, haddock, hake, and scallops)

6–8 large potatoes, peeled and sliced

32 oz chopped tomatoes

1½ cups dry white wine

1 tablespoon hot chopped pepper sauce (pimenta moída) optional

1 teaspoon paprika

Salt and pepper to taste

3–4 cups water, or *enough to cover the fish*

Directions:

Make sure to get all your ingredients together and prepped before starting.

In a large stockpot, pour enough olive oil to cover the bottom of the pot. Then over medium heat add the onions and sauté until they are translucent. Then add the garlic, hot pepper sauce, paprika, and salt and pepper to taste.

Stir everything together, and then add the parsley, potatoes, tomatoes, wine, and just enough water to cover.

Cover the pot and simmer for about 25+/- minutes or until the potatoes are almost cooked (*depending on the potatoes*). At this point, add the pieces of fish and adjust water level if needed, again making sure that there's enough liquid covering the fish .

Cover the pot and continue to low simmer for 15+/- minutes or until the fish is cooked.

Serve with fresh bread and a nice glass of wine.

Salted Codfish Preparation

Preparação de Bacalhau Salgado

Because our islands are surrounded by the Atlantic Ocean, fish has always been in abundance and a big part of our diet. Even though salted cod is the national dish of Portugal, cod is not fished in our waters. Codfish like the cold waters of Norway, and Newfoundland, Canada; Portugal's waters are much warmer.

Bacalhau is a salt-preserved codfish. Salted cod is mostly sold as cod-filets that have been heavily salted to draw out the moisture and then air-dried to preserve it. I'm not going to go into the history of it or give you directions on how to salt and hang them on the clothesline, but I do remember seeing that in some yards as well as in the fish markets around the corner from my home when I was very young. My parents would go to the local fish markets to pick out large filets for our Friday night dinners. Sometimes my mom would make codfish with rice but more often she would make a dish consisting of boiled cod and potatoes with a parsley sauce over it. It was a staple in my home, but when I married and tried making the same dish I was very intimidated for quite a few years by the whole process of cooking with it. I thought I could substitute it with fresh cod and no one would know better; boy, was I wrong! The flavors cannot be compared; salted cod has a slightly salty, more intense flavor than fresh cod. Once I got past my fears I realized it was a very simple process. If you haven't cooked with salted cod, here are my helpful hints on preparing it and getting ready for a wonderful dish.

When purchasing salted cod make sure to pick out a piece that has a thick center. Avoid the filets that contain more tail than anything else as that part is very flat and has little meat. Also, check to see if the cod has bones or not. I prefer the boneless and skinless portions, but bear in mind that it usually costs more for that convenience. Some people will disagree and say that salted cod with bone has an even more intense flavor. I personally don't notice a difference in flavor, but you can experiment and decide for yourself.

Once you have the dry salted cod at home, you need to soak the cod in water overnight up to a full twenty-four hours, depending on the thickness of the fish as well as your preference of a salty flavor. Since I like it fairly salty, I usually do the overnight routine. I rinse the salt off first, then I place the salted cod in a bowl large enough to

hold the cod. Then I pour cold water to cover the cod completely. Soak the cod for 12 or more hours depending upon its thickness (refrigerate in hot weather), changing the water 2–3 times daily. On the last soak before cooking, you can substitute milk for water. This last step is important; both my mom and aunt would say that using milk for the last soaking will make the cod more moist, and I agree. When I have just soaked it in water the cod is not nearly as moist or flaky.

I hope this helps you and now you're ready to cook some delicious salted cod dishes.

Salted Codfish Tart

Tarte de Bacalhau

When visiting family in São Miguel last year, I was taken on a day trip to visit the northern side of the island. Along the way we stopped for an afternoon picnic. It wasn't the typical picnic that I've had before. Besides the typical meat and cheese sandwiches, out came these delicious assorted savory tarts. First was the vegetable tart, then the chouriço tart, and last, but not least, the salted cod tart. My cousin Ana said these are like quiches, but they didn't taste like any quiche I have ever had before: they were so much better! My favorite was the salted cod tart. My cousin explained that she used leftover codfish from a previous meal. Trust me, leftovers never tasted so good! I have now made this several times for my family and each time I'm brought back to the amazing picnic by the cliffs.

Ingredients for dough:

2½ cups all-purpose flour
1 egg yolk
8 tablespoons butter
2 tablespoons ice cold water
¼ teaspoon salt

Ingredients for filling:

1½ pound desalted and cooked salted cod, shredded
1–2 large onions, chopped
4 large eggs
1 cup milk
1 cup heavy cream
½ cup black olives, sliced
4 tablespoons olive oil
2 tablespoons butter
2–3 garlic cloves, minced
1 bunch parsley, chopped
Salt and pepper

Directions for the dough:

Using your fingertips, mix the flour and butter together until it forms a crumbly consistency. Add the salt and egg yolk and continue mixing, then gradually add the ice water to bind everything together. Once its shape has formed, you can roll it out into the tart/pie pan. If you want to try a quicker route, you can use a store bought 10" frozen pastry shell or refrigerated pie dough.

In a large deep skillet, heat the butter and oil, add onions and sauté until the onions are translucent. Add the garlic, parsley, shredded cod and season everything with salt and pepper. Continue to sauté everything together for another 5 minutes, and remove from the heat.

continued on page 98

Small individual tarts

Salted Codfish Tart continued from page 96

In a large bowl, beat the eggs, milk, cream, salt, and pepper very well. Add it to the skillet and mix everything well together. Pour it into the prepared tart/pie pan and add the sliced olives on top.

Bake in a preheated 350°F oven for 50–60+/- minutes depending on your oven or until golden.

On a side note: You don't have to make just one big pie. If you prefer individual servings, I have made them in smaller tart pans as shown in my picture.

Creamed Cod

Bacalhau com Natas

This recipe of creamed codfish is a dish that my mom never made, but one I've enjoyed several times at my cousin João and Ana's home in São Miguel. Their daughter Daniela, who also loves to be in the kitchen creating so many delicious dishes, made this dish for me several years ago. Since then, she shared the recipe with me, which she got from her mother-in-law Rosa. I've made this recipe several times since for my family, and it is, hands down, one of my favorites. The only difference from the original recipe is that Rosa would fry the potatoes for this dish, but in my cousin's home they make it with boiled potatoes. It's a little different, but since I've only enjoyed it being made with boiled potatoes, that's how I'm going to share it with you too, but you are more than welcome to fry your potatoes instead of boiling them.

Ingredients:

10 oz salted cod (that's been desalted)
1 pound potatoes, peeled but kept whole (about 3 large potatoes)
1 large onion, chopped
1 garlic clove, minced
2 bay leaves
Olive oil
Salt and pepper to taste
4 cups heavy cream
4½ tablespoons all-purpose flour
4 tablespoons salted butter
Pinch of nutmeg
⅓ cup plain breadcrumbs
2 tablespoons parsley, minced

Directions:

Using a Dutch oven pan, add the desalted cod, potatoes, bay leaves and enough water to cover everything. Over medium to high heat, bring the water to a boil and then reduce to a simmer for about 8–10 minutes. Remove the cod from the pan and place in a bowl to cool down enough so that you can remove all bones, skin, shred it and leave aside.

Meanwhile, continue to parboil the potatoes until they are almost done, it usually takes another 10 minutes, especially if they are large potatoes—smaller potatoes take a shorter time. Test by sticking a fork into the potato, it should be fork-tender but not falling apart. Once they reach that point, you need to remove the pot from the heat and remove the potatoes from the water and let them cool down before you can handle them. Once you can, cut the potatoes into small cubes, and leave aside.

In a large deep-frying pan, add enough olive oil to cover the bottom of the pan, and over medium heat add the chopped onions,

continued on page 100

Creamed Cod continued from page 99

sprinkle with salt and cook until they are translucent. Once they reach that point, you want to add the minced garlic and combine well together.

Next you're going to add the shredded cod into the pan and mix. Now add the cubed potatoes and once again, mix and combine everything together. Then remove the pan from the heat and set aside.

In a large saucepan add the heavy cream, butter and bring to a boil. Once it begins boiling, lower to a slow simmer and start whisking with one hand while the other hand adds flour a little at a time. Keep whisking until it begins to thicken, then add nutmeg and whisk together. Now the cream sauce is complete, remove from heat and leave aside.

Next, I put a large soup ladle into the cream sauce, and I take one full ladle and add it to the large frying pan and incorporate the cream sauce into the cod mixture. Leave the remaining cream sauce for the last step.

Grease your baking dish (I used a 11" round 3" deep baking dish).

Add all the cod mixture into the baking dish, and then pour the remaining cream sauce over the cod mixture. Lastly, sprinkle the breadcrumbs on top and place into a 350°F preheated oven and bake uncovered for 30 minutes, or until the top has a golden color. Once you remove from the oven, make sure to sprinkle the top with the minced fresh parsley before serving.

Spiritual Codfish

Bacalhau à Espiritual

When a recipe has Spiritual in its title you can expect that the dish is going to be heavenly, and with this recipe you would be correct. I was finishing up the final edits of my recipes for this book when I remembered enjoying this dish that I was served at my cousins' quinta (small farm) when visiting last year. My cousins Ana and João both know how much I love the salted cod dish called Bacalhau com Natas, which means creamed cod, but this dish goes one step further by adding shredded carrots and finely grated São Jorge cheese. Once again, just like the Bacalhau com Natas, the recipe called for fried potatoes, but my cousin Ana instead boils the potatoes. You are more than welcome to fry the potatoes, but personally I think boiling them is just as delicious. A special thanks to my cousin Ana for sharing this recipe with me.

Ingredients:

11 oz salted cod, that has been desalted
2 pounds potatoes, peeled but kept whole (about 5–6 large potatoes)
3 cups finely chopped onions
3 cups grated carrots (use the medium grate)
2 garlic cloves, minced
2 bay leaves
Olive oil
Salt and pepper to taste
4 cups heavy cream
4½ tablespoons all-purpose flour
4 tablespoons salted butter
Pinch of nutmeg
⅓ cup plain breadcrumbs
¼ cup grated São Jorge cheese

Directions:

Add the desalted cod to a large Dutch oven pan, along with potatoes, bay leaves, and enough water to cover everything. Over medium to high heat, bring the water to a boil and then reduce to a simmer for about 8–10 minutes. Remove the cod from the pan and place in a bowl to cool down enough so that you can remove all bones, skin and shred the cod, then leave aside.

Meanwhile, continue to parboil the potatoes until they are almost done, it usually takes another 5–10 minutes especially if they are large potatoes—smaller potatoes take less time. Test by sticking a fork into the potato: it should be fork tender but not falling apart. Once they reach that point, you need to remove the pot from the heat and remove the potatoes from the water and let them cool down before handling them. Once you can, cut the potatoes into small cubes, and leave aside.

continued on page 104

Spiritual Codfish continued from page 102

In a large deep-frying pan, add enough olive oil to cover the bottom of the pan, and over medium heat add the chopped onions, sprinkle with salt and pepper and sauté until they are translucent. Once they reach that point add the shredded carrots and continue to sauté together for a couple of minutes, then add the minced garlic and combine well together.

Then you're going to add the shredded cod into the frying pan and mix. Next, you're going to add the cubed potatoes and once again, mix and combine everything together. Then remove the pan off the heat and set aside.

In a large saucepan, add the heavy cream, butter and bring to a boil. Once it begins boiling, quickly lower to slow simmer (if not the cream might continue to boil and overflow) and start whisking with one hand while the other hand adds flour a little at a time. You can remove the pan off the heat, and keep whisking until it begins to thicken, then whisk in the nutmeg and leave aside.

Next, you're going to take about half of the cream sauce and ladle it into the large frying pan and incorporate the cream sauce by mixing it into the cod mixture. Leaving the remaining half of the cream sauce for the last steps.

Grease your baking dish. (I use a large and deep 4-quart size dish.) Add all the cod mixture into the baking dish, and then pour the remaining cream sauce over the cod mixture. Sprinkle the breadcrumbs on top, and lastly top off with the grated cheese. Then place in a 350°F preheated oven and bake uncovered for 30 minutes, or until the top is golden color.

Make sure to serve it with a side of roasted vegetables or a side salad, and don't forget the wine too! Enjoy!

On a side note, this was a perfect dish to offer at a large family dinner or bring to a party, but if I was to make it just for Bob and I, I would have no problem cutting the recipe in half.

Cod Stuffed Cornbread

Pão de Milho Recheado com Bacalhau

This is such a delicious codfish dish. The first time I had it in the Azores it was served with a side salad along with fried potatoes. It was so different from the usual bread bowls filled with soup that I've had. After getting the recipe from the cook, I knew that I would have to try it out at home for my husband and me. Except instead of fried potatoes, I roasted them. I was happy with my results with this dish, and I hope that you get to make it too.

Ingredients:

1 small, round Portuguese corn bread, or any other round bolo of bread

1 pound salted cod, desalted

1 onion, chopped

2 bay leaves

4 garlic cloves, minced

1 tablespoon red-hot chopped pepper (pimenta moída)

½ bunch parsley, minced

Olive oil

Salt

Pepper

Directions:

Begin by preheating the oven to 350°F. Line a baking sheet with parchment paper or foil.

Place the desalted cod in a pot with enough water to cover the fish and add 1 bay leaf. Bring the water to a boil then reduce to a simmer until the codfish is cooked.

Once it's cooked and cool enough to touch, flake the cod into small pieces, making sure to remove any bones and skin from the cod. Leave aside.

Take the cornbread and cut off the top of the bread, as if it was a lid and put it aside. Then carefully remove as much of the bread inside, but make sure to leave enough to allow the bread to keep its shape. In a bowl, save all the pieces of bread you've dug out and add ½ cup of warm water and let the bread absorb the water, then squeeze out the water and save the moistened bread aside. Note: The staler the bread, the more water and time you'll need for it to soak up the water.

In a large skillet, add enough olive oil to cover the whole bottom of the pan. Add the chopped onion, add salt as well as a bay leaf and sauté until the onions are translucent.

Then add the minced garlic and continue to sauté together until the onions turn golden color. Plus, you don't want to burn the garlic; if you do, it could taste bitter, so keep mixing while sautéing.

continued on page 106

Cod Stuffed Cornbread continued from page 105

Add the small pieces of cod, then season with pimenta moída, salt and pepper to taste.

Sauté everything together, add a little more olive oil to the pan, then add back the small pieces of the moistened bread you dug out, and the minced parsley and continue to sauté everything together. If the mixture is too dry, and not coming together like a stuffing, you can always add a little more olive oil.

Once everything comes together, you're going to stuff the corn bread back with the codfish stuffing. Cover it using the top part (the lid) back on top.

Place cornbread with codfish stuffing inside on a baking sheet and bake for 30 minutes.

Even though everything is cooked, by placing it in the oven to bake, the crust gets toasted and crispy.

Once it's time to serve, I just cut into the bread bowl. The bread bowl now has absorbed all the flavors of codfish stuffing and is delicious!

Serve with a side salad and garden vegetables, as well as some fried or roasted potatoes. Plus, don't forget a nice glass of wine too!

My Cousin João's Roasted Octopus

Polvo Assado

Ingredients:

Serves 4–6

6–7 pounds octopus
3 onions, chopped
7 garlic cloves, chopped
3 tablespoons sweet red pepper paste
3 tablespoons tomato paste
2 tablespoons red hot pepper sauce (pimenta moída)
1 teaspoon ground white pepper
3 heaping teaspoons kosher salt
3 bay leaves
2 cups white wine
2 cups olive oil
10 large white potatoes, peeled, cut in half or quarters

Directions:

Preheat your oven to 300°F. If using freshly caught octopus you will need to tenderize it by freezing it for at least three days before using it. If you're in a hurry and don't have time to freeze it you'll need to tenderize it with a food mallet before cooking it, just hit it a few times. If you're buying the octopus at your local market chances are that you're buying it already frozen and all you need to do at this point is to defrost it.

Once the octopus is defrosted, make sure to clean it really well with water. If you find that the octopus is very slimy, use vinegar to help remove most of the slime. Once it's clean you can proceed to cut around the hood/head of the octopus and cut off each tentacle. Next, under running water again, clean each tentacle very well until it's clean of any slime.

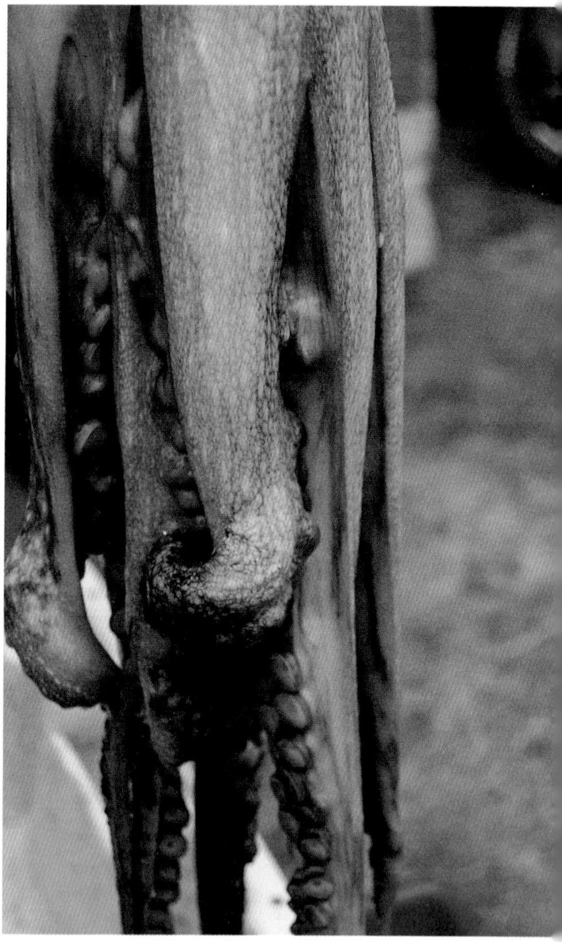

Fresh caught octopus

Using a large stockpot, add all the clean tentacles and all the ingredients except for the potatoes and mix it well together. Place the pot on the stovetop and cook for 30 minutes over medium heat.

After 30 minutes, remove all the tentacles and place them into a large roasting pan, leaving all the liquid in the stockpot. Leave the roasting pan aside. Now, add all the potatoes into the stockpot with the remaining liquid, cover, and cook on medium to high heat until the potatoes are cooked. Once the potatoes are cooked add them to the roasting pan by placing them around the outside perimeter of the octopus. Using a ladle, skim and remove the very top of the stockpot liquid and pore just enough to cover the bottom of the roasting pan . . . but not enough to cover the octopus.

Place the roasting pan into the oven, uncovered, and roast for 10–15 minutes. Serve with a nice glass of wine . . . enjoy!

My Tia Lilia's Stewed Octopus

Polvo Guisado

Ingredients:

3 pounds frozen package octopus, thawed
½ cup olive oil
2 large onions, chopped
1–2 bunches parsley, finely chopped
1–2 bunches scallions, chopped
2 tablespoons hot chopped red peppers (pimenta moída)
3 garlic cloves, chopped
2 tablespoons tomato paste
2–3 cups red or white wine
1 pound potatoes, diced
Salt and pepper to taste

Directions:

Start by cutting the tentacles from the head, or as my Aunt Lilia called it, the hood. I know you can use certain parts after removing the ink sac, but since I am afraid to have the ink sac break on me I just keep the parts I do want to eat and that's the tentacles. Also, the one thing I didn't do was tenderize the octopus with a mallet. As my aunt explained it to me, if the octopus has been frozen, somehow that tenderizes the octopus so there is no need to beat it up! Next, you need to make sure to wash the octopus tentacles really well. After they are washed, you'll need to bring a large pot of water to a boil. As soon as the water begins to boil, submerge the octopus tentacles and let them boil for at least 5 minutes. Then remove them and let them cool off. Once they have cooled off, cut them into small 2" size pieces. Once they cook they will shrink in size, so don't cut them too small. Leave aside.

In another large pot, add olive oil and onions, scallions, parsley, chopped red peppers, garlic, tomato paste, salt and pepper and sauté for 4–5 minutes. Add the cut up octopus tentacles and the wine and stir it all together. Bring to a boil, then reduce to medium low simmer and let it cook for 1½ hours making sure that during that time you continue to stir. You'll notice that as the octopus is cooking, it releases lots of liquid, so no need to add any at this time, but if the liquid does start to cook away, you can always add more wine.

After 1½ hours add the potatoes and continue to cook until the potatoes are cooked through. Once everything is cooked, taste and see if you need to adjust the seasoning and add salt and pepper if needed.

Now it's time to ladle into a nice bowl with some crusty Portuguese bread on the side . . . Oh and don't forget the wine!

Pork Ribs

Costelas de Porco

Ingredients:

Serves 4–6

4 pounds pork ribs, cut into serving size pieces
1 cup water
¾ cup wine or wine vinegar
3 tablespoon lemon juice
1 garlic clove, crushed
1 tablespoon red hot pepper, chopped (pimenta moída)
1 teaspoon salt
1 teaspoon cumin
1 teaspoon cinnamon
½ teaspoon grated lemon peel
¼ teaspoon pepper

Directions:

In a large bowl, combine all ingredients except the ribs; mix well to form a marinade. In a large tray, place the ribs and cover all thoroughly with the marinade. Refrigerate for at least 6 hours, but preferably overnight.

Once the ribs have marinated, remove them from the marinade and set the marinade aside.

Preheat the oven to 350° F.

Place the ribs in a large roasting pan and pour the marinade over them, ensuring all the ribs are well-coated. Cover the pan and roast for 1½ hours. Then, uncover and roast for an additional 30 minutes.

Tip: To speed up the cooking process, my mom sometimes boiled the ribs in the marinade with enough water to cover them for about 40 minutes. Then, she transferred the ribs to a roasting pan and roasted them uncovered for 30 minutes.

Marinated Pork Slices

Bifanas

Bifanas are one of the most popular and traditional pork sandwiches in Portugal. It is a seasoned pork sandwich and is actually considered to be Portuguese fast food. You can get this sandwich virtually anywhere in Portugal and at any Portuguese event. Its counterpart, the prego no pão, which translates to "nail in the bread sandwich," is similar to the bifana sandwich but made of sliced beef rather than pork. It's understandable to think, but some people get confused with these sandwiches initially because it sounds like bifana is beef and wouldn't be pork! Trust me when I say that you'll understand the love for this sandwich as soon as you bite into it.

Ingredients:

2 pounds pork loin, cut into thin slices
4 garlic cloves, sliced thin
2 cup beer or white wine
¼ cup vinegar
1–2 tablespoons hot crushed red pepper sauce (pimenta moída)
½ cup milk
Portuguese Rolls (Papo Secos)
Olive oil for frying
Salt
Pepper
Paprika

Directions:

Slice the pork tenderloin thin. If needed you can use a meat mallet to pound the meat to the right thickness. You can actually have your butcher do this for you, if you feel uncertain about slicing it really thin.

Place the pork slices in a large container and season with salt, pepper, paprika, hot red crushed pepper, and garlic. Combine everything together, and make sure to cover all of the pork. Pour vinegar and beer over the pork and allow marinating overnight in the refrigerator for best results. Some people like to marinate it for a few hours, but I recommend it overnight.

In a large frying pan, heat oil over medium heat. Fry the pork slices in batches until they start to brown, making sure to flip them so they cook evenly on both sides. This does not take long. A few minutes on each side is usually enough and it won't over dry the pork. As soon as they are cooked, remove from the frying pan, and leave aside on a plate. Once you have fried up the last batch add the ½ cup of milk to the leftover oil and meat drippings. Then return all of the pork slices and any juices back into the frying pan so that they are well coated with the sauce. Now you're ready to serve!

You can serve this as a dinner along with some rice and vegetables or with the usual fried potato slices. Or you can serve this as a sandwich with a thin slice of hot red pepper. Trust me, one way or another, it will be amazing!

On a side note:

Some people love to add mustard to the bread/roll (pop).

Some like to add sauteed onions instead or in addition to the sliced red hot peppers.

Roasted Chicken

Frango Assado

This roasted chicken recipe is totally unique and has changed the way I cook chicken forever! You must first clean the entire chicken, including removing parts stored in the cavity. Once this is done, turn it over and place it breast side down on a clean cutting board. With sharp kitchen scissors, cut to either side of the center spine from the neck to the tail, ensuring to remove the center spine. Turn the chicken so it is now breast side up. Using both of your hands, compress the chicken breast downwards and you will hear a crack. The chicken will flatten out and allow for an even cook. This method is also known as spatchcocking.

Ingredients:

6-pound chicken, cleaned and rinsed
1 cup olive oil
Juice of one lemon
3 cut lemons
1 tablespoon hot red pepper sauce (pimenta moída)
1 teaspoon garlic powder
1 teaspoon onion powder
1 teaspoon paprika
1 teaspoon dried thyme
Salt to taste
Pepper to taste

Directions:

Preheat your oven to 350°F. Spatchcock the chicken as described above, then line a large roasting pan with 3 sliced lemons and leave aside. In a large bowl, mix olive oil, lemon juice, hot red pepper sauce, garlic powder, onion powder, paprika, dried thyme, salt and pepper. Pour half of this mixture on top of the chicken; you'll use the other half in a bit.

Cover with aluminum foil and put in the oven for 2 hours. Remove from the oven and uncover the roasting pan. You will now pour the other half of the mixture over it. Then, put the chicken back into the oven, uncovered this time, for another 30–45 minutes or until your food thermometer inserted in the chicken reads 165°F. Serve it with a side salad and enjoy!

You can also barbecue the chicken on a grill for 45 minutes at 500°F. Both are just as delicious.

Chicken Mozambique

Frango Moçambique

If you have my previous cookbook, you know that I shared my family's Shrimp Mozambique recipe. This recipe is very similar, except this time I make it with chicken breast. My family loves it over butter rice, and leftovers get served inside a bread roll (pop). It's just as easy to make and just as delicious . . . and it's perfect for those that do not like to eat shrimp.

Ingredients:

- 4 lbs chicken breasts, washed and cut into cubes
- 1 cup water
- 1½ cup white wine or beer, +/- depending on how much sauce you prefer
- 2 sweet onions, chopped
- 8 garlic cloves, chopped
- 4 tablespoons flat leaf parsley, chopped
- 5 tablespoons butter
- 2 tablespoons olive oil
- 2 envelope packets Goya saffron seasoning "Sazon Goya con Azafran"
  *if not available see substitutions below
- 1–2 teaspoons hot crushed red peppers (pimenta moída) or a generous pinch of dried crushed red pepper
- Juice 1 lemon
- Salt and pepper to taste
- Extra parsley for garnishing

Directions:

Using a 4 quart pot or large deep skillet, melt the butter over medium-low heat. Add the olive oil, and sauté the onions until they turn a little golden in color.

In a separate bowl, dissolve the saffron packets with a cup of water. Pour the water into the skillet followed by the garlic, crushed red pepper, parsley, salt, and pepper. Cover and simmer for 3 to 4 minutes, allowing the spices and herbs to mingle well together.

Pour in the white wine or beer, and squeeze in the fresh lemon juice. Stir and cover. Raise the heat to medium-high and bring the sauce to a boil for a few minutes. Once this time has passed, reduce the heat to medium-low.

Toss in the cubed chicken and cook 7–10 minutes, or until the internal temperature reaches 165° F. Spoon chicken into bowls and serve with rice and plenty of crusty bread to dip in the delicious sauce. Garnish with parsley. Enjoy!

*Make your own seasoning:

Each packet contains ¼ teaspoons of seasoning, so 2 packets would equal ½ teaspoon of this mixture. To make the mixture, combine equal parts of saffron (or you can substitute

with the cheaper safflower, aka açafroa), paprika, turmeric, and onion powder.

Measure out the amount needed for the recipe and save the remaining mixture in a sealed jar for other future recipes.

Alcatra

Alcatra is a traditional Portuguese signature dish particularly from the island of Terceira, in the Azorean archipelago. As for the name, it comes from the Arabic word "al-katra," meaning "the piece" for a piece of meat. This reflects the Moorish influence, who occupied parts of Portugal in the Middle Ages. At its core, Alcatra is a slow-cooked, pot roast-style stew made from beef, though some variations may also use poultry, pork or fish. The meat is marinated and braised in a hearty mix of red wine, garlic, onions, bay leaves, and spices. What sets Alcatra apart is its distinctive cooking method. The ingredients are layered into a traditional unglazed clay pot called a "panela de barro," and then slow-cooked for several hours until the meat becomes tender, almost melting into the savory, wine-infused broth. It's traditionally served with sweet bread, but it can also be served with a side of potatoes or rice to soak up the flavorful juices. Alcatra is such a comforting, delicious dish, and I hope that you'll be making it. On a side note, when I made this dish in Terceira, I was told that they use enamel roasting pans to make it, too. So please don't think of not making it because you don't have the traditional clay pot.

Ingredients:

1 cured 4 quart clay pot or presoaked unglazed clay pot

Lard, to generously grease the inside of the clay pot

5 pounds assorted meats (I used 2 pounds of beef shanks and 3 pounds of bone-in chuck roast)

½ pound bacon, cubed, or smoked pork belly, cubed

2 large onions, finely chopped

3–4 garlic cloves, crushed

2 bay leaves

2 cups beef broth (other recipes suggest using water)

2 cups white wine

1 cup red wine

2 tablespoons +/- (adjust to taste) of crushed red hot peppers (pimenta moída)

1 tablespoon coarse sea salt

8 tablespoons butter, cut into pieces

10 allspice, whole

1 small cinnamon stick, or ½ of larger stick

½ teaspoon ground cloves

Directions:

The day prior to cooking, wash the meat and season with salt and leave overnight in the refrigerator. The first step the next day is to preheat the oven to 450° F.

Start by greasing the pot with lard and begin the layering process:

1st layer add your sea salt, 1 bay leaf, whole allspice, ground cloves, a couple of crushed garlic cloves and cinnamon stick.

2nd layer will be half of the onions and cubed bacon.

3rd layer will be the meat, making sure to add the meat bone first, then work your way up to make sure every piece of meat fits, almost like a puzzle.

4th layer will be the remaining half of onions, bacon, garlic, bay leaf, and the pieces of butter.

5th layer will be a mixture of the beef broth with the crushed red peppers. Pour this over everything in the pot.

6th layer will be your wines. First pour in the white wine, then red wine, making sure that all the meat is covered in liquid.

Cover the clay pot with aluminum foil, and with a fork poke some air vents on top. I also placed the clay pot on top of a cookie sheet before I placed it in the oven (I was afraid the pot would leak or crack as in my past experiences) but it's a great idea just in case any liquid spills during the cooking process.

Last but not least, place the clay pot in the oven and quickly decrease your oven's temperature to 400°F and cook for 4 hours. Finally, uncover the clay pot and cook for an additional 1 hour.

Enjoy!

Beef Stew

Carne Guisada

This beef stew is very simple; growing up this was one of my favorite dinners. We did not add any carrots, peas, or other vegetables to accompany the potatoes as with a traditional American pot roast. It was usually served with wine and a side of fresh Portuguese bread and I would always dunk some bread into the stew. It is a very hearty Portuguese dish that I'm sure you will love!

Ingredients:

Serves 6

1 pound of beef stew meat, cut in chunks
1 pound potatoes, peeled and chopped
1 onion, chopped
6 garlic cloves, minced
1 tablespoon hot crushed red peppers (pimenta moída)
1 tablespoon red pepper paste
1 tablespoon paprika
½ tablespoon cinnamon
½ tablespoon white pepper
Hot water
1 cup red wine
Salt
Olive oil

Directions:

Start by preparing and washing the meat with very hot water in a bowl. Once the blood has been cleaned out, remove the meat from the water and simply season it with just salt; leave aside.

In a Dutch oven, pour the olive oil to fully cover the bottom of the pan. Add in the onions and sauté them until they are fully translucent. Next add in the garlic, hot crushed red peppers, pepper paste, paprika, cinnamon, and white pepper. Place the meat into the dutch oven and mix and sauté everything together. After 3+/- minutes, add the red wine. Mix thoroughly and add enough hot water to fully cover the meat. Let it simmer until the meat is almost cooked. Add potatoes and let it cook until the potatoes are cooked and tender. Enjoy!

Pot Roast

Carne Estufada

Carne Estufada is a pot roast recipe that my mom made at least every other week. It was one of her go-to dinners that was hearty as well as comforting. As I discovered too often with her recipes, she had only written down a list of ingredients, so it was really wonderful to successfully recreate it! I actually knew it was spot on before I even taste tested it because the kitchen smelled just like I remembered. The aroma put me right back in my mom's kitchen, and just as I thought, the flavorful meat and vegetables tasted perfect! My mom would serve this with either rice or with boiled, roasted or mashed potatoes on the side.

Ingredients:

4 pounds beef chuck 7-bone steak
1 large onion, finely chopped
4 garlic cloves, minced
3 large carrots, peeled and rough chopped
1 bay leaf
2 cups chicken stock (my mom would use water, but chicken stock adds flavor)
1 cup white wine
1 tablespoon tomato paste
1 cup tomato pulp (plain sauce)
1 teaspoon cinnamon
4 tablespoons butter
Olive oil
Salt and pepper to taste
Fresh chopped parsley to garnish before serving (optional)

Ingredients for marinade:

1 garlic clove, minced
1 tablespoon hot chopped pepper aka pimenta moída (optional, and to taste)
1 cup white wine
1 teaspoon paprika
2 bay leaves
Salt to taste

Directions:

Please note: The day before you are intending to make this, please marinate the beef with some salt, garlic, paprika, bay leaf and wine. Place the beef in a container along with the marinade and place in the refrigerator overnight for best results.

Using a large dutch oven pan over medium heat, add enough olive oil to cover the bottom of the pan, then add the butter. Once the butter has melted, start adding the finely chopped onions, garlic, salt, and one bay leaf then saute everything together for a couple of minutes.

Once that's done, add the beef with its marinade and then everything else into the pot: the chopped carrots, the remaining bay leaf, wine, tomato paste and pulp, cinnamon and

continued on page 126

chicken stock (there should be enough liquid to cover the meat). Gently mix a bit, and over medium high to high heat, bring up to a boil, then reduce the heat to medium low, cover the pot and let it cook for 1½–2 hours or until the beef's internal temperature is 150°F and fork tender.

Halfway through cooking, uncover and check to see if there's enough liquid in the pot. Personally, I like it with more sauce, so at this point I might add another cup of liquid, and will add either another cup of wine or chicken stock if necessary. Again . . . this part is entirely up to you to decide.

Once the beef is cooked, I place the beef on a large serving dish and I place the boiled potatoes all around the beef, then with a ladle pour the sauce with the carrots over the potatoes and the beef. My mom would always finish it off with rough chopped fresh parsley on top. But the night I prepared this for this book I actually forgot to add it and only realized it after I had taken the picture and served it for dinner. So much for prepping all my ingredients so I don't leave anything out!

Now you're ready to serve. . . . Enjoy!

Added notes:

If you plan on serving it with either potatoes or rice make sure that you're cooking it alongside or beforehand. The last thing you want to do after cooking the Carne Estufada, is realize that you need to cook up your side dish.

I like using chicken stock for liquid, but my mom would use water. Although I would see her start with water, she would often add a chicken or beef bullion cube to it.

I love making this using a beef chuck 7-bone steak, but if you don't see it in your market, please make sure to ask your butcher for this cut. If by any chance they don't have it, look for a chuck roast that's well marbled.

Green Tea Cookies

Bolachas de Chá Verde

Ingredients:

4¼ cups all purpose flour
4 large eggs
1¾ cup sugar
1⅓ cup butter, softened
5 tea bags green tea (each bag contains 1 tsp of the green tea herb)

Directions:

Preheat the oven to 350°F and line a baking tray with parchment paper.

Open each tea bag and place in a small bowl; leave it aside.

In a large bowl, add the sugar and butter. With a hand mixer, mix until it forms a creamy consistency. Mix in the flour and eggs. Then mix in the green tea herb into the dough.

At this point, if the dough is too hard to mix with the hand mixer or spoon, you will need to knead it by hand. Make sure your green tea is well incorporated in the dough.

Using your hands or a small cookie scoop, make small balls the size of a ping-pong ball. Place the cookies on the lined baking tray and lightly press on each ball with a fork to make an imprint.

Bake for 20–25 minutes or until golden and serve with a cup of green tea!

Gorreana
O CHÁ DOS AÇORES

Dona Amélia's Queen Cakes

Dona Amélias

Dona Amélia pastries are a traditional dessert from the Azores, specifically from the island of Terceira. These delicate pastries consist of a sweet mixture of sugar, cinnamon, and molasses. The pastries are then baked until golden brown and dusted with powdered sugar. Dona Amélia pastries are known for their rich flavor and delicate texture, making them a favorite treat among locals and visitors alike. These pastries have a long history in the Azores, and their origin is said to date back to the visit of Queen Amélia of Portugal to Terceira in 1901. Today, they are a beloved dessert and a staple of Azorean cuisine.

Enjoy this dessert fit for a queen.

This recipe belongs to Filomena Corvelo, with whom I baked this in Season 2 of my TV series.

Ingredients:

1 cup sugar
3 eggs
¾ cup yellow corn flour
6 tablespoons melted butter
1 tablespoon molasses
1 teaspoon cinnamon
½ teaspoon nutmeg
Pinch baking powder
White raisins to taste

Directions:

Begin by creaming the sugar and eggs together using a hand mixer until it reaches a soft consistency. Toss in the melted butter and continue mixing. Add in flour, baking powder, cinnamon, and nutmeg and mix thoroughly. Lastly, add in the molasses and mix.

Grease and flour the cupcake/muffin forms and pour the batter to fill each form ¾ the way up. I toss 2–3 raisins into each cupcake before baking, but feel free to omit them if you're not a fan of raisins! Bake your cupcakes at 350°F for 20 minutes.

When done, finish them off with a dusting or roll them in powdered sugar and enjoy!

Pumpkin Scones

Broas de Abóbora

It's funny how family recipes get lost or forgotten, only to be rediscovered again: that's exactly the case with this recipe. I was going over recipes that my mom kept together in a large 3-ring binder. The recipe came from a coworker of hers at the factory she once worked at, but she did not mark down who shared it. Fortunately, my mom left notes about making it and liking it, but it wasn't until I made them that the taste and smell brought back memories of enjoying them, especially during the Christmas season.

My mom would use leftover cooked pumpkin, or she would make it with roasted sweet potatoes. Either way is delicious, so it's really what you have on hand, as well as what you prefer. I always thought they were bread rolls but when I looked up the translation of Broas, what I found surprised me. . . . They are considered scones!

Personally, I have made Irish scones using my father-in-law's recipe for as long as I have been married to my husband. But it's wonderful to make these in a different shape than the usual triangle; these, as you can see, are in football shape. If you love baked goods with dried fruits along with seeds and nuts, this recipe is for you!

Ingredients:

Serves 12

- 3⅓ cups all-purpose flour
- 2 cups cooked, mashed pumpkin or sweet potato
- 1 cup firmly packed brown sugar
- 3 large eggs
- ½ cup mixture of assorted dried fruit of your choice such as raisins, cranberries, chopped figs, chopped prunes
- ½ cup mixture of nuts or seeds of your choice such as pumpkin, sunflower, chopped walnuts
- 2 tablespoons brandy or rum
- Zest of 1 orange
- 1 tablespoon cinnamon
- 1 tablespoon baking powder
- ¼ teaspoon salt
- ½ cup flour for shaping

Directions:

Preheat oven to 350°F.

Line a 11" X 16" baking sheet with parchment paper, leave aside.

In a medium bowl, add the 3⅓ cups of all-purpose flour, baking powder and salt. Using a whisk mix everything together, then mix in the dried fruits and seeds, and leave aside.

In a smaller bowl, add the mashed pumpkin, brown sugar, cinnamon, brandy, orange zest, and mix well, then leave aside.

continued on page 138

Pumpkin Scones continued from page 136

In a large bowl, whisk the eggs until creamy, then add all the contents of the mashed pumpkin bowl. Beat everything well together, then add all the contents in the flour bowl. I start mixing everything using a wooden spoon, then as it gets harder, I usually mix by hand. At this point, the dough is slightly sticky to the touch . . . you'll think you need to add more flour to the mix but don't do it. When I did, the dough became very dense. Just start by taking a small handful of dough and mold the broas into shape with a little flour. Other times I flour my hands or I toss the dough into the flour then shape into a football shape . . . or should I say American football shape.

Once they are floured and shaped to your liking, place on a baking tray.

Depending on how small or big you make your broas, you can make from 9 to 12 broas . . . but with equal amounts of dough, you should have 12 pieces.

Bake for 50–55 minutes depending on your oven or until inserting a cake tester that comes out clean. Then cool completely before enjoying.

Note: I have made this recipe so often now that I have made it using every possible combination of different dried fruit or seeds . . . as well as using lemon zest when I realized I had no oranges at home. It's a family favorite and delicious with a cup of coffee or tea.

If we have any left after a couple of days . . . my husband likes to cut it in half lengthwise and toast in the toaster, then slather it with butter! It's amazing!

Cakes for Company

Bolos de Visitas

When I was growing up, my mom would bake a cake every Saturday. It was made specifically for the company that we received or when we were the company doing the visiting. She specifically had her favorites; Vanilla and Cream Cake, Water Cake, Carrot Cake, and Rosa's Cake. These delicious cakes made their rotation, and every Saturday evening our home smelled heavenly. I have to say, as a little girl it was very difficult to wait for Sunday company. My sisters and I would sometimes try and steal little bites from the bottom or the sides, but nevertheless, I was always caught! As a child, I would always hope that we wouldn't receive any company so that we could have the entire cake to ourselves, especially when my mom made the Vanilla and Cream Cake. Here are the recipes my mom made each Saturday. Now it's up to you, to share with your own *visitas*.

Vanilla and Cream Cake

Bolo com Baunilha e Nata

Ingredients for cake:

1⅓ cups granulated sugar
1 cup heavy cream
2 teaspoons pure vanilla extract
3 large eggs
1½ cups all-purpose flour
1 teaspoon baking powder
Pinch of salt

Ingredients for glaze:

3 cups confectioners' sugar
4–5 tablespoons milk
Zest of 1 lemon

Directions for cake:

Preheat oven to 350° F.

Grease a small pan or a small bundt pan and dust with flour and leave aside.

In a medium bowl add the flour, baking powder and salt, whisk together and leave aside.

In a large bowl, add the eggs, sugar and using a hand mixer, cream them together. Then add the heavy cream and vanilla, and continue to mix together until well blended. Once this is done, mix in the remaining dry ingredients. Beat together until everything is well mixed.

Pour the mixture into the pan and bake for about 35–45 minutes depending on the oven. Insert a toothpick or a skewer to ensure it is cooked all the way through. If it comes out clean, then it's done! Remove from the oven and let cool slightly before unmolding.

Once unmolded, let it cool completely before adding the glaze, but if you don't want a glaze you can always dust the cake with confectioners' sugar instead of having it plain.

Directions for glaze:

In a medium bowl mix (whisk) together the confectioners' sugar and milk. You can always adjust the thickness of the glaze by adding more or less milk. I usually start with 4 tablespoons. Then add the lemon zest and mix well together. Pour the glaze on top of the cake.

Also, I like glazing a few hours before serving. That way the glaze slightly hardens, and adds another delicious twist to just glazing and serving right after.

Serve and watch everyone enjoy it!

Water Cake

Bolo de Água

This cake is what I make when I just feel like baking. Besides being quick, easy, and delicious, it's also another childhood favorite of mine. I can see my mom baking this cake for our weekend; we always needed to be prepared for company!

Hope this brings back wonderful memories for you too.

Ingredients:

- 3 cups all-purpose flour
- 2½ cups granulated sugar
- 4 large eggs at room temperature and separated
- 1 cup warm water
- ¼ teaspoon salt
- 2 teaspoons baking powder
- Zest of 1 lemon

Directions:

Preheat oven to 350° F. Grease and flour tube pan and leave aside. In a medium bowl, whisk together the flour with salt and baking powder and leave aside.

Separate the eggs into two medium bowls. Using a hand mixer at high speed, beat the egg whites until they form high peaks and then leave aside. Again using the hand mixer, beat the egg yolks together with sugar and water, and then add the flour mixture a little at a time into the bowl until well beaten together.

Using a wooden spoon, mix in the lemon zest, and then fold in the egg whites. Pour mixture into the greased and floured tube pan, and bake for 60 minutes or until the inserted toothpick comes out clean.

Enjoy!

Carrot Cake

Bolo de Cenoura

Ingredients:

4 large eggs
3 cups flour
3 cups grated carrots
2 cups sugar
1 cup raisins
1 cup nuts (optional)
1 cup melted butter
2 teaspoons baking powder
2 teaspoons baking soda
2 teaspoons cinnamon
1 teaspoon salt

Directions:

Using a medium-size grater, grate the carrots. Leave aside.

Preheat the oven to 350°F. In a large bowl, combine flour, baking powder, baking soda, salt, cinnamon, and raisins, whisk thoroughly. Adding raisins, or any fruit, to a dry flour mixture will allow them to be evenly distributed rather than falling to the bottom of the cake. If you choose to add nuts to your carrot cake, you will also add them to the dry flour mixture.

In a separate bowl, beat together the eggs, sugar, and melted butter until creamy. Using a wooden spoon, mix in grated carrots. Slowly add the flour mixture into the egg mixture, continuing to mix together with a wooden spoon until fully combined.

Grease a bundt pan with butter and flour. Pour in the cake mixture and bake for 75 minutes (1¼ hour).

Make sure to cool slightly before removing from the cake pan and let it cool completely before dusting the top with confectioners' sugar.

Rosa's Cake

Bolo da Rosa

Ingredients:

4 large eggs, separated
2 cups flour
2 cups sugar
¼ cup milk
2 teaspoons baking powder
Pinch of salt

Ingredients for glaze:

1 cup confectioners' sugar
2 tablespoons milk

Directions:

Preheat the oven to 350°F.

In a large bowl, beat the egg yolks, milk, and sugar until creamy. In a separate bowl, beat the egg whites until they form stiff peaks. Set aside.

In a large bowl, add flour, baking powder, and salt. Whisk well together. Within this mixture, create a well, similar to making pasta. Inside of the well, add in the egg yolk and sugar mixture and beat well together. Once thoroughly mixed, fold in egg whites and stir until fully combined.

Grease a bundt pan with butter and flour. Bake for 45 minutes. Make sure to keep an eye on the cake since there is very little liquid in this recipe and it can quickly overbake!

Once the cake has cooled, you can add the glaze. All you do is mix confectioners' sugar and milk together. Drizzle the glaze over the cake and let it rest a few minutes before eating. This step is optional, so the choice is yours!

Sponge Cake

Pão de Ló

This recipe is from my Tia Lilia, but I think every Portuguese home has a slightly different recipe for sponge cake. It's the go-to cake for a light dessert and most of the time fruit soaked in wine and sugar would be served over it or maybe served plain with a nice cup of tea. I am very lucky that my aunt shared with me the secret to making the lightest sponge cake. The secret is weighing the 8 eggs as the rest of the recipe is based on this. You must match the weight of the sugar with the weight of the eggs, and half the weight of flour. I was a bit skeptical when I made it the first time, afraid it would not turn out great, but I should have known by now my Tia Lilia would not steer me wrong! It turned out as wonderfully light as ever, and it reminded me of my mom's Bolo de Água / Water Cake. It even formed a crusty crunching top layer too . . . It's also a delicate cake to cut, but please don't be as afraid to try it as I was, it really works!

Ingredients:

Please note that you will need a kitchen scale to make this recipe

8 eggs
Granulated sugar
All purpose flour
Zest of 1 lemon

The weight of the eggs equals the weight of the sugar and half of the weight of the flour.

For example, my eggs weighed 1 pound, so I used 1 pound of sugar and ½ pound of flour.

Directions:

Preheat the oven to 325° F, grease and flour a large deep bundt pan or an angel food cake pan and leave aside. Separate the eggs by the whites and the yolks. In a large bowl, mix the egg yokes, lemon, and sugar and beat until very creamy.

In another large bowl, whip the egg whites until they form high peaks. Start to add and alternate into the creamy egg mixture both small amounts of the flour and then the egg whites . Continue to alternate until everything is added and well incorporated. Pour the mixture into the greased and floured bundt pan and bake in the oven for 1 hour. Using a toothpick or skewer, insert into the cake and if it comes out clean the cake is done.

Orange Cake

Bolo de Laranja

If you love oranges, then this cake will become a favorite in your home. This recipe is from my cousin Laureana. She made it for me and served it with tea in the middle of the afternoon on one of my visits to São Miguel. It absolutely hit the spot after a busy morning, but this definitely would be wonderful any time of the day.

Ingredients:

Cake:

2 cups all purpose flour
1½ cups sugar
4 eggs
1 tablespoon potato starch
1 teaspoon baking powder
⅔ cup boiling water
Juice and rind zest of 1 orange
Dash of salt

Glaze:

Juice of 2 oranges
1 cup confectioners' sugar

Directions:

Preheat the oven to 350°F. Grease and flour a 13x9 inch pan. In a bowl, mix together the flour, baking powder, salt, and potato starch. Leave aside.

In two different bowls, separate the eggs and beat the egg whites until they form stiff high peaks and leave aside.

Beat the egg yolks, sugar, orange juice, and rind zest well and add in small amounts of boiled water, beating on high nonstop until creamy. Then start to add flour little by little until everything is well mixed.

Lastly, mix in the egg whites very gently, being careful not to beat into the mixture. Pour the batter into the pan and bake for 30 minutes or until a toothpick inserted comes out clean.

After the cake comes out of the oven, begin to make your orange glaze by mixing the sugar with orange juice. Pour over the cake while it's still hot. The cake will absorb it, giving it that special twist.

Salazar's Cake—The One Egg Cake

Bolo de Salazar

It's funny that every time I go through my mom's notebook of recipes I find a new recipe to try. The last thing I thought I would bake is a cake named after Portugal's Dictator António de Oliveira Salazar. I looked it up and don't you know, the dictator had this cake every day with his midday snack. It's a simple and modest cake, which makes perfect sense since some cooking supplies were sometimes rationed or very expensive if available at all. My mom made a note that they didn't call it by his name, instead they called it "The One Egg Cake." So, I proceeded to make it more for curiosity than anything else.

The recipe was a few lines long with no directions . . . 250 grams of flour, 250 grams of sugar, 1 small bowl of milk, 1 tablespoon of soft butter, 1 teaspoon of baking powder and 1 egg. Mix everything, put it in a greased pan and bake. That was it. . . . So, I took the recipe and tried my best to recreate it. Here's what I came up with.

Ingredients:

1¼ cups sugar
2 cups all-purpose flour
1 cup milk
1 full tablespoon butter, softened
1 teaspoon baking powder
1 large egg
Pinch of salt

Directions:

Preheat the oven to 350° F.

Grease and flour a small 8-inch cake pan. I used a small bundt pan.

In a bowl, add the flour, baking powder, salt and whisk together and leave aside.

In another bowl, add the egg and using a hand mixer, beat the egg at high speed for a good 5 minutes, so that the egg will have lots of air in it and help the cake rise.

Then add the sugar, milk, butter and mix well together for another 5 minutes. Next, start adding the flour mixture a little at a time into the egg mixture, always beating well with every addition of flour. Finally, when all the flour has been added, beat everything on high for a good 10 minutes.

Pour the batter into the greased pan and bake for 45+/- minutes depending on your oven. Make sure to test by inserting your cake tester, and if it comes out clean . . . it's done. Remove the pan from the oven and let it cool down a bit before removing onto a plate. Then cool further before cutting into it.

continued on page 154

Salazar's Cake—The One Egg Cake continued from page 152

I really had low expectations, but I was wrong. It's a small cake, on the dense side, but the flavor is like a pound cake and it was delicious. I can absolutely see this cake being served with an afternoon tea or even served with some fresh fruit. Both my husband and I enjoyed it so much that it didn't leave our house for our usual taste testers.

I hope that you get to make it, no matter what you call it!

Chocolate Maria Cookie Cake

Bolo de Bolacha Maria de Chocolate

When I was growing, up this cake was a must on everyone's dessert table. It's the easiest dessert to make since no oven is used. The original recipe uses traditional vanilla Maria cookies, and in between each layer you could find different fillings from an egg cream to vanilla frosting infused with lemon zest. Every family does it a little differently, so there's really no right or wrong way. When I decided to share my usual recipe, I went to a local Portuguese market to pick up all the ingredients needed and it so happened that they were selling both the vanilla and chocolate Maria cookies made in the Azores by the brand Moaçor. I have no idea when they started making the chocolate Maria cookies and up until then I had only seen them on my trips to the Azores . . . because it's rare to see these chocolate cookies at my market I decided to buy them and redo the recipe using them along with a different filling. I chose a mocha frosting to go in between all the layers of cookies. . . . I love coffee and chocolate combinations! But if you don't like coffee, feel free to use any substitution for your filling!

What started as an experiment turned into delicious goodness that everyone in the family just loved. It's sweet and rich, and a little goes a long way, but I highly recommend making it especially for family or friends that love chocolate.

Ingredients:

3 packages chocolate Maria cookies
1½ cups softened butter
2 packages of 15 oz boxes of confectioners' sugar
1 tablespoon vanilla extract
½ cup unsweetened cocoa powder
½ cup heavy cream
½ teaspoon salt
¼ cup boiling water
3 tablespoons instant coffee

Directions:

In a small bowl, add the boiling water and instant coffee and mix well together. Then leave aside. In a large bowl, beat the butter until creamy, then keep beating as you add the cocoa powder, salt, vanilla, powdered sugar and the coffee. Then add the heavy cream a little at a time to desired consistency.

On a serving dish, add the first layer of cookies; I use 7 in each layer. Lay them out with one in the center and six surrounding the center: it looks like a pretty chocolate flower. I also add a dab of frosting to the bottom of each cookie on the first row. By doing that the cookies stay in place as you build up the

continued on page 156

Chocolate Maria Cookie Cake continued from page 155

layers. Once the cookies are placed, spread a thin layer of the frosting, then add another layer of the cookies, then frosting and repeat. I did 10 layers, but you can definitely do more or less. Once you have your layers set, I like to frost the very top and decorate with crushed cookies on top.

I also recommend that you cover the cookie cake and place in the refrigerator for an hour before serving. This made the frosting harden up a little and made it easier to cut into without it falling apart.

I actually saved the remainder in the refrigerator overnight, and the next day I took it out for 15 minutes before cutting into it again. Even the next day, it was delicious and my daughters and my sons-in-law finished the rest of the cake!

Maria cookies in both vanilla and chocolate. If you can't find them in your market, you can substitute with another type of vanilla tea biscuits and chocolate wafers. I always thought that Maria biscuits were originally Portuguese, but they were actually created by the London bakery Peek Freans in 1874, to commemorate the marriage of the Grand Duchess Maria Alexandrovna of Russia to the Duke of Edinburgh.

Coconut Tarts

Queijadas de Côco

I just love coconut desserts, and every time I visit my family in São Miguel they introduce me to different desserts made with coconut. This recipe was given to me by my cousin Helena. I remember how much I enjoyed these tarts and how I made sure I left with a written recipe! I bake mine in regular cupcake tins, but if you're having a party and want to make them bite-sized I suggest using mini cupcake pans, it will give you 36 perfect bites.

If you love coconut you definitely need to make these!

The recipe makes 18 tarts in regular sized cupcake tins.

Ingredients:

Filling:

1½ cups sugar
2½ cups coconut
4 eggs
Zest of 1 lemon

Pastry:

1½ cups flour
½ cup softened salted butter
½ cup sugar
2 eggs
Alternatively, you can use a store-bought refrigerated pie crust

Directions:

Preheat the oven to 350°F and grease each cupcake tin, then begin to make the dough.

Combine the flour and sugar then work in the butter and eggs. Mix first, then knead by hand until smooth and forms a ball. Let the dough rest for about 10–15 minutes. Then, on a floured surface, roll the dough with a rolling pin to as thin as you can get it. Cut a 3½ inch circle of dough to line each pan or tin. If you're in a time crunch, you can always use store bought refrigerated pie crust.

Once the dough is made, you can begin to make the filling. Beat together the sugar and eggs until creamy, then add lemon zest and coconut, and with a wooden spoon mix everything together. Fill each pan or tin about ¾ of the way. If using tins, place them on a baking sheet before putting them in the oven and bake for 40–45 minutes or until the top is a golden color.

Remove from tins and let cool completely. Finally, dust them with confectioners' sugar before serving and enjoy!

Chocolate Tart with Maria Biscuit/Cookie Crust

Torta de Chocolate com Crosta de Bolacha Maria

Oh My Goodness . . . this dessert is hands down amazing. The first time I had a slice of it was at my cousin João Manuel's home. His daughter Daniella made it for our dessert one evening and it was love at first bite. The combination of the Maria biscuit crust with the silky chocolate and the cream topping is simply divine. For those not familiar with the Maria Biscuit, it's a wheat biscuit flavored with vanilla that's not too sweet. You can pick this up at any grocery store in their international aisle. But if you still can't find it, these biscuits are comparable to arrowroot cookies and can be used as a substitute. Also, a food processor is needed for this recipe.

Ingredients:

Cookie tart crust
2 (7.5 oz packages) Maria Biscuit cookies
2 large eggs
1½ soft sticks butter

Chocolate Filling:

1 can (14 oz) sweetened condensed milk
1 pint (16 oz) heavy whipping cream
12 oz of 60% cacao bittersweet chocolate baking bars (3 bars), broken

Cream Topping

1 pint (16 oz) heavy whipping cream
4 tablespoons granulated sugar

Directions:

Crush and grind the Maria Biscuits to very fine crumbs in the food processor, one package at a time. Then, change to the dough blade and add the eggs and softened butter. Mix well and transfer to a greased 12-inch loose bottom fluted tart pan. Press the dough into the bottom and up the sides of the pan. Bake at 350° F for 13–15 minutes. Let cool completely.

Place the chocolate and the sweetened condensed milk into a heavy saucepan over very low heat and stir constantly until chocolate is melted. Then, using a wire whisk, add the whipping cream and whisk until well blended. Pour the filling into the tart shell and refrigerate for at least 2 hours before you add the cream topping.

With a hand mixer, whip together the whipping cream and sugar and beat until soft peaks form. Spread over the tart filling and refrigerate overnight for best results. Before serving you can add chocolate shavings over the top to give it that extra special look everyone will remember *or* no one will forget!

Malassada Bread Pudding

Pudim de Pão de Malassada

I can honestly say that this malassada bread pudding recipe was a result of having too many leftover malassadas! Growing up, there was never a time I can remember having any malassadas left over. I think as soon as my mother would let us eat them they would be all gone! We would eat them so fast . . . almost like we were inhaling them!

So this year, like every year, I made malassadas at Carnival time for my family to enjoy. To my surprise everyone was on a diet! So I had 12 malassadas left on the platter. Malassadas are to be eaten the same day they are made because otherwise you'll find that the next day they will be hard and dry. So I figured why not try and make them into a bread pudding.

The results are truly delicious, and I might just make another double batch of malassadas just so I can have leftovers . . . it was decadent but absolutely amazing! I even served it with a scoop of vanilla ice cream, which brought it to another level. A must try . . . you will not be sorry.

Ingredients:

1¼ cups whole milk
1 cup granulated sugar
6 large eggs
1 tablespoon pure vanilla extract
One dozen day-old malassadas (I've substituted donuts, which were also awesome!)
2 tablespoons brown sugar mixed with 1 tablespoon of ground cinnamon

Directions:

Preheat the oven to 350°F. Grease an oven-proof-baking dish, preferably a 9x7 Pyrex dish.

Cut the malassadas into pieces (it's up to you on the exact size) and fill the baking dish to the very top . . . leave aside.

In a medium bowl, beat together the milk, sugar, vanilla, and eggs until creamy.

Pour the creamy mixture slowly over the bread, making sure to stop in-between pours to allow the bread to absorb the liquid. Once you pour all the mixture into the pan, let it rest for about 15 minutes. Also, make sure to use your fingers and press down on the bread in areas where it looks a little dry so that the creamy mixture can be absorbed. Last but not least, sprinkle the cinnamon sugar over the whole top of the bread and bake in the oven for 45–60 minutes, depending on your oven. Let it cool before serving . . . enjoy!

Fruit Salad

Salada de Frutas

Growing up Portuguese our desserts were often just a piece of seasonal fruit or a simple fruit salad. What we got was always a surprise as the fruits would change depending on the season. Sometimes there would be a mixture of apples and pears, melons, bananas, and anything else you can think of. If we had *visitas*, my mom would sometimes add just a tablespoon of sugar or Port wine to make the fruit salad sweeter.

This dessert is entirely up to you and your family. If you use apples or pears, make sure to squeeze some lemon juice on top to ensure they don't turn brown before serving.

Ingredients:

5 cups your choice of fruit
½ cup Port wine
Fruit juice
Sugar

Directions:

Mix your fruits of choice in a large bowl. Pour the Port wine, fruit juice, and sugar and mix thoroughly. Feel free to add as much liquid or sugar as you and your family like. This dessert is tailored to your taste! Enjoy!

Hot and Cold—
No Churn Homemade Ice Cream
Quente e Frio

This recipe I'm sharing with you was something I definitely did not have growing up, but I wish I did! When visiting my cousin João Manuel's home, his daughter, Daniela, shared several dessert recipes with me. She told me that this one was one of her favorites, especially during the summer.

When I finally experimented and tested it out on my family, I couldn't believe just how easy and delicious it was. It really is our version of cookies and cream ice cream. This recipe can easily be substituted with any cookie of your choice. We've experimented with chocolate chip cookies and my girls loved those, too. You really can't go wrong, but my favorite is the original, with Maria Biscuits or "Bolacha Maria." (The wonderful thing about Bolacha Maria is that they recently came up with a chocolate version!) Of course I needed to experiment with them in this dessert! Instead of using a bundt pan as my cousin taught me, I used a loaf pan. This way I didn't have to take it out of the pan to serve, but instead just scoop it out.

Ingredients:

1 pint container of heavy cream
1 14 oz can of sweetened condensed milk
1 7 oz package of Maria Biscuits (vanilla or chocolate)

Directions:

Grease pan of choice with butter. I used a loaf pan and left it aside.

In a medium sized bowl, crush the Maria Biscuits into small-sized pieces and leave aside. In a separate bowl, use a hand mixer to whip the heavy cream at a high speed until it's nice and firm. Then mix in the condensed milk and the crushed biscuits. Pour into the greased pan and put in the freezer for at least 4 hours.

While waiting for the mix to freeze, you can prepare the chocolate hot sauce to pour over your ice cream. I was given 2 recipes, one is a thin sauce and the other is much thicker, almost pudding-like. My family couldn't decide which one was best since they loved both. So it's up to you to decide which is your favorite!

continued on page 172

Hot and Cold—No Churn Homemade Ice Cream continued from page 170

Thick Chocolate Sauce:

1½ cups whole milk
2 tablespoons butter
4 tablespoons sugar
4 tablespoons cocoa powder
1½ tablespoons cornstarch
½ teaspoon vanilla extract

Thin Chocolate Sauce:

¾ cup whole milk
2 tablespoons sugar
3 tablespoons cocoa powder
1 tablespoon cornstarch

For the thick chocolate sauce you will need to whisk together the milk, sugar, cocoa powder, and cornstarch in a small saucepan. Bring to a boil, reduce the heat and simmer for 2 minutes. Add the butter and vanilla and continue to stir until the butter has melted.

For the thin chocolate sauce you will need to whisk together the milk, sugar, cocoa powder and cornstarch in a small saucepan. Bring to a boil, reduce the heat and simmer for 2 minutes.

When it's time to serve, remove the pan from the freezer and scoop out to enjoy.

If you used a bundt cake pan, when you remove the cake pan from the freezer you will need to insert the pan into a large bowl of hot water (but don't submerge it!). This will loosen the ice-cream and make it easier to remove it from the pan onto a dish for serving. (The first time I did this I left it too long in the hot water and the ice cream cake started to melt, so be careful.)

Using a serving dish, place the dish over the cake pan and flip the cake pan onto the dish and serve immediately. Cut into slices and drizzle with lots of hot chocolate sauce. Enjoy every yummy bite!

Menino Mija

Menino Mija is a holiday tradition unique to the Azores and something that needs to be shared and passed down to next generations. Between Christmas Eve and Epiphany (Dia dos Reis) communities of families walk through their villages visiting their friends and family. Upon arriving at their home, it is typical to ask whoever answers the door "O menino mija?" or, "Does the boy piss?." Although this expression might raise a few eyebrows, it has been a tradition for many decades in the Azores and something that I grew up with in our Portuguese community in the United States. "O menino mija" is a symbolic tradition that represents opening our homes for our family and friends, expected or unexpected. No matter how much or how little you have to offer, you will always be welcomed with something.

I remember when I was a teenager and would join my brother-in-law's family in this tradition every Christmas eve, right before going to midnight mass. It would be a large group of us, some with musical instruments, some with makeshift instruments. Each house we visited we would sing a song and wait for the door to open and once we finished we would ask the most important question, "O menino mija?." The person answering the door would respond, "Si. Na minha casa, o menino sempre mija," or "Yes. In my home, the boy always pisses." This in reality means that the drinks flow freely in the home. We would be welcomed inside the homes of those we visited and given drinks of different kinds of liquors, and of course, some sweets! Many will make liquor year round in preparation and will pair it with figs, bolo do rei, and more holiday sweets. This cycle of singing and drinking is repeated all night, until midnight mass. So as you can imagine, once we were at midnight mass, some of us would fall asleep. . . . I won't mention any names. But I was elbowed many times to wake up.

Christmas Cake

Bolo de Natal dos Açores

I have many fond memories of the Christmas season growing up. One of my favorites was watching my mom prepare a feast for the family celebration that would follow midnight Christmas Eve services. As soon as we got home the table would already be set with delicious foods and desserts. Each year my mom would bake a different cake especially for the center of the table, and it was always raised high on a tall cake stand to showcase above everything else. If she could have added a spotlight to it she probably would have, too!

The following recipe is for a special Christmas cake (Bolo de Natal) that would be one of those that took its turn being in the center of the table.

This cake is filled with three types of dried fruits. You may notice that crystallized fruit is missing from this recipe. My dad was not a fan of fruit, and my mom would substitute with whatever dried fruit she could get her hands on. Every year it would be a different combination of three dried fruits. You can really customize this recipe to your liking by using any mixture of dried figs, currants, raisins, dates, cherries, plums and dried mixed berries. There is no right or wrong, and any combination will give you a delicious moist cake.

Ingredients:

2⅓ cups granulated sugar (500 grams)
1 cup and 6 tablespoons butter (300 grams)
2½ cups all-purpose flour (300 grams)
2⅓ cups raisins (300 grams)
1⅔ cups chopped dried plums (250 grams)
2 cups chopped dried dates (250 grams)
6 large eggs at room temperature and separated
2 teaspoons baking powder
1 cup Port Wine (can substitute with Brandy)
1 tablespoon honey
Zest of 1 lemon
Pinch of salt
¼ cup confectioners' sugar

Directions:

In a medium bowl, mix together the raisins and the cup of Port wine, and leave aside for at least 1 hour so that the raisins can plump up with the wine. After an hour, strain out any wine that was not absorbed by the grapes and leave aside until the cake comes out of the oven. Save that extra Port, you will be pouring it over the warm cake once it comes out of its pan.

Preheat oven to 350° F.

continued on page 176

Christmas Cake continued from page 174

Grease and flour a large 10-cup bundt cake pan and leave aside.

In a large bowl, add the flour, baking powder, and salt and whisk everything together. Add the lemon zest, all the chopped dried fruit, and the Port-infused raisins and toss. Make sure that the fruit is covered in flour. Leave aside.

In another medium bowl, add your separated egg whites and beat on high until it forms high peaks. Leave aside.

In another large bowl, cream together the granulated sugar with butter. Once they are well combined and creamed, add the egg yolks and the honey and continue to beat together until well incorporated. Then, using a wooden spoon, start to add and mix in the dried fruit and flour. Stir everything together thoroughly and once everything is mixed, begin to fold in the egg whites. Once everything is folded in, you can spoon out the batter into the greased and floured pan and place in the preheated oven and bake for 60–70 minutes depending on your oven or until the inserted cake tester comes out clean.

Once it's done, let it cool in the baking pan for at least 10 minutes, then remove onto the cake dish and gently pour the remaining Port wine you have left over from soaking the raisins. Dust lightly with confectioners' sugar. If you really love Port wine, you can add more to your cake. It's definitely something you can experiment with before serving to your friends and family. Dust lightly with confectioners' sugar.

Other Favorites

Cake Toppings

Coberturas para Bolos

With every cake recipe I was given from aunts and cousins, I was told I could add different cake toppings to them if I wanted to make a simple cake look a little more fancy and decadent. Here are a few of them:

Chocolate Topping—*Cobertura de Chocolate*

1 cup granulated sugar
1 cup whole milk
1 tablespoon butter
2 tablespoons cocoa powder

In a medium saucepan, combine all the ingredients and bring to boil then lower the temperature for 10 minutes. Remove from the heat and then pour the topping over the cake to cover it. The cake will absorb this topping only if the cake is still warm from the oven.

Coconut and Nut Topping—*Cobertura de Coco e Nozes*

3 cups granulated sugar
3 cups whole milk
1 tablespoon butter
½ cup coconut
½ cup chopped nuts (your choice of nut)

In a medium saucepan, combine the sugar with milk and bring to a boil. Lower the temperature and continue to stir for about 30 minutes or until you can insert a spoon and create a string after lifting it from the mixture. At that stage you remove from the stove and add the butter, coconut and nuts. Pour the topping over the cake to cover it.

Orange or Lemon Topping—Cobertura de Laranja e de Limão

3 large eggs
1½ cups granulated sugar
1 tablespoon butter
Juice and zest of 1 orange or lemon; depending on your mood

Beat all ingredients and place them in a double boiler. Be sure to constantly whisk until it thickens. This will take roughly about 20–25 minutes. Let it cool to lukewarm and pour the topping over the cake to cover it.

Pumpkin Jam

Doce de Abóbora

One of my favorite things about the fall season is the arrival of pumpkins. I personally enjoy them cooked in so many different ways. I love them in my soups, roasted in the oven, and baked into desserts. But the one recipe that is such a special treat and not as common is pumpkin jam.

Growing up, my mom would make jam out of almost every fruit and sometimes vegetables . . . there really isn't much you can't make into a jam or compote. The memories I have of enjoying freshly made jam on warm buttered bread are something that makes my mouth water just thinking about it. The other great thing about making this recipe is that it also makes a wonderful hostess gift.

Ingredients:

2 pounds chopped pumpkin
2 pounds granulated sugar
Juice of 4–5 oranges, enough to fill 1 cup
1–2 cinnamon sticks
1 tablespoon pure vanilla extract
1 teaspoon salt

Directions:

Cut, peel, de-seed, and chop the pumpkin into small pieces. The smaller the pieces, the faster they will break apart in the sugar.

In a heavy bottom pan over medium heat add the pumpkin, sugar, salt, orange juice, cinnamon sticks, and vanilla. Stir everything together and bring to a boil. Then lower the temperature and let it simmer. Keep stirring the pot every few minutes until the jam starts to thicken in consistency. This should typically take about 45–60 minutes. You don't want to overcook it. The jam will harden as it cools.

Last but not least, spoon into sterilized mason jars. Let it cool and store the jars in the refrigerator. Since this is all natural with no preservatives, it should keep for two months.

This recipe yielded 5 8-oz. mason jars.

Oranges

Laranjas

Azorean oranges trace their lineage back to Asia. You'll find they are a delectable treat thanks to growing in the climate of the Azores archipelago. The region's unique weather provides the perfect setting for these citrus wonders to flourish. When visiting Portugal and the Azores, you will find oranges everywhere. In backyards, parks, farms, and even in the city. Oranges are very popular among Portuguese people. However, it's important to know that the best spots for orange trees in the Azores are not too high up or too close to the coast, as they can be affected by frequent fogs, strong winds, and insufficient sunlight. This clever tactic has allowed the cultivation of oranges to thrive in the coastal areas and the more sheltered valleys of the islands. What's remarkable is that the high humidity in the Azores eliminates the need for excessive watering, ensuring the oranges here are of the highest quality.

Now, let's explore the mouthwatering varieties of Azorean oranges. The "land orange" or "temporã" has its roots in the Orient. It is a beloved Mediterranean type celebrated for its early ripening, typically occurring between December and January. Another star is the "select orange," which was introduced from Brazil in the mid-19th century and boasts a maturation period from March to June. You'll also encounter navel oranges ripening between January and February. These orange orchards have thrived on multiple Azorean islands, including São Miguel, Terceira, and Faial. And there's more! The Azores have embraced other orange varieties over the years, including blood oranges, silver oranges, and lime oranges, which were introduced during the 20th century but on a smaller scale. These diverse citrus gems have played a significant role in Azorean agriculture and culture for centuries, even contributing to the region's trade and exports in the 19th century. For many Portuguese, it is common to find oranges in your stocking on Christmas. Although there is not a direct reason to why this may have started, there are a few ideas. One theory is that the oranges represent the story of St. Nicholas's gold. Other theories believe that oranges were seen as a rare luxury in difficult financial times, so many enjoy continuing the tradition. In your culinary adventures, you'll discover how these Azorean oranges add a burst of flavor to your dishes, whether in salads, desserts, or refreshing beverages.

Orange Jam

Doce de Laranja

This jam is a winner and a great addition to my jam list for gift ideas. I grew up with both my mom and my grandmother making it, and I think it's a perfect use for when you have some leftover oranges! This can be made with oranges, mandarines, or tangerines. Before making this, you want to make sure to peel off the skin, remove seeds and then weigh the fruit. Whatever the weight of the fruit, use half of this weight for the sugar. By the way, this is also a perfect time to buy a kitchen scale if you don't already have one! It makes everything much easier.

Ingredients:

789 grams (1¾ lbs.) oranges, cut into small pieces
391 grams (⅞ lb.) granulated sugar
1 tablespoon vanilla
Juice 1 lemon
1 teaspoon salt
Pinch of cinnamon

Directions:

In a heavy duty Dutch oven pan, over medium heat, add the sugar and mandarin/orange/tangerine pieces and start mixing together. Then, add salt, vanilla, lemon juice, and cinnamon, and keep stirring it all together. Continue to stir on medium heat until it is brought to a boil, then lower the heat and continue to stir until all the liquid is absorbed to your liking.

It actually took about one hour, but every stovetop runs differently . . . so keep an eye on it and make sure it doesn't overcook or burn.

After an hour, I'm generally happy with the consistency but I still like to leave a little syrupy liquid to keep the jam moist. Also, since this recipe has no preservatives, you must store it in the refrigerator. It will keep for several weeks, but I don't think this will last much longer than that.

Roasted Tomato Jam

Doce de Tomate Assado

My tomato jam is a summer staple at my house. Similarly, my mom would make this whenever she had an abundance of tomatoes, and now I do the same. For this recipe I prefer to roast them first as it not only gives a richer flavor, but it also helps make peeling easier. Enjoy, my friends!

Ingredients:

2 pounds tomatoes
1 pound granulated sugar
Juice of 2 lemons
1 teaspoon salt
Zest of 1 lemon

Directions:

Begin by washing the tomatoes. Cut them in half and toss them in a roasting pan, seasoning with salt and olive oil. Bake them in the oven for 30+/- minutes at 350°F. Make sure to face the tomatoes cut side down. You will begin to notice the skin of the tomato shrivel.

After roasting, peel the skin off the tomatoes immediately. In a heavy bottom pan over medium heat add the tomatoes, sugar, lemon juice, and lemon zest. Stir everything together and bring to a boil. Then lower the temperature and let it simmer. Keep stirring the pot every few minutes until the jam starts to thicken in consistency. This should typically take about 45–60 minutes. You don't want to overcook it, the jam will harden as it cools.

Last but not least, spoon into sterilized mason jars. Let them cool and store the jars in the refrigerator. Since this is all natural with no preservatives, it should keep for two months.

This recipe yielded 5 8-oz. mason jars.

Infused Butter

Manteiga Infundida

I was shocked to realize how easy it was to make this! The first time I had this was while I was vacationing in the Azores, and it was served along with fresh bread. One day they served butter infused with minced black olives, and the following day it was infused with hot red pepper sauce aka pimenta moída. I also saw there was butter infused with parsley and garlic, as well as rosemary infused butter. As soon as I got back home, I wanted to recreate it for my family, so I made both the black olive and the pimenta moída infusions. I especially like the briny taste of the olives coming through in the sweet butter. I also felt the same about the spicy and sweet blend that came with pimenta moída. Everyone just loved it! It's actually a perfect gift to bring to any party and you will most definitely impress. You can also customize it to your and your guests' taste preference.

Ingredients:

Butter
Herbs or spices of choice or
Minced olives of choice

Directions:

Bring butter to a soft room-temperature-like consistency. Blend in the herbs and/or spices of choice until fully mixed. Begin molding butter either into a rectangular or cylinder shape. Place butter in the fridge to harden, preferably for 1–2 hours and enjoy!

Chouriço Butter

Manteiga de chouriço

Here's another wonderful butter spread that I enjoyed while in the Azores. I was served this as an appetizer along with assorted breads. Even though they used chouriço sausage in their recipe, you can absolutely substitute with any other favorite sausage of yours. The recipe is very simple, and it will be a hit in your home too.

Ingredients:

1 pound chouriço sausage
½ pound salted butter, softened

Directions:

In a medium saucepan, add the chouriço. (I like to remove the casings.)

Add enough water to cover the sausage. Over medium to high heat, bring to a boil then simmer for about 20 minutes. Remove from the saucepan, and when it's cool enough to handle, roughly cut them in pieces and place in a food processor or chopper and quickly blitz it.

At this point it should be finely chopped. Leave aside. In a medium bowl, add the softened butter then add the chopped sausage and mix. Now spread some of this butter on some fresh bread, or crackers and enjoy!

Portuguese Seasonings

The Portuguese spice trade truly changed international cuisine. Portugal was one of the first European nations to create direct trade routes to Asia, Africa, and the Americas, as early as the 15th century. These trade routes made spices and other culinary ingredients and techniques a new aspect of trading.

Vasco da Gama, a Portuguese explorer, specifically played a significant role in bringing spices (black pepper, cloves, cinnamon, and more) from Asia to Portugal. These spices and new culinary techniques revolutionized Portuguese cuisine and created the infamous delicious gastronomy of Portugal.

Starting in Asia, the fusion of Indian and Portuguese food had a profound impact on Goan cuisine. The integration of both cultures created flavorful dishes, one being vindaloo, or "vinho d'alho." In East Timor, spices cultivated from the Portuguese, like cinnamon and cloves are used in several curries, spice infused rice, and stews. Macanese cuisine also incorporates spices into dishes like minchi (meat-potato hash) and African chicken alongside authentic Chinese flavors.

Portuguese influence in Brazil is a fusion of Portuguese, African, and indigenous flavors. Paprika, chili peppers, and more are integrated into dishes like feijoada and many seafood dishes. Many staple pieces in Brazilian gastronomy, such as watercress, cabbage, coriander, chives, rice, and many fruits also came from Portuguese influence. In countries like Mozambique, Cape Verde, Angola, and even South Africa, they incorporate piri-piri chili pepper sauce as a seasoning for marinating many meats for roasting. It is a beautiful way for so many different cultures to unite under the same shared love of food.

Saffron vs Safflower

The phrase "worth its weight in gold" in the spice world defines saffron. It is, by all means, the world's most expensive spice. It is derived from the stamens of a particular variety of crocus. Each flower produces only three tiny stamens (the three crimson colored "threads" protruding from the center of the bloom), each of which must be collected by hand. The fact that it takes some 50,000 to 75,000 flowers to yield a pound of the spice, makes it no surprise that in some local markets prices start at $60.00 per ounce. Thankfully, though, a very little goes a long way and just a tiny pinch will lend a dish a beautifully vivid orange color and a taste that is all but indescribable.

Fresh Safflower from São Miguel

I grew up with dishes seasoned with safflower, aka açafroa. Safflower is a common flower grown on our Island, and some people call it our paprika or our "fake saffron." Even though both add a great golden-orange color to our food, the two flowers are not related. Saffron (*Crocus sativus*) is a perennial and safflower (*Carthamus tinctorius*) is an annual and the cost between the two is obvious at the market. Safflower can be bought for as little as $4.00 per ounce. Compared to saffron, safflower is much less expensive.

All this information on the differences between the two never really mattered to me while sampling the wonderful dishes prepared by my family. I now find myself cooking with safflower instead of paprika or in addition to it. I feel it adds a much deeper taste to the special dishes, and the aroma always brings me back to my childhood.

Make your own Seasonings

Mozambique Seasoning

To make the mixture, combine equal parts of saffron (or you can substitute with the less expensive safflower, aka açafroa), paprika, turmeric, and onion powder.

Measure ¼ cup for each ingredient and combine in a mason jar for future recipes.

Classic Portuguese Rub

Unlike the Mozambique Seasoning, the Classic Portuguese Rub has a variation of different seasonings. This rub can be used for any dish and can be altered to your own personal taste.

It goes as follows:

4 tablespoons salt
1 tablespoon garlic powder
2 tablespoon paprika
2 tablespoons cumin
½ tablespoon cinnamon
½ teaspoon red pepper flakes

You can absolutely multiply the ingredients several times, and combine in a mason jar.

It's the best, so that you'll always be prepared with the seasoning mix.

Homemade Vanilla

Baunilha Caseira

A few years ago I read something about making my own vanilla. After we put away the Christmas decorations in January, I bought some vodka from the local store and ordered some Madagascar vanilla beans. The process is pretty simple, but can be a little time consuming. You can really go crazy making vanilla because as easy as it is to make, there are a variety of types of beans to choose from with different characteristics. I used Madagascar beans, but there are Tahitian beans, Ugandan beans, New Guinea beans, etc. Besides that, you can choose to use vodka or rum or bourbon or pretty much any type of alcohol (the alcohol extracts the oils from the bean). Some vanillas are better for baking, some better for frostings, you name it. Feel free to make more or less depending on how much you use vanilla in your baking.

Ingredients:

5–6 vanilla beans
2 cups vodka

Directions:

Spilt the beans in half lengthwise so that the seeds are exposed. Pour the vodka over the seeds and make sure it covers all of the beans. If needed, you can cut the beans in half if using a shorter jar. You don't want any beans above the alcohol line when you seal it up in the Mason Jar.

Let it sit for an extended amount of time, but at least a month; I've let some sit for a whole year before bottling. The longer it sits the stronger the flavor! Store it in a cool dry place and shake it every once in a while. Once you take some out from your bottle, you can top it off with some more vodka and add a few more beans to continue the vanilla making process.

If you do this, you'll never run out of pure vanilla extract again.

Vanilla Sugar

Açúcar Baunilhado

Have you ever heard of Vanilla Sugar? If you're an avid baker, you probably already have a container of it in your pantry. But for those that have never heard it before . . . let me tell you that it's definitely a baker's secret ingredient. Vanilla infused sugar is incredible and your baking will be elevated to another level . . . plus it's so easy to make.

All you need is:

4 pounds granulated sugar
2 vanilla beans
Container for storage

Directions:

Before you start putting together your ingredients, you'll notice that there's different types of vanilla beans to choose from, but the most familiar type and readily available is the Madagascar vanilla bean.

Here are the simple steps:

Pour the sugar into the container, then on a cutting board using a sharp knife gently slice the vanilla pods down the center. Gently scrape out the seeds.

Once you do that, you're going to add the pods and seeds in with the sugar. Make sure that you place them in the center and that the pods are covered with sugar.

Now cover the container and wait at least two weeks before using. Actually the longer you wait the better, since the vanilla flavor in the sugar intensifies the longer you wait. I like to shake the container a few times a week while waiting, that way the vanilla seeds are well dispersed in the sugar.

After waiting as long as you can, you're now ready to bake using your vanilla sugar instead of plain granulated sugar.

You can absolutely use it in all your recipes that call for sugar and once you do that you'll wonder why you've never done this before.

Remember that I said it's a baker's secret ingredient? Well, I guess I can share with you!

Tea Time

Chás

As soon as I have booked my flight to São Miguel in the Azores, sometimes months before, I start planning all the places I want to see and all the activities I don't want to miss. A must see for me is visiting Gorreana Tea Plantation in the village of Maia; it is the oldest commercial tea plantation in all of Europe. There is another tea plantation nearby, Porto Formoso, which is very charming and also has a rich history.

Gorreana is a family-operated business since 1883, and now is run by its seventh generation. The tea leaves are all grown organically and are picked and sorted by hand, and this whole process has remained the same from the beginning to the present day. To be honest, I love both plantations and usually visit both!

Tea was introduced to the Portuguese in the 16th century by the Chinese in Macau. The Portuguese have implemented tea into their lives ever since because of the variation of delicious flavors. It was introduced to Portuguese missionaries, but later made its way to royalty and even the common people. Shortly after regaining independence from Spain, the former Princess of Portugal, Catherine of Braganza, married King Charles II and introduced tea and tea time to England! It was an expensive luxury for the wealthy, which is why the British only drank it for its medicinal purposes. The love for tea only continued to spread throughout Europe.

The Azores created their tea plantations in the 19th century to boost the local economy after rapid disease wiped out the lucrative orange trade. The Gorreana Tea Factory, one of the original plantations, has since remained the only tea plantation in all of Europe and has been a leading factor in the economy of São Miguel. Because Gorreana still manually processes their teas, they are considered to be some of the best in the world.

Teas in my house were always the first option when one of us was sick. The tea O'Poejo, aka Pennyroyal, which is in the mint family, was great for our stomach aches; lemon tea was used for any illness or body aches. You could drink either in the morning or before bed. However, if we had a cold there was a much different solution: you would drink the tea along with an added shot of brandy before bed to "sweat it out." Despite how crazy it may sound, it really seemed to work!

Lemon Tea

Chá de Limão

Ingredients:

Hot water
Preferred herbs/tea

Directions:

Heat the water until boiling. If you're making lemon tea, you would peel the lemon, and then steep the peel until the water turns a bright yellow color and the scent gives off a citrus aroma. Steep tea until desired.

Feel free to use honey, sugar, or leave it natural.

This can be used as a medicinal drink or just for pleasure!

Index

Alcatra, 120
Baked Beans, 24
Beans
- Baked Beans, 24
- Bean Soup, 9
- Quick Stewed Beans, 22
- Young Fava Broad Bean Stew, 20

Beef Stew, 122
Beer Biscuits, 128
Biscuits
- Beer Biscuits, 128
- Pumpkin Spice Biscuits, 130

Bread
- Cod Stuffed Cornbread, 105
- Crackling Bread, 66
- Easter Sweet Bread, 68
- Homemade Bread, 60
- Olive Bread, 55
- Sweet Bread, 72

Bread Pudding with Pineapple & Meringue Topping, 164
Butter
- Butter Rice, 28
- Infused Butter, 188
- Chouriço Butter, 190

Cake
- Cake Toppings, 178
- Carrot Cake, 144
- Chocolate Maria Biscuit Cake, 155
- Christmas Cake, 174
- Dona Amelia's Queen Cakes, 134
- Orange Cake, 150
- Rosa's Cake, 146
- Salazar's Cake, 152
- Sponge Cake, 148
- Vanilla and Cream Cake, 140
- Water Cake, 142

Charcuterie Board, 44
Chicken
- Roasted Chicken, 116
- Chicken Mozambique, 118

Chickpea Tuna Salad, 88
Chocolate Maria Biscuit Cake, 155
Chocolate Tart with Maria Biscuit Crust, 160
Chouriço
- Chouriço Butter, 190
- Chouriço Croquettes, 39
- Flame Grilled Chouriço, 42
- Homemade Chouriço, 36

Christmas Cake, 174
Classic Portuguese Rub, 195
Cod
- Cod Stuffed Cornbread, 105
- Codfish Rice, 32
- Creamed Cod, 99
- Salted Codfish Tart, 96
- Spiritual Codfish, 102

Coconut Tarts, 158
Cookies
- Green Tea Cookies, 132

Creamed Cod, 99
Crackling Bread, 66
Dona Amelia's Queen Cakes, 134
Egg
- Scrambled Eggs with Tomatoes and Onions, 84

Easter Sweet Bread, 68
English Muffins
- Portuguese English Muffins, 63

Flame Grilled Chouriço, 42
Fruit Salad, 168
Green Soup, 12
Green Tea Cookies, 132
Grilled Tuna, 90
Holy Ghost Soup, 7
Homemade Bread, 60
Homemade Chouriço, 36
Homemade Vanilla, 196
Hot and Cold—No Churn Homemade Ice Cream, 170
Ice Cream
- Homemade Ice Cream, 170

Infused Butter, 188
Jam
- Orange Jam, 184
- Pumpkin Jam, 180
- Roasted Tomato Jam, 186

Linguiça Bake, 82
Linguiça Rolls, 58
Malassada Bread Pudding, 166
Marinated Pork Slices, 114
Milk Soup, 14
Mozambique Seasoning, 195
Octopus
- Roasted Octopus, 108
- Stewed Octopus, 110

Olive Bread, 55
Orange Cake, 150
Orange Jam, 184
Orange Tarts, 162
Pennyroyal & Medicinal Teas, 198
Pork
- Marinated Pork Slices, 114
- Pork Ribs, 112

Porridge, 16
Portuguese English Muffins, 63
Pot Roast, 124
Pudding
- Bread Pudding with Pineapple & Meringue Topping, 164

Malassada Bread Pudding, 166
Pumpkin
Pumpkin Jam, 180
Pumpkin Scones, 136
Pumpkin Spice Biscuits, 130
Quiche
Tomato Quiche, 80
Quick Stewed Beans, 22
Rice
Butter Rice, 28
Codfish Rice, 32
Tomato Rice, 30
Tuna and Tomato Rice, 86
Roasted Chicken, 116
Roasted Octopus, 108
Roasted Tomato Jam, 186
Rolls
Linguiça Rolls, 58
Taro Root Rolls, 52
Rosa's Cake, 146
Saffron and Safflower, 194
Salads
Chickpea Tuna Salad, 88
Fruit Salad, 168
Salazar's Cake, 152
Salted Codfish Tart, 96
Scones
Pumpkin Scones, 136
Scrambled Eggs with Tomatoes and Onions, 84
Seasoning
Classic Portuguese Rub, 195
Mozambique Seasoning, 195
Saffron and Safflower, 194
Sopa de Netos, 2
Soup
Bean Soup, 9
Green Soup, 12
Holy Ghost Soup, 7
Milk Soup, 14
Sopa de Netos, 2
Spiritual Codfish, 102
Sponge Cake, 148
Stew
Beef Stew, 122
Stewed Octopus, 110
Tia Lilia's Fish Stew, 92
Young Fava Broad Bean Stew, 20
Sugar
Vanilla Sugar, 197
Sweet Bread, 72
Taro Root Rolls, 52
Tarts
Chocolate Tart with Maria Biscuit Crust, 160
Coconut Tarts, 158
Orange Tarts, 162
Salted Codfish Tart, 96
Tea
Lemon Tea, 199
Tia Lilia's Fish Stew, 92
Tomato Quiche, 80
Tomato Rice, 30
Tuna
Chickpea Tuna Salad, 88
Grilled Tuna, 90
Tuna and Tomato Rice, 86
Vanilla
Homemade Vanilla, 196
Vanilla and Cream Cake, 140
Vanilla Sugar, 197
Young Fava Broad Bean Stew, 20
Water Cake, 142

The Immigrant Heart

I stand on the shoulders of those before me

And I will be the starting point for those that come after.

My father always said that he immigrated for his children, grandchildren and those that follow.

It's the struggle that they suffered that keeps us pushing along to make sure that what they battled is won.

How amazing it is to come from people who
are not afraid and are brave for us.

They showed us that there is nothing we can't do.
We not only succeed for ourselves but for them as well.

—*Maria Lawton*

Maria Lawton, affectionately known as the "Azorean Green Bean," stands as a culinary luminary and beloved host of the acclaimed series "Maria's Portuguese Table" on PBS. Born on the stunning Azorean island of Sao Miguel, part of the Portuguese archipelago nestled in the middle of the Atlantic Ocean, Maria's culinary journey began amidst the vibrant flavors of her homeland.

At the tender age of six, Maria's family emigrated to the United States, like many new Americans, carrying with them the rich culinary traditions of the Azores. Food and cooking became central pillars of Maria's family life, nurturing her love for Portuguese cuisine and sparking a lifelong passion for sharing its beauty with the world.

Driven by an unwavering desire to preserve her cultural and culinary heritage, Maria wholeheartedly embraced these invaluable lessons, eventually sharing them with a broader audience through her award-winning PBS Series, "Maria's Portuguese Table." Each episode serves as a tantalizing voyage through Portugal's diverse regions, exploring the nuances of local cuisine, traditions, and historical significance.

Maria's endearing persona, culinary expertise, and profound reverence for her heritage have endeared her to viewers worldwide. Beyond her television acclaim, she is also a celebrated author, with her first best-selling cookbook, *Azorean Cooking: From My Family Table to Yours*, serving as a cherished testament to her roots. Through a tapestry of personal stories and authentic recipes, Maria offers readers a poignant glimpse into the rich cultural landscape of Azorean cuisine.

Her warm spirit and steadfast dedication continue to inspire audiences and food enthusiasts alike, elevating Portuguese cuisine onto the global stage of gastronomy. At home, Maria finds solace with her husband Bob, Co-Executive Producer of the show, and their beloved cockapoo, Gracie. Embracing her role as a grandmother, Maria eagerly awaits the day when her grandchildren join her in the kitchen, ensuring the legacy of culinary traditions thrives for generations to come.

In addition to her current projects, Maria is also in the process of penning several other books to be published soon, further enriching the world with her culinary wisdom and heartfelt narratives.

For further information on Maria Lawton and her culinary endeavors, please visit her official website at www.azoreangreenbean.com.